The Death of the Church Victorious

The Death of the Church Victorious

Ovid E. Need Jr.
Assistant Editor: Peter Pellegrin

Order From: **Biblical Examiner**
5130 Danville Road
Lynchburg, OH 45142
www.BiblicalExaminer.org

Or From: Sovereign Grace Publishers, Inc.
P.O. Box 491
Mulberry, IN 46058
www.sgpbooks.com

Death of the Church Victorious
Copyright © 2002, 2004
By Ovid Need
All Rights Reserved

ISBN 1-58960-301-X

*Printed In the United States of America
By Lightning Source, Inc.*

**Dedicated
to**

The Lord Jesus Christ
whose sovereign grace alone
made this book possible.

**Special Thanks
to**

The People of the Linden Baptist Church
who patiently endured the many hours their pastor spent on this project.

Evangelist John Weaver
who urged this writer to the research into print.

Dr. Paul Cates
whose wife's family was deeply involved in the early days of the movement discussed herein. Bro. Cates spent many hours checking the manuscript for historical accuracy.

Table of Contents

Foreword i

Foreword iv

Introduction 1

Part I, Overview 5

Chapter 1, The Importance; 2, Morgan Edwards; 3, The Brethren; 4, The Mystics; 5, The French Revolution; 6, Who's Who

Part II, In the Beginning 27

Chapter 7, Death Introduced; 8, Edward Irving; 9, Death and Dates; 10, The Terrors of Satan

Part III, Ben-Ezra 41

Chapter 11, Rome's Gain; 12, Rome and Ben-Ezra; 13, Lacunza and Ben-Ezra; 14, The Jesuits; 15, Irving and Ben-Ezra; 16, Irving and Ben-Ezra Unite; 17, A New View of Revelation; 18, New Doctrine Introduced; 19, Zionism; 20, National Israel Exalted; 21, Jewish Hope Christianized; 22, The Defeated Church; 23, Everything Around National Israel; 24, The Advent of the Lord; 25, The Millennial Reign; 26, The Resurrection of the Dead; 27, A Motive for Holiness; 28, Death for Victory; 29, Prophecy; 30, Novelties; 31, Law; 32, Christ; 33, Satan; 34; Redemption

Part IV, Prophecy Conferences, 125

Chapter 35, Christ and Prophecy; 36, Henry Drummond; 37, The Albury Park Conferences; 38, Zionism and Joseph Wolff; 39, Powerscourt Conferences; 40, Powerscourt and the Rapture; 41, Tongues and the Rapture; 42, Tongues, Irving and his Church; 43, The Rapture

Part V, The Men and Times, 163

Chapter 44, The Anglican Church; 45, Social Climate; 46, Irving, Cornin, Bellett; 47, Anthony Norris Groves; 48, John Nelson Darby; 49, Darby, Continued; 50, Newman and Newton; 51, G.V. Wigram, P.F. Hall; 52, George Müller; 53, Hudson Taylor and Others

Part VI, Development and Doctrine, 203

Chapter 54, Millenarianism and Money; 55, Millennialism Develops; 56, Chiliasm and Premillennialism; 57, The Imminent Return; 58, Against the Future; 59, Zeal Corrupted; 60, Church with no Earthly Function; 61, Just Wait; 62, Unity in Death; 63, Developing Doctrine; 64, Prophecy and the Church; 65, Darby vs. Newton

Part VII, World-Wide Conquest, 237

Chapter 66, The Foundation of Conquest; 67, Primary Areas of Conquest; 68, Switzerland Invaded; 69, Darby's Switzerland Lectures; 70, Various Nations; 71, Millennialism and Marxism

Part VIII, War Against Orthodoxy, 263

Chapter 72, Resistance to Millennialism; 73, Baptist and Presbyterian; 74, Against the Baptists; 75, Against Obedience; 76, For Two Gospels; 77, Significant Millenarian Victories; 78, Bible Readings; 79, Moody's Conversion; 80, Moody and Darby; 81, Moody and Moorehouse; 82, Moody and Bible Readings; 83, Moody's New Message

Part IX, America Conquered, 301

Chapter 84, America Invaded; 85, The War Between the States; 86, Key Events; 87, Millenarian Bible Conferences; 88, Northfield; 89, Keswick; 90, Millenarian Training Institutions; 91, C.I. Scofield; 92, Various Men;

Part X, Darbyism-Millennialism, 335

Chapter 93, Starting Over; 94, Dispensationalism; 95, Paul's Writings; 96, According to Darby; 97, Daniel; 98, The Great Tribulation; 99, Antinomianism; 100, Sin; 101, Sin Defined; 102, Sin and Judgment; 102, Conscience and Guidance; 104, Corrupted Words; 105, The Great Escape; 106, Phenomenal Growth; 107, Conclusion

Appendix A, Letters of Explanation, 385
Albury Park (1826)
Darby's Letters

Appendix B, Various Meanings 427

Appendix C, 465
Manuel De Lacunza (Ben-Ezra)
Joseph Wolff

Works Cited 469

Various Other Works 473

Scripture, General Index 477

Introduction

No system of thought remains simply thought, for a person's ideas about God — his faith — will control his actions. Moreover, most people tend to embrace doctrines they are taught with little or no thought of their origins, implications, conclusions, or even of their contextual Scriptural soundness. More than a few good men have embraced doctrines because of the personalities of their teachers, because of peer pressure, or simply because the doctrines were appealing.[1] William Law (1686-1761) spoke of those who defend opinions based on things other than Scripture:

> ...[H]ow many have studied the words of Scripture for a lifetime, without receiving that humility of Christ which produces the very mind of Christ and turns fallen man into a son of God! Academic degrees they hold in plenty from the best centers of religious learning—but know so little of Spirit of Christ! What a paradox to see the professed Church of the Lamb filled with great numbers of champion disputants, who from age to age have been up in arms to support and defend a set of opinions, doctrines, and practices, all of which may be most cordially embraced without demanding the least degree of self-denial, and most firmly held fast without bestowing the least degree of humility!

Why is it that we see Bible scholars equally pleased with and contending for the errors and absurdities of every system of theology under which they happen to have taken their education? Because natural genius and human wisdom can feed on no other food than the deceptive fruit of that ancient tree of knowledge. What

---

1. Proverbs 18:17 tells us that the first one to plead his cause seems right until he is challenged. I have found that committed dispensationalists basically teach what they were taught, for the doctrine cannot be supported through systematic Bible study. Unless, of course, that study is always done with the pre-conceived belief in the church/Israel distinction. Accordingly, they refuse to listen to any teaching that might challenge what they had been taught. Humility should make one willing to learn, but many are unwilling to consider anything else. In dispensational churches, the pastors protected us from being challenged by non-dispensational ideal. If mentioned at all, other views were mocked. This author's experience has been that dispensational pastors apparently fear to have their teaching challenged before their people. It is a folly and a shame to take a Biblical stand without checking out all sides, Proverbs 18:13. See *Revelation*, 4.

a gross ignorance, both of man's need and Christ's salvation, to run to Greek and Hebrew schools to learn how to put off Adam and to put on Christ! How absurd to seek to be wise in scholarship concerning the letter of Scripture in order to obey Christ's command that we must become like a little child to enter into His kingdom! How came the learned Greeks by their pride and vanity, and inability to come under the humility of the cross? It was because the false glory of their own cultivated abilities blinded them in the same way that a letter-learned knowledge blinded Jewish scribes and Pharisees. And so it often is in the Church today.[2]

Many Christians profess to be followers of the humble Lamb of God, yet refuse to give up a system of theology because they happened to have taken their education under that system. Though exalting the word of God with their mouths, they exalt friendships and traditions with their actions. They are, accordingly, identified with the "letter-learned knowledge blinded Jewish scribes and Pharisees," for whom Christ had no good words.

Many of the modern teachings we will discuss are considered basis for fellowship by some who hold them vehemently, when the basis of fellowship should instead be converting faith in Christ, the necessity of the convicting power of the Holy Spirit and the application of God's total Law-Word and grace into all society through the word of God. The soundness of the doctrine of redemption — the most important of all doctrines — is many times overlooked as long as there is a common teaching in other areas, like Eschatology.[3]

This present study was initially motivated by this pastor's contact with a book by Dave MacPherson. Questioning MacPherson's

---

2. *Power*, 50, 51, 52.

3. Dispensational millennialism/"Pre-trib" rapture became the "shibboleth" for fellowship at the start of the twentieth century "because of its tremendous fund-raising potential." Biola College was among the first to discover its potential, *Plot*, 222, 223. The Believer must hold to some basic points to be considered a Bible Believing Christian: the inspiration of Scripture, the virgin birth of Christ, Christ's substitutionary death (vicarious atonement), his literal resurrection. Obviously, "Liberty of Conscience" must operate within sound Biblical parameters. See *Systematic Theology*, 899. See also *The London Baptist Confession of 1689*, chap. 21.

conclusions because they were so contrary to what this pastor had been taught, his reference materials were obtained and checked where possible. As MacPherson's documentations were examined, this pastor was saddened and surprised to find that a very large portion of current "Christian" doctrine, over which many modern Christians will part company, was less than theologically sound.

There were so many new and unique theological opinions developed by talented and powerful men in the early 1800s, which now control modern Christian thought, that we cannot deal with them all. Consequently, the inclined reader is strongly urged to examine for himself the points brought up, yet overlooked. In fact, I suggest readers do as this pastor did — research material unobtainable through used book stores was obtained through libraries and inner-library loans. Thus what started as an effort to dismiss some facts, to which this author did not want to admit, developed into an examination of the origin and spread of a modern theology that encourages the Christian to withdraw from society to become more "spiritual," *i.e.,* "Heavenly-minded."[4]

We urge those desiring to take an honest look at the modern dispensational *system* to check E.R. Sandeen and G.E. Ladd.[5]

Our objective is to establish the source of many modern, well-known doctrines that have led to the hopeless, helpless attitudes of Christians in general. We will attempt to restrict our study to just enough information to reveal the roots and fruits of the modern dispensational millennial faith.

Furthermore, one should be cautious about identifying size and physical growth with the movement of God's Spirit, or he will find himself defending many pagan systems of belief, *e.g.,* Muslims. (1 Tim. 6:1-7.) In other words, the zeal and explosive growth characterizing a system of belief are not necessarily the Spirit's

---

4. *Origins,* 301.
5. In his 1901 *History,* Neatby attributes the name "Evangelical" to the early Brethren dissidents against the Church of England, 34. Thus both *Fundamental* and *Evangelical* are names that originated to describe the followers of the unique doctrines developed in the Irvingite/Brethren movement.

stamp of approval. Only the totality of God's word and its overall effect upon the world for Christ and his kingdom can approve or disapprove any system of Christian life and thought.

Please examine the following with Scripture in hand and the attitude of *and if in anything ye be otherwise minded, God shall reveal even this unto you* (Phil. 3:15) — that is, with the desire that if any area of doctrine believed is contrary to God's written revelation, he will *reveal even this unto you*. Then the revealed truth according to God's word must be acted upon, or there will be even more deception. (Jas. 1:22, Mat.12:45.)

This pastor is convinced that if the church at large does not abandon its saltless, lightless and lifeless "Heavenly-mindedness" and "Other-worldliness" to again make Christianity relevant in society, God himself will remove the "Other-worldliness" thinking through some not so pleasant means.

This pastor desires to see the return of relevant, Biblical Christianity to the church and to society. New Testament Christianity that causes individuals to use their God-given talents for the cause of Christ in every area of their lives and thoughts can again "turn the world upside down."

Foreword

Ovid Need's study of *Death of the Church Victorious, Tracing the Roots and Implications of Otherworldliness* is a work of major importance. A false spirituality and an otherworldliness of anti-Biblical characters have long plagued the Christian Church and hobbled its progress.

There have been several sources of this evil and perverted interpretation of Christianity. *First*, and foremost, the ancient pagan views of Greece (and Rome) have long commanded the church. For neoplatonism most of all, spirit is good and matter is on a lower level and potentially evil. (In Manichean thinking, which greatly influenced St. Augustine and others, matter is fully evil and spirit is good.) Given this perspective, Greek and Roman pagans in great numbers forsook materialism to become desert hermits. This movement entered the church as asceticism. While Protestantism decries monasticism, it is still influenced by the spirit-matter dichotomy and perspective of medievalism.

From a Biblical perspective, it is clearly false to view spirit as good and matter as lower or evil. Both are God's Creation, and both are pronounced "very good" in Gen. 1:31. Satan and the fallen angels are obviously purely spiritual and yet purely evil. Morality is not governed or established by spirituality per se, but by obedience to God's law-word. Sin involves man's I whole being, material and spiritual, and our moral obedience to God similarly involves our heart, mind and being, every part of us. To flee the material realm is not Biblical, but a form of paganism. We are called to *Godliness*, not neoplatonic spirituality.

For centuries, however, neoplatonic spirituality has undermined Christianity. The remarkable vigor of English Puritanism, for example, was undermined by the Cambridge Platonism. What appeared as a "spiritual" advance was in fact a radical retreat from victory.

It is time for the church to break with spirituality in the name of Biblical Christianity. How each spirituality has warped and distorted the faith can be seen in such patristic writings as St. Gregory of Nyssa's work on the books of Moses. He rejected any literal and historical meaning for wildly absurd allegorical meanings.

One consequence of this evil spirituality is antinomianism, an abandonment of God's law in favor of "spirituality." Somehow an abstract spirituality is supposed to provide moral impetus, something experience has shown to be false. *Second*, otherworldliness means a contempt for creation. Scripture tells us clearly that marriage is for time only, that there is neither marrying or giving in marriage in heaven. But this does not make marriage any the less important! Preaching the Gospel is for time only, but that does not make it meaningless. Creation is God's glorious work. It is man's training ground for eternity. Man must exercise dominion and subdue the earth and make it God's Kingdom (Gen. 1:26-28; Mt. 6:31). Time and creation must be man's concern while here. We can have no part of God's heaven if we do not take His creation seriously.

Otherworldliness runs away from God's requirements of us here and now. If Protestants find a monk's retreat from the world wrong, is their otherworldliness any the less objectionable?

I know pastors who, in the name of spirituality and other-worldly "holiness," have evaded every critical moral issue all their lives. What will their Lord say to them when they plead that they have believed His every word?

Third, another false view has been one common to many from abbot Joachim of Flora through Hegel. The Spirit is invoked, in Joachim in semi- Christian fashion, to Hegel's pagan *Geist* or Spirit, to justify a non-Christian spirituality that jettisons God's law-word. Modernism rests firmly on Hegel's view and sees a progressive 'revelation' or development, while the Joachimite perspective views the God of justice and law replaced by the God of grace, and now by the God of love.

In this perspective, there are no eternal truths, only "truths for the times," and spirituality means being in tune with the spirit of the age. The otherworldliness of this view is its refusal to believe that God's creation is not malleable by man and his own vision. The world and history are seen as the potential re-creation of spiritual man. These three perspectives are notable in their influence, but other views also exist that seek to create a new other-worldly and spiritual religion.

Pastor Need analyzes those views in evangelical circles which are working against the future of the faith. His study is a summons to a Biblical faith and power. It is written with grace and insight. Its timelessness cannot be overstated. It is a joy to read, and a work that the Christian community should be grateful for.

Rousas John Rushdoony
October 1, 1996

Foreword

I was grateful when my friend and fellow crusader, Indiana pastor Ovid Need, shared his new manuscript on *Death of the Church Victorious* with me. And honored when I was asked to compose this preface.

Throughout the past century far too many scholars, including evangelical ones, have assumed that John Nelson Darby of the Plymouth Brethren deserves credit for the pretribulation rapture idea. Need proves, with more than enough evidence, that this simply isn't so; he shows that others preceded Darby and that Darby unethically "borrowed" their thoughts and then gave the impression that he alone deserved adulation for the same escapist doctrine.

The thrust of *Death of the Church Victorious* demonstrates, with painstaking detail and documentation, that pretrib dispensationalism has been incredibly destructive since its birth and development in the 1800's.

Pastor Need brings to light dispensationalism's dire effects: pessimism instead of prevailing, cowardice instead of conquering, isolation instead of involvement – a system offering a "rapturous" sneaking away at "any moment" instead of encouraging the saints to subjugate and subdue the enemy until victory is obtained!

But there's still hope that the death of victory will someday become the resurrection of victory—and Ovid Need's *Death of the Church Victorious* is needed to bring this about!

Dave MacPherson

Part I

Overview

Chapter 1
The Importance

Early in the 1800's — as the second wave of the great western revivals reached its zenith — a tiny religious sect in Britain began to publicly teach a new end-of-the-world view. It was a complicated, pessimistic, disruptive view which, since then, has weakened Christian unity, spread abroad a pall of pessimism, and gradually dampened the spirit and evangelism that had pervaded Christianity for nearly a century.[1]

The average Christian reader may consider this present study unimportant, if not completely irrelevant, to situations in his Christian life. Probably the best way to stress its importance is to quote the back cover of Henry Allen Ironside's (1876-1951) book, *A Historical Sketch of The Brethren Movement*:

> Perhaps very few Christians who hold to fundamental truths realize how much the church is indebted to a somewhat obscure group of believers which began in the early part of the nineteenth century, known generally as Plymouth Brethren, though they themselves prefer to be called simply "Brethren," "Christian Brethren," or "Believers."... A wealth of literature, opening up the Scriptures, emanated from this group, and has had far-reaching influence around the world.... Dr. H. A. Ironside was connected with the Brethren for over forty years...

In addition, we find this statement in Ironside's opening remarks:

> ...Because of the far-reaching influence of this *distinctive school of Christian thought* it may not be unprofitable to inquire into the causes of the movement... By far the great majority of outstanding

---

1. *Plot,* back cover.

fundamentalist leaders readily acknowledge their indebtedness, in measure at least, to the oral or written ministry of the Brethren... For though the Brethren assemblies have never been large in numbers as compared to the great denominations of Protestantism, their *propaganda has been world-wide, and thousands have accepted their views* on many lines who are not openly identified with them...[2]

The doctrines of the new millennialism were collected by and organized in the mind of one man in particular — John Nelson Darby. (See "John Nelson Darby, p. 179.")

Where did the view start? Why was it started? What motivated its rapid spread? Who was involved? Why were its tenets so gladly received by the overwhelming majority of the Protestant Christian world when its teachings were so contrary to then orthodox Christian teachings? What are the modern implications of the teachings developed by this "tiny religious sect"?

In this first part, we will introduce the major propagators of the "new end-of-the-world view." Though not initially developing the *system*, it was the "Brethren" who adapted it, and converted the Christian world to it. The popular *Scofield Reference Bible* is a "Brethren" book.[3]

Chapter 2

Morgan Edwards

Premillennialism, *i.e.*, a literal thousand year reign of Christ, has been taught from the beginning of Christianity.[4] So we will only mention in passing, Morgan Edwards (1722-1795). Edwards offered

---

2. *Sketch,* 7, 9. Emp. added.
3. "Scofield's reference Bible represents a lifelong study of Scriptures, and is hailed in all the world by Brethren as setting forth their views on the interpretation of Scripture, especially of prophecy and 'dispensational truth.' And naturally: Scofield was for a generation an assiduous and admiring student of Darby's writings." *Advent,* 19.

a millennial system well before the Roman Jesuit, Manuel Lacunza (1731-1801), offered his 1790 document under the pseudonym, *Ben-Ezra* (Manuel De Lacunza Y Diaz; see "Rome and *Ben-Ezra*," p. 45), which is the apparent basis of modern millennialism. Though this writer found no link between Edwards and the "Brethren," we should consider him, for he played an important role in Baptist history — he spent many years collecting early American Baptist history, and his history is the basis of all Baptist history since.[5]

While a student at Bristol Academy (England), 1742-1744, young Edwards wrote *Two Academical Exercises on the Subjects Bearing the Following Titles: Millennium and Last-Novelties*. It was not published until 1788 in America after providence moved Edwards to Philadelphia in 1761.[6]

---

4. See *The Lost Books of the Bible*, Barnabas 13:1-9. It is believed that Paul's companion, Barnabas, wrote for the benefit of the Christianized Jews. Barnabas held the six days creation and seventh day rest taught that after six thousand years, "the Lord God will bring all things to an end." Then there would be a thousand year rest (seventh day), followed by "the eighth day, that is, the beginning of the other world." According to Ladd, "Support for belief in the rapture has been claimed from Victorinus, of the fourth century, and from Joseph Mede of the seventeenth. Whether this is so or not, it is clear that no group of Christians made it a matter of faith before the nineteenth century." *Hope*, 286, n35. Berkhof tells us that "According to some (Barnabas, Hermas, Papias) its [the Kingdom of God, ed.] final form is preceded by a millennial kingdom." However, far greater emphasis was on the coming judgment. Berkhof, *History,* 41. However, the goal of this present work is not to document the origin of millennialism, but to follow its results. The (c. 1530) belief that the Spirit's illumination "superceeded the need of the written word of God" led to the belief that Christ would soon to set up his Kingdom with a sword. This belief led to John of Leyden's horrible 'kingdom' at Münster. See Thomas Armitage, *A History of the Baptist*, I.268-368, and *Ethics*, s.v. "Anabatism."

5. *Morgan Edwards*, 160-188. Hearing of Backus' design to write a Baptist history, Edwards sent a great amount of his collected material to him. Though Edwards requested its return, it never was. All major Baptist historians after Edwards, knowingly or unknowingly, used his material, *ibid*, 157. Benedict at times and without credit quoted Edwards word for word, *ibid*., 170. "...William Sprague, William Cathcart, Thomas Armitage and Ruben Guild... held Edwards in high esteem as a person to be praised for his contribution to Baptist historiography." *Ibid.*, 208.

In 1788, Edwards began to lecture throughout the Middle Colonies:

> The lectures were probably based upon the subjects contained in two books published in 1788, Res Sacrae: An Academical Exercise Composed in Latin in the Year 1742; and Now Translated into English and Two Academical Exercises on the Subjects Bearing on the following Titles; Millennium and Last-Novelties.[7]

Edwards' millennial ideas were based upon taking Scriptures literally, except when such understanding leads to contradiction or absurdity. In doing so, he ignored the warnings of past godly men. John Trapp (1601-1669) had warned of the error of taking things too literally:

> The Jews hold that this whole prophecy [Ez. 38-39, *ed.*] shall be fulfilled at the coming of their long-looked-for Messiah, and whilst they take all things therein according to the letter, they run into many very great errors.[8]

---

6. *The Academical Exercises* was "written to fulfill requirements at Bristol Academy between 1742 and 1744." *Morgan Edwards*, 68, note 199. Thus he was only 20-22 years old when he offered his *Millennium, Last-Novelties*. Edwards offered nothing new; from about the eleventh century, Roman Jesuits had offered the millennial system to counter Protestant attacks against the papal system. See "Rome's gain," p. 41. To make his system work, Edwards added some words to his proof text, "Rev. xx. 4, 5": "The saints shall reign with Christ [on earth] a thousand years." Then he used his changed proof text to say that a "*Literal millennarianism* alone will do justice to these texts...", *e.g.*, "Dan. vii. 18, 27". Also during this time, the saints must reign throughout the world (even over angels), for Christ will be in Jerusalem. *Novelties*, 11. Edwards placed "the abomination mentioned by Daniel" as a prelude to Christ's reign yet to come. He said that Elias' coming is to restore the *Mosaic economy*, a necessity for a literal fulfillment of Ezekiel 43, 44 (the temple). He said that St. John [author of the Gospels and the Revelation, *ed.*] "(like Elias) was caught up to paradise," in order to literally fulfill Jn. 21:22, Mat. 16:28. *Novelties*, 15-18. Edward's old English spelling is changed for ease of reading. "Another event previous to the Millennium will be the appearing of the son of man [sic] in the clouds, coming to raise the dead saints and change the living, and to catch them up to himself, and then withdrawing with them..." *Ibid*, 21. In other words, a *rapture*— "Will not they spring up to meet him in the air?" *Ibid*, 53.

7. *Ibid.*, 51. Apparently, Edwards' *Novelties* remained "dormant" until published in America. His influence in Europe was probably minimal, though he did some fund raising there to start Brown University.

Edwards also exalted a restored Jewish nation over the Blood-Bought Church, a view that was not new. Already *in the air*, he may have simply offered the old Jewish hope. Many years before Edwards, Trapp said concerning Isaiah 11:11, *shall set his hand again a second time*:

> Not to bring them back to the promised land, to Palestina, as once he did out of Egypt; that is but a rabbinical dream, not unlike that other—viz., that all Jews, in what country soever they are buried, do travel through certain underground passages till they come to their own country of Jewry...[9]

Though God destroyed the nation with the Roman army, the "rabbinical dream" of a restored, exalted Jewish nation to rule the world again as it did under David and Solomon never died — through it alone could God complete his work on earth. Apparently, the "Jewish" offer was made many times to the Protestant church before the *Ben-Ezra* offer was accepted. Whenever Trapp is close enough, he warns the church against accepting that old Jewish dream. (See Historic Chiliasm, p. 439.)

Conclusion

Edwards offered his *Millennium and Last-Novelties* (1742, 1788) before *Ben-Ezra* was released in Spanish (1790). It seems, however, that though Edwards lectured extensively throughout the Middle Colonies on the *Millennium and Last-Novelties* several years before *Ben-Ezra* was published in Europe, his novel millennial ideas did not find the fertile ground for the deep roots they found later with Darby. There may be a good reason for the disparity, *viz*. the dates:

---

8. Trapp, on Ezekiel 38:3. "At that time [when the twelve Hebrew tribes were chosen by God, *ed.*] the Jews bore both names [the People of God and the People of Israel, *ed.*]; now they bear neither. They who have long since put aside the worship of God cannot be called the People of God..." *The Governance of God*, III. 91.

9. Trapp, on Ezekiel Isaiah 11:11. Trapp saw "those last enemies of the Church" as "the Turks [Muslims, *ed.*] and Popelings" joining forces "to root out the true religion." Trapp on Ezekiel 38:2. The Muslims are even now gaining world dominance.

(1) Edwards publicly offered his *Millennium and Last-Novelties* in America, not in Europe, in the wake of a successful American War for Independence (and before the French Revolution) — the public mood, undoubtedly, was victorious; (2) Irving successfully offered the *novelties* (*Ben-Ezra*) in Europe in the wake of the devastating French Revolution (1789-1799) and Napoleonic Wars (1803-1815) — the public mood, undoubtedly, was man's hopeless corruption; (3) Darby successfully offered the *novelties* in America during and after the devastating War Between the States (1861-1865) — the public mood, undoubtedly, was man's hopeless corruption.

Though Edwards greatly influenced the colonial era Baptist Church, the time was not right for the American church at large to accept the millennial gospel. Many years later, the War Between the States would prepare America for that hopeless gospel which says man's only answer for his corruption is the Lord's intervention with a sword.

Chapter 3

The Brethren

This writer found no evidence that Morgan Edwards' *Novelties* had an influence on either European or American Christian culture. But Lacunza's influence is easily traced to the Plymouth Brethren *Scofield Reference Bible*, through which it became orthodoxy. Hence, we will follow the system as it emanated from *Ben-Ezra*. Lacunza's system appears to be basically what was presented by Edward Irving (1792-1834; see "Edward Irving," p. 29). However, Lacunza took two large volumes to develop the basic points Edwards presented in his short college *Academical Exercises*. Irving summed up Lacunza's massive work into his 200 page introduction.

Lacunza's developed system was introduced to the European Protestant English world by a Presbyterian pastor, Edward Irving. It was popularized by a former Anglican, John Nelson Darby. It was systematized by Cyrus Ingerson Scofield (1843- 1921). Thus from one man, Lacunza, the system became the standard for Christian thought for many generations. Because the Brethren were the ones to convert Christianity to the millennial system, we will primarily follow the system's journey through them to the far reaches of the world.

The influence of the Plymouth Brethren (who adapted the system, c. 1830) upon Christianity after the late 1800s is readily apparent as one reads later Baptist creeds, confessions and messages. The Presbyterians suffered the same death blow from the system as did the Baptists.[10]

The Irvingites, Darbyites, Brethren and Scofieldites have the same basic system of faith, *viz.,* dispensational millennialism — Irving's tongues and faith healing excepted. (Dispensationalism: a philosophy that divides history into a number of distinct eras in each of which the mode of God's operations, if not nature's, is unique. C.I. Scofield used seven.) While many good, sincere people claim to be Christians of various stripes (Baptist, Presbyterian, Pentecostal, &c.), in reality, they cling tenaciously to a common system having deep roots in *Ben-Ezra.*

Though the view had been offered several times before, the successful offering was a 1790 Spanish manuscript published by Rome in 1812. In 1827, it was translated and published in English by Edward Irving. To Lacunza's basic system, Irving added a "pre-trib rapture," an idea he may have obtained from a Scottish lass, Margaret Macdonald. However, it was under Darby's name (Darbyism) and skilful guidance that the system spread over the whole earth. It became the foundation for Plymouth Brethrenism. In the early 1900s, it was codified by Scofield. Irving's system was

---

10. Sandeen traces the "conversion" of the both the Baptists and Presbyterians from orthodox, world-changing Christianity to the modern hopeless, useless state typified by far too many Baptist and Presbyterian pastors, teachers and schools, *Roots,* chaps. 6 & 7. So does Marsden, *Fundamentalism.*

adapted by various denominations with only minor differences among them.

The Darbyite/Brethren ranks contained talented writers who were allowed to establish a new *orthodox* Christian theology in almost every area of life and thought.

Looking at the teachings spread world-wide by men later known as the Plymouth Brethren, a few points will be obvious: First, the modern day infiltration of the beliefs of this small group of men into almost every Christian denomination, and second, the striking contrast between what they taught and what was typical, orthodox Biblical teaching of their day, *viz.,* one general resurrection before which the gospel of Christ would conquer the nations for the Kingdom of God. We must say, however, that the smell of the *Death of the Church Victorious* was already in the air, making people extremely receptive to the withdrawal offered by Irving's system. No doubt the men involved did not consciously set about to turn society over to anti-Christian forces, but the implications of their ideas did just that. As we will see, they became passive and indifferent to surrounding evils despite the fact that Christians are commanded to be "light" and "salt" in the world around them. In fact, Christ sends his followers into the world with the prayer that they be kept from imbibing the world's evil life-style. (Jn. ch. 17.)

The developed ideas of these few men, spread by consistent hard work, were readily accepted by the vast majority of Christianity.

Chapter 4

The Mystics

The modern millennial system was founded in what could be called, "Christian Mysticism." Mysticism is a modern term that originally meant the direct, secret and incommunicable knowledge of God received in contemplation — as opposed to "natural

Theology" (the knowledge of God obtained through creatures), and "dogmatic Theology" (the knowledge of God as revealed in his word). Mysticism, in a "Christian" sense of the word, is the belief that one can have direct knowledge of God, spiritual truth, through subjective experience, *e.g.*, intuition or insight.

Christianity absorbed from Judaism the belief in mystical theology and its connected phenomena, where God dealt with his Old Testament prophets through angelic meditation, visions, dreams, trances, revelations and extraordinary gifts of the Holy Spirit. We can say that mysticism is a belief that God deals with man through means other than through his Spirit acting in accord with his revealed word. Montanus (155 A.D. See "Montanism," p. 450) was one of the earliest to claim mystic ability under the name of Christian.[11]

Mysticism in the Christian religion finds its primary roots in a personal, inward experience, and thus is closely connected with Pietism.[12] Mysticism exalts the inward, living, invisible Word of God above the outward, written word of God, the Scriptures:

> The greatest of all early Protestant mystics was Jacob Boehme (born a few miles from Gorlitz in Sielsia, 1575, died 1624)......The living and permanent core of Boehme's message, however, sprang out of his own deep experience and his own vivid apprehension of the meaning of Christianity as a way of life. In the year 1600, as in 'a flash of lightning,' he felt that 'the gate of his soul was opened' and that he saw and knew what no books could teach. Under much persecution and struggle and with frequent successive 'openings,' he slowly matured his message and gave it in a long series of books, hard to comprehend but, nevertheless, containing much real insight.[13]

---

11. *Ethics*, s.v. "Mysticism."
12. Pietism emphasizes personal devotion and personal feelings over sound doctrine. See "Pietism," p. 459.
13. A good example of mysticism is Scofield's notes for Galatian 3:24, p. 1245 where he refers to feelings rather than the revealed Law-Word of God. See *Biblical and Theological Studies*, chapter XVI, "Mysticism and Christianity." Benjamin Warfield (1851- 1921).

Studying the early millennial material (1830-1880), one will find that there is more to millennial mysticism than basing theories on individual intuition or insight. Many times, mystical describes the early premillenarians' attitude towards a world in turmoil. Therefore, the early men who developed a vast portion of modern Christian millennial thought were mystics; they taught both "other-worldliness" as one waits for a rapture and millennial reign of Christ to deal with problems, and they taught according to their feelings, intuitions and insights, which were exalted over Scripture.[14]

One must not overlook the fact that the Holy Spirit was promised to guide Christians into all truth, John 16:13, &c. And without the continual inspiration, or guidance, through the indewlling Spirit in accord with the written word of God, the Christian is left with a religion that is no better than that of the Pharisees of old. But that is not the subject of this present study.[15]

Accordingly, mystical many times means "heavenly-minded" or "other-worldliness" — detached from and unconcerned about the surrounding events of this life, particularly unpleasant events, *e.g.*, the French Revolution caused Christians to want to be emotionally unattached from this world of sin, mystical.[16]

---

14. "Pseudo-mystics" might be a better term, for a "mystic" claims direct apprehension of God, bypassing all intermediaries, *i.e.*, Scripture. Accordingly, feelings must be examined in the light of God's word, as must be the fruits of the actions taken based upon the feelings. Obviously, if the fruit is spoiled when compared to God's word, the feelings are not from God. See *"Premillennialism,"* p. 428.

15. For an excellent study on the Holy Spirit's proper place in the life of the Believer, see *The Power of the Spirit*, by William Law (1686-1761).

16. "'Separation,' to many of them [the early founders of millennialism, the Brethren, *ed.*] often meant standing aloof, in some spiritual quarantine, from the dirt and squalor of the world; there were few who saw it as meaning engagement, if God so called a man, in that world's affairs, but with a mind and motives separated a world apart from those which characterized its victims." Coad, *History*, 266.

Overview 15

Chapter 5

The French Revolution

The system absorbed and developed by the Darbyists would not have been destructive to Christianity if it had remained obscure, but obscurity was not to be the case.[17] Unlike Morgan Edwards' time, the early 1800s saw Europe prepared for a gospel of defeat, so the theology that found its development in the mystical insight of a few men had very wide appeal, attracting men of great stature and wealth.

As are all movements, the millennial movement was a *child of its time*. Understanding a little of what Europe was like in 1800, one can see why people were ready for the millennial doctrine of escape. The European community had been prepared for "Christian Mysticism" by the French Revolution and the Napoleonic Wars, events that took place just a few years previously.[18] The Revolution and wars "proved" that human nature was corrupt beyond hope, even beyond reaching by the Spirit of God. Therefore, the only option left to the faithless, *i.e.*, those who do not believe God's Spirit of Grace can conquer the world for Christ, was for the Lord to subdue mankind with his physical, literal, supernatural, cataclysmic intervention with a literal "rod of iron":

---

17. Alexander Reese uses the term "Darbyist" to describe those who follow Darby's system, as one would use the term "Calvinists," *Advent,* 310. Scofield was a "Darbyist."

18. "The French Revolution (1789-99) violently transformed France from a monarchical state with a rigid social hierarchy into a modern nation in which the social structure was loosened and power passed increasingly to the middle classes." "The Napoleonic Wars were those waged between France under NAPOLEON I and various combinations of European nations from 1803 to 1815. They were a direct continuation of the FRENCH REVOLUTIONARY WARS (1792-1802). The object of the Allies was to curtail French expansion, but only with overwhelming numbers did they finally defeat Napoleon in 1814-15." *Multimedia Encyclopedia,* ver 1.

The apparently complete and precise fulfillment of biblical prophecies during the French Revolution had a direct impact upon biblical interpretation generally. It became a hallmark of the millenarian party that literal rather than figurative or spiritualized fulfillments should be sought for every biblical prophecy. When "kingdoms" were prophesied, for example, literal, historical events involving flesh-and-blood kings ought to be expected rather than the triumph of one or another virtue. Millenarians became convinced that allegorical and spiritualized interpretations of prophecy were a manifestation of unbelief and a denigration of the authority of Scripture.[19]

Many men in those days believed that the prophetic sections of the Bible were intended to provide a divine summary of future human history, from which it would be possible for the enlightened of later ages to draw firm information on the course of current historical events. It was not a new idea. Study of the prophetic Scriptures had in earlier centuries fascinated minds as diverse and gifted as those of the explorer Columbus, of Napier the mathematician, and the great Sir Isaac Newton. Such studies had reached a point of great excitement in the years following the French Revolution, largely because, about a century before, several expositors had made prophecies on the basis of Biblical statements, which were taken to have foretold the French Revolution and its aftermath. Earnest British preachers and teachers of many denominations were convinced that the world they knew was shortly to see dramatic and direct divine intervention, and several went so far as to date these happenings for the middle decades of the nineteenth century. Alongside such wild expectations, new ideas on the interpretation of the Biblical prophecies were abroad.[20]

...[D]ispensationalists insisted that the only proper way to interpret Scripture was in "the literal sense," unless the text or the context absolutely demanded otherwise. All dispensational interpreters agreed on this. Prophecies must mean exactly what they said ("Israel" must mean the Jews, never the church). Prophetic numbers referred to exact periods of time. Predictions would come true as real events, although the Bible might use images to describe them— as "The Beast" of Revelation 19 for the earth's last and worst political tyrant.[21]

---

19. *Roots*, 13.

20. *Code, History*, 109. Not only the French Revolution, but also the Napoleonic Wars provided ideal conditions for the intense study of unfulfilled prophecy, Neatby, *History*, 38. Edwards' *Novelties* was offered before the Revolution.

The French Revolution was more than simply a revolution against a constitutional monarchy. It was open warfare against Christian culture, and could be defined as the modern revolution and triumph of humanism and humanistic law over Christianity and Christian law. Its war against Christianity succeeded, generally destroying the faith that had prevailed to that time — faith that God's Spirit could subdue kings and kingdoms to Christ from the inside out. In Europe, it expunged any hope of spiritual victory from the general Christian population.

A major instigator in the Revolution was Robespierre. After his death, "The war went on with its revolutionary rhetoric; its talk about Liberty and Equality; its fight against the Christian religion; its worship of efficiency no matter what the human cost."

Though the French church was Roman, the Revolution was against EVERY vestige of Christianity. Taking place only a few short years before Irving and the early millenarians appeared in history, it prepared Europe's *secular and religious* societies to readily and gladly imbibe a hopeless and defeated gospel, Lacunza's *system*.

Many important concepts developed in the Revolution, and those concepts influenced every corner of European society as they spread "across the face of European culture." The Revolution provided a ready audience for the newly developing millennial views. The Revolution was encouraged by a liberal church which itself fell victim to the Revolution.

In the Revolution, Louis the Sixteenth was guillotined, January, 1793, and buried without a funeral. His Queen, Marie Antoinette, was guillotined in October, 1793, and uncounted tens of thousands of innocent people perished in the name of "the Rights of Man."

The religion of Patriotism replaced the church and Christianity: Patriots were seen as the social changing force rather than preachers proclaiming the Biblical, Christian Gospel of Christ; the "Republic,"

---

21. *Fundamentalism*, 61.

France, became the new god, so, accordingly, sin and blasphemy were defined as any move against the State; the mark of the true Patriot was swearing allegiance to the new god, the "Republic's" Constitution; Left, Right and Center became political terms; "purge" changed from a medical to a political term; poverty was considered proof of one's sincerity and virtue, and thus "lack of success was not due to inability but to injustice"; conspirators were the source of all the nation's ills, so vague charges of secret conspiracies at work were used to unite the people to follow those making the charges.

The "Rights of Man" were exalted above everything, and multitudes of innocent people died in the name of "the People"; equality was equated with liberty; "spontaneous," nation-wide demonstrations sprung forth at key times in key places to further the Revolution's goals, *viz.,* to destroy Christianity; propaganda was used to change social ideas, *i.e.,* words were seen as weapons of warfare, so truth was of no concern; innumerable pamphlets and journalists mysteriously appeared, speaking in a united voice to mold public opinion, and truth was unknown from fiction; the mandatory tithe was outlawed; the duty of the State was to support the poor at the expense of the rich; every vestige of Christianity was abolished, churches destroyed, priests killed, the metric system imposed and the calendar changed.

The Revolution was seen as the means to bring the people to Paradise. The Revolution had to be spread world-wide for world-wide Paradise to arrive ("...the rest of the world would soon topple its monarchs and nobility, defrock its religious leaders, and create a new world society."); the Government was only interested in controlling "Political crime", and finally, for our mention here, children over five were considered state property. "'What we learn from the study of the Great Revolution is that it was the source of all the present communists', anarchists', and socialists' conceptions,' said Prince Peter Kropotkin in *The Great French Revolution* (New York: Putnam's Sons, 1909)"[22]

The Revolution also introduced "Liberalism:"

This was the spirit which had burst out of the French Revolution, but was at work in 1833 in the universities of Germany, unknown to most Englishmen... In England in 1833 Liberalism was the view that education, civilization, and reason would cure the evils and sorrows of mankind. Religion, in this view, was apt to be regarded as 'the rubbish of superstition.' By Liberalism the followers of the Oxford Movement meant 'the tendencies of modern thought to destroy the basis of revealed religion, and ultimately of all that can be called religion at all.'[23]

Multitudes fled the horrible situation in France, taking with them the news and influence of the Revolution. Thus European society and the early promoters of Lacunza's millennial *system* were greatly influenced by what had just happened. The early 1800s were heavy with the concepts of the Revolution, and the Revolution and Napoleonic Wars developed ideal conditions for militant, world-changing Biblical Christianity to be replaced by powerless, mystical Christianity, conditions that did not exist in Edwards' time. Men came upon the scene who would make that destructive change. How they felt, what they believed, the way they reacted to surrounding events and the public's general attitude at the time of their arrival must all be considered in the light of the times. They, as are men of all ages, were *children of their time.*

Edwards' 1788 *Novelties* book and lectures apparently had little lasting influence on America's Christian Culture. However, the War Between the States prepared the way for Lacunza's hopeless, defeated gospel to be readily accepted in America through immigration and through Darby's visits.[24]

---

22. See *Robespierre*, 76, 92, 107-110, 114, 117, 124, 125, 131, 135, 140, 147, 148, 161, 163, 167, 168, 186, 188, 194, 200, 213, 215, 216, 223, 224, 227, 233, 258.

23. *Encyclopaedia*, ix. 586.

24. The events from the early 1800s leading up to the *War Between the States* closely paralleled the events in Europe — including militancy against an educated clergy and the conversion of America from Calvinism, in which the "revivalist" Charles Finney (1792-1875) played a great part, and America's conversion from traditional post-millennialism [see "Postmillennialism," p. 429], exemplified by the Reverend William Miller (1782-1849). See *Secret,* 78, &c.

Chapter 6

Who's Who

The list of men involved in developing and spreading the new millennialism reads like a "Who's Who in Christian History From the Early 1800s." Whereas some did not stay with the original founders or even with the Brethren, they retained the basic Brethren millennial *system*. Many of the men are well known to all Christians, and some are totally unknown to most Christians. Though relatively little known, the Brethren have cast an exceedingly long shadow through their writings. The church is just now starting to come out of their shadow, but not by choice. The state is forcing the church to abandon its Monastic position that all but extinguished the Christian light. (See "Monasticism," p. 455.)

The early men were reacting against organized religion of their day, primarily the Anglican and Romanist. However, they included other established groups in their reaction — Baptist, Presbyterian, Methodist, &c. Most of the time, the opinions they developed were their personal beliefs apart from the study of the Scriptures. In other words, they *felt this is the way it should be*, then Scriptural support was found for what they already had concluded. Thus the vast majority of the Brethren millennial opinions originated in a subjective fashion rather than from consistent, systematic Bible study.

As we identify the major men in the Brethren (and Keswick - see "Keswick," p. 314.) movement, we are not suggesting that they were anything but godly men with great insight into particular areas, having a tremendous love for souls. We do need to keep in mind, nonetheless, that their main emphasis was — either intentionally or unintentionally — to remove Christianity from society. Though greatly revered throughout Christianity, the following men were not Baptist, Presbyterian, &c.; they were Irvingite/Darbyite/Plymouth Brethren. Among the better known persons involved either in the original doctrinal development of the movement, drawn into it as it grew, or directly influenced by those directly involved, were:[25] *J.N. Darby; *A.N. Groves; *Edward Cronin; Henry Drummond; Watchman Nee; *George Müller; [26] Hudson Taylor — China Inland Missions; C.H. MacKintosh; [27]G.V. Wigram — author of the *New Englishman's Greek* and *Hebrew Concordances*; W.E. Vine — *Vine's Expository Dictionary*; S.P. Tregelles — author of *Tregells on Daniel*, &c.; J.G. McVicker;[28] William Kelly;[29] W.F. Grant; [30] "the mystical Andrew Jukes"; [31] Henry Moorhouse — "The man who moved the man [Moody, *ed.*], who moved millions...;"[32] P.F. Hall; Charles Stanly — author of the C.S. Tracts; G.H. Lang; R.C. Chapman; *B.W. Newton; *F.W. Newman; J.H. Newman; *Edward Irving; [33] and Lady Powerscourt.

---

25. These are not listed in the order of involvement, * denotes the original formulators, and this is not a complete list. Others of importance will be added as we proceed in the text, and each of the listed will be developed. The basic opinions coloring all these men's theories were developed in the Irvingite movement. Irving was a man the Brethren denied acquaintance with.

26. Coad, *History,* 245. Müller was known for his orphan work and his Scriptural Knowledge Institution. Though Müller separated from the extreme Darbyite theories, his SKI was a very great influence in spreading the newly developed dispensational millennial *system* of militancy against the world's conversion to Christ. On the break between Darby and Müller, see *Advent,* 318-320.

27. (1820-1896) "Mr. Mackintosh had been a school master, but he subsequently devoted himself exclusively to the ministry. He had a very marked popular gift, both as a speaker and a writer, and became by means of his notes on the Pentateuch, the principal interpreter between Darbyism and the church at large. Unfortunately, he was an interpreter and nothing more. His thought was loose and unsystematic. He was profoundly unoriginal, and carried no compensating weight of authority." Neatby, *History,* 262. CHM was thus not trained in theology. He popularized Darby's dispensational theories, and his writings had a great influence upon D.L. Moody, *Roots,* 173. Quoting CHM, Reese gives an insight into CHM's thinking: "The great object of the enemy is to drag down the Church of God to an earthly level — to set Christians entirely astray as to their divinely appointed hope — to lead them to confound things which God has made to differ, to occupy them with earthly things...," *Advent,* 20. Thus CHM, parroting Darby, saw the church as having no earthly use. Hastings tells us that CHM "wrote *Notes on the Pentateuch,* which has had a wide circulation, and has greatly popularized Darby's views." *Ethics,* s.v. "Brethren (Plymouth)."

28. Coad, *History,* 171.

Moreover, Inter-Varsity Fellowship and Sudan Interior Mission came out of the Plymouth Brethren movement.[34]

Though not among the *founding fathers* of the Brethren who developed its doctrines, the following are among those who were extremely important in spreading Brethrenism: H.A. Ironside; Donald Grey Barnhouse; D.L. Moody;[35] R.A. Torrey; J.W. Chapman;[36] Sir Robert Anderson;[37] W.A. "Billy" Sunday;[38] E.M. Bounds and Andrew Murray (both Keswick teachers); and, lastly

---

29. At age twenty-four, he identified himself wholeheartedly with the body of doctrine held by J. N. Darby, with whom he worked for many years. Undoubtedly he was one of the best scholars in the Darbyite movement. *Who*, s.v. "Kelly, William." Around 1878, Mr. Kelly broke with Darby over a marriage issue of really no importance. Kelly took a very strict stand. As matters over the issue developed, Darby found it expedient to "follow" the other side if he would still lead. Kelly was the major leader of the Exclusive Brethren after Darby's death in 1882. Neatby, *History*, chap. 14. Kelly, with Darby's approval, edited Darby's writings to credit him with many ideas that were not his.

30. "Mr. F. W. Grant of Plainfield, New Jersey, [was, *ed.*] probably the most accomplished Theologian amongst the Brethren of the American continent." Mr. Grant was excommunicated for heresy, Jan. 4, 1885. He taught: (1) "the O.T. [Old Testament] Saints were 'in the Son,' and had 'eternal life in Him,' in virtue of being born again;" (2) "that when thus born we are at that moment forgiven, justified, no longer in the flesh, but in Christ, and dead to sin and the law;" (3) "that this new birth gives us the full position of sons of God, and being sons we are sealed with the Holy Ghost, faith in Christ's work not being necessary to 'sealing;'" (4) "that Romans vii. is the experience of one who is justified in Christ, sealed, seeking to abide in Christ, and to be fruitful and holy," & (5) "that souls may have peace and not know it, be justified and not know it, have the Holy Ghost and be in bondage." Neatby, *History*, 314, 315.

31. Coad, *History*, 79. He identified with Darby and the Brethren around 1842.

32. (1840-1880) *Who*, s.v. "Moorhouse, Henry (Harry)." *Advent*, 310.

33. A Presbyterian minister who founded the Irvingites, or the modern Pentecostal movement, including the Catholic Apostolic Church, Coad, *History*, 63, 109. We have included him here though elsewhere we show that he was not a Brethren: He introduced what the Brethren claimed as their own.

34. *Roots*, 245.

35. Coad, *History*, 189; *Hope*, 198. Moody's "conversion" to Brethrenism is quite well documented: He "converted" under the influence of Brethren evangelist, Henry Moorhouse, *Advent*, 310. Moorhouse/Moorehouse, both spellings are used: *Life* uses Moorehouse, *Who* & Coad, *History*, use Moorhouse. Henry Moorehouse is also referred to as Harry. We will use Moorehouse unless in quotes.

36. A major leader in the Millenarian movement, *Roots*, 239.

and most importantly, C.I. Scofield, whose Bible notes have done more to spread Irvingism/Darbyism than anyone since Müller's SKI:

> Among the many who absorbed Darby's teaching was Henry Moorhouse, an evangelist among the Brethren, who, in turn, influenced D.L. Moody. Before the end of the nineteenth century Moody was probably the most esteemed evangelical figure on both sides of the Atlantic, and the Bible College named for him at Chicago became a seminary of ardent premillennial belief. The impact of Darby on another American, C.I. Scofield, was still more momentous, for Scofield's notes made his master's teaching on prophecy an integral part of the Reference Bible first published in 1909 and thereafter wedded to Scofield's name. Within fifty years, approximately three million copies of the *Scofield Reference Bible* were printed in America, a proportionate number were issued by Oxford University Press in Britain, and the volume had vast influence in making Darby's prophetical beliefs the norm for evangelicals in the English-Speaking world.[39]

However, the new millennialism did not rise without opposition. There were sound Bible scholars who expressed grave concern over the doctrines being developed and spread by the newly emerging dispensational millennial movement. Among those who saw the danger and spoke out against the *system* were: R.L. Dabney of Virginia; Rev. Thomas Croskery of Londonberry; Rev. William Reid, D.D.;[40] C.B. Bass; Patrick Fairbairn; B.B. Warfield; George Smeaton; C.H. Spurgeon;[41] and "the well-known Baptist theologian," Dr. A.H. Strong.[42] In fact, "It became the custom in the more respectable Calvinist works of erudition of this period to take the old sniper's long-shot at the Brethren." The theological system

---

37. (1841-1918) Coad, *History*, 224. He was trained at Trinity College, Dublin, and entered the legal profession in Ireland, 1863. Among many other things, he was a frequent speaker at Mildmay Conferences. *Who*, s.v. "Anderson, Sir. Robert."

38. J.W. Chapman's assistant, *"Billy" Sunday*, 45.

39. *Hope,* 198. Darby "and his writings fired Henry Moorhouse, who fired D. L. Moody, one of the three or four religious geniuses of America, and Moody moved the world." *Advent,* 130. See *"Premillennialism,"* p. 428.

40. See Strong's quote of Reid.

that was developing in the early days was seen as "a menace to the Orthodox."[43]

The warning against the *system* being developed within the Brethren movement not only came from many Calvinists of the day, but from within their own ranks: J.G. M'Vicker said, "Of the many evil spirits which have gone out in these last days, the proud and lying spirit which has seduced the poor Darbyites is one of the most dangerous."[44]

The names of C.H. Spurgeon, Patrick Fairbairn, B.B. Warfield and R.L. Dabney stand out. As Spurgeon, Fairbairn and Warfield presented the truth of God's word, they were not overly harsh in their stand against the new millennialism. As we know, their warnings went unheeded.

In the days of restrictive and oppressive religion in the established church, the freedom offered by the Brethren movement attracted young, talented and energetic men. They longed for the individual freedom to be all they felt God would have them to be, but the very freedom which drew them together was destroyed by Darby by 1850.

The basis of fellowship in the early days of the Plymouth Brethren movement was "unity in Christ." It was not doctrine that initially attracted followers, for the Brethren took no doctrinal stand as such. Concerning doctrine, Darby said in an 1866 letter, "I should deplore as ruinous, slipping into the place of followers of a system of doctrine." An 1880 letter said, "Truths are sometimes simpler,

---

41. Coad, *History,* 212, 264. Spurgeon said, "'Ye men of Plymouth, why stand ye here gazing up into heaven —' The fact that Jesus Christ is to come is not a reason for star- gazing, but for working in the power of the Holy Ghost. Be not so taken up with speculations as to prefer a Bible reading over a dark passage in the Revelation to teaching in a ragged-school or discoursing to the poor concerning Jesus. We must have done with day-dreams, and get to work…" *Lectures,* 36. See also Spurgeon's *Treasury of David,* Ps. 89:9, &c.

42. In 1907, Dr. A. H. Strong called Brethren doctrine unscriptural and heretical, invoking a strong reaction from Ironside after Strong was dead, *Sketch,* 205.

43. Coad, *History,* 228, 229.

44. *Ibid.,* 214.

when we take them simpler and do not make a system." Of course, he was not referring to his own system, for he never forgot to compliment those who "arrived" at seeing things his way. He went on in his 1880 letter to decry those who left his system of doctrine.[45]

The common trait of the original men who formulated basic "Scofield" doctrine was their overwhelming personalities. Most of the time, their personalities completely over-shadowed their theology. Therefore, though newcomers to the movement were not forced to believe a particular system of opinion, the strength of character of its leading men caused the followers to 'convert' to their understanding of Scripture. Thus as young, energetic, intelligent, freedom loving men were drawn into the movement, they were also drawn into Darby's offered dispensationalism.[46]

The strength of the "dangerous" Darbyite movement lay in the British Isles where the presence of a large number of Calvinistic Baptist Churches made Calvinism very strong. As a rule, the strong Calvinistic churches — especially the Baptist — stood against the developing millennial system, though most of the founders of the "sect" were Calvinists. Some Darbyists even retained Calvinism.[47]

But as the strong Calvinistic pastors who stood against the new system passed from the scene, it engulfed not only Baptist theology, but general church theology. It is not hard, consequently, to understand why confessions of faith — especially Baptist — written after 1875 or so, reflect so much of the millennial faith. In fact, A.C. Dixon, who assumed Spurgeon's pulpit, embraced what Spurgeon had stood firmly against: Monasticism and other-worldliness. As a result, the vast majority of Christian material developed after the rise of Darbyism — mid 1800s — is essentially Darbyite material.

Not only did the system attract men of tremendous thinking, oratory and persuasive abilities, but it also attracted wealthy people willing to promote the new millennial faith by financing extensive

---

45. *Letters,* I.455, III.79.
46. Coad, *History*, 246.
47. *Ibid.,* 228, 229.

Bible conferences and publishing houses. Thus the influence of one man, Irving, on a very small group of men was and is far greater than would appear possible.

Though still in the death-grip of Monasticism, we are seeing a renewed spirit of involvement, a willingness to take godly precepts into areas previously *off limits* to God. Christians are becoming involved in social areas as Christians, if for no other reason than *self-defense, e.g.*, the Home School movement.

Part II

In the Beginning

Chapter 7

Death Introduced

The enemy may have been stabbed at the heart; yet will he get up, and renew the fight. Thou must walk — yea — sleep — in thine armour. It must be worn, not laid up. There is "no discharge from this war," till the body of sin and death is laid in the grave. Meanwhile victory is declared, before the conflict begins. Let every day then be a day of triumph. The promises are to present victory. With such stirring, stimulating hopes, thou shalt surely have rule, if thou wilt but dare to have it. And if thou hast not courage enough to be a Christian, thou must be a slave for life to the hardest of taskmasters. This bloodless victory, so contrary to the turmoil of war (Isa. ix. 5), is the crown of Christian grace. (Rom. xii. 19.) No other grace of the gospel can be exercised without its influence. Yet the daily conquest anticipates the final victory, the spoils of which will be reaped throughout eternity.[1]

"Christ the Victorious" was being proclaimed from Christian pulpits in the early 1800s; the saints were being assured of their election, their adoption and their fellowship in their victorious Redeemer. They were being prepared by Christian preachers to follow the Captain of the Lord's Host into the daily battles of life, confident they would come out victorious for their Captain.

The message of "Christ the Victorious" during this present *gospel dispensation* greatly distressed a certain Scottish Presbyterian minister:

> The ministers of the gospel, as captains of the Lord's host, do not present unto the people or seek to keep continually before them the terrors of Satan, the weakness of the flesh, the powerfulness of the

---

1. *Proverbs,* 251, 252.

world; but keep before them Christ the victorious, the Spirit the quickener, the Father Almighty, their election unto salvation, their adoption unto the communion of the blessed trinity, their fellowship with all the saints who have endured and overcome.[2]

Now, forasmuch as the church, labouring under her present dimness concerning the future advent of Christ and his glorious kingdom, hath been much taken up with the former advent, and led greatly to exaggerate the importance of the out-pouring of the Spirit at Pentecost, that first act of the priestly office of Christ, under which we now live; it is hardly to be expected that much should be found needing here to be reformed by the views which we now offer [in *Ben-Ezra, ed.*]. But as no important error in the system can long exist without being everywhere felt, I shall be able to show, in respect to the giving of the Holy Spirit, some very important changes which the scripture [sic] view of that subject hath undergone, through hiding of the light of the glory of his second advent and kingdom.[3]

There is universal belief in the church, that an age, a very long age of blessedness, of at least a thousand years duration, is to run, before the end of the world, and consequently before the coming of Christ. And who will speak of the uncertainty or the nearness of the Lord's coming, to men, who thus believe?...[4]

Edward Irving found it dreadful that Christians were looking for "Christ the Victorious" in history this side of the second advent. He identified such victorious thinking as a "vague notion which Satan hath substituted in its stead."[5] In other words, "Christ the

---

2. *Ben-Ezra*, I.lviii. Showing the hold Lacunza, the author of *Ben-Ezra*, had over Irving, Irving, in his *Preliminary Discourse,* complained that the church was entirely occupied with the effects of the first coming of Messiah, and thus ignoring the glories of the second advent and the Jewish nation, *ibid.,* 26. Irving sought to change the church's emphasis from the victories of the first advent to the "millennial blessedness" of the second advent.

3. *Ibid.*, ciii.

4. *Ibid.,* li. Darby considered the prevailing thought of his day a great error, *viz.,* that the gospel would convert the world, *Writings,* II.185, c. 1852. He condemned those who desired to convert the world to Christ, *Letters,* I.257, 1858. He justified his accusation of that *great error* — faith the world would be converted — by saying that Daniel's stone had not yet struck the image, and would not until the millennial reign of Christ, which is clearly the "Ben-Ezra system."

Victorious" doctrine was Satan inspired — Satan substituted it for the truth of the millennial *faith*, which Irving will go on to define.

Chapter 8
Edward Irving

Irving's background was in the Presbyterian Church of Scotland. At thirteen, he went to Edinburgh University, graduating in 1809, where he did "not appear to have been a remarkably distinguished student..." He obtained "a license to preach in June 1815..." In 1819, he became an assistant to Dr. Chalmers at St. John's, Glasgow. After two successful years of labor under Dr. Chalmers, feeling entirely eclipsed by Chalmers and "with increased confidence in his own powers to stimulate the ambition which had always been a leading trait in his character," he answered a call to pastor a little chapel in Hatton Garden, London, the Caledonian Presbyterian Church (of Scotland), 1822. He moved to London in July of the same year.

Until he could get settled, he remained in the home of Mr. Basil Montagu, who introduced him to a life of glamour, and introduced him to Mr. Coleridge.[6] From Coleridge, Irving "received the first idea of the prophetic growth of God's word: as what have I not received from him..."[7]

Intellectually, Irving,

[W]as weak, to say nothing of his deficiency in judgment and common sense; his voluminous writings are a string of sonorous

---

5. *Ben-Ezra*, I.lxiv, lxvi. Darby complained that the prevailing Christian opinion of his day was of one common, general resurrection, an idea he found utterly repugnant, *Writings*, II.175, 1843.

6. *Life*, 68, 69, 91. No first name given for Mr. Coleridge. Irving married in 1823, *ibid.*, 86. Nor is there a first name given, other than O.W., for Mrs. Oliphant, the author of *The Life of Edward Irving*.

7. *Ben-Ezra*, I.lxxv. One is hard pressed to find a clear definition of "the prophetic growth of God's word." Irving speaks a lot in generalities, apparently learning a great deal from Coleridge.

commonplaces, empty of useful suggestion and original thought. This poverty of matter is in part redeemed by the dignity of the matter...[8]

Clearly not a theologian, it was Irving's eloquence that "transformed his originally small and poor congregation into a large and rich one, and at this time the fact became externalized in a new church in Regent Square, then regarded as the handsomest of any not belonging to the establishment in London. There, Sunday after Sunday a thousand persons assembled to hear Irving expound for three hours at a stretch..."[9]

Irving's reputation and church increased:

> Byron scarcely leapt into fame with more suddenness than Irving. The new preacher's oratory was pronounced worthy of his melodious and resonant voice, noble presence, commanding stature, and handsome features, which were marred only by a slight obliquity of vision. The little chapel was soon crowded, and the original congregation was almost lost in the influx of the more brilliant members of London society. His celebrity is said to have been greatly aided by a compliment paid him by Canning in the House of Commons, but, however attracted, his hearers remained. One great source of magnetism in Irving was undoubtedly the tone of authority that he assumed. Others might reason and expostulate, he dictated. The effect of Irving's success on his own character was unfavourable: it fostered that "inflation" which Carlyle had already remarked in him in his obscure Kirkculdy days, and, by encouraging his belief in his own special mission, made him a ready prey to flatterers and fanatics. His first important publication, "An Argument for Judgment to Come," published along with his "Orations" in 1823, is in its origin almost incredibly silly, being a protest against the respective Visions of Judgment of Southey and Byron, which Irving thought equally profane. It is no wonder that he himself soon became a mark for satirists, but their attacks only served to evidence his popularity.[10]

---

8. *DNB*, s.v. "Irving, Edward." Though Irving's "Discourse" is in an "exalted pitch," he is quite difficult to follow. "He was spotless in manners and morals at all times; but not without faults of temper..." *Life*, 37.
9. *DNB*, s.v. "Irving, Edward."
10. *Ibid.*

In The Beginning 31

Arriving in London with an inflated opinion of himself, Irving proclaimed the "imminence of the second advent." He did so at least five years before Darby and the Brethren appeared. Irving later found his teaching was identical to the system of the Jesuit, Lacunza:

> While Irving's extravagant assumptions in the pulpit served to provide frivolous society in London with a new sensation, the student of ecclesiastical history may see in them a premonition of the great sacerdotal reaction which occurred ten years later, a reaction grounded on very different postulates and supported by very different arguments, but equally expressive of a tendency in the times. Indeed, when Irving arrived in London in 1822, partly by inevitable reaction from the lukewarmness of the eighteenth century, partly from the marvellous political history of the preceding thirty years, a great revival of enthusiastic religious feeling was beginning. People could hardly be blamed for seeing a fulfillment of prophecy in the events of the French Revolution; and, this granted, the corollary of an impending end of the world was but reasonable. The Apocalyptic tendency expressed itself in the poetry and art of the time; in Byron's "Heaven and Earth" and Moore's "Loves of the Angels;" and in the pictures of Danby and Martin. It was inevitable that Irving should go with the current, and equally so that he should be entirely carried away by it. His entire absorption in the subject may be dated from the beginning of 1826, when he became acquainted with the work of the Spanish jesuit Lacunza, published under the pseudonym of Aben Ezra, "The Coming of the Messiah in Glory and Majesty." Deeply impressed, he resolved to translate it, and the intimacy which this task occasioned with Henry Drummond [q.v.] and others of similar sentiments gave birth to the conferences for the study of unfulfilled prophecy which for many years continued to be held at Drummond's seat at Albury. The translation was published in 1827, with a long preface, which has been reprinted separately.... In May of [1828, *ed.*]... he undertook a journey in Scotland, with the object of proclaiming the imminence of the second advent. The experiences of this tour were of chequered character. Chalmers thought his Edinburgh lectures "woeful," but he brought the Edinburgh people out to hear them at five in the morning.... On this tour he contracted a friendship with Campbell of Row, soon about to be tried for heresy, which gave support to the suspicions of heterodoxy where were beginning to be entertained against himself.... Early in 1829 the "Morning Watch," a journal on unfulfilled prophecy, entirely pervaded, as Mrs. Oliphant remarks,

by Irving, was established by the members of the Albury conference...

Irving had never been on cordial terms with the religious world, and since the delivery in 1826 of a powerful sermon advocating the prosecution of missions by strictly apostolic methods, he had been regarded by it with suspicion and dislike. An attempted prosecution for heresy in December 1830 had failed for the time in consequences of Irving's withdrawal from the jurisdiction of the London presbytery, but he was now helpless. The church trustees, who disapproved of the tongues, were clearly bound to take steps for the abatement of what they regarded as an intolerable nuisance, and as Irving was not prepared "defendre a Dieu de Faire miracle en el lieu," no course but his removal was possible. He defended himself with an imperious haughtiness little calculated to conciliate his judges, most of whom were probably inimical to him on other grounds, but the most friendly tribunal could hardly have come to any other decision, and he was removed from the pulpit of Regent Square Church on 26 April 1832..."[11]

Under Irving's leadership, his Presbyterian Church saw the first outbreak of modern "tongues," over which the church excommunicated him, and locked him out. (See "Tongues and the Rapture," p. 148.) Deposed from the Presbyterian ministry in 1832 as a heretic, he, Drummond, Cardale, Taplin, and about eight hundred others went down the street and formed the Catholic Apostolic Church, *i.e,* the Irvingite Church.[12]

Chapter 9

Death and Dates

Sunday, October 11, 1825, Irving's son's life was "cut short by Satan..." and "seeing it was in the season of thy sickness and death, the Lord did reveal in me the knowledge and hope and desire of his

---

11. *Ibid.,* 490-492.
12. *Who,* s.v. "Irving, Edward." Irving was not, nor had been much of a reader. *Reminiscences,* 82

Son from heaven — Glorious exchange! He took my son to his own more fatherly bosom, and revealed in my bosom the sure expectation and faith in his own eternal Son!" — "no other event of his life penetrated so profoundly the depths of his spirit."[13] Irving discusses the death in great detail in the CONCLUSION AND SUMMARY of his translation of *Ben-Ezra*, seeing death and a millennial reign of Christ as one's only hope. (See "Irving and Ben-Ezra," p. 59, and "Chiliasm," p. 439.) All other hope, said he, was "some false refuge,...a fatal delusion of Satan." "[T]here is not a spot to flee to [breathe, *ed.*] the liberty of God," nor to find deliverance "from the thraldom of Satan" apart from a millennial reign of Christ.[14]

Though his absorption with unfulfilled prophecy may be dated from the beginning of 1826, Irving actually started studying *Ben-Ezra* as early as 1823, for he said it came into his possession three or four years prior to 1827. Irving was proclaiming the *imminent return of Christ* and "the blessedness of that millennial kingdom," and was gathering very large crowds to hear his prophetic speculations as early as 1822, so he evidently was already proclaiming some of *Ben-Ezra's* millennial ideas when he acquired the document.

During deep involvement in his attempt to translate it into English, his son died. While in his hopeless state of mind after his son's death, the millennial system overwhelmed his being. Emboldened by Lacunza's *Ben Ezra*, he began publicly proclaiming the system from his pulpit, Christmas Day, 1825.

Irving,

[L]oved the mysterious — "loved to see an idea looming through the mist." And once captured by such an idea, once seized by its mystery, he would become its slave, never asking what contradictions or complications might follow.[15]

---

13. *Ben-Ezra*, I.lxxiv. *Life*, 112, 115. The date is given by Mrs. Oliphant.
14. *Ben-Ezra*, I.clxxiiff. (clxxviii.) Reading Darby, one cannot help but be overwhelmed by his emphasis on death, *e.g.*, *Writings*, II.452, *Letters*, II.424.
15. *Roots*, 16. "Loved to see...," "Irving used the words himself (Drummond, *Edward Irving*, p. 67.)" Sandeen's footnote.

In 1826, this 34 year old's mind became overwhelmed with the thought of the second advent:

> The thought of seeing his Lord in the flesh cast a certain ecstasy upon the mind of Irving. It quickened tenfold his already vivid apprehensions of spiritual things. The burden of prophetic mysteries, so often darkly pondered, so often interpreted in a mistaken sense, seemed to him, in the light of that expectation, to swell into divine chorus of preparation for the splendid event which with his only bodily eyes, undimmed by death, he hoped to behold.[16]

Irving's preaching was contrary to the public opinion of his day which said that Christ is the victorious Saviour this side of the second advent.[17] Christian leaders mocked and ridiculed him, and other pastors accused him of presenting heretical ideas, but, in his mind, Lacunza's writings cleared him of the charges. In fact, the exciting ideas concerning unfulfilled prophecy found in *Ben-Ezra* strengthened Irving's commitment to "The new revelations of doctrine which had already illuminated his path."[18]

Note the date of the first Albury Park Conference on Unfulfilled Prophecy — "the first week of Advent, 1826." It, "more than any other event, gave structure to the British millenarian revival, consolidating both the theology and the group of men who were to defend it."[19] Advent begins on the fourth Sunday before Christmas. Irving attended the first Albury conference with Lacunza's millennial system heavy upon his mind — it was only 11 months after he started proclaiming it from his pulpit and just four weeks before he dates his *Discourse*, "Christmas Day, 1826." At Albury he found a group of Protestants who would help develop and defend the

---

16. *Life,* 198. His very strong tendency toward mysticism (feelings and impressions over the word of God) was a common trait among all the developers of the newly emerging millennial system.

17. Irving complains about the "idol, PUBLIC OPINION," *i.e.,* one general resurrection, *Ben-Ezra,* I.xxi, xxii.

18. *Life,* 199, 200.

19. *Roots,* 18.

system over which he had been ridiculed for so long. They were marvelously successful.

We must, accordingly, assume that Irving went to Albury heavy with his views of: the Christians' hopelessness in the church age; death and the grave; the unrestrained reign of Satan during the present age; the soon coming of Christ to start another glorious dispensation of victory over death and Satan; the exaltation of national Israel; and the exaltation and glorification of man during a millennial reign. His views matured after he came into contact with Lacunza's document and during his terrible distress over the loss of his son. Though no documents other than Scripture were allowed at that first meeting on unfulfilled prophecy, it is logical to assume Irving came overflowing with Lacunza's system in which he had been completely engrossed. He would have promoted his soon to be released English translation, and those attending would have been first in line to obtain a copy.

As evidenced in Irving's *Preliminary Discourse* to *Ben-Ezra*, the death of his son allowed him to be overwhelmed with Lacunza's hopeless system. Reading Irving's *Conclusion and Summary,* one gets the distinct impression that his belief that Satan killed his son led him to the conclusion that Satan now has unlimited reign over every area except the spiritual, and Satan's reign of terror will continue until a millennial period of Christ's literal reign yet to come. It follows, therefore, that Christians suffering under Satan's oppressive heel during this present dispensation just need to be patient, and wait for the thousand year millennial reign when they will be exalted[20]—Irving's system said that the purpose of man's redemption was to exalt and glorify him, man, during a millennial reign of Christ.[21]

---

20. *Ben Ezra,* I.clxxviii, clxxxi.
21. *Ibid.,* clxii. Darby held quite firmly to the same idea, though adding to it: Only those who remain unconcerned about current social affairs while suffering during this present age will reign with Christ, *Writings,* II.135, 368, 483, 1852.

Irving's opposition failed to see the second advent as he saw it — they saw it not as the world's conversion, but as its destruction. Many mocked his views, ridiculed his ideas, and joked about him: he suffered "magazine raillery, newspaper abuse, ribald poems and silly reviews." However, he saw Lacunza confirming that his view of the second advent was actually the orthodox view. In fact, Lacunza's document gave Irving courage to ridicule those who had ridiculed him. He compared himself to Christ, *viz.*, one man suffering for the whole — that is, suffering for the welfare of the church. The Christian thought of his day totally dismissed his idea of a restored Jewish nation, "Zionism." (See "Zionism," p. 72.) He defended his teaching as not being "fancy," yet admitted his system of interpretation was new and was very much against the common, popular system of his day.[22] Irving often exhibited *anger* and mockery against those who disagreed with his views; he called those who opposed his system, fools and possessed by Satan.[23]

Chapter 10

The Terrors of Satan

Irving's mockers have long ago faded into the background. His system of "the terrors of Satan, the weakness of the flesh, the powerfulness of the world" — modern dispensational millennialism — overwhelmed a large portion of the Christian community. All but a dim spark of hope in "Christ the Victorious" was extinguished by

---

22. In order of usage: *Ben-Ezra,* I.xxii; *DNB,* s.v. "Irving, Edward." *Ben-Ezra,* I.xv, lxxix, xxii, xviii, l, xviii, xli, xlviii, xcii, cvi, clvi, cxxix, xlii.

23. Clearly repeating Irving's millennial ideas, Darby, who knowingly and intentionally went against orthodoxy in the church of his day, also called those who opposed his opinions tools of Satan, unfaithful to God, blinded by Satan and attacking God. In order of usage: *Life,* 99, *Ben-Ezra,* I.xlviii, xcliii, clxviii, clxxvii, lvii. *Letters,* I.366, II.152, III.74, I.370, 1864, *Writings,* II.133, 1852, *Letters,* I.90. The "Ben-Ezra system" was established by considering all opposition Satanic. Darby also saw himself suffering, as Christ did, for the welfare of the church.

Irving's ideas, which were supported by Lacunza and, as we will see, popularized by Darby. Those who hold to "Christ the victorious" are now the ones who suffer the "magazine raillery, newspaper abuse, ribald poems and silly reviews."

Irving had no useful suggestions for confronting "the horrors of the French Revolution — battle and murder and sudden death — [that, *ed*.] floated before the terror-stricken eyes of all who had anything to lose."[24] Both the French Revolution and the Napoleonic Wars provided ideal conditions for an intense study of unfulfilled prophecy.[25] "During 1827-1830, the years of intense millenarian excitement, the Oxford evangelicals, like many others, speculated about the coming judgment and the coming Christ."[26] Irving's English translation of *Ben-Ezra* was published in 1827, and could well have been a cause of the intense millenarian excitement. The Albury Park conferences could also have been a cause.

The millennial system's escape into prophetic study and its view that the second advent of Christ as the only hope for straightening out man the sinner — proved by the French Revolution and the Napoleonic wars — were met by mockery and scorn until two key events took place: The first Albury Park Conference on Unfulfilled Prophecy, and the release of Irving's English translation of the 1790 Spanish Roman document, *The Coming of Messiah in Glory and Majesty*, written under the pen name, *Ben-Ezra*.[27]

At the 1826 Albury Park conference (see "Prophecy Conferences," p. 125), Irving,

---

24. *Life,* 53. The French Revolution was believed to literally fulfill Rev. 13 and Dan. 6, and it was a key in changing the general Christian view of the millennium from post to pre: In the wake of the Revolution, "Converts to premillennialism abandoned confidence in man's ability to bring about significant and lasting social progress in the church's ability to stem the tide of evil, convert mankind to Christianity, or even prevent its own corruption." *Roots,* 6, 13. The obvious fallacy is that "Christians" abandoned *faith:* They abandoned the word of God which continually teaches that God's Spirit of Grace is stronger than all man's sins combined.
25. Neatby, *History,* 38.
26. *Roots,* 30.

[C]hanged the common superficial idea of the world's conversion — that belief calmly held or earnestly insisted on in the face of acknowledged disappointment in many missionary efforts, and the slowness and lingering issues of even the most successful, which is common to most churches. "That error," he himself says, "under which almost the whole of the Church is lying, that the present world is to be converted unto the Lord, and so slide by a natural inclination into the Church — the present reign of Satan hastening, of its own accord, into the millennial reign of Christ. For this doctrine he learned to substitute the idea of a dispensation drawing towards its close, and — its natural consequence in a mind so full of love to God and man — of an altogether glorious and overwhelming revolution yet to come, in which all society, churches, kingdoms, fashions of this world, galvanically kept in motion until the end, should be finally burned up and destroyed.[28]

Embolden by Lacunza, Irving learned to substitute his system of hopelessness under the oppressive heel of Satan for the "idea of the world's conversion."

Lacunza's millennial ideas (sometimes called Irvingism, and can now be called Scofieldism) had been public property for quite some time before the Brethren started their sweep of church history with it, c. 1830.

Irving's influence is overlooked:

> The men of this generation have very little idea of the vast influence exercised by the weird, majestic eloquence, the sheer-like utterances, and the colossal person of the famous Scotch preacher. Ministers of State, noblemen, theologians, literary men, all ranks and conditions of society, were led captive by him. His teaching, which was closely modeled upon the style of the old Hebrew prophets, dealt very largely with the subject of unfulfilled prophecy and the speedy manifestation of the Second Advent of Christ. Irving

---

27. A common trait of millennialism is its lack of practical answers for surrounding turmoil. Darby's answers involved becoming more personally *spiritual* and escape into prophetic study. The Niagara conferences also offered the same answer. One of Darby's most repeated points was that the faithful will miss the Apocalypse and be kept from judgment: "I am more than ever confirmed..." that the faithful will escape judgment, *e.g., Letters,* I.58, 1843.

28. *Life,* 92, 93. (*Life* left the quote open.)

infected his hearers with his views and expectations. Meetings for the study of prophecy became the fashion.[29]

Edward Irving died of turberculosis in 1834, but his hopeless system was passed on to a small group of men who covered the earth with it. We are walking in the shadow of a man of whom most people have never heard:

> The standard view of the second advent held in eighteenth-century England was derived from Daniel Whitby (1638-1726), rector of St. Edmund's Salisbury, and an erudite controversialist. Whitby argued that the thousand years of millennium were still future. This final era of the world's history would commence with the conversion of the world as a result of a new outpouring of the Holy Spirit, would involve the restoration of the Jews to Palestine and the overthrow of both pope and turk, and would be followed by the Second Advent. This view, which became known as the post-millennial interpretation, necessarily excluded the possibility that the return of Christ could occur during the lifetime of anyone living and caused pious people to regard death as the eschatological hope of the Christians... In the early nineteenth century, the question was raised whether the Second Advent should not be expected prior to the millennium.[30]
>
> Belief in a pre-millennial advent of Christ, which as we have earlier noted found some advocates in the mid-seventeenth century, practically disappeared from the main-stream of evangelical thought in the century which followed. Those who maintained it might still be found, particularly in some backwaters of Nonconformity, but the belief had no place in the creed of the leaders of the eighteenth-century Revival, nor in that of the men who led the missionary movement which followed. Consequently, when the nineteenth century dawned the cause of pre- millennialism was at a very low ebb...
>
> The leader of this change of direction [back toward pre-mill, *ed.*] was Edward Irving... with a frank acknowledgment of

---

29. *Plot,* 17. MacPherson takes this quote from George T. Stokes, "John Nelson Darby" (*the Contemporary Review,* Oct., 1885).

30. *Origins,* 12-14. Studying the Darbyite movement, one will be impressed by its emphasis on death. Is it any wonder "death education" has become so popular in secular education? Millenarians have for years emphasized and longed for death. See "*Futurism,*" p. 434

indebtedness, to Hatley Frere, a layman of pre-millennial convictions.[31]

---

31. *Hope,* 187-189. A little later, Reverend William Miller lead an attack against "traditional post millennialism" in America, c. 1837.

Part III
Ben-Ezra

Chapter 11
Rome's Gain

From about the eleventh century, Protestants, because of Rome's growing corruptions, begin to hold the Antichrist as the papal system, past and present.

In order to counter those attacks, in the 1500s, a Roman Jesuit, Francisco Ribiera, (see Francisco Ribiera, p. 43) developed and introduced the *Futurist* system, which said that Revelation was yet future, placing the Antichrist where he would not be a threat to the church. (See *Futurism*, p. 429.) The Jesuit's countered the Protestants' charge by saying Revelation was yet future.

However, the *Futurist* system did not have its full impact on the Protestants until its introduction by another Roman Jesuit, Lacunza. His document (*Ben-Ezra*) would also have died a natural death as had Rome's previous efforts if it had not come into the hands of Edward Irving, who introduced it to the Protestants. Thus, we cannot ignore the fact that the "Roman Catholic commentators", *i.e.*, the Jesuits, took Protestant pressure off of Rome, and the average Roman Catholic has remained free of "millennial fever."[1]

John Trapp (1601-1696) expressed it this way — the "damned Popery" personifies the devil, the smoke out of the bottomless pit is Popish doctrines of devils, and "monks, friars, Jesuits, &c., are fitly called" the *locusts upon the earth*. (Rev. 9:3.)[2] Even the

---

1. A supprising number of those commentators were "converted" Jews, and their documents exalted the Jews.
2. *Trapp.* V.754, 755.

Millenarians were, without exception, stoutly anti-Catholic. They viewed every agitation by English and Irish Catholics as confirmation of the increasing corruption of the world and thus of the increasing likelihood of the second advent.[3]

Thus, the futurist view of the Revelation did not originate with Darby nor with the Plymouth Brethren. Rather, it came from Roman Catholic commentators countering Protestant attacks upon the papacy as the Antichrist by insisting that none of the events relating to Antichrist had yet occurred. Lacunza's *Coming of Messiah in Glory and Majesty* (1827), the work of the Spanish Jesuit whose testimony to the premillennial advent of Christ Edward Irving considered so valuable, belonged to that tradition.[4]

Better known among those who identified the Papacy as the Antichrist already seated in churchly temple of God (2 Thess. 2) were: Eberhard II (1200-1246), archbishop of Salzbürg; John Wycliffe (1320-1384); John Huss (1369-1415); Martin Luther (1483-1546); John Calvin (1509-1564); John Knox (1505-1572); John Napier (1550-1617); Huldreich Zwigli (1484- 1531); William Tyndale (1484-1536); John Bradford (1510-1555); John Hooper (1495-1555); Thomas Becon (1511-1567); John Jewel (1522-1571); King James (1566-1625; the translators of the KJV saw their English translation striking *such a blow unto that Man of Sin as will not be healed* [*Introduction* to the 1611 KJV]; they saw *the Man of Sin* not future, but presently reigning — the Papacy); Sir Isaac Newton (1642-1727); Johann Albrecht Bengel (1687-1725); John Wesley (1703-1791); John Cotton (1584-1652); Cotton Mather (1663-1728); Jonathan Edwards (1703-1758) and Timothy Dwight (1752-1817, Edward's grandson). "The *futurist* view of an *individual...* Antichrist was unknown among the Protestants of North America prior to the nineteenth Century."[5]

---

3. *Roots,* 17. The Geneva Bible notes are anti-Rome, calling "Pope Gregory the seventh, a most damnable necromancer and sorcerer, whom Satan used..." Rev. 20:2.

4. *Ibid.,* 37. See also *Plot,* 254. Irving was probably enamored by the Jesuit's system, not by the Roman Church.

There are *two* great truths that stand out in the preaching that brought about the Protestant Reformation: (1) the just shall live by faith (not by the works of the Romanism); and (2) the Papacy is the Antichrist of scripture.[6]

The pressure was on Rome, especially with the word of God in the hands of the average person. "So in order to turn the blame away from the Papacy, the Roman Catholic Jesuits started teaching that the Antichrist was some future individual that would come at the end of time."[7]

Francisco Ribera

[The Jesuit, *ed.*] FRANCISCO RIBERA (1537-1591) of Salamanca, Spain, published a 500 page commentary on the grand points of Babylon and Antichrist, the object being to set aside the Protestant teaching that the Papacy is the Antichrist. In his commentary, he assigned the first chapters of Revelation to the first century. The rest he restricted to a literal three and a half years at the end of time. He taught that the Jewish temple would be rebuilt by a single individual antichrist who would abolish the Christian religion, deny Christ, pretend to be God, and conquer the world.[8]

According to Schaff:

The events of the Apocalypse from ch. 4 to the close lie beyond the second advent of Christ. This scheme usually adopts a literal interpretation of Israel, the Temple, and the numbers (the 3 1/2

---

5. *Great Prophecies*, 182-195. Woodrow quotes from Leroy Froom, *The prophetic Faith of Our Fathers* (four volumes), III.257.

6. *Ibid.*, 196. Commenting on 2 Thess. 2:3, John Gill (1696-1771) said: "...nor is this to be understood of a certain Jew, that is to be begotten by the devil on [sic] a virgin of the tribe of Dan, and who is to reign three years and a half, and then to be destroyed by Christ, which is a fable of the Papists..." The idea of a future, literal antichrist is a Papists' fable. *Online Bible*, v. 8.01.

7. *Ibid. Encyclopedia Britannica*, XXIII. 213 (11th Edition), attributes the *Futurist* system to Ribera. Biederwolf attributes "The Preterist System," *i.e.*, "the Revelation has largely been fulfilled" in the destruction of Jerusalem to "the Jesuit Alcazar in 1614." Biederwolf leans toward the "The Historical System," *i.e.*, "the prophecies of Revelation embraces the whole history of the Church and its foes from the time of its writing to the end of the world." This view "originated about the eleventh century among those who began to protest against the growing corruptions of the Church of Rome." *The Second Coming Bible Commentary*, 566, 567. Both the "Preterist" and the "Futurist" systems took pressure off Rome.

times, 42 months, 1260 days, 3 1/2 years). So Ribera (a Jesuit, 1592), Lacunza (another Jesuit, who wrote under the name of Ben-Ezra "On the coming of Messiah in glory and majesty," and taught the premillennial advent, the literal restoration of the ancient Zion, and the future apostasy of the clergy of the Roman church to the camp of Antichrist), S. R. Maitland, De Burgh, Todd, Issac Williams, W. Kelly.[9]

Ribera's commentary laid the foundation for the great structure of *Futurism*, which would be built upon and expanded by those who followed. Ribera's teaching was further popularized by Robert Bellarmine (1544-1621), an Italian cardinal and the most renowned of all Jesuit controversialists.[10]

After accepting the Jesuits' *Futurist System* (and the *Preterist System*, we must add; see "*Preterism*," p. 432, and "*Futurism*," p. 434), millenarian Protestants no longer saw Rome as a present but

---

8. *Great Prophecies,* 196-197. "This school was launched in 1580 by the Jesuit Ribera, who, as Guinness says, 'moved like Alcazar, to relieve the Papacy from the terrible stigma cast upon it by the Protestant interpretation (the Historical School), tried to do so by referring these prophecies to the distant future, instead of like Alcazar to the distant *past.*'" *The Second Coming Bible Commentary,* 569. There are at least two ways of spelling Ribera's name, and both are used in herein.

9. Schaff, *History,* I.838. Rowdon says that "Alcazar (1554-1613), [a Spanish Jesuit, *ed.*], had contended that the prophecies of the Apocalypse had been fulfilled in the early centuries. Nero was Antichrist, pagan Rome was Babylon, and the millennium commenced with the triumph of Christianity over Pagan Rome." *Origins,* 14. If the implications of this teaching are followed through, it permits Rome's pope as the "Vicar of Christ" during the present millennium; all people need to submit to him. The benefits of millennialism appear to be on Rome's side. Accordingly, the ideas presented by Morgan Edwards in 1742 were already floating around in Europe. Trapp applies all of Rev. 13 to the pope and Rome. Olson, a Romanist himself, clearly lays modern millennialism at the feet of Rome trying to take the pressure off of the pope. He traces Rome's efforts from Peter Olivi (c. 1248-1298) to Manuel Lacunza, "a renegade Chilean Jesuit, under the alias of Jaun Ben-Ezra..." He points out that John Hus (1371-1415) was burned at the stake for saying the pope was the Antichrist. *Catholics,* 149-153. However, Olsen fails to make the "Jewish" connection, *i.e.*, several Jesuits were "converted" Jews.

10. *Great Prophecies,* 198. Catholic writers also claim that the *futuristic* system was founded by the Jesuit Ribera in 1591. "Hitchcock, the Beasts and the Little Horn, p. 7." A former Catholic priest, Joseph Zaccchello attributes the futurist system to the Jesuits. *Ibid,* 198.

only a distant future threat.[11] We should also mention that Irving's system saw no hope of victory over the present forces of evil except "by the brightness of his coming" in the second advent. With no hope, why try to conquer all things for Christ?

Chapter 12

Rome and Ben-Ezra

Ben-Ezra — The Coming of Messiah in Glory and Majesty — played a key role in supporting Edward Irving's message of defeat. Because the *"Ben-Ezra* system" (a term used by Fr. Paul, p. 46.) is easily traced to the *Scofield Reference Bible* notes and to important Protestant leaders of the past 150 years (which will be done in this present work), *Ben-Ezra* can be considered the fountainhead of the modern dispensational millennial system. (See "Millennial Views," p. 428.) As we will see, Irving was the key in making the *"Ben-Ezra* system" a Protestant system of theology; therefore, we will spend a considerable amount of time discussing his view of and involvement with *Ben-Ezra.*

This writer tried to restrict quotes from both Irving and *Ben-Ezra* to just those "millennial" points he, as a former follower of the millennial faith, is familiar with. In other words, the quotes, though maybe more extensive and redundant than they should be, are quotes that many followers of that faith will recognize as modern millennial doctrine. Many quotes are offered in their larger context to emphasize their importance to the millennial faith. Though we will

---

11. *Ben Ezra*, I.xxxii. Darby claimed he developed the idea of a coming personal Antichrist, making the connection between 1 Thess. 2 and a personal Antichrist yet to appear, *Writings,* II.294,331, 339. See *The Parousia, A careful look at the New Testament doctrine of our Lord's Second Coming,* by James Stuart Russell, for a complete treatment of the preterist view of Bible Prophecy. Though *Preterism* does not offer a personal Antichrist yet to come, it does not see the papal system as the present Antichrist. See

not discuss *Ben-Ezra* itself (Irving sums it up well), there are several points leading up to the document that should be examined.

The document was "finished in 1790" by a Roman Catholic Jesuit priest named Manuel De Lacunza Y Diaz.[12] Evidently, it was written without Rome's knowledge, for the Church itself commissioned a critique of *Ben- Ezra,* which Irving left in his translation.

Fr. Paul

The "CRITICQUE OF THE WORK by M.R.P.FR. PAUL, of the conception of the order of the Barefooted Carmelites," is addressed to "My Lord Vicar General, ('Señor Provisor Vicario Capitular')." It is dated, December 17, 1812. Fr. Paul said that after first reading the manuscript 21 years previous, he determined to get a copy to carry with him — "I have read it over as often as I could." Fr. Paul was very familiar with *Ben-Ezra*, and his conclusions are important for those in the millennial faith:

First, Fr. Paul tells us that Lacunza did not publish under his name, but "published under the pseudonym of Aben Ezra." Lacunza's manuscript was titled *"The Coming of Messiah in Glory and Majesty,* by Juan Josafat Ben-Ezra, a Converted Jew." However, Fr. Paul tells us that,

> Few things entrusted to my care, have occasioned me so much perplexity and pain, as the criticism which your Excellency requires me to give upon the first volume of the work entitled "The coming of Messiah in glory and majesty;" written, as appears, by Juan Josafat Ben-Ezra, who takes the character of a Jew converted to our holy religion of the Catholic Apostolic Roman Church.[13]

Accordingly, "a Converted Jew" meant a Jew converted to Romanism, not to Protestantism. The *Ben-Ezra* document circulated in manuscript form just 13 years after the French Revolution.[14]

Second, Fr. Paul defines Lacunza's system of millenarianism:

---

12. Irving described Lacunza as one of Roman Catholicism's "most gifted and dutiful sons," *Ben-Ezra,* I.xxi. See p. 465 a description of Manuel Lacunza.
13. *Ben-Ezra,* I.3.
14. *Ibid.,* xxi. And thus Lacunza lived during the Revolution.

Two capital points, among many others of inferior importance, form the foundation and key of Ben-Ezra's system: the first that Jesus Christ, with all the state of majesty and glory described to us in the divine books, is to come to our globe, not only to pronounce here definite sentence upon all the sons of Adam, but also, before the time of that judgment arrives, to reign in this world, and be acknowledged of all the nations of the earth together; that our world may enjoy a period of blessedness, wherein all it's [sic] inhabitants endowed with reason, shall know and adore Jesus Christ the Son of the Living God, and his Father who sent him for our salvation, with all the other mysteries which are taught by our holy religion. The second, that in the beginning of this happy period, the Jews, whom by such a wonderful providence we see preserved, though dispersed and oppressed among the nations, will be converted to Jesus Christ, and acknowledge him for their Messiah, will return and become the people of God, and worship him in spirit and in truth, to the universal promotion of the whole world.[15]

Church/Israel Distinction

Modern dispensationalism relies upon a "distinction between the church and Israel. Dispensationalism defines 'Israel' as those who have ethnic ties to Abraham, Isaac, and Jacob, or those who are part of Judaism."[16] Darbyites contend that Darby's "'distinction' evolved into his pre-trib rapture view."

Though credit was taken by and given to Darby for "a church/Israel distinction," it was clearly found in Lacunza's system before 1790.[17] Fr. Paul called what is known today as dispensational millennialism, the "Ben-Ezra system." The system at this point apparently lacked a clear "pre-trib rapture" idea, which was added c. 1830 by Irving and Darby. (See "Powerscourt and the Rapture," p. 145.)

---

15. *Ibid.,* 6, 7.

16. It is utterly impossible for anyone to trace any blood line even to Jacob-Israel. A Jew is simply one who follows the Jew's religion, which is as much against Christ today as it was in Christ's day. An Israelite is no more than one who lives in the nation of Israel. Dispensationalism must reject any principle of hermeneutics that would allow a blending of Israel and the Church. *Israel,* 25.

17. See *Plot,* 88, 90, 95. Young Morgan Edwards also made this point as early as 1742.

Following closely Lacunza's system and along with the "ruin of the church," Darby developed Lacunza's "distinction between the earthly hope of the Jewish church and the heavenly hope of the Christian church." "[L]eading dispensationalist Charles Ryrie...wrote that the church/Israel distinction is the *best* way to determine whether or not someone is a dispensationalist — the most important criterion."[18] Lindsey goes as far as to say that any teaching that "the church has been given the promises made to Israelites" is "demonic and heretical".[19]

The "church/Israel distinction" is a key plank in the millenarian platform, as well as a necessary doctrine in supporting the modern Protestant Zionist movement.

Rome found nothing wrong with Lacunza's system. After many years of intensive study of the document, Fr. Paul said,

> That in this work there is not contained any thing repugnant to our holy faith, but that it may be of good service in making known, and publishing abroad, many truths, whereof the knowledge, though not absolutely necessary in the first ages of the church, is become indispensable in the times in which we now live.
>
> And with respect to customs, not only does it contain nothing contrary thereto, but on the other hand tends much to reform them by the motives which it brings forward... [Motives to stimulate the soul "to fear and love of him." *ed.*][20]

It was finally banned by the "Holy Office" on Sept. 6, 1824, and again on July 11, 1941, this time with specific reference to the book's moderate "millenarianism" — its praise of Judaism, or Zionism.[21] *Ben-Ezra* required an exalted, glorious Jewish state to be

---

18. *Plot*, 88. See *Catholics*, 217ff. Accordingly, the "church/Israel distinction" must be protected at all costs, or the system falls apart.

19. Hal Lindsey, *The Rapture*, [New York:Bantam Books, 1983], 35. Quoted by Olson, *Catholics*, 182. Without the church/Israel distinction, dispensationalism collapses. Dispensationalism studies Scripture, but all Scripture must be studied in light of the "church/Israel distinction." *Ibid.*, 213.

20. *Ben-Ezra*, I.7, 8. By *Ben-Ezra* removing the papacy from the present danger of God's judgment and transmitting it to a future prospect of that judgment, the papacy was thus permitted even by its followers to do as it pleased in the present dispensation.

reestablished by God; that state would then rule the world as it did under the Warrior-King, David.

Fourth, Fr. Paul claimed that, basically, the *"Ben-Ezra* system" was not new:

> Nevertheless, when I take into consideration the number of ages which have elapsed in the church, without even the mention of this system, otherwise than as a fabulous opinion; and advert to certain fathers and doctors, as Jerome, Augustine, Gregory, and to all the theologians since their day, who treat it with aversion, and some of them as positive error; I cannot help quaking and trembling, under the impression that there is less risk in erring with so many learned and very holy masters, than in venturing to aim at the mark by one's own inclination and judgment. [It is safer to take the high ground and stick with established doctrine, *ed.*] True indeed it is, which somewhat tranquillizeth me, that the matter in dispute preserves the faith of the holy church inviolate, [though on thin ice, the document does not undermine Romanism: a thought in which Fr. Paul finds comfort, *ed.*] whichever side you embrace: there being between the two parties but one faith, and one Christ Jesus, whom they believe in and adore as their God. All of us believe and confess, as it is in the creed, that this Sovereign King will come to judge the quick and the dead. The faithful of the catholic church, or any of her children in this article, hath never been, nor can ever be unhinged. No, the controversy, merely turning upon the mode and circumstances of that advent which all believe, stands thus:-the common opinion of the doctors of our times restricts the coming of Jesus Christ to the single and terrible, and most solemn act of finally judging the whole race of mankind, and publicly assigning to every one through all eternity the reward or punishment which their works deserve: while our author, without excluding, or at all doubting the truth of this judgment, extends it to a period of time antecedent to that last testimony of the sovereignty and divinity of our Lord Jesus Christ, plants his throne and his tabernacle for a time amongst men, while yet sojourners upon the earth, makes him to dwell with them who became his people, and he their only God, known and adored of them all. — We know that this opinion is not new, but was held by the fathers of the first four centuries of the Christian church,

---

21. This could account for why the "poor Romanists" gladly received Darby and his teachings. Also, Rome's actions could have been simply a facade, so the Protestants would accept it. The ramifications of Protestant acceptance of the system appear on Rome's side.

amongst whom we count certain of the disciples of the apostles themselves; who yet did not condemn those who thought differently; as may be collected from the expressions of Justin Martyr in his dialogue with Trypho the Jew.

That the opinion, or judgment of these first fathers should have been abandoned, and that the contrary should have obtained from the fifth century forward to our times, with such force and constancy, there is to be taken into account, on the one hand, that the heretics of the third and fourth century did intermingle gross errors with the sound doctrine of these saints, and on the other, that the universal erudition and venerable authority of that great doctor, St. Jerome, who openly declared himself against the Millenarians, without distinguishing between the catholics and heretics, might bring it about that they should be all involved in the indiscriminate condemnation of their doctrines. This, however, appears certain, that the opinion of the Millenarians, unpolluted with the errors which the heretics introduced into it, was common, and held by very many Catholics, as St. Jerome himself gives us clearly to understand, in the introduction to the xviiith book of his Commentaries upon Isaiah... Whereby it is clearly manifested, that the opinion which the holy doctor contravened was widely spread. And when it is observed, that the commentaries upon Isaiah, of which the xviiith book is the last, were entered upon in the fifth century, towards the year 409, the proof is complete, that at this date there prevailed very commonly in the church this idea of the reign of Jesus Christ upon the earth, which is the foundation of the opinions of the Millenarians. But when the immense learning, authority, and deserved reputation of St. Jerome had declared itself against the notion, wherein he was followed by the great doctor St. Augustine, it came to lose ground, and at length to be given up as a point no wise concerning the purity of the faith; and which was to be looked upon as very remote, wherewithal had been mixed up gross errors, deservedly condemned by the ecclesiastical doctors and by the church herself... So that the opinion has against it only the authority of the fathers and theologians from the end of the fifth century onward....[22]

Lacunza revived and refined a millenarian system that had been dismissed and dormant for better than 1,400 years; it had been replaced by a system holding to a "single and terrible" coming of Jesus Christ. Fr. Paul said the *Ben-Ezra system* "is become indispensable in the times in which we now live" — that is, the

French Revolution prepared the world for its reintroduction. The system did not undermine Rome, so Fr. Paul closes his critique: "From all which judge, that it may and ought to be allowed to be printed."

Chapter 13

Lacunza and *Ben-Ezra*

Lacunza himself tells us about his document:

First, in his dedication, he defined three goals of the document: (1) to motivate "the priests to shake off the dust from their Bibles" and be more attentive to "that Divine Book"; (2) to promote holiness among the many he saw falling into the gulf of infidelity (though never defined, infidelity was a term frequently used by Irving and Darby)[23]; and (3) to restore the Jewish hope "to my own brethren the Jews." Lacunza's complaint against the church of his day was its failure to teach Jews the truth of the Messiah:

> [H]ow are they to know Him unless the doctrine be opened to them? and how, in the state of ignorance and blindness in which they are actually found, can that doctrine be sufficiently discovered, while you show them only the one half of Messiah, while the other half is concealed, and even positively denied? — if there be preached to them only what is to be found in the scriptures, pertaining to thy first

---

22. *Ibid.*, 4-6. Lacunza argued that though his system (Premil) was only dominant for four centuries and the opposing opinion (Postmil) had been dominant for 14 centuries, it did not mean his was wrong, *ibid.*, 14, 15. However, the millennial faith had never been a prevalent faith, not even in the early church, *Dogmatic Theology*, IIB.642, 643. "[D]espite its overall similarities to older Christian views of history," Lacunza's system was not the same as passed away 1,400 years previously: "it was a product of nineteenth-century thought," *Fundamentalism*, 64.

23. Darby spoke great, swelling words against sin without defining sin, *e.g.*, "sin is taken abstractedly, the thing, sin, even personified, which is the highest figurative form of abstraction." *Letters*, II. 101. From Lausanne, June, 1850. Also 139, 170, 272, III.42, 97, I.170, 1849. He was confident, however, that sin had nothing to do with the Mosaic law.

coming in suffering flesh, as Redeemer, as Master, as Example, as High Priest, &c.- and there be denied to them without any reason, what, according to the same scriptures, though with ideas little worthy, and even gross, they believe, and hope, pertaining to thy second coming.[24]

The problem Lacunza saw was that the church only proclaimed half of the Messiah, and that half did not exalt the Jewish "race", of which he claimed membership.[25] *Ben-Ezra* was motivated by Lacunza's concern about the depressed state of the Jews:

> By the consideration of these words (Rom. 9:2.), it was not long before the very feelings of the apostle awoke in me; and perceiving that my heart was oppressed by the reawakened and renewed force of that grief, which I do almost always bear about with me, I shut the book (Bible.), and hastened into the fields to relieve my heart. Where, the first burst being over, and my grief a little subsided, various reflections began to succeed.[26]

The foundation of the modern dispensational millenarian system was a "burst" of emotion — "the very feelings of the apostle awoke in" this "miserable Jew" — while he was musing on the Jew's sad estate. His various reflections were no doubt what developed into *Ben-Ezra*. Lacunza's account of the origin of the system of supposed millennial glories of the Messiah and the resurrected Jewish nation to great glory is quite similar to the account Margaret Macdonald gave of her vision, the vision to which the rapture idea has been attributed. Both came as an overwhelming feeling — a burst of emotion.

---

24. *Ben-Ezra,* I.9. "To The Messiah Jesus Christ, the Son of God, Son of the Most Holy Virgin Mary, Son of David, and Son of Abraham." Clearly, one purpose of Lacunza's manuscript was to support the "miserable Jews" — that is, lift them from their then oppressed state, *ibid.,* 15, 16. Irving's description of the "Ben-Ezra system" sounds as though Lacunza intentionally wrote a theological document to change the then accepted Christian view of the Jews to one that would exalt a Jewish nation.

25. *Ibid.,* 29. There is absolutely no way to trace a supposed Jewish race with blood ties to Abraham. *Commentary,* III.421.

26. *Ibid.,* 21.

Irving saw the same problem — that is, the church emphasizing "Christ the victorious," the first advent of Christ, and failing to emphasize the second advent and an exalted, restored, glorified Jewish nation. The men who followed in Irving's steps also saw the same problems.

Lacunza also sought to instill general holiness into the church through knowledge. Though the knowledge was of the "Divine Person" and was from "the Sacred Scriptures," the problem still remained: Holiness and purity do not come from knowledge, but from God's Spirit of Grace working through the preaching of his Law-Word. (Jn. 17:17, Ps. 19:7ff., 119:9ff., 119:151.) It is the daily application of God's Law-Word that promotes holiness among his people.

Lacunza's incomplete manuscript was unintentionally circulated — "those copies were circulated beyond all reasonable bounds; and one of them, I am assured, made its way across the ocean, where they say it has caused no small stir." He asks his readers to not dismiss his manuscript as dangerous and cast it away simply because of its "novelty." Though his ideas "until this present time have not been understood," the time was right, so the Lord, he was confident, was bringing the system to light through him. He asks the critics to submit his novel ideas to:

> [T]hese three rules, which are the only infallible tests of faith — 1st. Divine scripture in its proper and literal sense: — 2d. Divine tradition: — 3d. The express and clear determination of the church assembled in the Holy Spirit.

By these three "only infallible rules," he was convinced the Roman Church would find no fault in him, for he conformed well within its "Divine tradition." He said his manuscript was for the Roman Catholic Church, and if in any manner his novel system undermined established Roman dogma, he would "at once yield as conquered, and readily acknowledge my ignorance."[27]

Chapter 14

The Jesuits

Lacunza credits a previous Italian work, "The Second Epoch of the church," by another Catholic and religious writer, Euodio Papia (ND), with containing much of what he covered, particularly the notes on Revelation 20. He defended himself against charges of plagiarism by saying that he had never read all of Papia's work, and that Papia supposed three comings of Christ. Lacunza admitted that he did read Papia's exposition of Revelation 20, in which Papia referred to "The Second Epoch..." Lacunza makes a point worth quoting:

> Euodio seems to steer this last course [a "space of time between the Antichrist and the glorious coming of Christ," *ed.*], and would not be chargeable with any novelty, did he not, at the beginning of this epoch, suppose a middle coming of Christ to destroy iniquity, and to order the church and the world after another and a better fashion; making him to come once more at the end of the world, to judge the quick and the dead: upon which point, it seems to me, he should have explained himself more fully.[28]

The "secret rapture" solved the "three comings" problem: (1) coming in a secret rapture, (2) coming to set up a millennial kingdom after the personal appearance of an Antichrist, and (3) coming in final judgment. Lacunza said that though agreeing with Papia "in some

---

27. *Ibid.*, 11-13. Several times, Lacunza confessed his system was contrary to the then current, common and universal public opinion concerning the second advent, arguing that universality of an opinion does not make it right. He confessed that he departed "from the common sentiment, or the common judgment of the Expositors, and to a certain extent also, from that of the Theologians." He also knew his system would create "the tempest of strong and violent censure, which I anticipate." He felt he was entering into combat against the established system as he turned his back on the 1,400 years of church history. *Ibid.*, 14, 29, 31. Irving's rejection by the church invoked the same attitude. Morgan Edwards had already published and taught the system in America some time before Lacunza's document was released.

28. *Ibid.*, 18.

things either general or particular," he followed no established system. He simply followed "that article of divine faith, which says, *From thence he will come to judge the quick and the dead.*"[29]

Going back further than Papia, Lacunza identifies another Jesuit:

> Omitting whatever is extraneous, his general system appears to me the same as was proposed in the last century by the learned Jesuit Antonio Vieira, in a work entitled, *Concerning the consummation of Christ's kingdom on the earth* (De regno Christi in terris consummato). And this system again appears to me the same in substance with that of many holy fathers and other doctors therein cited, as also of others that have written since; who all hold it for certain, that one day the whole world, with all the peoples and nations and even individuals thereof, shall be converted unto Christ, and enter into the Church; which being come to pass, they add, that the Jews also shall then enter in, that it may be fulfilled which is written by St. Paul (Rom. xi.25), *that blindness in part is happened unto Israel, until the fullness of the Gentiles be come in; and so all Israel shall be saved:* And by the evangelist, (John x. 16) *there shall be one fold and one Shepherd.* Consequently they suppose there is to be another state of the church, much more perfect than the present, wherein all the inhabitants of the earth will be true believers, and great peace and righteousness and observance of the divine laws, &c. will reign in the bosom of the church.[30]

Note: First, Vieira was a Jesuit; second, he called for the exaltation of the Church (Roman) and conversion of the world to take place in a "much more perfect" time yet to come; and third, the "much more perfect" age would be closely connected with the Jews.

It is interesting that the 1,400 year dead millenarian faith (revolving around a restored glorified Jewish nation, Zionism) was resurrected by at least three Roman Jesuits writing to enlighten the Church — Antonio Vieria, Euodio Papia and Lacunza. That faith now generally controls Christian thought.

There is apparently yet another Romanist involved in offering the millennial system to the Protestants, Joseph Wolff (1795-1862; see "Zionism and Joseph Wolff," p. 136, and "Joseph Wolff," p. 465),

---

29. *Ibid.,* 16, 18. Papia also exalted the Jewish nation.
30. *Ibid.,* 17, 18.

whom we will meet later. He was a close friend of both Drummond and Irving. He alone was allowed to establish the proper understanding of prophetic Scriptures at Albury Park.

Several times Jesuits offered the Protestants a system of faith, teaching that Christ himself must come to straighten out the social chaos; it will be accomplished through an exalted Jewish nation from a literal throne in a dispensation yet to come. Believers in such a system give up their faith in "Christ the victorious" who can convert the world to himself through his Spirit of Grace. Can such a millennial faith seek to Christianize all nations as commanded by the Lord Jesus in Matthew 28:19, 20?[31]

Irving developed the church/Israel distinction found in Lacunza's document, adding at Revelation 4:1 a secret rapture according to 1 Thessalonians 4:16-17, and the return of Christ and his saints to judge the earth after the "outpouring of divine judgment upon the earth."[32]

Modern dispensational millennialism thus has deep Jewish and Roman roots. Lacunza was the third or fourth Romanist to present the dispensational system before it made its way into modern "orthodox" non-Roman theology. If providence had not placed it in Irving's, and then in Darby's, hands, *Ben-Ezra* would have remained a Roman Catholic document, relegated to obscurity as had been the fate of Vieira's and Papia's documents. In fact, Lacunza expressed fear that his document would simply be consigned to the *"Index Romanus*: [i.e. the Roman list of proscribed books]" as Papia's had been, and thus "transmitting it from the womb to the grave without discretion or mercy."[33] The Presbyterian minister was the one who

---

31. The purpose of the gospel is to make all nations obedient to the faith, Rom. 16:26.

32. "...the Brethren view that, prior to the open return of Christ in judgment, He will return secretly in order to remove His people from a doomed world." *Origins*, 16. For an excellent treatment of 1 Thess. 4:16, 17, see *Biblical and Theological Studies*, XVII, "The Prophecies of St. Paul."

33. *Ben-Ezra*, I.16. Maybe Rome counted on the document "dying," so she did not stand against it at the first.

made Futurism — the *"Ben-Ezra* system" — a Protestant system. Lacunza justified viewing the new Israel literally rather than spiritually — as the Protestants were doing — by saying that though Agar and Sarah are clearly stated by Paul to be an allegory, the fact that they literally existed did not change. Thus he implied that though Israel is identified spiritually in the New Testament as the church, it did not change the fact that Israel is still a literal nation that must be regathered and glorified as God's chosen people on earth.[34]

Though there is no firm evidence that the Roman Church officially had anything to do with introducing Futurism to the Protestants, one cannot deny the advantages Rome gained from Futurism:

First, the historic Protestant view of the papal system was stoutly anti-Rome, seeing it as the present Antichrist, which was a serious problem for Rome. As long as that view prevailed, there was no hope of uniting the Protestants back to mother Rome. Futurism placed the dangers of the papal system and the Antichrist in the distant future, so they are of no concern during the present dispensation.

Second, the Reformation caused the Protestant church to apply biblical Christianity to all the world with faith that the world would be Christianized — that is, made Protestant Christians. Conversion was followed up by training the converts to infuse God's word into every area of society, *e.g.*, Christian (Protestant) welfare agencies, education, national and local civil governments. Lacunza and his disciples changed the Reformation faith by convincing Christians

---

34. *Ben-Ezra,* I.27. Darby was quite firm at this point also: Israel must be reestablished and glorified, *e.g., Writings,* II.355, *Letters,* II.443, &c. This "church/Israel" distinction is a key in the millennial system, *Plot, 88*ff. In works defending modern Fundamentalism, this writer has noticed a significant absence of any serious effort to tie Lacunza's work with the modern millennial dispensational system. Though *Ben- Ezra* is mentioned, it is mentioned only in passing as dispensationalism is traced to Irving and/or Darby and the Plymouth Brethren. One wonders why Fundamentalism is not attributed to its rightful owner, the Jewish Roman Jesuit, Lacunza.

there is no hope of Christianizing the nations in the present gospel dispensation.

The Protestant church generally now sees no hope of conquering anything (other than souls) for Christ this side of a millennial reign with a *rod of iron*. The Protestant church has no desire to *rule the world, e.g.*, train men in "Christ the victorious" to take dominion by his enabling grace in Christ's stead. According to Lacunza's system, only during Christ's millennial reign will the saints have social, economic, religious and civil authority.[35]

Third, Lacunza clearly exalted the Jewish nation. Would Futurism have been accepted without Christianizing the old Jewish hope? Did the Jews have a hand in offering the system? We know that there were several Jews involved in laying the foundation of modern dispensational millennialism, including financing Scofield, *q.v.*

Fourth, Lacunza, and many millenarians following him, emphasized the study of prophecy over the study of doctrine, believing that study will purify the saints of sin. The average non-Roman seems to know more about supposed *prophetic* passages than he does about serious doctrinal passages. The lack of serious doctrinal study leaves people open to whatever wind of doctrine is blowing the strongest. How can Protestant Christians stand upon the word of God against false doctrines when all they know is that the Lord is supposed to take care of the difficulties some day in the future? Faith comes by hearing, and hearing by the word of God. How can one have the faith to stand without serious doctrinal study of the word of God? How can one *refuse profane and old wives' fables* when he is only grounded in "prophecy?"[36] Studies in Futurism admittedly attracts people, but that emphasis leaves Believers with no weapons to counter false doctrines.

---

35. It is worth noting that the Protestants were many years behind the Romanists in establishing Christian schools for their children, and then only because the state schools became so corrupt.

36. See Rom. 10:17, 1 Tim. 1:19, 4:7, 2 Tim. 2:15, 26, 3:16, Heb. 6:1, 2.

Fifth, where do the many men who united with Futurism as it grew fit in, *e.g.,* Irving, Darby, Müller, Moody, and Scofield? Only the Lord knows.

As we saw, Lacunza admitted that Jesuits offered the *futurist* system at least three times, and maybe four, apparently refining it as it was offered. Though he said he offered it to encourage the Jews and the Roman priests, it was the Protestants who accepted it.[37]

Though faded well into the background, many of Lacunza's ideas were as old as the church itself. Irving never tired of saying that the ideas he was being ridiculed over were confirmed by the *Ben-Ezra* document. Irving probably had a martyr's complex, seeing himself more alone and persecuted than he was.

Dates worth noting:

Ribera (1596), Papia (ND, but well before Lacunza) and Morgan Edwards (1742-1744) all presented the system before the French Revolution. Europe was not ready until after the Revolution; America was not ready until after the War Between the States. *Ben-Ezra* came at the right time.

Chapter 15

Irving and *Ben-Ezra*

About 1816, the Buenos Ayres government sent the *Ben-Ezra* manuscript to England to be printed. Fifteen hundred copies were printed for use in the Spanish colonies, but Irving neither saw one nor heard of anyone who was familiar with them. Irving arrived in

---

37. One should also note that today's lax emigration policy into the U.S. allows untold multitudes of Spanish people into the U.S. The Spanish people are predominately Romanists; thus Protestant America may soon be a thing of the past. *Ben-Ezra* repeatedly called for a time of "great antichristian trouble" led by "the personal infidel Antichrist" and for an exalted Jewish church in a dispensation yet to come, *e.g., Ben- Ezra,* I.xxx,xxxi.

London in July, 1822. Early in 1823, he came into contact with a translation of an old 1812 version of the manuscript. A parish priest received a copy of the 1812 Spanish edition from a Catholic friend, and brought it to England. The priest gave the document no publicity beyond a small circle of his immediate friends and visitors, one of whom was a close friend of Irving's. The friend was intrigued by what was reportedly in *Ben-Ezra,* so he asked to borrow it while he went to London. "Deeply impressed with the truth and the importance of the doctrines contained in it, concerning the glorious advent of the Lord," the friend sought counsel from others on how to bring the document to the church's attention. They decided one would translate the document, and another would revise it, and then they would send "specimens of the work" to important Roman churchmen.[38] During the time the men were seeking to get the document into circulation among the Protestants,

> ...I [Irving, *ed.*] was obeying the call of God's Spirit to set forth from the pulpit those thoughts whereof I have given an abstract above; and it began to be noised abroad, as every thing is in this city and age of news- mongers, and was brought to the ears of a dear brother in the ministry of Christ, now most dear, though then unknown to me, save by his report, which was in all the churches, for his labours of love and munificence in behalf of the dispersion of Judah...[39]

In his document,

> Lacunza rejected the Augustinian view that the Millennium is co-extensive with the present era and that Christ will return at the end of this period to judge the living and the dead. Instead, he postulated the coming of Christ prior to the millennium and before the general resurrection. At His coming, Christ would receive in the air the risen saints and the faithful among the living. These would be kept from the judgment that would then fall upon the earth. Most of those left

---

38. *Ibid.,* I.xvi, xvii.

39. *Ibid.* Irving complained that for some time, his was the lone voice, except for one other Anglican voice, proclaiming the millennial faith, *i.e.,* "the blessedness of that millennial kingdom," and the foolishness of any hope in "Christ the victorious." He proclaimed his teaching amidst the mockery, ridicule and charges of "propagating heretical errors" by the Christian community, *Ibid.,* xv, cxxiii.

on the earth would perish in these judgments, but enough would survive to constitute the millennial kingdom which would follow.[40]

The man who was concerned about the "dispersion of Judah" heard a report of what Irving was preaching. Unable to attend one of Irving's meetings, he asked a friend to take notes of what Irving was saying. The man desiring the notes was one of the men trying to get *Ben-Ezra* into Protestant churches. And thus,

> [T]he pages of Ben-Ezra and the substance of my discourses met together upon the same table in London, on their passages to two different destinations. The truth which he had been taught in the midst of Catholic superstition, and had written with fear and trembling under the walls of the Vatican, met with the truth which God's Spirit had, during a season of affliction, taught me, in the midst of the intellectual pride of my native country; and which I was preaching in the midst of the contemptuous derision of the church in these parts, their scoffs, their insinuations, their magazine raillery, and their newspaper abuse."[41]

Though Irving knew it was a Roman Catholic document, he was quite excited over *Ben-Ezra*. It supported the ideas for which others had derided him.

Chapter 16

Irving and *Ben-Ezra* Unite

> For when it was perceived that the substance of what he had written and I was preaching was the same, and the feelings which we expressed the same, and even the expressions sometimes the same, they thought it good to bring the book to me for my perusal.[42]

---

40. *Origins*, 15. "Lacunza postulated the idea of two resurrections, that of the saints prior to the millennium and that of the wicked after it." *Ibid.*, 30, note #107.
41. *Ben-Ezra*, I.xvii, xviii. Irving is unclear in identifying which of the two were then working with *Ben-Ezra:* the one wanting the notes or the one taking the notes.
42. *Ibid.*, xviii.

Four months previous to acquiring the Spanish *Ben-Ezra,* Irving had started Spanish lessons. After a few lessons, he tried reading the Scriptures. After several days, he perused *Ben-Ezra.* Before he finished "reading the Dedication," he became convinced that the Lord had brought this Roman document to his attention for the specific purpose of translating it for the Protestant church. Irving suggested to those trying to get it to the Protestants that it should go as one piece instead of "piece-meal, as had been suggested." At the time, the two Romanists who desired to get it to the Protestants agreed to translate and review the manuscript, committing its circulation to Irving.

Attempting to identify Ben-Ezra in order to "inform the church who this Hebrew-Christian or converted Jew" actually was, "and what was known concerning him," Irving sent a letter to the one who brought the document to his attention. Shortly thereafter, he received the reply to his letter that Ben-Ezra was Lacunza, a Jesuit,

> [W]ho, along with the rest of his order, had been exiled from the Spanish colonies of South America, whereof he was a native, and had taken refuge in Italy. Also, that the character of converted Jew was assumed for the same reason; but of this I confess that I am still sceptical [sic]... Now let this book be read as a voice from the Roman Catholic Church, and let the Palingenesia and Basilicus' Letters of my friend be read as a voice from the Church of England, and let the substances of my discourse for the last year, as given above, be read as a voice from the Kirk of Scotland; and when the coincidence of sentiment and doctrine is perceived in the diversity of personal character and particular interpretations, let any one, if he dare, reject the whole matter as the ravings and dreamings of fanciful men.[43]

Irving suspected that Lacunza *was* actually a "converted Jew."[44] The second man, his friend, "a voice from the Church of England," was

---

43. *Ibid.,* xix, xx.

44. From the documents' clear and strong promotion of the old Jewish hope, Lacunza could well have been a Jew with the specific purpose of influencing the church for Zionism.

the one whom Irving heard was preaching the same views as his on the second advent.

To his surprise, two men from Irving's Presbyterian Church engaged a summer place where he could get some rest, permitting him to devote everything to translating *Ben-Ezra*. (He was not proficient in Spanish at that time.) He was only interrupted one time from his seclusion — that was the 1826 Albury conference on unfulfilled prophecy, attended by another converted Jew, Joseph Wolff. (See "The Albury Park Conferences," p. 132, and "Joseph Wolff," p. 137)

Though no writings, including *Ben-Ezra,* were permitted at that conference, Irving's heart obviously overflowed with his master's document on which he had labored so hard and so long. (Irving called him "my master," *q.v.*) Irving, undoubtedly, introduced Lacunza's millennial system at Albury, and promoted his soon to be published translation. From Albury on, the prophetic conferences centered around developing and defending the millennial system that made such a huge impact at Albury Park.

Being the son of a Jewish rabbi, there can be no doubt that Wolff promoted the rabbinical dream at Albury Park. Since Wolff alone was allowed to establish the *proper understanding* to questionable prophetic passages, the restoration of an exalted Jewish nation, even exalted over the blood-bought church, became a firm plank in the prophetic systems that came out of these prophetic meetings.[45]

With only a few sheets left in his effort, he heard of and acquired a more complete version of *Ben-Ezra*; however, he did not change his version. He simply added the index from the other version:

> But I did not think this a matter of sufficient importance to delay the publication; and I count it well that it has been so ordered, because the members of the Roman Catholic Church, for whose sake I undertake this labour, as for all others who believe in the two

---

45. The reason why only the "converted Jew" Joseph Wolff was allowed to give the proper understanding to Scriptures will be developed. Because the *Ben-Ezra* system is so easily traced to modern millennialism, we are tracing it from that source.

advents of Christ, would have ill brooked [sic] that an edition prepared in London, under the eyes of those they know not, should have been preferred to the edition published under the authority of the Spanish church..., the work of one of her most gifted and most dutiful sons.[46]

He did not try to hide the fact that *Ben-Ezra* was a Roman document, published at one time under the authority of the Spanish church. Though urged to warn readers of the Roman character of *Ben-Ezra*, Irving did not want to take "advantage of the honest, well-meaning" Manuel Lacunza. However, Irving never missed the opportunity to warn his readers against the common doctrines permeating society in his day. Irving had a far kinder spirit toward Romanists than he did toward the Protestant leaders, for they ignored his prophetic opinions:

> [I]n the interpretation of the various texts and contexts of the prophetic Scriptures, (and to him [Lacunza, *ed.*] all Scripture is prophetic), there is no Protestant writer whom I know of, to be at all compared to him. His book is the finest demonstration of the orthodoxy of the ancient system of the millenarian which can be imagined; indeed I may say perfect and irrefragable. I never expect to see an answer to it, nor do I believe an answer will ever be attempted.[47]

> ...having contented himself [Lacunza, *ed.*] with establishing the orthodoxy and Biblical truth of that system of opinions, upon which we are now to try conclusions with the opposite prevailing system...[48]

He determined to send portions of his translation to various Christian leaders, asking them to review and comment on his work. To entice them to respond, he promised to place their comments at the end of the document. However, in response, Irving,

> [R]eceived nothing but the highest approbation of the spirit of the writer and the power of his argument. This ought to be known and

---

46. *Ibid.*, xxi.
47. *Ibid.*, xxvi. This writer finds it strange how Irving kept fleeing back to *Ben-Ezra* to define orthodoxy. Since Irving, the "Ben-Ezra system" has become "orthodoxy." However, he may have felt *Ben-Ezra* revived very early orthodoxy.
48. *Ibid.*, lxvii, lxviii.

spread abroad as some covert, the only one which I could construct, against the evil report which a thousand ignorant and sectarian pens will, in the plenitude of their all-comprehending ignorance, immediately set abroad against him [*Ben-Ezra, ed.*]. Oh, but I do rejoice that, from the moment I began to use a pen for the instruction of my countrymen, I did, without any compromise, expose the character of the Protestant Inquisition, and make war against it.[49]

The refusal to even consider the new millennial system started Irving's war against the second advent as understood by the general Christian thought of his day, c. 1825. His chief weapon was his pen, and he *shot forth* the arrow of *Ben-Ezra* to the heart of the Christian faith. The result has been that the then common view of "Christ the victorious" in this present *dispensation* was replaced with the "terrors of Satan."

According to Irving, Lacunza preached in America. Lacunza himself mentioned the spread of his system overseas, even before he presented it to the public in 1790. Morgan Edwards had already published the system in America in 1788. Thus the system, later brought to America by the Brethren, Darby especially, was already making inroads into American Christian culture before 1800.[50]

Chapter 17
A New View of Revelation

Ben-Ezra's view of the Roman Church basically changed Revelation from its historical orthodox position, history, to prophecy:

> We agree in perceiving that the papacy hath furnished, is furnishing, and will furnish the great strength and supply of the infidel power, that the infidel power will carry along with it the papal hierarchy and kingdom, that it will be supported by these in the persecution of the true church of Christ; that it will stand up against the Lord and his

---
49. *Ibid.*, xxii, xxiii.
50. *Ibid.*, xxiii, xxiv.

anointed, and not be destroyed but by the brightness of his coming. I may add, moreover, that his interpretation of the acting of this future infidel beast of ten horns, so exactly concurs with our interpretation of the acting of the past papal beast, that I oft fancied he was describing rather than anticipating; and a friend of mine in whose sound judgment I have much reliance, remarked to me that it confirmed him in the protestant interpretations, more than anything which he had ever read in their [protestant, *ed.*] own works.[51]

Lacunza took the Protestant understanding that Daniel's beast was the papal power past, present and future, and placed it all into the future, a new dispensation yet to come. Irving rejoiced that this "most dutiful son" of Rome saw Daniel's beast exactly as he saw it, with the only *minor* difference being the timing of the beast.

Though Lacunza presented a view of Revelation with which Irving did not agree totally, his system became the accepted view:

> Next with respect to the Apocalypse, for the above mentioned are the only two visions of Daniel which he treated at large, I must begin by observing that I perfectly concur with his ideal that the title of the book "The Revelation of Jesus Christ," is to be understood in an active, not in a passive sense, to signify as it doth in all the epistles "the revealing of Jesus Christ," or the manifestation of his promised coming. [Notice Irving said, "his promised coming," *ed.*] And it may be some confirmation of this idea to state that I had been convinced of this several months before I saw the work, and had suggested it to a friend, who is conversant in these matters. But though concurring with my author in this the germ of his system of interpreting the Apocalypse, I do by no means concur in his inference, that therefore it must wait for and immediately precede the day of the Lord's coming, and be all evolved with a rapidity of succession which will not fill many years; and that no part of the book from the fourth chapter to the end, has yet been accomplished. In his inference I do not concur, though I concur in the idea that the book is nothing but the manifestation of the Lord's coming, revealed for the teaching and consolation of his church. But such a manifestation as will comfort and sustain the church during the whole period of his absence, being to her what the succession of prophets was to the former church.... So while Ben-Ezra has most triumphantly refuted those who would make all the Apocalypse to

---

51. *Ibid.,* xxxi.

run out or terminate long ere this, he has laid himself open to the same sort of triumphant refutation by confining it to a short period towards the end of time, which is not yet arrived.[52]

Irving said Lacunza "triumphantly refuted those who would make" the Revelation history rather than prophecy. Thus he changed the orthodox view of the book of Revelation of his day. Lacunza placed everything from chapter four on, such as the "the apocalyptic seals, trumpets and vials," completely in the future.[53] Lacunza claimed it was all to take place within a short span of time just before the Lord's return to start the millennium. Irving differed slightly with Lacunza's view:

> For, according to his views, all from the fourth chapter forward unto the end of the book, remains unaccomplished, and will be rapidly evolved in a regular succession immediately upon the eve of the Lord's coming. In which case it is like no other prophecy that the Spirit of God ever indited; and wants the prophetic sanction of embracing what hath already come to pass, and therefore wants the irreversible claim upon the belief of the church.[54]

Lacunza's new system prevailed, and became the accepted prophetic understanding for the Protestant church, including the statement, "the things that are."[55]

Irving strongly implied that Lacunza's document was given "to conclude the canon, and serve the part of a prophecy to the Gentile church, leading in and pointing directly, like all prophecy, to the grand restoration by the coming of the Lord..." He also compared it with Isaiah and Daniel, who prepared the Old Testament church — the congregation of the Lord — for what was to come upon it. *Ben-*

---

52. *Ibid.*, xxxii. "Almost all believe that the 1260 days closed in the French revolution, and that the seven vials then began to be poured out upon those who had the mark of the beast." *Ibid.*, xl.
53. *Ibid.*, xxxiv.
54. *Ibid.*, xxxvi.
55. Darby assumed Lacunza's idea of the church leaving the earth before God judges the wicked, holding that God cannot act in judgment against sin until the rest of his body, *i.e.*, the church, is with him, *Writings*, II.545, &c. He also claimed as his idea that the church would be removed when John heard the trumpet in Rev. 4:1, *Writings*, II.362, c. 1852.

Ezra, he contended, prepares the church, suffering under Roman Paganism, for the coming "downfall of the Papacy":[56]

> And this, I assert, has been the case: during the first three centuries, the Apocalypse was known and cherished in the Church as the great assurance of the downfall of Paganism; during the sufferings of the Waldenses and the Protestants, it was cherished as the ground of belief, that the Pope and the papal empire was the beast...[57]

Thus he used the early persecutions by paganism to confirm Lacunza's system of a future fulfillment of Revelation over the prevailing view of a historical understanding of the book. (That view was that the Revelation prepared the early church for the coming destruction of the Jewish nation, Jerusalem, and the old Hebrew economy as described by the Lord in Matthew chapters 21-24.) Lacunza's system placed the fall of the papal system into a future dispensation. Intentionally or unintentionally, Lacunza took the Protestant pressure off Rome, defused and dissolved attacks upon the pope as the Antichrist, and allowed the pope to work unhindered to make the whole world popish.[58]

Chapter 18

New Doctrine Introduced

Lacunza's 1790 document is the apparent basis of the modern dispensational millennial system, including hints of a "rapture" at

---

56. *Ben Ezra,* I.xxxii. Darby, throughout his writings, implies that he was given by God to the church to provide further light, *e.g., Writings,* II.347.

57. *Ben-Ezra,* I.xxxiv.

58. Darby solved the history problem by saying that history is not to be used in understanding prophetic passages. He solved the exegetical problem with his new Bible study method, "Bible Readings." (See "Bible Readings," p. 281.) He worked at placing Mat 24, and thus the Revelation, in the future, *Writings,* II.319, 370, &c. By teaching that "history is not necessary in order to understand prophecy," for "history never explains prophecy," he was able to make passages, *e.g.,* Mat. 24, stand as prophecy from the time they are read rather than from the time they were given. *Ibid.,* 93.

Revelation 4:1. Those views have produced disastrous results as the implications of that faith have worked into society over the past 175 years. The following quotes from Irving's *Discourse* will clearly show the source of a great amount of what is currently taught by the millennial system.

Ignoring both the source and the authorship of the document, both serious considerations that should have caused him to dismiss it, Irving continued to translate the document while pastoring the Scottish Caledonian Church. He signed his *Translators Discourse,* Christmas Day, 1826. However, his edition was not sent to the printer until 1827, having been interrupted by the 1826 Albury Park Conference on Unfulfilled Prophecy.

The Translator's Preliminary Discourse is a lengthy 194 pages, giving an overview of his and Lacunza's thinking, which is important for our present study. In fact, Irving's 1826 *Discourse* confirms that the Christian faith was a victorious faith until the early 1800 rise of the Brethren.

One purpose for Irving's lengthy *Preliminary Discourse* was to answer the charge that he had been "propagating heretical errors":

> I have begun the preliminary discourse by giving an exposition of the doctrine which I have been teaching; first, to justify myself before the church of Christ in general, and especially before the church of Scotland, which ordained me to the ministerial and pastoral office, and against the crude misapprehensions which in a day of such theological ignorance, and the malicious misrepresentations which in a day of such sectarian bigotry and bitterness, have gone forth on all hands against me, as if I were propounding speculative notions, or propagating heretical errors. Secondly; to show the wonderful coincidence of the doctrine, which I had taught in ignorance that it was taught by any other, which the doctrine contained in this book which I now present to the churches using the English tongue, and I may say with doctrine which is now in all quarters beginning to take root and bear fruit in these parts.[59]

---

59. *Ben-Ezra,* I.xv. As previously noted, Irving was probably teaching his "novel" ideas as early as 1822, and maybe earlier. Irving gained "extravagant assumptions" of himself because of his popularity.

Irving openly stated that his novel ideas were based upon what appeared in surrounding society despite what the word of God said. Irving attempted to justify his novel view of Isaiah 9:6, *i.e.,* "The prophecy therefore waits still for its great accomplishment [in 'the restoration of the Jewish people at the future advent of Messiah,' *ed.*] in the Son of the Virgin, by the act and power of the Son of the Virgin" by saying:

> Whether this [Isa ix.2, *ed.*] was wholly accomplished in his first coming, to which it is applied in the gospel of Matthew, I leave every one to judge for himself; but to me it seems manifest that it was not... because they profited little by the light then afforded to them...[60]

The dispensational system is quite hostile toward any spiritual application of Christ's victorious reign as mentioned in Isaiah, Jeremiah, Ezekiel and Hebrews 8. It is hostile against Satan's defeat during this present dispensation and any kind of spiritual application of Daniel 7:13, 14. Irving argued from every angle for fifteen pages that Christ's reign must be a literal millennial reign over a literal, restored, exalted, glorified, warlike Jewish nation:

> If any one say, No; Jesus of Nazareth shall never sit upon David's throne, nor rule over the house of Jacob. Then I say, Jesus of Nazareth is not the person here prophesied of [Isa. ix, *ed.*], but some other. If they say, Yea, but he is the Emmanuel born of the Virgin, who now is spiritually filling the spiritual throne of David, and spiritually reigning over the spiritual house of Jacob, and spiritually holding universal spiritual empire. Then all I have to say is, I do not know what the spiritual throne of David means. It is the throne of a believer's heart. Where learned you to call a believer's heart the throne of David? It is the throne of the Majesty on high. How dare you blaspheme, and call the throne of God the throne of David?...[61]

Patrick Fairbairn (1805-1874) states:

---

60. *Ibid.,* cxl. Irving admitted he was militating against the general Christian consensus of his day: Geneva's 1599's Isa. 9:2 note, "This captivity and deliverance were figures of our captivity by sin and of our deliverance by Christ through the preaching of the Gospel, Mat. 4:15,16."

61. *Ibid.,* cxliii.

But presently afterwards [after Peter questions Christ, Acts 1:6, *ed.*], when the Spirit has descended with his enlightening and elevating influences, he proclaims Christ as already "exalted to sit on the throne of David" (Acts ii:30); or, as it is again expressed, anointed by God, according to the terms of the second Psalm, and now meeting the opposition of ungodly men, which was there predicted respecting the Lord's anointed King (chap. iv:24-28).[62]

Christ, according to the clear words of God's Spirit, ascended to the throne of his father, David. (Acts 2:27-36.) When Peter preached that Christ ascended to David's throne, as prophesied, to rule over his enemies, the Jews cried out, *Men and brethren, what shall we do?* One wonders, consequently, if a reason we do not see men today *pricked in their heart* is because Christ is not presented as he was by the Spirit to the first church — enthroned as the King with total power and authority over God's enemies. But the system seems to hold that when the Spirit does not speak according to appearances, the Spirit is ignored.

Hatred for any thought of Christ's spiritual reign leads to the next conclusion: that Psalms 45 and Psalms 149:7-9 are yet to be fulfilled literally by Christ sitting on a literal throne of David at Jerusalem. Irving justified his literal understanding of Psalms 45 by saying that Christ must yet earn the "right to the title of, Gebor [sic. Hebrew, Irving's term, *ed.*], the mighty one...", and that he must yet "conquer the love of his Spouse....by great exploits of war and conquest, wrought on her behalf."[63] Furthermore, he contended that the victories spoken of in 1 Corinthians 15:53-57 must be understood literally, and will not come to pass until a literal, millennial reign of Christ.[64]

The reader should note that Lacunza and Irving overlooked the fact that the Lord forbade David from building the temple because David had *shed much blood upon the earth in* the Lord's sight:

---

62. Fairbarn, *Prophetic Prospects of the Jews*, 107.
63. *Ben Ezra*, I. cxxxvi [sic — this page is misnumbered; it should be, cxxxvii] - clii (cxlvi, cli). Rather than dealing with Ps. 45, we urge the reader to examine Spurgeon's *Treasury of David*.
64. *Ben-Ezra*, I.clxxxiii.

> But the word of the LORD came to me, saying, Thou hast shed blood abundantly, and hast made great wars: thou shalt not build an house unto my name, because thou hast shed much blood upon the earth in my sight. (1 Chron. 22:8)
>
> This declares how greatly God detests the shedding of blood, seeing David for this cause is prevented from building the temple of the Lord, though he enterprised no war, but by God's command and against his enemies. (Geneva)

Since the Lord has expressed his utter contempt for building his glorious temple with bloody warfare, how can one imagine that Christ will use the literal blood of his enemies to build a future millennial kingdom? The promise of 1 Chronicles 22:8ff., was that one *Greater than Solomon,* the Son of David, would build the temple of the Lord through his conquering Spirit of peace.[65] The Jews found such an idea to be totally contrary to what they had hoped for and dreamed of for generations.

Chapter 19

Zionism

Ben-Ezra, Irving, Darby and about all who worked at developing the millennial faith, continually exalted the Jews and national Israel over the Gospel Church.[66] This writer found it difficult to cover any of the millennial topics as they developed from *Ben-Ezra* on without encountering the Jews and Israel. In fact, it is so difficult to avoid that the reader may think this document is emphasizing that one point. The place of national Israel and the Jews in God's plan (which seems to replace Christ and the church for which he died) is a key plank in the modern millennial system.

---

65. See Mat. 12:42; 1 Cor. 3:16 and 2 Cor. 6:16.
66. The Ben-Ezra/Darbyite system makes national Israel the heart of all Old Testament Scripture, and places the church as an after-thought. It revolves Scripture around a restored, carnal Israel, rather than around Christ. Scripture is about Christ, not a restored Israel. See *Israel*, chapter 1.

The obvious common thread throughout the rise of millenarianism is its exaltation of a restored nation of Israel, known today as Zionism.[67] Modern Zionism can be traced to a concern about the depressed condition of the Jews in the early 1800s. "Protestant Zionism" and "Political Zionism" are terms used by Sandeen to describe the renewed Jewish hope introduced by Irving and Joseph Wolff.[68]

Concerning a literal understanding of Ezekiel 39 (specifically burying the dead, vv. 12-16), Fairbairn said:

> It bids defiance to all the laws of nature, as well as the known principles of human action; and to insist on such a description being understood according to the letter, is to make it take rank with the most extravagant tales of romance, or the most absurd legends of Popery.[69]

Did Fairbairn have in mind the millennial system that was gaining popularity in its insistence that everything be understood literally? Regardless, he did say that insistence on literal understandings smelled of Popery.

---

67. *Zionism:* "An organized movement of world Jewry that arose in Europe in the late 19th century with the aim of reconstituting a Jewish state in Palestine." *American Heritage Dictionary*, CDROM. It could also be referred to as *Jewish Chiliasm:* "Klieforth, Keil, etc., speak of the views expressed by Koehler and Hoffmann in their works on Zechariah, that this chapter [Zech. 14, *ed.*] refers to a yet future siege of Jerusalem after the return of the Jews in a condition of unbelief, and of their deliverance by the appearing of Christ, as 'Jewish Chiliasm,' but Jewish Chiliasm was not *all* wrong. *There is* a Messianic Kingdom — a literal reign of peace and righteousness on the earth, with Israel as its center; but where Jewish Chiliasm erred was that it overlooked, or explained away, the sufferings of the Messiah which precede the glory." *Zechariah*, 490. Thus we have Baron propagating "Protestant Zionism." In his work on Zachariah, Merrill F. Unger is also a strong "Protestant Zionist," *Zechariah*, Zondervan, 1963. We will use *Political Zionism* as non Christians rebuilding a national Jewish state, and *Protestant Zionism* as Christians seeking to rebuild a national Jewish state.

68. *Roots*, 10-12. In 1891, successful American business man turned evangelist, William E. Blackstone, (1841-1935) "sent a memorial to President Harrison asking the president to use his office to bring about an international conference to consider the Jews and their claims to Palestine." *Who*, s.v. "Blackstone, William Eugene."

It was their false hope of deliverance from Rome by the promised Messiah that caused the Jews of 70 AD to fight against Rome:

> But now, what did the most to elevate them in undertaking this war [against Rome, which led to their total destruction, ed.], was an ambiguous oracle that was also found in their sacred writings, how, "about that time, one from their country should become governor of the habitable earth." The Jews took this prediction to belong to themselves in particular and many of the wise men were thereby deceived in their determination. Now, this oracle certainly denoted the government of Vespasian, who was appointed emperor in Judea. However, it is not possible for men to avoid fate, although they see it beforehand. But these men interpreted some of these signals according to their own pleasure; and some of them they utterly despised, until their madness was demonstrated, both by the taking of their city and their own destruction. [70]

The hope of a Messiah to exalt a restored Jewish nation over the world still lived as the rebellious Jews perished in the flames that engulfed the Temple and then Jerusalem. Lacunza revived that hope. Throughout *Wars,* Josephus says that Rome moved against Jerusalem because of the Jews' rebellion against God.

---

69. *Ezekiel,* 423. The view that Ezekiel chaps. XL-XLVIII speak of a literal restoration of a literal nation in Palestine is the revived "Jewish-carnal view" (*Ben Ezra,* I.cxxxviff. - Lacunza admits the papal power is the Antichrist, but is not during the present dispensation), 434, 435. In Fairbairn's "Preliminary remarks" to Ezk. 40, he proves the absurdity of trying to view that section literally, *ibid.,* 431-450. Scofield clearly teaches the "Jewish-carnal" view, *Scofield,* 885. Trapp called the Jewish literal interpretation of this passage a "fanatical notion... the fool's paradise of a sublime dotage." *Trapp,* III.643. William Law (1686-1761) called the hope of an "outward Messiah... [with an, ed.] outward kingdom" a dream of carnal Jews. *Power,* 93.

70. Josephus, *Wars,* Bk VI, Chap. V.4. See Hengstenberg's *Christology of the Old Testament,* 1201, for further study on the restored "Jewish Hope," Zionism. The early church fathers contended Christians the true Jews, *e.g.,* Justin, *Ante-Nicene Fathers,* I.207ff., *e.g.,* "CHAP CXIII. — RIDICULOUS INTERPRETATIONS OF THE JEWS. CHRISTIANS ARE THE TRUE ISRAEL," 261. Hastings also points out that Israel's dream was that Jahweh [sic] would reign in Zion over his people: "It is not something quite new, but a glorification of the old." *Ethics,* s.v. "Kingdon of God." That hope kept the insurrection alive despite Rome's armies surrounding the Temple. That ancient hope is alive today in dispensationalism, *i.e.,* "Protestant Zionism."

Darby solved the problem of honest history failing to support the dispensational system by separating history from theology; accordingly, he made history a series of unrelated facts, a totally unscriptural view of history. In 1881, Darby defined Zionism thusly: "He comes from heaven to destroy the beast, and takes the kingdom, and then out of Zion establishes His kingdom on earth, the Assyrian [being destroyed]."[71] The renewal and *Christianization* of the Jewish hope was not original with Darby. Lewis Way (see under "Henry Drummond," p. 129), Joseph Wolff (see "Joseph Wolff," p. 465), Edward Irving and Lacunza were key figures in its modern renewal. The Albury and Powerscourt prophecy conferences were where these men and ideas merged.

In the midst of his argument placing Isaiah 9 into a future reign of Christ, Irving attempts to use a long-lived Jewish hope to justify his "novel" ideas:

> Time by the Jews was divided into two great portions, the age that is, and the age that is to come; meaning by the former the duration of their captivity, affliction, and waiting for Messiah; and by the latter, the eternity of their triumph and rejoicing, and kingdom, in the presence of Messiah.... For it was a universal opinion among the Jews, that at the commencement of the future age the dead should be raised who had lived and died in the fear of God, and in the hope of Messiah: who, they believed, would not disappoint their faithful expectations, but bring them along with him. Of this age it is here said that he is to be the Father, even as Satan is the father of this age, and all save those begotten unto Christ are his children....[72]

As noted above, however, his total argument self-destructed, for it was based upon appearances rather than what is clearly stated by the Spirit of God. In his fifteen page argument, Irving continually flees to appearances over Scripture:

---

71. *Letters,* III.137, 138.
72. *Ben Ezra,* I.cxlvi, cxlvii. As previously mentioned, one of the purposes of *Ben-Ezra* was to exalt the Jewish nation. Note the hint of a "rapture." Darby was dogmatic concerning the necessity in God's plan of a literal, triumphant, militant Jewish Messiah to reestablish and glorify an Israelite, Jewish nation — he claimed the doctrine originated in his mind, *e.g., Writings,* II.355, 355, *Letters,* II.443, &c.

For I agree with my author [Lacunza, *ed.*] in thinking that we are not yet in possession of that new covenant, described in Jeremiah and Ezekiel, and quoted by Paul in the eighth chapter of the Hebrews, which was made to Israel, and, in her, to all the world; (for she is, as it were, the mediatrix and mistress of the nations, at the time of her restoration) for the fourfold blessing of the covenant will by no means apply to any visible body at present on the earth; and only in the way of an earnest will apply to the spiritual Church, which is invisible, and cannot be said to contain Israel, or, as little, to contain all men...[73]

Consumed with the system, Irving repeatedly summed it up, continually pointing out that it was contrary to the accepted Christian thought of his day:

> That system of opinions with respect to the coming of Christ, which at present holds possession of the churches.... We add this to the present popular creed [referring back to a Prophet, Priest and King "words of the Catechism of our church," *ed.*] of the church, from which we take nothing away. We say that the day of the Lord which is the face of Peter's warning, they interpret of a natural day, but which we in the spirit of his warning, and of John's exposition, interpret of a thousand years, is the period during which this manifestation will be made. We interpret the conflagration of the earth to be its purification or baptism with fire, and not its annihilation. We doubt whether annihilation be an idea contained in the scriptures at all; for we perceive that the second death is not annihilation; nor are wicked men annihilated; nor is Satan, nor is death, nor is..., the place of separated spirits, which are all cast into a lake of fire. We believe that our Lord shall reign a certain limited time with his enemies under his feet, that is in a state of subjection; and afterwards that he shall reign for ever, with his enemies under the dominion of the second death. That there shall be a period of Satan's imprisonment and of death's subjection, and of the earth's protection, government, and blessedness, in despite of all the powers of darkness; and that after this there will be an eternity of Satan's second death, and death's second death, and the second death of all wicked men and wicked angels, and their fruits of wickedness; which shall be to the earth an eternity of infallible blessedness, of God's immediate presence, of the concentration of his love, of the peculiar abode and government of his Son. And that

---

73. *Ben-Ezra*, I.cl.

this immortal earth for ever, and the redeemed saints inheriting for ever their inheritance incorruptible and undefiled and that fadeth not away, and the Son of God their king, united to human nature ever, shall be for ever the monument of God's love and mercy to believing sinners, the enduring proof unto the universe of the incredible power of faith in the word of God, which when all the unfallen creatures of God behold, they may adore the triumphs of faith, and hold fast their allegiance, and delight in the glory of redeeming love, and in the victory of almighty grace over sin....'[74]

Lacunza offered, among other things, new understandings concerning (1) a thousand year "day of the Lord", as opposed to the general idea of a single, natural "day of the Lord"; (2) a literal, limited reign of Christ over his enemies with a rod of iron; (3) Christ's literal reign with military might from a restored Jerusalem; and (4) grace's victory over sin yet to come. Note the striking similarities with Morgan Edwards' much earlier *Academical Exercises*.

Though the statement above came after his discourse on Isaiah 9:6, it is part of his conclusion to that discourse. Therefore, it was based upon his denial that the Spirit of God knew what he was talking about in Matthew 4:15, 16; Irving used what appeared to the natural eye concerning Isaiah 9:2.

Darby solved the exegetical problem that confronted Irving with Matthew 4:15, 16 — that is, New Testament authors understood and applied Old Testament prophetic passages spiritually rather than literally. The ability of committed millenarians to completely ignore the Spirit's New Testament spiritual application of Old Testament prophetic passages is amazing. Apparently, they are unconcerned about what God's word says if it does not support their position or interpretation. Darby's Bible study method, "Bible readings," permits dispensationalism to claim to believe Scripture while, at the same time, denying the obvious intent of the Author.

A second statement made by Irving that we should note:

---

74. *Ibid.*, clii, cliii.

> Now this third province of our High Priest's work I find to be thus written in the Scripture. That at the coming of the Lord there will be such a purification of the earth by fire, and amelioration of its condition by other means, known perhaps to God only, though our author [Lacunza, ed.] hath well, yea, magnificently speculated thereon, as shall realize the blessedness of that millennial kingdom, whereof some part of the delineation is set down above. This will take place by the casting out of Satan... and by subjugation of all things to the Prince of Peace, and to the saints who shall be raised to be partakers of his government and kingdom...[75]

Not only does Irving throughout his *Discourse* continually tell us that his ideas are based upon his observations and Lacunza's speculations, but he also tells us that they are based upon his opinions: "but to me it seems manifest", "I have my suspicion", "my own conviction", "while I feel assured". He wrote, "Nay, more, though it is very presumptuous to speculate upon these things by the way of natural reason", then proceeded to justify his opinions with many arguments appealing to the "natural" man.[76]

How much of Irving's "blessedness of the millennial kingdom" was simply the prophetic speculations of Lacunza and how much was already being proclaimed by Irving, we cannot say. We do know, however, whether from Irving or from Lacunza, that a vast portion of what follows is speculation *according to appearances*, quite contrary to John 7:24.

---

75. *Ibid.*, cxxiii. He admitted that the view of the future glorious millennial kingdom of the restored Israel and warlike Messiah was Lacunza's, *ibid.*, cxxix.

76. All these quotes are just on one page, *ibid.*, xcl, except his use of "natural reason," clxii. At least nine times, Darby tells us that his view of Mat. 24 was according to the way he felt it should be, *e.g.*, "seems to me,... I think,... I believe," &c. *Writings*, II.355.

Chapter 20

National Israel Exalted

The church of the Lord Jesus Christ is now the depository of God's word. The word of God revolves around Christ, not around a Jewish state. But in reading the *Discourse,* one wonders where Christ is in the millennial scheme of things, for it revolves around a renewed national Israel, not around the victory of Christ. *Watch Israel, for it is God's timetable,* is the cry of millennialism.[77]

Irving said that while preaching from 1 Thessalonians 5:4-7:

> ...I was found maintaining the doctrine of the *second advent.* It was this day twelve-months, a day to be remembered in the history of my ministry; for which, not I only, but many souls now walking in the hope of thine appearing have reason to bless thee, oh thou great Head of thy Church!
>
> The doctrine which I maintained, was, that "the coming of the Lord in judgment, from the time of Enoch, the first of inspired preachers, until the time of John, the last of them, had been upheld before the elect church as the great object of their hope and desire; and for these three great reasons. — 1st. That then the number of the elect is accomplished; 2nd. That then their warfare is ended; and 3rd. That their kingdom is come: while on the other hand, it had been equally upheld before the reprobate and unbelieving, as the great object of fear and argument of repentance; 1st. because then their kingdom is ended, 2ndly. their day of grace concluded; and 3rdly. their judgment, i.e. of the quick is accomplished, and the fate of all their generations sealed until the judgment of the dead, which cometh not till after the reign of the saints and the elect, designated in scripture, "a thousand years," and among divines, *the millennium."*
>
> Having broken ground in this great controversy, I found it necessary to maintain myself, and to that end took up certain great and strong positions, which seemed to me the keys of the whole debatable laud; of which positions these three were the chief.

---

77. Does the Word of God revolve around Christ or around a renewed Jewish state? That subject is worth another book in itself. See LaRondell's *Israel.*

First; that the present visible church of the Gentiles, which hath been the depository of the oracles and the sacraments, and the ordinances, since the Jewish state was dissolved, I mean the mixed multitude who are baptized in the name of the Father, and the Son, and the Holy Ghost,... this body of baptized men, which I call the Gentile church, who should every one of them have been a saint; being "by baptism ingrafted into Christ Jesus to be made partakers of his justice, whereby our sins are covered and remitted;" ([Irving's footnote, *ed.*] Confession of Faith of the Kirk of Scotland, ratified and established A.D. 1567. And I may refer to all the Articles, Confessions, and Catechisms, from the Augsburg to the Westminster.) standeth threatened in the Holy Scriptures because of its hypocrisies, idolatries, superstitions, infidelity, and enormous wickedness... (Isaiah xxiv.) with such terrible judgment, as hath not been, nor ever shall again be seen upon the earth... -which fearful consummation I judge to be close at hand...[78]

Observe:

First, Irving understood the Gospel Church, the Body of Christ, only in the form of a visible church of the Gentiles. Looking, hence, to the fallen nature of man revealed in the visible church, he saw nothing of God's hand in the affairs of men, especially wicked men. His *Discourse* implies that he and Lacunza knew very little of the converting grace of God that creates a new man from the inside out: *For if any man be in Christ, he is a new creation...*

Second, he placed the time of the change of "the depository" of God's word with Old Testament Israel to the "visible church of the Gentiles" with the *death* of "the Jewish state", rather than placing it at the time of Christ. The system revolved around a renewed nation of Israel, a Jewish church. In fact, it held to three churches: Old Testament, New Testament and a future Jewish church, with the prophetic Old Testament passages of a victorious church (*e.g.* Isaiah) referring to a future Jewish church[79] — a church/Israel distinction.

Third, the church, failing to carry out the Lord's will on earth, is now fit for nothing except the judgment of God, resulting in its

---

78. *Ibid.,* iv, v.

desolation: "which fearful consummation I judge to be close at hand".

Chapter 21
Jewish Hope Christianized

Lacunza and Irving *Christianized* and gave to the church the Jewish hope of a renewed, glorious, national, millennial reign of the Messiah over Israel. Lacunza either gave Irving the Jewish hope, or confirmed Irving's existing idea.

Irving saw "Christ our Prophet, preparing for the coming of Christ our Priest." He was against applying spiritual truths, *e.g.,* Christ our Priest, to the visible world, as was then being done in magazines, sermons and newspapers. Christ our Priest, he held, must be used prophetically only, for that alone "would purify the heart, enlarge the soul, and exalt the discourse of the common people in a most wonderful degree..."[80]

Irving called looking back to Christ's victory at his first advent an "unnatural position."[81] Using his reasoning for not looking back, he justified the millennial system of a renewed Jewish state, *i.e.,* Zionism:

> [N]o prophecy is of a private or limited application, so as to run out before the end, but every one, or almost every one, hath something in it yet unaccomplished, they [the church of his day, *ed.*] make but

---

79. *Ibid.,* xxxviii. According to the system, Revelation is for Gentile church, and will all be fulfilled in her. Among Darby's many "Irvingite" points, he held that the church is removed in Rev. 4:1 and is not heard from again until Christ returns to set up his literal throne, *Writings,* II.20. Irving was certain that the Gentile church was ruined, and had to be replaced with a Jewish church, *Ben-Ezra,* I.cxxxiv. Darby was known for his "ruin of the church" theory and its soon-coming judgement by God of spewing it out of his mouth, *Writings,* II.11, 186, &c. "As to the ruin of the church, the theory came to me...," *Letters,* I.42, 1840.
80. *Ben-Ezra,* I.lxxxvi, lxxxvii.
81. *Ibid.,* lxxvii, lxxviii.

bungling, blundering work in providing the accomplishment of any of them to be perfected: insomuch that in the great question of Messiah's former advent, I should undertake to hold the Jewish side, against a goodly number of our Christian divines, interpreting the prophecies according to the canons of sound interpretation applicable to all other books...[82]

He openly confessed that he sided with the Jewish hope of a renewed Zionist state against the standard view of the Christian divines of his day. He admitted that his view of a renewed Jewish state in power and glory was a Jewish idea. His definition of "no prophecy is of a private or limited application," permitted him to ignore history. Irving was, hence, able to hold to Lacunza's hope of a renewed Jewish state despite what Christ and the apostles said.[83] Accordingly, one ignores history, including how the early church viewed Scriptural matters, as one studies *prophetic* passages: *So what if the early church fathers saw Matthew 24 and the Revelation basically fulfilled in the destruction of Jerusalem and did not hold to a renewed Jewish state? We must not look back. We must look forward to a future literal fulfillment of those passages.*

We encourage the reader to check some important references from Josephus — historical records that are totally ignored by Lacunza's system. Honest history shows the fulfillment of events that Lacunza and Irving sought to place into the future.

First, the three and a half years of Daniel 2:27 — when Titus, the Roman general who destroyed Jerusalem after the seven year war, gave orders to his soldiers to dig up the foundations of the tower of Antonia, Josephus informed him, "that on that very day, the seventeenth day of Panemus, the sacrifice called 'the Daily Sacrifice' had failed, and had not been offered to God for want of men to offer it."[84]

Second, the "Abomination of Desolation" was fulfilled.[85]

---

82. *Ibid.,* lxxvii, lxxviii. Claiming he alone was using "the canons of sound interpretation," others who were not following his lead were wrong.
83. Darby: "History never explains prophecy." *Writings,* II.93, 1854.
84. *Wars,* Book VI, Chap II, § 1.

Third, according to his promise (Mat. 23:36), Christ returned in 70 AD in judgment upon the generation that put him to death. He did not return unannounced.[86]

Josephus said, "Accordingly the multitude of those that therein perished exceeded all the destructions that either men or God ever brought upon the world."[87]

Chapter 22

The Defeated Church

Irving offered an extremely defeated view of the church, holding that the church is hopelessly ruined. He taught that the church's responsibilities before its millennial reign with Christ are strictly spiritual, as are Christ's:

> But though in this spiritual way ["And the church fulfilleth the office of king only in the same spiritual sense in which Christ presently fulfilleth it; that is, by dispensations of forgiveness and excommunication, of binding and of loosing," *ed.*] the church doth show forth all these three offices [prophet, priest and king, *ed.*], yet, in none of them is she completely invested. She doth but see as through a glass dimly; she hath forgotten that she was purged from her old sins; and she exerciseth no kingly discipline over her members, but is under bondage to every low and crafty influence. She hath been so from the first, and will be so unto the last, growing

---

85. *Seige*, 453.
86. *Wars*, Book VI, Chap. V, § 3.
87. *Ibid*, Chap. IX, § 1 and § 4. "The whole multitude of Jews that were destroyed during the entire seven years before this time...," § 3, footnote. "[T]hey were ejected out of them [the strong towers, *ed.*] by God himself..." Book VI, Chap. VIII, § 5. Taking into account the number of pascal lambs used the year Jerusalem was destroyed, it is estimated that no less than 2,700,000, but nearer 3,000,000 Jews perished in 70 AD, Book VI, Chap. IX, § 3, footnote. Also see Book VI, Chap. III, § 3, footnote. Matthew Henry (1706), with many proof texts and Josephus, understood Jerusalem's destruction fulfilling Matt. 24. See his comments on Acts 2:14, III. [3]. Accordingly, dispensationalists had to claim *new light* for the last days.

worse and worse, until utterly wearied out, and casting away all hope of her amendment, her King shall come and judge her. Yet, all sunk and degraded as the church of Christ hath become, she is the only visible Prophet, Priest, and King of the earth....[88]

Irving held, however, that the ruined church can be spared God's judgment if it acted the part of a Priest and offered "prayer, and praise, and thanksgiving, and holiness, and painful intercession, fasting, weeping, and lamentation" to restrain the wrath of God.[89]

Having reduced Christians, the Gospel Church and Christ to strictly *spiritual* functions during the present *gospel dispensation*, Irving denied Christian social and civil responsibility to exercise Godly instruction and authority in society. He maintained that neither Christians, the church, nor Christ could exercise any Godly influence over God's material creation until the millennial reign of Christ. Only then would Christ exalt his people as rulers over cities.

His vision of the failed, ruined church, led to the next supposition. Quoting Irving:

> Secondly; When the Lord shall have finished the taking of witness against the Gentiles, and summed up the present dispensation of testimony in this great verdict of judgment, and while the execution is proceeding, he will begin to prepare another ark of testimony, or to make the whole earth an ark of testimony; and to that end will turn his Holy Spirit unto his ancient people the Jews, and bring unto them those days of refreshing spoken of by all the holy prophets since the world began: in the which work of conveying to them his Spirit by preaching of the word, he may, and it is likely will, use the election according to grace, who still are faithful amongst the Gentiles... This outpouring of the Spirit is known in scripture by "the latter rain," of which I deem the religious revivals of the last thirty years [back from 1826; Lacunza released his document, 1790, so its public acceptance fit within "the latter rain" period, *ed.*] to be as the first droppings of the shower..., it will be given to those who will receive it, both Gentiles and Jews, and will prove the touchstone of both; — amongst the Gentile church...; in the Jewish church accomplishing that refining and passing through the fire

---

88. *Ben Ezra,* I.cxxxiv. Maybe a reason Rome banned *Ben-Ezra* was its reduction of the church to strictly *spiritual* functions!
89. *Ibid.,* cxxxiv, cxxxv.

which is spoken of immediately on their restoration. (Mal. iii.3. Zech. xiii. 9.) Which Antichristian spirit among the Gentiles, and enraged infidel spirit among the Jews, may amalgamate with one another, to produce a spurious restoration of the nations to their own land, and occasion that great warfare in the neighbourhood of Jerusalem, when Antichrist shall fall, and his powers be broken in the battle of Armaggeddon. But the faithful among the Jews now brought to believe on him whom they have pierced, shall in the mean time be prepared by much sorrow, and distress, and supplication, for the coming of the Lord to settle and establish them surely and for ever in their own land; and the faithful among the Gentiles shall be expecting the Lord to deliver them, according to the promises which he hath made to his elect church of being raised from the dead, or changed among the living at his coming, and all gathered to him in that day. It was my second proposition, that in this way the Lord will be preparing for himself an ark of testimony in the Jewish nation, through whom to make the whole world one great and universal ark of faithful testimony.[90]

... I sought very diligently to define from the scriptures what was the precise place and purpose of the present spiritual dispensation, which God hath interposed between a dispensation of a local and typical character upon the one hand, and a dispensation yet to be, of a universal and real character upon the other; both centering in and radiating out from the Jewish people.[91]

According to the millennial system:

First, having failed, all the Gentile church inherits is the wrath of God; hence, the Lord must "prepare another ark of testimony." This he does by turning his "Holy Spirit unto his ancient people, the Jews," as referred to "by all the holy prophets since the world began," *viz.*, "the latter rain."

Second, a latter rain is to yet to be conveyed "to them [the Jews, *ed.*] by the preaching of the word." Later, when tongues took over his ministry, Irving supposed tongues to be the latter rain.

---

90. *Ibid.*, v, vi. Trapp saw the falling star of Rev. 9:1 as "the bishop of Rome," a view the Jesuits worked to change. *Trapp*, V.754.

91. *Ben Ezra*, I.ix. Every point of the above Jewish "system" can be found in Darby, *e.g.*, Darby held that the Jews were the people of God's choice, and though laid aside for a season, had to be retaken in order for God to complete his work on earth, *Letters*, I.124, *Writings*, II.265, 266, &c.

Third, he supposed that latter rain would bring "unto his ancient people the Jews" the "refreshing spoken of by all the holy prophets" — that is, God's blessings as supposed in the Old Testament upon the nation of Jews. Moreover, the Gentiles might even be included when the rain comes.

Fourth, despite the inspired word of God — *There is neither Jew nor Greek* in Christ (Gal. 3:28) — the system makes a clear and firm distinction between the Gentile church and the Jewish church.

Fifth, the system required "the coming of the Lord to settle and establish them surely and for ever in their own land." It called for a permanent reestablishment of a national Israel, replacing the church in God's plan for the ages.

Chapter 23
Everything Around National Israel

The system confused the promises of God — the Old Testament promised wrath against his disobedient people (national Israel, see Mat. 23, 24), was given to the church, and the promised blessing for the church, (those in Christ), was given to a supposed, renewed, national Israel. In Lacunza's new dispensation to come, the Lord might still work among the Gentiles, but he will do that work through a renewed national Israel. The victory of Christ seems to have no part in Lacunza's system of future events. The system, "both centering in and radiating out from the Jewish people," revolves everything around a renewed national Israel, "Protestant Zionism":

> This much I draw from our Lord's discourse with Nicodemus, that we are still conversant with the earthly things, and have still the heavenly things to expect; that as much as the Jews, ought we to look forward to the glory which is to be revealed, and that it is an utter error fraught with evil consequences, to consider the incarnation of Christ as the ultimate end of the prophecies, and the utmost satisfaction of the wants of the world. All that hath yet been

revealed in the Providence of God to his church, is the last half of what is promised in the word of God, and what his church should hold fast with assured faith.[92]

However, in Isaiah 11, the Messiah is compared to both a *root* and an *ensign*. From the very foundation of everything to the sum total of everything, Christ is *all in all*; everything revolves around Christ; Christ is from the undermost to the uppermost of all; Christ works under, or behind, everything that takes place; Christ covers all areas.[93] All history has worked, is working and will work to exalt Christ, *that in all things he might have the preeminence*. What kind of men replace Christ with a literal nation, and revolve the word of God and all history around that nation?

Despite the Lord's words that all Scripture (*i.e.*, law, prophets and the psalms, Lk. 24:44ff.) pointed to himself and his redemptive work, Irving, with Lacunza's support, contended that a glorified national Israel was the theme of all prophecy, and not Christ. He maintained that a restored Jewish nation alone would satisfy the desires and needs of the world. In other words, the work of Christ was not finished at his first advent. Christ's work must yet be completed: "But for us who stand midway in the work, and see but one half of it..."[94]

The system continues with no hope for a peaceful solution for a troubled world through the Spirit of Grace. Its cure is fire and blood:

> Thirdly. That these judgments upon the Gentile nations and all the earth, he will finish by his own personal appearance in flaming fire, taking vengeance on those who know not God, and obey not the gospel of our Lord Jesus Christ; raising those who sleep in Jesus, and changing those of the Gentile Church who still abide in life, and preserving the mourning Jewish church, as Goshen was preserved in the plagues of Egypt: and when the promised land shall have been cleared of all intruders, and they themselves by suffering perfeeted [sic] for the habitation of it, he shall lead them into it with a mighty and outstretched arm: and sit upon the throne of David, judging and

---

92. *Ben Ezra*, I.xcviii.
93. *Christology*, I.454-482. See Eph. 1:23, Col. 3:11, 1:18, &c.
94. *Ben-Ezra*, I.xcvi.

seeking judgment, and hasting righteousness; and send forth the law from Zion, and the word of the Lord from Jerusalem; and rule among the nations, and be the Prince of universal peace; using in this judgment and government of the earth his risen saints, who shall be his ministers to execute whatever his pleasure is. And thus, Satan being cast out, and the Prince of light, and the heavenly Jerusalem, the dwelling place of his elect church being present, the Jerusalem on earth, with the house of Jacob, and all the nations shall enjoy that fulness of peace and joy, that millennial reign of righteousness, for which we all hope and pray, and diligently labour.[95]

Accordingly, Christ must literally "sit upon the throne of David" in Jerusalem, in a renewed Jewish nation. Only from that throne can Christ (1) clear "the promised land of all intruders" (Canaan); (2) exercise judgment on the earth; (3) "rule among the nations, and be the Prince of universal peace"; (4) exalt the "risen saints... [to, *ed.*] be his ministers to execute whatever his pleasure is." Then through his reign from David's throne, "all the nations shall enjoy the fulness of peace and joy" during "that millennial reign of righteousness." He stated many times that Satan has yet to be cast out of heaven. This would not take place until the second advent and Christ's millennial reign through the Jewish church, the restored Jewish nation.[96]

The system held that only when Christ returns and sits on his throne will Satan's bondage cease:

> I say almost of course, yet not altogether of course; because though Satan shall then be cast out of the world, and his active temptations wholly at an end, men will still be in the flesh and heirs of death, during the whole period of the millennial kingdom. And therefore they will need government, both civil and ecclesiastical, a law of righteousness which we now possess, administered according to the

---

95. *Ibid.*; vi, vii. Satan, in his opinion, has yet to be stripped by Christ of his "usurped dominion." *Ibid.*, x. Concerning Satan, Darby was confident Satan is unhindered during the church age, not yet bound, and Christ can not reign until Satan is bound during a millennial reign, *Writings*, II.110, 133, 134, 140, 344, 502, &c. Darby saw the church's removal, as did the *Ben-Ezra system*, but as of 1852, he was not using the word "rapture." *Writings*, II.545, 546.

96. *Ben-Ezra*, I.xiii. Darby was very dogmatic in this area also: Applying Gen. 15:13 to the Jews, he taught that the Jews had to be restored to the "promised land," *Writings*, II.182.

wisdom of Christ and his reigning church, without any opposition or strife of Satan. Power shall then be holy; and the creation shall then be pure; and the bondage of Satan shall have ceased...[97]

Thus righteous laws can and will be enforced upon the earth only when Christ rules from a literal throne. Irving considered the true church during that millennial period to be a restored national Jewish church. He defended his ideas from charges of heresy:

> These three points of doctrine concerning the Gentile church, the future Jewish and universal church, and the personal advent of the Lord to destroy the one and to build up the other, I opened and defended out of the Scriptures from sabbath to sabbath, with all boldness, so far as the integrity of my own conscience was concerned, yet with fear and trembling, so far as the sweet harmony and communion of saints, in which I delight, was concerned; for at that time I did not know of one brother in the ministry who held with me in these matters; and of those to whom I broke the subject, I could not get the ear even for preliminaries. So novel and strange a doctrine, with respect especially to the outward visible churches, those great idols of Christendom, of which every one of us dreameth his own to be modelled after perfection, and to have in it the seed of eternity, and the power of universal application, if not the promise of universal conquest; such uncivil and implacable language, concerning overwhelming judgments upon the very eve of the millennial blessedness; above all, such low and derogatory ideas of the risen and exalted Saviour, as that he should ever again come to visit earth, and be visibly present in it for any length of time, could not fail, and certainly did not fail, to call down upon my head all possible forms and degrees of angry and intemperate abuse, of disappointed and sorely-afflicted expostulation. But the more I examined, the more I was convinced, and resolved, though alone and single-handed, to maintain these three great heads of doctrine from the Holy Scriptures, against all who should undertake to uphold the commonly received notion, that the present Gentile dispensation was about to burst forth with great verdure and fruitfulness, and fill the whole earth with the millennial blessedness, after which, to wind up and consume all, the Lord would come in the latter end, and depart with the same expedition with which he came.

---

97. *Ben-Ezra,* I.xiii. God's justice, Darby held, can only emanate from a literal throne of David in Jerusalem, *Writings,* II.158, *Letters,* I.22ff.

And, further, I maintained, that such ideas concerning the glorious efflorescence of this present dispensation into a universal fulness, is not only inconsistent with all the scriptures, but with the very nature and intention of the dispensation itself, as it hath been understood and is expressed by all orthodox divines...[98]

He continued to maintain the system's "three great heads of doctrine" despite the fact that orthodox teachers of his day not only refused to consider the doctrine, but rightly called down upon Irving's head "all possible forms and degrees of angry and intemperate abuse, of disappointed and sorely-afflicted expostulation." In fact, he compared the then prevalent hope that the church could conquer the world for Christ with the foolishness of a ship about to sink amidst the stormy ocean, and thinking it could "possess the whole ocean!"[99]

As already noted, Irving was dogmatic with Lacunza's system, and reiterated it *ad nauseam* throughout his lengthy *Discourse:*

> The restoration of the Jewish nation, to be again the Church of God, and their re-establishment in their own land, to be the head of nations, and the centre of the earth's unity, and the going forth from them of the Spirit of righteousness which is to bring all nations to the Church and bind the whole world in one great community of Christians, acknowledging the Son of God, as the Lord of all, and practicing [sic] the righteousness which is by faith, to constitute a worship and service which shall have in it the universality of the spiritual, combined in some way with the locality of Jerusalem as the centre, and the supremacy of the seed of Abraham as an example, and of David their king, as the head of all; this is only the fulfilling of that glory of Christ and blessedness of the whole earth, for which the whole dispensation and witness that hath been since Abraham, and now is present in the world, is but preparatory. We have had the variety of the wicked earth, we wait for the unity of the saved earth; we have had the humility of the suffering Church, we wait for the glory of the triumphant Church.

---

98. *Ben-Ezra*, I.xiii.
99. *Ibid.*, viii. He emphasized believers being partakers in Christ's suffering, not in his victory over the world, flesh and the devil, *ibid.*, xi. Darby also saw nothing but suffering for the church until the millennium, *Writings*, II.468, 1852, *Letters*, I.180, 202, &c.

Such is the skeleton of that body which God hath given to his great purpose of saving the world...[100]

According to this system, the Gentile church is so corrupt that it must be judged and cast off by God — it must be replaced with a restored Jewish nation that will then be (1) the Church of God; (2) the center of the whole earth; and (3) the source of world-wide missionary activity by which the Lord will fulfill "his great purpose of saving the world." This was a novel idea that permitted Old Testament prophetic passages that spoke of the world's conversion to be placed in a *dispensation* other than the church age, *e.g.*, Psalm 22:27. Darby's infamous "ruin of the church" idea was already in the *public domain* when he presented it.

Irving said that only "with a series of judgments" can the Lord bring the world to its knees before himself as King of kings. Of course, what other hope is there than a literal intervention by the Lord if the Holy Spirit is seen only as little more than "The Comforter" during this present *dispensation?* Questions: First, how can both Christ and David reign on the same literal throne of David in the same literal location, a restored, exalted, glorified Jerusalem? Second, did not the system ignore John 16:7-11, which clearly states that the entire world will be convinced of sin by the Holy Spirit after the resurrection?

Chapter 24

The Advent of the Lord

Most of Irving's opinions were opposite the then prevailing system, "Public Opinion." [Irving's term, *q.v.*]. Among many other things, Lacunza's system held that Daniel's kingdom of stone did not "begin with the former advent of Christ, and so avoid the second advent altogether...," and the smiting of the image is yet to come,

---

100. *Ben-Ezra*, I.xii. Darby applied the Psalms for the Jews only, *Letters*, I.123.

implying that the image will be smitten only when the millennial kingdom is established from the renewed Jewish nation.[101] Lacunza changed the typical meaning of the day of "time, times, and half a time," (Dan. 12) from symbolical to literal, "to mean three years and a half, or forty and two months, or 1260 days."[102] Irving found his master's ideas concerning the "imminent peril of infidelity" to be remarkably like his own as described in his tract, "Babylon and Infidelity Foredoomed."[103] Based upon Lacunza, Irving held that his opinions, though opposite the prevailing system, were indeed orthodox.

The opinions are important enough to the millennial faith that we will document their modern roots.

Irving's dedication opening his translation of *Ben-Ezra* reads:

DEARLY BELOVED IN THE LORD.

My soul is greatly afflicted because of the present unawakened and even dead condition of all the churches, with respect to the coming of our Lord Jesus Christ, which draweth nigh, and which, as I believe, is close at hand: and having, by God's especial providence, been brought to the knowledge of a book, written in the Spanish tongue, which clearly sets forth, and demonstrates from Holy Scripture, the erroneousness of the opinion, almost universally entertained amongst us, that He is not to come till the end of the millennium, and what you call *the last days,* meaning thereby the instant or very small period preceding the conflagration and annihilation of this earth; I have thought it my duty to translate the

---

101. *Ben-Ezra,* I.xxvii. Darby, covering the world with his "system," was dogmatic that the future smiting of the image by the stone was his idea, *e.g.,* "such as God has shown me," *Writings,* II.121, 185, 272, 315, 323, &c. "The crushing blow is still suspended." *Scofield,* 901; 898, Daniel prophecies "the apostasy of the Church..." *Geneva*: Daniel shows God's "singular mercy towards his Church..."

102. *Ben Ezra,* I.xxix. Though Darby claimed to have thrown out all past understandings of Daniel and to be the first to divide Daniel's 70th week in half ("I am inclined to suppose..."), the *Ben-Ezra system* had already made the break. Irving also laid claim for himself and Lacunza the discovery of 1260 *years* yet to be accomplished; he seems to use the 1260 at his convenience, *days* or *years.* See *Writings,* II.324, 377, 1843. Darby claims to be the one to formulate the 3 1/2 years idea, *Letters,* I.139, 1848.

103. *Ben-Ezra,* I.xxix.

same into the English tongue for your sake, that you may be able to disabuse yourselves of that great error, which hath become the inlet to many false hopes, and will, I fear, if not speedily corrected, prove the inlet to many worldly principles and confederacies, and hasten the ruin and downfall of the present churches. And now, forasmuch as it is to those *who look for him* that he is to appear without sin unto salvation, and those *who love his appearing* that the crown of glory remaineth, I do exhort you, dearly beloved in the Lord, and as a friend and brother I do entreat you, yea, as an ambassador of the great God our Saviour, whose servants you are, I do commend you, in that High and Holy name at which every knee shall bow, that you take leisure from your several avocations, lay aside your several speculations, and diligently apply yourselves to the Holy Scriptures and to the throne of the Heavenly Majesty, that by the Holy Spirit, whose office it is to show you things to come, you may come to some light of divine knowledge, and determination of holy purpose, upon this subject of Messiah's advent, which until now hath ever been wont to be cherished as the great and darling hope of the believer's soul. Whereby we know that it is the last time, because it is written (2 Pet. i. 3.), there shall come in the last days scoffers, saying, Where is the hope of his coming.

From your brother in the common faith, and servant in the Ministry of the Gospel, a Presbyter of the Church of Scotland.

Edward Irving[104]

First, the common Christian understanding of the Lord's second advent of Irving's day was that Christ would come "at the end of the millennium." His purpose in translating *The Coming of Messiah in Glory and Majesty* was to change the common Christian understanding of the second advent to his understanding. He called the system's novel view of the second advent, "the coming of the Lord."

Second, the term "awakening" referred to awakening Christians to the soon coming of the second advent. It had nothing to do with lost souls awakened by the redeeming, converting grace of God.[105]

---

104. *Ibid.,* i, ii.
105. Darby defined conversion and awakening as conversion to and awakening to his system, *Letters,* I.53, 55, 58, 1843, II.306. In 1862, he excitedly reported that the USA was being "awakened" to his system, *ibid.,* I.336.

Third, the term *the last days* was changed in meaning. It was changed from the period from Christ to the end to "the instant or very small period preceding the conflagration and annihilation of the earth."

Irving was awakened from his ignorance and from the "erroneous idea which prevailed," and he was delivered from the "darkness" he "received from the fathers" well before reading *Ben-Ezra*. Fear of going against then accepted Christian doctrine, however, prevented him from publicly proclaiming his thoughts, which he later placed in a discourse, "Babylon and Infidelity Foredoomed." The time of judgment, he held, was "near at hand." He set about to awaken the church, "to make known that sure conviction to which I had now attained."[106]

Throughout Irving's *Preliminary Discourse,* he spoke as a martyr for the restored hope of a very soon return of Christ — a second advent — that was prevalent in "the church in the best times of her existence": "I wot you utilitarian Christians rail against prophesyings, and well may you, because ye are become prophets in your several spheres, trying all conclusions by your foresight of their future effects and fruitfulness of God..."[107]

Irving lashed out against those who repudiated his ideas. Drawing courage from Lacunza's writing, his *Discourse* seems to be a 200 page, 'I told you so!' to the church that had mocked his views. He exhibited the same spirit toward those who had ridiculed him that he evidently had experienced from them. He identifies "the two views of the second advent," using Lacunza's *Ben-Ezra* to justify his argument against the standard view of his day:

> ... There is no question, nor ever hath been, nor ever can be, concerning Christ's personal re-appearance in human form upon the earth; although I perceive the faith of the Protestant churches to be so withered by absolute infidelity or by intellectual demonstration, which is the egg of infidelity, that they start when you say that Christ

---

106. *Ben-Ezra,* I.iii. Also, vii.
107. *Ibid.,* xlviii. Nor did Darby weary of telling of the *abuse* he *suffered* for his *new* system. See also xviii.

will appear again in personal and bodily presence upon the earth: and I am sure, for as often as I have heard the judgment discoursed of, in this age of moth-eaten and undervalued creeds; and for as often as I discoursed of it myself, before I had insight given me into this mystery, I have never found it treated as a personal act of Christ, or rightful attribute of his mediatorial office; but as a thing personal to us, a whip to scourge our lethargy, a spell to break our sleep, a thunder-note to awaken our terrors; treated as a metaphysical part of the metaphysical idea of moral responsibility, rather than as the grand demonstration of the power and majesty of the humbled Son of God, the grand act of the justification of Christ's injuries and the injuries of his suffering church upon those who had done them wrong. And I am sure the judgment hath become almost a dead letter in our creed and in our preaching, form being thus abstracted away from the personal act and bodily presence of Christ the judge. In proof of the fact that it [the second advent, *ed.*] hath been so abstracted away from the personal act and bodily presence of the Lord, I need only to state, that I have hardly conversed with one minister or preacher of the gospel, who had thought at all upon the subject of the second advent, excepting that small number who have adopted these views of his kingdom; and I have hardly met with one private Christian of the thousands to whom I have preached it, who had ever heard it treated of as a great head of doctrine, or even had a conception that it was such. And at this moment, I believe, that of Protestants by far the greater number have not even a faith, or if they have a verbal faith, founded on the standards of their churches, have no actual faith in the personal advent of Christ at any time.[108]

He continues:

And we may see into what indifference and contempt the whole subject has come, and how it hath passed into the domain of poetical imagery, and forms of the fancy, when it has become the theme for ribbald [sic — ribald, *vulgar, lewd humor, ed.*] poems and silly reviews.[109]

The future coming of Christ and the reign of the saints for a thousand years over the material world, Lacunza's system contended, is what the saints should look forward to. Without that "hope," death is a victory for "Satan and triumph of his power." It is in that future reign

---

108. *Ben-Ezra,* I.xlix, l.
109. *Ibid.,* l.

that the inheritance upon the earth promised to Abraham will be fulfilled. At that time,

> [W]e shall behold all enemies put under his feet, Satan the accuser of the brethren cast out of the earth, and with him all his evil angels which dwell in the natural man, and rule the world. And we shall see the prison doors of death unbarred, and the grave yield up her dead, and then shall come to pass that saying of the prophet, Death shall be swallowed up in victory.... [W]e shall be for ever with the Lord, partakers of his throne, partakers of his crown, and partakers of his government; his assessors in judgment, his deputies in power, ruling over the cities of his dominion, and judging the tribes of the sojourners of the earth.... And so shall we in the exercise of that government and sovereignty which we shall then be permitted to hold of the earth, be as Adam, a king in his majesty... [Then, *ed.*] the earth shall be full of the righteousness of the Lord, as the waters cover the channels of the deep.
>
> Such, in few words, is that which is comprehended under the term, "the Coming of the Lord," to which we invite the hope of the church, instead of that which you desire them to look to...[110]

Writing in 1868, Darby claimed to be the source of several ideas in just one paragraph: the soon "coming of the Lord," the exaltation of "the Jewish nation" and another "dispensation" when Christ reigns in righteousness:

> The coming of the Lord was the other truth which was brought to my mind from the word, as that which, if sitting in heavenly places *in* Christ, was alone to be waited for, that I might sit in heavenly places *with* Him. Isaiah xxxii. brought me to the earthly consequences of the same truth, though other passages might seem perhaps more striking to me now; but I saw an evident change of dispensation in that chapter, when the Spirit would be poured out on the Jewish nation, and a king reign in righteousness.[111]

Darby claimed "the coming of the Lord" idea originated with him.[112] But he, apparently, simply developed Lacunza's system. He

---

110. *Ibid.*, lxi-lxiv. Note that *Ben-Ezra* makes no provision for those saved during the thousand years. It also requires that sinners live righteously during that time, or they will be put to death. From Rev. xix, Darby taught that God does not exercise his power in direct government before the second advent, for sin now totally controls the world. *Writings*, II.113, 1852.

111. *Letters,* I.516. He used "the coming of the Lord" in the true *Ben-Ezra* sense.

held that the hope of the soon coming causes the church to ignore surrounding corruption (Rev. xvi. 10): "If we give up waiting for Him, we prepare ourselves a part with the hypocrites. The waiting for Jesus was that which at the beginning detached the heart from the world, and rendered faithful [Christian obedience, ed.]. The Christian religion has made its way into the world. [sic] in consequence of this faithfulness, and of this detachment from it." According to the system, the only hope for the believer in the surrounding darkness is the soon "coming of the Lord," a hope that separates him from all earthly and worldly cares. In fact, Satan's goal is to get the Christian's mind off the soon coming of the Lord.[113]

The system taught that faith in "the coming of Christ" recovers the apostolic "strength and primitive separation from the world." Irving called any opinion contrary to his view of the "coming of the Lord" a "vague notion which Satan hath substituted in its stead." Man's ills, it contended, come "because we watch not continually for his coming."[114] Concluding his lengthy argument justifying Lacunza's doctrines, Irving said:

> Such are the true arguments, such as the true demonstrating, even these passages of scripture, and this constant invocation of the word of God, to be in expectation of the coming of the Lord, and these to a believer, should be all sufficient to stir up the soul to look daily for the coming of the Lord in power and glory, and the cock crowing, at the first watch, or at mid-day. For myself I can aver, that resting upon these Scriptures hath more availed to set me loose from worldly cares and attachments, to comfort me under worldly trials, to fill me with watchfulness and patience...[115]

---

112. By 1879, Darby was taking credit for developing the idea of the soon coming of the Lord: "When I began to preach these ['the Lord's coming and the resurrection,' ed.], fifty years ago, I was held to be... [a, ed.] heretic..." *Ibid.*, III.19. Darby assumed the system as his own at Powerscourt.

113. *Ibid.*, 479, 85, 498, 417. *Ibid.*, II.417.

114. *Ibid.*, lxvi. The study of prophecy, Darby taught, will solve the world's ills by causing Christians to be unconcerned about the surrounding darkness, *Letters*, I.330.

115. *Ben-Ezra*, I.lxvii.

Lacunza's system claims to set one "loose from worldly cares and attachments," making him "otherworldly," *i.e.*, unconcerned about the social chaos around him.

The church of 1825 stood against Lacunza's system and its meaning of "the coming of the Lord," holding the "opposite prevailing system." Nevertheless, Lacunza's system overwhelmed both the church and society as both can now only long for death and a future reign with Christ. If death is the Christian's hope, then what is left for the unbelievers except death education and a terrible suicide rate among young people?

In accordance with Lacunza's and Irving's hostility against a far off second advent, the millennial system urges Christians to be unconcerned about present turmoil; it discourages the training and equipping of Christians to work for the benefit and blessings of their children and heirs in the faith (after all, during the millennial reign, the restored Jewish nation will send forth missionaries to convert the world to Christ and disciple the nations); in effect, it turns the future over to the very anti-Christian powers Irving complained against. He offered withdrawal and defeat to a church that was preaching "Christ the victorious." At Albury Park, Irving found kindred spirits and help to convert the non-Roman church to Lacunza's system.[116]

Chapter 25

The Millennial Reign

Lacunza was very dogmatic on the point of Satan's power, emphasizing it many times. The enemies of the Lord and his Christ,

---

116. Darby and others who followed the system were firm against preparing for any future physical welfare (contrary to 2 Cor. 12:14) of one's children, *e.g., Serve God, and he will take care of your children. Letters*, I.268. Though Rome repudiated the *Ben-Ezra* document, this writer found no evidence that it repudiated Lacunza. It appears the only influence millennialism made into Rome is what has spilled over from the noisy Protestants in this area.

including Satan, are not placed under the feet of Christ nor under the feet of the saints until the thousand year reign, quite contrary to Ephesians 1:20ff. At that time, the saints would,

> [S]hare his kingdom, to take part in the judgment, to advance righteousness, to glorify God with every faculty, and command the earth with what nobel vicegerency Adam heretofore commanded it.[117]

The millennial faith leaves its faithful followers helpless victims of Satan, captive to Adam's transgression. They are left with no hope of the Second Adam being formed in them — as promised by Romans 5:14, 1 Corinthians 15 (vv. 22ff.) — this side of "the coming of the Lord," a millennial reign of Christ.

Irving contended that a Christian's hope for death and the joys following it as he reigns with Christ permits him to be lifted above the present world. The system even placed 1 Corinthians 10:31 — Whether therefore ye eat, or drink, or whatsoever ye do, do all to the glory of God. — into the future, holding that King Jesus rules not over one's physical body, but only in and over the spirit during the *gospel dispensation.*

Irving shows how the then prevalent and millennial systems agreed:

> We are agreed therefore, I say, upon the personal advent of Christ to this earth, to judge the quick and the dead, and to apportion of their eternal destinies.

Chapter 26

The Resurrection of the Dead

"Public Opinion" agreed with *Ben-Ezra* and Irving concerning the personal, visible return of Christ, but not concerning the resurrection. "Public Opinion" believed that there was only one

---

117. *Ben-Ezra,* I.lxv. See also vi., x, xiii, lxiv, lxv, &c.

general resurrection at the end. However, Irving clearly saw "two advents of Christ" — one at the beginning of the millennium, and another at the end of the millennium, as well as an exalted Jewish nation. *Ben-Ezra* was his proof that his ideas were not "heretical errors":

> During the progress of the work, the more I discovered its great weight and value, as an all-sufficient argument for the orthodoxy of the ancient system, and the heterodoxy of the commonly received one [one general resurrection at the end, *ed.*], the more desirous did I become that it should have a fair and free introduction to the Church: and, perceiving that it bore hard against the stream of common opinion, I thought within myself, how I might best defend it from the storm which would be raised against it on all hands by the British inquisition, whose ignorance of truth I knew to be equalled only by their malice against every thing which touched the infallibility of their idol, PUBLIC OPINION.... I mean the ignorant, unprincipled, unhallowed spirit of criticism, which in this Protestant country is producing as foul effects against truth, and by as dishonest means, as ever did the Inquisition of Rome. Perceiving well that my worthy master Ben-Ezra had in his own right nothing to expect but the most vehement abuse and ridicule of his opinions, and, in my company, still more, I weighted well how I might obtain for him a fair hearing from the church which has become review-ridden to a most alarming degree...[118]

Irving exalted *Ben-Ezra* as the Christian standard for the historic, orthodox Christian faith. He compared the former Roman inquisition against those who would not admit Roman Catholic doctrine to a British inquisition, for it would not admit his doctrine of more than one resurrection. Through the untiring efforts of Irving and the following committed millenarians, the then common Christian view of the second advent with "Christ the victorious" and one general resurrection, was changed to the *"Ben-Ezra* system."

Irving calls attention to the points of difference between "Public Opinion" and the *"Ben-Ezra* system." They differed on "whether that advent is to conclude the existence of the habitable earth, or to begin the period of its peace, and righteousness, and blessedness;

---

118. *Ibid.,* xxi, xxii. Emp. his.

whether he is to come to destroy, or to reign over the earth; whether his presence is to be brief, and as it were momentary, or abiding and everlasting."[119]

Chapter 27
A Motive for Holiness

Though all agreed that his people "will be raised or changed at the moment of his coming, or rather the instant before, in order to come along with him," Irving asks the question as to which serves "the ends of Christian doctrine, spiritual living, and personal holiness more?" Would that end be served more by the "idea of the personal advent of Christ, with all his risen saints that sleep in him and are changed, to order the earth in righteousness [premillennialism, *ed.*]; or the idea of his personal advent at the universal judgment, to destroy the earth, and remove all that have dwelt therein to heaven or to hell..."[120]

Faith in one general resurrection, said Irving, does not seize hold on the affections to lift one above the cares of this world, purify feelings, emotions and motives, nor does it cleanse one from sin, *i.e.*, motivate to holiness.[121]

---

119. *Ibid.*, l, li. He argued strongly against the general resurrection as was generally held in his day, and for two resurrections: There must be, he contended, two resurrections, so the saints can return and literally reign with Christ.

120. *Ibid.* Irving's whole question is based upon error, for the word of God tells us that it is the preaching of the law that stops every mouth, and makes the whole world guilty before God. The result is man's conversion and holy living brought about by the Holy Spirit. Rom. 3:19-30. Converting faith establishes the law in the life of the Believer — that is, makes him want to live above sin as defined by the Spirit; however, this is not the concern of this treatise. 2 Cor. 5:17, Phil. 2:13, 1 Jn. 3:4.

121. *Ben-Ezra,* I.lx, lviii, lix, lx. Irving hints strongly at *soul-sleep, ibid.,* lix. Keeping one's mind on heaven, Darby repeatedly said, detaches him from the cares of this world, *Letters,* I.91 (1846) & 460.

Many times, Irving complained that the Protestant pulpits of his day held to a general resurrection — the first resurrection being spiritual, giving life to those who were dead in their trespasses and sins. Irving argued that the first resurrection "denoteth the whole blessedness of the righteous thereafter..."[122].

Irving also mentioned personal holiness in the above statement:

> First: That the commonly received opinion... There is universal belief in the church, that an age, very long age of blessedness, of at least a thousand years duration, is to run, before the end of the world, and consequently before the coming of Christ. And who will speak of the uncertainty or the nearness of the Lord's coming, to men, who thus believe?...[123]

The common opinion was "post-millennial," which Irving held could not motivate to holiness. He was convinced that only Lacunza's system of an imminent return and literal millennial reign of Christ would motivate people to holiness. He thought that by postponing "the resurrection of the body indefinitely", *i.e.,* a general resurrection at the end, man would be controlled by materialism, laboring for things here on earth.

> Yes; ever since we discovered the 1260 years to be accomplished, we have been observing the series of events which are to run, before our Lord's coming, and we do expect certain events, such as the destruction of the Antichristian powers, and the spiritual vocation of Israel.... We are living amongst the signs of our Lord's coming [1827, *ed.*], we have seen six, and are waiting for the seventh and last..., we are all active to get the house in order...[124]

But the system he proposed "to pious people of this generation of the church," was "met with the most faithless and unprofitable answer," moving him "with great anger against the artifice of Satan to blind so many souls."[125]

---

122. Ibid, liv. See Eph 2:1, 5; Col. 2:13; 1 Pet. 2:24.
123. *Ibid.,* li.
124. *Ibid.* "Spiritual vocation," *i.e.,* Jewish missionaries to convert the world to Christ. Darby taught that the hope of Christ's soon coming purifies saints from sin: he makes no mention of God's grace in that holy task, *Writings,* II.417. "[W]e discovered..." evidently refers to Lacunza and Irving.

The Apostles Paul and John, he held, had the hope of the immediate return of Christ, but the church lost that hope, and was looking for "smooth seas." He did not miss the opportunity to shoot at those who had been shooting at him:

> While you are dreaming of smooth seas and a harmonious crew, and a haven hard at hand, we see the gathering of the clouds, and the curling of the waves, and a rebellious mutinous crew, and a fearful shipwreck, from which a few, a very few, of the wise and prudent will escape....
>
> But I do not tempt myself and my reader into minor discussions, but rest firmly upon this, that the common system ["post-mil," *ed.*] having cast out the expectation of Christ's coming, has cast out the special and peculiar reward of the resurrection....
>
> Now in consequence of the far off and indefinite distance to which they have postponed the coming of the Lord... [126]

Irving did not miss an opportunity to call the doctrine of one general resurrection unscriptural, saying that his system was the only scriptural system:

> But such views of a material world after the resurrection of the body, whencesoever proceeding, are looked upon as fanciful though they be the only ones contained in scripture. [127]

Lacunza redefined two terms: First, he defined *faithless* as refusal to believe the millennial system of future events, *e.g.*, the imminent return of Christ, and second, he defined *Satan's work* on earth as blinding souls to the soon return of Christ and a literal millennial reign. However, Scripture defines both *faithlessness* and *Satan's work* in terms of conversion from sin to Christ. (Acts 26:18, Eph. 4:17ff.)[128]

---

125. *Ben Ezra,* I.lvi. lvii.

126. *Ibid.,* liii, liv, lv. Irving lamented that the common system of his day did not expect an imminent return of Christ, nor a separate resurrection for the just. It taught a general resurrection. Lacunza's millenarianism, accordingly, required two resurrections: First, the resurrected saints to rule the material world with Christ during his literal reign from the restored Jerusalem in its gory, and second, a general resurrection, consisting of those saved during the millennial reign.

127. *Ibid.,* lvi.

Irving admitted he broke the ground that led to the general Christian departure from the then established orthodox Christian doctrine concerning the second advent, which was one general resurrection at the end of the millennium. That he replaced with a two part resurrection. In addition, according to Irving's system, one cannot pray, "Thy Kingdom come" in this present dispensation.[129]

Chapter 28

Death for Victory

While the church preached "Christ the victorious," Irving proclaimed death:

> Do you every morning think within yourself, this day may be my last, therefore, let me be watchful. Do you say every evening, I am one day nearer my death, now let me be thankful — I ask you, is the idea of death before your soul continually, darkening the brightness of worldly joys... Doth the knowledge of your certain death work such a constant and blessed effect upon your life: Doth it?[130]

Fearing death and not looking forward to it, said Irving, were results of "sin's great conquest, and Satan's chief work." Rather than looking forward to the great conquest of Christ, *i.e.,* "Christ the victorious," in one's life on earth, one must look forward to death, expecting it tonight or tomorrow. Christ's victory was in the resurrection, and only after the resurrection can the Christian expect any victory and joy. Life, according to Irving's system, is empty, joyless and defeated, endured only because of the heavenly joy awaiting after death.

---

128. Darby defined faith as faith in the "system:" the literal, soon coming, millennial reign of Christ and all it implied, *Letters,* I.176, *Writings,* II.310. Thus *faithlessness* is in terms of the millennial faith.
129. *Ben-Ezra,* I.iv, v.
130. *Ibid,* lvii. Darby not only looked forward to his own death, but urged others to look forward to their deaths, *Letters,* I.245, 254, 1855.

In fact, he castigates any thought of "Christ the victorious" before death. It is in the context of his teaching on death that Irving said,

> The ministers of the gospel, as captains of the Lord's host, do not present unto the people or seek to keep continually before them the terrors of Satan, the weakness of the flesh, the powerfulness of the world; but keep before them Christ the victorious, the Spirit the quickener [giver of life, *ed.*], the Father Almighty, their election unto salvation, their adoption unto the communion of the blessed trinity, their fellowship with all the saints who have endured and overcome.[131]

A vibrant, faithful belief in "Christ the victorious" empowers a Christian to live in the present and work for the future. Meditating day and night on death is not only anti-Christian (Josh. 1:8, Ps. 1:2, &c.), but it surely strips the individual of any desire to plan and work for the future in any way. It turns the future over to the spirit of Antichrist.

Chapter 29

Prophecy

Irving continued to compare the two dramatically different systems — the then common system taught that the world would be converted before the second advent; Irving's system taught that the world would not be converted. Previously, he compared the usefulness of the two systems, saying that Lacunza's emphasis on death, the nearness of the coming of the Lord and the future reign of the saints with Christ, would cause people to serve the Lord more effectively in life than would the thought of a distant return of Christ. He then analyzed the difference between the two systems: "CONCERNING THE BEARING OF THE TWO OPINIONS UPON THE DOCTRINE OF CHRIST'S PROPHETIC OFFICE."

---

131. *Ben-Ezra*, I.lviii.

Christ, Lacunza held, is revealed by both the past record of his word and by the fulfillment of prophecy: "[I]t is a good canon of prophetic interpretation, that its accomplishment must be looked for in visible objects, not in invisible or spiritual states..." Despite the Spirit's clear spiritual application in Matthew 4:15, 16, he taught that when one reads prophetic passages from both Old and New Testaments, he is to look for a literal fulfillment rather than the spiritual fulfillment as was common in the early 1800s.

The *Ben-Ezra system* denies that Christ can come in judgment against wickedness except by coming literally with a physical sword in his hand. However, Christ clearly told Caiaphas, before whom he stood, that Caiaphas personally would see Christ return in judgment. (Mat. 26:64, Mk. 14:62.) Many followers of Lacunza's system do not believe that Christ actually meant what he said in Matthew 23:36 (*Verily I say unto you, All these things shall come upon this generation.*). They meet Christ's words with the same unbelief and charges of blasphemy as were his words in his day. (Mat. 26:65, Mk. 14:64 & Lk. 22:67.) It is sad that secular historians face truth better than many millenarian Christians.[132] Because millennialism revolves around a restored national Israel, it requires prophetic passages to be understood literally if at all possible:

> ... And I observe still further, that the series of answering events is not completed, for the spiritual church being still lost in the wilderness, not yet having become visible, but waiting for it till the day of the manifestation of the Son of God: also the Jewish dispersion hath to be gathered again into a church and a nation, and the throne of David to be established, his tabernacle to be set up, and the whole earth to be brought under his dominion of which future

---

132. *Secular* means "without God." Therefore, there are NO *secular* areas for Christians, 1 Cor. 10:31. We will use *secular,* however, in its common understanding. The Devil has convinced Christians that there are *sacred* and *secular* areas of life. In doing so, he has persuaded Christians to turn everything except *spiritual* activity over to the antichrist crowd. *Literal,* actually taking place and limited to the explicit meaning of a word or text. *Spiritual,* symbolizing or representing something. *Physical,* tangible or bodily.

visible events as I find the promise and prophecy to be always given in language derived from the history of the Jewish people...[133]

In addition to a reestablished, glorious Jewish nation under David, the system called for "his tabernacle to be set up." (The wording is confusing: Whose tabernacle is he talking about — Christ's or David's? David used the tabernacle erected by Moses, for the glorious Temple was erected by Solomon.) Moreover, the church must endure persecutions "until the resurrection..." Not until the millennial reign of the church with Christ and the rod of iron will the prophecy, "thou shalt bruise his heel" be fulfilled. Irving then blatantly misquotes a passage:

> Wherefore it is written, both of Christ and of his church, that they shall rule the nations with a rod of iron, and dash them in pieces like a potter's vessel, and have all their enemies under their footstool.[134]

In order to support his idea of a literal millennial reign of the saints with Christ over the earth, Irving changed the word of God. (Is it any wonder he was charged with heresy?) Though Irving said, "Wherefore it is written," it is not as he said—it is not "written, both of Christ and of his church, that they [Christ and the saints, *ed.*] shall

---

133. *Ben-Ezra*, I.lxx. We should add that his "doctrine of the second advent" (lxxi) understood many passages prophetic from the time they are read, not from the time they were written, *e.g., Mat. 24 is yet to be fulfilled because we are just now reading it*, rather than saying it was prophetic from the time it was given by Christ. Darby was confident that Christ's kingly reign over the nations must be from a literal throne in the reestablished Jewish nation, and only then will the nations be judged by righteous judgment, *Writings,* II.139, 561. Millennial reign has yet to be given to Christ, for it is his reward: Only then will he have the power and authority to reign, *ibid.,* 140, 171, 1841. Implied, obviously, is that the ungodly nations are presently exempt from God's righteous judgment against their sins. Darby spoke a great deal of the church being in the wilderness of this world, *e.g., Letters,* II.203, 455, c. 1873.

134. *Ben-Ezra*, I.lxxii. Believing Christ's reign was yet to come, Darby thereby placed Psalm 2 and Christ's rule with a "rod of iron" off into the future, *Writings,* II.482, 588, 1852. In fact, he taught that all men would not be subject to Christ until the "millennial" reign of Christ, *Letters,* I.361, 1863. Darby also called for a literal temple to be built during a millennial reign, and a literal sacrifice to be instituted, *Letters,* II.469, 1878, *Writings,* II.267, 270. He dogmatically stated that Psalm 2 and Revelation 19 "Cannot be the gospel," *Writings,* II.121.

rule the nations with a rod of iron..." Psalms 2:9, "rod of iron," clearly refers to only the Son—*thou shalt break them... thou shalt dash them*—with no reference to "his church," *i.e.*, the saints. The wicked rulers are urged to *be wise,* and *kiss the Son, lest he be angry,* v. 12. They are not urged to kiss the saints lest they be angry. Vengeance belongs only to the Lord, and never are the saints given the right to seek and take vengeance. Irving also said "that they [the saints, *ed.*] shall rule... and have all their enemies under their footstool." The prophecy is from Psalm 110:1, and is one of the most quoted in Scripture. (Mat. 22:44, Mk. 12:36; Lk. 20:43; Acts 2:35; Heb. 1:13 and 10:13) It makes no reference to the saints. We must admit, however, that the saints are seated with Christ in *heavenly places,* but there is no hint that the wicked will be ruled by the saints with a rod of iron, nor that "their enemies" will be placed "under their footstool."[135]

The church, "from Abraham till now," was in its immature state, but Lacunza's prophetic document convinced Irving that the church would mature. From his "kind and honoured instructor, Mr. Coleridge," he "received the first idea of the prophetic growth of God's word..." He taught that "... prophetic is the only proper method of a divine revelation." His strange view of prophetic growth led to even stranger ideas, "the evidence of our religion [rests not, *ed.*] upon the miracles which attended the ministry of the Lord and his apostles", nor upon the writings of Christian scholars. Rather, it rests upon the fulfillment of prophetic passages: "All other causes of infidelity put together, are but as a feather in the scale compared with the evil effects of the books which have been written in defence of the Christian religion."[136]

---

135. With no hope of "Christ the victorious" in this life, is it any wonder many dispensationalists are inactive and depressed, detached from and unconcerned about the surrounding social turmoil? With no hope for righteous social change through preaching Christ, they are left with only a political hope, and then they believe it is sin to be involved in politics!

136. *Ben-Ezra,* I.lxxiv, lxxv, lxxvii.

Lacunza's system desired Christianity to rest on fulfillment of prophecy. The system would have said, "We know the Christian religion is true because prophecy is being fulfilled right before our eyes." Although we hear the same statement today, we are not told that almost 200 years ago Irving taught that the French Revolution fulfilled the 1260 days mentioned in Revelation 11, and that he taught and expected the soon coming of the Lord based upon that Revolution.[137] If Irvingism were true, then there is no logical basis for Christianity — the French Revolution was not the fulfillment of the Revelation 11 prophecy as Irvingism taught.

Chapter 30

Novelties

Note some novelties of Lacunza's system:

...In no other character doth Peter declare him after the day of Pentecost, and James in the council of Jerusalem, and the two shining ones on mount Olivet, and Paul and all the apostles, than as THE KING who ascended on high without seeing corruption, waiting and expecting, till the Father shall accomplish the times and the seasons, and bring in the days of refreshing spoken of by all the prophets, the restitution of all things waited for by the whole creation of God. In no other way doth John see him in the Apocalypse than as a child, the seed of the woman caught up to God and his throne, and there abiding until after certain sore warfares and persecutions of his church, he cometh again with many crowns upon his head, and followed by all the armies of heaven, in order to break the confederacy of Satan's powers to bind the old serpent himself, and cast him into the bottomless pit, to keep him in subjection for a thousand years, and afterwards turn him into hell with all the nations that forget God...[138]

The Ben Ezra system taught: First, Christ and his people are powerless in the church age, so they must wait for a day yet to come,

---

137. *DNB*, s.v. "Irving, Edward." *Ben-Ezra,* I.xl.
138. *Ben-Ezra,* I.lxxii.

i.e., his millennial reign, to exercise his power over creation; second, Christ is not presented as the all powerful Creator of heaven and earth during the church age — he is presented as a child who must be cared for by his mother; third, the church has nothing now but persecutions while Christ waits helplessly in heaven; fourth, Satan's powers were not broken at the first advent, and they will not be broken until Christ's millennial reign; and fifth, Satan will be bound for a literal thousand years while peace and righteousness flourish, and then he will be released. There is no healing of the nations until Christ's millennial reign.[139]

Lacunza's and Irving's system held that a reason for infidelity was because the Christian leaders failed to study and propagate prophecy:

> The infidelity of the present day is the fruit of our poverty in the knowledge and preaching of Christ's prophetic office and the prophetic character of his word.[140]

> The question not being to search the Scriptures for the *substance* of the dogma; which is already known, presupposed as known, believed, expressly and publicly professed in the whole Catholic Church, but simply to search therein for certain things accidental to the dogma, whereof the sure and certain knowledge, though not absolutely necessary to salvation, may yet be of the utmost importance, not only with respect to Catholics, but with respect to Christians in general, and also with respect to the miserable Jews.[141]

The call of the millennial system was not to search Scripture for the substance of dogmatic theology and how to apply the victory of

---

139. *Ibid.,* lxxiii, lxxiv. Darby held that only during a future millennial reign of Christ will the saints reign as kings and priests, *Writings,* II.135, *Letters,* III.55, 1879. A key point of Darbyism: Since Christ helplessly waits in heaven for his millennial reign while the saints suffer on earth, his saints must helplessly wait here on earth for that day yet to come, *Writings,* II.135, 484, 1852. Furthermore, Darby held that the Christian only has enough grace from God during this dispensation to keep him from falling, *Letters,* I.50. In other words, there is no present grace from God to overcome the surrounding social ills. Moreover, Lacunza held that Christ is now behind the veil in the heavenly temple making intercession for the saints, implying that he is unconcerned about matters now on this earth.

140. *Ben-Ezra,* I.lxxvii.

Christ to society. It issued calls to search Scripture for prophecies concerning the Catholic Church, Christians in general and concerning the coming exalted state of the Jews. It held prophecy conferences rather than application conferences. It said that because the church is looking back to Christ the Victorious instead of to the future reign with him in a coming dispensation, it is powerless in the present, and is, accordingly, controlled by infidelity — "If people were taught about and believed in the soon coming of the Lord, they would remain pure."

If the church wants to deal with infidelity, it must take its attention from the present and seriously study the future second advent. ("Infidelity" is a word much used by both Irving and Darby, making them sound as though they are against violations of the Ten Commandments, which is not the case. Neither man present the Commandments as God's righteous requirements for man. They do, however, imply that "infidelity" means rejection of the systems they were promoting.) The church must change its emphasis (from present usefulness in knowledge of Scripture), and must study its future prospects with Christ.

> Whereas, if the expectations with which Christ for ever endowed his Church were again to become her belief, she would look forward to his second coming, and diligently inquire into and carefully guard every part of Scripture which beareth thereon: whence it would come to pass that the prophetic character of all Scripture would come to be recognized, for it all pointeth to that glorious event; and the prophetic office of Christ restored, and a barrier, the only effectual barrier, placed against the deluge of infidelity which hath swept over the church under the disguise of intellectual illumination and expedient usefulness. It was the expectation of Messiah which made the Jews to set such a value upon their prophecies; it is the absence of such an expectation, or indifference to it, which hath made us to set so little value upon them.[142]

---

141. *Ibid.,* 15, 16. Darby held that the preaching of prophecy would strengthen faith in Christ and increase and establish one's sanctification, *Writings,* II.194. This writer must admit that many advertisements used to draw crowds to "prophecy conferences" sound more like the occult (*e.g.,* know what the future holds) than they do like Christian services.

The following are various points concerning prophecy taken from Irving's *Discourse:*

Irving considered *Ben-Ezra* part of God's prophecy to the Gentile church as Isaiah and Daniel were to the Jews. Christ was revealed not only in his word, but also in prophetic revelation. The church was immature from Abraham, but now it is maturing through prophetic growth, *i.e.,* study prophecy and discover more hidden things (however, prophetic growth is not clearly defined). Prophetic passages must be understood literally. As Christians look ahead to the prophesied coming of the Lord, problems will be solved — in fact, failure to study prophecy is injurious, and leads to a worldly church. The weapon to combat Satan is the study of prophecy — the millennial hope will conquer all problems and situations. Prophecy proves man cannot subdue the world until a literal reign of Christ. Everything from Revelation 4:1 is yet literally to take place here upon the earth. A personal Antichrist yet to come (2 Thess. 2) was offered by Lacunza. (Irving implied Lacunza caused him to change his views back to the traditional view of a future, personal Antichrist.)

Lacunza held that Christ's kingdom of stone, as recorded by Daniel, will not be established until the second advent. Accordingly, he had to hold that Daniel's four kingdoms exist in the church age of grace. *Ben-Ezra,* accordingly, changed the standard Protestant understanding of the ten horned past Papal beast to a future infidel beast. Lacunza's system took Protestant pressure off of Rome.[143]

---

142. *Ben-Ezra,* I.lxxxv.
143. Order of use: *Ben-Ezra,* I.xxxvii, xxxii, lxviii, lxxiv. lxxv, lxx, lxxviii, lxxxii, lxxxiii, xxxvi, xli, xlii, xxix, lii, xlii, xliii, xxvii, lxxvi, xxxi.

Chapter 31

Law

One of the most important and devastating points of the millennial system is its view of God's law as given through Moses:

> Now in respect to the revelation of the law, it properly belongeth to his prophetical office, and consisteth of all those parts of the word of God, which being wholly independent of space and time, apply themselves to the pure reason; while by being presented imbedded in the circumstances of space and time, they give demonstration and satisfaction to the lower faculties of our nature as they pass inward to the reason.[144]

The reader's guess is as good as this pastor's as to what he said. However, Irving's continued statement is not quite so hard to follow:

> But the pure and perfect law [Ten Commandments, ed.] serveth at the best no higher end than to slay the self-righteousness of man, and can never be used for a higher end.[145]

> By the coming of the Spirit the tables of stone were broken, and the writing was transferred to the fleshly tables of the heart...[146]

Thus he claims that the Commandments are not a rule of life. In fact, Irving claimed that using the Lord's Old Testament law as a standard leads men to self-sufficiency. His idea, along with his idea

---

144. *Ben-Ezra*, I.ciii.
145. *Ibid.*, civ. Darby also clearly dismissed the Commandments as a rule for righteous living, saying, "we are dead [in Christ, *ed.*] and the law cannot apply to a dead man... The absolutely perfect and living rule is the life of the Lord Jesus Christ...," *Letters*, II.108. Scofield called the Commandments, "deathful tables." See "C.I. Scofield," p. 322.
146. *Ben Ezra*, I.xcv. Christ fulfilled the law. Through Christ, there is no need to worry about law because we have his righteousness, *ibid*. This "system" saw a law/gospel conflict: Christ saved us from the law; Old Testament law cannot be compared to the New Testament law, for the Old Testament law was for the immature church, *ibid.*, cviii. Irving speaks strongly for obedience, but the obedience is to the life of Christ, thus avoiding the Commandments, *ibid.*, cxi. He also contrasts law and love rather than uniting them, clxxxii.

concerning Christ the King who would not be "a King" until the millennial reign, stirred up anger against him (Irving):[147]

> And here I may go back a step and make a similar remark upon the divorcement of the law from the lawgiver, and of both from Christ. This inquiry in which I am engaged, needeth a sagacious spirit, and a single eye, and a delicate hand, requiring me to make a continual estimate of the current theology, and bringing me into the midst of the prejudices of living men, and present times; the more may the Lord deliver me from all malice and unrighteousness, and enable me to discern truly between *His word* and *His people,* between *His church* as it ought to be, and *His church* as it actually is. Well then; I do certainly feel persuaded that Moses is some way regarded as our law-giver, and Christ as our Saviour from the law; or rather that the law under which we are placed holdeth of the former dispensation, and the gospel of the latter dispensation. "For the priesthood being changed, there is made of necessity a change also of the law." Heb. vii. 12,[148] and his argument in the viith and ixth chapters of the same epistle, where he sets himself to prove the faultiness of the former testament and its need to being set right or reformed by another testament, which was made unalterable by the death of the testator: but from whence ariseth an antagonist feeling between law and gospel which confuseth many people, and in Satan's hands is made an open door to antinomianism. Now, however necessary it was for the apostles when showing the impossibility of justification by the works of the law, to rest their argument upon the mosaic law in which the party with whom they reasoned, did repose their trust, I think, for us Christian divines, who have not the same form of antagonist, to do the same, is greatly to weaken our own argument, and to prejudice the cause of godliness which is committed to our trust. Because no one will say that the law written upon the two tables of stone, though sufficient in its kind, and perfect in its end, as all God's revelations must be, is at all to be compared in respect to the force of its precepts and the spirituality of its application, with those laws delivered by our Lord to his disciples in the days of his flesh, or to those which the Holy Spirit spake by the mouth of his servants the apostles. The moral law of the old dispensation, is to the moral law of the new dispensation, what the gospel under the former, is to the gospel under the latter; a writing of the same for a younger period, even the infancy of the church. Now, no one would

---

147. *Ibid.,* cvi.
148. The law that was changed was Levi's priesthood law. Geneva, 1599.

return to their rudiments of knowledge and conscience received in infancy, but press forward to a higher, and a purer, and a more comprehensive, and more manly form of the same. Yet this is exactly what we do when we rest our laws upon that form which was given by Moses, instead of resting them upon that form which was given by Christ in the days of his flesh, or rather I should say at Pentecost, when in his character of Lord, he shed down the Spirit, and the power, and the law of holiness upon his church. Christ is my law-giver, and the words written by the Holy Spirit in the books of the New Testament are my written law; but my living law is the Holy Spirit in my soul bearing testimony to every case as it ariseth. We have a law-giver, and a written law, and we have an interpreter of it, and there needeth no casuistry nor casuists. The Holy Ghost serveth us in that capacity. To convince the natural conscience of a sinner therefore, of its sinfulness, I would not be for going to the ten commandments, whereof he may have kept the very letter, and be a greater sinner than he who hath kept none of them (as the Pharisee was a greater sinner than the publican); but I would take him to the words of Christ and his apostles which express it spiritually, and directly address the conscience and say, Brother, feelest thou thus to thine enemy, dost thou thus to thine enemy; feelest thou thus to him that hatest thee? &c. And I would take him to the life of Christ and say, Brother, livest thou thus? thus communest thou with God? thus bearest thou a world's indignity? thus art thou in agony for a world's salvation? thus bemoanest thou the hidings of thy Father's countenance? And so would I find law and life, precept and example combined together, and come down with all the power of a personal case upon the person with whom I treated.[149]

Irving defended Lacunza's system against charges of heresy with, "But the system whereof our author [Lacunza, *ed.*] showeth the orthodoxy..." Lacunza and Irving planted the seeds for several new doctrines concerning the law.

Amidst the confusing wording (and archaic English) above, we find these points: First, Irving taught the new millennial system despite the prevalent theological prejudices against it; second, Moses' law, *i.e.*, the moral law that seeks to control outward actions with threats and promises, was for the former dispensation; third, Christ is "our Saviour from the law," or he removes us from

---

149. *Ben Ezra.*, I.cvi-cviii.

responsibility to Moses' law; fourth, Paul proves in Hebrews that the law of the covenant, the Ten Commandments, was faulty, and had to be replaced by another law; fifth, the "law written upon the two tables of stone" cannot be compared to the New Testament law given by Christ to his disciples; sixth, Moses law was for the immature church, so the mature church in Christ is no longer under that law; seventh, when the basis of law is Moses instead of the words of Christ, we go back to immaturity; and eighth, the written law is found only in the New Testament, and it is written in the soul of the believer by the Holy Spirit. Irving used a lot of confusing words to say, basically, that a mark of Christian maturity is not needing the Old Testament law to distinguish between good and evil. He tells us that the mature Christian is controlled by his conscience rather than by the written Law of God.[150]

One of the most devastating and unscriptural points made by Irving and imbibed by the church is that the life of Christ (a very ambiguous statement) is what convicts of sin rather than the Commandments. However, the Spirit dogmatically tells us that the knowledge of sin comes from the Commandments, not from the life of Christ.[151]

Chapter 32

Christ

Millennialism left even Christ at the mercy of man and Satan during this present dispensation. Irving reduced Christ's present rule to a strictly spiritual rule:

---

150. Scofield called it "the divine will... inwrought," *Scofield*, 1245.

151. Rom. 3:20, 1 Jn. 3:4. The continued Christian's responsibility to the moral law, the Ten Commandments, is not our subject. However, we urge the reader to do some research, for he will surely be held accountable to God's law. See A.W. Pink on Hebrews 8:6-9, Barnes' Notes on Hebrews 8 and Matthew Henry on Romans 11. Any author who wrote before Darbyism became orthodox is worth checking into.

This kingly office having received from God at his ascension, he doth even now exert in granting these two things, repentance and remission of sins to all who believe; and moreover, in bestowing the Holy Spirit to regenerate and build up the new man after the image of God in righteousness and true holiness. And it is very sweet to me to know, and feel, that my Saviour is become King, and is presently exercising kingly sovereignty over the spiritual world, being able, and being willing to grant the blessings of his priesthood to all who believe on his incarnation, and desire the righteousness which cometh of that faith...[152]

Irving's proof that Christ is not literally King of the whole earth is that during the *gospel dispensation* Christ does not literally,

> [O]verthroweth kings and setteth them up, and bindeth princes in fetters of iron, or enlargeth them to wider conquest and dominion, blesseth the cottage with plenty and contentment, or, as now, sendeth everywhere niggard famine, and puny, miserable wretchedness...
>
> That this however is still but an aim or a tendency, and hath not yet been realized upon the earth, will appear no less manifestly from the slightest observation and reflection. We are yet in the state of the embryo, having the rudiments of that perfection, and hasting to the birth....[153]

Irving's *Discourse* has very strong Romanist undertones, showing the great influence Lacunza had upon him. Rather than using the Protestant King James translation, he uses the Vulgate translation for Isaiah 9:1, 2, presenting Christ and his church as helpless victims of Satan's dominion over the earth during the *gospel dispensation*.[154] The present suffering, afflicted church, he held, is as weak and powerless as an unborn child waiting, as Christ now waits with the Father, for a glorious, exalted time yet to come:

> And so also it is with his church, which deriveth from his Spirit no more power than is sufficient to follow his footsteps: prophesying in part (responsible to prophesy of the coming millennial reign,) and in part fulfilling both the office of kings, and priests, but only in part. The Holy Spirit given at Pentecost doth set us in the way of our

---

152. *Ben-Ezra*, l.cv, cvi.
153. *Ibid.*, cxxxv.
154. *Ibid.*, cxxii, cxxxvi [sic], cxxxviii.

Lord's suffering, and enable us to be conformed to his death; He doth no more.[155]

Emphatically Irving held that the only power available to the Christian is power "to be conformed to his death." The Christian is thus left a helpless victim in every area of life, so he can only be unconcerned about the social turmoil around him. Accordingly, Irving's dispensationalism limited Christ's kingly sovereignty during this dispensation to salvation, the conscience of man and *spiritual* things. Moreover, he implied strongly that man is the one who makes the choice, and, accordingly, Christ is only King over those who choose him, thus limiting Christ even more. He contended that the Old and New Testament passages speaking of Christ as King referred to "his second advent when he shall be revealed as a King."[156]

As we give some various opinions about Christ from Irving's *Discourse*, one should be struck by its open proclamation of the Jewish hope. It holds that Christ is not much more than the spiritual ruler over those who choose to let him rule over their spirits in the present Gentile dispensation.

The millennial system holds that Christ's only kingly office now is exercised in giving repentance and remission of sin. It holds that the Old Testament passages referring to the King are after the second advent and during the millennial reign, and are not for the *gospel dispensation*. Christ is King at this time only over his church, for he is the mediatorial, or priestly king only, *i.e.*, spiritual king. Lacunza's view of Christ the King is true, Irving held, because we do not now *see* Christ acting as King over the wicked, establishing and putting down worldly powers. The view that he is King only over his church, those who believe on him, strongly implies that Christ is only King over those who allow him to be their King. In other words, Christ is not yet the Prophet, Priest and King as

---

155. *Ibid.*, cxxxv, cxxxvi. "Footsteps!" The system had/has no firm *rule of action* other than an ambiguous "like Christ."
156. *Ibid.*, cvi. Notice, "a King," not THE King!

prophesied, because wicked men are still in high places. His rule over his people is only spiritual, implying strongly that Christ only rules the conscience, or spirit, in this dispensation, and that he does not rule the believers' bodies. Christ is king only over the "invisible powers." He will not be King over all creation until the millennium when he sits on David's literal throne in Jerusalem as a bloody king, as was David.[157]

Lacunza held that Christ will not be the Prince of Peace until the millennial reign, and then peace will be enforced with the sword:

> After which there will be peace, but till then never. For till then Satan shall rack the bowels, and tear the heart-strings of human peace, and stir up wars to the end of the earth for ever, until God, born of the virgin, shall again be with us.[158]

We should mention that before the great shift from victorious Christian living to powerless, spiritualized religion, American Christians went into all the world to work out their own salvation (many still do, but the general temper has changed). The outworking of their salvation sent them confident in the knowledge that the gospel of Christ would convert the world to Christ and his peace — they went as a Christian army armed with the *gospel of peace.* Today, powerless Christians stand mutely by as "peace keepers" with guns and tanks go into nations to "keep the peace." Christians, generally, have accepted a system that teaches that not even Christ can keep the peace among fallen men without the threat of death with his literal *rod of iron.* (We will develop the change in the motive for mission work; it changed from Christianizing the nations to simply spreading the gospel.)

Lacunza's system, as presented by Irving, holds that looking forward to the coming reign will restore proper Christianity, giving a "more sure light in dark places." In other words, prophetic

---

157. In order of use: *Ibid.,* cv, cvi, cxi, cxx, cxxxiii, cxxxvi, clvi, clxi, xlviii, clxx, clxxi, clxxii. David was a *bloody* king, having shed much blood in war; therefore, could not build the temple. See 1 Chron. 22:8, 28:1-3.

158. *Ibid.,* cxlviii.

opinions are added to the word of God. Only during the millennial reign can man exercise proper dominion under Christ, proved by the French Revolution, so Christians must wait. The system is, hence, against educating Christians for godly dominion this side of the millennium. The millennial hope is that every area of creation, including man and Satan, will be conquered then. Meanwhile, man is a hopeless victim of Satan. It holds that all prophecy will be fulfilled literally, to the letter, in the millennium, (*e.g.*, Ps. ii [heathens for the Son's inheritance]; Ps. cii; Isa lxv, lxvi, xi.6, xxxv. 1, 2; Heb. xii. 27-29; 1 Cor. xv. 24-28). Christ will not be the Prince of Peace until the millennium, and the saints will reign then and only then as part of his government and kingdom. The millennium will open a new book about God's character. The kingdom will not be cleaned up and offered to the Father until after the millennium. And finally, Irving admitted that the millennial glories he postulated were based upon Lacunza's speculations.[159]

Chapter 33

Satan

The millennial system, however, does not leave the earth without rule. Rather than judging righteous judgment according to the word of God, Irving judged according to appearance:

> [B]ut Satan the enemy of Christ still ruleth over the powers of this world, whose kingdoms are not yet become the kingdoms of our Lord. In no sense can Christ therefore be said to have been invested with the kingdoms of this world, otherwise he would not surely trouble and afflict his own church which he hath purchased with his own blood. The times and seasons which were to elapse before the kingdom should be restored to Israel, the times of the Gentiles during which Jerusalem was to be trodden under foot, have not yet run their appointed course. Our Priest is still detained in

---

159. Order of use: *Ibid.*, I.lxxviii, lxxxi, lxxxii, lxxxiv, cxxii, cxxv, cxxi-cxxiii, lxxxv, cxxvi. clxxii, cxxiii.

expectation, at the right hand of his Father, and waiting while the Lord hideth his face from the house of Jacob. Giving all weight to the kingly style with which he was born, and with which the superscription was written over his cross, and to the present kingly office of his church, as I have stated it above, I cannot see how with any propriety he can be said, either during, or since the days of his flesh, to exercise the office of a King, save in the initial and partial sense which hath been already explained. The office and function of a King is that of exaltation, but Christ's life, and the life of his church, are of the lowest humiliation. No one is greater than a king in that dominion over which he ruleth; and yet Christ was lower than all. He was "a man of sorrows and acquainted with grief," smitten, stricken, and afflicted. He was not in the form of a king, but in the form of a servant. He was the heir of the throne, and making his way to it by the cross, but he was not crowned, he was not enthroned, he had not assumed the power. Satan in his hearing said, These the kingdoms of the earth, and all the glory of them, are mine; and Christ did not challenge the usurpation; if indeed it may be called usurpation, for Satan had achieved them by his potent subtlety. He held them in virtue of the curse of God: and he must hold them till that curse can be removed consistently with the holiness of God. Immediately before Christ was taken up, he was asked if he would then restore the kingdom to Israel, but which it was manifest that he had not yet fulfilled that great object of his mission.... And the Apocalypse, in chap. xx, declareth that it shall continue so until the beast and the false prophet — that is, the personal Antichrist and the papal power, with all that follow them shall have been destroyed in the battle of Armageddon. And this we do not yet perceive, for the personal Antichrist is not yet made manifest, and the false prophet still sitteth as God in the temple of God. On every ground, therefore, I hold it to be a contradiction of all language, and a confounding of all distinctions, to say that Christ hath begun to exercise his office of a King....[160]

Irving admitted ("I hold it to be..."), that against the then common Christian thought, the system presented some more novel ideas: First, Satan still rules the earth, the kingdoms of which are not our Lord's — proved by appearance; second, Satan will rule until Israel is literally restored as a nation and Jerusalem exalted as the center of

---

160. *Ibid.,* cxxxvi, cxxxvi [sic]. Note again, "a King," not THE King! See Jn. 7:24. On Irving's anger toward the idea of Christ's spiritual reign, see cxliii.

the whole earth; third, King means literal, physical exaltation, and neither Christ nor the church can be seen exalted in the gospel dispensation, proving his point;[161] fourth, the fall gave Satan ownership of the earth, to do with as he pleases; fifth, Christ's mission was to exalt the nation of Israel, which he failed to do; sixth, there must yet arise a "personal Antichrist," for "the personal Antichrist and the papal power" will not arise until after Revelation four in Lacunza's timetable;[162] seventh, the system requires a literal battle of Armageddon to destroy the beast, false prophet, the personal Antichrist and the papal power that will arise in the next dispensation (there is no need to worry about any of those things until then); and finally, all the preceding points, Irving was confident, proved him right and that the then prevailing Christian opinions of the present victorious rule of Christ the King, his second advent, and one general resurrection were wrong.

We urge the reader to compare the following view of Satan with Lacunza's view of Christ as he relegates Christ to second class citizenship in the present dispensation. Lacunza's system holds that Satan usurped the world from the Godhead and had victory over Christ, implying that Satan put Christ to death. Satan is not subdued, nor will his usurped dominion be interrupted until Christ is on his throne. Despite the Spirit's words that the power of the devil is broken, (1 Jn. 3:8) the millennial system left the saints in the present dispensation at Satan's mercy with no hope of victory over Satan until a literal millennial reign of Christ. Only during the millennium will Satan's binding power over man be broken. Only then will he be subdued, cast out, defeated and literally chained. But until then,

---

161. "And he shall be King in the manifestation [the millennial reign, *ed.*], when he cometh forth in his robes of state, or in his glorified body, to destroy his enemies and take possession of the earth." Darby was dogmatic that Satan now governs the world, *Letters*, II.286.

162. We must mention that the rise of a "personal Antichrist" was a key topic at the 1833 Powerscourt Conference on Unfulfilled Prophecy, and has inundated the church since. See "Powerscourt Conferences," p. 141.

the saints helplessly suffer according to Satan's will. Satan's present work is to cause disbelief in the newly offered millennial system.

It is likely that Irving's distress over his son's death permitted such a corrupted view of Satan to grip him, but modern Christians have no excuse.[163]

Lacunza's system held that Satan usurped all the material creation from God in the fall, and now all nature does according to Satan's will. The millennial reign, however, will reclaim these areas for Christ. Adam's fall placed all the saints at the mercy of Satan until Christ's millennial reign.[164]

Chapter 34

Redemption

C.H. Spurgeon opens his catechism with:

> 1. Q. *What is the chief end of man?* A. Man's chief end is to glorify God, and to enjoy Him forever.[165]

One of the more serious corruptions of God's word is the system's view of redemption. At the very least, Lacunza implied that Christ failed in his efforts to accomplish fallen man's redemption:

> Now the redemption of man from the threefold degradation of ignorance, unrighteousness, and oppression, and the establishment of knowledge, righteousness, and liberty over the earth, is the end which the Son of God proposed to accomplish by the second perilous procession from the bosom of his Father's love. He purposed to restore man to his primitive birthright, and the world to

---

163. In order of use: *Ibid.,* clxix, clxxv, vi, lxiv, lxv, clxxix, xiii, cliii, clvi, cxxiii, x, xiii, lxiii, clxxv, clvi, lxvi, cxxvii, cxxxvi, cxxii, cxxiii, clxiv, clxxxi. Darby said openly that Satan put Christ to death.

164. *Ibid.,* x, xiii, lxiii, cxxii, clxix, cxxvii, cxxxvi. Darby held that Adam gave everything to Satan, so Satan now is unhindered on the earth, raising up and putting down whomsoever he will.

165. 1 Cor. 10:31, Ps. 73:25, 26. *A Catechism.* Spurgeon's Catechism follows closely the *Westminster Catechism.*

its primeval blessedness. I say not that this is all, but do rather believe that it is but a very small part of all which shall come out of this great demonstration of the divine love, to his own infinite glory and to the wonderful exaltation of man for ever and ever. It is, however, distinctly contained in the mediatorial undertaking, and completely accomplished when the kingdom is given up to the Father...[166]

Millennialism changed the redemptive purpose of man from *Glorifying God and enjoying Him forever* to *God glorifying man and enjoying him forever.* The heretical system believes that Christ failed to accomplish the purpose of redemption — falsely understood as *restoring man* (especially the Jews) *and exalting him for ever and ever* — in his incarnation, death and resurrection. So he must return in a millennial reign to finish the job.

God help us! *Who shall deliver us from the body of this death,* the system offered by Lacunza and Irving? In stark contrast to millennialism's hopelessness, Scripture declares: *But thanks be to God, which giveth us the victory through our Lord Jesus Christ.* (1 Cor. 15:57)

---

166. *Ibid.,* cxxxi. Ruling for the Lord in that millennial reign "over all the regions of the universe, which I [Irving, *ed.*] conceive to be our high destination," clxii. He admitted he argued his point "by way of natural reason," *i.e., This is the way that seems right to me.* "...I see the supremacy of man's nature over all natures..., clxviii.

Part IV
Prophecy Conferences

Chapter 35
Christ and Prophecy

Two critical events salvaged Lacunza's system from the fate of Vieira's and Papia's documents.[1] The first event was Irving's translation of *Ben-Ezra* from Spanish into English. The second event was the 1826 Albury Park conference for the study of unfulfilled prophecy.

Curious inquiry into the future — prophecy conferences — was the primary tool for replacing "Christ the victorious" with "the terrors of Satan." Such inquiry was not new.

Following the life of Christ, we find that Christ's death had been a great disappointment to the disciples. They had fully expected the Lord to reestablish David's earthly throne in a glory greater than Solomon's. (Mat. 20:21, Lk. 24:21.) Christ's forty days with them after his resurrection had greatly encouraged them, restoring their Jewish hope. Hence, they asked the question, "When will you reestablish David's kingdom making Israel the chief of nations?" (Acts 1:6.) Christ's answer to them is extremely significant as we consider the Prophecy Conferences movement. A *Particular Baptist* pastor of two centuries ago, John Gill (1669-1771), made this extremely pertinent comment concerning the Lord's answer to the disciples' question:

> *Which the father hath put in his own power;* and not in the power of creature, no, not of the angels; see Mat. 24:36 wherefore it is vain and sinful, as well as fruitless, to indulge a curious inquiry into these

---

1. Roman Jesuits who presented the system some years before Lacunza, *q.v.*

things, or into the times and seasons of what is future; as of the time of a man's death, of the end of the world, of the second coming of Christ; only those things should be looked into which God has revealed, and put into the power of man to know by diligent search and inquiry.[2]

Thus it is not only foolish but sinful to seek to know the time of the Lord's return. The contrast given by the Lord to prophetic speculations is receiving power from the Spirit to bear witness to the gospel throughout the world. He did not tell them to go home, lock themselves in a room, search Scripture and develop speculations about his return. Hence, the concern of God's people is not with the return of Christ in one manner or another, but on spreading the gospel of the Kingdom of God unto the uttermost part of the earth. "Prophecy Conferences" with the expressed purpose to know and understand the future are, accordingly, sinful. Many men have made and are making excellent livelihoods and many followers by speculating about the future.

Millenarianism and Money

Olson comes down hard on modern authors who appear to write to the purse, *e.g.*, Dave Hunt, Salem Kirban, Chuck Smith, Jack Chick, John Hagee and Grant Jeffery.[3] He quotes extensively from Dave Hunt, Hal Lindsey, Tim LaHaye and Jerry B. Jenkins, pointing out their terrible double standard and lack of theological knowledge. I must confess, I never had the inclination, the courage, nor the time to wade through the thoughts of those who seem to present themselves as God's advisers as to how the world will end.

Olson rightly calls attention to the hypocrisy of these men who level charges against Rome about being "apostate" and "false", yet they hold a theological system full of rifts, divisions, and competing groups who disagree with one another, sometimes viciously.[4]

---

2. Gill, *Online Bible*. See also: Keil on Ez. 20 (IX.265); Geneva, Gill and Matthew Henry on Deut. 29:29. *Particular Baptist, i.e.*, Calvinistic Baptists—*The London Baptist Confession of Faith of 1689*.
3. *Catholics*, 45, 46.

Moreover, "No Biblical writer ever revealed the future merely for the sake of satisfying curiosity: The goal was always to direct God's people toward right action in the present... The prophets told of the future only in order to stimulate godly living",[5] and the Revelation is no exception.

> Lindsey's obsession with Bible prophecy has taken him into strange territory. Because he believes that the main purpose of biblical prophecy is to predict the future, he often compares the Bible to people such as Nostradamus, Jean Dixon, and fortune-tellers... In his later books Lindsey compares the accuracy of Bible prophecy to the druids of Stonehenge, astrologers, and assorted clairvoyants, and chapter headings that have included 'Polishing your Crystal Ball' and 'John's Chain of ESP'.[6]

---

4. *Catholics*, 46. This writer is not defending Rome, for he is inclined to agree with the Reformers. However, note the double standard of those who condemn Rome, yet do far more damage to God's Word than Rome. As shown in the present document, dispensationalism has done more social damage than Rome could ever do. This writer has typically found antagonism against and fear of any non-dispensational doctrine from dispensational followers, antagonism similar to that exhibited by Rome toward Protestants over the years. It appears that modern publishers determine what they think the Christian public will purchase, and then they find men to write toward that market, *e.g.*, the *Left Behind* series. Those who write to the purse are the worst kind of hypocrites and false teachers; they rightly criticize Rome for developing doctrine to gain a following, yet they develop doctrine to sell books. They will not escape in the day of judgment as they write science-fiction and pass it off as Biblical theology in order to sell books. Furthermore, Rome says that all Scripture must be understood according to Rome, yet modern dispensationalism says that all Scripture must be understood according to Tim LaHaye, Hal Lindsey, or any number of "profiting prophets." Because a major foundation of dispensationalism is the church/Israel distinction, book sellers must support carnal Israel, Zionism, if they will continue to make their millions from prophetic science-fiction. It seems that profits outweigh the billions of US dollars going to support carnal Israel, and outweigh the thousands of Christians being persecuted by *Israel*. Hal Lindsey goes so far as to say that any teaching that says that "'the Church has been given the promises made to the Israelites' is 'demonic and heretical'." Hal Lindsey, *The Rapture*, p. 35. Quoted by Olson, *Catholics*, 182.

5. Dave Chilton, *Days of Vengeance*, p. 27. Quoted by Olson, Catholics, 99.

6. *There's a New World Coming*, back cover, *The Late Great Planet Earth*, pp. 1-8. Quoted by Olson, *Catholics*, 268, 269.

Here we see that there are modern *Biblical* prophecy teachers who see themselves as better prognosticators than are in the world, and see the Bible as not much more than a "Crystal Ball."

What started at the 1826 conference on unfulfilled prophecy, and grew through the many conferences since, has developed into a very profitable money making machine. These conferences to develop unfulfilled prophecy were basically meetings in violation to the clear instructions of our Lord. James 1:22 tells us these early developers of prophetic speculations were open to collective self-deception. *But be ye doers of the word, and not hearers only, deceiving your own selves.* And considering the world-wide effect the conferences had against "Christ the victorious," some spirits may have met with them.

The conferences for the development of unfulfilled prophecy were held in a religious climate conducive for prophetic speculations to be developed and accepted:

> The early part of the nineteenth century has been regarded as a period when the corporate implications of Christianity were neglected. Indeed C.C.J. Webb argued that the happiness and salvation of individual souls as the supreme concern of religion was one of the outstanding assumptions of English religious thought in the first part of the nineteenth century. It has become customary to lay the major share of responsibility for this upon the evangelicals, not only because they taught that religion is an individual matter, but also because they acted on the principle that "differences in external polity" are "compatible with a more fundamental spiritual unity," by founding societies, such as British and Foreign Bible Society, whose committees included clergy of the established and descending churches.[7]

The religious atmosphere of the time of the conferences saw the primary concern of religion as the happiness and salvation of individual souls. It also saw religion as an individual matter.[8] The world changing Christian faith was withdrawing from its powerful social influence. That withdrawal laid the foundation for the modern Christian goal of *personal peace* and *affluence*:

---

7. *Origins*, 7.

Personal peace means just to be let alone, not to be troubled by the troubles of other people, whether across the world or across the city— to live one's life with minimal possibilities of being personally disturbed. Personal peace means wanting to have my personal life pattern undisturbed in my lifetime, regardless of what the result will be in the lifetime of my children and grandchildren. Affluence means an overwhelming and ever-increasing prosperity—a life made up of things and more things—a success judged by an ever-higher level of material abundance.[9]

Chapter 36

Henry Drummond

The first of many conferences to study unfulfilled prophecy was the Albury Prophecy Conference, sponsored by a wealthy 40 year old evangelical banker and member of Parliament, Henry Drummond (1786-1860). The French Revolution and its aftermath convinced "Earnest British preachers and teachers of many denominations" that they would "shortly see dramatic and direct divine intervention..." The "wild expectations, new ideas on the interpretation of Biblical prophecies" resulted in a "ferment of excitement," leading to various meetings to study prophecy. "One series, held annually from 1826 to 1830 at the Albury, Surrey, home of the banker Henry Drummond, became the centre of wild speculation, and from them developed the pentecostalist movement of Irving's Catholic and Apostolic Church."[10]

---

8. "Self-Esteem," is not new. Note: First, God tells us that the primary duty of all religion is to please him, Ecc. 12:13, 14, 1 Cor. 10:31; and second, the word of God is extremely clear — that is, man's relationship with his Creator according to his law affects all society. Adam's disobedience to God's Law-Word was not an individual matter, cf. Deut. chaps. 28-32, &c. Darby saw prophecy as a guard preventing "him from being mixed up with the spirit of the world, whose judgment is announced." The Millenarians promoted prophecy as an escape from the reality of surrounding evil, *Writings,* II.488, &c.

9. *Live,* 205. Emp. his.

In the early 1820s he was prominently associated with both the Continental Society and the London Society for Promoting Christianity among the Jews, a friend of Lewis Way and the sponsor of Joseph Wolff's missionary activities. Also a friend of Irving's, Drummond eventually left the Anglican church and joined his congregation.[11]

Henry Drummond was "a man born to great riches." Thus he was free from the restraints of most men, for they find it impossible to put their own will into full execution. Drummond exercised an ever increasing influence over Irving.[12]

Though the Powerscourt conferences played a crucial role in developing and spreading the newly proposed, futuristic, prophetic assumptions and theories, they actually started with the Albury Park conferences. And the time was right for wild prophetic speculations. Everything apparently pointed to,

> [T]he expectation conveyed in this Spanish book, to which his own mind and that of many others had been directed... If the advent of the Lord were indeed close at hand [1826, *ed.*]; if events were visibly marching forward to that great visible era of doom and triumph, as so many students of prophecy concurred in believing — it was but natural that a hope so extraordinary should bring the little brotherhood into a union far more intimate than that of mere concurrence in belief...
> "A desire to compare their views with respect to the prospects of the Church at this present crisis" naturally arose among them, as

---

10. Coad, *History,* 109. *Origins,* 16. See also *Who,* s.v. "Drummond, Henry." He was a member of Parliament, 1810-1813 and 1847-1860.

11. *Roots,* 19. The modern millennial system, "Protestant Zionism," can be directly traced to Drummond's support of Way and Wolff. He also supported J.H. Evans, Coad, *History,* 70-73. It was his considerable wealth, gained from the banking industry that financed Lacunza's (a "converted" Jew) system. Jews also financed Scofield, *q.v.* Millenarianism has always had abundant financing.

12. *Life,* 203, 204. Drummond is credited with "founding" Irving's church. Thomas Carlyle, after meeting Drummond in his home, describes Drummond: "A man of elastic, pungent decisive nature, full of fine qualities and capabilities, but well nigh cracked by an enormous conceit of himself, which, both as pride and vanity (in strange partnership mutually agreeable), seemed to pervade every fibre of him, and render his life a restless inconsistency. That was the feeling he left in me; nor did it alter afterwards when I saw a great deal more of him..." *Reminiscences,* 246.

Irving informs us in the preface of *Ben-Ezra;* and after several meetings during the summer, a serious and lengthened conference on the subject was arranged to take place at Albury, the residence of one of the most remarkable of the little prophetic parliament, the late Henry Drummond.[13]

At Albury, well before Darby left the Anglican Church, Irving at last found Protestant churchmen who gladly accepted the newly developing millennial system. These churchmen set about to refine and spread the system to all Christendom. The Albury Park conferences laid the groundwork for the 1831 Powerscourt conference, which was repeated in 1832 and 1833.[14]

Therefore, the significance of the Albury conferences cannot be overestimated. Two very important events took place at the first conference: The introduction of a key player (Joseph Wolff) in the development of the basic premises of Brethrenism, and the introduction of a document that became the basis for general Christian beliefs to the present day:

> Very closely linked with what might be called the "haphazardism" of the Brethren is their attitude towards the question of unfulfilled prophecy. Brethrenism may even be held to derive its very existence in part from the new prophetic studies to which the unsettlement of men's minds, consequent of the long agony of the Napoleonic wars, gave rise. Prophetic meetings were established in 1827 at Aldbury Park, Surrey, the seat of the well-known Henry Drummond. At these meetings Edward Irving took part, and to Aldbury Irvingism traces its rise. Lady Powerscourt attended these conferences, and "was so delighted with them that she established a similar series of meetings at Powerscourt House near Bray, in the County Wicklow"....[15]

---

13. *Life,* 202, 203. Irving's translation of *Ben-Ezra* was not complete by the first conference.

14. *Roots,* 18-41. Darby's letter, reproduced herein, explains what took place at the 1832 conference, which laid the ground work for the important 1833 conference.

15. Neatby, *History,* 38. Neatby gives a different spelling and date for the meetings, Aldbury vs. Albury and 1837 vs. 1826. But dates and places are not our primary concern. Moreover, though some following dates may contradict at times, we give the dates as recorded by our sources. (Irving dated the Albury conference, 1827. His was a leading role in it.)

The social and religious chaos of the day was perfect for the wild "prophetic speculations" developed in these meetings to be "merged with Darby's foreboding concerning the Established Church," which took place at Powerscourt. The prophetic speculations from these meetings have been preached by such renowned men as Moody and Ironside. They were codified many years after Albury by C.I. Scofield.

Chapter 37

The Albury Park Conferences

Drummond invited about twenty interested laymen and clergy to attend for an extended discussion on "prophetic truth." Those who gathered at this first conference planned a full week-long debate of the great prophetic questions that most concerned Christendom. Special letters of invitation were sent to all who were thought to be interested in prophecy. Men of all stripes (and the wealthy widow, Lady Powerscourt) came, and according to Irving, for eight days, they met, spending "six full days in close and laborious examination of the Scripture..." Their emphasis was upon the second advent.[16]

With no outside influence in this meeting other than Scripture and the Zionist, Joseph Wolff (see "Joseph Wolff," p. 137), the participants became secure in the hope of the very soon "personal appearance of our Lord at a period which some actually fixed, and all regarded as close at hand, [they, *ed.*] looked also, as a necessary preliminary of that appearance, for a personal development of evil, more remarkable and decided than anything that had preceded it;

---

16. *Life*, 204. "Some members of the Albury conference spoke confidently about the second advent happening in 1843 or 1847, but, whether they set dates or not, all the participants expected Christ's return within a few years." *Roots*, 22. *Origins*, 86, 87. Coad, *History*, 109, 111. Irving's account of this conference is reproduced in App. A.

and had so identified and concluded upon the source from which this Antichrist was to come...".[17]

Irving was a child of his time, a time of hopelessness left by the French Revolution and the Napoleonic wars. At Albury Park, Irving's opinion that any "idea of the world's conversion" was an "error" found a ready audience and many followers. But Irving was not alone in his hopeless state of mind, his views of prophecy and his feelings of urgency. There were many like- minded present, and providence would unite them and their thoughts through the many following conferences on unfulfilled prophecy.[18]

It was the personalities of those involved that influenced others to receive their teachings. Though not well-read, Irving was scholarly, well disciplined and well liked, and possessed tremendous speaking ability.[19] His oratory skill is attested to by the fact that in May of 1824, Irving was "selected to preach one of the anniversary sermons of the London Missionary Society. The invitation to do this was presumed to be a compliment to Irving, and voucher of his popularity, as well as a prudent enlistment of the 'highest talent,' to give attention to the yearly solemnity of the Society." A full hour before the appointed time, the Presbyterian minister packed the tabernacle that had been built for Whitfield in Tottenham Court Road.[20] "In the opinion of De Quincey, he [Irving, *ed.*] was 'by many degrees the greatest orator of our times.'"[21] Though he was an immensely popular preacher, he was not a serious student of Scripture.

"The soon return of Christ" became the most discussed topic at these prophecy conferences, and was a basic, common motive for soul-winning and mission work within the early millenarian (Brethren) movement.

---

17. *Life,* 206.
18. Does Deut. 13 apply?
19. *Reminiscences,* 82.
20. *Life,* 94, 96.
21. *Hope,* 188.

Second Albury Conference

The second Albury conference on unfulfilled prophecy took place in 1827. Though there are no written records of this conference, Irving spoke of it in a letter to Dr. Chambers of Edinburgh University: "We have had another Albury meeting, and are more convinced than ever of the judgments which are about to be brought upon Christendom, and upon us most especially, if we should go into any league or confederacy with, or toleration of, the papal abomination."[22]

Third Albury Conference

The third Albury conference on unfulfilled prophecy occurred November 30, 1829. Though there are no written records, for they intentionally kept none, we have an idea of what was discussed and developed from Irving's later writings: They were to develop the new prophetic speculations, and what was developed is not unlike accepted prophetic doctrine today. By 1829, *Ben-Ezra*, through Irving's English translation, was well known among those attending these conferences. Lacunza's system is clearly present in Drummond's summary of the 1829 conference:

> 1. This "dispensation" or age will not end "insensibly" but cataclysmically in judgment and destruction of the church in the same manner in which the Jewish dispensation ended.
>
> 2. The Jews will be restored to Palestine during the time of judgment.
>
> 3. The judgment to come will fall principally upon Christendom.
>
> 4. When the judgment is past, the millennium will begin.
>
> 5. The second advent of Christ will occur before the millennium.

---

22. *Ibid.*, 255. The pressure was off, so the great swelling words thereafter against Rome were sounding brass and tinkling cymbals. By placing God's judgment against Rome into a future dispensation, the Protestants delivered the nations to Rome. The Protestants lost the Christian faith that required them to Christianize all nations.

6. The 1260 years of Daniel 7 and Revelation 13 ought to be measured from the reign of Justinian to the French Revolution. The vials of wrath (Revelation 16) are now being poured out and the second advent is imminent.[23]

All the founders of modern dispensationalism were confident that the French Revolution was the key to prophetic understanding and fulfillment. Their many speculations have proved wrong, but that has not discouraged those retaining the millennial faith. They simply design new charts with new dates and events when old ones fail.

Though the Albury conferences introducing millenarianism took place before Brethrenism, Brethrenism derived its existence in part from the new prophetic studies that were taking place at these conferences.[24]

The Albury conferences "brought together almost every British millenarian scholar of note... [whose primary concern was, *ed.*] to discuss and develop the new pre-millenarian theories" as presented by *Ben-Ezra*. The Albury conferences on unfulfilled prophecy laid the foundation for the many prophecy conferences to follow: Mildmay and Powerscourt in Britain, Niagara and Northfield in North America.[25] The results of the emphasis on prophetic speculation and the supposed nearness of the second advent are quite obvious: Christianity became little more than an ascetic experience looking for personal peace and prosperity, withdrawn from public life.[26]

The purpose of the conferences was not to develop proper ways to apply God's Law-Word to the surrounding social chaos. Rather, the purpose was to study and develop a new system of prophetic speculation — how to escape the surrounding social chaos. Those

---

23. *Dialogues*, 1.ii-iii, which were written after the third conference in 1828. *Roots*, footnote on p. 21.

24. Neatby, *History*, 38.

25. *Roots*, 18. Until Moody and Northfield, the ideas developed from these early prophecy conferences were regarded as departure from the historic, orthodox Christian faith, heresy. It was through Moody and Northfield that the new system became accepted in North America.

26. Neatby, *History*, 40.

attending felt the basic millennial doctrines were new, and it was their responsibility to further develop the new theories.

Though Darby was not listed among those attending the Albury meetings, he later claimed as his own many of the conclusions reached at Albury Park.

Certainly, by the time the Albury meetings were concluded, Irving had well perfected the new *Ben-Ezra* ideas when he took it to the 1833 Powerscourt conference — the loose ends were tied together. As if to confirm the *Ben- Ezra* ideas and to prepare the way for the Powerscourt conferences to study unfulfilled prophecy, an event took place in Scotland:

> At the last of the Albury meetings for study of unfilled prophecy, held in July, 1830, the exciting news of the appearance of the miraculous gifts in Scotland was discussed....[27]

Margaret Macdonald was the source. (See "Tongues and the Rapture," p. 148.)

Chapter 38
Zionism and Joseph Wolff

As we have seen previously, though offered several times, Zionism did not make inroads into Protestantism until Irving introduced Lazunza's 1790 document at the first Albury Park prophecy conference. There it found ready hearers who would develop the idea and cover the world with it.

Lacunza's system insisted that only half of the Lord's work was completed on earth, so he must reestablish a national Israel to complete his work. Because the church failed to reach the world for Christ, Christ must work through a reestablished, glorified national

---

27. *Origins*, 10.

Israel (the Jews restored to Palestine as God's chosen people), *i.e.,* "Protestant Zionism."

In the "P.S." on Irving's *Preliminary Discourse,* he mentions some events that took place at the first, 1826, Albury conference. Extremely interested in prophecy and able to finance conferences, Henry Drummond

> [T]hought well to invite by special letter all the men, both ministers and laymen, of any orthodox communion whom he knew or could ascertain to be interested in prophetic studies; that they should assemble at this house of Albury Park, in Surrey, on the first day of Advent, that we might deliberate for a full week upon the great prophetic questions which do at present most intimately concern Christendom. In answer to this honourable summons, there assembled about twenty men of every rank, and church, and orthodox communion in these realms; in honour of our meeting, God so ordered it that Joseph Wolff, the Jewish missionary, a son of Abraham and brother of our Lord, both according to the flesh and according to faith, should also be of the number...
>
> ... And when we assembled, and had shortly sought the Divine favour to continue with us, an office generally performed by our reverend Moderator, he proceeded in due course to ask each man for his convictions upon the subject which had been laid before us in the morning: and the rest diligently used their pen in catching the spirit of what dropped from each other's lips. No appeal was allowed but to the Scriptures, of which the originals lay before us; in the interpretation of which, if any question arose, we had the most learned Eastern scholar perhaps in the world to appeal to, a native Hebrew — I mean Joseph Wolff...."[28]

Out of this meeting came the idea of the soon "personal appearance of our Lord...".

Joseph Wolff

Who was Joseph Wolff (1795-1862), the 31 year old *scholar* who exercised tremendous influence in this conference? His story starts with a man named Lewis Way, another of Drummond's friends. Way inherited a large sum of money in 1804, freeing him from the

---

28. *Ben-Ezra,* I.clxxxviii-cxciv. For the entire P.S, see App. A. Mrs. Oliphant also quotes this entire section about Wolff, *Life,* 204-206

"drudgery of work." In 1811, while visiting in Devonshire, Way "was told about a grove of trees which were not to be cut down until the restoration of the Jews to Palestine." The owner's will read in part:

> "These oaks shall remain standing, and the hand of man shall not be raised against them till Israel returns and is restored to the Land of Promise."[29]

His interest aroused in Jewish prophecies, Way investigated prophecies relating to the restoration of the Jews, and looked for contemporary agencies whose attention was directed to Jewish restoration:

> He discovered the existence of a faltering group named the London Society for Promoting Christianity among the Jews [Drummond was connected with this society, *ed.*], founded in 1809 and led by a converted Jew, Mr. Joseph S. C. F. Frey. When Way became concerned with it in 1815, the society was deeply in debt and troubled by rivalries between church and dissenting supporters. Way, who had by this time been ordained as an Anglican, settled the obligations of the society at a cost of over twelve thousand pounds, virtually buying out the deserters and converting the society at the same time into an Anglican agency and a vehicle for his own ministry. Way turned the LSPCJ, previously concerned only with proselyting London Jews, into a missionary society devoted to the training and support of Jewish converts to Christianity, who were then sent into eastern Europe, Russia, and the Middle East.... Way made a journey to Russia for the purpose of settling one of these men and, at the same time, obtaining a first-hand picture of the condition and beliefs of European Jews. The Climax of this venture occurred when Way was introduced to Czar Alexander I and influenced him to submit a memorandum on the condition of the Jews to the European powers assembled at the Congress of Aix-la-Chapelle in 1818.
>
> The Jews Society, as it was referred to by its members, achieved its greatest success as an advocate of Protestant Zionism. The efforts to evangelize the Jews had little success... Only Joseph Wolff, a flamboyant Prussian Jew who became an Anglican after having previously become a convert to Catholicism, could play the role of the missionary hero; and he, it must be said, played it with such flair

---

29. Quoted by Sandeen, *Roots*, 10.

that one suspects he must have been half adventurer and imposter. But the restoration of the Jews to Palestine — the return of the chosen people to the promised land — became firmly established in the millenarian creed. Through the monthly issues of the *Jewish Expositor,* the LSPCJ journal, and in dozens of other books, this question was discussed in never-wearing detail. The Zionist cause won rather wide sympathy at this time; the Jews and the Greeks seem to have been classed together as heroic but downtrodden people. But millenarian interest in the restoration of the Jews stemmed explicitly from the interpretation of prophecy. The prophetic text which described the cataclysmic events apparently fulfilled in the French Revolution also predicted the second advent of Christ and the restoration of the Jews. The prophetic timetable had joined these expectations inextricably. The millenarian accepted both events as the will of God, prayed for the coming of both, and, if he could not work for the accomplishment of the second advent, did what he could to aid the cause of Palestine resettlement.... [T]here is no question that the millenarian movement played a significant role in preparing the British for political Zionism.[30]

The preacher of the millenarian creed ("Protestant Zionism") at the first Albury conference was Joseph Wolff. Wolff, a son of a Jewish rabbi, converted to Christianity, *i.e.,* Roman Catholicism, and was baptized, 13 Sept., 1812. Arriving in Rome in 1815, he was introduced to Pope Pius VII. He went on to Collegio Romano, 5 Sept., 1816, and transferred to Collegio di Propagands. He later entered the monastery of the Redemptorists at ValSainte. Disliking the system at the monastery, he visited Henry Drummond — whom he had met in Rome — in London. He soon thereafter declared himself a member of the Church of England.[31]

Joseph Wolff laid the foundation for modern Protestant Zionism. History tells us that this 31 year old man met with the pope, "publicly attacked the doctrine of infallibility," was "expelled from

---

30. *Ibid.,* 10-12. Sandeen's footnote at "impostor," Joseph Wolff, *Missionary Journal and Memoir,* 2ed ed. (London, 1827); Joseph Wolff, *Travels and Adventures of the Rev. Joseph Wolff* (London, 1861); H. P. Palmer, *Joseph Wolff* (Heath Carnton, 1935).

31. *DNB,* s.v. "Wolf, Joseph." *DNB*'s account of Wolff, which the reader should review, is reproduced in App. C.

the city for erroneous opinions," had a "mission work among the Christians," searched for "the lost ten tribes," named his first-born "after his earliest English friend" (Henry Drummond), and knew Irving.[32]

Joseph Wolff, *a converted son of a Jewish rabbi,* is the one mentioned by Irving at the first prophetic conference where the new millennial system was introduced by Irving.

One should note that Wolff and Drummond quite possibly met in Rome when Wolff met with Pope Pius VII. The dates are interesting — Drummond and Wolff were both in Rome in 1815. Drummond called and financed the 1826 prophecy conference where the Roman Jesuit's system was introduced by Irving, who was a close friend of both Drummond and Wolff before the conference. (Wolff met his first wife through Irving.) Those attending that first 1826 conference intentionally dismissed all past Protestant understanding of the prophetic questions before them. Probably because Wolff claimed to be "a son of Abraham" and "a native Hebrew," and because those present considered him to be "the most learned Eastern scholar perhaps in the world," Wolff alone was allowed to give the proper understanding to the questionable *prophetic* passages which were before them.[33]

Wolff had traveled widely propagating Zionism well before the first 1826 Albury conference.[34] So when questionable passages of Scripture were encountered at the first conference on unfulfilled prophecy, rather than seek the historical orthodox Protestant church's understanding, they sought proper interpretation from Joseph Wolff, the "flamboyant Prussian Jew... half adventurer and

---

32. *Ibid.*
33. *Ben-Ezra,* I.clxxxviii-cxciv, *q.v.* Drummond's and Irving's close association with Wolff probably played a big part in allowing him alone to be their *expert.*
34. We have an idea of what kind of man Wolff was: "On his way [to Tinnevelly, *ed.*], he [Groves, *ed.*] stayed from 27 October to 6 November, 1833, at Cannanore. The missionary community there had recently been visited by that rather eccentric preacher of the Second Advent, Joseph Wolff, whose views had caused dissension. Groves was able to restore harmony and build upon the foundation of adventist teaching that Wolff had laid." *Origins,* 196.

impostor" trained by "The Jews Society" in "Protestant Zionism"! And the new *unorthodox* prophetic understanding established in that first conference is now *orthodox* Protestant prophetic understanding.

Thus the Jewish hope that had been laid to rest by Christ and the early Church fathers is resurrected by Jews.[35] It was resurrected with new strength and vigor to became a solid plank in the millenarian platform; the "church/ Israel distinction," that is, "Protestant Zionism," which goes hand in hand with "political Zionism." (See "Zionism," p. 72, FN.)

Chapter 39

Powerscourt Conferences

The wealthy widow, Lady Powerscourt — "more than a little touch of the mystic" — had attended the first Albury Park conference, and was greatly impressed with Irving's speaking.[36] She then held prophetic conferences at her estate to develop the prophetic system. Her conferences played a crucial role in developing and spreading the emerging millennial system.

Though several Powerscourt conferences were held, we will only touch on two in order to show their themes: 1832 and 1833. The 1832 Powerscourt conference laid the foundation for the important 1833 conference.

Following is a summary of the (September 24th, to 28th) 1832 Powerscourt conferences, which William Kelly believed Darby wrote:

---

35. The Jews would be restored in power and glory, and one of their own would "become governor of the habitable earth," ruling from their gloriously restored city, Jerusalem.

36. "One who knew her well said that 'she seemed as if she lived in heaven, and barely touched the earth'." *Origins*, 86. It was said that Darby and the young, attractive widow, Lady Powerscourt, had contemplated marriage, but the engagement was broken off by mutual agreement because of Darby's commitment to a traveling ministry. Coad's *History*, 110, *Roots*, 34.

Tuesday. - The Prophetical character of each book in the Bible; including the three great feasts of the Jews, the blessings pronounced on Jacob's sons, the Parables in the Gospel, and the Epistles to the Seven Churches in Revelation.

Wednesday. - Should we expect a personal Antichrist — If so, to whom will he be revealed? Are there to be one or two great evil powers in the world at that time? Is there any uniform sense for the word *Saint* in the Prophetic, or New Testament scripture? By what covenant did the Jews, and shall the Jews, hold the land?

Thursday. - An inquiry into, and a connection between Daniel and the Apocalypse.

Friday. - What light does scripture throw on present events, and their moral character? What is next to be looked for and expected? Is there a prospect of a revival of Apostolic churches before the coming of Christ? What the duties [sic] arising out of present events? To what time, and to what class of persons do 1 Tim. iv.; 2 Tim. iii.; Jude; Mat. xxiv. 23, 24; and 2 Peter iii. refer?[37]

The question of "the gifts" was also raised at the 1832 meeting along with other prophetic themes. There was an under-current against the direction in which Darby took these meetings. Rev. P. Roe, an evangelical clergyman who was present, "noted in his diary for 29 September, 1832, that he had found the conference unprofitable 'upon the whole'. He continued: 'Many of the subjects were evidently difficult to be understood. The most extravagant assertions were made, and dogmas quite opposed to each other maintained with the greatest pertinacity. The duty of seeking for miraculous gifts was strongly insisted upon! Oh! what a fool man is!'"[38] Thus we see that, among other things, the idea of the appearance of a personal Antichrist developed, and dogmatic assertions made at this meeting which were "quite opposed to each other."

We should mention that Darby answered the question, "Is there a prospect of a revival of Apostolic churches before the coming of Christ?"

---

37. *Letters*, I.5, 7. Because the system developed at the Powerscourt meetings became the basis of modern dispensational millennialism, we have reproduced the complete letter in App. A.

38. 34*Origins*, 93.

> What we are about to consider will tend to shew that, instead of permitting ourselves to hope for a continued progress of good, we must expect a progress of evil; and that the hope of the earth being filled with the knowledge of the Lord before the exercise of His judgment, and the consummation of this judgment on the earth, is delusive... Truly Christendom had become completely corrupted; the dispensation of the Gentiles has been found unfaithful: can it be restored? No! impossible.[39] The saint could no longer occupy himself with the hope of the restoration of the Church as a professing whole, and therefore the coming of the Lord is placed before it as its only resource...[40]

And thus Darby swept away eighteen hundred years of developed, accepted orthodox Christian doctrine. However, he was not the first preacher of death. Irving had, in 1826, already "changed the common superficial idea of the world's conversion."

The 1832 meeting laid the foundation for the 1833 meeting that established the basic millennial system with which the Brethren would conquer the world.

The 1833 Powerscourt Conference was held from Monday 23 September to Saturday 28 September. Among those who attended these meetings, setting its temper, were (note their youth): Darby, 33; Müller, 28; Bellett, 38; B.W. Newton, 26; P.F. Hall, 29; V.G. Wigram and Henry Craik, 28, who became a Baptist minister. Here their basic principles and concerns were discussed and developed. Darby, in particular, took a very prominent part in them, throwing "himself wholeheartedly into this fervour of prophetic expectation and discussion."[41]

> Newton expressed himself forcibly in his reminiscences. "I went", he said, "and never was more disappointed. An amazing lack of both intelligent understanding and of devotedness." He regarded the

---

39. *Hope,* 201. The quote is from Darby's *Collected Writings,* prophetical, I.471, 486.

40. *Writings,* II.558. As one reads Darby's letters, he will clearly see that Darby dogmatically taught that Christians have no hope of restoring any kind of godly social order; their only hope is very soon to be raptured out of the surrounding chaos, *e.g., ibid.,* 515, *Letters,* I.329.

41. Coad, *History,* 110.

Powerscourt Conferences as the instrument whereby Darby essayed to end private judgement in the interpretation of prophecy and looked upon the 1833 meetings as "really the commencement of Brethrenism."[42]

These men had common concerns: the importance of the authority of Scripture as well as the sad condition of the church. "They were convinced that the hope of Christ's return should figure more prominently in the thinking of Christians," a major theme of Lacunza's system. The main topics at this conference were the condition of the religious world and prophecy. There was also opposition among these dissenters to the obligation of paying tithes and to the involvement of the clergy in *secular* affairs.

It was a reactionary group. In their opposition to those they reacted against, they went to the opposite extreme. In their stand against the mandatory tithe, undoubtedly they swung the other way with the doctrine that the tithe is not required by God in this *age of grace.*

Another point of discussion in 1833 was the practice of the organized church, both Anglican and Roman, that excluded the laity from sharing in spiritual duties except in menial and semi-administrative matters. As a reaction to the established churches' policy, they turned almost everything over to the layman.[43] And thus we have the Congregational form of church government — democracy where policy decisions are made by the members through their elected representative, the board, and then a *pastor* is hired as little more than the corporation's CEO. (Most churches this writer knows of are *Congregational* in their operations.)

Irving came to Powerscourt with the new millennial system; according to Harold Rowdon, he also came with a concern over the disunity of the Body of Christ and with "his conviction that the absence of the pentecostal gifts of the Holy Spirit was a significant

---

42. *Origins,* 96.
43. *Origins,* 97-99.

mark of her [the church's, *ed.*] plight." That conviction was not so readily received.

Chapter 40

Powerscourt and the Rapture

Powerscourt saw the teaching of a pretribulation rapture introduced. It developed into its full bloom at these meetings:

> It was at Powerscourt that the teaching of a pretribulation rapture of the Church took shape. Tregelles, a member of the Brethren in these early days, tells us that the idea of a secret rapture at a secret coming of Christ had its origin in an "utterance" in Edward Irving's church, and that this was taken to be the voice of the Spirit. Tregelles says, "It was from that supposed revelation that the modern doctrine and the modern phraseology respecting it arose. It came not from Holy Scripture, but from that which falsely pretended to be the Spirit of God." This doctrine together with other important modifications of the traditional futuristic view were vigorously promoted by Darby, and they have been popularized by the writings of William Kelly.[44]

> ... Set in impiety, the doctrine of the Lord's secret Coming, before the manifestation of the Man of Sin and before the Great Tribulation, was then first openly promulgated in England. It was adopted by the late J.N. Darby, and was caught up far and near, and hailed as enchanted teaching.[45]

Though others, *e.g.*, Irving, offered a secret rapture idea, its origin has since been attributed to Darby by most scholars. (Darby denied the teaching developed outside of himself.)[46] Rowdon quotes William Kelly's *The Rapture of the Saints: Who suggested it, or rather on what Scripture?*: "Kelly quoted Darby as saying that the

---

44. *Hope*, 40, 41. Ladd footnotes his quote from Tregelles, "S.P. Tregelles, *The Hope of Christ's Second Coming*, first published in 1864, and now available at Ambassadors for Christ, Los Angeles, California." Kelly "edited" Darby's writings to credit *pre-trib* to Darby. We have already seen that Darby was not the originator of the *pre-trib* theory, e.g., Edwards, *q.v.*

45. "E.P. Cachemaille, *The Prophetic Outlook To-day* (London: Morgan & Scott, 1918), pp. 19, 20." Quoted by MacPherson, *Plot,* 189.

idea that the rapture of the saints would take place prior to the return of Christ to earth came to him in 1830 through his study of II Thess. 2:1, 2."[47] Before Irving, common historical *premillennialism* held simply that Christ's coming will precede his millennial kingdom — Chiliasm (see "Historic Chiliasm", p. 439):

> [T]wo modern forms of premillennialism: *pretribulationism,* introduced by J. N. Darby and Plymouth Brethrenism about 1830, places the tribulation as future... and not potentially present... and divides the first resurrection and Christ's coming into 2: one for the church before the tribulation..., another for Jews after the tribulations: and with *post-tribulationism,* which places the tribulation [in the, *ed.*] future..., so that the rapture is no longer an imminent hope.[48]

Darby's views of the "ruin of the church," rapture and the future view of the Revelation were not based in Scripture, but in his *mystical* insight. He watched and listened to what was taking place around him (at Powerscourt especially), then molded Scripture with "Bible readings" to fit the ideas gleaned from others. Rowdon

---

46. Coad, *History,* 111-136. In 1885, George T. Stokes wrote, "From Irving, then, Darby derived his prophetical system, which became one of the most prominent features of his system...," *Plot,* 17. Darby's 1833 & 1834 letters simply mention his expectation of "the near coming of the Saviour," *e.g., Letters,* I.12, 31. It was not until 1855 that Darby "saw in that word the coming of Christ to take the church to Himself in glory," *Letters,* III.299.

47. *Origins,* 30, note #115. According to Mr. Payne, "Dispensationalism generally affirms that the restraint must be the Holy Spirit of God, in the Church, *Scofield Reference Bible,* 1272, and that its being 'taken out of the way' refers to the rapture of the church, prior to the lawlessness of the great tribulation. The Thessalonian context, however, suggests nothing about the Holy Spirit, or why such veiled language should be used if He were the one meant. Though he may indeed do so, the Spirit is never mentioned in Scripture with the function of restraining lawlessness; and vv. such as John 16:8, Eph. 6:18, or I John 4:4 cannot be adduced as strictly germane to such an activity, though cf. the effort of J. F. Strombeck. *First the Rapture,* p. 101. Scripture, moreover, gives no hint of the Holy Spirit's ever being removed from the world — Strombeck's citation of Gen. 6:3, *ibid.,* p. 102, misinterprets its reference to the termination of life by the flood; cf. G. Vos, *Biblical Theology,* pp. 61-62. Modern dispensationalists concede that the Holy Spirit continues in the world after the rapture, convicting men of sin and judgment, and opening their hearts to the message of salvation. Thus the only thing really removed would be His presence as indwelling the church; cf. J. D. Pentecost, *Things to Come,* pp. 262-263, which would appear to be an interpretation dictated by pretribulationist preconceptions." *Prophecy,* 565.

recounts Craik's summary of the subjects discussed at the 1833 Powerscourt meetings:

> Reflected in the subjects for each day's discussion... was the implication that the era of the Christian Church is to be distinguished from all that has gone before and all that will follow. The Christian dispensation (i.e. the administration of God's purposes during the Christian era) was therefore distinguished from the Jewish dispensation on the one hand and the 'further dispensation' on the other.
>   This distinction was the means by which Darby related the idea of the "rapture" of the Church to the unfulfilled prophecies of Scripture. Darby stated that the basic idea came to him as he studied Isaiah 32, but he may also have been influenced by a human agency. In a tract on the subject, W. Kelly referred to an incident which took place in the summer of 1845 when Newton told him that, many years before, Darby had written him a letter saying that a suggestion made to him by Mr. T. Tweedy (a former clergyman who had joined the Brethren in Ireland and was subsequently to serve as a missionary in Demerara) had cleared up a difficulty which he had previously felt. Newton related the same story in his reminiscences where he dated the letter 1832 or 1833. Darby's new-found solution was apparently to regard the Christian era as a parenthesis between the sixty-ninth and seventieth "weeks" of Daniel's vision (Daniel 9. 24-27). The seventieth week (of years) would not commence until after the rapture of the saints of the Christian era. The fulfillment of those prophecies regarding God's judgment of the nations, and the earthly blessings promised to His earthly people, Israel, would then — and not till then — be fulfilled.[49]

Though Darby clearly "derived his prophetical system" from Irving, both Darby and Irving said the secret pre-trib rapture was a new,

---

48. *Prophecy,* 596. The modern speculations concerning "the last or apocalyptic Week of Daniel" was claimed by Darby about 1830; it was further developed and propagated by many men since, *e.g.,* C.H. Mackintosh. Though there was a historical premillennial position in Christian thought, the new and novel idea of a "secret rapture" and the restoration of Israel at the close of Daniel's week had "never been heard of in the whole history of the Christian Church since the Apostolic Age." The "new and novel" ideas can be traced only to Darby and the work of the Plymouth Brethren, *Advent,* 19, 29. Both Reese and Payne attribute the *secret, pre-trib rapture* to Darby. However, it was not new with Darby, though he certainly popularized it.

49. *Origins,* 97. Emp added. See *Letters,* III.299.

novel and unique idea incorporated at Powerscourt into the system that came out of the Albury Park conferences.

And so, through ideas gleaned by Irving from the writings of Lacunza, and reinforced by Margaret's vision, then subsequently claimed by Darby as his own discovery, the war of the millenarians against the papacy was defused. For if a personal Antichrist must yet come after a secret rapture, how could the present papacy be the Antichrist, as historically claimed by the Protestants? Non-millenarians now became the enemy.

Chapter 41

Tongues and the Rapture

It appears strange to combine *tongues* and the *rapture*, but their close connection requires we mention tongues in passing. One cannot trace the origin of today's other-worldliness without encountering tongues, and the importance that the desire for the *gifts* played in the millennial movement. Though their relationship is not commonly known, both are easily traced to Edward Irving.

This present study is not about the modern tongues movement, but because of its common root with modern pre-mil eschatology, we should consider some things about tongues:

> The 'unknown tongues' — the crowning development of Irving's ministrations — were first heard on 28 March 1830, from the mouth of Mary Campbell, 'in the little farmhouse of Jernicarry, at the head of the Gairloch.' On Irving's theories of the second advent, this and the miraculous cure of Miss Campbell, which was believed to have occurred shortly afterwards, were events to be expected, and he can scarcely be excused of excessive credulity of having rather encouraged than repressed the manifestations which rapidly multiplied.... The manifestations have been described by many, both speakers and hearers. The best descriptions are vivid accounts of Robert Baxter, himself an agent, who ended by attributing them to diabolical possession, and that by Irving himself, who, obliged to

maintain the Pentecostal affinities of the phenomenon, is exceedingly indignant with 'the heedless sons of Belial' who pronounced the utterances mere gibberish; and protests that, on the contrary, 'it is regularly formed, well proportioned, deeply felt discourse, which evidently wanteth only the ear of him whose native tongue it is to make it a very masterpiece of powerful speech.' But whose native tongue was it? Miss Campbell conjectured, for unknown reasons, the Pelew Islanders'. The whole story is a curious instance of religious delusion.[50]

The first successful millenarian voice in Scotland, Irving, was also the first to have tongues in his congregation. Accordingly, the two modern movements — millenarian and tongues — have a common source, Edward Irving. Mr. Thomas Carlyle said that,

> The "Gift of Tongues" had fairly broken out among the crazed and weakliest of his wholly rather dim and weakly flock. I was never at all in his church during this visit, being at once grieved and angered at the course he had fallen into; but once or twice poor Eliza Miles came running home from some evening sermon there was, all in a tremor of tears over these same "Tongues," and a riot from the *dissenting* majority opposing them.[51]

Irving permitted the "miraculous gifts" at his Presbyterian Church, causing the elders to excommunicate him and lock him out. He then formed his Catholic Apostolic Church down the street in 1831.[52] Though Darby accepted most of Irving's ideas, including the new millennial view of Daniel's 70th week and a personal Antichrist, he stoutly resisted Irving's tongues, calling them devilish, and Irving lost his influence.[53] Throughout history, from the time of Montanus, the *supernatural appearance* of tongues has been common when dispensationalism is taught. When one appears, so does the other. We will look at the 1800's development first.

---

50. *DNB,* s.v. "Irving, Edward."
51. *Reminiscences,* 251, 252.
52. *Roots,* 26, 27.
53. *Letters,* I.23, 1833, III.198. He also stood strong against faith healing, *ibid.,* 209.

After the third Albury Conference, 1829, Mrs. O.W. Oliphant records this account of Irving's association with Mr. Alexander Scott of London, England:

> Mr. Scott, like many others both in that day and this, entertained the belief that the supernatural powers once bestowed upon the church were not merely the phenomena of one miraculous age, but an inheritance of which she ought to have possession as surely and richly now as in the days of the apostles. A similar idea had already, in a kind of grand prophetic reverie, crossed the mind of Irving. So far back as 1828, he himself says he had become convinced that the spiritual gifts so largely bestowed upon the apostolic age of Christianity were not exceptional, or for one period alone, but belonged to the church of all ages, and had only been kept in abeyance by the absence of faith.[54]

Mrs. Oliphant quotes Irving's narrative of the *facts connected with recent manifestations of spiritual gifts*, published in *Fraser's Magazine* for Jan., 1832:

> "And as we [Irving referring to Mr. Scott, *ed.*] went in and out together he used often to signify to me his conviction that the spiritual gifts ought to be exercised in the church; that we are at liberty, and indeed bound, to pray for them, as being baptized into the assurance of the 'gift of the Holy Spirit,' as well as of 'repentance and remission of sin'...."

Irving proceeded to say that the more he thought on this subject, the more he agreed. He then preached it at every opportunity.[55] Mrs. Oliphant continues:

> The influence of Mr. Scott's opinions did not end here. His arguments opened still more effectually in another quarter, as Irving went on to describe:
> "Being called down to Scotland upon some occasion," continues Irving, "and residing for a while at his father's house, which is in the heart of that district of Scotland upon which the light of Mr. Campbell's ministry had arisen, he was led to open his mind to some of the godly people in these parts, and, among others, to a young

---

54. *Life*, 275.
55. *Ibid.*, 275-276. Note the surfacing of the requirement for the exercise of the "spiritual gifts" for assurance of one's salvation.

woman who was at that time lying ill of a consumption, from which afterwards, when brought to the very door of death, she was raised up instantaneously by the mighty hand of God. Being a woman of a very fixed and constant spirit, he was not able, with all his power of statement and argument, which is unequalled by that of any man I have ever met with, to convince her of the distinction between regeneration and baptism with the Holy Ghost; and when he could not prevail he left her with a solemn charge to read over the Acts of the Apostles with that distinction in her mind, and to beware how she rashly rejected what he believed to be the truth of God. By this young woman it was that God, not many months after, did restore the gift of speaking with tongues and prophesying to the Church."[56]

Thus the common root of the modern charismatic movement and modern dispensational view is established.

Irving went to every corner of England with his subject of prophecy and the second advent. Europe was ready, and he found support for his system in every church he entered. He wrongly viewed the growth of his following as God confirming his unique prophetic system of the pre-trib rapture, second advent and his doctrine of tongues.[57]

On a Sunday evening near the end of March, 1830, Irving met the young woman whom Mr. Scott had met in Scotland a few months previously. According to Irving, she was seriously ill, and her sisters had come to her home to spend

> [T]he whole day in humiliation, and fasting, and praying before God, with a special respect to the restoration of the gifts... While in the midst of their devotion, the Holy Ghost came with mighty power upon the sick woman as she lay in her weakness, and constrained her to speak at great length, and with superhuman strength, in an unknown tongue, to the astonishment of all who heard... She had told me that this first seizure of the Spirit was the strongest she ever had; and that it was in some degree necessary it should have been so, otherwise she would not have dared to give way to it.[58]

---

56. *Ibid.*, 276.
57. *Ibid.*, 282. Darby viewed the growth of his following as proof of God's hand upon him. However, he viewed the growth of other's following as proof they were using the flesh, *Letters,* II.258, 262. See 1 Tim. 6:5, 6.
58. *Life,* 287.

This young lady was taken with a strong seizure that overcame her own will! This statement alone should cause great alarm.

Mrs. Oliphant pointed out that this opened "The agitating and extraordinary chapter in the history of the modern church, which we have hereafter to deal with..." She identified this first speaker in tongues as Mary Campbell. Mrs. Oliphant then traced the experience to Port Glasgow, Scotland, and the home of two sober, quiet brothers who were

> [I]n no way likely to be the subjects of ecstatic emotions. But with results more startling and wonderful still, the newly-awakened power glided over the loch and river, to the devout and prayerful house of the Macdonald's.Touching first upon an invalid sister, it then burst upon the elder brother with impulse more extraordinary than any mere utterance... "At dinner-time James and George came home as usual," says the simple family narrative, "whom she then addressed at great length, concluding with a solemn prayer for James, that he might *at that time* be endowed with the power of the Holy Ghost. Almost instantly, James calmly said, 'I have got it.' He walked to the window, and stood silent for a minute or two. I looked at him, and almost trembled, there was such a change upon his whole countenance. He then, with a step and manner of the most indescribable majesty, walked up to ----'s bedside, and addressed her in these words of the 20th Psalm, 'Arise, and stand upright.' He repeated the words, took her by the hand and she arose."[59]

She, later identified as Margaret Macdonald, then ate supper with them. She wrote Mary Campbell about what took place, inspiring Mary to rise up and declare herself healed. Mary then went on the speaking circuit — she "spoke, expounded, gave forth the utterance of her power in crowded assemblies, and entered into the full career of a prophetess and gifted person."[60]

The early church clearly spoke concerning "prophetic utterances" such as Margaret's. Dealing with Montanus, the first recorded person teaching dispensational views *and* encouraging prophetic utterances, Asterius Urbanus wrote (c. 232):

---

59. *Ibid.,* 288-289.
60. *Ibid.,* 289.

Now the attitude of opposition which they have assumed, and this new heresy of theirs which puts them in a position of separation from the Church, had their origin in the following manner. There is said to be a certain village called Ardaba in the Mysia, which touches Phrygia. There, they say, one of those who had been but recently converted to the faith, a person of the name of Montanus, when Gratus was proconsul of Asia, gave the adversary entrance against himself by the excessive lust of his soul after taking the lead. And this person was carried away in spirit; and suddenly being seized with a kind of frenzy and ecstasy, he raved, and began to speak and to utter strange things, and to prophesy in a manner contrary to the custom of the Church, as handed down from early times and preserved thenceforward in a continuous succession. And among those who were present on that occasion, and heard those spurious utterances, there were some who were indignant, and rebuked him as one frenzied, and under the power of demons, and possessed by the spirit of delusion, and agitating the multitude, and debarred him from speaking any more; for they were mindful of the Lord's distinction and threatening, whereby He warned them to be on their guard vigilantly against the coming of the false prophets. But there were others too, who, as if elated by the Holy Spirit and the prophetic gift, and not a little puffed up, and forgetting entirely the Lord's distinction, challenged the maddening and insidious and seductive spirit, being themselves cajoled and misled by him, so that there was no longer any checking him to silence. And thus by a kind of artifice, or rather by such a process of craft, the devil having devised destruction against those who were disobedient to the Lord's warning, and being unworthily honored by them, secretly excited and inflamed their minds that had already left the faith which is according to truth, in order to play the harlot with error. For he stirred up two others also, women, and filled them with the spurious spirit, so that they too spoke in a frenzy and unseasonably, and in a strange manner, like the person already mentioned, while the spirit called them happy as they rejoiced and exulted proudly at his working, and puffed them up by the magnitude of his promises; while, on the other hand, at times also he condemned them skillfully and plausibly, in order that he might seem to them also to have the power of reproof.[61] And those few who were thus deluded were Phrygians. But the same arrogant spirit taught them to revile the Church universal under heaven, because that false spirit of prophecy found neither honor from it nor entrance into it. For when the faithful throughout Asia met together often and in many places of Asia for deliberation on this subject, and subjected those novel doctrines to examination, and declared them to be spurious, and rejected them as heretical, they were in consequence of that expelled from the Church and debarred from communion.

III. FROM BOOK II

Wherefore, since they stigmatized us as slayers of the prophets because we did not receive their loquacious prophets – for they say that these are they whom the Lord promised to send to the people, – let them answer us in the name of God, and tell us, O friends, whether there is any one among those who began to speak from Montanus and the women onward that was persecuted by the Jews or put to death by the wicked? ... But they will never be able to show that any one of the Old Testament prophets, or any one of the New, was carried away in spirit after this fashion. Nor will they be able to boast that Agabus, or Judas, or Silas, or the daughter of Philip, or *the woman* Ammia in Philadelphia, or Quadratus, or indeed any of the others who do not in any respect belong to them, were moved in this way.... For if, after Quadratus and the woman Ammia in Philadelphia, as they say, the women who attached themselves to Montanus succeeded to the gift of prophecy, let them show us which of them thus succeeded Montanus and his woman. For the apostle deems that the gift of prophecy should abide in all the Church up to the time of the final advent. But they will not be able to show the gift to be in their possession even at the present time, which is the fourteenth year only from the death of Maximilla.[62]

In A.D. 232, the "prophetic utterances" exhibited by Miss Macdonald would have been considered by some demonic utterances.

---

61. Footnote in text: "Montanus, that is to say, or the demon that spake by Montanus, knew that it had been said of old by the Lord, that when the Spirit came He would convince or reprove the world of sin; and hence this false spirit, with the view of confirming his hearers in the belief that he was the true Spirit of God, sometimes rebuked and condemned them. See a passage in Ambrose's *Epistle to the Thessal.*, ch. v. (Migne)."

62. *Fathers,* VII.335-7. Though this early work against the Montanus has been attributed to Asterius Urbanus, there is no clue to its authorship.

Chapter 42
Tongues, Irving and his Church

Word of the outbreak reached Irving from many sources. Evidently both Mary Campbell and Margaret Macdonald wrote papers describing their "revelations" and experiences, because on June 2, 1830, Irving referred to having read them. Having already lost two children to illness, these reports of the supernatural healings were especially important to Irving. At that time a third son, Samuel, was gravely ill. Mrs. Oliphant gives an account of how he wrote, with his concern heavy on his heart, "Oh, my dear A, tell me when this distinction of the works of the Spirit into ordinary and supernatural arose? There is no such thing in the Scriptures. I believe the Holy Ghost is as mighty in the church, and, but for our unbelief, would be as apparent, as ever He was."[63]

Mrs. Oliphant continued, making this observation: "Such seems to have been as yet his attitude in respect to the supernatural commotions in the west of Scotland. And there is no evidence that as yet they had extended to London, or appeared in his own immediate surrounding."[64]

Irving attended the fourth Albury Prophecy Conference, July 1st, 1830, and returned home to his sick child July third. Three days later, Samuel died. Though his own son was not healed, Irving's confidence in a new miraculous dispensation was not shaken. He continued to seek, and promote publicly, the experience; in a letter, July, 1831, he said, "Two of my flock have received the gift of tongues and prophecy."[65]

---

63. *Life,* 293.
64. *Ibid.,* 295. Mrs. Oliphant says, "New friends, bound together by the close and peculiar links of prophetic study..." People were thus united around the study of prophecy, which is not a very firm foundation. Sadly, the same spirit continues to prevail in millenarianism.
65. *Ibid.,* 317.

Irving, a Presbyterian minister, was called into account a year later before "the London Presbytery." He said, "I, as Christ's dutiful minister, standing in His room and responsible to Him (as are you all), *have not dared to believe that, when we asked bread, He gave us a stone, and when we asked fish, He gave us a serpent...*" — in other words, "We prayed for it. Therefore, it must be of God." Rather than judge the experience according to the word of God, he judged it by appearances.

Four months after its first outbreak, the new wonder exhibited itself publicly, but it was so disorganized that Irving would not permit its manifestation in his presence nor in his church. "Then, in the process of time, perhaps at the end of a fortnight, the gift perfected itself, so that they were made to speak in a tongue and to prophesy; that is, to set forth in English words for exhortation..."[66] After "trying the spirit" to his satisfaction as he understood Scripture, Irving permitted it to proceed in the public assembly of his Presbyterian church. Once he "determined it was of God, he stuck with that determination even at the cost of his church." Irving also viewed these supernatural manifestations as a sign that God was answering their prayers concerning the low state of the church.[67]

Once permitted, the *gift* spread quickly throughout his flock. Though Irving wanted it used in an organized manner, it turned his services into confusion. There is an account of a woman who could not restrain herself, so she rushed into the vestry, and gave vent to utterance. Another woman ran down the side- aisle and out of the church to give her utterance. Though the *gift* appeared primarily in women, men were also involved. "One witness speaks of it as 'bursting forth,' and that from the lips of a woman, 'with an astonishing and terrible crash;' another (Mr. Baxter), in his singular narrative, described how, when 'the power' fell suddenly upon

---

66. *Ibid.*, 318. Notice that this supposed work of the Holy Spirit was so imperfect and disorganized at the first that Irving would not permit it in the church, nor would he for some time. The refusal was in spite of the fact that they had been praying for the "gift."

67. *Ibid.*, 318-322.

himself, then all alone at his devotions, 'the utterance was so loud that I put my handkerchief to my mouth to stop the sound, that I might not alarm the house;'..."[68]

Though Irving attempted to retain control, those practicing the gifts could not control themselves. The personal accounts of others involved also mentioned that the experiences were uncontrollable even by the ones doing the uttering, *e.g.,* Mary Campbell said that the experience was an uncontrollable seizure, forcing her to speak.[69] Below is an excerpt from an account given by "a believer and actor in the transactions which he describes, but at the time that he wrote, rejecting their [tongues in Irving's church, *ed.*] Divine, though still maintaining their supernatural (though diabolical) origin."

> "... My persuasion concerning the unknown tongue, as it is called (in which I myself was very little exercised), is, that it is no language whatever, but a mere collection of words and sentences; and in the lengthened discourse is, most of it, a jargon of sounds; though I can conceive, when the power is very great, that it will assume much of the form of a connected oration."[70]

At every corner and in every way, the gifts (tongues and prophetic utterances) were totally unscriptural, yet Irving defended their appearances.

Unable to tolerate the chaos, the trustees of Irving's Presbyterian church removed him:

> "First. — That the Rev. Edward Irving has suffered and permitted, and still allows, the public services of the church in the worship of God, on the Sabbath and other days, to be interrupted by persons not being either ministers or licentiates of the Church of Scotland.
> "Second. — That the said Rev. Edward Irving has suffered and permitted, and still allows, the public services of the said church, in

---

68. *Ibid.,* 323-328. By Nov. 1831, worship services in Irving's church had become chaotic.

69. *Ibid.,* 318-355. Mrs. Oliphant gives a very good overview of what took place with this new phenomena.

70. "Narrative of facts characterising the Supernatural Manifestations, in Members of Mr. Irving's Congregation and other Individuals, in England and Scotland, and formerly in the writer himself, by Robert Baxter: 2nd edition, Nisbet, London, 1833, pp. 134, 135." Quoted by Stanley, *Corinthians,* 265.

the worship of God, to be interrupted by persons not being either members or seatholders of the said church.

"Third. — That the said Rev. E. Irving has suffered and permitted, and also publicly encourages, females to speak in the same church, and to interrupt and disturb the public worship of God in the church on Sabbath and other days.

"Fourth. — That the said Rev. E. Irving hath suffered and permitted and also publicly encourages, other individuals, members of the said church, to interrupt and disturb the public worship of God in the church on Sabbath and other days.

"Fifth. — That the said Rev. E. Irving, for the purpose of encouraging and exciting the said interruptions, has appointed times when a suspension of the usual worship in the said church takes place, for said persons to exercise the supposed gifts with which they profess to be endowed."[71]

In May of 1831, Irving was removed from his position as pastor of Caledonian Presbyterian Church in Regent Square by the Presbytery of the Established Church of Scotland in England. Being locked out by the trustees, on May sixth, Irving and about 800 followers met in a small room in Gray's Inn Road. There Irving continued the emphasis on the "manifestations."[72]

Chapter 43

The Rapture

Around 1845, there was a dispute between B.W. Newton (1805-1898; see "Benjamin Wills Newton," p. 190) and Darby over Darby's developing system of theology. They both held to a basic "pre-mil, historic Chiliasm" view, yet Newton stood against Darby's acquired, *secret pre-trib* rapture theory. Neatby's record of Newton's account of Darby's rapture theory is worth repeating in full. Newton was so upset at the implications of Darby's theory that he said the church would be far better off in ignorance about it:

---

71. *Life.*, 355-356.
72. *Ibid.*, 369-372.

The chief question in dispute was the relation of the Christian Church to the Great Tribulation. Both parties were futurists, that is, they held that the fulfillment of the bulk of the Apocalypse is still future, and belongs to "the times of the end"; and they therefore both maintained that a great and unprecedented persecution awaits the faithful immediately before the revelation of the Son of God in glory. But whereas Newton held that the faithful in question were simply those members of the Christian Church that would be on the earth at that time, Darby insisted that the whole Christian Church would be removed to heaven by a rapture unobserved by the world, shortly before the outbreak of the Tribulation. He accordingly found the victims of the Tribulation in "another semi-Christian or semi-Jewish body," as Newton put it, who "will be called out as witnesses to God before the end of the age". Now this dispute seemed of immense practical consequence to men who anticipated the immediate end of the age. Were they to warn their disciples of an impending trial, far more terrible than the worst that the blood-stained annals of the Church record, or were they to comfort them with the assurance of their total immunity from it? Nor was this all. It is clear that the doctrine of the secret rapture is inconsistent with the descriptions given of the Second Advent in the prophetic passages of the Gospels. Darby, therefore, taught that these descriptions were given to the apostles, not as the founders of the Christian Church, but as the representatives of a faithful remnant in the midst of apostate Judaism,-- to which character the witnessing body at the time of the end (composed as it will be of semi-converted Jews) is to answer. This involved a different view of the Gospels from that which had previously obtained among Christians, and materially altered the relations of the Church to the principles declared by Christ during his earthly ministry. A tendency accordingly grew up to treat large portions of the Gospels as "Jewish". In particular, the law of Christ in the Sermon on the Mount was to a great extent transferred from the Church to the rather shadowy "remnant". This tendency in turn linked itself with a growing repugnance to associating the idea of law in any shape with Christian standing--a repugnance that has widely given rise to a plausible (though not altogether just) charge of antinomianism against the Brethren.

Darby's doctrine, exempting the Christian Church from the judgments that both parties agreed in anticipating, was connected with a general disposition to magnify unduly, as Newton thought, the special privileges of the Church as compared with the faithful of the older dispensation. Newton strenuously upheld that Abraham and the rest of the faithful of old would form in heaven an integral part of the Church, the Bride of Christ. Darby resisted this as a view derogatory from the Church's special glory, and roused apparently against Newton a great enthusiasm on behalf of her invaded prerogatives..."[73]

This was not the only area of disagreement. Newton also clashed with Darby on other important points of doctrine: The ideas of a space between Daniels' sixty-ninth and seventieth weeks — where prophecy is suspended and God is an absentee landlord — and of a future Antichrist. Though Darby and almost all the Brethren held to a future rather than an historical interpretation of the book of Revelation, they were not the first to do so.[74] The ideas clearly supported popery, and had been used by sixteenth century Romanist commentators countering Protestant attacks against the papacy as the Antichrist; they insisted that none of the events related to the antichrist had yet occurred. However, Darby refused to admit that the ideas had developed outside of himself.[75] Newton remarked concerning Darby's "parenthesis" notion, "The secret rapture was bad enough, but this is worse."[76]

Newton's complaint against Darby's system was valid, for Darby's unconventional understanding of Daniel hinged on his changing one word in Daniel 9:27. Using the marginal reading "a" for "the," he changed the verse to say "a covenant" rather than "the covenant": "If it had been said, *the* covenant, one might suppose it of some covenant already existing, whereas there is no such thought in the expression."... "'And he shall confirm a covenant with the

---

73. Neatby, *History,* 104-106.

74. Rowdon, using the Fry MS as his source, also refers to the early Brethren — including Irving — as the source of a secret rapture before the second advent. *Origins,* 82. 1 Jn. 2:18-22, 4:3, tells us that the antichrist started work in the church at the start.

75. *Writings,* II.270, 272, 287, 315, 323, &c. On page 328, he mocks any understanding of Daniel outside of his. See also, Letters, I.131. The future view of Revelation grew out of Rome's defence against claims that the Pope was the Antichrist, *Roots,* 37. Ben-Ezra presented the parenthesis and future Antichrist ideas.

76. *Roots,* 37-38.

many for one week.' This is the week which still remains..."[77] Evidently, Darby's many translations of Scripture were done in order to support his theories.

It is interesting to note that the early Brethren changed James' formula, "If the Lord will," to a formula of their own, "If the Lord tarry."[78]

In previous chapters we saw how Edward Irving presented Lacunza's millennial system to the Protestants at the 1826 Albury Park conference, where it was excitedly received. We then see the system taken to Powerscourt. Securely attached to the system there were the "secret pre-trib rapture" theory and a parenthesis in prophetic fulfillment between Daniel's sixty-ninth and the seventieth weeks.

The evolving system emerged from the Powerscourt conference with a new "founder" — John Nelson Darby, who worked to claim the system for his own.

---

77. *Writings*, II.269. The simple change of one word that changes a doctrine is a major complaint against the many modern versions of Scripture.
78. Neatby, *History*, 22, 7.

Part V

The Men and Times

Chapter 44

The Anglican Church

Though speaking against everything already established, the early millenarians primarily used the Anglican Church to justify their departure from orthodoxy. Therefore, it is not unprofitable to consider a few things concerning that church.

The 1800s saw many Anglicans developing and defending the victorious Biblical faith, seeking to instill godliness into every area of life and thought. During the time of the development and growth of dispensational millennialism, the Anglican Church was at its strongest point in history, producing some of the greatest orthodox Bible scholars in the history of the church. It produced men such as: Augustus Montague Toplady (1740-1778),[1] Charles Simeon (1759-1836),[2] Charles Bridges (1794-1869),[3] Edward Bouverie Pusey (1800-1882),[4] Richard Chenevix Trench (1807-1866),[5] Arthur Penrhyn Stanley (1815-1881),[6] John Charles Ryle (1816-1900),[7]

---

1. He wrote some hymns, one of which was *Rock of Ages*, *Who*, s.v. "Toplady, Augustus Montague."

2. He wrote, among other things, Horae Homiletica, or Discourses upon the whole Scripture. They were widely circulated, and have been reprinted. *Who*, s.v. "Simeon, Charles."

3. Better known literary works are his expositions on Ecclesiastes, Psalms 119 and Proverbs, considered by Spurgeon as "The best work on the Proverbs." *Proverbs*, inside the dust cover, Banner of Truth Trust, 1981 reprint. See Bridges' statement of Christian victory at the opening of ch. 4.

4. He was a descendant of the old Huguenot family of Bouverie. *Who*, s.v. "Pusey, Edward Bouverie." Pusey's superior notes on *The Minor Prophets* are found in *Barnes' Notes*.

5. *Ibid.*, s.v. "Trench, Richard Chenevix."

Alfred Edersheim (1825-1889),[8] Andrew Robert Fausset (1821-1910),[9] Brooke Foss Westcott (1825-1901),[10] Joseph Barber Lightfoot (1828- 1889),[11] Frederic William Farrar (1831-1903),[12] Robert Baker Girdlestone (1836-1923),[13] and Alfred Plummer (1841-1926).[14] John Newton ("Amazing Grace," 1725-1807), a pronounced Calvinist, was ordained an Anglican deacon in 1764.[15] Moreover, the great English lawyer, Sir William Blackstone (1723-1780) studied at Oxford, where he returned to teach. In 1753, he introduced at Oxford courses in English law. The Christian foundation of English and American law laid by Anglican trained Blackstone is one of the things that fell victim to Darby's millennial movement which gained such great momentum in the late 1800s.[16]

---

6. *Ibid.*, 386. Klock & Klock reprinted his commentary on the Epistles of St. Paul to the Corinthians, 1981.

7. *Ibid.*, 358.

8. Though ordained to the Presbyterian ministry, "In 1875 he took orders in the Church of England, and was curate of one Anglican Church for a year and vicar of another for six years." *Ibid.*, 129.

9. Fausset collaborated with Jamieson and Brown to produce the J.F.B. Commentaries. Fausset wrote the third, fourth and sixth volumes of the six volume set. Ibid., 140.

10. "Westcott's commentaries on John, Ephesians, Hebrews, and the Johannine Epistles have never been superseded [*sic*]." *Ibid.*, 434.

11. *Ibid.*, 249

12. Klock & Klock reprinted his commentary on *The Second Book of Kings*, 1981. He also prepared commentaries for the *Expositor's Bible*, &c. "His biographer says, 'The man was known to the world as a great preacher, a profound scholar, and a man of unparalleled literary activity...'" *Ibid.*, 140.

13. *Ibid.*, 166

14. He wrote, among other things, the *Expositor's Bible,* and *The Pulpit Commentary. Ibid.*, 335.

15. *Ibid.*, 306.

16. His Oxford lectures were published in Blackstone's distinctly Christian Commentaries on English Law, 1765-1769. Nearly ten thousand citations of Blackstone in American courts (1789-1915) reveal that he was accepted as an authority on common law well into the 1900s. "Blackstone is the spirit, at least, to which the American law schools owe their life." U.S. Supreme Court justices Kent, Story and Marshall were only few of his many U.S. disciples. "Harvard, Yale, Columbia, California, and Michigan, are in a real sense the fruit of his work and of his ideas." *Jones' Blackstone*, I.xv-xxix.

In addition, the Anglicans mentioned above taught that sin was a violation of the Ten Commandments, and that all men are accountable to God accordingly. They taught causality — that sin has dire physical consequences against both the world's nations and against individual sinners, whether saved or unsaved.[17]

Throughout history, there have been supposed spiritual leaders — more concerned with worldly amusements, power and money than with faithfully proclaiming the word of God — like those mentioned in Jeremiah 23. The Anglican clergy had its share of apathy, ignorance, inconsistency, improper walk, pride and worldly-mindedness. They, as well as the Romanists, had more than their share of creeds and cold, dead formalism substituted for the word of God and Christian conversion. Both had the mandatory tithe, which Darby and others (most notably A. N. Groves) abhorred and taught against.[18]

The Church admittedly was cold and dingy, with many worldly clergymen fighting for power in both the church and civil government. However, the Oxford Movement of 1833 — Pusey was its "guiding spirit" — brought about a change for the better. By 1845, a major motive of the Movement was to counter the assault of "Liberalism" against "Christianity," brought about by the French Revolution.[19] The Movement sought to call the clergy back to self-discipline, unworldliness and personal devotion to the Lord Jesus Christ as a living Friend.

---

17. Example: Bridges comments on Proverbs 22:3, 27:12.
18. *Origins,* 49. The French Revolution brought down the mandatory tithe in France, *Robespierre,* 76, 77. Did their dogmatic attitude against God's Law cause them to stand against the tithe? The church was wrong in demanding the tithe, but so were the millenarians for dismissing the tithe.
19. *Ethics,* s.v. "Oxford Movement." Darby complained against the "superstition" of the church, and dogmatically separated history from any interpretation of Scripture, *q.v.* Also during the Oxford Movement period, the new millennial movement, led by Müller, changed missionary effort from trying to Christianize the nations to simply spreading knowledge about Christianity, an obvious result of the French Revolution, *q.v.*

The Oxford Movement with its passionate devotion, its appeal to Christian history and to authority, brought back the old conception that the Church, not as a mere human institution and a department of the State, but as the Body of Christ, with life-giving sacraments and a ministry reaching back through the Apostles to the Lord, a society which 'takes its origin not in the will of man, but in the will of the Lord Jesus Christ'...[20]

Therefore, we must raise these questions: First, was the problem actually over the efforts of men like E.B. Pusey to instill godliness into every area of life and thought, including claiming the Church and civil government for godliness? Darby was vehemently against the "Puseyites," speaking against them at every opportunity. In the Oxford Movement, the "Puseyites" were calling for godly reformation in the Established Church — Darby said the only hope was for people to leave any established church and join his new millennial movement. Second, was the problem actually over the efforts of men like Charles Hodges to hold all mankind, including Christians, to the standard of the Ten Commandments? (See 1 Jn. 3:4.) As we will see, Darby had more, and harsher, words to say against the Baptists than against either Rome or the "Puseyites," and his problem with them was not that they were in bed with the state.[21]

Even a casual examination reveals that the early millenarians (Darby, Müller, &c.) were against being bound by the orthodox faith — that is, by the Law-Word of God. They wanted to go their own way, establishing a new, lawless path for following generations. They also militated against all responsibility to confront *spiritual wickedness in high places*, and militated against any effort to convert the world to Christ. The millenarian goal was never to call society to godliness, but to escape from its problems and its Christian responsibility to deal with those problems with God's applied word.

---

20. *Ibid.*, 589.
21. Darby found the Baptists horribly under the law, *q.v.* The "law and grace" issue is not the theme of this current study. See a tract by this writer, "Law and Grace: Is there a difference?" Rom. 6:14.

The millennial movement involved an overreaction against the state church's requirement that ministers submit written sermons for approval before delivery. The antagonism against written messages resulted in a stand against studying for messages to be delivered to the congregations:

> Its founders, as we have seen, were all clergymen. But these must soon give place to men less cultivated and with fewer gifts of ministry... What else can be expected if men are true to the principle that previous preparation is sinful and dishonoring to the Spirit? The fact is, there is no originality, variety, or durability in the ministry of the Brethren...[22]

The foundation of the movement (Brethrenism), accordingly, was a deliberate departure from what the millenarians claimed was evil, both in organized religion and in orthodox theology. Ten basic points developed within the millennial movement:

> Dr. Wm. Reid, Plymouth Brethren unveiled, 79-143, attributes to the sect the following Church-principles: (1) the church did not exist before Pentecost; (2) the visible and the invisible church identical; (3) the one assembly of God; (4) the presidency of the Holy Spirit; (5) rejection of one-man and man-made ministry; (6) the church is without government. Also the following heresies: (1) Christ's heavenly humanity; (2) denial of Christ's righteousness, as being obedience to the law; (3) denial that Christ's righteousness is

---

22. "Rev. Thomas Croskey, *Plymouth-Brethrenism: A Refutation of its Principles and Doctrines* (London: William Mullan & Son, 1879)." Quoted in *Plot,* 143. The founders may have been "all clergymen," but their backgrounds were not in theology. Rather than using Scripture as their foundation, they used their feelings and opinions. Just a few years previously, 1790, the Roman Church in France tried to organize to protect itself from what was taking place in the Revolution. "The move worked in reverse by extending the question of the clergy into the political arena. Suddenly the nation became embroiled in a whole complex of arguments about the proper conduct and the right rules for priests." The move failed, and all church property was confiscated, and the leaders of the church who did not flee for their lives were butchered. *Robespierre,* 107. The established churches of the day required all their clergy to submit their messages in writing for approval. Rather than simply not requiring the messages to be submitted, the Brethren (millenarians) *reacted* by forbidding all written messages. One should question, however, if the stand against serious study and education was a precaution against the danger that a well educated clergy would see the unorthodox doctrine of the leaders, Eph. 4:14.

imputed; (4) justification in the risen Christ; (5) Christ's non-atoning sufferings; (6) denial of moral law as rule of life; (7) the Lord's day is not the Sabbath; (8) perfectionism; (9) secret rapture of the saints,—caught up to be with Christ. To these may we add; (10) premillennial advent of Christ.[23]

We must conclude that the Protestant restrictions hated by the millenarians had to do basically with a strict understanding of Scripture. They rebelled against the idea of a victorious Christian faith, *i.e.*, "Christ the victorious." They rebelled against the idea of Christian responsibility to Christianize the nations through the preaching of the gospel. They rebelled against the idea that Christians should obey the Ten Commandments, *i.e.*, sanctification. Their desire was to be free, free from the bands and cords of God's word, so they could do as they pleased.

Chapter 45
Social Climate

Ireland of the early 1800s was heavily Roman Catholic, making it fertile ground for distributing Scriptures.[24] There were many schools and societies organized to both distribute Scriptures and to teach people how to read so they could read the Scriptures. However, the corruption and love for money in the organized churches, both Anglican and Roman, gave sufficient cause for small groups (1800-1825) to separate from the organized churches in the English speaking nations.[25] These groups had two things in

---

23. "On the Plymouth Brethren and their doctrine, see... H.M. King, in Baptist Review, 1881:438-465... J. C. L. Carson, The Heresies of the Plymouth Brethren;..." *Systematic Theology*, 896. "Perfect" would be defined by Brethren without regard to God's law, *i.e.,* pure motives.

24. Three locations figure predominately in the newly emerging millennial (Brethren) movement: Dublin, Plymouth and Bristol. Neatby, *History*, 4.

25. Some of these small groups later became organized as Baptist, although more probably became Plymouth Brethren. *Origins*, 26.

common: First, they shared a common dislike for the cold, dead organized church. Second, they had a love for the Scriptures. "They followed no theological system, since they regarded the Scriptures alone as authoritative, but their religious beliefs were characteristically evangelical." Their anti-clergy reaction with its consequent anti-intellectual spirit developed into an outright disdain for an educated clergy. "'They consider the existence of such an order among disciples as utterly incompatible with holy Scriptures, and with the character and interests of the churches of God.'"[26]

Because it has no firm, dogmatic theological foundation from which to examine nor challenge unorthodox ideas, an anti-intellectual spirit encourages strange, unorthodox doctrines. Hence, the anti-established church spirit soon led to dismissing all past orthodox theology.

In the aftermath of the French Revolution and the Napoleonic Wars, "the ideas that went to make up Brethrenism were 'in the air,' and were extensively obtaining embodiment."[27] Largely because of this, these groups shared a determination not to get involved in "secular" affairs, which "represented a retreat into a shelter of spiritual monasticism..."[28] "No part was played by them in politics, except the giving of submission and honour to 'the powers that be,' and the offering of prayer for them."[29] Thus we see that rather than attempting to *convert* the nations to Christ through the gospel, the movement reacted by withdrawing.[30] These small groups devoid of spiritual leadership started in the British Isles, and the hopeless *faith* was brought into the U.S. through immigration.[31]

---

26. *Ibid*, 18-25. Irving drew great crowds during this time as he traveled England propagating his prophetic theories. The mood of the people was right for unorthodox teaching. Scofield said that one of the things that has destroyed the church is "the division of an equal brotherhood into 'clergy' and 'laity.'" *Rightly Dividing the Word of Truth*, 12.
27. Neatby, *History*, 24.
28. Coad, *History*, 104.
29. *Origins*, 25.
30. See *The London Baptist Confession of Faith of 1689*, Chapter 24, "2 It is lawful for Christians to accept and execute the office of a magistrate."

Because they only reacted against sin instead of acting upon the word of God, theirs was a serious over-reaction against all social involvement, an educated clergy, a systematic interpretation of Scripture, and any involvement in civil government — they threw out the baby with the bath water. This overreaction provided an excellent foundation for men with strong personalities to appear and unite the small groups.[32] Providence provided the foundation, and around 1830, the strong men appeared to build upon the foundation.

> The Brethren sought to effect a fresh start without authority, precedent, or guidance beyond the letter of Holy Scriptures. For them, essentially, the garnered experience of eighteen Christian centuries were as though it were not. It thus became the law of the Brethren to disown all regularly constituted authority, all orderly arrangement, &c. These small groups of people who loved God and His Word were united by a common dislike, even hatred, for organized religion of their day and its corruption. Accordingly, it was not a common Bible doctrine, but a common distaste that caused them to separate from the organized state church. The fruit is ripe for the picking; Darby had a keen eye for favorable circumstances; he picked the fruit.[33]

---

31. *Origins*, 23-25. Rowdon quotes from letters sent by one of these churches in New York: "'Without any thing in the state of civil society to operate upon the hopes or the fears of Christ's disciples: without any renowned leader or leaders for their guidance; without any representative body to organize them into a distinct sect, or to establish a uniformity among themselves; and without any patronage from the learned or the great, these churches arose at various places at nearly the same period of time.'" *Ibid.*, 33. The same spirit was thus surfacing on both continents.

32. They united with deliberate departure from everything the established churches stood for, including their system of Scriptural interpretation. *Ibid.*, 252, 255.

33. Neatby, *History*, 3, 38, 77.

Chapter 46

Irving, Cornin, Bellett

In this chapter and the following chapters, we will look a little closer at the men behind the millennial movement. Most of the founders are largely unknown to the modern reader; however, all will recognize the unothodox doctrines they developed and propagated worldwide.

Whether these men were familiar with "the *Ben-Ezra* system" and simply expanded it further, only the Lord knows. Though some of the beliefs—both truth and errors—held and developed were as old as the Church itself, it is obvious that many of these men regarded them as new.[34] Whatever their motives might have been, it is clear that they refused to build upon the past foundations of Christian belief

Edward Irving

Though Edward Irving was not an early Brethren leader, he is the apparent fountainhead of modern dispensational millennialism. Irvingism — minus tongues and healing — later became identified with the Brethren. As seen previously, he was proclaiming the millennial faith and gathering large crowds to hear his opinions as early as 1822, even before he encountered *Ben-Ezra*. He introduced and publicly taught the millennial system, particularly the *imminent return of Christ* and a literal *millennial reign* with his saints. He also added the ideal of a pre-trib rapture to the system, c. 1830.

---

34. Irving had already laid a foundation before the Brethren came along. Though the Brethren sought to claim originality, their prophetic opinions were already present. Moreover, Hastings points out that Richard Brothers (1757-1824), who laid the foundation of the modern ANGLO-ISRAEL movement, taught as a key to his movement, "the imminent restoration of Israel to the Holy Land, and the elevation of himself as prince of the Hebrews and ruler of the world." He "was confined as a lunatic, but succeeded in obtaining many admirers..." *Ethics,* s.v. "Anglo-Israelism." Thus many ideas claimed by the Brethren as original, such as Israel's restoration, were already public domain.

Hence, the concepts of a defeated church — whose only hope is its soon escape from a chaotic world — and a Messiah to reestablish a glorious Jewish state (Zionism) were already in circulation several years before Cronin held his first meeting.

Edward Cronin

Edward Cronin (1800-1880), a converted Romanist slightly younger than Darby, went to Dublin for his health in 1826. He sought to join in communion with various small groups, but was denied because he would not "accept membership in one of the dissenting churches." He believed, "That the Church of God was one, and all that believed were members of the one Body." In response to the closed communion, this 29 year old man started his own group, "apparently in Nov., 1829."[35] Darby, though he claimed otherwise, was not in attendance at the original meeting of the group that became known as the Brethren.[36]

As time progressed, and men of strong personalities emerged to assume control, clear and firm *shibboleths* were established, such as an imminent return of Christ, a "church/Israel" distinction and a pre-trib rapture. Those who did not agree with their prophetic schemes were not welcome among them. (The same attitude is common today. See 2 Tim. 2:22.) The common unifying motive was not the preaching and teaching of God's word, nor a collective desire to obey God's word; it was basically a desire to withdraw from society and Christian responsibility, and to have fellowship apart from a doctrinal standard.

John Gifford Bellett

John Gifford Bellett (b. 1795) was another man of great significance in the movement. Bellett was probably the link between Darby and the Dublin movement in its earliest days. A scholar, Bellett attended Trinity College with honors. Around 1822, this

---

35. Neatby, *History*, 20.
36. *Origins*, 37, 38.

twenty-seven year old man was called to the Bar in Dublin, but practiced very little. In Neatby's words, "Probably he was under no necessity in the matter, and his attention was becoming thoroughly preoccupied with religious interests." Bellett's brother's reasoning for Bellett's lack of interest in worldly matters is important to our study:

> "It is likely," according to his brother, the Rev. George Bellett, "that the strong religious feeling which he afterwards, through God's mercy, so deeply imbibed, may not only have made him indifferent to honors [which he obtained at Trinity, *ed.*] of this sort, but have caused him *to look upon them as unlawful.*"[37]

So, in Bellett, we see developing the millennial view that God-given scholastical abilities must be used only in the "ministry." Such thinking withdraws Christian influence from all fields requiring intellectual skills and abilities, such as law, science, medicine and civil government. This perspective became a solid plank in the dispensational system, and has become an indispensable part of twentieth century Christian thinking.

"The study of unfulfilled prophecy was a prominent feature of the movement from the first; or perhaps it would be more correct to say it was one of the main foundations of the whole system." Later, upon meeting Darby, Bellett found that their minds and souls travelled rapidly in the same direction.[38] "Their study of prophecy was a powerful factor in determining the attitude of the Brethren towards life in the world. Since they were convinced that the world, as well as the professing church, was ripe for God's judgment, they deemed it necessary to steer their own course as far clear of it as possible."[39]

---

37. Neatby, *History*, 10, 11. Ital. added. Note that this formulator of millennial doctrine had no theological training. He was a lawyer, as were several others attracted into the movement, including Darby. They had tremendous natural abilities to sway people to their ways of thinking.
38. *Ibid.*, 12.
39. *Origins*, 301.

Chapter 47

Anthony Norris Groves

A.N. Groves (1795-1853) was a dentist who gave up his successful practice to go to the mission field. On Oct. 16, 1826, thirty-one year old Groves travelled to Dublin to attend an Anglican College — Trinity — to prepare for the field.[40]

He described himself as a "high churchman," but in Dublin, which was full of dissenters and in close proximity to Romanism, his prejudices gave way: "I saw those strongly marked distinctions that exist in England little regarded; the prevalence of the common enemy, Popery, joined all hands together."[41] (Again we see that the foundations laid by these men did not stem from deeply-held Biblical convictions, but rather around their opposition to the established churches).

In 1827, some things happened to break his connection with Trinity and the Anglican Church.

First, he was a pacifist, unable to subscribe to the article, "It is lawful for Christian men to take up arms at the command of the civil magistrate..."[42] With that realization on his mind, he gave up any plans of ordination by the Church.

Second, because Groves continued in his desire to go to the mission field, he approached the Society about going as a layman. He was told that if he went, he would not be allowed to partake of the Lord's Supper unless there was an ordained minister to give it, nor could he give it to others. Apparently, he still believed some ordination was necessary and did not want to make a complete break and become a "sectarian." "But one day the thought was brought to my mind, that ordination of any kind to preach the gospel is no

---

40. *Ibid.*, 39.
41. Coad, *History*, 7, 8.
42. Neatby, *History*, 9.

requirement of Scripture..." From that time, he never had any doubt of his liberty in Christ.[43] This was a key point in his unity with Darby.

Mr. Neatby makes this very important statement:

> To us, whether we think Groves right or wrong, his new point of view has become so familiar that we have difficulty in entering ever so little into the feelings of those to whom it came as a flash of supernatural illumination. This immense disparity between our feelings and theirs is, in great part, a measure of the influence that Plymouth Brethrenism has exercised.[44]

And thus "as a flash of supernatural illumination," the door is opened for untrained and undisciplined leaders to counter orthodoxy and to define and develop new *orthodox* Christian doctrines.[45]

We do not mean to imply that all Anglican or Roman training was proper; however, we are explicitly saying that Groves opened the door for the novice to take control of the church and establish doctrines based upon personal feelings and supposed "supernatural illumination." (1 Tim. 3:6.)

One of the more important events leading to Groves' abandonment of any promise of physical blessings and earthly hope for the church or Christians in general was his wife's death in Baghdad, 1833. "Groves had expected, on the basis of the promise of Psalm 91, to be preserved from physical harm, but the loss of his wife made him think that this was an unwarranted assumption: The

---

43. *Ibid.,* 9. As a result of his confrontation over the Lord's Supper, he came to the "Scriptural conviction" that all ordination of ministers was wrong, Coad, *History,* 20- 22.

44. Neatby, *History,* 10.

45. We are not implying that a background of theology or language is necessary to understand and/or teach Scripture, for understanding comes from the Spirit, 1 Cor. 2:14. Joseph Parker (1830-1902) missed the privilege of a college education. He "gathered his education by much reading, by attending lectures, by seizing upon any information, principle, or data he could come upon." *Who,* s.v. "Parker, Joseph." See also *Power,* 54. But when teachers intentionally separate from centuries of developed Christian doctrine, basing their ideas upon emotions and opinions as did the first millenarians (Brethren), corruption must follow. Let the buyer beware!

promise must be understood in a 'spiritual sense.'" This idea became a solid plank in millennialism.[46]

Groves was very self-conscious about his prosperity, so he studied Scripture to determine the proper use of his goods. The conviction he came to was to give it all to the poor and take a vow of poverty.[47] Accordingly, he renounced all thought of providing for his children, depending on God to take care of them, and "This is the general state of mind out of which Brethrenism arose."[48] In the aftermath of the French Revolution, poverty was considered a mark of sincerity and virtue. Hence, European Christianity was ready for Groves' theory that it was somehow holy and pious to forsake one's children.

Accordingly, Darby found a kindred spirit in Groves. Some time later, Darby used Satan's tempting words to Christ, "all is delivered to me," to prove that all worldly wealth, power and authority now belong to Satan. So anyone who has worldly wealth got it from Satan.[49] On the other hand, he held that the supply of money to propagate his doctrines proved the faithfulness of God toward those "he sends forth."[50] In other words, finances prove the soundness of doctrine only if the doctrine is "dispensational." Darby also held that it was sinful to prepare for one's children.[51] Thus developed the common 'mega-church' mentality — simply put, if a person follows God's will, God will take care of that person's children. Then God's will is defined as spending all one's time actively involved in the

---

46. *Origins,* 192.
47. Coad, *History,* 17.
48. Neatby, *History,* 36, 37.
49. *Writings,* II.461. An uncle left Darby some money, so he had no financial worries. The same words of Christ were used to justify Lacunza's contention that Satan controls this present age, and that Christians are simply helpless victims at this point in time.
50. *Letters,* I.203.
51. *Ibid.,* 268. This pastor has personally heard probably the best known Baptist pastor of the 1900s say that if you will do God's work, God will take care of your children. He defined God's work as teaching Sunday School, working a bus route, and/or otherwise engaged in religious activity building a 'mega-church' while ignoring the family. That pastor lost all his children.

ministry of *soul winning* — that is, increasing the numbers who attend church.

Despite their erroneous belief that a prosperous person cannot be a good Christian, and despite their disdain for involvement in worldly pursuits, many wealthy people — doctors, lawyers, publishers, &c. — looking for something to do, were attracted to and financed the millennial movement, especially their prophecy conferences. The wealthy, *e.g.*, Drummond and Lady Powerscourt, were drawn by the zeal of the young men involved in the movement, its freedom from organized religion, its lack of a firm doctrinal position, and by its mysticism.[52]

Groves' — and later Brethren — militancy against Proverbs 13:22, gave abundant grounds for the rise of the modern, all-powerful welfare state. The state quickly gains power in areas abandoned by a withdrawn church. Groves, and many who followed him, denied responsibility for their families, giving their approval *as Christians* to the French Revolution's contention that the care of the poor is the state's responsibility. They placed the "church's" blessing upon the modern practice of placing one's parents in a nursing home for the sake of convenience.[53]

A third point that brought about Groves' break with the Anglican Church and drew others to him was his conviction that Christ alone

---

52. Code, *History,* 178. Personal note: If the modern *Reconstruction Movement* had the same committed financing as the *Deconstruction* millennial movement, the world would have be won to Christ. This author finds it strange that professed Christians will invest vast sums of energy and money to remove Christianity from society, but the same people will fight tooth and nail to keep Christianity from being reintroduced into society. Pre-trib, as promoted by Darby & Co., has "1. Made a few promoters wealthy at the expense of trusting supporters who've regularly been disillusioned after numerous rapture date-setting fizzles. 2. Diverted millions of dollars away from reaching the ones who, in a variety of ways, now threaten to destroy the western Christian civilization that has benefitted even the would-be destroyers..." *Plot,* 233, 234.

53. Upon close examination, one will find that not only does the average church condone the welfare state, but there are many "church/Christian" organizations that actively seek state financing for what they consider just causes. The lack of Christian social responsibility in this *dispensation* was insisted on by Irving's master, Lacunza.

— not the inspired word of God — was the basis of fellowship. Groves' conviction was carried to such an extreme that he permitted neither pulpits nor ministers in the early days of the movement, trusting in the Lord to minister to them as he saw fit.[54] This conviction, typical of so much of what these early millenarians did and taught, was based upon feelings and mystical experiences.[55]

Neatby gives this account of a conflict that took place some years later: "Moreover, the [Exclusive, *ed*.] Brethren had a horror of discourses prepared before hand for delivery at an open meeting..." In fact, after the split around 1848, one of the charges leveled by Darby against Newton, who had joined with the Plymouth Brethren, was that "before coming to the Lord's table, he did not see it at all wrong to be prepared with what to say to the saints".[56]

Darby held pre-preparation to be a denial of the presence of the Holy Ghost in the church. The militancy in the early, formative years of the millennial system against prepared messages permitted vast amounts of erroneous expositions and speculations to be established in its foundation.

Through a series of circumstances, Müller, whom we will soon meet, married Groves' sister, October 7, 1830.[57]

Let us now summarize some of the "fundamental truths" of this "obscure group" — which spawned a host of prolific writers to cover the earth with their new opinions — that we have surveyed thus far:

(1) Unity in Christ is not based upon a common desire to obey God's word, but upon a common desire to withdraw from society and to fellowship apart from a firm doctrinal standard; (2) intellectual, scholarly abilities are considered unlawful to use outside of *full time Christian service*; (3) prophetic study

---

54. *Origins,* 40. Thus men with strong personalities found it easy to lead sincere people down whatever path they chose.
55. Coad, *History,* 28, 29. Mysticism basically exalts the inward, living, invisible Word of God over the outward, written word of God, the Scriptures. See "Revivalism," p. 463.
56. Neatby, *History,* 206.
57. *Trust,* 81.

emphasized; (4) intentional casting away of eighteen hundred years of developed Christian thought of the day; (5) common hatred for and reaction against any organized religion, though *they* soon became organized; (6) all earthly hope abandoned, and Bible promises are *only spiritual*; (7) pacifism; (8) ordination and training of clergy rejected, though they soon rejected any clergy not trained in millennialism; (9) no organization, no clergy and no prepared messages in meetings; (10) Scripture searched to support personal opinions and personal convictions; (11) prosperity and concern for one's children's future welfare renounced; and (12) feelings, emotions, mystical experiences, observations and *supernatural illumination* used as the basis for doctrine rather than God's inspired word. The stage is set, the way is prepared, and Europe is ready for a man to pull it all together.

Chapter 48
John Nelson Darby

Though multiplied tens of thousands of Christians world-wide believe and teach the dispensational, millennial system propagated by John Nelson Darby (1800-1882), he is virtually unknown to most of them. Much of Darby's theology was gleaned from others, but he had an unique ability to make it his own. It is impossible to overestimate his importance to and influence on modern Christian thought. This unknown Irish clergyman set out to change 1800 years of Christian thought — he marvelously succeeded.

He was unquestionably the most influential man in the millennial movement, both in developing basic millennialism and in its spread. It was Darby who — through extremely hard work and strong personality — covered the earth with the newly developed millennial system. Christianity accepted the system under Darby's name: "Above all, the Brethren made their appearance in the person of Darby."[58]

Darby was a man with tremendous zeal and intellectual ability, and he can probably be credited with single-handedly destroying the orthodox Biblical Christian faith ("Christ the victorious") that had previously *turned the world upside down* (Acts 17:6). C.I. Scofield attempted to systematize Darby's theories.[59]

Feeling the Scriptures of his day were inaccurate, he sent forth several translations, including English, German and French.[60] The English translations of his day were the Geneva and the King James Version. Though the reader may say, "So what?," he should realize that Darby's influence over 150 years later is incalculable.[61]

Alexander Reese, commenting on Revelation 3:10, makes this point in a footnote: "Darby's rendering ('out of evil') is not according to his usual literalness and accuracy, for he ignores the force of the article." Thus Darby translated Scriptures in ways supportive of his theories.[62] "Curiously, Darby built on foundations laid by another Britisher..." The degeneration of Calvinism in Switzerland (Geneva) helped develop conducive conditions for Brethrenism.[63]

Darby was an extremely talented man with exceptionally keen logical powers. "[H]e proceeded to Trinity College, Dublin, which

---

58. *Origins,* 205. We have reproduced some of Darby's letters, and have tried to give an overview of the thoughts of this key man in this present document. Darby did not originate much of what William Kelly credited to him.

59. *Roots,* 61.

60. *Letters,* II.65.

61. Not only are the theories propagated by Darby the basis for *The Scofield Reference Bible,* but all the computer Bible programs on CDROM this pastor is familiar with offer Darby's translation as a legitimate translation. He is thus being promoted as one of the major Bible scholars of the 1800s.

62. See *Advent,* 203-204, and *Letters,* I.534.

63. *Origins,* 204, 205. Studying about Darby and reading some of his writings, this pastor must confess that he considers Darby one of the most, if not the most, dangerous teacher, i.e., false prophet, ever to appear in history since the death of the last apostle, St. John. Darby spiritualized Christianity. In doing so, he removed its life, and killed its victory. Darby's life, zeal, actions and doctrine evidenced genuine Christianity. However, the seriousness of the destruction caused by the system he spread, "otherworldliness," and his tireless zeal in promoting the destructive system cannot be overstated. He gave people what they wanted.

is thus as much the academic parent of Plymouth Brethrenism, as Oxford of the Evangelical revival a hundred years earlier." Trained to be admitted to the Irish Bar, "Darby abandon his career for the church, being ordained a deacon by Archbishop Magee in 1825, and priest in 1826." Though Darby's resignation from the Anglican Church may safely be assigned to 1828, it may have been as late as 1834.[64] Groves and Darby met around 1827.[65]

Though lame, he traveled day and night over all kinds of terrain in order to teach the Scriptures. "I quite trust the Lord sent me there; I was about 2,000 miles in the last four weeks, besides preaching and walking." In Darby's words:

> I was a lawyer; but feeling that, if the Son of God gave Himself for me I owed myself entirely to Him, and that the so-called christian world was characterized by deep ingratitude towards Him, I longed for complete devotedness to the word of the Lord; my chief thought was to get around amongst the poor Catholics of Ireland... As soon as I was ordained, I went amongst the poor Irish mountaineers, in a wild and uncultivated district, where I remained two years and three months, working as best I could.[66]

Darby then recounts his riding accident. (See under "Benjamin Wills Newton," p. 190.) Reading Darby's letters, one will be struck by the many times Darby mentions his long hours, "working day and night," his suffering of extreme conditions as he traveled presenting his view of Scripture, his self-professed humility and the many times he uses the word *judge* as he assesses people and situations. Darby was convinced that a *completely devoted Christian* could be nothing but a minister or missionary. His conviction was spread world-wide through his travels.[67]

---

64. Neatby, *History,* 13, 17. 1828-1834 is well after Lacunza's millennial system was public domain in English.

65. *Origins*, 41.

66. *Letters,* III.297. His complete letter is reproduced in App. A. The first quote is from *Letters,* I.352. 2,000 miles in four weeks in 1863 was a busy travel schedule.

67. More than once, Darby compares himself to the Apostle Paul, *e.g., Letters,* II.291.

Because of his poor physical condition and the dedication he displayed, "the 'poor Romanists' looked on him as a genuine 'saint'." He is said to have given up almost all reading except Scripture. About 1850, F. W. Newman (see "New and Newton," p. 189) said of Darby:

> [T]his gentleman has everywhere displayed a wonderful power of bending other minds to his own.... Over the general results of his action I have long deeply mourned, as blunting his natural tenderness and sacrificing his wisdom to the Letter, dwarfing men's understanding, contracting their hearts, crushing their moral sensibilities, and setting those at variance who ought to love: yet oh! how specious was it in the beginning! he only wanted men 'to submit their understanding to God,' that is, to the Bible, that is, to his interpretation!..."[68]

As did Groves, Darby had a background of "extreme high churchmanship."[69] However, his writings show that he was *not* a systematic theologian, a charge made by all who examined his life and writings.

Darby's overpowering personality and character made him the leader. His tone of voice and power over men persuaded others to follow him. Darby's physical appearance was shabby and neglected — he, no doubt, wanted to reflect his disdain of all things worldly. Despite his appearance, he had a tremendous power to bend other minds to his own.[70] His self-sacrifice was his greatest influence.[71] Able to identify with the common people, he made himself at home wherever he went. He got along well with those he could influence, yet there were great conflicts with those he could not. Neatby describes Darby's theological abilities thusly:

> It is impossible to consider Darby a very precise divine. Though he had undoubted power, it was rather as the mystic than as the systematic theologian.[72]

---

68. Neatby, *History*, 46-48.
69. *Origins*, 39, 46.
70. Neatby, *History*, 46, 38.
71. Coad, *History*, 106.

Hence, Darby, like Irving before him, was incapable of analyzing problems and formulating solutions from a systematic study of God's word. Darby's following was built on his strength of character, not on soundness of doctrine.[73]

> J.N. Darby was a very subtle man. He had been a lawyer, or at least educated for law. Once he wanted his Archbishop to pursue a certain course, when he (J.N.D.) was a curate in his diocese. He wrote a letter therefore saying he had been educated for the law, knew what the legal course would properly be; and then having written that clearly, he mystified the remainder of the letter both in word and in handwriting, and ended up by saying: You see, my Lord, such being the legal aspect of the case it would unquestionably be the best course for you to pursue, etc. And the Archbishop couldn't make out the legal part, but rested on Darby's word and did as he advised. Darby afterwards laughed over it, and indeed he showed a copy of the letter to Tregelles. This is not mentioned in the Archbishop's biography, but in it is the fact that he spoke of Darby as "the most subtle man in my diocese."[74]

Darby's strength of personal character and personal influence was overpowering. When Darby visited Oxford in 1830, F.W. Newman introduced him to many university men. "He immediately became a sort of evangelical father confessor..., ...day after day there was no end to the secret closetings with him." Many of these Oxford men

---

72. Neatby, *History,* 171. Anyone who tries to read any of his writings will readily see that Darby's "doctrine was chaotic." Whereas Irving based his opinions on the way things appeared to the natural eye, Darby based his opinions upon the way he felt things should be.

73. The movers behind the French Revolution faced the same problem. They could easily place their fingers on the obvious problems, and were thereby able to get multitudes to follow them to their destruction. But they were incapable of formulating serious answers for the problems they pointed out. Therefore, their answer was simply revolt against the established order, but they had nothing to replace it with. Having no answers only compounds problems. Revolution solves no problems, for the problem is sin. Only the new creation in Christ solves that problem. Neither Lacunza, Irving nor Darby dealt with problems other than to urge Christians to wait for the next *dispensation* — the Lord will return and correct the problems.

74. *Plot,* 136, 137, "Max S. Weremchuk, *John Nelson Darby,* p 142."

were led in the same direction as was F. W. Newman.[75] Darby, writing some years later, said,

> Two years later (1830) [after his accident, *ed.*], I went to Cambridge and Oxford. In this latter place, some persons who are still engaged in the work, shared my convictions, and felt that the relation of the church to Christ ought to be that of a faithful spouse.[76]

B. W. Newton said "that Darby may have been sent to Oxford to watch the evangelical movement on behalf of popery and that he had not read a line of Darby's writings which a papist might not use."[77]

Darby often displayed a haughty, imperious, peremptory and ungovernable spirit in public. A controversy arose with a local pastor in Lausanne, Switzerland, and "the stress of conflict appears to have told on Darby's temper. A conference of the Dissenters of Lausanne was held in September, 1842, to examine his doctrine of the apostasy of the dispensation. With great difficulty, Darby was persuaded to attend, and he went only to protest against the meeting as not having 'the approval of God.'" Herzog, a local college professor, said of the meeting:

> "Especially he [Darby] obstinately refused to take part in the discussions; but they pressed him, putting it to him as an obligation of Christian charity to declare himself on matters of such importance. In the end, as if weary of contention, he submitted to the desired conference, but only to astonish his very partisans by the rashness of his assertions, often contradictory; by the vagueness of his expressions, and by his wretched stratagem of jumping off from one subject to another. The discussion quickly lost all regularity, and degenerated into a regular uproar which put an end to the meeting. But however bewildering this strange scene might be, people left it

---

75. *Origins,* 66.
76. *Letters,* III.301.
77. *Origins,* 65, 66. F.W. Newman invited Darby to Oxford; Newman had already introduced Newton to the "study of prophecy..." He now was acquainting "him with the man who was to mean so much to him..." It was Newton who made the statement about Darby. The millennial system, with its pre-trib rapture theory, took the pressure off "the Catholic papacy as 'Antichrist'," *Plot,* 254. Admittedly, Newton and Darby were at odds with each other, but should we, therefore, dismiss Newton's charge against Darby? Following through the conflict between the two, Darby was the one who acted wickedly in the matter, and Müller told him so, *q.v.*

profoundly impressed with the haughty, imperious, peremptory, ungovernable spirit that Darby had displayed. The thoughts of his heart had come to light, and this discovery of a blemish in the character of a man surrounded until then with so profound a veneration fully opened the eyes of some even amongst his admirers."[78]

From this point, Darby's influence declined.

Chapter 49

Darby, Continued

Though a millennial system, which might be construed to include a pre-trib rapture, was already being proclaimed (and even published in America in Morgan Edwards' 1788 work and in the "'Morning Watch,' a journal on unfulfilled prophecy") well before Darby came out of the Anglican Church, Darby claimed it as his own.[79]

Refusing to admit that any of his dispensational ideas originated outside of himself, even the most superficial comparison of Irving's *Discourse* (and *Ben-Ezra*) and Darby's system reveals that the two systems are so obviously identical that it cannot be coincidental.[80]

Darby had very little connection with the early Brethren, though they were not yet known as Brethren. But in his typical manner, Darby took credit for the foundation of the Brethren, discounting any influence of Groves, Cronin and Hutchinson. Darby is credited with being "'used of God to bring cosmos out of chaos.'" The chaos was the fighting of the Anglican and Roman Churches for temporal

---

78. Neatby, *History*, 85-86. Darby did not like confrontations; rather, he would "let things work out," *Letters*, II.120, 1871. His excuse for non-involvement was that he did not want to use his individual influence to settle matters, *ibid.*, 381. However, he readily used his individual influence to promote his opinions and to destroy men who disagreed with him, *e.g.*, Newton. *Ibid.*, 389, 391.

79. *Ben Ezra*, I.clxxviii, clxxi. The journal, established in early 1829, was entirely pervaded by Irving's ideas, *DNB*, s.v. "Irving, Edward." See "Chiliasm and Premillennialism," p. 210.

power from which many who loved God fled. "Noel asked, 'Could every person who had watched the steam raise the lid of a boiling tea kettle claim to be the inventor of the steam engine?'"[81] In other words, the tempest was brewing and coming together (social conditions were right, and there was intense millenarian excitement at the time); Darby was at the right place at the right time to guide it with his strong personality, his newly acquired system of theology and with his strange, new method of Bible study, "Bible reading."

Darby "looked around... for some body which might answer his aspirations after a spiritual communion based on New Testament and religious principles, and not on mere political expediency, and soon found it in a society, or rather an unorganized collection of societies, which had been for many years growing and developing, and which under his guidance was destined to take final shape in the sect now called the Plymouth Brethren..."[82] Those *bodies* were the dissenters of the early 1800s who had separated from the organized Anglican and Roman Churches.

Among other things, Darby taught that the Church Age has no place in prophecy, fitting between Daniel's 69th and 70th week where prophecy is suspended — "the gospel times entirely left out" of the Bible.[83] Thus according to Darby's system, the church was given no Old Testament promise of anything — It "is not the subject of promise; though the church is heir by her union with Christ of the

---

80. See *Plot,* 88, 90, 95. MacPherson quotes 21 identical points from Darby's writings that are not only verbatim in Lacunza's document, but appear in the same context, 89, 90. Darby, evidently, claimed as his own what he found in "the *Ben-Ezra* system." William Kelly, with Darby's permission, edited Darby's works to attribute to him many things that were not his ideas. *Plot,* 136, 155ff. This writer, using a 1971 reprint of Darby's letters, has no way of knowing what Darby actually said and what Kelly wanted him to say. Darby was uninterested in honest history; his concern was getting people to follow his system. "[H]istory is not necessary in order to understand prophecy," for "history never explains prophecy." *Writings,* II. 93. Though there is no mention of Darby's ability with Spanish, he was very proficient in several languages, including German.

81. *Origins,* 44, 45. Harold Rowdon is quoting from N. Noel's "rather tendentious *History of the Brethren...*"

82. Neatby, *History,* 26.

promises which are in Him as the true seed of Abraham..."[84] Having no promise of victory on this earth, the church failed. Therefore, it must be spewed out of God's mouth. Then God will establish his throne in Jerusalem and literally reign, doing what the church failed to do, for it had no grace from God to make her different from the world. Darby was quite dogmatic — the church cannot be restored in strength to reach the world.[85] With no grace from God, the church has no power to overcome sin. The early church failed, and, therefore, has only God's judgment against it.[86]

Darby took several shots at the Postmil Reformers, at one point saying that sin is being captive to superstition and errors through education that believes evil can be conquered by another means than by Christ's literal, supernatural intervention.[87] The apostles, taught Darby, never looked for a long continuance of the church; rather, they looked for the Lord's soon return.[88] Accordingly, the only thing left for the church is to realize its lack of responsibility. It has no worldly concerns upon this earth, for it is forbidden to try to set evil right.[89] The corruptions Darby found in the established churches simply justified his thoughts both to himself and those to whom he spoke.

Darby's power was as a mystic, not as a systematic theologian, for he was incapable of analyzing or solving problems from Scripture.[90] Darby knew the value of the mysterious. He placed the church on the mysterious level, making excommunication the

---

83. *Letters,* I.131, 308. According to E. W. Bullinger, "Closely connected with this foregoing point, that the book [Rev., *ed.*] is Hebrew in character, and intended specially for Hebrews, is another undoubted fact, that the Church of God is not the subject of the Old Testament, either in history, type, or prophecy." *The Apocalypse,* 7.
84. *Letters,* III.242.
85. *Writings,* II.11ff., 186, 515ff., 585. Irving introduced this idea around 1822, and it was found in Lacunza's 1790 document.
86. *Ibid.,* 359ff.
87. *Ibid.,* 311. Irving also mentioned that he had been held by the superstition from the fathers.
88. *Ibid.,* I.512.
89. *Ibid.,* I, 164, 165, 314, 483. No concerns, *ibid.,* 131.

greatest terror a person — rich or poor, educated or uneducated — could have. He effectively used fear to keep his followers 'in line,' gaining as great a hold over people as the Church of Rome ever held. As part of his hold, he stood against any local oversight of congregations, elder or pastor, seeing any local leadership as a threat to his central authority.

As Darbyism developed, it became as 'high church' as any organized religion ever was. The Brethren movement built on toleration was destroyed by Darby himself because of his own lack of toleration. Around 1850, the Brethren split into Open and Exclusive factions. Darby issued a decree concerning what he felt was a heresy, demanding that everyone depart from the man he considered a heretic, Newton. Those obeying the decree were known as the Exclusive Brethren, while those who did not were known as the Open Brethren. Accordingly, as the years progressed, the basis of fellowship was over whether individuals followed man-made — Darby's — decrees. The fellowship that started around Christ's death being remembered at the communion table became fellowship around Darby's opinions. His exclusivity was worse than that in the organized churches that he — joined by multitudes of others — had reacted against.

Darby left 1,500 Exclusive Brethren Churches at his death. With no strong leader to take his place, the Exclusive Brethren, which became very introverted and mystical, lost much of its zeal and influence.[91] However, Lacunza's seed was planted in both the Open and Exclusive Brethren.

In Europe, both the *secular* and *spiritual* societies were in turmoil. Some of Groves' and much of Newton's and Darby's thinking represented a retreat into a shelter of spiritual monasticism to escape that turmoil. The turmoil opened wide the door for someone of Darby's character to radically reform Christianity from

---

90. Neatby, *History,* 31. He *felt* his way through situations, and then persuaded others he was right.
91. *Ibid.,* chap. 10.

its intended world-changing force into a monastic withdrawal: "the extraordinary personality and genius of John Nelson Darby" led the reform that brought the Brethren Church to "the brink of ruin."[92] We must add that "the extraordinary personality and genius" of many millennial leaders have not helped to bring the church in general back from "the brink of ruin."

The Brethren's other-worldliness, pacifism, withdrawal from civil government as well as from society in general, and their system of prophetic speculation which was basic to both, has since become definitive church theology, primarily through the works of Brethren such as C.I. Scofield and H.A. Ironside.

We will extensively develop Darby's system as we proceed, for he, with his then unorthodox ideas, laid the foundation for what is now generally accepted orthodox theology. Few Christian institutions have avoided his influence.

Chapter 50

Newman and Newton

Francis William Newman

In 1827, Darby had a riding accident. While convalescing at his brother-in-law's home (Darby remained single), two important events took place: First, he met F.W. Newman, and, second, in his own words, "During my solitude, conflicting thoughts increased; but much exercise of soul had the effect of causing the Scriptures to gain complete ascendancy over me. I had always owed them to the word of God."[93]

Lacunza said his system developed as he mused on the depressed condition of the Jews, and his emotions overwhelmed him. Irving

---

92. Coad, *History*, 104.
93. *Ibid.*, III. 298. See also Coad, *History*, 27. Darby's account of his accident is reproduced in this document.

said his system developed in his depression over his son's death, and his emotions overwhelmed him. Groves' system developed after his wife's death.

Benjamin Wills Newton

B.W. Newton (1805-1898, a *distinguished theologian*) "Held a place of influence in the Plymouth 'gathering' until 1845 when he and Mr. Darby came to a definite variance with each other as regards prophetic teaching (especially Darby's 'secret rapture' theory) and church order."[94] "During 1827-1830, the years of intense millenarian excitement, the Oxford evangelicals, like many others, speculated about the coming judgment and the coming Christ."[95] Note the dates "of intense millenarian excitement" — Irving's English translation of Lacunza's system was published in 1827, and was thus released to the public during the intense excitement. The dates imply that the 1826 Albury Park conferences may have caused the excitement.

F.W. Newman, who met Darby in 1827, was a private tutor to 22 year old B.W. Newton back at Oxford where Newton was a student. Newton became a major figure in the Brethren movement both at Plymouth and world-wide. Newman had temporarily left Oxford in the autumn of 1827 to act as a tutor to the family of Sergeant Pennefather, Darby's brother-in-law. Though Newman was with Sergeant Pennefather where Darby was recuperating from his accident, his influence continued upon Newton — still back at Oxford — through correspondence. Newton had been trained in strong Calvinism, but at Oxford, he began to doubt his training. Near the end of 1828, F.W. Newman returned to Oxford from Ireland where he had been deeply influenced by Darby at Sergeant Pennefather's. He also returned with some new convictions:

---

94. *Who*, s.v. "Newton, Benjamin Wills." Though *Who* places Newton's birth at 1805, Sandeen places it at 1807, *Roots*, 30. Sandeen thus makes him 20 years old at Exeter College, Oxford.

95. *Roots*, 30.

The Men and Times 191

Convinced that the New Testament provided warrant for the expectation of the approaching return of Christ to this earth, he saw the force of Darby's argument against working for objects in the distant future. The desire to take Christianity to the heathen, which, he averred, had been with him since childhood, was stimulated. Though he had scruples about receiving Anglican ordination and regarded dissenting ministers with such distaste (thinking them pompous, narrow-minded and sectarian) that he was not desirous of becoming one, he nevertheless felt free to take Christianity to the heathen.

It was Newman's apparently new found interest into the study of prophecy which captivated Newton [whom Newman was privately tutoring at Oxford, *ed.*], and a series of meetings for the discussion of the subject was held in his room. Newton has left conflicting accounts of the immediate development of this new interest which was to play so important a part in his latter life that he was to say that 'it turned the whole current of my life.[96]

The movement grew, adding men of stature, abilities, zeal and wealth. Many were men considered today as the *fathers of our faith*. Their unity, however, was not around a common doctrinal stand resulting from serious and thorough Bible study. It was around common dislikes and common feelings.

Darby encountered several groups of like-minded people in Plymouth who were upset over the Church of England. His strength of personality and zeal united them to himself.[97] These people provided a ready made, extremely fertile field for the seeds of Darby's acquired millennial opinions. The turmoil, deadness and the restrictions of the organized churches left many who loved God starved for zeal, Bible teaching and freedom to serve God. Darby's genius filled their hunger.

Darby's zeal attracted multitudes to him, permitting him to teach the starved masses his hopeless millennial *faith*, justified by the

---

96. *Origins*, 63. Darby and B.W. Newton were both orphaned at an early age, Code, *History*, 62. Note the attraction to study prophecy. The reader will find the major strength and financing of the *dispensational* movement comes from its emphasis on *unfulfilled* prophecy, rather than on development and application of God's word into present society.

97. Coad, *History*, 34.

corruption in the organized churches of his day, which he pointed out. One cannot deny the corruptions any more than he can deny corruptions today, but how much of what Darby pointed out was to increase his own following? His ability to attract so many followers seemed proof to him that all who opposed him were in error against the Godhead.[98]

Darby's personality, his personal example and enthusiasm, contrasted with the well-known corrupt clergy, along with the *spell* he cast over others, caused his ideas to be accepted and others to follow him. Some of the greatest men in the last 150 years of Christian history were captivated by his spell. It was not the emphasis upon Bible doctrine, but the emphasis upon prophecy that attracted the huge following to men like Darby, Newton and G.V. Wigram.

Chapter 51

G.V. Wigram, P.F. Hall

George Vicesimus Wigram (b. 1805) was the twentieth child of Irishman Sir Robert Wigram, a wealthy London merchant. Another son of Sir Wigram was to become Bishop of Rochester. At Oxford, Wigram was a close friend with B.W. Newton. After experiencing conversion, Wigram resigned his commission in the Guards, and "entered Queen's College with the purpose of taking orders."

At this time, Wigram was an eccentric character, prodigal with his wealth in some respects, yet affecting a slovenliness in dress as a means (Newton alleged) of self-mortification. Newton (who later had reason to regard his erstwhile friend rather sourly) recounted

---

98. *Ibid.*, 88, *Letters,* II.182, 187. Darby was confident that his understanding of Scripture alone was proper, *ibid.,* I.179, 182, 187, 453, 463, 505, for he alone had the truth. Not even the Reformers achieved his level, for he considered himself God's special messenger on the level of Jeremiah and Paul, *ibid.,* II.386, 504. He said he was God's answer to the enemy, and all opposition to him was the devil's work, *ibid.,* 430, 454, 463. He insisted that departure from his system actually departed from the faith, *Ibid.,* 465. He even compared himself to Christ, who watched over the Seven Churches, *ibid.,* 224.

how he would rub a new coat on the wall to make it shabby: adding tartly that the self-denial was on the part of those who were seen out with him! Wigram was said by Newton to have had a wide selection of friends...

Whatever Wigram's connexions and friendships, they were all sunk in the loyalty he now gave to the new friend and leader he found in Darby: a loyalty so strong that it was later to lead to the complete sacrifice of older friendships, and even of courtesy and of fair judgment in controversy.[99]

Percy Francis Hall

At Plymouth, 30 year old Darby and his companions met a 26 year old man named Percy Francis Hall (b. 1804), who was already preaching extreme pacifistic views. Because Hall's views corresponded so well with his, Darby's and Groves', Wigram established a chapel for Hall to preach in. Hall preached that a Christian could not be a civil magistrate because God is a God of mercy and grace, not of law.

Hall's pacifism was very consistent with Darby's opinion that Christ is *waiting* to judge the world, so Christians must also wait. Therefore, Christians cannot be civil judges.[100] Hall published a pamphlet giving the reasons for resigning his Plymouth Coast Guard commission:

> [T]hat powers, distinctions, honours and riches of the world are not for the Christian. Though the New Testament requires submission to rulers, it enjoins the exercise of authority only as father, husband and master. Hall felt it inconsistent for a Christian to serve as a magistrate and to enforce law, instead of that grace to which he should be a witness. Hall drew the touching picture of a magistrate who must condemn a guilty man though he be broken-hearted and plead for his wife and starving family. Old Testament usage cannot be invoked since its revelation was partial; the teaching of Jesus is of paramount importance. Coming to the practice of war which was his particular problem, Hall maintained that the precepts and example of Jesus forbade the use of force, and that not merely in private relationships. Love, which is the fulfilling of the law, is to be

---

99. Coad, *History*, 60, 61.
100. *Writings*, II.484, 1852.

the characteristic of the Christian and is to be shown to all men. Though he denied the concept of a Christian nation, yet professing Christian nations go to war with each other with the unseemly possibility that Christians might be in combat with fellow-Christians. Finally, even if it is unlikely that Christians in the military profession would ever be called upon to fight (he was probably thinking of his own position) yet they should withdraw from any association with those who do, for was not Eli held responsible for the sins of his sons?[101]

Wigram's chapel did not emphasize Bible doctrine, emphasizing instead prophecy and withdrawal from society.[102] Darby and other early millenarians pointed out the many and quite obvious problems around them, but they offered no solution to the chaos. All they offered was withdrawal, leaving them with not much more to study than how they felt the chaos fit together in their prophetic schemes.[103]

One of the outstanding points common in all these early men — Groves, Newton, Darby, Wigram, Müller, Hall — is that they were all young, vigorous men with extremely strong charismatic personalities which drew people to them. There was very little, if any, emphasis on systematic biblical theology. Their unity was around the communion table, which represented death to them, freedom from the restraints of organized religion (*i.e.*, dogmatic doctrine) and the study of prophecy. Multitudes were attracted to them.

---

101. *Origins,* 75. Justice and mercy must be in terms of God's holiness, not man's. "Hall had attained the rank of naval Commander, but had resigned his commission and sold his possessions. Like Groves, he had put forward his views in a booklet entitled *Discipleship,* in which he adopted extreme pacifist grounds, which caused him to go so far as to insist that a Christian could not be a civil magistrate, and thus be obliged to pass sentence upon persons found guilty in his court...," Coad, *History,* 61. The meeting took place c. 1830. Note the open militancy against orthodox Christianity: *The 1689 London Baptist Confession* held that "It is lawful for Christians to accept and execute the office of a magistrate when called thereunto...," Chapter 24, OF THE CIVIL MAGISTRATE., point 2. These men were well financed in their war against the Biblical Christianity that had *turned the world upside down.* Note the rejection of the Old Testament except where it suites a purpose, *e.g.,* Eli.

102. Coad, *History,* 34, 60-62. Services started at the chapel in 1831.

103. *Ibid.,* 68.

Chapter 52
George Müller

Another very important man drawn to Groves and Darby was George Müller (1805-1898), "who may well be called the most illustrious man ever associated with the Brethren." Müller's story is too well known to be told again in detail. The son of a tax collector, he grew up in a grossly wicked manner. He attended a religious meeting in the home of an acquaintance of one of his friends and was converted, November, 1825. Müller met Groves through a common friend, another pillar in the millennial movement, Henry Craik (1805-1866). Müller married Groves' sister, October 7, 1830.

In November, 1830, twenty-five year old Müller accepted a call to pastor a Baptist church at Teignmouth, England. "For some time, Müller continued a Baptist pastor. But, little by little, he began to develop views which were to cause him to become more and more associated with the Brethren." Probably influenced by Groves' view of wealth (it was unspiritual), Müller renounced his regular salary at the end of October, 1830. Müller's link with the Brethren is well established:

> More germane to our immediate purpose, it provides [the marriage, &c., *ed.*] further evidence that Müller was imbibing the spirit of Groves not only through the reports that were coming from Baghdad, but through personal contact with those who had been influenced by, and had influenced, him.[104]

Groves had a great influence over Müller.[105] The beliefs that united Müller, Groves and Darby were common desires for freedom from the creeds of organized religion, common fellowship around the communion table, and their common spite for the organized ministry of the church. Müller did not necessarily unite with them around

---

104. *Origins,* 118. See also Neatby, *History,* 53ff., *Origins,* 114ff., and *Who,* s.v. "Müller, George."
105. Neatby, *History,* 55.

doctrine, although he was in basic agreement.[106] Though Müller developed his views concerning living by faith at Teignmouth, he did not impose them on others. His views, though, were and are still common among the Brethren.[107]

The early days of the Brethren saw Müller unite with Henry Craik to pastor a church in Bristol that greatly prospered under their leadership.

> In October, 1832, Darby preached in both chapels occupied by Müller and Craik [both 27 at the time, *ed.*] and wrote appreciatively of the work that was being done there, his only adverse comment being the one frequently on his mind in those days: 'I should wish a little more principle of largeness of communion'.[108]

In Müller, however, we see that the extreme views of withdrawal from society were not totally shared by all who united with the Brethren. He is known for his social work with orphans. Nevertheless, Müller founded the Scriptural Knowledge Institution (SKI), which did more to spread the destructive tenets of Brethrenism than probably any one other event of his time. Müller's Institution was a main-stay of Hudson Taylor's China Inland Mission in its early days.[109] In his February 25, 1834, journal entry, Müller gave six reasons for forming "a new Institution [SKI, *ed.*] for the spread of the gospel." Although this writer certainly agrees with five of Müller's reasons, he must take serious exception with Müller's first reason:

> The *end* which these religious societies [then in existence, *ed.*] propose to themselves, and which is constantly put before their members, is, that the world will gradually become better and better,

---

106. Coad, *History*, 38.

107. *Ordained*, 95. Because the pastor's salary came from "pew-rents," which Müller was convinced were wrong, he wanted nothing to do with them. *Faith*, 81.

108. *Origins,* 121. "I dread narrowness of heart more than anything for the church of Christ, *especially now."* Letters, I.8, 1832. But Darby became so narrow that he destroyed the movement he basically founded.

109. Coad, *History,* 52, 53. The millennial system of passivity, otherworldliness/non-involvement in "worldly matters," and their distinctive, unique prophetic views. The system neutralized Christianity wherever it went.

and that at last the whole world will be converted [sic.] To this end, there is constantly reference made to the passage in Habakkuk ii. 14: "For the Earth shall be filled with the knowledge of the glory of the Lord, as the waters cover the sea;" or the one in Isaiah xi. 9: "For the earth shall be full of the knowledge of the Lord, as the waters cover the sea." But that these passages can have no reference to the present dispensation, but to the one which will commence with the return of the Lord, — that in the present dispensation things will not become spiritually better, but rather worse, — and that in the present dispensation it is not the whole world that will be converted, but only a people gathered out from among the Gentiles for the Lord, — is clear from many passages of the divine testimony, of which I only refer to the following: Matt. xiii. 24-30, and verses 36-43, 2 Tim. iii. 1-13, Acts xv. 14.

A hearty desire for the conversion of sinners, and earnest prayer for it to the Lord, is quite *scriptural*; but it is *unscriptural* to expect the conversion of the whole world. *Such an end* we could not propose to ourselves in service of the Lord...

1. We consider every believer bound, in one way or other, to help the cause of Christ, and we have scriptural warrant for expecting the Lord's blessing upon our work of faith and labor of love; and although, according to Matt. xiii. 42-43, 2 Tim. iii. 1-13, and many other passages, the world will not be converted before the coming of our Lord Jesus, still, while he tarries, all scriptural means ought to be employed for the ingathering of the elect of God.[110]

The then operating missionary societies "constantly put before their members" the hope of Christianizing the world before Christ's return. That goal of Christianizing the world Müller found unscriptural. Lacunza's "dispensational" view of Matthew twenty four, which became popular in his lifetime, caused Müller to abandon any hope that the gospel could change the world for Christ. It also caused him to say that those expecting the Gospel of Christ to Christianize the nations are not serving the Lord. Müller, therefore, led in changing the goal of missionary endeavors from Christianizing the world's nations to simply "soul saving." Accordingly, the missionaries trained by the SKI went over the world to "save souls," yet they were convinced that it was unscriptural to hope that the gospel message could bring about godly

---

110. *Trust,* 109, 110, 113. See *Origins,* 129.

social change. The expectations of their faithless gospel were met. Müller's ideas united with Darby's, who, echoing Irving's words, condemned all who desired to convert the world to Christ.[111]

Müller attended the 1833 Powerscourt prophecy conference in Ireland.[112]

Chapter 53

Hudson Taylor and Others

Hudson Taylor's influence for powerless, other-worldly Christianity cannot be overlooked.

> The early decades of the twentieth century were perhaps the years of greatest enthusiasm for foreign missions and in this area Keswick's record was indeed strong. J. Hudson Taylor (1832-1905), a Britisher who founded the China Inland Mission in 1865, had become deeply committed to Keswick views. The China Inland Mission became a model for independent and self-sacrificing missionary work as well as a source for much of the later fundamentalist agitation against liberalism in the mission field. The Student Volunteer Movement, originating out of Moody's Northfield conference, also had close Keswick ties. Many impressive young men of the era responded to these teachings by consecrating their lives to missionary service.[113]

We do not question Mr. Taylor's love for God nor his Godliness. However, we must question his deep commitment "to Keswick views" that "social service programs were particularly dangerous." (See "Keswick," p. 314.) We must also question Taylor's close tie with Müller's SKI and its message that it is sin to seek to

---

111. *Letters*, I.257, 1858. *Writings*, II.185. Apparently, these men, Müller included, believed the gospel of Christ is powerless when it comes to bringing about godly social change through individual conversion. See 1 Cor. 1:18-2:5, Jude 3. Is the literal sword, which is expected forcefully to subdue sinner, stronger than the Spirit of God? Müller was a key figure in *the death of victory*.

112. Coad, *History*, 45.

113. *Fundamentalism*, 97.

Christianize the world (a neutralized, powerless gospel). Taylor "became a protegé of C.I. Scofield," and he fully embraced the dead message of withdrawal from all society to become personally more spiritual.

"The early decades of the twentieth century were perhaps the years of greatest enthusiasm for foreign missions..." However, notice that the message taken to the four corners of the world was one of hopelessness and defeat. Taylor and his mission work, though saving many souls, delivered to the Chinese a hopeless message of defeat — Taylor, with the help of Müller's SKI, neutralized Christianity, leaving the Chinese "helpless against the military onslaught of the Communists." Fully expecting an imminent "rapture," multitudes of Chinese Christians were tortured and slaughtered. On the other hand, non-millenarians fled. Hiding safely in the mountains, they kept Chinese Christianity alive.[114] Moreover, China's modern attitude toward forced abortion must, at least in part, be attributed to those who taught a generation of Chinese Christians that it was sin to be involved in social programs and issues.

When Christians withdraw from involvement in social programs, they give them to the ungodly by default.

Robert Cleaver Chapman

In 1832, Robert Chapman (1803-1902), a very important figure in the mystic Christian movement, was added. He gave away his wealth and law practice to become the pastor of a strict Baptist Church, Ebenezer Chapel. "Chapman's long life and simple holiness of his character made him an outstanding patriarch and counselor of nineteenth century open Brethren." Chapman had been converted in 1823 under J.H. Evans, who was supported by the wealthy banker, Henry Drummond, a major figure in the conferences to develop the millennial system.[115]

---

114. *Cult*, 75, 76.

Samuel Prideaux Tregelles

Another key and highly regarded figure acquired by the movement by 1835 was Samuel Prideaux Tregelles (1813-1875). Though he was reared a Quaker with very little formal education, he had a phenomenal memory and a flair for languages. He was to become one of the more outstanding textual critics of his day.

During an 1832 visit to Plymouth, 19 year old Tregelles visited B.W. Newton, who had married Tregelles' cousin. He was fascinated by Newton's unique prophetic views. "He experienced an evangelical conversion through hearing Newton preach, and threw in his lot with the Brethren." Tregelles joined with Wigram in producing an exhaustive concordance of the Greek New Testament, and played a major role in producing a similar concordance of the Old Testament.[116]

We can safely assume that Tregelles' writings reflect the dispensational millennial system that had been adopted from Irving a few years earlier by the then twenty-seven year old Darby.[117] Newman imbibed Darby's theories. He then taught the system to the student he was tutoring, B.W. Newton. Newton's preaching lead to Tregelles' conversion in 1832. Thus Tregelles was a product of Darby as Darby's influence and teachings continued to gain momentum and committed followers.

---

115. Coad, *History*, 70-73. Note the close connection between and mixture of the Brethren and Baptist. Men such as Müller and Chapman initially identified themselves as Baptist, but they clearly followed the Brethren's system. In other words, they were not Baptists.

116. *Origins*, 160. See also Coad, *History*, 66.

117. Irving was absorbed in Apocalyptic tendencies as early as 1826, presenting his views at every opportunity. "Early in 1829 the 'Morning Watch,' a journal on unfulfilled prophecy, entirely pervaded, as Mrs. Oliphant remarks, by Irving, was established by members of the Albury conference." *DNB*, s.v. "Irving, Edward." *DNB's* complete account of Irving is reproduced in this document. In other words, not only were the ideas Darby claimed as his own in 1827 or 1828 being widely propagated by Irving, but the "Morning Watch" was publishing them far and wide. See *Life*, 257, 258, for Mrs. Oliphant's remarks.

But we must not overlook the fact that the freedom offered in these early years was also freedom from any dogmatic doctrinal stand. In Darby's words:

> The history of these times [the Seven Churches in Revelation, *ed.*] proves that the living power and truth in the Church was not in its doctors, but in its martyrs.[118]

According to Darby, the church's power does not lie in doctrinal purity but in its the martyrs; its power is not in serious systematic study of Scriptures but in those who give themselves to service. The common ground with the key figures in the Mystical Christian Movement was not a common doctrinal stand. The unity was their common opinions and feelings about subjects dear to their hearts, primarily against the doctrines, restrictions and actions of the organized churches of their day. They were able to unite with one another because there was no dogmatic doctrine to unite around. Our conclusion must be that wealthy people could unite with them without having to depart from sin as defined in the Commandments, for sin was very seldom, if ever, defined by them in terms of God's word.

The key figures in the developing millennial system were quite young considering they were formulating a radically unorthodox system of theology. Many were captivated by their own persons, and all possessed unique and overwhelming abilities to attract multitudes to themselves regardless of what they taught. The millennial leaders were considered false teachers of their day, and though they were all well educated, they were NOT systematic

---

118. *Writings,* II.455, from his seven lectures on THE PROPHETICAL ADDRESSES TO THE SEVEN CHURCHES, 1852. Darby does, however, call for doctrinal purity, but the purity he demands is purity in believing in his system: "It seems to me that what I have said will be received by every true Christian," *Letters,* II.71, 72. He defined faithfulness to God as faithfulness to his unique ideas concerning Scripture; unfaithfulness to his ideas he defined as unfaithfulness to the Lord, *Letters,* I.200, 217. He taught that the Christian's *strength* lay in his unconcern about worldly matters, *Writings,* II.585.

theologians.[119] They did not — could not — develop their new ideas from serious study of God's word.

Their unity was around the study of unfulfilled prophecy and around Irving's conviction that any faith in the world's conversion through preaching the Christian gospel is a false hope, yes, even presumption.

The stage is set. The men are gathered. Millennial excitement is high. A world, remembering the French Revolution and Napoleonic Wars, is ready. The basic system is formulated and has been in print for some time.

Christianity will be reduced to a mystical rather than a practical experience. Faith will be reduced from obedience to every word that proceeds out of the mouth of God to a mere mystical experience of prayer. By reducing Christianity to the mystical realm, "being filled with the Spirit" will be equated to an emotional — even mystical — experience.[120] It will transform Christianity from its New Testament Biblical power that turned the world upside down, conquering paganism from the inside out, to little more than a mystical, emotional experience and personal salvation.

It will effectively neutralize Christianity; it will willingly give the world over to the forces of evil.

---

119. Many of the system's founders were lawyers, as Scofield had been, *q.v.*

120. Millennialism tends to reduce Christianity to a personal, emotional experience, which is in contrast with the clear teaching of God's word in passages like Ex. 28:3, 31:3-6, 35:31-36: compare with Lev. 25:18, 26:3-13, Jos. 1:7, 8, &c. The Old Testament must establish the basis for every thought and action. No New Testament author gave anything contradictory to already established Old Testament precepts and laws. Exodus tells us that fullness of the Spirit is wisdom, knowledge and understanding from God, enabling the individual to work hard at God's calling for himself. Spirit filling is the ability to use one's God provided skills and abilities for God's glory — hard, consistent and dedicated work. Thus it is the wisdom, knowledge and understanding from God to 'dig a ditch' for God's glory if ditch digging is one's God given ability and calling. See "Revivalism," p. 463.

Part VI
Development and Doctrine

Chapter 54
Millenarianism and Money

The modern millennial system remained neither Lacunza's nor Irving's for long. The millenarians worked and continue to work hard to see that Darby is attributed with the basic system. Led primarily by Darby, it was the Brethren who converted the modern Christian world to dispensational opinions.[1]

Darby traveled the world promoting the millennial system. Hardly a nation under heaven did not receive a visit from Darby and/or from his followers. His message of "just wait for the Lord's soon return" and no social responsibility was right for the time. "Things are breaking up fast," said Darby in 1871, evidently referring to the breakdown of historic Christianity. People were thirsting "for the word," meaning that they were abandoning the historic victorious Christian faith that held them accountable to the firm standard of God's word. In its place, they were gladly receiving Darby's millennial message of escape.[2] Dissolution with the established churches was also on all sides, and Darby was able to take advantage

---

1. There are excellent books tracing the history of what has been called, "Fundamentalism" as offered by the Brethren. See *Plot,* 198, *Roots,* 13. The basis of Morgan's 1740 system was a "literal rather than figurative" fulfillment of prophecy. See also *Origins,* 207. Darby's 1840 lectures delivered in Lausanne, Switzerland, developed not only the hopeless millennial message, but many more, *e.g.,* "the view that the Jews had been given the land of Israel unconditionally."
2. *Letters,* II.129. In another letter, he says, "...some who could not walk the same side of the street with me a few years ago, have come and said, What you told us thirty years ago is all coming true. The shaking of the world has moved them." *Ibid,* 144. In other words, social conditions made it appear that the end was near, so people were converting to his view.

203

of the dissolution with the new ideas that people were ready to receive.[3] Even Darby expressed amazement at the speed with which his opinions were accepted everywhere he went. [4] Probably no other teaching in Gospel Church history has ever gained such wide acceptance so quickly. Though Darby saw the explosive growth of his system as God's Spirit working, he saw any growth outside of his circle of influence as proof others were using the flesh.[5]

The early dispensationalists believed that the failure of the church 'dispensation' meant that there must come another dispensation to take the church's place — a reestablished Jewish nation, Zionism, filled the need.

Brethren writers, especially Darby, edited the writings of past saints — including the Reformers — and hymns to support their theories.[6] The apparent reason was to make the millennial system appear orthodox when it clearly was not. Darby readily admitted that his new truths changed the orthodox understanding of multitudes of Scriptures as he intentionally went against the orthodox Christian doctrines of his day.[7] He changed meanings of words, passages of Scripture and even the Scripture itself by issuing new translations to support his prophetic opinions.[8] Among other things, he boasted that his unique prophetic views changed the entire book of Psalms from its historic understanding of the past eighteen hundred years.[9] For example, Darby defined "sovereign grace" as a God-given ability to remain heavenly minded, detached from earthly things.[10] He

---

3. *Ibid.*, I.178, 1849. Growth in London, 209.

4. See *Letters*, I.54, 297-305, 1843. Darby's unique ability allowed him popularize other's ideas as his own. Coad, *History*, 111-136. This ability has been a common trait in millennialism.

5. *Letters*, I.258, 262ff., II.330.

6. *Plot,* 145, 146. Darby tells of his hard work in changing the words of the Reformers and of then existing hymns. *Letters,* I.413, III.45.

7. *Writings*, II.493, 494.

8. *Letters*, I.55, 380, 382, 402 — he convinced American Christians that the Old Testament is not for today, 534, II.32, 48, 65, 420, &c.

9. *Ibid.*, I.243ff., II.561. His views were not unique with him. Though Edward's views and Lacunza's system had been public domain for several years, it was, apparently, not generally known.

translated, studied and taught all Scripture in light of the opinions he propagated around the world.

Despite opposition from established churches, Darby's ideas — gleaned from others and developed into his own system[11] — overwhelmed the church at large. The pre-trib rapture idea, united with Lacunza's renewed millennial hope and presented by Irving and Darby, has become to many the shibboleth that separates. Meanwhile, the basic tenets of the Christian faith — such as the Verbal Inspiration of Scripture, Virgin Birth, Vicarious Atonement, Victorious Resurrection — have fallen into the realm of the unimportant. A reason, according to Dave MacPherson, for the antagonism against those who do not hold to pre-trib is "its tremendous fund-raising potential."[12]

MacPherson concludes:

> The real test is ahead. If pretrib promoters ignore or twist this book's documentation, and if their only bottom line is a continuing flow of funds, then I won't be surprised if God views them collectively as an "Achan" (Josh. 7) and allows a national or even international money collapse!
>
> I'm not expressing any particular end-time view by saying this. I'm only stating the principle Jesus gave when He said that we can't put money on an equal level with serving God...[13]

Irving supplied the system, and Darby supplied a supposedly Scriptural foundation for the system, *i.e.,* "Bible Reading." (See "Bible Readings" p. 281.)

> Millenarianism has grown out of a new "school of Scripture interpretation;" and its laws of interpretation are so different from the old, that the Bible may almost be said to wear a new visage and speak with a new tongue—a tongue not very intelligible, in many of its utterances, to the uninitiated. The central law of interpretation by which Millenarians profess always to be guided, is that of giving the literal sense.[14]

---

10. *Writings,* II.381, 425.
11. *Plot,* 109.
12. *Ibid.,* 223.
13. *Ibid.,* 234.

There is money in millenarianism:

> These views [the "prophetic theories that have gained a large acceptance among Evangelical Anglicans, Fundamentalists in all Protestant Churches, Plymouth Brethren, Keswick and similar movements, free-lance Bible-teachers and evangelists," *ed.*], which began to be propagated a little over a hundred years ago in the separatist movements of Edward Irving and J. N. Darby, have spread to the remotest corners of the earth, and enlisted supporters in most of the Reformed Churches in Christendom, including the Mission field. They are held and spread with conviction and tenacity, and occasionally with overbearing confidence. They have had the advantage of being outstanding tenets in all sections of a denomination, which has had the satisfaction of seeing the peaceful penetration of other communions by their theories of the End. So much so that an increasing number of pastors feel called upon to leave the ordered work of the pastorate, to stir up interest in what is called the "imminent" or impending Coming of Christ. Some of these at a few hours' notice can fill the largest Churches with audiences anxious to hear of the latest signs of the times, though it is a fundamental presupposition of the school that the Imminent Advent awaits the fulfillment of no signs whatever. Some of this interest is wholesome; more of it would be if all of what is taught were true.[15]

Reese makes a good point: "...fill the largest Churches..." *Pre-trib Millenarianism* has the ability to raise tremendous amounts of money. Fortunes were and are made with "Dispensationalism."[16]

In 1866, Spurgeon was preaching against the millennial *prophets* for *profit* who shuffled texts of Scripture, *e.g.*, Bible Readings, to make them say what they wanted them to say. Speaking on 1 Corinthians 11:25, 26, he said:

> "Till he come." I must not say anything about that, except that he will come, and I think that ought to be enough for Christians. To my

---

14. "*Princeton Review* 25 (1853):68." Quoted in *Roots,* 107.
15. *Advent,* xi, xii.
16. *Plot,* 208, 223. This pastor has heard more than one speaker tell his listeners not to leave their money for the antichrist. Rather, the money should be given to the speaker's worthy cause. In addition, we hear church debt justified: "Borrow now, and let the devil's crowd pay it off." Well, the devil's crowd is now paying it off — those who pressed the church to go into debt.

Development and Doctrine 207

great sorrow, I had sent to me, this last week, two or three copies of a tract purporting, according to the title-page, to have been written by myself, prophesying the coming of the Lord in the year 1866. Now, you may expect to hear of me being in Bedlam, whenever, by my tongue or my pen, I give countenance to such rubbish. The Lord may come in 1866, and I shall be glad to see him; but I do not believe he will; and one reason why I don't believe he will, I have told to you before: it is because all these false twopenny-halfpenny prophets say that he will. If they said he would not, I should begin to think he would; but inasmuch as they are all crying as one man that he will come in 1866, or 1867, I am inclined to think he will not come at any such time. It seems to me that there are a very great many prophecies which must be fulfulled before the coming of Christ, which will not be fulfilled in the next twelve months; and I prefer, beloved, to stand in the position of a man who knows neither the day nor the hour in which the Son of man cometh; always looking for his appearing, but never interfering with those dates and figures, which seem to me to be proper amusement for young ladies who have nothing to do, and who take to them instead of reading novels, and for certain divines who have exhausted their stock of knowledge about sound doctrine, and therefore make up, and gain a little ephemeral popularity by shuffling texts of Scripture as the Norwood gypsies shuffled cards in days gone by. Leave the *prophets* to divide the *profits* which they get from simpletons; and as for you, watch for Christ's coming, whether it shall be to-day, or to-morrow, and set no limits, and no dates, and no times. Only work while it is called to-day; work so that, when he cometh, he may find you, as faithful servants, ready to come in to the wedding with him. "Till he come," then, the Lord's supper is to be a showing forth of this death.[17]

In other words, men like to speak on "prophecy" because of the money they can get "from simpletons." Few seem to care that "proof" texts must be shuffled as a deck of cards to make them fit together according to the speaker's desire.

Because the "shuffling" system of exegesis has been taught by men of outstanding character and abilities for well over a hundred years, many of those now caught in it cannot see past their emotions nor the great men of the past who propagated the system in which

---

17. C.H. Spurgeon, Sermon, *The Lord's Supper, Simple but Sublime.* Lord's day evening, 1866.

they have been trained. Truth, many times, falls into the background when emotions and personalities are involved.

Chapter 55

Millennialism Develops

The first and primary formulators, including Irving, leaned toward Calvinism, so Calvinism was not really the shibboleth between the Brethren and orthodox Christianity of the day. Rather, the primary division was Scripture vs. mysticism, *viz.*, the early men 'felt' their way through situations, and then they sought and developed Scriptural support for the way they felt things should be, or to confirm the way things appeared to them.[18]

The destructive implications of the millennial system that the Brethren made part of orthodox Christian doctrine are easily followed.[19] Starting after 1827 with a professed desire for unity based only upon the death of Christ, by 1841 Darby's movement was already facing disarray.[20] By 1873, Darby was more "Popish" than the pope himself, claiming the same authority as Christ to judge what went on in all Brethren assemblies. He fully expected each to accept his judgment as the final word in all matters of faith and

---

18. Darby continually refers to his feelings concerning matters, referring to Scriptures in only a few cases when he finds it convenient, *Letters,* I.85, 96. However, he does warn people against depending upon dreams when we have the word of God, *ibid.,* 76. He seems to use Scriptures to turn people, ladies in this case, toward himself, *ibid.,* 215, 217. Though Darby's standard was the way he felt about matters. (*ibid.,* II.40, 73, 450), he condemns others for depending upon their feelings, *ibid.,* 453, *e.g.,* "...that the Spirit of God be the source of all our thoughts and desires, to live Christ." *Ibid.,* 460. Darby thus held not the word of God as the final authority, but how the "Spirit" within him felt about a matter. "I feel I have the Lord with me," *ibid.,* II.471. (Several times, he gives the impression he is trying to claim the same apostolic authority as St. Paul by applying the Apostle's phraseology himself.) Darby acts according to conscience, not according to the word of God: "My conscience does not reproach me...," *ibid.,* I.74, 215. Irving continually refers to appearances to justify the "Ben-Ezra system."

practice. One of his complaints against the Brethren assembly at Bethesda was that it did not seek nor abide by his judgments in various matters. In a letter passing his judgment upon Newton and the Brethren assembly at Bethesda, Darby justified calling Newton a heretic and Bethesda a work of Satan.[21]

Many pastors, especially in America, had to start teaching millennialism out of self-defense — that is, their people were so strongly influenced that the pastors had to teach the system or lose their people. Writing from Boston in 1874, Darby rejoices that many American pastors were teaching Brethren doctrines. He laments, however, that they were only taking from the Brethren what they wanted — they had to drop his "ruin of the church" theory (actually, they Americanized it), or they would no longer have their local congregations:

> ...there is a great effort to keep souls in the various systems while taking advantage of the light which brethren have and preaching their doctrines. They do not even conceal it. One of the most active who has visited Europe told ministers that they could not keep up with the brethren unless they read their books, but he was doing

---

19. The Brethren's understanding of prophecy seems to be developed and published primarily by non-theologians. If this author understands right, neither Harold Camping nor Dave Hunt claims a theological background. The same lack of theological ability is detectable in many of the dispensationalists fathers, such as Irving and Darby. The Brethren many times militated against sound theological training, even knowingly and intentionally dismissing all past understandings of the passages they used to support their views. Darby's new theory of the Lord's soon coming frightened people: "...the thoughts are new... and all the old habits are against their feelings... we must not be surprised at its effect being slow on the mass [sic], the ordinary instruments of acting upon others having been trained in most opposite habits." *Letters,* I.26, 1834. Though Darby claimed the thoughts were new, Irving had already popularized them.

20. "The Plymouth Brethren would 'unite Christendom by its dismemberment, and do away with all sects by the creation of a new sect, more narrow and bitter in its hostility to existing sects than any other.'" *Systematic Theology,* 895, 896.

21. *Letters,* II.224 (1873). He told Newton, who pastored Bethesda, what to do in a matter, and Newton would not do it. Darby called on Newton to repent for disobeying God as God spoke through him. Hardly a letter by Darby fails to mention his personal judgment about some matter in an assembly of believers or in a person's life.

everything he could to prevent souls leaving their various systems called churches.[22]

Being a reactionary movement, the early millennial leaders went too far. Rather than Scripturally addressing the problems and influencing the problem areas for God that forced their reaction, they separated from those areas.

The Brethren movement itself shattered, lost momentum and faded into the background, but its millennial message continued to develop. The message was spread through prophetic conferences sponsored by wealthy individuals and through the writings of, if not Biblically sound, then exceptionally talented men, well-known to the modern Christian world.

Chapter 56

Chiliasm and Premillennialism

According to William Shedd (1820-1894),

> Premillenarianism was the revival of the pseudo-Jewish doctrine of the Messianic Kingdom, as this had been formed in the later periods of Jewish history by a materializing exegesis of the Old Testament. See Neander: History, I. 650 sq. Its most flourishing period was between 150 and 250. Its prevalence in the church at that time has been much exaggerated. That it could not have been the catholic and received doctrine, is proved by the fact that it forms no part of the Apostles' creed, which belongs to this period, and hence by implication is rejected by it. "Chiliasm," says Neander (I. 651), "never formed a part of the general creed of the church. It was diffused from one country [Phrygia], and from a single fountainhead." In the preceding period of the Apostolic fathers, 100 to 150, it had scarcely any currency. There are no traces of it in Clement of Rome, Ignatius, and Polycarp. In Barnabas, Hermas, and Pipias it is found; but these are much less influential names than the former. The early Apologists, Tatian, Athenagoras, and Theophilus do not

---

22. *Letters,* II. 304. "One of the most active" could well have been D.L. Moody. Also, 306, from NY, 1874. "The ruin of the church" idea is found in *Ben-Ezra.*

advocate it. Alfore (On Rev. 20:4, 5) is greatly in error, in saying that "the whole church for three hundred years from the apostles understood the two resurrections in the literal premillenarian sense.[23]

Fr. Paul said in his critique that Lacunza's system simply revived after 1,400 years the millenarian faith; Shedd tells us that though there was a "premillenarianism" faith in early church history, it was not the prevalent faith. In contrast to Chiliasm, Baptist theologian, Augustus Strong (1836-1921) said:

> *(a)* Through the preaching of the gospel in all the world, the kingdom of Christ is steadily to enlarge its boundaries, until Jews and Gentiles alike become possessed of its blessings, and a millennial period is introduced in which Christianity generally prevails throughout the earth.[24]

Strong compares the premillennial view of history, *i.e.*, the Lord must return suddenly to straighten out sin's mess (millennial reign), to drilling rocks and blasting and to a flame suddenly ignited by gas — this theory, he said, is quite contrary to the seed to which God's kingdom is compared.[25] In the opinion of a great many living in the early 1800s, the French Revolution dashed any hope of a general, world-wide movement of God's Spirit. Hence, the new idea that only a "catastrophic return of Christ" could change society found a ready audience — a thought prevalent among Christians at the end of this millennium.

An important point made by both Mr. Roy Coad and Mr. Ernest Sandeen is that no matter how hard one tries to trace Darby's (Lacunza's) system back to Apostolic times, it cannot be done. But even if it could be traced, the developers did not know that they were following a well worn path. In other words, if their ideas were not new, the men did not realize they were not new. As far as they were concerned, they were breaking new ground and making an

---

23. *Dogmatic Theology,* II B. 642, 643. See "Chiliasm," p. 439
24. *Systematic Theology,* 1008. Strong goes on to amplify the development of evil during a time period and its restraint. He does not present a *bed of roses*.
25. *Ibid.,* 1010.

intentional break with the past centuries of developed Christian doctrine.[26]

Modern millenarianism was basically developed in Britain, which had been prepared by the French Revolution.[27] It was swept into the United States by the flood of immigrants in late 1800s and early 1900s. Christians, left without hope in Christ the Victorious, withdrew their social influence. Biblical, world-changing Christianity was effectively neutralized, and the world was delivered to the many enemies of Christ, including Communism.[28]

Chapter 57

The Imminent Return

One of the most destructive themes promoted by the millenarians (Irving initially) was the conviction of Christ's soon return — "The imminent return of Christ" is a Brethren phrase. It colored all Christian thinking from the time of its introduction. The logical implications of this view were developed and spread world-wide with tremendous evangelistic fervor, primarily by Darby. Christians were ready for a promise that they would soon be gone from such a blood-thirsty world. However, Lacunza's renewed millennialism, with the rapture idea added, did not spread without resistance from Bible scholars of the day.

---

26. "[I]f the early Brethren were treading in paths which had already been well worn by earlier radical spirits, they did so in ignorance of their predecessors..." Coad, *History,* 93. The point is that these men were confident they were formulating a new system of theology. Darby intentionally threw out past understandings of Daniel, replacing them with his own — he started over again with the things "such as God has up to this shewn me," *Writings,* II.323, 324, 1852. Lacunza offered Darby's view at least 50 years before Darby claimed it.

27. Coad, *History,* 103, 109.

28. The only conspiracy, or plot, this writer is pointing out is the one started in the Garden, Jer. 8:6ff., Ps. 2, &c.

From Geneva in 1842, Darby gives the millenarian definition of the soon coming of the Lord:

> Nothing urges more to the plainest and most faithful evangelization, than the thought that Jesus is coming quickly. On the other hand, if you are wishing for money, or seeking to make provision for placing your children in the world, or if you have any plans for the future, you cannot wish for the Lord Jesus to come; and if you cannot, then your hearts are not right with Jesus. For Christians, it is a melancholy state. And if any one does not own the Lord, nothing is more awful than the coming of Jesus: it is judgment for such a one.[29]

There would have been little or no problem with Darby's opinion if he had not traveled so widely and influenced so many people. He traveled to America, and, like Irving, rejoiced as Christian leaders awakened to the truth of Christ's soon coming as he saw it: *Jesus is coming quickly...*[30] When Darby said people accepted that truth, he also meant they saw the need to enter into a "melancholy state."

Darby was quite militant in his views about the Imminent Advent of Christ. His view was very fundamental to his theology — if the second advent is soon, why be involved in *secular* activities? Though also holding to Darby's view, Müller was a sensible enough theologian not to make it an issue.[31]

Let us briefly mention six points derived from the idea of "Christ's imminent return." These points will be further developed as we proceed:

First, it is useless to work for things in the distant future.

Second, it is sin to be involved in such worldly pursuits as math, art, science, history and, of course, civil government. The imminent

---

29. *Writings,* II.164-165.
30. *Letters,* I.53, 55, 58. He rejoiced over the "awakening" in America as America started seeing things his way to be uninvolved in surrounding social matters, *e.g., Letters,* I.53, 55, 58, 1843, I.306, 336, 1862. Irving defined awakening as awakening to the soon coming of the Lord. Darby thus used Irivng's definition for awakening — awakening to his *truth* of just waiting for the Lord to come.
31. Coad, *History,* 156, 119.

return doctrine led to teaching that anything not having the immediate and direct *spiritual* result of winning souls is sinful.

Third, though it developed a tremendous evangelistic zeal, there was a corresponding zeal to withdraw from society. If Christians have only to wait for Christ's return, then the only Scriptural instruction needed is how to become personally more spiritual, and how to *win souls to Christ.* This teaching echoed the assertion made by the leaders of French Revolution — social concerns are the state's responsibility.[32]

Fourth, the system led to a new sin being defined and developed: any effort to convert the world was sin.[33] The millenarians' new idea of sin was a major influence in the great evangelistic explosion and missionary movement that took place from c. 1850 on. George Müller, a product of the Brethren movement, was one of the first major exporters of the new doctrine of sin. He was followed by such well known men as D.L. Moody and R.A. Torrey.

Fifth, the system taught that true unity and spirituality can only be obtained by renouncing all material possessions, stripping the Kingdom of God of wealth to carry on the work of Christ here on earth.[34] Thus a materially prosperous person cannot be a good Christian, which is, of course, a logical implication of "the imminent

---

32. The French Revolution, they believed, proved their point. Darby saw the church's mission not as converting the world to Christ, but spreading the message of his soon coming and the Christian's lack of earthly responsibility, *Writings,* II. 164, 165. The rough edges of the early Brethren's beliefs were smoothed, however, to make them palatable to American Christians.

33. *Writings,* II.185. Darby condemns "...mere evangelicism [sic], which, pretending to convert the world, mixes with the world it pretends to convert." *Letters,* I.257. See "Sin Defined" p. 361

34. Like Groves, Darby exalted poverty, teaching that true unity could only be accomplished when all material possessions were renounced. Coad, *History,* 33. However, Darby lived from the wealth left to him by an uncle. Recounting some 1847 events, Coad says: "The Bristol/Barnstaple leaders deduced their principles from Scripture, and seemed able to do so with the minimum of pre-conception. Darby, for all his attempt to do the same, seems perpetually to be imposing on Scripture a pre-conceived system of interpretation," *ibid,* 124. His system can be found in Scofield's notes and in far too many churches.

return of Christ." This teaching also echoes a basic premise of the French Revolution — poverty was proof of virtue and sincerity.

Finally, missionary endeavors were reduced to simply spreading knowledge and reaching as many as possible before the "Lord's soon return." The belief in "the imminent return of Christ" led the Brethren to change James' formula, *If the Lord will,* to a formula more in conformity to the new system, "If the Lord tarry."[35] Moreover, reaching others was many times simply persuading people to accept the millennial system of Christian thought.

The developers and propagators of the millennial system were convinced that the answers to the surrounding social ills of their day were to become more personally spiritual, win more souls and awaken other believers to the sin of being involved in *worldly, secular matters* — such involvement, they said, was a sin of faithlessness. Their belief caused them to further withdraw Christianity from society. (Prophecy was presented as a means of withdrawal.) The result of their view of *soul-winning* and withdrawal from social issues was increased social deterioration.[36] Then as they observed increased social deterioration, they withdrew even further rather than worked harder to increase Christian influence. Without the Christian salt and light, social conditions continued to deteriorate. The continued deterioration brought about by the Christians' withdrawal confirmed the system's view of prophecy — God must literally and supernaturally intervene in the affairs of man with a *rod of iron.* They saw that intervention as imminent because of the deterioration of society. Proof — The French Revolution.

---

35. Neatby, *History,* 228.
36. As Darby's view of the church and of the future gained popularity, he complained about deteriorating social conditions and increased acceptance of sin — which he saw as motivation to work harder to spread his message of withdrawal, *Letters,* II.307, from NY, 1874. Christianity was thus effectively neutralized as the Darbyites saw the social decay as proof of the imminent return of Christ to "rapture" his saints. Social decay, to them, meant they had nothing to worry about. *Cult,* 37. In fact, increased evil is a cause for rejoicing, for the "rapture" is near.

The prophecy conferences developed the millennial hope, but the men involved missed the obvious. The degeneration of society is not God's fault, although certainly history works his sovereign plan. Rather, degeneration is man's own fault for withdrawing the salt and light from the world.[37]

Chapter 58

Against the Future

Assuming Irving's argument against any hope for the future success of the gospel,

> ...Darby taught that the expectations of Christ's return '*totally forbids all working for earthly objects distinct in time*', including the pursuit of learning. But Darby evidently made this important exception: 'so far as any of these things might be made useful tools for immediate spiritual results.[38]

The Christian's attention was thus moved away from the promises of God in regard to the future to his present tumultuous circumstances. However, Scriptural faith is based on the future promises of God, not in present unpleasant circumstances.[39] Darby's argument was developed after his 1827 riding accident.

Darby associated spiritual peace with his departure from the previous eighteen centuries of developed orthodox theology, not with following God's word. He was

> 'a very exact churchman.'... The terms of Darby's own account show that he had practiced 'what is now called Puseyism' as a

---

37. Mat. 5:13-16, Hos. 13:9.
38. *Origins,* 52. Also forbidden is working for one's children's future.
39. The command of God that Moses was expected to obey in the face of impossible odds was based on a future promise of success. When Moses refused to believe that future promise of God, he made excuses. The result was the anger of God toward him. (Ex. 3:12; 4:14.) Can one likewise refuse to believe God's promises concerning the future and expect any different action today than what Moses received, or did God change?

layman,[40] but his statement that he passed out of the system at the time of his [riding] accident dates the transition c. 1827 rather than 1825. Darby did not regard this spiritual change as his evangelical conversion, which he placed six or seven years earlier, but as the time when realizing the truth of the union between the believer and Christ he came into the possession of spiritual peace.[41]

He argued for a soon return of Christ and against working for objects in the distant future. In fact, he took a strong stand against any education that might influence society for Christian law and order. His stand even led Darbyists to consider the study of mathematics a sin, for

> ...they firmly believed in the proximity of the Second Advent, and this belief coloured all their spiritual life, and was profoundly influential on their outward conduct.
> In private, it made them for many years markedly ascetic; and it was probably by far the most potent of the influences that withdrew them from all connection with public life, and that even led them to regard participation in politics as an act of treason against the heavenly calling of the Church. The late Professor Newman's account of his intercourse with Darby illustrates both tendencies. He writes as follows: "My study of the New Testament at this time had made it impossible for me to overlook that the apostles held it to be a duty of all disciples to expect a near and sudden destruction of the earth by fire, and constantly to be expecting the return of the Lord from heaven..."
> The importance of this doctrine, is, that it totally forbids all working for earthly objects distant in time; and here the Irish clergyman threw into the same scale the entire weight of his character. For instance, if a youth had a natural aptitude for mathematics, and he asked, ought he to give himself to the study, in hope that he might diffuse a serviceable knowledge of it, or possibly even enlarge the boundaries of the science — my friend would have

---

40. Neatby, *History*, 13. "I know the system [Puseyism]. I knew it and walked in it years before Dr. Newman, as I learn from his book, thought on the subject; and when Dr. Pusey was not heard of... I held apostolic succession fully, and the channels of grace to be there only. I held thus Luther and Calvin and their followers to be outside..." *Ibid.*, 13, 14.

41. *Origins*, 46. Pusey's writings can be found in *Barnes' Notes* on the Minor Prophets. "...It is clear from his correspondence that he passed through some great crisis of belief in 1825..." Neatby, *History*, 14.

replied, that such a purpose was very proper, if entertained by a worldly man. Let the dead bury their dead; and let the world study the things of the world... But such studies cannot be eagerly followed by the Christian, except when he yields to unbelief. In fact, what would it avail even to become a second La Place after thirty years' study, if in five and thirty years the Lord descended from heaven, snatched up all His saints to meet him, and burned to ashes all the works of the earth — ... [42]

However the hold which the apostolic belief then took of me, subjected my conscience to the exhortations of the Irish clergyman, whenever he inculcated that the highest Christian must necessarily decline the pursuit of science, knowledge, art, history, — except so far as any of these things might be made useful tools for immediate spiritual results."[43]

During his recovery, Darby came to the conclusion "that there was still an economy to come, of His ordering; a state of things in no way established as yet."[44]

Though not original with Darby, he was the most effective figure of the 1800s to stand against the prevalent Calvinistic view of his day concerning the millennium — Post. Reacting to the corruption

---

42. Darby said, "I am anxious about a rumour I heard of your becoming a doctor, and I am sure you will forgive my anxiety for the Lord's sake and yours.... I look to the principle... That is well.... But when I set about to learn a profession or trade, it is not merely the time, but Christ, and Christ's work, is put in a second place, and faith is set aside as to that, and the church encouraged in want of devotedness. All this seems to me evil..." *Letters,* II.6, 7. Also *Letters,* I.471. Though Darby held it sin to learn a trade, he allowed one to continue a trade if the person already had it before "conversion" to his opinions. Moreover, Darby considered taking a salary a sign of unbelief though his own "faith was never tried in that way, as an uncle left me something before I was run out [of funds, *ed.*], or very soon after..." *Ibid,* 7. Brethren evangelists lived on very meager fare, *e.g.,* "... a devoted pioneer, who pushed into unbroken ground in France. He fed on nettle tops, which they use much as spinach, not to give up an open door..." *Ibid.* From Barbados, Darby rejoiced that many people came to understand that serving Christ and learning "a profession or trade," did not mix. *Ibid.,* 8. Nor was it original with Irving. Edwards had taught it many years earlier.

43. Neatby, *History,* 40, 41. Obviously, these men used the Lord's words telling of his imminent return in judgment against the wicked men of Jerusalem who killed him — Mat. 21:41 — for his return in judgment of the whole world.

44. *Roots,* 33. Darby's letter (*Letters,* III.297-305) summing up his life and calling, including his accident, is in App. A.

he identified in other churches, he further developed, added to and spread to the far reaches of the earth, the theory "That the Christian era would be terminated by the exhibition of divine vengeance."

Darby's study of unfulfilled prophecy "brought about his conviction that the Kingdom of God would be established on earth as a result, not of the exertions of men on its behalf, but of the direct intervention of Christ Himself, and that in judgment combined with the belief that the Jewish nation rather than the Christian church was the instrument which God would use for the establishing of His kingdom on earth, to discredit the concept of the established church."[45] Darby's theory that only "the direct intervention of Christ Himself..." simply renewed the Jewish hope that the Messiah would return and again exalt the Jewish nation, Zionism.

The basic premise is established: abandon all hope that the Church of the Lord Jesus Christ on earth can bring about any lasting social change through the preaching of the Christian gospel. These early men saw society's only hope as Christ's return in wrath and judgment,[46] which became a plank to be developed by the millenarians. They turned society over to the ungodly.

Ernest Sandeen gives a good reason for and summation of Darby's theology after his accident in 1827:

> In opposition to the worldliness of the church, Darby advocated a church so spiritual that it existed outside of history. The church in this new dispensation of grace was so much a mystery that it had been hidden even from the prophets of the Old Testament, Israel had been a worldly kingdom with material promises and blessings. The Messiah had come to fulfill that worldly kingdom but had been rejected by his people. When that happened, God had broken the continuity of history, stopped the prophetic clock, and instituted the church. When the church is raptured out of the world, this clock will start again and God will return to the task of dealing with the earthly

---

45. *Ibid.,* 52, 53. He taught it was a sin to attempt to convert the world to Christ. He strongly implied that those who did not see the end as he did — only hope is Christ's literal return — were caught in the devil's lie, *Writings,* II.83. He leveled that charge against Newton.
46. *Roots,* 13.

problems of Israel. Only then will the final events predicted in Daniel — the events of the seventieth week — occur. Since for Darby the ministry of Jesus was divided into two parts (his early appeal to the Jews as earthly Messiah and his later role as founder of the church), the exegesis of the Gospel required a careful separation of passages referring to Jewish or to churchly promises and admonitions. The task of the expositor of the Bible was, in a phrase that became the hallmark of dispensationalism, "rightly dividing the word of truth."[47]

Concerning 2 Timothy 2:15, Scofield said,

> The Word of Truth, then, has right divisions, and it must be evident that, as one cannot be "a workman that needeth not be ashamed" without observing them, so *any study* of that Word which ignores those divisions must be in large measure profitless and confusing. Many Christians freely confess that they find the study of the Bible weary work. More find it so, who are ashamed to make the confession.[48]

Dispensationalism requires careful division of passages from their contextual meaning by, in Spurgeon's words, "shuffling texts of Scripture as the Norwood gypsies shuffled cards in days gone by." Those who fail to understand Scripture as required by the dispensational faith are many times accused of being unable to "rightly divide the word of truth."

---

47. *Ibid*, 67. Hengstenberg: "Let us examine now, in what sense the building of a temple is ascribed to the Messiah. Under the Old Testament, the temple was the seat of the kingdom of God; it was in this, and not in the walls, or any other outward thing connected with it, that the very idea of the temple consisted. And for that reason, it was admirably adopted to be the type and figurative representation of the kingdom of God itself, that is of the Church, which did not commence with the coming of Christ, but was essentially the same under both the Old and New Testaments.* (*"The temple of God is one, namely the Church of the saved, originating in the promise given in paradise, and lasting to the end of the world." *Cocceius*.) Solomon and Zerubbabel had helped to build this temple; inasmuch as their outward efforts proceeded from faith, and was directed not to the outward edifice, to the shell merely, but to the kernel, which continued to exit, when the shell had long been destroyed." *Christology*, 998. Is it any wonder these early Brethren had to cut themselves off from all past development of Scripture — Reese attributes the term referring to "the Blessed Hope" as immunity from the Great Tribulation to the Darbyite movement, *Advent*, 28.

48. *Rightly Dividing the Word of Truth*, 3. Emp. his.

Chapter 59

Zeal Corrupted

The prospect of the soon return of Christ translated into an evangelistic zeal to take Christ into all the world and to waken sleeping Christians to their peril of imminent judgment.[49] Their soul-saving zeal took the forceful millenarian preachers into all the world, but included with their soul-saving zeal was zeal against godly efforts for things in the distant future. Their zeal against working for "earthly objects distant in time" spelled disaster for the cause of Christ as their new gospel was spread by fiery young men. The obvious result of their millennial message was a neutralized Christianity. Many zealous, elite, wealthy and well educated intellectuals were attracted by the millenarians' zeal.[50]

Darby's argument against working for things in the distant future was passed from Darby to Newton, whom he had never met, by Newton's private tutor, F.M. Newman. Apparently, Darby's ideas did not yet contain his thoughts on a secret rapture, for when Darby introduced the novel idea a few years later, Newton stood against it.[51]

Understanding the millennial idea as a major Bible doctrine to be studied and sought out, Newton's whole life was turned; his new-

---

49. *Roots,* xxi. Compare this with the command to go into all the world to teach all nations the totality of God's word, and thus subdue all things to the Lord by applying his word to everything. Darbyism spread rapidly, but it grew by proselytizing — that is, by converting multitudes of Christians to its millennial system. Irving's chief concern in his *Dedication* was that sleeping Christians would be awakened to the soon return of Christ. It was not with the conversion of sinners.

50. Coad, *History,* 178.

51. "[Newton] Held a place of influence in the Plymouth 'gathering' until 1845 when he and Mr. Darby came to a definite variance with each other as regards prophetic teaching (especially the 'secret rapture' theory of Darby) and Church order." *Who,* s.v. "Newton, Benjamin Wills." Darby had many very harsh words to say against Newton after the split, *q.v.*

found zeal for prophecy, soul-saving and withdrawal from society was spread to everyone he met, *e.g.*, J.L. Harris and Dr. William Marsh.[52]

Chapter 60

Church with no Earthly Function

During this time, the Church of England was in a bitter conflict with the Romanists. In 1827, Archbishop Magee of Dublin asked Parliament to require all converts from the Church of Rome, "600 to 800 a week," to take oaths of allegiance and supremacy to the Anglican Church. Darby's riding accident gave him plenty of time to think about the required oath of allegiance. His reaction was to say that the church had no business being in any way involved with such worldly matters.[53] He saw the church as a "heavenly society" with really very little if any earthly function. In Darby was "a young curate of short experience but strong conviction..." His response to Magee's move was to print and circulate his protest: "In his paper, he deprecated the appeal to the secular power on the ground that the church is a heavenly society."[54] "...There is a spiritual supremacy independent of civil government; the spiritual supremacy of Christ, of which the clergy are ministers — not an earthly dominion, but the very contrary..."[55]

Certainly, the Anglican Church was wrong to influence parliament to enforce the oath, yet the reaction to its move by Darby and his followers was just as wrong when they said that the Church

---

52. *Origins*, 58-69. Mr. Rowdon presents the information found in the Fry MS, a manuscript in the possession of Mr. C.E. Fry of Newport, Isle of Wight. It was written by Mr. Fry to preserve the tradition of Newton's teaching after his death. It was compiled from several sources, including letters and Newton's written papers. MacPherson refers to it also.
53. Coad, *History*, 27.
54. *Origins*, 47.
55. Neatby, *History*, 16.

Development and Doctrine 223

has no business whatsoever in worldly matters.[56] Their early conviction was not developed from Scriptures. Rather, it developed in reaction to the battle between the Anglican and Roman Churches for temporal power and influence. Consequently, there was no solid Scriptural Plum-Line to prevent the pendulum from swinging to the other extreme — from total involvement in and fighting over temporal power (Anglicans and Romanists) to total uninvolvement (millenarians).

The conflict between the Anglican and Roman Churches only strengthened Darby's hostility against the established churches and all they stood for. There were a great many others who shared Darby's disdain for the established religions, starting him on his long and successful path of separating the church (Christianity) from all worldly matters — "Separation of Church and State."[57]

Darby misused Christ's words — when Christ said that his kingdom is not of this world, Christ did not mean that his Kingdom is *not in this world.* Darby neutralized Christian resistance to tyranny:

> In a highly informative book about the Conspiracy entitled "Karl Marx, Capitalist", June Germ observed in 1972 concerning religious neutralism: "Although much of the Bible has been challenged by agnostics and antagonists, it is of more than a passing significance that this one issue should be singled out for unswerving acceptance. Christ said His Kingdom was not of this world but the political manipulators who are promoting world government use every method imaginable to con people into accepting the idea of global dictatorship. They will even attempt to make it look like Bible prophecy, if possible."[58]

---

56. Darby was dogmatic that one cannot be involved in *worldly matters* and religion without denying Christ, *Writings,* II.451, 476. He strongly condemned any worldly goods, *Ibid.,* 575.

57. *Origins,* 44. Darby wrote, "So far as men pride themselves on being Established, Presbyterian, Baptist, Independent, or anything else, they are anti-Christian." Neatby, *History,* 33. This author is against a church controlled state; however, he is for the church training Christian men to exercise proper civil leadership in offices of authority.

58. *Cult,* 52.

224 *Death of the Church Victorious*

The idea that Christians are *not of this world* was thus misused in an attempt to persuade the Christian community that worldly affairs were not important to them – they are as strangers in a strange community. The idea was used to help neutralize Christian resistance to those promoting world government.

Chapter 61
Just Wait

While recuperating from his riding accident and with the conflict between the established churches heavy on his mind, Darby put together his basic opinions; some extremely important views develped

> The Christian, having his place in Christ in heaven, has nothing to wait for save the coming of the Saviour, in order to be set, in fact, in the glory which is already his portion in Christ.[59]

Darby's view of Christian duty left the traditional concept of the church, and replaced it with his "characteristic mystical insight." His view, therefore, that Christian duty is simply to wait for Christ's return was not based upon Scripture, but upon his typical "mystical insight." "Was there not all the material here for a merely ascetic definition of Christianity, and for a still more frightening recurrence of that spirit of 'he followeth not with us' which Darby himself had condemned?"[60] Darby took the material, and he turned Christianity into little more than an ascetic, "mystical experience" which is still very much with us today:

> Thus, in the only practical hint he had to give, conformity to the death of Christ was equated by implication with asceticism, with an

---

59. *Letters,* III.298. See also Coad *History,* 28. When one attempts to put the dates together concerning what Darby claimed and what actually happened, they do not work out properly.

60. Coad, *History,* 33. "Mystical" — action based upon *intuition* and *insight* rather than on God's word.

outlook that rejected the material for the spiritual... He had given a theological and mystical answer to a matter of practical Church action — with no plain indication as to how that devotional answer is to be translated into deed.[61]

Neatby ably describes Darby's ability:

> In 1828, when, as already related, he issued the first document of the new movement, *Considerations on the Nature and Unity of the Church of Christ,* he failed as signally as Cronin to raise any definite issue. The tract is an appeal to Christian feeling against the divisions of the Church. As such it is far from contemptible. The tone is fervent and lofty, and though the style is not good, there are passages of no little dignity and beauty. The characteristic faults of the author's later polemical writings are scarcely, if at all, to be found. He is not censorious or Pharisaical; he writes in no spirit of detachment from the Church he condemns, and when he speaks of the virtues with which the denominations were adorned he appears to bear his witness with cordiality. But we look in vain either for any thorough analysis of the evil complained of, or for an intelligible suggestion of any possible remedy.[62]

The millennial system's only answer to the turmoil of the world was to wait for the Lord to come straighten it out.

Examples: Darby's only answer for distressed souls was otherworldliness — hope for Christ's imminent return, and that the distressed person should "Occupy yourselves with Christ..." We belong to another world, we feel dead and risen with Christ; therefore, said Darby in answer to life's difficulties, we are detached from problems here. He could see nothing from Scriptures except "heavenly things," so his only answer to problems of life was that we are in heaven with Christ — *don't worry, be happy.* In fact, the surrounding social troubles only motivated him to become more mystical, *i.e.,* detached from the world, urging the saints to occupy themselves more with Christ's suffering. When feeling pressed, said Darby, look away to Christ at once.[63] With no practical answers, he could only emphasize the necessity of a life of self-denial, stressing

---

61. *Ibid.* "Mystical experience" — what makes one feel good vs. what is required by God.
62. Neatby, *History,* 30-31.

the Holy Spirit.[64] However, the self-denial of these early developers of modern dispensationalism was not nevertheless, not my will but Thine be done (self-denial for the Lord's will). Rather, self-denial to them meant denial of material goods as they reacted against the lust for material goods they perceived in other churches.

With no practical answers to the degenerate conditions of society around them, the dispensationalists had no choice but to make Christianity an emotional experience.

Presenting problems with no sound solutions leads to even greater problems. The distressed seekers, though sincere, are left open for many harmful influences, as happened in the French Revolution:

> While some of his fellow deputies squirmed and others leaned forward in genuine interest, Robespierre would proceed to apply the reasoning of Rousseau to the situation; to stress equality of the People, the rights and needs of the People, and in general to claim the People as his special constituency. Michelet, irritated even after the passage of years, said, "He said what ought to be done but rarely, very rarely, how one ought to do it."[65]

If Bible believing churches and preachers see only problems and no answers of hope from God's word for the surrounding social chaos, then they only have two messages for their people in order to have something to preach: First, how to become more spiritual (dealing with the inner man), which would include prayer, Bible reading, *soul-winning,* and being more like Christ in his death. Their second message must, therefore, emphasize eschatology, future events, the end-time, and the return of Christ to deliver his people from the hopelessness of the present life. These two messages are also the logical implication of the *imminent return,* for preachers have no need to deal with social issues. The primary concern, therefore, of

---

63. *Writings,* II.419ff.; *Letters,* III.8, 35, 52, 57, 82, 88, 157. This pastor was told by a *Christian*: "I praise the Lord that things are getting bad. That means the Lord will soon come back to get us."

64. *Origins,* 48, 49.

65. *Robespierre,* 73.

religion is little more than the happiness, prosperity and salvation of individual souls. The gospel of the Lord Jesus Christ is thus destitute of any need for social concern.

Under Darby, the church was given supposed Scriptural grounds to accept the new religion developed in the Revolution only a few years previously — the religion of Patriotism replaced the Christian Gospel of Christ. Man is a hopeless sinner and the church is ruined, so there is no hope of a general spiritual Christian victory over the whole world. Therefore, patriotic action is the social changing force rather than the gospel of Christ.[66]

Chapter 62

Unity in Death

The name of the Lord is the center of unity; Christ's death is the rallying-point of communion; conformity to Christ's death in terms of a life of self-giving is the pre-requisite for unity; believers should live in the light of the approaching return of Christ.[67]

A main emphasis in the system was Christ's death. It offered very little, if any, teaching on his life of victory over the world, flesh and devil in this present life through his people. Christ's ascension to his Father's right hand far above all principalities, powers and every name that is named was at least ignored, if not outright denied. The message of no possible victory in this life against the gates of hell led to a totally spiritualized view of Christianity. Strong took a very strong stand against "the premillennial theory," saying that it

> ...begets a passive and hopeless endurance of evil, whereas the Scriptures enjoin a constant and aggressive warfare against it, upon

---

66. Though one of the most remembered theories of Darby is his "ruin of the church," the idea is based upon Lacunza's *seven church ages in Revelation* theory, which was later promoted by Irving, and both well before Darby claims the idea in 1827, at the earliest. However, Darby certainly popularized the idea of defeat.
67. *Origins,* 48.

the very ground that God's power shall assure to the church a gradual but constant progress in the face of it, even to the time of the end.... In both these figures [Dan. 2:34, 35 & Mat. 13:31, 32, *ed.*] there is no sign of cessation or of backward movement, but rather every indication of continuous advance to complete victory and dominion. The premillennial theory supposes that for the principle of development under the dispensation of the Holy Spirit, God will substitute a reign of mere power and violence. J.B. Thomas: "The kingdom of heaven is like a grain of mustard seed, not like a can of nitro-glycerine." Leighton Williams: "The kingdom of God is to be realized on earth, not by a cataclysm, apart from effort and will, but through the universal dissemination of the gospel all but lost to the world." E. G. Robinson: "Second Adventism stultifies the system and scheme of Christianity." Dr. A. J. Gordon could not deny that the early disciples were mistaken in expecting the end of the world in their day. So we may be.... Yet a just view of Christ's coming as ever possible in the immediate future may make us as faithful as were the original disciples.

The theory also divests Christ of all kingly power until the millennium, or, rather, maintains that the kingdom has not yet been given to him.... On the effects of the premillennial view in weakening Christian endeavor, see J.H. Seelye, Christian Missions, 94-127; *per contra,* see A.J. Gordon, in Independent, Feb. 1886.[68]

Christianity today appears to be living in the death of Christ as it sits back as a dead person — that is, dead to the surrounding social chaos with no desire to bring order out of that chaos through the applied word of God. We should not be surprised at modern society's fascination with death — it simply reflects the average Christian's fascination with death and heaven rather than what he should be fascinated with, life and service to God and his fellow man.

---

68. *Systematic Theology,* 1012, 1013.

Chapter 63

Developing Doctrine

The unity desired by the millenarians was not around the preaching and teaching of God's word and sound doctrine — breaking of Spiritual Bread — but around the Lord's Supper — breaking of physical bread. A professed reason for departure from the Anglican Church was over its closed communion, not over its doctrine.[69] However, we know that a major premise of the movement was against any strict doctrinal stand. Such a basis of unity left the movement extremely vulnerable to shallow, curious and new unorthodox ideas in the name of Christianity.

The early Brethren meetings played an important role in the development and spread of their millennial opinions. Arriving in Vevey, Switzerland, in early 1838, Darby established a permanent meeting. Two years later, March, 1840, he "got a footing in the far larger and more important town of Lausanne." His "keen eye to favouring circumstances" enabled his influence to "spread with startling rapidity over the whole of the Canton and far beyond", largely by aid of tracts. J.J. Herzog, a professor in the Anglican Church's Theological College at Lausanne, points out that Darbyism worked at "ecclesiastical levelling" — reducing ordained ministers to the level of the average layman.[70]

Spring of 1841 saw a local Lausanne Methodist pastor, Henri Olivier, renounce Methodism, and "unite his flock to Darby's." Henri's brother, Francois Olivier, not being "wholly satisfied with the course things were taking... began in the winter of 1842-3 to hold meetings independently of Darby." Though Oliver planned his meetings not to interfere with Darby's, Darby was less than pleasant toward him, probably because Francois "Oliver was a rival on the spot."

---

69. Coad, *History*, 30.
70. Neatby, *History*, 83.

Oliver, who had watched the experiment for a long time at Lausanne, charged the worship with vagueness and uncertainty; complained of "frequent, prolonged, freezing pauses"; of a "want of Christian dignity in the attitude" of the worshippers, and "especially in the observance of the Lord's Supper"; of a lack of teaching, owing in part to a scruple about preparing beforehand — a scruple that gave rise, in Olivier's opinion, to "discourses deficient in compass, offending either by a defect in ripeness and fullness, or by a constant and extremely wearisome recurrence of favorite ideas". He considered (as many perfectly friendly observers have done since) that the meetings of the Brethren, in order to be profitable, generally required the presence of some persons of commanding superiority. Darby, in reply, did not deny these blemishes; indeed he seems to allow that there was truth in the allegations...[71]

Accordingly, the new theological system was not a result of in-depth study of Scripture, for prepared studies were forbidden. Rather, the power of the system depended upon the commanding personalities of the speakers. The implications of such methods of teaching are too obvious to develop.

About this time, there was a tremendous amount of speculation concerning the Lord's second advent. Darby's tract, issued at the beginning and spelling out the basic theology of the millennial movement, emphasized not only the death of Christ, but made special reference to his approaching return.

Darby watered the already planted the seed — Lacunza's imminent return teaching. Because of the chaotic state of affairs and the unwillingness — or inability — of the church in general to deal with the chaos (nor could Darby deal with it), it was to be expected that the attention of some of the clergy would be "turned to the eschatological hope which was being proclaimed from the

---

71. *Ibid.*, 85, 86, 92. Oliver's observation leads one to believe that a reason the early leaders were so antagonistic against preparation, scholarship, leadership, &c., in individual assemblies was that such things could undermine their authority in the Brethren assemblies and ability to lead the assemblies in the way they wanted them to develop.

housetops."⁷² Lacunza's seed has indeed brought forth some exotic fruit in the Protestant Church.

Chapter 64

Prophecy and the Church

The system's answer to the social ills was not practical action from and application of God's law-gospel. Its answer was to withdraw from those ills by studying prophetic Scripture and becoming more spiritual while conforming more to the death of Christ. Darby had nothing from God: "He had given a theological and mystical answer to a matter of practical church action — with no plain indication as to how that devotional answer is to be translated into deed."⁷³ Concluding his study on Revelation 8, Darby said,

> It is absolutely necessary that we should renounce everything. We shall have to do so sooner or later, either with joy by the Spirit of Christ, or with shame when the judgments of God shall break every tie that is still keeping us back. We must then leave everything, or else be burnt up with Sodom. Prophecy has a special power to separate us from this present evil world, which the patience of God can bear, because He is taking His own out of it, but which is judged already nevertheless.⁷⁴

It was not Scriptural soundness that caused Darby's theories to be accepted and enabled him to win debates. Rather, it was his force of character, tone of voice and power over men.⁷⁵ His tremendous self-sacrifice was his greatest influence. His thoughts were rarely systematic, and his approach to truth was subjective as he searched Scripture to support theories such as the "ruin of the church."⁷⁶

---

72. *Origins,* 49.
73. Coad, *History,* 33. That is, the answer is to become more emotionally detached from the problems, or an answer to make one feel good.
74. *Writings,* II.44.
75. Coad, *History,* 142.

To say that the true church is now invisible, Darby continued, is an admission of its apostasy and departure from its true condition. He was equally firm in his repudiation of the gathered church idea, for two reasons which go to the heart of his thinking. First, he declared, the state of things pictured in the New Testament has ceased to exist, and no authority or power is given by God to restore the failed economy. The church is in ruins, and to attempt to re-establish pure churches is an act of presumption...[77]

Thus Darby's *mystical insight* caused him to teach, among other things, that the true church can only be visible (his church obviously). Because the earthly church failed, it has only judgment against it. Therefore, there is no hope of the church being restored in strength, and any such attempt is useless, even sin. Darby placed the church between Daniel's 69th & 70th week where, according to his theory, prophecy is suspended.[78] The Christian church is in ruins, he contended, so God must spew it out and reestablish Israel — a Jewish church — to complete his work on earth.[79] His theory was based upon what he felt, his *mystical insight,* rather than upon reason or sound Biblical exegesis.

Darby stated his millennial hope thusly:

> Through prophecy we feel our nearness to him, and our faith in him is strengthened and our sanctification is increased and established... For the Christian is informed of the result of the politics of this world, and, being "warned of things not seen as yet," he separates himself, whether in heart or in action, from all that of which the *denouement* will be so sad. Besides, an acquaintance beforehand with all that is to take place keeps him tranquil and composed. There is no need that he should give his heart to the world with surrounds him, for he knows by the written revelation of God both its course and its end.[80]

---

76. *Ibid.*, 124.
77. *Ibid.*, 127.
78. *Writings,* II.361, 585.
79. Coad, *History,* 126. *Writings,* II.266.
80. *Writings,* II.193, 194.

Development and Doctrine 233

In other words, God is going to straighten sin's mess all out someday, so the Christian, knowing prophecy, remains totally unconcerned, *mystical*, about the conditions around him:

> ...[T]he Lord's coming is not a question of prophecy, but my present hope. Events before His judging the quick are the subject of prophecy; His coming to receive the church is our present, heavenly hope... The government of the world is another thing; prophecy lights up that as a candle in a dark place.[81]

Prophetic study, hence, causes Christians to be unconcerned about society's ills, *mystical*. All the early major figures in the movement had Darby's philosophy. They used their great abilities to reform Christianity from victory — go and claim every area of life and thought for Christ — to pietism-mysticism — become more *personally spiritual* and wait. (See "Pietism" p. 459.) The movement produced a great many Bible conferences for the sole purpose of learning how to become more spiritual, deal with the inner-self and study prophecy. The founding millenarians purposely avoided any social application of the gospel as they waited to be *snatched from the present evil age*. Their gospel of *wait to be snatched away* attracted vast multitudes who fled from their Christian responsibility to stand against evil and conquer all things for Christ and his Kingdom through preaching and teaching the Christian gospel.

Strong's warning fits well at this point:

> ...The fact that every age since Christ ascended has had its Chiliast and Second Adventists should turn our thoughts away from curious and fruitless prying into the time of Christ's coming, and set us at immediate and constant endeavor to be ready, at whatsoever hour he may appear.[82]

Darby's thinking could not be followed from Scripture, for "his doctrine was chaotic." Nor did he have Scriptural answers for the

---

81. *Letters*, I.329, 330.
82. *Systematic Theology*, 1008. On the wickedness of "curious and fruitless prying into the future," see: *Ezekiel*, Fairbairn, 209, 210, 221, 222. On Deut. 29:29, see comments by Geneva & John Gill (*Online Bible*); Joseph Parker, *Preaching Through the Bible*, IV.325-332; and *Matthew Henry's Commentary*, I.850. See quote by Spurgeon, *q.v.*

difficulties and questions he raised. He had to be accepted by faith, not by Scriptural standards.[83] Yet this man's chaotic doctrine is taught in almost every Protestant Bible school and controls the vast majority of missionary endeavors of our day.

Chapter 65

Darby vs. Newton

Around 1847, some of Darby's best friends, including Newton, separated from him, believing that he was departing from historic Christian orthodoxy.[84] Newton held that Darby was not subject to the word of God, and that he could not Scripturally defend his system of theology, especially the new, any moment, secret rapture theory:

> ...Newton posed the question, 'Is the church directed in Scripture to expect a secret coming of the Lord Jesus Christ —' and answered with a resounding no. Claiming that it was a new doctrine, he stated, 'the whole testimony of Scripture is against it.' The church had never anticipated the return of Christ at any moment, Newton argued, for the apostles themselves had clear intimations of intervening events, such as the predictions of Peter's death in John 21 and 2 Peter 1. Furthermore, the Scriptures themselves contain the refutation of the idea of a secret rapture, Newton claimed, as he turned by way of illustration to the parable of the wheat and tares in Matthew 13 where Jesus said, 'Let both grow together until the harvest.' If one accepted Darby's view of the secret rapture and any moment coming, Newton pointed out, then many Gospel passages must be 'renounced as not properly ours.'[85]

Unable to defend his system, Darby had to embrace a radical dispensational teaching to support his ideas. His "exegetical problems... forced him to adopt the radical solution of consigning

---

83. Coad, *History*, 33, 106, 111.
84. *Ibid.*, *History*, 136.
85. *"Five letters* (London, 1877), 72-73." *Roots,* 65, 66.

some parts of the New Testament exclusively to the Jews and others exclusively to the church." Dispensationalism was shared by many, including many of Darby's opponents, some of whom were not millenarians. Darby's uniqueness was his rapture theory and the radical dispensationalism he developed in its defence.[86]

Though the Brethren movement claimed to be built on toleration, when Newton challenged Darby's Scriptural soundness over the pre-trib rapture, Darby retaliated not by Scripturally defending his position, but by charging Newton with moral dishonesty. Darby, with some followers, then devoted the next ten years to destroying Newton, using many unscriptural means to accomplish the task. V. G. Wigram — *The New Englishman's Hebrew & Greek Concordances*, who was not a theologian — sided with Darby while Dr. Tregelles told Wigram that he, Wigram, had acted wickedly in the matter. Darby, who sought Müller's support against Newton, was told by Müller, "I have this moment only ten minutes' time, having an important engagement before me; and as you have acted so wickedly in this matter, I cannot *now* enter upon it, as I have no time."[87]

An expert at making generalized statements with no substance, it was Darby's overwhelming personal character (his "power over a public assembly," which included a trait of not giving up on an issue unless he came out victor) that prevailed over Newton, not his Scriptural soundness. His inability to address distressing situations and circumstances from the word of God reveals that he understood

---

86. *Roots,* 67, 68. The *dispensational* system was not new with Darby. Others had started a new *dispensation* after Rev. 4:1.

87. Neatby, *History,* 124, 176. Neatby records the whole wicked matter, 106-190. Müller was a key man in the Brethren movement, imbibing all their doctrine several years previously. Darby's tirades against Newton for not following Darby's thinking are worth recounting — Darby calls him a liar and a heretic, accusing Newton of being wicked, blasphemous, evil and an enemy of the soul, just to name a few epithets hurled by Darby, *Letters,* I.88, 120, 162, 175, 200, 201, 269, 270, 433, 441, 443-4, 478-9, 482, 496, *ibid,* II.223. Darby traveled the country seeking other Brethren assemblies to agree with his charges against Newton, never once abiding by Mat. 18, nor defending his position from Scripture.

nothing of textural criticism. His traits are not uncommon today among the followers of his system.

Part VII
World-Wide Conquest

Chapter 66
The Foundation of Conquest

Though not a prevalent system, millenarianism had been public domain since earliest church history. After many centuries of inactivity, the time was right, and the system was revived. From Lacunza to Irving to Albury Park to Powerscourt — where it acquired a new wrinkle, a pre-trib rapture — the system traveled, gaining much enthusiastic support. It left the Powerscourt prophecy conferences under a new leader, J.N. Darby, and with a new name, Darbyism. It went on to inundate Christianity as notes in the *Scofield Study Bible*. The rapid, world-wide acceptance of the system is quite amazing.

"Escape into prophecy to avoid Christian responsibility to win the world for Christ," appears to contradict the obvious fact that the millenarians were extremely zealous evangelistically. However, the millennial movement did not grow through Christian conversions; rather, it grew through proselytism:

> Proselytism is a recognised principle with the Brethren — a principle openly avowed. The Church, according to their view, is in ruins, and their mission is to gather together its scattered members under the banner of Brethrenism. Nor are they at all scrupulous in the accomplishment of their object.[1]

---

1. "Rev. William Reid, DD., *Plymouth Brethrenism Unveiled and Refuted* (Edinburgh: Wm. Oliphant &Co, 1880)." Quoted in *Plot,* 144. Brethren infiltrated established churches to undermine pastors and win the congregation to their way of thinking: "Not a few ministers by means such as these, have been driven from the scene of their labours, and the gathering of the Brethren has taken the place of a properly constituted dispensation of Divine ordinances (p. 13)." *Ibid.,* 144.

Their zeal took them and their message of *Christian Escape* and *otherworldliness* world-wide, seemingly overnight. Christians loved and gladly accepted the theory, for it released them from their responsibility to convert the world to Christ by hard work and preaching the Christian Gospel. Examining the millenarians' ideas, we easily answer the apparent contradiction of zealous evangelism and *Christian Escape* from responsibility to evangelize (Christianize) the world. The pieces come together when we consider a primary reason why Müller started his mission outreach organization — other institutions "had as their object the conversion of the world, an object which Müller had not been able to find in Scripture."[2] Müller's militancy against any idea that the gospel could convert the world was common to the early millenarians.

Müller is best known for his work among England's orphans. In praising his work, we tend to overlook a precedent he established:

> Yet the overriding consideration in Müller's mind was the conviction that the success of such a project as he had in mind would be a testimonial to the faithfulness of God in answering prayer. He felt that he had a particular gift *'in being able to take God at His word and to rely upon it'* and that if he 'a poor man, simply by prayer and faith, obtained, *without asking any individual,* the means for establishing and carrying on an Orphan House: there would be something which, with the Lord's blessing, might be instrumental in strengthening the faith of the children of God, besides being a testimony to the consciences of the unconverted, of the reality of the things of God'. In the event, it became possible to speak of Müller's orphanages as a witness to the power of prayer in a day of unbelief and materialism.[3]

Not down-playing the importance of faith and prayer, we wish to note that Müller identified the Christian faith as an ecstatic, mystical experience of feeling. He separated Christianity from active obedience to the total of God's word in order to receive God's blessings. (1 Jn. 3:22.) Müller, regarded as the apex of Christian faith, thus removed the blessings and curses of Deuteronomy

---

2. *Origins*, 129.
3. *Ibid,* 131.

chapters 28, 29, from Christianity.[4] Müller's vow against debt is certainly in accord with Romans 13:8, yet how many claim to follow Müller's faith while disregarding Romans 13:8. They claim Müller's faith to repay the debts incurred contrary to God's established laws.

Müller noted "with implicit approval, the gift of £10 from one who had put the money into a saving bank against sickness or old age but had come to see that he should give it away and trust God for the eventualities of life."[5] Did not Groves take the same attitude some years earlier?

The spread of the system is quite interesting and significant; it must be attributed to the unusual and tremendous zeal of its developers.

The intentional ignorance of orthodox Christian teaching led to several seriously destructive worms in the seed of the powerful movement that conquered the church. Among the many worms were: other-worldliness; withdrawal from society and social responsibilities by retreating into prophetic speculations; pacifism; Imminent Advent of Christ, withdrawing Christian salt and light from society;[6] the ruin of the church; and new definitions of sin, *e.g.*, any attempt to purify the church or win the world to Christ. Probably the most serious worm was the use of strong, persuasive personalities, tremendous zeal and sometimes wild human reason to influence others, *e.g.*, "This is the way we feel it should be, so now let's find Scripture to justify these new theories concerning God's Revelation to man." The system's supposed church/Israel distinction led to the heretical idea of two approaches to the Heavenly Father — offering one approach for the Gentiles, the work of Christ, and one approach for the Jews, the renewed sacrifices. Thus Christ's finished work was only for the Gentiles.[7]

---

4. See Heb. 4:11, margin, Ps. 1 and Josh. 1:7, 8.
5. *Ibid*, 133.
6. Darby set Christ's return date as 1842, Coad, *History,* 119. Date setting has been and is a common millenniarian trait.
7. See *Letters,* II.51, 52.

All these worms, and more, were combined with tremendous zeal for evangelism — that is, proselytizing people out of the ruined, non-millennial churches. Then the seeds of the millennial system were sown throughout the world in the name of Biblical Christianity. We see around us the fruits of the seeds. Though resisted by many orthodox Christian leaders at the time of Irving's introduction, Christian Monasticism (withdrawal) now dominates Christian life and thought.

Chapter 67

Primary Areas of Conquest

Through extensive immigration during the latter part of the Nineteenth Century, the millennial system went into every English speaking nation, especially into North America. For practical reasons (they wanted to keep their people), the American church rejected the "ruin of the church" idea. The results of the system are obvious in these nations today.

Millenarian authors filled the new millennial hunger for Christian literature.[8] Furthermore, this period of time saw Müller's Scriptural Knowledge Institution expanding its reach world-wide, including into the West Indies. Its expansion insured the spread of Müller's basic teachings — any attempt to win the world for Christ is sin, the theory of withdrawal to become more spiritual, prayer with no mention of obedience for claiming God's promises, and the new millenarian prophetic system.[9]

From the beginning, millenarians stood strong against any political involvement.[10] With the zeal and energy that found outlets in Brethrenism and the natural appeal of the new millennial system,

---

8. Coad, *History,* 192-193.
9. *Ibid.,* 198.

the system spread like wild-fire, influencing everyone it touched with its dogmatic monasticism.

Many British Isles Baptists and Mennonite were closely identified with the Brethren — the influence was especially strong upon Baptists. Most of the strong Calvinistic churches stood against Darby's influence, but many others were not so wise.[11] The Congregational and Pentecostal denominations fell to Darbyism also, more out of self-defense (to keep their people who loved the new system) than anything else. The early millenarians intentionally undermined the established churches, including the Anglican, Baptist and Presbyterian, robbing them "of the *elite* of the flocks."[12]

The Brethren's missionary zeal was first and foremost a missionary zeal to convert the saved to its millennial system. Its zeal was also toward *soul-saving* and persuading its converts into a monastic attitude of withdrawal. Christian growth in maturity, it held, was growth in unconcern about matters going on in society.[13]

Three areas into which the early millennial movement spread with great influence were: 1) Germany — Müller; 2) India — Groves; 3) Switzerland — Darby: Canton de Vaud was his area of influence c. 1838-40.

Germany

In May, 1843, Müller received a letter from a lady at Stuttgart to whom he had recently been serviceable when she was on a visit to

---

10. *Ibid.,* 206. Darby was very dogmatic in his condemnation of American involvement in politics, *Letters,* I.402, 1865. In fact, he considered voting a sin, and God would provide sufficient grace to prevent one from committing the *voting* sin, *Ibid.,* 130, 1848. A *voting* letter is reproduced in App. A.

11. Coad, *History,* 228-229.

12. Neatby, *History,* 92.

13. *Letters,* I.318, II.413, *Writings,* II.493, 509. The major thrust of Darbyism was to convert the saved to its new, unique school of Christian thought, especially its idea of withdrawal. Unquestionably, the Anglican Church had its share of corruption, so the early men probably used the obvious corrupt individual clergymen to justify doing all they could to get members out of all churches, no matter what denomination. They stood against denominations in general, except, of course, the Brethren denomination.

Bristol. During the visit she had adopted Müller's religious opinions, and on her return to Stuttgart she went to the Baptist Church, was baptised and received into membership. Her letter was accompanied by one from a leading member of her church "a solicitor or barrister to the Upper Tribunal of the kingdom of Wirtemberg". He "wished to have upon Scriptural grounds" Müller's "views about open communion".[14]

Müller's party arrived in Stuttgart, August 19, 1843. Müller spoke at the Baptist Church several times before conflict arose. The Baptist Church forbade its members from taking the Lord's supper with unbaptized believers or with those who belonged to any state church. Müller could not agree with that, so there was soon a division between the elders of the Baptist Church and Müller.

Müller started a separate meeting similar to Darby's Brethren meetings in Switzerland. He spent just over six months teaching them "what was meant by meeting in dependence upon the Holy Spirit," and left about twenty-five behind who had been "breaking bread with him." He drew several out of the Baptist Church:

> Herzog raises the cry that has been raised ever since in every land, that Darbyism robbed the pastors of the *elite* of their flocks; and, though the expression is too general, there is a great deal of truth in it.[15] This was the small beginning of a fairly considerable movement in Germany.[16]

Müller's stated reason of why he went to Germany was because he,

> knew not of one single body of believers who were gathered on Scriptural principles.[17]

Müller's stated motive for his work was that other Christian works of his time "had as their object the conversion of the world, an object

---

14. Neatby, *History*, 96.
15. *Ibid.*, 92. As late as 1875 as the strong Darbyite movement was falling apart, it still attracted large numbers of the "most spiritual, intelligent, conscientious, decided, and devoted, from all the churches: a startling fact, especially for ministers," *Ibid.*, 283.
16. *Ibid.*, 95-100.
17. *Ibid.*, 96. Christians are commanded to disciple all nations, Mat. 28:19, 20.

which Müller had not been able to find in Scripture." Moreover, he desired to promote his brand of *Christian Mysticism.*

India

The expansion of the millenarianism world-wide through evangelistic zeal must be kept in its context — its *soul-winning* zeal contained strong hostility against winning the world for Christ, considering any such effort sin. The motives for expansion was their conviction that the Scriptural prophecies concerning the Second Advent of Christ would shortly be fulfilled. If the early millenarians had been told the Lord would not be back by the start of the Tweny-first Century, they would have considered the teller a poor, faithless, unlearned Christian, if Christian at all.

> Thus, A. N. Groves wrote in his journal for 13 December, 1833: 'I consider the testimony of Jesus is to be published through every land, before the Bridegroom comes; this makes my heart feel an interest in heathens, that we may hasten the coming of the Lord'. Groves was particularly drawn to the Near East because he felt that the final drama was to be enacted there. At the end of 1831, contemplating the arrival of reinforcements in Baghdad where he was working, Groves exclaimed, 'Oh how happy shall we be to await the Lord's coming on the banks of those rivers, which have been the scene of all the sacred history of the old church of God, and are destined still, I believe, to be the scene of doings of yet deeper interest at the coming of the Lord; and whilst I should not hesitate to go to the farthest corner of the habitable earth, were my dear Lord to send me, yet I feel much pleasure in having my post appointed here, though perhaps the most unsettled and insecure country beneath the sun'.
> Darby also gave clear expression to the view that the conviction of the certainty of judgments soon to fall upon the earth provides a powerful 'motive for missionary exertion'. Similarly, Müller felt impelled to undertake itinerant missionary work 'through *the recently received truth of the Lord's second coming'*.[18]

Their evangelical zeal removed Christianity, *i.e.*, godly influence, from the world of their day. They especially removed Christianity

---

18. *Origins,* 187.

from the area of civil government. Neutralizing Christianity, they willingly turned the world over to the wicked one. Groves took every possible step to avoid even the appearance of being politically involved.

Though Groves' successful mission work in Baghdad included a school, even his mission school reflected millenarian thinking. The purpose of Groves' school work was "not on the ground of attending to the rising generation, but to aid him in language, attach young scholars to him, give him opportunity of 'trying his wings' (as he called it) against Christian errors, and exciting the attention of Moslems."[19]

The purpose of Groves' educational work was not training future generations to take dominion of all things for Christ according to 1 Corinthians 10:31. Its purpose was to help him learn the language, to "attach young scholars to" himself and to counter what he considered Christian errors, *e.g.*, Christian involvement in social and civil issues.

Groves, Müller, Newton and Darby all traveled quite extensively with the same basic motive and message — *soul-winning* (proselytize!) and waiting for the Second Advent of Christ. Not only did these men travel widely with their monastic ideas, but they also motivated numerous others to take their newly developed messages into the furthest reaches of the world. Groves traveled extensively in India and even expressed his "desire to visit Judson's mission in Burma in the hope of seeing 'some one Mission carried on in unison with the principles I feel to be right.'"[20]

---

19. *Ibid.*, 191. Note the missed opportunity to reach the Muslims; a sin for which we are now paying a very high price.
20. *Ibid.*, 196, 197.

Chapter 68

Switzerland Invaded

Darby was requested by an influential member of the Free Church to come to Lausanne, Switzerland, in 1840 to stop "the rapid spread of Wesleyan Methodism amongst the Dissenter." With his keen eye for favoring circumstances, the next five years saw Darby's influence spread with startling rapidity over the whole Canton (any state in the Swiss Republic). Largely by tracts, he carried on a successful campaign against Methodism — it "vanished before him." Darby charged that "Wesleyanism...hardly contained any real Christians, and that it set aside, in its doctrine and its discipline, 'all that is most precious in the truths of salvation'."[21] Though Herzog thought Darby's movement would run a short course in Switzerland, "French Switzerland has ever since remained the stronghold of Brethrenism abroad."[22]

Professor Herzog, an eyewitness to Darby's success, provides this insight into Darby's great evangelistic zeal:

> "Notwithstanding that Mr. Darby seeks less to convert souls than to unite under his direction souls already converted, we gladly acknowledge that he deserved to a great extent the compliments that were paid to him... But when in his teaching he broaches ecclesiastical questions, when he appears as head of a party, and when he endeavors to unite under his banner souls already converted, then he decidedly falls below his own level."[23]

---

21. Neatby, *History*, 76-80. Darby said, "I have served negatively in some measure, for Satan would have seized this moment of crisis by the means of Wesleyanism, and that as a system or generality, has not taken place..." *Letters*, I.43. He expressed great joy when people left Wesleyanism, or any other non-Darbyite movement, and submitted to his way of thinking.

22. Neatby, *History*, 93.

23. Quoted, *ibid.*, 78, 79. The logical conclusion of Darby's "ruin of the church" theory was to use every means to get believers out of all other churches and into his newly developing church and system.

Darby's main effort was to gather the already converted into his millennial system. The same situation applied to Groves — his main goal in India was not to start new works, but to infuse his ideas into existing works.[24]

In Vaud, Switzerland, "Following English precedent, Darby made the study of prophecy the pivot of his work; and his delineations of millennial glory dazzled the minds of his hearers." The Free Church had been a disappointment to the dissenters, thus leaving favorable circumstances for Darby's message. During 1840, Darby delivered a series of eleven lectures in Lausanne in which he "introduced the new insights which he had developed during the previous decade and which would have the effect of deepening dissatisfaction with existing forms of church life":[25]

> He saw as the key, the distinction between Israel as the earthly people of God and the Christian Church as His heavenly people. The present age will close in two stages, with the removal from earth of the genuine members of the Christian Church at the secret coming of Christ, and the judgment of apostate Christendom when He comes in glory with His saints. Then, and only then, will God's plan for the earth begin to be implemented through the agency of the Jews who will have recognized their Messiah at His coming in glory. Two corollaries came to be drawn: the coming of Christ for His Church may be expected at any time; those passages in the Gospels in which Christ spoke of His coming in open glory — such as Matthew 24 — must have been addressed to His disciples as Jews, not as Christians.[26]

---

24. *Ibid.*, 66. Darby made abundantly clear that his primary goal was to "convert" already established Christians and churches to his way of thinking.
25. Origins, 207
26. *Ibid.*, 230, 231. This "new insight" was clearly presented in Lacunza's system.

His opinions threw Lausanne into confusion.[27] Darby followed up his lectures with a pamphlet on prophecy that proved, to him anyway, the Christian dispensation was a dismal failure, so the Lord must yet develop another dispensation if he would complete his work on earth.

> According to Herzog's account, it would appear that Darby followed up his lectures on prophetical subjects with a forthright pamphlet on apostasy. In it, he set out to show that each dispensation of God's dealings with men had ended in failure, almost as soon as it had begun. Though there might be subsequent partial revivals, a fallen dispensation was never restored. As for the Christian dispensation, it had failed, even in apostolic days, though Paul was raised up as apostle to the Gentiles, and a remnant had remained faithful throughout. Darby almost implied that this constituted a new dispensation, and certainly insisted that the restoration of 'old things and earthly arrangement' (for example, detailed church order) was out of the question since it would be an attempt to restore a dispensation that had fallen.[28]

Newton reacted sharply against Darby's views, but his only real objection to Darby's theories was the idea of a secret return of Christ for his saints — he saw it as a novel idea with no Scriptural warrant. Nor was Newton as strong as Darby on a church/Israel distinction. Newton was convinced that Darby's views were not only wrong but also dangerous to the church and would lead to its destruction:[29]

---

27. *Origins*, 208. Rowdon's account of what Darby's eleven lectures contained is reproduced herein. Reading his 1845 letters from Lausanne, one can easily understand why the Christian community was distressed over Darby's novel, unique, unorthodox ideas. Though accepted today as *orthodox*, at the time of their introductions, they were so astoundingly unorthodox that they caused riots so serious that the police had to be called. See *Letters*, I.82, 83, 227 & 251.

28. *Origins*, 209. The church failed to do the Lord's work on earth, so it must be spewed out of the Lord's mouth and replaced with a nation Israel, through which the Lord will continue his work on earth. See *Writings*, II.11, 182, 186, 359, 563. Scofield said it thusly: "Each of the dispensations may be regarded as a new test of the natural man, and each ends in judgment—marking his utter failure in every dispensation." *Dividing*, 12.

29. *Origins*, 231-133. Newton had been taught Darby's ideas by Newman before Darby added the secret rapture and the church/Israel distinction.

Newton denied both the view that there would be a secret coming of Christ prior to His revelation in glory, and the distinction between Israel and the church that lay behind it; though he held that a godly remnant of Israel, converted at the glorious appearing of Christ would form the nucleus of Christ's millennial kingdom on earth, while all God's believing people from all ages would share in heavenly glory.[30]

Darby was openly very hostile to Newton's position. Wigram sided with Darby against Newton, even threatening not to eat with Newton.[31]

Darby's personality drew multitudes to him from both the national church and the dissent element. He assumed authority over all who were drawn to him, stressing absolute freedom, yet he "would have no center but himself."[32] As elsewhere, Darby's strength lay not in his ability to present a consistent Biblical argument for or against a point, but "in the reality of the abuses he attacked."[33]

An excellent example of Darby's ambiguity — and ability to grasp favoring circumstances — is seen "in his central doctrine of the 'Ruin of the Church.'" The dissenters readily identified this vague phrase, but Darby never clearly defined his meaning, nor did anyone ask him to. Regardless, the phrase drew many dissenters to him. But deep in the midst of Darby's writings we come "to understand that it was of the church as the company of the elect that Darby predicated the ruin."

Darby's keen eye for favoring circumstances is also seen in the situation at Vaud: Herzog observes that "People had already begun to regard the church as destroyed, and its relations with the state as incompatible with the very idea of the church; to regard the

---

30. *Ibid.*, 238-239.
31. *Ibid.*, 239.
32. Neatby, *History,* 83. In Darby's letters, he talks a great deal about *love among the brethren,* yet his letters reveal a terrible malice against Newton.
33. *Ibid.*, 87.

ordination of ministers as a mere matter of human expediency that had no connection whatever with a divine ordination."[34] Darby arrived preaching hard and revealing error. People were drawn to him because he put his finger on problems. But rather than offering Biblical solutions, Darby offered his Theology of Withdrawal from problems by studying prophecy.

> There existed in Vaud a certain religious *malaise,* of which the growth of Methodism in an otherwise uncongenial soil had been a symptom. The Free Church had yielded less satisfaction than its promoters had hoped, and the minds of its adherents were prepared to hail the charms with which the certain future — doubtless it was said, the near future — was invested in Darby's prophetic dissertations. He was never "weary," Herzog tells us, "of urging on his hearers this decisive word: 'Prophecy tends to snatch us from the present evil age; that is its principal effect'."[35]

His vagueness shows the inability of Darby to think logically. Darby fought hard against any distinction between a visible and invisible church. His early molding — age twenty-five to thirty — resulted in "a curious blending of Puseyite with ultra-evangelical elements." He was unable fully to depart from the Catholic Church Theology of episcopal succession. Thus, "he often took refuge in very vague generalities." To Darby, Christianity was dependent upon the preservation of an external unity.[36] Darby lived long enough to see his work toward unity go to pieces, destroyed by his own hands — he could tolerate no disagreement with his authority.[37] Darby's heart revealed itself, showing that the only unity he desired was unity around his opinions, for he moved very wickedly against those who disagreed with him, especially Newton.[38]

---

34. *Ibid.,* 94. One of the major common points of agreement among all the early Brethren was the militancy against any kind of ordination.
35. Neatby, *History,* 76-81.
36. *Ibid.,* 88-91.
37. *Ibid.,* 308.
38. *Origins,* 227ff.

Chapter 69

Darby's Switzerland Lectures

Because of the importance of Darby's Geneva lectures, we will quote some of Mr. Harold Rowdon's excellent summary of them. Though Darby presented the theories in these lectures as his own, they were clearly found in Lacunza's 1790 *Ben-Ezra system,* and they were quite contrary to the previous 1400 years of orthodox church teachings.

Rowdon invested a great amount of labor to root through the very muddy waters of all of Darby's quite extensive writings to find the gems he used from Darby's *Collected Writings* and *Letters* to put together his summation of the lectures. One cannot help but admire Rowdon, for Darby's letters are extremely redundant, repeating over and over the same few themes. All of his letters tell of his hard work, his humility, his avoidance of controversy (when the controversy was not to his advantage, that is), and his ESCAPE from reality. Not one letter among his three 500+ page volumes of letters offers any kind of practical solution for surrounding social problems. His letters and messages would fit quite well in the average modern "fly away", "fluff and stuff" church, for they were designed to make those under his influence "more heavenly-minded," detached from worldly cares and responsibilities, mystical.

Moreover, when this writer attempted to read Darby's *Collected Writings,* he was overwhelmed by the obvious fallacies found in Darby's messages, such as the following:

> We are His fullness, that is, we complete the mystic man, Christ being the Head. For the Church is that which completes and displays Christ's glory in the world to come; and then there will be not only Christ in heaven, known to the believer, but Christ ruler over the earth, over all things. It is a blessed thought, that it is not merely God as God who fills all things, but that Christian redemption and mediatorial fullness in grace and righteousness fills all things. "He that descended is the same also that ascended up far above all

heavens, that he might fill all things." Everything from the dust of the earth up to the throne of God has been the scene of the accomplishment of, and witness to, Christ's glory. But when He does actually thus "fill all things," and it is not merely known to faith, it will not be alone, but as the Head of the body which is now being formed, taking the Church to share in His dominion and glory. All things will be subject to Him in that day; but the Church will be associated with Him...[39]

Observe: First, Christ's glory is *now* displayed through the church (Eph. 3:10), and second, Christ is *now* head of all things and all things are *now* subject to him (Eph. 1:22, 23). Therefore, out of compassion for this writer, the reader and the length of this document, we will restrict ourselves to Rowdon's account:[40]

> During 1840, Darby delivered a series of eleven lectures which excited great interest among dissenters and members of the state church alike. Herzog commented somewhat tartly that, having done what he had been asked to do, Darby commenced his own business. This was to introduce the new insights which he had discovered during the previous decade and which would have the effect of deepening dissatisfaction with existing forms of church life.
>
> By now, Darby had come to see clearly that the key to understanding the unfolding revelation of the Bible was the distinction between the Jewish dispensation and that of the Christian Church. In a lengthy pamphlet entitled 'Divine Mercy in the Church and towards Israel', he had drawn the distinction between the Jews as God's earthly people and the Church as God's heavenly people. Further elaboration of this view had come in Darby's 'Notes on the Book of Revelation, to assist Inquirers in searching into that Book', in which he had argued that the Church would be removed from the earth before the outpouring of the judgments enumerated from the beginning of the fourth chapter of Revelation.

---

39. *Collected Writings,* II.419, 420. *Letters,* II.102, 1850, from Lausanne. Darby says that Christ's government, authority over all creation, of the earth is yet to come.

40. *Origins,* 207-208. "'The Hopes of the Church of God, in connection with the Destiny of the Jews and the Nations as revealed in Prophecy' (Eleven Lectures delivered in Geneva, 1840), *Collected Writings,* II. 420-582. According to Herzog, the lectures were delivered in Lausanne... They may have been given more than once." *Ibid.,* 221.

In the lectures delivered in Switzerland in 1840, Darby spoke of the heavenly character of the Church; the passages in the New Testament which seemed to him to support the idea of a Second Advent of Christ; those which he understood to mean that there is to be a resurrection of the just, prior to that of the unjust; those which he took to mean that evil will develop on the earth and, therefore, that the world will not be converted by the preaching of the Christian gospel;[41] The ecclesiastical apostasy which had already taken place in principle, and the civil apostasy which was yet to take place; God's judgement of the nations of the earth, signs of the imminence of which were already appearing; the view that the Jews had been given the land of Israel unconditionally, and that, although they had temporarily forfeited it, they had been given the promise of restoration. In the final lecture, Darby attempted a synthesis with special reference to the events to be expected in the future. The view was put forward that both 'call' and 'government' had been entrusted to Israel, but that consequent upon Jewish apostasy, government had been entrusted to the Gentile nations while the divine calling remained in abeyance. While government is in the hands of the nations, the Christian Church is being called out from Jews and Gentiles to form the heavenly people of Christ.

When the number of the Christian Church is complete, Darby continued, it will go 'to join the Lord in the heavenly places'.[42] The nations of the earth, including the Jews, will be incited by Satan himself to rebellion against God under the leadership of Antichrist. This rebellion will be quelled by the direct intervention of Christ whom the Jews will then recognize as their Messiah. Israel — from the Nile to the Euphrates — will be possessed by the Jews who will have returned from the four corners of the earth, and Jerusalem will become the centre of Christ's government of the world. Then will follow earth's golden age when the earthly glories of the Jews will be matched by the heavenly glories of the Church, the heavenly Jerusalem. This will be the climax of God's purposes for the earth; though it will not be of endless duration. It will be terminated by another period of crisis which will usher in 'the world to come', the eternal state.

---

41. *Collected Writings*, II. 470-486. "Towards the end of this particular lecture, Darby admitted that 'many a cherished feeling' had been shocked that night (p. 483) and concluded by saying that, as the Jewish dispensation had been cut off, so would the Christian (p. 486)." *Origins*, 221.

42. *Writings*, II.576. "This is clearly an allusion to the 'rapture' of the Church." *Origins*, 221.

In this way, Darby outlined his solution of the problem as old as Christianity — the relation between the Jewish nation and the Christian Church. By insisting that the characteristic promises made to the Jews related to the earth and that the promises made to the Church were chiefly heavenly, and by positing a future time when both sets of promises would be fulfilled to the letter simultaneously, he reconciled the two without resorting to the argument that the earthly promises to the Jews must be understood in such a way as to find their fulfillment in the spiritual blessings given to the Church. Darby's method of interpretation doomed any attempt to give to the Christian Church earthly status or power...

Darby mentions the riots that broke out here when he presented his new theories. He pleaded for Christian liberty so he could continue presenting what the people then considered heresy. Darby not only did "what he had been asked to do," stop Wesleyanism, but his unique ideas won the church's heart and soul, and killed the hope of a victorious Christianity apart from a literal intervention by Christ himself. Darby, almost single-handedly, robbed the Church of the Spirit's power (faith, Mk. 11:23, 24) to convert the world to Christ.

Faith in the victorious gospel as presented in Acts and defined by Paul in 1 Corinthians chapters one and two and hope in a victorious church upon this earth were effectively put to death by the efforts of one man, John Nelson Darby. His message of escape from Christian responsibility appealed to the masses and brought about the modern *Death of Victory*.

Chapter 70

Various Nations

The following is but a partial list of countries where the early millenarian missionaries went with great success. There were many Brethren churches in these countries, but the basic motivating zeal was to *convert* the peoples to the millennial system, especially the idea that "A Christian shouldn't be involved in worldly pursuits," expressly politics. With the firm withdrawal from worldly pursuits went their idea that Christians must form a separate society.

As a parenthesis, let us make this point: "In principle, the two [Brethren and Pentecostal-type churches, *ed.*] have much in common..."[43] Hence, the Pentecostal denomination has Brethrenism's same basic beliefs — withdrawal from society and Pietism. (See "Pietism" p. 459.) Consequently, nations are captive to socialism despite Pentecostalism's inroads in those nations.

Considering what took place in the following nations since their millennialism influence, the list is quite amazing. The following nations are the better known of those influenced to one degree or another by millennialism in the late 1800s through about the time of WWII. Nations such as French-speaking Switzerland, Germany and India were influenced far more than nations such as Mexico.

Müller's Scriptural Knowledge Institution was quite successful. It supported twenty-one missionaries abroad, nineteen in Great Britain and Ireland, and had missionaries in British Guiana and India. Müller attracted many missionary candidates from Germany and Switzerland to be taught in his institutions.[44] They were trained in Müller's militancy against any effort to win the world for Christ, in his Christian monasticism and in his mystical view of prayer, which required no disciplined obedience to God's word. (See Jn. 14.)

But, as we have seen, there was *death in the pot*. The commendable missionary zeal for *soul-winning* contained, among other destructive seeds, at least equal zeal against Christianizing the nations, and for the withdrawal from society and just waiting for the

---

43. Coad, *History,* 207. Darby, however, early on stood very adamantly against Irving's "Tongues" & "Faith Healing," calling them works of the devil, *Letters,* I.23, 1833, III.198, 209. Darby's stand prevented both from becoming basic millenarian doctrine. The Pentecostal *gifts* are not emphasized in Scofield's notes, for Darby rightly dealt with them, and Scofield followed Darby's system.

44. *Origins,* 192-204. This author finds events in these two countries after Müller's influence highly disturbing and significant: Germany started two World Wars, and the Swiss have provided some strong anti-Christian laws.

Second Advent of Christ. Moreover, faith was equated with prayer rather than obedience according to James chapter two, 1 John 3:22.

Nations influenced with millennialism include: Zambezi, Angola, Zair, Northern Rhodesia, Thodesia, Pakistan, Thailand, Argentina, Brazil, Mexico, Guatemala, Honduras, Venezuela, New Zealand, Ecuador, Zambia, Iberia, West Indies,[45] U.K., Canada, U.S.A., Holland, Faroe Islands (Danish Islands about midway between Scotland and Iceland), Germany,[46] France,[47] Italy, Belgium, and Switzerland.

Whole areas were affected by millennialism. The Brethren's strong influence was felt in Central Africa (F.S. Arnot) and East and West Africa.

Though millennialism influenced South and Central America, its greatest influence was in Eastern Europe and Russia before and after WWII.[48] Its message of otherworldliness and withdrawal went into the Baltic states and into the Slav countries: Czechoslovakia, Poland, Yugoslavia, Hungary and Romania. It went into Egypt, Mozambique, and China via China Inland Mission and Watchman Nee. It went into Australia, New Zealand, Malaysia, British Guiana,

---

45. "The leading personality in this movement was Leonard Strong, and ex-naval officer turned clergyman who went out in 1826... He was put in touch with early Brethren (he came from Herefordshire and had been curate at Ross-on-Wye), for whom British Guiana (or 'Demerara') and the West Indian Islands soon became a prominent interest, fostered by Müller's Scriptural Knowledge Institution." Coad, *History,* 198. Darby speaks of the very large increase in followers upon his visit to the West Indies, *Letters,* I.533, 1868.

46. "In both France and Germany the Darbyite movement has been stronger than the independents and, indeed, has probably retained the essence of Darby's teachings with far less corruption than British and American 'exclusives.' It is of interest that Evelyne Sullerot, the French feminist, was born on her mother's side of a Darbyite Family.... Influenced by a visit of Baedeker to Berlin in 1875, she [Fraulein Toni von Blucher, *ed.*] was responsible for a mission work in that city during the next thirty years, itself associated with a new wave of Pietism, the *Gemeinschaftsbewegung,* which swept Germany at that time under the influence of the English-speaking revival movement and is still influential in all denominations." Coad, *History,* 197.

47. Darby carried on a very "effective" work from Guelph, reaching into America with his letters.

Spain, and Portugal. Japan and Korea also had Brethren missionaries as early as 1888.[49]

Motivated by their zeal, the millenarians went into all the world, taking with them their various doctrines of pietism, withdrawal from society (monasticism), otherworldliness and no social nor political involvements. They considered all believers who might be involved in trying to reclaim any area for Christ as weak in faith.

Significantly, the millenarians went into the many areas of the world listed above with great power and influence, starting c. 1830. The great missionary movement lasted about seventy-five years, which should have been long enough to prepare the peoples of the world for what was coming in the early 1900s: the Bolshevik Revolution, Hitler and the second American revolution — a revolution away from its distinctly Christian roots. The millennial system, rather than producing strength to stand against the evils of the early 1900s, made Christians in places such as China, Russia, Germany and America indifferent to what was taking place around them — Christian resistance world-wide against the evils of the "New World Order" (Communism) was effectively neutralized.

---

48. "Lord Radstock... engaged in a remarkable evangelistic work among aristocratic circles in Russian and Eastern Europe, and introduced Baedeker to his friends in those countries. Despite the persecution of evangelical groups, Baedeker succeeded in winning the confidence of many of the highest officials, and in obtaining a prison visitor's permit valid throughout Russia... (Baedeker's travels, ed.) took him throughout Russia, and right across Siberia into Sakhalim Island. Coad, *History*, 195.

49. Coad, *History*, 188-208. "Even more interesting was the entirely indigenous and independent movement of the 'Little Flock," a Brethren-type movement which grew up in China between the wars under the leadership of the saintly Watchman Nee (Nee to-sheng). Despite its similarities to the Brethren movement, this movement remained a separate entity from European missions but Nee was influenced by Darby's writings and adopted his view that there could be only one local church in any one town, comprising all believers there. Since the Communists gained power in China, Watchman Nee has been imprisoned, and his churches suppressed." *Ibid.*, 201, 202. However, Nee rejected the extreme exclusiveness of the Darbyite movement, *ibid.*, 213.

Thus there can be no recovery from the evils set about in those revolutions until there is a recovery from the evils set about in the dispensational millennial system.

Chapter 71

Millennialism and Marxism

What is known today as *Dispensationalism* — God working in different ways in different periods of time — was a solid plank in the rising millennialism. Clearly, "it as a product of nineteenth-century thought." Supporting the explosive growth of Marxism, it taught that a new age of peace and freedom can only be accomplished by the sword.

Dispensationalism and Marxism have some striking similarities:

> Despite its overall similarities to older Christian views of history, dispensationalism has a number of peculiarities that identify it as a product of nineteenth-century thought. These have to do especially with its explanation of how dramatic historical change takes place, a common preoccupation of the thought of the era. In the prevailing naturalistic explanations of change the principal model was development through conflict. This is apparent in the work of the two most influential theorists of mid-century, Darwin and Marx. Marxism in fact has some formal similarities to the nearly contemporary development of dispensationalism. History is divided into distinct periods, each dominated by a prevailing principle or characteristic. Each age ends in failure, conflict, judgment on those who rule, and the violent introduction of a wholly new era. History thus proceeds in dramatic steps toward a final age of peace. The crucial difference is that in the Marxist scheme the scientific approach to history assumes that the laws of change are governed by wholly natural factors of human behavior; in dispensationalism science discovers revealed principles of supernatural laws that have guided historical change.[50]

---

50. *Fundamentalism,* 64. Pierce, in *The Rapture Cult,* shows how millennialism neutralized the enemies of Communism.

Serious charges were leveled against the millenarians in 1918:

> In "The Premillennial menace," (an article published in the *Biblical World, ed.*) Case surpassed the standards being set in the journal and produced so distorted a portrait of the millenarians (led by R.A. Torrey, speaking in Carnegie Hall, Nov. 25-28, 1918, *ed.*) that one is tempted to believe he was being satirical. These men, Case argued, were subversive to the American war effort, "fundamentally antagonistic to our present national idea." "Premillenarianism is a serious menace to our democracy," it "throws up the sponge... raises the white flag," is a "spiritual virus," and the "most helpless of all gospels." As if these epithets were not adequate, Case noted that the millenarians operated with a "thoroughness suspiciously Teutonic" and implied that they were financed by German secret agents. As the frosting on the cake, Case insisted that millenarians were indistinguishable from the Russellites and lent themselves to the same purposes as the IWW. The Fundamentalists, apparently, never cornered the market on invective.[51]

Millennialism threw in "the sponge." It effectively yielded America's Democratic Republic to the forces that sought to overthrow it.

The millennial system neutralized Christianity world-wide. The millennial conquering of the nations permitted Marxism (the "New World Order," Communism) to march in its world-wide conquest with no significant Christian opposition. The millennial expectation of an imminent, any moment return of Christ to straighten out the mess with his *rod of iron* is justly charged with allowing Communism to prosper;[52] Marxism was a major beneficiary of millennialism. In fact, America's 1933 recognition of the Communist USSR government would never have happened if the *Moody Monthly* had not said that the Second Coming would solve the problem.[53]

---

51. *Roots,* 236. Russellites, a Protestant sect begun in 1874 by Charles Taze Russell (1852-1916), called Jehovah's Witnesses. Among many things, they believe all allegiance is owed only to God and to nothing of this world. They refuse military service, and are excluded from having to salute the flag in public. They grow primarily by proselytizing.

52. *Cult,* 42, 51, &c.

53. *Ibid.,* 38. "Dec. 1933, p. 208. Quoted by Spann (Ref. 13)."

The national media, *e.g., US News & World Report*, appears to favor the premillennial view of Christianity. In doing so, they tell Christians that resistance to the "New World Order" is useless, for it is prophesied in Scripture:

> Premillennialists, who include most evangelical and fundamentalist Christians, take a much more pessimistic view of history. For them, says Grenz, the world will grow nastier. Only "the catastrophic return" of Christ, he says, will "inaugurate the golden age on earth."
> ...While there are differences of opinion within the tradition, the dominant view, called dispensationalism, has its roots in the teachings of John Nelson Darby, a 19th-century Englishman and founder of the Plymouth Brethren...[54]

Socialism, *i.e.*, centeralized government control of everything within its reach, is a result of Christians withdrawing from society to become personally more spiritual. One can, therefore, assume that the system the millenarians took with them in their missionary zeal was a major reason the nations of the world fell into the clutches of the wicked one. Clearly, when Christians are taught not to be involved in an area, that area will be delivered to the forces of antichrist by default.

The emphasis of the early millenarians was on a heavenly calling at the expense of their earthly responsibility:

> The attitude they adopted is summed up in the phrase 'heavenly-mindedness', the title of a paper contributed by J.L. Harris to the October, 1853, issue of *The Christian Witness*. They regarded the world of men as being opposed to the plans and purposes of God: there was inflexible hostility between the world and the true Church. Therefore, they concluded, in the words of B.W. Newton, that 'so far as we identify ourselves with the world, we surrender our claim to the peculiar and distinctive privilege of the Church, we lose the present discipline and the future reward, and plant ourselves in a world which, though not neglected, but often visited with goodness, remains still a barren field in the sight of God, and necessarily inherits judgment at the last'.[55]

---

54. *U.S.News & World Report*, Dec 19, 1994. See *Cult*, 48, 50.
55. *Origins*, 302.

Very early, Darby compared the Christian life in the world to a person traveling through a strange community. The person sees problems and turmoils in the community. However, because he is a stranger simply passing through, he has no responsibility nor desire to do anything, for his mind and desires are totally on the glory waiting for him ahead. In fact, Darby held that if the person takes his eyes off that glory and tries to do something about the problems in the community, he has departed from the Lord: "If I have any object on this side of the glory, even the welfare of the Church in detail, my soul will suffer from it." His message was simple — ignore the problems, and it appealed to the natural man, "...Christians have no business..." being involved in anything other than *soul-saving*. They are unconcerned, for they believe that "The Church of God has been taken entirely out of the world to be associated with God's Prince in heaven..."[56] We should point out that this kind of thinking means that the Good Samaritan was a sinner for getting involved in a social issue, caring for the sick.

Their mystical attitude of "heavenly-mindedness" resulted in overlooking the practical affairs of life, as they developed and promoted the heavenly aspect of the Christian's life and of the church. They withdrew the Christian influence from ordinary life, defining sin as any involvement in worldly matters.[57]

> It is difficult not to feel that in their retreat into "other-worldliness" some of those leaders of early Brethren, from their upper-class Anglican backgrounds, were all too unconsciously grasping at that which would enable them to avoid facing these ugly realities of life: just as something of the same sort lay behind the retreat of the Tractarians into the ancient Catholic traditions. The immense peril of this retreat is that it confines the expression of Christian devotion to religious excercises – a limitation against which the whole example and teaching of the Lord Jesus Christ Himself cries aloud.[58]

---

56. *Letters,* I.51, 1842; *Writings,* II.152, 153. 457, 549, about 1852.
57. Coad, *History,* 364-365.
58. *Ibid.,* 265.

The result was to confine the expression of Christian devotion to a mystical, religious, emotional experience. Reacting against what they pointed out as wrong in the surrounding churches of their day, they went to the opposite extreme. They wrote off the world as incapable of turning to Christ, so it was only fit for judgment. But they forgot that the Creator still works in his physical world, using men to do his work. Basically, they gave the kingdom of God a strictly spiritual meaning as they emphasized its future aspects and ignored its present reality and importance.[59]

Though the more outlandish aspects of Darbyism were dropped in the revival of 1859, his dispensational system is well entrenched.[60]

Honestly observing the modern results of the millennial message, one will admit that the change the message brought to Christianity is not for the better. For with the *soul-saving* (conversion to the millennial system), missionary zeal went the doctrine of defeat. It withdrew the Lord's salt from the world's corruption and the light from the world's darkness. Since the rise of millennialism, corruption has spread and darkness increased. It is time to overthrow the otherworldliness that makes Christians useless to God and man in this present world. God promises that saltless, lightless and lifeless Christianity will be cast out and trod under the foot of man.

Modern dead Christianity must again grasp the fact that *we are more than conquerors through him that loved us,* and that conquering victory takes place in time and space as God, with his Spirit of Grace, uses people to conquer the world for King Jesus.

---

59. *Ibid.,* 264. Darby was extremely dogmatic, teaching that the church and the world are both in complete and irreversible ruin, and both fit only for judgment, *Letters,* II.242.
60. Coad, *History,* 247.

Part VIII
War Against Orthodoxy

Chapter 72
Resistance to Millennialism

As a young, unmarried, Anglican priest, Darby's wide travels had already drawn many to him. After departing from the Anglicans, his travels increased. Though based in feelings and mysticism rather than sound Bible study, his message against the restrictions of organized religion and for the *freedom* he offered in his new movement drew many groups of Non-Conformists to him. As his followers grew in numbers throughout Europe, he established many Bible study groups that emphasized prophecy — the *system* saw prophetic study resulting in Christian purity. His movement grew rapidly through genuine hard work and evangelistic effects.[1]

Though Europe was prepared by revolutions and wars to welcome the "pessimistic, millenarian world view" and escape into prophetic speculations, America was not as prepared. Hence, when Darby's millennial *system* was introduced in America, millenarians had to fight hard to convince,

> [T]he rest of American Protestantism that it was neither heretic, lunatic, nor unpatriotic. Millenarians argued that they correctly understood Bible teaching regarding the second coming of Christ and that their doctrines were taught by the apostles and believed by the church fathers. They sought to distance themselves from the traditions of William Miller's adventism and protested against being pictured as a band of fanatics ready to don ascension robes.[2]

William Miller's (1782-1849) views were remarkably similar to what developed in Britain between 1816-1840:

---
1. Coad, *History*, 88.

Miller, after years of labor, somehow reversed the sequence, and came to believe there would be a Second Coming first, then a Day of Judgement, the ascent and descent, and a thousand years of Eden...[3]

Conservative leaders, particularly within the Baptist and Presbyterian denominations, stood against the mystical Darbyites until the rise of Modernism.[4] Because the millenarians held so firmly to the inspiration of Scriptures, the Conservatives joined with them against the common enemy, Modernism.[5] The new alliance culminated in D.L. Moody's conferences at Northfield, Massachusetts, which provided the mystical millenarians previously unknown respectability in America.[6]

---

2. *Roots*, xx., 50. "The most famous millenarian in American history, William Miller, was far from being a fanatic. A self-educated farmer from Low Hampton, New York, he showed no interest in prophecy during his early years and was, in fact, something of a skeptic until converted [and joined a Baptist Church, ed.] in 1816. During the next few years, precisely at the time that British prophetic interpretation began to stir, Miller became fascinated with interpretation of prophecy. Depending almost entirely upon his own exegesis of the Bible, Miller developed a system of prophetic interpretation that came remarkably close to duplicating that being developed by the historicist premillennialists of Britain..." Miller set his date for the end as 1843 according to his understanding of Dan 8. He, like every date setter since, such as Edgar Whisenant and Harold Camping, was wrong. Some at the first Albury conference set the second advent date as 1843 or 1847, *Roots*, 22.

3. *Secret*, 130. A brilliant comet appeared in early 1843, to which the Adventists (followers of Miller) pointed as proof of Millers' predicted imminent doom. The evangelists used the comet to urge people to conversion in order to avoid the doom. The Adventists' millennial movement was strong in upper New England, the hotbed of the Abolitionist Movement. *Ibid.*, 146.

4. Modernism: Any of several movements variously attempting to redefine Biblical and Christian dogma and historical teachings in the light of modern science, historical research, &c., *e.g.*, attempts to make Biblical dogma and evolution comparable were at the foundation of Modernism. In 1907, Rome condemned Modernism as a denial of the Christian faith.

5. The "higher criticism" movement made itself felt during the rise of millennialism. All who held the inerrancy of God's word joined forces against the "higher criticism." And thus the millenarians became identified with orthodox Christianity though they destroyed it. *Cult*, 36.

6. *Roots*, xxi.

Chapter 73

Baptist and Presbyterian

Well-known men such as H.A. Ironside, C.H. Mackintosh, R.A. Torrey, Watchman Nee, George Müller, Hudson Taylor, D.L. Moody, G.V. Wigram, W.E. Vine, S.P. Tregelles, J.G. M'Vicker, D.G. Barnhouse, J.W. Chapman, "Billy" Sunday, E.M. Bounds, Andrew Murray and C.I. Scofield, have been exalted as great men of the faith. Yet many of these men stood against the Baptists of their day, and initially the Baptists stood against what these men propagated. Though he had no Scriptural support, Ironside railed against A.H. Strong, and, it seems to this writer, the Baptists have since sided with Ironside.[7]

Apparently, America's, the Baptist's and the Presbyterian's conversions happened about the same time.

The Change, Post to Pre

Postmillennialism, by far the prevalent view among American evangelicals between the Revolution and the Civil War... Articulated as a distinct view in early eighteenth-century England, postmillennialism was promoted in America during the Great Awakening, notably by Jonathan Edwards... They saw human history as reflecting an ongoing struggle between cosmic forces of God and Satan, each well represented by earthly powers, but with the victory of righteousness ensured...[8]

After the Civil War the more liberal evangelicals, whose basic epistemological categories were profoundly altered by the new naturalism and historicism, began gradually to abandon the dramatically supernatural aspects of the postmillennial view of history. In particular they ceased to take seriously the idea that history was determined by a cosmic struggle between the armed

---

7. This writer has found Ironside's books more popular in bookstores and among Baptists than Strong's. Ironside did write far more books than did Strong.

8. *Fundamentalism,* 49. We will deal more thoroughly with America's conversion in Part IX.

forces of God and Satan and that these supernatural powers might directly intervene at any moment.[9]

Strangely, the major figures in America's conversion to Christian Monasticism were Presbyterian Calvinists:

> In fact the millenarian (or dispensational premillennial) movement had strong Calvinistic ties in its American origins. The movement's immediate progenitor was John Nelson Darby... During his later career Darby spent a great deal of time proselytizing in North America. He found relatively little interest there in the new Brethren sect, but remarkable willingness to accept his views and methods of prophetic interpretation. This enthusiasm came largely from clergymen with strong Calvinistic views, principally Presbyterians and Baptists in the northern United States.[10]

The Calvinist denominations, Baptist and Presbyterian, were the most heavily influenced by the millenarians:[11]

> In 1876 a group led by Nathaniel West, James H. Brookes, William J. Erdman, and Henry M. Parsons, all Presbyterians, together with Baptist A.J. Gordon, initiated what would become known during the next quarter-century as the annual Niagara Bible Conference, which became the model for similar conferences held every decade or so until the end of World War I. These early gatherings, which became the focal points for the prophetic side of their leaders' activities, were clearly Calvinistic. Presbyterians and Calvinist Baptists predominated, while the number of Methodists was extremely small.[12]

> The many small Bible institutes and colleges that sprang up across the United States beginning in the late 1800s were major avenues of dissemination for Scofield's synthesis of dispensationalist thinking.

---

9. *Ibid.,* 50.

10. *Ibid.,* 46. Darby was Calvinistic in terms of God's sovereignty, *i.e.,* God had raised him up.

11. While Pentecostals have the same roots as all dispensationalists, the Baptist and Presbyterian were separate groups. The Pentecostal movement was founded in dispensationalism, but the Baptists and Presbyterians were converted to dispensationalism, with its heaviest influence in the Baptists. The Baptists were overwhelmed with the movement.

12. *Ibid.,* 46. William J. Erdman is listed by Scofield as a "Consulting Editor" on the opening page of *The Scofield Reference Bible.* Brookes could be considered *the father of the Scofield Bible,* Scofield being his protegé.

A leading figure in the educational movement was Lewis Sperry Chafer (1871-1952), a Presbyterian pastor and a pupil and colleague of Scofield who took up the dispensational torch after Scofield's death in 1921. Chafer, like Scofield, had no formal theological training, a fact in which he took apparent pride. Like his mentor, he was also a popular speaker, tireless in his efforts to spread dispensationalist beliefs throughout America. In 1924 he helped found the school in Dallas, Texas, that would become Dallas Theological Seminary; along with Moody Bible Institute in Chicago it developed into a major center of dispensational teaching in America. ... [Chafer] insisted that unless a person held dispensationalist beliefs he was doomed to teach a false gospel: ... 'Chafer taught that the Scriptures addressed specifically to the Church are the Gospel of John (especially the Upper Room discourses), the Acts, and the Epistles.'[13]

Strangely, the Presbyterians seem to have been the major promoters of dispensationalism. Irving was a Presbyterian, as were the major organizers in America, but the denomination as a whole seems to have been better immune to its influence.

Calvinists, particularly Presbyterians, tend to stress intellect, the importance of right doctrine, the cognitive aspects of faith and higher education, so we find it strange that the first men at Niagara were swept up in the winds of the time. Though Niagara, which led in Americanizing the millennial *system*, was controlled by Presbyterians, the Presbyterian denomination, with its emphasis on scholarship, appears to have better withstood the *wind of doctrine* the millennial Presbyterians set in motion. (Several Keswick conferences were held at the Presbyterian stronghold, Princeton.)

The Baptists, seemingly, were not as well equipped. They tend to be more independent, and are disposed to overlook scholarship, sound doctrine and ability with the word of God in their leaders. Thus they were more in line with the early Brethren who emphasized personal charisma and strong personalities. Groups failing to emphasize sound Biblical scholarship and ability with the word of God are more likely to *lay hands suddenly* on unqualified men for

---

13. *Catholics*, 178, 179.

Christian leadership (as long as they can build a church — that is, add numbers to it). But the strong wind was blowing, and many Calvinists, both Baptist and Presbyterian, were blown along, replacing "Christ the victorious" with "the terrors of Satan."

However, we are now seeing serious students of the Word again finding Irvingism and Baptist (and Presbyterian) doctrine as incompatible as it was from 1825-1875. They are returning to the historic Baptist faith delivered by Baptists of the past, *e.g.,* John Gill and Augustus Strong. However, it must be admitted that not all Baptists were nor are "Particular" Baptists, *i.e.,* Calvinistic.

Accordingly, Baptist Confessions of Faith written after the Baptists converted to Darbyism reflect the antinomianism and defeatist attitude of the Irvingites. Many Baptists desire to claim C.H. Spurgeon as one of theirs, but they deny the confessions he used, both his strong Calvinist confession and the *1689 London Baptist Confession.*

Chapter 74

Against the Baptists

Because the Baptists have apparently been the most mesmerized by Darbyism, believing it their heritage, we will document Darby's continued hostility toward them. However, not only would Darby today speak very approvingly of modern Baptist, but he would so speak of Christianity in general.

Though Darby spoke strongly against Anglicanism, Puseyism, Romanism and Methodism, his harshest words were against Baptists. Hostile against the Baptist view of baptism, he was also resolutely against the Baptist's thought that a Christian could be under any kind of obligation to the Lord's commands and/or that a child of God should be involved in any kind of work for the future here on this earth.

In 1855, Darby "had an opportunity of preaching to a large assembly of strict Baptists, who are dreadfully under the law..." He was "able to set a full gospel before them... [who, *ed.]* had never heard a simple gospel–it is law and experience." He tells of the many conversions in the area.[14] Darby's gospel consisted primarily of just waiting for the Lord's very soon return, with no law binding the believer.

Initially, both European and American Baptists stood strongly against Darby's unorthodox ideas, including his theory concerning the Lord's "imminent return," which released believers from earthly responsibility. Darby saw the Baptists who stood against his unorthodox ideas as simply poor, mistaken people groping in the dark. In 1856, Darby complained:

> At ------ they [Brethren labourers in Nismes, where Darby's theories were experiencing wide acceptance, *ed.*] have been harassed by the ardent Baptist party.... But if I had needed anything to convince me that it is all wrong, this would have sufficed. Such a display I have rarely witnessed, or evidence of a fleshly work. It was deplorable. I have, however, declined controversy, and sought only to calm and claim liberty of conscience. But while desiring and wishing before God and men this liberty for Baptists, and feeling that God can allow in the midst of abuses that this point should be brought on the conscience and before the church, as a means of proving its state, and examination of the point this has occasioned has more than ever convinced me that the whole Baptist principle is a mistake from beginning to end, and nothing more than conscientious want of light... I trust now, save with a very few, all are disposed to leave people free in conscience...[15]

Trying to take the high road, Darby claimed to be too spiritual to be involved in any controversy, yet he saw nothing wrong with using controversy to destroy those who disagreed with him. Darby considered all opposition to his unorthodox ideas as, at the least, "evidence of a fleshly work." He considered any growth outside of his followers (such as Baptists), "works of the flesh." In the situation

---

14. *Letters,* I.242. To a Darbyite, conversion was primarily conversion to dispensational millennialism.
15. *Ibid.,* 251, 252.

with the Baptists and at the times when riots broke out because of his teaching unorthodox doctrines, he pleaded for religious liberty and freedom to present his ideas. Yet when others presented teachings contrary to his, it was quite a different matter:

> Those who agreed with him were the Church of God upon earth. Those who disagreed with him on any point of doctrine, he excommunicated at once, and regarded as outside the covenanted mercies of God.[16]

The initial conflict between Darby and the Baptists was apparently over *believers baptism,* though Darby was against "the whole Baptist principle... from beginning to end." In 1863, writing from Canada, Darby repudiated his former attendance at a Baptist meeting as he further describes his antagonism against the Baptists:

> I can conceive nothing more false than a baptist testimony--more poor than a baptist church: the whole thing is a mistake. We are, according to 2 Timothy ii., purging ourselves from evil in a great baptised mass, thinking to begin and found, as with heathen, in a false position... Dear ----- assumed this position in ---- that they baptised believers (himself the most inconsistent of men as to it) but admitted others. I said at once I could not go in that case: I went in the unity of the body, not on sufferance to a baptist meeting, and the thing was withdrawn, and said not to be meant in this way. Nothing would induce me to go to a baptist meeting; I would as soon go to popery... If the *assembly* takes the ground of being baptists, of course I should not go...[17]

In his letters, Darby writes probably more on the one subject of baptism and the Baptists in general than on any one other subject

---

16. "George T. Stokes, 'John Nelson Darby' (*The Contemporary Review,* July-Dec., 1885), pp. 537-52." Quoted in *Plot,* 146.

17. *Letters,* I.364, 365. Darby's words never softened toward the Baptists. Vol. II of Darby's *Letters* contains 26 pages of letters explaining why he considered the Baptists wrong, 275ff. One of the ways of proving himself right and Baptists wrong was to say of Acts 8:36, "the following verse, I apprehend, is not authentic scripture, though I doubt not in such a case right, but not the then way of dealing, however..." *Ibid.,* 281. He commonly dismisses as "not authentic" passages that might create problems for his opinions. Darby was hostile toward all religious groups that did anything more than "occupy till He come" — that is, wait for the imminent return of Christ. *Ibid.,* 272.

other than *just wait for the Lord's return*, with several letters devoted entirely to those subjects. Though at times Darby's thinking is fairly easy to follow, his view on baptism is not one of those areas. Rarely using Scripture to confirm his opinions and judgments elsewhere, Darby used more scriptures to support his often contradictory and confusing view of baptism than he used to support everything else combined.

Though Darby held that baptism "is a symbol of death and resurrection (for which reason John Baptist's baptism was nothing for Christianity as such)...," he implied that water baptism actually washes away sin:

> We are baptised to Christ's death and raised in Baptism — not baptised because we are dead and risen. It is objective: what is represented in Baptism? I am figuratively buried into death and rise again, not as a witness that I am. The principle is false and mischievous. "Arise and be baptised, and wash away thy sins," not because faith has washed away. It is the outward public sign of that whereto Christ's death and resurrection are available, a witness of that — not that the person has availed himself of them: that may or may not be true. To receive of the Lord's supper, I do not go because I have remembered Christ's death, or have fed upon Him, but to remember Him there.
>
> No one can read the statements of scripture and not see these statements of the Baptists are wholly contradicted by those of Scripture.[18]

Darby apparently broke with the established religions in every area except infant baptism. Though admitting there was "no *command* for infants to be baptised," he "supposed a moral effect" for the practice. But he did not suppose the same moral effect for adults.[19] He was greatly distressed over the Baptists' effort to convert people to their way of thinking:

---

18. *Letters,* II.287. "Baptism signifies, undoubtedly, death and resurrection, but it is then and there, as to the meaning of the form, we die and rise again." *Ibid.,* 282.

19. *Ibid.,* 283.

My objection to the Baptist action is not that they act on their consciences as to it: I would not seek to hinder them; but they have a feverish activity and propaganda about it, which is not Christ. And clearer views so set one on Paul's ground — that he was not sent to baptise — and sets it in the background, that we lose our intelligent place when we propagate it.[20]

The Baptists' "feverish activity" cannot even begin to compare with the Darbyites' "feverish activity" to convert Christianity to the millennial *faith*. Vacillating in most other areas, he did not vacillate in opposing the Baptists. He stood with the Establishment he had fought so hard against otherwise.

The major distinction between the 1800s' Irvingites and the Baptists at the end of the 1900s seems to be not much more than the necessity and mode of baptism.[21] Working hard, Darby converted the Baptist denomination, to a large extent, to the millennial faith — the Baptists have become the greatest defenders of Darby's version of the *Ben-Ezra system*.

Chapter 75

Against Obedience

Darby was quite firm that the Christian is under no obligation of *obedience* to God in anything, except maybe the Lord's Supper:

> ***The first principle commonly stated is that of obedience [in baptism, *ed*.]. My answer to this is an absolute denial of obedience

---

20. *Letters*, II. 275, 276, from London, July 1st, 1874. Speaking of the Baptist practice of re-baptizing, he said, "...I, with my whole heart, allow liberty of conscience,....," but he calls the Baptist position that the act of baptism speaks of unity, absurd and sin. *Ibid.*, 291. Unity, he said, is in the Lord's Supper. He based his opposition to baptism upon the fact that Paul said he was not sent to baptise."I believe it is a rite established at the beginning; but I was not sent to baptise, nor was Paul." *Letters*, II.291.

21. Baptism speaks of the trust of the candidate in the finished work of Christ in his place, and it speaks of commitment to obey his Commander and Chief, the word of God.

to ordinances in Christianity. It is a mischievous anti-christian principle, called "subject to ordinances," and deteriorates the whole character of a person's Christianity. As regards baptism in particular, it is perfectly certain that according to scripture it is not a matter of obedience... [Baptism, *ed.*] was a privilege desired or conferred, and not an act of obedience — admission amongst Christians, the act of the baptiser on behalf of the assembly, not of the baptised. The truth is that there is no command of Christ to be baptised — there was *to* baptise, and it could not be otherwise. Christ could not as to Christianity give a command to those without. If the man is within it is by baptism, so that there can be no command to be baptised. The importance of this is that it shews that the baptist system falsifies the whole nature of baptism. Hence the apostles were not baptised. They — the twelve, not Paul — were sent to baptise, to admit into God's house. They could not be admitted...

Hence Paul who was sent a minister of the church to complete the word of God was not sent to baptise.... The twelve who, though the church existed, had not this mission, but had been sent forth by Christ in connection with the kingdom... But this mission was not a mission for believers' baptism as it is called. They were sent to disciple all nations, baptizing them in the name of the Father and of the Son and of the Holy Ghost.

...the scriptures never speak of baptizing believers, nor any one, because they are dead and risen again in baptism.[22]

Darbyism sees the nature of Christianity not as any kind of *obedience principle* to the Lord and his word, but as a *privilege principle* of doing what pleases the Lord.

> In the first place, I am quite clear that the whole system of Baptists is wrong in principle from beginning to end, and in their idea of the import of the act. They speak of *obedience;* now, obedience to ordinances is setting aside the whole spirit and character of the gospel and of Christianity itself. In all cases it is unscriptural... Hence there is no command to be baptised, but to go and baptise; and this marked in a very signal manner, as the twelve apostles never were baptised...[23]

---

22. *Ibid.,* 276, 278. Letters of unknown dates, of which this is one, were inserted after the one from London, July 1st, 1874, because their subjects all concerned baptism. Typical of Darby, his wording is confusing.

23. *Ibid.,* 281, 1874. Darby held dogmatically that the apostles were never baptised. *Ibid.,* 290.

274   *Death of the Church Victorious*

But if any one thinks that he ought to be baptised, or that he has not been, surely he ought, or he will have his conscience ill at ease about it, and that is evil, no matter what the subject is, only he would do well to search the mind of God first. *Obedience to an ordinance* is, I am satisfied, wrong; and there is no command for it in scripture. It is not the act of the baptized nor a public testimony. All this I believe to be most unscriptural, and in its principles unchristian, though often most honestly done.[24]

Darbyism defines sin as supposing any command upon a Christian — sin is a violation of the conscience rather than a violation of the written word of God.[25] That false idea is common today.

Chapter 76

For Two Gospels

The Baptists (c. 1869) also stood against, among other things, Darby's efforts to reestablish a literal Jewish nation with its temple, sacrifices and its unique plan of entering into God's blessings:

> The truth Baptists have to learn is that there is a place, a system established by God, where the blessings are found--the olive-tree of fatness--without the questions of conversion being settled, in which heathen, Mohammedans, and now for a time Jews are not, but in which these last will hereafter again be, though not on our footing. I know it is said you are bringing us back to Judaism... [26]

Though normally confusing, Darby writes with uncharacteristic clarity here — he maintains that Baptists were in error by believing there is only one gospel, the gospel of Christ. Accordingly, the

---

24. *Ibid.*, 284. "The great evil of their [Baptists, *ed.*] system is, that they occupy themselves with ordinances instead of with the Lord, and one is obliged to do the same when speaking of it." *Ibid.*, 289.

25. *Ibid.*, 141. "The principle of being required to obey an ordinance Christianity rejects, [baptism, *ed.*] because it makes an act of the outer man a condition for entering into the enjoyment of the privileges of grace..." *Ibid.*, 290. Thus Darby held that the "privileges of grace" are available to the most lawless "Christians."

26. *Ibid.*, 51, 52. Vol. II contains a whole letter against the Baptists, 47-52, *e.g.*, "Another important principle destroyed by the Baptist system..."

"church/Israel" distinction requires two plans of salvation. *Though not on our footing*, the Jews are brought into God's blessings — that is to say, apart from faith in Christ's finished work, the Jews will be brought back into fellowship with the Father. Note Darby's comment concerning the rending of the veil, Matthew 27:51:

> The ancient state of things was ended, whether as the relations of man with God, or in that which concerns the very creation. In the rejection of the Son of God, all relationship of the first man and of the first creation with God has been ended for ever. A new basis has been laid down in righteousness and by the full revelation of God in sovereign love, for the eternal joy of man, in the last Adam, and in the new creation.[27]

In other words, God has two different plans of salvation in history, with the old plan different from the new. He fails to mention, however, that faith has always been the condition of righteousness. From Adam on, no one has come to the Father apart from repentance and faith, exhibited in atoning sacrifices that looked forward to Christ. Abraham believed God and it was counted unto him for righteousness.

It is a recent heresy to say that there are two plans of salvation, and that the work of Christ (the "Church") was hidden from the prophets of old. Writing in about 185, *Against Heresies*, Irenaeus (c. 130-c. 202) said:

> [W]e have not been taught another God besides the Framer and the Maker of all, who has been pointed out to us from the beginning; nor another Christ, the Son of God, besides Him who was foretold by the prophets. 3. For the new covenant having been known and preached by the prophets, He who was to carry it out according to the good pleasure of the Father was also preached; having been revealed to men as God pleased; that they might always make progress through believing in Him, and by means of the [successive] covenants, should gradually attain to perfect salvation. For there is one salvation and one God; but the precepts which form the man are numerous, and the steps which lead man to God are not a few...[28]

---

27. JND CW 30.310. *Online Bible*.
28. *Fathers*, I.472, 473.

Baptist doctrine and the dispensational system were incompatible in the early years. Writing from Guelph, Canada, June, 1867, Darby says:

> We are at our Guelph meeting. I am a great deal better, though weak. Our meeting, somewhat of a new character, has been very happy-- new, because we had many from the States in different degrees of progress, of getting into liberty (indeed they had got that, but) to see the church, and other truths we are accustomed to rejoice in, the Lord's coming and others. They all broke bread, though some had been closed Baptist. How far they will break loose, or be among brethren, I cannot tell. Some--one Baptist minister in particular-- have left their systems, are just out, and have taken no further step. The Spirit of God has been working in them, and is, and the meeting has been a help to them, but there are many adverse influences, and one waits to see the result of His work. Such a scene was all new to them: as to the truths, they had been gradually growing into them when I was in New York, but I greatly trust that the meeting will have been a real blessing. It has been less simply among brethren, [Plymouth Brethren, *ed.*] but a quiet, diligent study of the scripture, and the brethren happy...[29]

One could either be a Darbyite or a Baptist, and Darby rejoiced when he was able to convert any Baptist to his *faith*. Throughout the 1800s, Baptists had to depart from Baptist fellowships and doctrines to unite with Darbyists (Alexander Reese's term for followers of Darby). But now Darby's *faith* has become key *Baptist faith*, e.g., imminent return of Christ, pre-tribulation rapture and uninvolvement in social issues is now found in most Baptist Church doctrinal statements. And hence the greater part of an entire denomination converted to Darbyism.

The denomination lost its vision for Christian victory over the world in the late 1800s and the early 1900s. The modern Baptists' defeated attitude is expressed by *The 1878 Niagara Creed*, an outgrowth of the strong dispensational millennial move that overwhelmed Christian thought after the middle 1800s.[30]

---

29. *Letters,* I.508. See also 198, 242, 251-2, 296, 328.

Chapter 77
Significant Millenarian Victories

There were some significant events that culminated in the conversion of the Baptists and Presbyterians to the dispensational millennial faith. Because the Presbyterian chain of command held local pastors accountable to a higher human authority, the Darbyite spirit did not seem to overwhelm the Presbyterians as it did the Baptists with their loose and independent spirit.

The conducive conditions for millennialism were the results of several events:

First, the English naturalist, Charles Robert Darwin (1809-1882): His *Origin of Species* was welcomed by those who hated God and his inspired word. Darwin offered "scientific proof" that God's account of creation was not true, and if not true, then God's pronouncement against man's sin was not true. If the Bible's account of creation was true, evolution "proved" it could not be taken literally. Grappling with Darwin's theory of evolution, Henry Ward Beecher (1813-1887) presented his solution — leave the truth of science to scientists, economics to the economists, and the invisible, spiritual things to the Christian ministry.[31]

Second, the rise of Modernism: As we know, among the many tenets of Modernism is its denial of Divine Inspiration of God's word.

Third, "the secularization of the culture:"

---

30. Point XIV: "We believe that the world will not be converted during the present dispensation, but is fast ripening for judgment, while there will be a fearful apostasy in the professing Christian body; and hence that the Lord Jesus will come in person to introduce the millennial age, when Israel shall be restored to their own land, and the earth shall be full of the knowledge of the Lord; and that this personal and premillennial advent is the blessed hope set before us in the Gospel for which we should be constantly looking..."

31. *Qv*. Beecher's heretical solution was completely contrary to 1 Cor. 10:31.

With the rapid process of secularization throughout the nineteenth century, inevitably some people questioned the continued close identification of the church with the culture... In America, later in the century [from Darby's influence in Britain, *ed*.], increasing secularization was more often perceived as the failure of postmillennial promises concerning the growth of the kingdom in this age.[32]

Darwinism, Modernism and Secularism motivated those believing in the inspiration of the Scriptures (premillennialists, postmillennialists, dispensationalists, non-dispensationalists, Baptists, Presbyterians, &c.) to unite against their common enemy — that is, against those who denied God's word. The mixing up against the common enemy never got unmixed. The mixing combined with other factors, and the millenarians gained greatly in the mix-up.

Fourth, revivalism and emotionalism:

Charles Finney (1792-1875)

Converted in 1821, Finney almost immediately resolved to give up law to accept a call to preach. It was in "the [closing, *ed*.] days of great learned preachers, whose congregations listened in awe to descriptions of the mysterious workings of an inexplicable Providence" that Finney came upon the scene:

> The surge of revivalism associated with the rise of Charles Finney in the 1820s which developed in the "New School" tradition certainly did not forsake intellect, but it did create new channels for emphasis on emotion throughout American evangelicalism. Sandra Sizer in her analysis of the rise of the gospel song in nineteenth-century America has suggested that Finney's revivals marked the beginning of the attempt to build a new Christian community united by intense feeling.[33]

Entering the Presbyterian Church, he was licensed to preach in 1824:

---

32. *Fundamentalism,* 54. Secularization, *i.e.*, the removal of God from areas of life, was not a new problem. It has been growing rapidly since the Middle Ages. The secularization of the nineteenth century, however, led to redefining the then prevalent faith, postmillennial.

33. *Ibid.,* 45.

As a preacher forceful, direct, personal, and dramatic. Wherever he went revivals prevailed. He initiated the "anxious bench" and dwelt upon the importance of the hearers coming to immediate decision and of raising in public attestation of their decision. His novel methods and his departure from certain Calvinistic emphases called for the criticism of the more conventionally and doctrinally conservative leaders of the Church. Unique methods of preaching prevailed and he continued revival labors. It is estimated that more than half a million people were converted through his ministry... As a revivalist, as a theologian, and as college president, he left the impress of his character upon thousands of lives and contributed not a little toward shaping of Christianity in the American republic.[34]

"People wanted to hear that God was a reasonable being with whom it was possible to bargain and cajole. The evangelist was His agent, and could explain the rules." Finney also attacked "virtually all the tenets of Calvinism that still bounded most Americans together..., he scorned both theology and the educated ministry..." Revivalism, led by Finney, "argued that a sinner could attain salvation through his own will; one need only turn toward God."[35]

> VI. The human will is free, therefore men have power or ability to do all their duty.
> 1. The moral government of God everywhere assumes and implies the liberty of the human will, and the natural ability of men to obey God...[36]

---

34. *Who*, s.v. "Finney, Charles Grandison."

35. *Secret*, 77, 78. This writer has found this attitude all too common among the Baptist pastors with whom he is familiar: the decision is in the sinner's hands, leaving God at the mercy of the sinner. Not only did Finney's preaching prepare America for the millennial system, but it played a large part in bringing about the War Between the States. The preachers of war learned and used Finney's methods to fan the flames of war. Finney also helped the Abolitionist Movement — Finney's northern converts linked slavery to sin that had to be removed immediately and at any cost. *Ibid.*, 113.

36. *Finney's Theology*, 261. Finney's hostility against Calvinism is evident throughout his *Theology* lectures. A key point of Calvinism is that the natural man has no ability to please God. See Rom. 3:11, 1 Cor. 4:7, &c. But this is not the theme of this present study. For an excellent treatment of Finney's theology and Orberlin Colleges' impact on America, see Warfield's *Perfectionsim*.

Revivalism's unity around *intense feeling* permits unity with those who might even deny God's word; it stresses an emotional experience with Christ, but ignores the fact that the emotions are many times *worked up*; it de-emphasizes sound Biblical doctrine and emphasizes personal piety, personal emotions and feelings. Millennialism offered a Christianity based upon feelings: "This is the way I feel it should be, so let us search Scriptures to justify it."

Finney was noted for attacking academic institutions that "gave young men intellectual strength, to the almost entire neglect of cultivating their moral feelings."[37]

Revivalism took the emphasis from sound Biblical doctrine, which should have been applied personally and socially, and placed the emphasis on emotions. It stripped American Christianity of its intellectual strength, leaving it vulnerable to the millennial system that was about to invade the nation in the late 1800s

Fifth, the appeal: The average Christian loved the new message of no Christian responsibility, so he was attracted to "Bible readings" making that offer. Pastors and Christian leaders who might have otherwise stood against the unique system emanating out of millennialism saw their people drawn to the new Bible teachings of no social responsibility. Hence, many pastors felt they had to teach the millennial system if they would keep their people.

Sixth, the War: The War Between the States prepared America for millennialism's hopelessness as the French Revolution had prepared Europe.

Seventh, the money: Both Bible school and church leaders learned quickly that the prophetic speculations in dispensationalism were a rich source of funds. Seeing the hand writing on the wall, more than a few schools and pastors started preaching to the purse.

---

37. *Fundamentalism,* 27. Admittedly, institutions need to be attacked for exalting human wisdom and skill over the leading of the indwelling Spirit and the word of God: "Many men seek after qualifications to be pastors of Christ's sheep by chasing after the wisdom of learned religious scholars." *Power,* 49.

War Against Orthodoxy 281

Eighth, the Bible Conference movement: D.L. Moody's influence and his Northfield Conference influence cannot be overestimated.

The above-mentioned points, along with other things, all came together, leaving extremely conducive conditions for millennialism's hopeless spirit to overwhelm any thought of a victorious gospel. The once dominant victorious Christian spirit was smothered to death by millennialism's anti-Christian spirit of defeat.

Chapter 78

Bible Readings

American Christians were involved in changing society through Christ-centered, Biblically-based social activity during the period of great immigration to America from Europe. Though Darby had an extremely abstract definition of sin in about every other area, he found American Christian activity and social involvement reprehensible — he clearly saw it as sin. Thus his work was cut out for him if he would make the American church see things his way. Conversion, according to Darby, basically was conversion to his "truth," *i.e.*, his monastic, pietistic view of Scripture that he *proved* through "Bible readings." Writing from Lexington, Kentucky (Jan., 1873), Darby said,

> My work here has been a new one, and pretty much sowing, but with the comfort of seeing plainly the Lord's dealing. It has been among Americans proper, that is, born. Some have come in here and there, but the work in the States was essentially among settlers; my present, among real Americans, God opening the way distinctly. Some new gatherings are formed, weak, but still a testimony, and wholly of such, and I have had large readings, and some lectures in various places......there are doors open to truth, and I have been able in various places and circumstances to bring the whole truth before ministers and people, and they [sic] interested in it. It is a work of

patience, and grace and a plain gospel almost unknown or denied...[38]

American Christians initially rejected Darby's version of the millennial system, but patience and persistence won out in the end. Writing from Concord (1873), Darby comments, "fresh souls were coming in seeking the truth... Now the Lord is working in the States — now evidently, all feel it — awakening souls to seek something better, and to feel that there are those who soberly seek, and in some respects have found in the word and sought in their walk something real..."[39] From New York (April, 1873), he writes,

> The work of God is going on in the United States; the convictions extending that we possess something that they do not possess. Preachers, elders, etc., have come to Boston for the daily Bible readings. They acknowledge also that we understand the scriptures better than they do; they often oppose, but often defend, so that in some aspects brethren are entering on a new phase of work. Our whole work remains always the same, to present Christ and the truth, accomplished salvation, and His coming; but this makes the responsibility of brethren still greater. God is opening doors; but His power alone can work upon hearts, to make them walk with Christ, and give up the way of this world. But the movement in every way is remarkable. The Lord is about to come.[40]

"Bible readings" convinced people of Darby's superior knowledge, and that the new understanding of Scripture was "the truth." However, Darby complained from New York that though his ideas were catching on, evil was greatly increasing.[41]

"Bible reading" was a new system of interpretation. It consisted of taking a *Cruden's Concordance* and following a word through the Bible with a comment or two on each passage. "Bible reading" acquired the term, "rightly dividing the word of truth." The system had to be formulated to support the emerging unique, unorthodox ideas.[42] Its development did not go unnoticed in the seminaries of

---

38. *Letters,* II.201.
39. *Ibid.,* 210, 211.
40. *Ibid.,* 212.
41. *Ibid.,* 307, 1874, from NY.

that day. Francis L. Patton of Princeton Seminary (1890) warned against "their arbitrary and unhistorical system of interpretation."[43]

"Bible reading" gained its strength in the early 1800s as teachers looked at the French Revolution and saw how, in their opinion, it fulfilled all the prophetic verses. It came to America during the time of the War Between the States. Though both wars have faded into history, the same passages used back then to say *prophecy is being fulfilled,* are now used to say *prophecy is being fulfilled.* Those same passages continue to be used to raise vast sums of money and to attract many who want to speculate about the future.

The "Bible reading" method is dangerous for at least two reasons: First, there is little, if any, in-depth Scriptural preparation required for this type of preaching. And, second, it begs for false assumption by removing the 'Reading' verses from their contexts.

Interpretation of verses in this manner allows a teacher to use verses either literally or spiritually as needed at the time to support whatever opinion he desires to present and/or defend. It encourages looking for isolated passages to fit whatever the winds of current events might require. It allows "Spiritual Truths" to be gleaned contrary to the clear intent of the Author. It allows "defence" of unorthodox ideas.[44]

With this manner of study, numerous false doctrines have developed over the years. But when "Bible reading" teachers are challenged over false doctrines, they claim their doctrines are Scriptural while ignoring the fact that their proof texts are out of context. The intent of the Scriptures' Author can be completely ignored, and the one challenging the text out of its context is accused by the teacher of denying the word of God. This tactic of defending

---

42. From the earliest, Darby talks about *readings,* the Brethren's unique method of studying Scripture, and the large crowds attracted to the readings. *Letters,* I.18 [1832], II.55, 105, 271, 374, 385, III.29, 78, 95, 96. The millennial system was so haphazard that a new system of study had to be developed for its support.

43. *Roots,* 137, 138.

44. This problem with the millenarian movement finds its roots in Irving and Darby. *Ibid.,* 110.

out of context passages has been a basic strength of the Darbyite movement.[45]

This study method solved the exegetical problem Irving faced when he separated Isaiah 9:2 from the plain word of God in Matthew 4:15, 16. Appearances demand, in Irving's opinion, that Isaiah 9:2 be literally fulfilled in the future despite the Spirit's words of Matthew 4:15, 16. "Bible reading" permits applying passages, *e.g.*, Isaiah 9:6, literally despite their required spiritual New Testament understanding.

Bible readings solve the Prophetic Puzzle:

> [Dispensationalism] has changed the Bible from being a mass of more or less conflicting writings into a classified and easily assimilated revelation of both the earthly and the heavenly purposes of God, which purposes to reach on into eternity to come.[46]

Thus, Dispensationalism, or Fundamentalism, sees the Word of God as a series of facts that must rearranged in a more scientific way for the understanding of the average reader. (See C.I. Scofield, chapter 91.) Rather than let the context interpret *facts,* the facts are collected like "pieces in a jigsaw puzzle that need to be sorted and then fit together to possess a finished picture of divine truth..."[47]

> Hal Lindsey often writes about the "prophetic puzzle", stating that "the prophecies [of Scripture] can be pieced together to make a coherent picture, even though the pieces are scattered in small bits throughout the New and Old Testaments."[48]

Lindsey gives us few options with his prophetic puzzle" statement. First, God was confused when he gave his word, and men like Lindsey and Lahaye must fix what God's error. Second, God does not want the average person to discover his prophetic secrets, so he

---

45. *Ibid.,* 108.
46. L.S. Chafer, "Dispensationalism", *Bibliotheca Sacra,* 93 (October 1936): 446-47.) Quoted by Olson, *Catholic,* 252.
47. Noll, *Scandal of the Evangelical Mind,* pp. 126, 127. Quoted by Olson, *Catholic,* 253.
48. *Catholic,* 253. Olson quotes Lindsey, *Late Great Planet Earth,* p. 33.

scattered them throughout his word. He then raises up men who can take the literal facts as found in their historical, grammatical and Biblical context, and rearrange those facts with no regard to their contexts. They then fit them all back together to offer a teaching that appeals to the natural mind. Those who want to know what God said in his puzzle must purchase the books, for they are unable to study the puzzle out for themselves.

Regardless, these writers seem to think that the average man is not intelligent enough to read and understand the word of God as it is given, and he must purchase books by the "profiting prophets" in order to understand God's secret prophetic code.

> 3. Another obvious similarity between canonical Apocalypse and its uninspired counterparts is the *use of vivid images and symbols* (monsters and dragons, symbolic numbers and names, etc) *in depicting the conflict between good and evil*. A failure to take full account of this feature has led to some of the most outlandish teachings on this book by some whose rule of interpretation is 'literal, unless absurd.' Though this is a good rule when dealing with literature written in a literal genre, it is the exact opposite in the case of apocalyptic literature, where symbolism is the rule, and literalism is the exception.[49]

Note that Daniel's interpretations of dreams and his own dreams are not taken literally, even by those who hold to "literal, unless absurd," yet the same people want to make the Apocalypse all literal.

Many who teach Dispensationalism have offered some extremely outlandish ideas, for their rule of interpretation is "literal unless absurd." Though such a manner of literal Bible interpretation is no where even suggested by the Word of God, it is the life-blood of dispensationalism.

Olson points out the many double standards in dispensational writings, e.g.: The basis of the Church/Israel distinction, without which dispensationalism would fail, is the reliance upon "the so called 'literal' method of interpretation..." But the "literal" method will not work unless the passages are pulled out of their historical

---

49. *Revelation*, 11

and Scriptural contexts—that is, *rightly divided* from their context and placed where the teacher or reader wants them. Scofield says that "any study of that Word which ignores these divisions must be in large measure profitless and confusing."[50] Admittedly, dispensationalism studies Scripture, but Scripture must always be studied in the light of the Church/Israel distinction.

Accordingly, all Bible study before dispensationalism discovered its divide and conquer technique (divide up Scripture, and reassemble it to fit current events in order to conquer the opposition and the pocketbook of the hearer) was basically "profitless and confusing."

The above idea of study is as bad as Rome's, that says all Scripture must be understood according to Rome's understanding. In this case, all Scripture must be understood according to Tim LaHay, Hal Lindsey, or any number of "profiting prophets".

Chapter 79

Moody's Conversion

> During The Last two decades of the nineteenth century the unordained Dwight L. Moody was the most influential "clergyman" in America.[51]

Millennialism could have remained a uniquely European brand of Christianity without Dwight Laman Moody's (1837-1899) *conversion* to Brethrenism. It took place after he heard Henry Moorehouse, a Brethren evangelist, speak in 1868 when Moorehouse visited Chicago and preached for Moody. His conversion is the basis of much of today's fundamentalism. He was a key transitional figure in changing American Christianity from its world-conquering force into a culture-denying, soul-rescuing

---

50. *Catholics*, 213. See "Scriptures according to Scofield," p. 328
51. *Roots*, 173.

influence.[52] Moody led in America's "departure from the dominant tradition of American evangelicalism..." George Marsden identifies these important men in spreading Moody's brand of millenarianism: R.A. Torrey, J.M. Gray, C.I. Scofield, W.J. Erdman, G. Needham, A.C. Dixon, and A.J. Gorden.[53] We must also add H.A. Ironside.

Though some evangelists developed novel methods in certain directions (awakening interest before their arrivals, uniting the religious forces of the place for a general effort, securing the public testimony of converts and getting the results which have been harvested well preserved after their departure), nearly all the prominent evangelists since Moody may be regarded as his disciples and imitators, *e.g.*, G.F. Pentecost, B.V. Mills, R.A. Torrey, J.W. Chapman and W.A. "Billy" Sunday.[54]

Moody's influence for making the millennial system acceptable is evident to this day. The school bearing Moody's name continues to propagate his millenarian faith, but let us not overlook its radio ministry. Through the Moody Broadcasting Network, his dispensational, millenarian philosophy reaches every corner of America.[55]

The view that "the world" would "grow worse and worse" was an important departure from the dominant tradition of American evangelicalism that viewed God's redemptive word as manifested in the spiritual and moral progress of American society.[56]

---

52. *Fundamentalism*, 6, 33. "Fundamentalism:" The term originated to describe those who held to the dispensational, millenarian system. The term, *Fundamentalism*, has since enlarged to embrace far more than just the millenarians — generally, all who hold to the inspiration of Scriptures and profess to live by their belief.

53. *Ibid.*, 37. J.M. Gray is listed as a "Consulting Editor" on the opening page of *The Scofield Reference Bible*.

54. *Ethics*, s.v. "Revivals of Religion." Though *Ethics* was published in 1913, Hastings clearly describes modern revivalism. After 1868, Moody was using "Bible reading" to preach Brethren doctrine, millennialism.

55. Local MBN radio stations are true to Moody's position. A local MBN station refused to accept state wide, Christian oriented lobbying spots until it was threatened with loss of revenue. In our rural area of Indiana, we can clearly receive at least three MBN stations.

D.L. Moody set the stage for the modern evangelist-revivalist — he passed down methods and messages acquired from others.

Moody's Christian Conversion is recounted by Mr. Kimball, Moody's Mount Vernon Congregational Church's (Boston, Massachusetts) Sunday-school Bible class teacher:

> I simply told him of Christ's love for him and the love Christ wanted in return. That was all there was. It seemed the young man was just ready for the light that then broke upon him, and there, in the back of that store in Boston, he gave himself and his life to Christ.[57]

In 1855, young Moody presented himself for membership in the Mount Vernon Church at the age of eighteen:

> At his examination, however, it was felt that the applicant was not sufficiently instructed in Christian doctrine to be taken into membership. In answer to the question: "What has Christ done for you, and for us all, that especially entitles Him to your love and obedience?" Young Moody replied: "I think He has done a great deal for us all, but I don't know of anything He has done in particular."[58]

Seeing nothing to be "considered satisfactory evidence of conversion", the examination committee deffered recommending him for admission to the Church. Young Moody was persistent, and presented himself again March 12, 1856: The committee reported: "'...At last we saw some faint evidence of conversion which justified us in recommending him to the church.'"

When Moody went to Chicago from Boston, he united "with the Plymouth Church, of which Rev. J.E. Roy, D.D. was then pastor..." William Moody, Mr. Moody's son, notes that Mr. Moody, "as he remembered his success in childhood as a recruiting agent for the Sunday-school at Northfield, conceived the idea that he had a special talent for this work..."[59] Providence placed him into *full time* ministry before he was twenty-five. His only "Bible training" was what he picked up from his attendance at Sunday church services.

---

56. *Fundamentalism*, 38.
57. *Moody*, 41
58. *Ibid.*, 44.

Moody considered his natural ability to attract people to himself his qualification to enter into the *ministry*. It was not the ability with Scripture that attracted people to either Darby or Moody; rather, it was their charisma characters. And one must not overlook the implications of *natural ability* to attract followers, an ability that must be submitted to God:

> Dwight L. Moody, the great American evangelist, used to be accompanied on his tours by the singer, Henry Drummond. Originally Drummond was able to influence and hypnotize people at a distance of fifty miles. After his conversion, he had difficulty in overcoming these occult powers. While ministering at Moody's meetings, he occasionally noticed that the audience was being influenced by his psychic powers. He was very troubled about this and asked the Lord to free him from these occult powers. The Lord answered his prayer.[60]

Psychic powers are real, even in "Christian" circles, and can be used to obtain many followers and a good income.

Though D.L. Moody talks about trusting Christ or accepting Christ, his son William gives quotes from an 1873 letter by Mr. Bennett: "I don't know how many, but over fifty gave their hearts to

---

59. *Ibid.*, 45-47, 55. "...Sunday he arrived at school leading a procession of eighteen little 'hoodlums' that he had gathered. This success made his special calling clear to him..." *Ibid.*, 56, 57. Moody, who had been a good salesman, used his ability to attract crowds to persuade people to his point of view. In the eight months previous to leaving *secular employment* (c. 1850), it is said that twenty-three year old Moody made five thousand dollars, *Who*, s.v. "Moody, Dwight Lyman." Typical of the early developers of the millennial *system*, he was not a theologian. Moody's son makes no mention of Moody placing his faith in Christ, or even knowing about it, at his *Christian Conversion*. The term used for the conversion of a sinner was *yielding to Christ*. However, though not spoken, the *spirit of the time* could assume that faith in Christ was common knowledge. When the War broke out, Moody, having an "ardent abolitionist" training, enlisted as a Unionist. He took many of his young followers with him into the War effort. He was one of the first to be shot down, *ibid.*, 81ff. Finney was also a strong abolitionist. These men must bear some of blame for the War Between the States. It was a religious war — a war against Calvinism, among other things.

60. *Occult*, 297-298. Henry Drummond (1851-1897) accompanied Moody in his meetings. Thus one wonders how much of modern church growth is the Spirit's work, and how much is men using the spirits renounced by Drummond? See 2 Cor. 10:4, 5.

Christ."[61] Accordingly, becoming a changed man is attributed to a personal choice of giving one's heart to Christ rather than the convicting and converting power of the Holy Spirit.[62] Consequently, Moody was a key figure in reducing the Biblical Gospel of Christ to its present, powerless, low estate — commonly called "easy believism."

A major key to Moody's success in drawing people to himself was the new methods he introduced into evangelism.[63] He emphasized sentiment rather than sensation (something done by both Irving and Darby), and he brought a businesslike air and a degree of middle-class respectability to American revivalism.[64] One of his new methods was having people in the meetings turn to those beside them and ask if they are saved.[65]

Enemies leveled charges against Moody to undermine his efforts in Europe; however, upon close examination, even they had to admit that Mr. Moody and those with him were above reproach in every area. The good that was evident from his efforts overcame the charges of his critics.

Chapter 80

Moody and Darby

The massive immigration in the 1800s brought many Brethren and Brethren evangelists to America, motivating Darby to visit the continent. He worked in America among the immigrants, but by

---

61. *Moody*, 162.
62. *Ibid.*, 312. Such thinking was a key in the Revivalists movement, led by Finney. See Jn. 6:44, 65, &c.
63. *Ibid.*, 158.
64. *Fundamentalism*, 32.
65. *Moody*, 168. Moody also introduced what is known as *The Wordless Book*; "a book with four leaves, black, red, white, and gold..." It is used today to explain the gospel to children. *Ibid.*, 220. Moody was easily influenced by those he felt he could trust. *Roots*, 173.

1873, he found greater influence in the larger cities of the Midwest and East.[66] Darby was in North America off and on from 1862-1877. He gained many proselytes, especially from among the Baptists and Old School Presbyterians:

> The aim of the Brethren is to "gather churches out of churches;"... and, accordingly, they prowl unceasingly round all our churches, seeking to reap where they have not sown, and leaving to the denominations generally the exclusive privilege of evangelizing the masses.[67]

Darby visited Chicago at least five times, and met with Moody once. Though Darby's 1873 report of that one meeting was not complimentary of Moody's theology, by 1875, Darby's opinion of Moody changed. He then "felt that Moody had 'greatly got on in the truth.'" In 1868, R.T. Grant commented to Darby that many of Moody's workers were converting to Darby's *system*. Thus Darbyism was built out of already established churches.[68] In 1874,

---

66. *Ibid.*, 72. *Letters*, I.352, II.201.

67. Quoted in *Roots*, 73, 74, from "The Plymouth Brethren," *Princeton Review* (1872). See also *Roots*, 71, 73. Darby refused to be identified with any sect — denomination — holding all sects to be wrong, *Letters*, I.329. Darby mentioned several times that his views on the imminent coming of Christ were warmly received among the Baptists and Presbyterians, *ibid.*, II.183.

68. *Roots*, 75. Darby refers to the inquiry into his "truth" taking place in "in Chicago," *Letters*, II.193, 1872. He was very much against Moody's methods. Darby spoke with Moody in Chicago, and mentions that Moody was greatly influenced by M.'s (Moorehouse's) tract. The tract was a good *"resume* of brethren's teaching...," *ibid.*, 259, 1874. In 1875, Darby says, "...though I hear M. had got on."... "M., I am told, had made progress; but when I knew him he denied openly all grace in conversion...," *ibid.*, 327, 328. Darby defined Moodyism as work instead of Christ, *ibid.*, 356, 1875. Darby does, however, compliment Moody: "he has got on in truth unquestionably...," *ibid.*, 359, and by 1876, Moody is credited with "greatly got on in truth...," *ibid.*, 369. Darby felt that Moody pressed people into the work far too soon after their *conversion*, calling it a "most mischievous" practice, *ibid.*, 375, 1876, from Toronto. It is clear that any approving words toward Moody were because Moody was perceived moving toward Darby's *system* of "truth." It was as Finney was gaining popularity that "The Bible was replaced by 'tracts,' in which writers wove little inspirational stories based on single Bible passages or on personal experiences." *Secret*, 77. All of these things worked together to leave America open to millennialism, which could only be supported by "Bible readings."

Darby did, however, correctly stand against Moody when Moody was in Edinburgh: "...I dare say there may have been conversions, and one must bless God for that. But Moody, before he came to England, denied openly all work of grace in conversion and denounced it as diabolical in his own pulpit."[69]

In November, 1876, Darby makes this comment about Moody:

> Activity is everywhere: this, not any direct blessing, is the effect of Moody's work. Fifty years ago that was more in brethren's hands — efficient lasting work they have to look to.[70]

Thus Moody becomes a major promoter of the doctrines that for fifty years had been uniquely Brethren.

Chapter 81
Moody and Moorehouse

Though Darby said of Moody, "I know the man well,"[71] he was not the one to *convert* Moody to Brethrenism. Henry Moorehouse is the major connection between the Plymouth Brethren and Moody.[72]

Moody had gone to Great Britain for a short time in 1867 not only to meet George Müller and Charles Haddon Spurgeon (1834-1892), but also to aid his wife's health.[73] At that time, the revival — very much a part of the millennial movement — was going strong in the British Isles. While there, Moody not only met Spurgeon and Müller, but also had an opportunity to attend some of the revival meetings. There he encountered the newly developing method of preaching among the Plymouth Brethren called "Bible reading."

---

69. *Letters,* II.259.
70. *Ibid.,* 385.
71. *Letters,* II.257, 1874.
72. *Hope,* 198.
73. *Moody,* 130. Moody met Charles H. Spurgeon, and some time later, Spurgeon assisted him in a London campaign, *ibid.,* 135, 243.

Moody also had the opportunity to speak in some of the revival meetings where a very energetic young man named Henry Moorehouse heard him. At twenty-four, Moorehouse was one of many notable men who threw their lot in fully with the Brethren, and at twenty-seven, he was already a veteran Brethren preacher in the revival. Coad points out that these men,

> [B]rought outstanding personality and energy to the service of a simple clear cut message, which made up by its direct appeal to the crowds who came to hear them, for all it might have lacked in Theological finesse. There was a joyous abandon in their revivalism which added a colour and zest to life that more than compensated for that which their Puritan ethic was accused of destroying.[74]

Thus personality replaced theology in attracting the multitudes.

Moorehouse was drawn to Moody from the first, and wanted to come to America to preach for Moody; Moody resisted. Nevertheless, the next year (c. 1868) when Moorehouse came to America, he came to Moody again. Because of his persistence, Moody allowed him to preach in his Chicago church one Thursday night while Moody was out of town. Moody's people loved the young man's preaching and invited him back. Moody heard him the following Saturday and was completely won over to the young man.

Moody recounts Moorehouse in his pulpit:

> "Sunday came, and as I went to the church I noticed that every one brought his Bible. The morning address was to Christians. I had never heard anything quite like it. He gave chapter and verse to prove every statement he made..."... "It's pretty hard to get a crowd out in Chicago on a Monday night, but the people came. They brought their Bibles, and Moorehouse began, 'beloved friends, if you will turn to the third chapter of John, and the sixteenth verse, you will find my text,' and again he showed another line, from Genesis to Revelation, that God loved us. He could turn to almost any part of the Bible and prove it..."

Preaching on John 3:16, Moorehouse took the text and ran it through "the Bible from Genesis to Revelation to prove" the point of God's

---

74. Coad, *History*, 170.

love. He preached seven sermons on this one verse, all in the same manner, and Moody was *converted*. Not only did Moody have Moorehouse back many times from 1869-1878, but he took Moorehouse on a seventy-two meeting tour in various American cities. Moody's preaching was changed forever: "Mr. Moorehouse taught Moody to draw his sword full length, and fling the scabbard away, and enter the battle with the naked blade."

Moorehouse and Moody held joint meetings in Great Britain in 1873.[75]

> At the end of [the meetings], Dwight L. Moody's own speaking methods and message, had been changed for good. ... This influence on Moody-vital to his later evangelistic preaching-was perhaps the most spectacular indirect result of a Brethren evangelist, and Moorehouse by that week of sermons on one verse of Scripture probably accomplished indirectly a greater work than that which resulted from the remarkable campaigns of his own short life (he died in 1880 at the early age of forty).[76]

Through his Northfield Bible Conferences, Moody taught Christian leaders both the Brethren's millennial *system* and the new Brethren method of preaching, "Bible reading."

Chapter 82

Moody and Bible Readings

Adopting the "Bible reading" method of preaching, Moody used it well. Moody's first attempt (1872) at "Bible reading" with others was in a private home in Brooklyn:

> The method of study ["Bible readings," *ed.*] was quite new to all, even to the leader. A theme was taken, or a single word, such as *grace, hope, adoption, assurance, love,* etc. The Bible was searched by means of concordance and topical text-book for all passages bearing on the theme:

---

75. *Moody*, 137-140, 167.
76. Coad, *History*, 189.

These were emphasized and illustrated. None were more impressed with the wonderful interpretation of the Scriptures by the Scriptures than Mr. Moody. This plan gave a new direction to his study and his preaching.[77]

Ernest Sandeen tells us that, as in Moody's case, the use of the "Bible reading" method of preaching can often be traced to an encounter with a Brethren preacher. Moody said, "I study more by subjects than I do by texts..." He collected subjects, and then he collected illustrations to fit the subjects.[78] His theology was ambiguous to the point of seeming not to be theology at all.[79]

All that is necessary with the "Bible reading" method of teaching Scripture is to string a list of verses together, and add a few comments to each:

> Moody's sermons virtually abandoned all pretense of following conventional forms of explicating a text, and were closer to "layman's exhortation" filled with touching anecdotes with an emotional impact comparable to that of a personal testimony.[80]

Notice how close this method parallels the original Brethren resistance against pre-prepared messages. From the time of the Chicago meetings with Moorehouse, Moody's preaching was patterned after this new method of preaching. He practiced and taught this method to whomever would listen at Northfield as well as the rest of Moody's schools. Moody thus made this new method of preaching with no regard to the context standard for American preaching.

Moody's later work in Great Britain in 1873 is recorded thusly:

> Mr. Moody's manner of expounding the Scripture at once attracted attention. The Bible readings, which he had given in Brooklyn and other cities, were continued with great effect. Believers were aroused to a new interest in the Sacred Word. Bibles were seen at every meeting and new methods of Bible study were

---

77. *Moody*, 438, 439.
78. *Ibid.*, 441.
79. *Fundamentalism*, 32.
80. *Ibid.*, 45.

suggested......His Bible school and the Chicago seminary have filled hundreds of young minds with the same enthusiasm.[81]

Moody's school sent hundreds of Plymouth Brethren world-wide with the hopeless millennial faith and a very unorthodox Bible study method to support that faith.

Chapter 83

Moody's New Message

In addition to winning Moody over to the new method of preaching, Moorehouse changed Moody's view of God: "I used to preach that God was behind the sinner with a double-edged sword ready to hew him down. I have got done with that. I preach now that God is behind him with love, and he is running away from the God of love."[82] Moody's message from the time of Moorehouse's meetings was the love of Christ to draw sinners to the Saviour.[83]

In addition, Moody now stressed the necessity of conversion and the love of God, while avoiding hellfire and God's wrath. His theology in the area of eternal punishment was not far from Beecher's. Moody also dropped any social involvement that threatened to hinder his evangelism. Marsden identifies c. 1870 as the turning point of Moody's preaching to the new version of holiness and premillennialism,[84] corresponding with his involvement with Moorehouse.

Ironside remembers hearing Moody at an 1888 Los Angeles meeting: "Three things impressed themselves upon the lad (twelve

---

81. *Ibid.,* 163.
82. *Moody,* 139.
83. *Ibid.,* 439.
84. *Fundamentalism,* 32, 35, 37. Concerning hell, Beecher asserted that the Bible "employs not the scientific reason, but imagination and the reason under it." While not openly denying the doctrine of hell, he implied that it is an imagined fear. *Ibid,* 23.

at the time) that night, although he was still an unsaved, if religious, boy. Moody spoke for only thirty-five minutes; he quoted many Scripture passages, illuminating them with moving illustrations that were homely and tender..."[85]

Moody was also so influenced by the Darbyite writer, C.H. Mackintosh, that he purchased all Mackintosh's writings, and stated that he would sooner give up his entire library, excepting his Bible, than part with them.[86]

Moody appeared in Edinburgh in the end of 1873. Although he had come previously in 1867 for private reasons, his later trips were to lead in great evangelistic campaigns. His meetings were soon full. Moody had a shrewd perception of character, and knew how to utilize all available forces; these things were coupled with a power to attract young men and inspire "hero worship." Next door to the place Moody held most of his meetings, there happened to be a theological college, and many of the students assisted in the meetings.[87]

Among the college students who assisted Moody in Edinburgh, the one destined to prove most useful was Henry Drummond (1851-1897). Drummond for years accompanied the American evangelist from one great city to another, devoting himself especially to meetings for young men. (He developed qualities of rare distinction for managing young men.) When settled subsequently as professor of Natural Science in Glasgow, Drummond became an evangelist to the universities of Scotland, working chiefly in Edinburgh. Drummond's evangelistic labors on behalf of young men, especially students, extended all over the world. Between Drummond and Moody, there remained a beautiful and life long friendship. Even after Drummond was charged with heretical views, Moody

---

85. *Ordained*, 42. Moody did not "illuminate" passages with other passages, using Scripture to understand Scripture. Rather, he used human experiences to understand Scripture. Moody helped prepare American Christianity to willingly accept "Christian" Psychology – interpreting God through human experiences
86. *Roots*, 173.
87. *Ethics*, s.v. "Revivals of Religion."

constantly said that he had heard Drummond far more than had his accusers, and had never heard anything with which he did not agree.[88]

The Irish revival of 1879 — which involved Moody and Drummond — was imported from America where it had already been prevalent for two years. Moody had learned his methods, many from Moorehouse, in his own country before going to the British Isles.

Moody returned to Great Britain in the fall of 1881. He preached in Glasgow for five months and made short visits to some of the large centers of Scotland. He also visited Switzerland, Swansea, Cardiff, Newport, Plymouth, Devonport, Paris, Bristol, Cambridge, Oxford, Torquay, Exeter, Southampton, Portsmouth, Brighton, Ireland, Birmingham, Leicester, Nottingham, Manchester, Leeds and Liverpool.[89] When he returned to America, his presence was required at the Northfield Seminary and Mount Hermon School, USA. He then returned to Britain, where he held large successful meetings.

Of Moody's London meetings, a critic said:

> The Pall Mall Gazette makes mention of this fact as they tell of the great crowds which gathered to hear Moody and Sankey. "Whatever we may think of them, however much their methods may grate upon the susceptibilities of these who have at length succeeded in living up to their blue china, these men are factors of considerable potency in the complex sum of influences which make up contemporary English life...
>
> "Mr. Moody's conduct of the entire meeting was a remarkable manifestation of the way in which the fervor of his zeal is helped by his extraordinary sagacity, and by the tact of a shrewd man.... He understands how much depends on details, and great care is given to the veriest trifle..."[90]

Note two points: First, it was Moody's methods that drew the crowds — it was estimated that he spoke to over two million in London

---

88. *Ibid.*
89. *Moody*, 299-301.
90. *Ibid.*, 304-305.

alone. When Moody wanted to reach the 1893 World's Fair crowds, his plan was to "...present the Gospel so attractively that the people will want to come and hear it."[91] Second, notice the tremendous zeal and seemingly endless energy, combined with tremendous charisma, that marked Moody, traits typical of the Brethren movement (he had been a good salesman). The early millenarians did not depend upon doctrinal soundness to sway the crowds to their theories; rather, they depended upon methods and zeal.[92]

Moody went to Europe in both 1873 and 1881 as a mentor of the fiery young Darbyist, Henry Moorehouse, which begs this question: How much of the "revivalists" *movement of soul* is God's Spirit working and how much is the result of well planned and executed methods designed to move the soul? The question does not downplay the importance of planning, but can we ignore that there is a difference? Methods designed to move the soul downplay, if not outright bypass, the work of God's Spirit of grace in converting the sinner.

As Moody went up and down in the States evangelizing until his death, his success in the Old Country gave him standing such as no evangelist before him had enjoyed.

---

91. *Ibid.*, 413.
92. Sadly, few people seem to care about sound theology, for it requires thinking and studying. Zeal is commendable, as long is it is according to sound knowledge, Rom. 10:2.

Part IX
America Conquered

Chapter 84
America Invaded

In 1859, the great revival that started in North America reached Britain, and the effects were felt in "all denominations."[1] During the time of American Revivalism, the millenarians did a great amount of eschatological writing. Their other-worldliness and pietism — withdraw from society into their local churches to become more spiritual — found a quick and ready readership and following.[2] The British revivals produced many new converts hungry for the Bread of Life, and the millenarians were there to give them bread. But their bread contained the destructive worms of mysticism, monasticism and defeat, as the converts were taught, in Irving's words, "the terrors of Satan" in this present dispensation.

The freedom offered in the movement, not the doctrine, attracted men of great ability who were subsequently influenced by the system formulated by Irving, Darby, Groves, Newton and Müller. In other words, after converts identified with the movement, they were overwhelmed by the personalities of a few basic men, Darby especially, and were thus persuaded to accept the new system of "Christian thought."

---

1. Moody's meetings in Europe were supported by both the Free and the Established churches. Moreover, the Roman Catholic paper in Ireland "was extremely friendly" toward Moody's work. The Catholics saw the danger coming from the direction of Huxley, Darwin and Tyndall, not from Moody. *Moody*, 187, 215.
2. Coad, *History,* 169.

Though monasticism and mysticism — other-worldliness — did not influence all who were attached to the movement completely to abandon all social action, the spirits of monasticism and mysticism were clearly passed on.[3]

Darby was extremely proud of his hard work, taking credit for things he really had very little, if anything, to do with, so consider the following accordingly.

His 1863 visit found Americans in the same frame of mind as had been Europeans when Irving introduced the millennial system. The War Between the States left Americans ready to accept the promise of escape from the troubles, sorrows and responsibilities of this world.[4] Darby's visit during that time of turmoil caused him to become more *heavenly-minded*, *i.e.*, separated from reality.[5]

Darby was also warmly received in Canada, drawing many pastors and laymen to his "Bible readings" from both Canada and the U.S.A.

Though Darby worked hard to convert America to his opinions, Moody was the key. Only after Moody's conversion to Americanized Darbyism did the millennial system start to receive a measure of respectability. Moody also prepared America for Scofield's introduction of Darbyism some years later.

As the revival spread, spiritual hunger increased, and providence provided intellectuals to develop a theological foundation for the developing millennial system. Providence also provided vast funds to publish millennial writings. The strength of the millennial movement was the vast amount of literature produced by Darby and many of the original millenarians. Their influence went world-wide in print, forever changing the face and character of Christianity.[6]

---

3. *Ibid.*, 179.
4. *Letters*, I.351, 1863, from Canada. See also, I.352, II.377.
5. *Ibid.*, II.372, 373, 1864
6. Coad, *History,* 210. One wonders if maybe Divine Providence allowed Deut. 13 to be placed into action?

Initially, American Christianity rejected Darby's system, but he did not give up. "New gatherings are formed," writes Darby from Springfield, Illinois, "but chiefly by those from Europe, though here all is American."[7] Writing from Nismes, Dec 9, 1849, Darby said,

> One thing is evident, God is working in the last days. Dissolution is on all sides, not only going on, but felt to be going on... there must be devotedness, practical devotedness as belonging entirely to Him. This is what I earnestly desire and pray for. We are bought with a price, and are not our own — happy and blessed to be so in a world stranger to life and God. To maintain such a position [of otherworldliness, *ed.*] Christ must be everything.[8]

The terms "Otherworldliness" and "Heavenly-mindedness" were not *invented* by Darby, but they effectively described his system of opinions. The terms he liked were "devotedness and unworldliness"[9]—that is, aware of but unconcerned about surrounding social and religious activities.[10] Quite often, Darby mentioned the conducive circumstances in the areas where he was presently located, and the willingness of the people to receive his message of escape — "I am in Ireland... Here I have found a number of young men in a very lively interesting state, recently converted, ever ready to feed on the word... Indeed the Spirit of God is at work around the country..."[11] About England, Darby said, "The agitation is very great in these countries, even in England..."[12]

---

7. *Letters*, II.193, Nov. 21, 1872.
8. *Ibid.*, I.178.
9. *Ibid.*, II.376.
10. *Ibid.*, 60, 1870. "We belong to heaven," Darby would no doubt say, "Therefore, don't worry about surrounding events." *Ibid.*, I, 318. From Elberfeld, 1861. The Christian is to be outside looking in, *ibid.*, 416, 1866. In fact, the Christian's unconcern gives strength, joy and happiness, *ibid.*, 480. Note the date — Unsettledness was in America's air, to say the least.
11. *Ibid.*, 233, from Dublin, May, 1854.
12. *Ibid.*, 245, 415. Canada, *ibid.*, 342.

Chapter 85

The War Between the States

As the French Revolution and the Napoleonic Wars prepared Europe for the Brethren's mystic brand of Pietistic Christianity, so did the War Between the States (1861-1865) prepare America. Darby visited America several times between 1862 to 1877. In a letter from Toronto, May 27th, 1863, Darby writes that he traveled,

> [A]cross the country [America, *ed.*] on the skirts of the war — though not feeling it, beyond soldiers being about, and encampment in sight where E. distributed tracts, &c., but a sad state of things.[13]

Accordingly, the unsettled War conditions left Americans in a hopeless state of mind. People wanted an escape from the realities of life. The American church leaders resisted the *truth according to Darby,* but the millennial message of escapism found receptive ears among the "souls who sigh[ed] over the state of things and long[ed] for something better."[14]

Arriving in the Americas during the War Between the States, 1862, Darby found that the turmoil gave him a ready audience. In 1862, writing from Hamilton, Canada, Darby said, "Here and in the U.S. the church and the world are more mixed up than even in England, so that the testimony of brethren is more definite and important as far as the sphere goes, and things seem to point to an awakening as to this in the States. I have been invited to more than one point..." "Mixed up" is Darbyism for Christian involvement in trying to influence society with the word of God. "Testimony of brethren" is Darbyism for the Lord's very imminent return and general millennial theories, including Christian monasticism.[15] Clearly, people loved his message of noninvolvement and no

---

13. *Ibid.,* I.351. Between 1862 and 1877, Darby traveled nearly seven years in the U.S. and Canada. *Roots,* 71.
14. *Letters,* I.352.

responsibility for Christian social change, especially in the wake of the War.

Seeing the social turmoil on all sides, he wrote from Canada in 1865:

> Here things are going on with wonderful rapidity, towards the end, though I know it is limited by the Lord's having gathered out His own, short or long as is needed for that. But it is a time not hard to discern; men's minds unsettling from what seemed established...[16]

Neither Lacunza's system — nor its child, Irvingism/Darbyism — offered any answer to the unsettled conditions except to be more heavenly-minded and study prophecy; the people loved it.

A small number of prophets of defeat went over the world with their visions of doom, escape and no Christian responsibility except just to wait for the Lord's soon return. Their primary effort was toward the already converted, particularly in America, to rescue them from doomed, organized religion. The prophets of death wrote multitudes of books, and the hearts of the people were won away from the gospel of "Christ the victorious" (which requires work, dedication and sacrifice) that had been *vox populi*, *i.e.*, popular opinion. Pastors who might have otherwise stood against the new theories, maybe even regarded them as heresies, saw their people rushing to the new, unorthodox, hopeless theories of escape, defeat and withdrawal from society with no responsibility except to wait. To complicate matters, the unorthodox ideas seemed to be justified by Scripture through "Bible reading."

Darby himself complained that the pastors started preaching what had, up to that point, been uniquely Brethren doctrines because they wanted to keep their people in their churches. He found it very unsettling that they preached his theories yet they failed to preach

---

15. *Ibid.*, 336. Also 343, 351, 365. Darby also found a ready audience among the Romanists and French. *Ibid.*, II.173, 1872. Darby's purpose in America was to stress the Lord's very soon return, and if Christians wanted to be right with God, they had to separate from worldly affairs. *Ibid.*, I.372, 472.

16. *Ibid.*, I.406. "...gathered out His own," is Darbyism for seeing things his way. He had good words only for those who agreed with him.

that the organized church was ruined and that the people needed to come out of them and join his movement. The non-Brethren pastors and schools felt they had to preach the millennial system or lose their people and finances. Pastors and the Christian colleges soon saw that there was money in millennial speculations, and their hearts were won to the system.[17] Thus a new, unorthodox, "chaotic" system of exegesis becomes part of Christian life and thought. We must add that no doubt many pastors like the idea that their preaching has no social consequences — they can proclaim from the house tops that they believe in *Family Values,* yet they never define what they mean. They can jump and shout against sin, yet neither define it nor offend anyone.[18]

The word of God was fulfilled in the system that swept the world after Irving published *Ben-Ezra*:

> *The prophets prophesy falsely, and the priests bear rule by their means; and my people love to have it so: and what will ye do in the end thereof?* (Jer. 5:31)

Chapter 86
Key Events

There were several key events after 1850 that caused the millennial system to be embraced by the American Church as orthodox Christianity. The change Darby longed for in America would have been impossible for one man to achieve, especially a European. However, providence provided key events to remove "Christ the victorious" from American culture and turn it over to defeat: 1) the abundant immigration of Darbyites to America from

---

17. MacPherson presents an excellent case that money motivated many ministries not only to adopt Darbyism, but promote it on a grand scale. See *Plot,* 232-234.

18. *Family Values* is a much used term today, but whose *family* is being referred to? The sodomites', the adulterers' or...?

Europe; 2) the introduction of Darby's method of Bible study, "Bible reading"; 3) the *conversion* of D.L. Moody; 4) the War Between the States; 5) the Bible conference movement at Northfield, Niagara, &c.; 6) the spread of Keswick's Christian thought by men such as "Billy" Sunday; and 7), the publishing of the *Scofield Reference Bible*. Scofield's book, beyond any doubt, did more to influence the English speaking world for the millennial system than any one other event. Moreover, Darbyism spread to the non-English world through the ensuing missionary effort by men carrying *Scofield Bibles*.[19]

Up to these events, American Christianity keep Darbyism at arm's length, viewing his opinions concerning dispensational millenarianism — including the idea of a pre-tribulation rapture — with great suspicion. Darby himself laments over American resistance to his system. Writing from Canada, Sept., 1872, he said,

> In the States there is some progress. They are going on happily enough in the east, some added, but no great progress in numbers; in the west a good many Presbyterians, several ministers among them, teach the Lord's coming, the presence of the Holy Ghost, that all sects are wrong, but as yet few move from their places. A few have - not of clergy yet, though one or two have been preached out. In one place there is a move, but I cannot but think when some move that the conscience of others will be stirred up. But many who now favour the truth I suppose would become opponents: to give up ease for the cross is not pleasant to the flesh.[20]

In fact, Darby said that American Christians were astonished at the *truth* he presented. In an 1872 letter from Chicago, Darby wrote:

> There is inquiry, and a good deal of it among those interested in the things of God, consciences awakened as to the state of the church and learning truth, astonishment at what is found in scripture; for

---

19. Note the working of providence — it provided victory in America's War for Independence; however, it provided defeat for victorious Christianity with the rise of millennialism and defeat for Calvinism and freedom in the War Between the States.

20. *Letters*, II.182. The same letter mentions the great increase in numbers: "...as numbers increase..." and later, "The work is spreading and enlarging in all quarters, and the need of mature labourers shews itself everywhere."

work, not truth, is the American line of things, and an activity which leaves the saints and the world all mixed up together.[21]

"[A]ll mixed up together" may have been Darby's reference to a worldly American Church, for he did make such complaints.[22] But having followed Darby's thinking for 50 or so years in his letters, we must say that Darby's heart was troubled greatly over the fact that American Christianity was involved — "all mixed up" — at the time of his visit in exercising Christian influence and dominion in its culture. It generally expected to convert the world to Christ. Darby worked tirelessly to convince the hardheaded American Christians that any effort to form society along godly Biblical guidelines was sin — all one was responsible to do was wait for the imminent return of Christ. Then it is Christ's responsibility to literally straighten things out with his "rod of iron."

Darby said that he had to present "the most elementary truths of Christianity. Man is set up, and Christians so used to it, that all God's thoughts [that is, *God's thoughts* according to Darby's opinions, *ed.*] have to be brought in as new things. A hundred truths which would be quoted to prove other points."[23] Darby's "elementary truths" were so radically new in America that he had to prove them with many Scriptures — that is, "Bible reading." Apparently, one of the greatest thrills to Darby's heart was church splits over his millennial system. Darby writes that in spite of American resistance to his "truth,"

> Still one works on, and there is a growing desire among Christians to know more of the truth. But everything has to be brought to the word — all indulge so wholly their own thoughts. I have daily meetings here, and even twice a day, besides visiting. In -----, a Presbyterian minister, by preaching what he had learned of the Lord's coming and truths connected with it, has broken up his congregation, and some thirty or forty are going to meet, waiting on the Lord to be guided - many of them, however, ignorant of sound principles of gathering [remember, Darby is speaking from the

---

21. *Ibid.*, 189. Darby's definition of "truth" centered in himself.
22. *Roots*, 73.
23. *Letters*, II.189.

Brethren view of gathering, *ed.*], but some very nice brethren. So one works on, only one has to look to the Lord continually, and not faint, for in this country the path is beset with difficulties [*i.e.,* American Christianity resisted Darby's mysticism, withdrawal from society, *ed.*]...[24]

He writes from St. Louis (Nov. 30, 1872):

> ... Three ministers have come out since I came over here, and two small gatherings, but very weak, have been formed, and there is some earnest inquiry... This is American work: some new gatherings round Boston, but I believe of emigrants. The native population is extremely difficult to reach; conscience has little power — activity, organization, man. In most places grace is hardly known, and mostly opposed: a few old school Presbyterians hold it, otherwise I know none — the state of things deplorable. The teacher of the Sunday school teachers openly denies the resurrection: so one of the pastors here — everything as loose as it can be: only God is above it.[25]

Reading Darby's letters, one will find that his definition of grace under "Paul's dispensation" is to be dead to this world and alive with Christ in heavenly places. But *dead to this world* meant absolute indifference to earthly matters. After all, are we not dead though we yet live here on this earth? In an 1872 letter from Springfield, Illinois, Darby laments over the fact that the American Church is more interested in action and "mending the world" — an action abhorred by millenarians — than in "Simple following the Lord." 1872 was about the time of Moody's conversion to Darby's "truth":

> We began yesterday to break bread at Springfield, Illinois, six; there may be one or two more from the country. Many more see the ruin [of the church, *ed.*], and that the state of things is unscriptural, but hope still to cling together, and think they are outside the camp.... In Chicago there was, in a certain circle, considerable inquiry after the truth, and many wished me to stay or return. I may do this. But one

---

24. *Ibid.,* 190-191.

25. *Ibid.,* 197-198. He had some legitimate complaints against American Christianity, but his major problem with it was Christian involvement in trying to win and/or influence the world for Christ. He was greatly distressed because American Christians were involved in social issues, *i.e.,* "worldliness." *Ibid.,* I.514. 1867.

will have it as a rule in the American churches. Old school Presbyterians, or some of them, have the most of it. It is otherwise resisted or unknown. The active man at Chicago, lately in England [obviously Moody, *ed.*], is deep in the mud of this. In our readings, three I think know something of grace, though not clear on other things; a few found it, but it is preached nowhere, but the contrary. But not a few souls got interested in truth. At present, if they go to church they hear what upsets and bewilders them. Loose action suits itself to all this.... But work in the U.S. is pilgrimage for me, and so best. Simple following the Lord is unknown; activity, organization, mending the world, mixing with it, is all that is known, hence also the word has little authority. Still, as I have said, there is inquiry, and godly people feel the state of things. Were I younger, I might look to more constant work. The loose brethren who may come, fall in with all this, and leave where it is. New gatherings are formed, but chiefly by those from Europe, though here all is America...[26]

Immigration

We cannot overestimate the importance that the immigration of the last half of the 1800s played in America's *conversion*. Darby previously had an extremely fruitful ministry in Switzerland; and the Swiss immigrants in America brought him over to minister among them. Accordingly, Darbyism initially arrived in America in the hearts of the immigrants; they invited and supported him while he planted his destructive seed of death in America.[27]

Darby's millennial "truth" was unacceptable to the average American Christian. It was imported by immigrants from Europe who had already been converted to millennialism. Thus the *Christian spirit* that immigrated to America from Europe with these dissidents was not the same *Christian spirit* that settled the nation many years previously. The *spirit* that settled this nation was a spirit of "Christ the Victorious" — conquer the world for Christ. On the other hand, the *spirit* that came with the millenarians was the spirit of "the terrors of Satan" — withdrawal from the world because it

---

26. *Ibid.,* II.193.
27. *Ibid.,* I.234, 369, 371, 352, 365 (1863).

belongs to the Devil. America was thus *converted* from a land of Christian hope to a land of defeat.

Though finding among the immigrants support, a ready audience and a foothold, Darby had to work patiently to make his opinions acceptable to those who were here in the spirit of "Christ the Victorious."

Chapter 87
Millenarian Bible Conferences

Moody was a crucial link between the early millenarians — with their "Bible reading" method of non-contextual, "mystical insight," Bible exegesis — and with American Christianity. Another crucial link was the American Bible Conference movement. It had as great an effect in North America as it did in Great Britain for developing and spreading the millennial system:

> During the last quarter of the nineteenth century, the millenarian movement assumed a different form and, especially in the United States, began to organize and proselyte through a series of newly founded prophetic and Bible conferences...[28]

Thus in America as in Europe, the new millenarian movement specialized in and grew through proselytizing, not through converting sinners to Christ.

Niagara Bible Conference

The first and most influential Millenarian Bible Conference in America was the Niagara Bible Conference. It started as an informal conference in 1868 in New York City, but "From 1883 to 1897 the conference met at Niagara-on-the Lake, Ontario, and thus acquired its customary name... The founding father and controlling spirit of the conference was the Reverend James Hall Brookes (1830-1897),

---

28. *Roots,* 132.

a Presbyterian minister from Saint Louis, Missouri."[29] "Dr. Brookes knew and loved many of them [Brethren, ed.]. His pulpit had often been opened to them. Darby, Malachi Taylor, Paul J. Loizeaux and others had preached in his church at various times.[30]

Niagara was also attended by George Needham. Needham (1840-1902) was reared in Ireland where he preached among the Plymouth Brethren, and later in life, joined the Baptists. As we saw previously, the organizers of the prophetic movement in America were predominantly Presbyterian Calvinists.

> [T]he Niagara conference represented J.N. Darby's concept of the church adapted to the American environment. Although they were intrigued by much of Darby's theology, ...most American ministers could not follow Darby in his denunciation of "systems" -- that is, denominations. But at Niagara denominations could be and were consistently ignored; the minister became the Bible teacher and the sermon was transformed into the Bible reading.[31]

Thus the "Bible reading" method of study used at Niagara allowed the men to develop arbitrary and unhistorical understandings of passages to support the developing millennial system. The teachers, meanwhile, could loudly proclaim that they believed and used God's inspired word.[32]

No one was intentionally invited to speak at the early Bible and prophetic conferences — including Niagara — who was not completely committed to the "premillennial truth." Later conferences after c. 1887, however, allowed conservatives to speak who did not necessarily hold "premillennial" views.[33]

---

29. *Ibid.*, 133, 134. Brookes was ordained in 1854 after one year at Princeton Seminary.
30. *Sketch,* 196. However, Ironside, writing in the 1940s, offers no documentation that Darby spoke in Brookes' pulpit at various times. *Loizeaux Brothers* could be considered the "official publishers" of Brethren material. This writer assumes P.J.Loizeaux was part of that publishing concern.
31. *Roots,* 136. Serious Bible exposition was replaced with "fluff."
32. *Ibid.,* 136, 137.
33. *Ibid.,* 165.

Accordingly, *The 1878 Niagara Creed* the conferences produced presents European millennial theories in a palatable form for American Christians. (Compare *Niagara's* mystical emphasis with the practical emphasis of *The London Baptist Confession of Faith of 1689*.) Point XIV clearly identifies *The 1878 Niagara Creed, q.v.,* as Irvingism Americanized.

Chapter 88

Northfield

But as important as Niagara was in Americanizing Irving's millennial system, Moody's Northfield conferences were the primary means of *converting* the American Christian culture to mystic monasticism. With these conferences, Moody changed the face and character of American Protestantism:

> As a result of Moody's efforts a new kind of pietistic holiness was brought from England to this continent... With Moody as an ally and convert, and with the Northfield conference as a sounding board for their views, the millenarians had an unparalleled opportunity to impress their own views of this world and the next upon evangelical Christianity.[34]

From Moody's first conference in 1880 through 1886, Northfield was fairly dominated by millenarians. Northfield permitted the millenarians to establish themselves nationally as reputable Protestant leaders,[35] which they had not been.

The millenarians transformed the Holy Spirit's role from conquering the world for Christ, which had shaped American Christian Culture, to little more than a personal, mystical experience and influence. America's Christian message was changed accordingly. F.M. Ellis, a Baltimore Baptist minister, spoke at the 1890, Baltimore millenarian Bible conference on the Holy Spirit, of

---

34. *Ibid.,* 172, 173.
35. *Ibid.,* 175.

which Rev. Amzi Clarence Dixon was an organizer. (In 1910, Dixon became pastor of Spurgeon's London Tabernacle.) At the conclusion of a discussion on the Holy Spirit's role in the church, Ellis said,

> Our best service towards the spiritualization of the church will be found, I am persuaded, in our becoming personally more spiritual.

Thus, the millenarians, though developing in part out of a desire to escape from the antinomian tendencies within the holiness revival of the 1850s, found themselves drawn back into the movement for personal sanctification.[36]

Chapter 89

Keswick

Keswickism — Perfectionism — holds that "the sincere man is the perfect man":

> As God therefore expects from every man, at any given moment, only the best that he can do with his impaired faculties, perfection is simply doing one's best. In other words, perfection is in full consecration, in an entirely surrendered will... *The moral law has been superseded by the law of faith.* [Emp. added, ed.] Thus the life of faith is the perfect life, and, when perfectly maintained, excludes the presence and power of sin. Moreover, this gift of faith which makes perfect is a distinct bestowment of the Holy Spirit--a 'second blessing' following the primary gift of faith (cf. 'Have ye received the Holy Ghost since ye believed?' [Ac. 19.2], and Mahan, *The Baptism of the Holy Ghost,* p. 34.). The prevailing teaching among those who to-day advocate the possibility in the present world of a perfect Christian life is to regard it as thus realized, *i.e.* in an entire surrender of the will to God, issuing in the power and joy of full consecration to His service and in the sustained habit of the life of faith. What is known as the Keswick school may be considered here as typical.[37]

---

36. *Ibid.,* 178.
37. *Ethics,* s.v. "Perfection (Christian)." See old *Scofield* edition of the Bible, 1244.

Keswickism helped reduce Christianity from being a new creature in Christ desiring to do those things pleasing in his sight according to all of his moral law, to little more than a mystical feeling, *i.e.*, feeling good about one's Christian experience — "The moral law has been superseded by the law of faith."[38] How many times have we heard the phrases, "No man is perfect," or "Just as long as the motives are pure" to justify sin? Both phrases are combined Darby and Keswick thought.

Biblically,

> Perfection means uprightness and maturity in terms of a goal or purpose, an end established by God. Our maturity in heaven will include sinlessness, but our maturity here is of a different sort.
>
> In this life, we can be perfect in the sense of being blameless in our faithfulness to God's purpose, but to be blameless does not mean being faultless.[39]

Keswickism — personal holiness at the expense of the world-conquering power of the Holy Spirit through obedience to God's total word — was brought into the Northfield conferences by Moody when, in 1891, he brought in the Keswick teacher, F.B. Meyer:

> On one occasion the millenarians objected to one of these British speakers strenuously enough to caucus and then send a representative to Moody to protest against the new heresy this man was teaching. The date was probably 1891, the man was the Reverend Frederick B. Meyer (1847-1929), a well-known Baptist minister whom Moody had met in York in 1872. Meyer's "heresy" was a doctrine of personal sanctification associated with the Keswick conferences in England.[40]

"Moody managed to pacify the disgruntled millenarian leaders," and Meyer returned in succeeding years, as did other Keswick teachers, Prebendary Webb-Peploe, Andrew Murray — a Dutch Reformed minister from South Africa, and G. Campbell Morgan. Through

---

38. See 2 Cor. 5:17, 1 Jn. ch. 3.
39. *Institutes*, 629. In his book, *Perfectionism*, Warfield deals extensively with then rising tide of the movement in the late 1800s and early 1900s, including Finney's theology.
40. *Roots*, 176.

these Northfield conferences, Moody successfully merged Keswick's personal holiness doctrine with American millenarianism. Northfield saw Keswick's holiness teaching "rooted firmly in millenarian soil and had the effect of broadening the character of the millenarian movement in accentuation of the trend begun in the Niagara conferences."[41]

Northfield instructed multitudes of preachers from around America "on methods of Christian work, Bible interpretation, and all other varied experiences of a wide and charitable conception of Christian thought and activity."[42] By 1891, Moody was well instructed in the millennial system. Northfield, consequently, quietly instructed American Christian leaders in millennialism's mystical Christianity as developed and matured in Brethrenism.

First Keswick Convention

The first 'Convention for the Promotion of Practical Holiness' was held at Keswick, London, 1875. The principle leaders included F.B. Meyer and Andrew Murray: "'The Keswick Convention has set up no new school of theology, it has instituted no new sect, it has not even formed a society, but exists for the sole purpose of helping men to be holy.'"[43] Moody's involvement with the Keswicks in America proved most influential in forming "other similar associations for the deepening of the spiritual life," *e.g.,* the Student Christian Movement. (How sad that these intelligent men did not meet for the purpose of influencing society for the Kingdom of God, *ed.*)

The Keswick's definition of holiness, though, advocated personal peace and purity through a mystical surrender in faith. The Keswick teachers emphasized the power of the Spirit to lead the believer away from evil and toward righteousness:

---

41. *Ibid.,* 179-180. Personal holiness would be defined as prayer, Bible reading, church attendance, personal piety, and maybe personal *soul-winning.* These personal things are commendable; the problem is when Christianity is reduced to just these personal things, as the millenarians did.

42. *Moody,* 370.

43. *Ethics,* s.v. "Holiness (New Testaament and Christian)."

In more popular statement, a 'higher life' or 'second blessing' of 'full salvation' may be experienced through a single act of perfect consecration to God, who in response completely neutralizes or eradicates the sinful nature so as to grant a present deliverance from the power of sin, on the sole condition of 'abiding' in an attitude of dependent life-union with the exalted Christ. ...How far some forms of it can go may be judged by the affirmation of pastor Paul, 'I have for a long time now seen nothing of my old nature' (*Gnadau Conference Report,* 1904, p. 298). Such a claim to perfect holiness, however, is to be interpreted in a religious rather than a moral sense.[44]

Keswickism mistakenly identifies holiness with asceticism, other-worldliness and introspection, going hand in hand with Darbyism. The Keswick doctrine of personal holiness confines the grace of God to strictly conversion and personal holiness — determined by an act of faith, not morality. The logical implication of Keswick thought is that if an individual desires to live outside of himself and influence society in any way, he must do it on his own without the power of God, the Holy Spirit.

Let us be quick to add that personal holiness is commendable. However, when sought at the expense of social, practical, everyday holiness, half of the power and work of the Holy Spirit as well as an extremely large portion of God's word is lost.

Moody, starting with his 1891 Northfield Conference, instructed America's Christian leaders in Keswick's doctrine and all its practical implications. Clearly, a major portion of the responsibility for the demise of the once victorious American Christian Culture must be borne by Moody.

Charles G. Trumbull

Charles G. Trumbull (1872-1941), "editor of the respectable and popular weekly, the *Sunday School Times,*" was converted to Keswick sanctification in 1910.

---

44. *Ibid.,* 749.

Trumbull used his influence to familiarize American Protestants with the teaching of "the victorious life." He also helped to formally organize the movement, initiating in 1913 an "American Keswick" conference, which settled permanently at Keswick, New Jersey, in 1923. That same year Robert McQuilkin, Trumbull's associate, founded Columbia Bible School, an important center for promoting Keswick views. Trumbull himself soon after his conversion became a protegé of C.I. Scofield.[45]

Trumbull had no small part in killing the remains of American's Christian spirit of victory:

> At the American Keswick conferences, true to the English model, the emphasis was almost entirely on personal experiences of joy, peace, and "victory," with the practical results seen in enhanced devotional life and zeal for missions. In contrast to earlier holiness movements in America, this seems to have lacked almost entirely a social message. For Trumbull this was a matter of principle. Writing around 1914 about Sunday schools for *The Fundamentals*, Trumbull argued that social service programs were particularly dangerous. They included many things "Christian in spirit," but put fruit ahead of roots. Trumbull pointed to the popular Billy Sunday as the proper model. Sunday said little about social services in the current progressive sense, but his evangelism, said Trumbull, "lifts society as the usual social service program can never do. Similarly, in response to criticism that the Keswick conferences had "no real objective outside of oneself and a personal experience," Trumbull's reply was that no one would make such a charge if he had seen the zeal for foreign missions shown at the conferences.[46]

Hence, Keswickism held firmly that involvements "in social service programs were particularly dangerous." Clearly, uninvolvement in "social service programs" by Christians must lead to involvement in them by the pagans, for the Lord himself said, *The poor you have with you always.* With a common voice from all sides, Christians of the early 1900s were overwhelmed with the idea that they must abandon "social service programs" to the pagans. And thus the tremendous rise of the Welfare State, for the Lord God will take care of the poor.

---

45. *Fundamentalism*, 96.
46. *Ibid.*, 96.

Other leaders in the Keswick personal holiness movement were: J. Hudson Taylor,[47] C.I. Scofield, Robert Speer, David Baron, W.H. Grillith Thomas — who taught at Wycliffe College in Toronto.

Hence we see that Keswick theology is almost identical to Irvingism-Darbyism. As the dispensational theories developed and the Keswick personal holiness gained strength, the world-conquering gospel of Jesus Christ was reduced to merely personal salvation, personal consecration and waiting for the personal return of Christ. Christian emphasis turned inward, and practical application of Christianity outside of self was at the least ignored when not considered sin. Moody was the key figure in uniting Irvingism and Keswickism for American Christians.

However, Keswick withdrawal did not invade America without resistance.

> When the Keswick conferences came to Princeton, from 1916 to 1918, they were entering the lair of the aging lion of strict Presbyterian orthodoxy, Benjamin Breckinridge Warfield [1851-1921, *ed.*] of Princeton Theological Seminary. Unlike most of his contemporaries, Warfield was not in the least distracted by the popularity, success, or practical results of a doctrine. True to the Princeton tradition, he spotted a doctrinal innovation and pounced. During the next several years, in a series of sharp and condescending criticisms, Warfield attempted to tear apart once and for all innovative holiness teachings of every sort.... Warfield found the popular writings of Charles Trumbull especially culpable on the score of shallowness. Trumbull often used the slogan, "Let go and let God." Thus Trumbull explained in terms of "Christ within us" who would control our lives so long as we did not resist him. This formula, said Warfield, made God wait for our act of faith (a common Calvinist objection to most modern evangelism). So Christ was supposedly let in and out of peoples' lives like a stream of electricity turned on or off.[48]

Observe: First, the Presbyterians became a primary promoter in America of Keswick's *luke warm* Christianity. Second, all doctrines

---

47. *Ibid.*, 97. Hudson Taylor "became deeply committed to Keswick views." All of his works, therefore, promoted the idea that social involvement was a sin.
48. *Fundamentalism*, 98.

MUST be compared with God's word, not to their apparent results. Third, the idea of *Christ let in and let out of one's life* permits a false gospel of *let the Lord into your life to save you.* Fourth, modern, shallow theological writings — *fluff and stuff* — can be easily traced to the Keswick invasion, invited by Moody.

Chapter 90

Millenarian Training Institutions

There were several unsuccessful efforts to establish millenarian schools for laymen. However, through persistent hard work, the millenarians saw the successful establishment of what became known after Moody's 1899 death as the "Moody Bible Institute." Reuben Archer Torrey (1856-1928), a Congregational evangelist, was its first superintendent when it finally opened in October 1889. There were many other millenarian institutes started about that time: Northwestern Bible Training School (Minneapolis) by A.J. Frost and William Bell Riley, both Baptist; The Bible Institute of L. A., by Thomas C. Horton; The Toronto Bible Training School; Philadelphia Bible Institute, &c.

Student Volunteer Movement

> Another tremendous influence for American millennialism was Moody's *Student Volunteer Movement* (SVM), started within the YMCA in 1886. The SVM was the start of the greatest demonstration "of missionary interest ever known in the United States. The SVM was not dominated by the millenarians, but they played a crucial" role in the world-wide propagation of Irvingism-Darbyism.[49] It was, however, fully committed to Keswick opinions.

The SVM millenarian "missionary challenge was conceived in terms of 'dispersing' information rather that Christianizing the whole world, and it was in that sense that they understood the word

---

49. *Roots*, 183.

'evangelization.' They did not expect that their preaching would produce mass conversions..." Their hopeless "outlook is not surprising, since the SVM originated in conferences completely dominated by millenarian speakers... There is no way of knowing how many missionary volunteers left America as millenarians or became millenarian converts in the field, but there seems little doubt that millenarians were better represented in mission fields than within the American churches."[50] The SVM clearly represented the millennial view that it is sinful to expect the conversion of the world. The missionary effort, accordingly, devolves to simply spreading knowledge of the truth — they were *faithless* missionaries, spreading the millennial message of hopelessness.

After Moody's death, the millennial system continued to spread under his name. The Moody Bible Institute held many conferences — in which Scofield took active parts — in the early 1900's which "clearly and forcefully advocated the Darbyite pretribulationist position." In 1914, on the eve of the First World War, "another in the long series of Bible and prophecy conferences was held at Moody Bible Institute." This conference was especially strong in the millenarian convictions, with the finer details of Darbyism emphasized:

> In the last address of the [1914, *ed.*] conference, R.A. Torrey linked the second advent to the Keswick doctrine of holiness in the fashion that had become customary since the turn of the century, speaking on "The Lord's Second Coming a Motive for Personal Holiness."[51]

However, Torrey was not the first to make such a link. Based upon *the Ben-Ezra system,* Irving was quite dogmatic that prophetic study of the Lord's soon return would purify one from sin. Rather than seeing God's Spirit of grace purifying one from sin, millenarians

---

50. *Ibid.,* 185, 186. Remember, Müller's motive for starting his mission work was that other missions had as their goal the conversion of the world. We need some missions now with the goal of converting the world to Christ.
51. *Ibid.,* 224-6. No doubt this conference calmed the nervous Christians, so they would not question the worldly matter of war.

taught it was the hope in the Lord's soon coming that purifies one from sin.[52]

The purpose of the Bible Institute movement was to provide a forum for the spreading of the millenarian doctrine among the laymen who desired to learn the word of God. The most famous of all, Moody Bible Institute, was a primary instrument for making the millennial system acceptable in America. It made mystical, powerless, defeated Christianity a major part of the "orthodox" faith in an American culture that had been built on a foundational faith that the gospel of Christ would change the world for God and godliness.

Millenarians become Fundamentalists

Finally:

> As a result of the 1919 World Conference on Christian Fundamentals, the millenarian movement had changed its name. The millenarians had become Fundamentalists.[53]

And thus the fox is in the hen house.

Chapter 91

C.I. Scofield

It is impossible to trace the destructive influence of millennialism without meeting Cyrus Ingerson Scofield (1843-1921), for he was a leader in the American Darbyite party.[54] *The Scofield Reference*

---

52. *Writings*, II.417, c. 1852. See also *Writings*, II.179; *Letters*, II.361. Man cleans himself up! — a very key point in revivalism.

53. *Roots*, 246.

54. *Ibid.*, 214. There are several good works on Scofield — J.M. Canfield, *The Incredible Scofield And His Book,* Asheville, N.C. Canfield points out that all references to Scofield in Mr. Moody's Biography are to Dr. Scofield, while all reference to D.L. Moody by Scofield are Mr. Moody. Thus, according to Canfield, Scofield's degree may have been "self-bestowed," p. 155. *Who* simply says Scofield was "privately educated." See also, *The Great Rapture Hoax.*

Bible is the primary method of the "peaceful penetration of other communions by" Irving's and Darby's "theories of the End."

> This ["peaceful penetration," *ed.*] is furthered by the world-wide circulation of the *Scofield Reference Edition* of the Bible (over a million copies). There is much sound divinity, admirably collected, in it; but it is a pity that an alternative edition is not available with the text of *The 1911 Bible,* which was about the best of all attempts made to correct the Family Bible of the English-speaking world... It is a pity also that highly-debatable theories of the End were set down alongside the sacred text as if they were assured results of modern knowledge...[55]

Thus the extremely popular *Scofield Reference Bible* is a Plymouth Brethren publication, finding its roots in the mind of J.N. Darby:

> Scofield's *Reference Bible* represents a lifelong study of the Scriptures, and is hailed in all the world by Brethren as setting forth their views on the interpretation of Scripture, especially of prophecy and "dispensational truth." And naturally: Scofield was for a generation an assiduous and admiring student of Darby's writings.[56]

Though Scofield has been greatly maligned, maybe with good reason, he simply attempted to systematize Darby's extremely haphazard, chaotic thoughts. By the time Scofield's book was released, the Christian world had been prepared for Scofield's notes and cross references. His book was an immediate best-seller. Thus a very large measure of what the average Christian believes is a direct result of the hard work of the Brethren.

The reader can easily see Brethren doctrine in Scofield:

> It may safely be said that the Judaizing of the Church has done more to hinder her progress, pervert her mission, and destroy her spiritually, than all other causes combined. Instead of pursuing her appointed path of separation from the world and following the Lord in her heavenly calling, she has used Jewish Scriptures to justify herself in lowering her purpose to the civilization of the world, the acquisition of wealth, the use of an imposing ritual, the erection of magnificent churches, the invocation of God's blessing upon the

---

55. *Advent,* footnote, xi.
56. *Ibid.,* 19.

conflicts of armies, and the division of an equal brotherhood into "clergy" and "laity."[57]

Among other things, Scofield held that the church must not attempt to civilize the world, *i.e.*, convert the word to Christ. He also held to seven dispensations, each ending in "utter failure." Accordingly, the "Man under Grace" dispensation ends in failure, meaning that Christ's work and God's grace is not sufficient to conquer man's sin. His definition of "grace" must lead to failure, for he calls it "the dispensation of pure grace—which means undeserved favor..." In other words, man can live contrary to God's divine law and still have God's favor.[58] In fact, he held it evil to use the Ten Commandments as man's rule of life:

> It was reserved to modern nomolators to wrench these holy and just but deathful tables from underneath the mercy-seat and the atoning blood, and erect them in Christian churches as the rule of Christian life.[59]

But, according to Scofield, even if God's law is man's standard, man is left on his own to obey it:

> 3. GALATIANISM, or the mingling of law and grace—the teaching that justification is partly by grace, partly by law; or, that grace is given to enable an otherwise helpless sinner to keep the law.[60]

Scofield's world-wide influence is incomprehensible, as multitudes of missionaries have gone forth with Scofield's notes in hand.

Scofield and the "Jews"

1900 saw a heated debate between the pre and post-tribulation, *i.e.*, any-moment coming of Christ (Darby's position), aspect of

---

57. *Rightly Dividing the Word of Truth*, 12.
58. *Ibid.*, 12, 14, 15.
59. *Ibid.*, 42
60. *Ibid.*, 36. Scofield does say that "men are required to live holy lives." But he defines holiness apart from "the law." See God's definition of grace, Phlip. 2:13. Finney held that God's power is not always required to enable man to obey God's commands. *Theology*, 278ff., under the heading, "*The doctrine of gracious ability is an absurdity.*"

millenarian doctrine — that is, will the rapture take place before or after the tribulation? This debate was basically a rehash of the Darby-Newton conflict in the 1840s. The post-tribulationists lost control of the millenarian movement, largely through the efforts of Arno C. Gaebelein (1861-1945).

"By 1902 Gaebelein was almost constantly holding conferences somewhat [sic] in the United States." The fatal blow, however, was the publishing of the *Scofield Reference Bible*:

> At the Sea Cliff conference in 1901, Scofield first discussed with Gaebelein his plan to write an annotated version of the Bible....
> The Bible which Scofield discussed with Gaebelein that night is perhaps the most influential single publication in the millenarian and Fundamentalist historiography. The Scofield Reference Bible combined an attractive format of typography, paragraphing, notes, and cross references with the theology of Darbyite dispensationalism. The book has thus been subtly but powerfully influential in spreading those views among hundreds of thousands who have regularly read that Bible and who often have been unaware of the distinction between the ancient text and the Scofield interpretation.[61]

Gaebelein was a German immigrant who arrived in the United States in 1879. He became a minister in the German conference of the Methodist church. "He learned Yiddish well enough to be accused of attempting to pass as a Gentile." (Thus Gaebelein was a "Jew.") He preached to large audiences of Jewish men on Saturday afternoons with considerable success. He began publishing a Yiddish monthly paper and, in 1894, established an English periodical called *Our Hope* to publicize his work, proclaim the imminent second advent, and alert Gentiles to the remarkable Zionist awakening among the Jewish population. After converting to Plymouth Brethrenism, he finally cut himself off from the Methodists in 1899. A heated conflict arose in 1900 between the pre- and post-tribulation positions.[62]

---

61. *Roots,* 221, 222.
62. *Ibid.,* 215.

In a special December issue of *Our Hope* devoted entirely to Christ's premillennial advent, in which appeared Scofield's "May the Lord Come at Any Time," Gaebelein said point blank: "No one can continue to give out a truth, scriptural, *edifying* testimony of the coming of the Lord who believes that certain events must come to pass before the Lord comes or that the church will pass through the tribulation." With that statement, Gaebelein had, in effect, excommunicated the post-tribulationists.

The controversy also involved who would be in apostolic succession from Brookes, who was a thorough Darbyite pre-tribulation rapture dispensationalist, and from Gordon, a historicist, *i.e.,* historic "Chiliasm." Each side had a publication, with Gaebelein (*Our Hope*) on the pre-tribulation side, and with Cameron (*Watchword and Truth*) on the historicist side. Both Gaebelein and Cameron sought to fill the void left by Brookes and Gordon. (Scofield was a protegé of J.H. Brookes.)[63] Brookes and Gordon were among the five organizers, four Presbyterian and one Baptist (Brookes), of the prophetic movement in America—the first Niagara Bible conference for prophetic study, 1876.[64]

The Gaebelein-Scofield-Darbyite party emerged from the struggle far stronger than its opposition. According to a 1943 issue of *Moody Monthly,* Gaebelein, who never seemed to lack funds, put Scofield in touch with several of his supporters, all of whom contributed toward Scofield's expenses during the next few years while he worked on his Manuscript:

> Lyman Stewart, president of Union Oil Co. of California; Francis E. Fitch, a member of the Plymouth Brethren and the head of a printing company which printed the New York Stock Exchange lists; Alwyn Ball, Jr., a real estate broker and member of the large New York real estate firm of Southack and Ball; John B. Buss, a St. Louis businessman; and John T. Pirie, owner and New York representative of Carson, Pirie, Scott & Col, the Large Chicago department store. Pirie owned a large estate at Sea Cliff on the north shore of Long

---

63. For A.J. Gordon's belief, see Strong's *Systematic Theology,* 1012, 1013.
64. *Fundamentalism,* 46.

Island, and it was there, in the summer of 1902, that the decision was made to proceed with the Reference Bible.[65]

Gaebelein was known for "prophetic vision of the needs of the Jews in this country" and "his effort in behalf of the Jewish people. [He was, *ed.*] Superintendent of the Hope of Israel Mission in connection with the City Mission of New York. (1894-1899)."[66] Rev. Arno C. Gaebelein, D.D., a "Jew" converted to Plymouth Brethrenism, is listed by Scofield as a consulting editor for his *Study Bible*. Evidently, it was "Jewish" money that financed the *Scofield Study Bible*.[67]

Scofield and Brookes

The connection between Scofield and J.H. Brookes, a leading Irvingite-Darbyite dispensationalist, is easily followed. Scofield considered Brookes one of his closest friends, as well as the one who established him in the faith.[68]

> What does Brookes have to do with Scofield? After Scofield's ... conversion in St. Louis, they became good friends. Scofield later reminisced in writing about Brookes: "During the last twenty years of his life Dr. Brookes was perhaps my most intimate friend, and to him I am indebted more than to all other men in the world for the establishment of my faith." Scofield thus was acquainted with Brookes as early as 1877 — the date of Darby's last visit to America.[69]

The connection between Moody and Scofield is not as clear. In Moody's Biography, Scofield is simply mentioned as being in

---

65. *Roots,* 215-220, 233. *Cult,* 40.

66. *Who,* s.v. "Gaebelein, Arno Clemen." "He was author of many books on Bible study, prophecy, and the Jews..." (16 listed). Gaebelein, therefore, was a key in developing, promoting and supporting modern *Protestant Zionism*. See also *Advent,* 19.

67. The most prestigious publishers in the English-speaking world published Scofield's book. Also of note is that the "Christian Identity" movement was rising about this time, c. 1870. It also helped neutralize Christianity. *Cult,* 40ff. Note the number of converted Jews at the start of the modern "Protestant Zionist" movement.

68. *Roots,* 217, 223.

attendance in one of Moody's meetings in Dallas in 1895. At the time of Moody's death, December 22, 1899, Scofield had been pastor at the Northfield church for close to four years, from 1895 to 1902.[70] Moody obviously would not allow anyone to pastor Northfield who was not in doctrinal agreement with him. We get some idea of Scofield's theology from his notes attached to the KJV Bible. Note some things Scofield tells us in his "INTRODUCTION (TO BE READ.)"

Scripture According to Scofield

First, Scofield's notes are a collection of works of "experienced Bible students and teachers, in England and the United States."

Second, he states that he felt that "the old system of reference, based solely upon the accident of the English words, was unscientific and often misleading." So in his edition of the Bible, he replaces that old, outmoded method with "a new system of connected topical references." No doubt he refers to the "Bible reading" method of study developed to support the millennial system.

Third, he refers to the previous fifty years of explosive interest in Bible study, which conforms with the explosive growth of Darbyism, 1850 on.

Fourth, Scofield significantly says, "The Editor disclaims originality." Scofield clearly tells us that he simply compiled the works of others from the previous fifty years:

> This apology was also his boast. To be original was not the mark of good millenarian exegesis. But Scofield also meant to acknowledge that he had done very little more than put his predecessor's work into a most ingenious and assimilable form. Scofield never demonstrated great ability as a biblical scholar, apologist, or

---

69. *Hoax,* 78, 79. "The pastor who delivered the sermon and presided at the funeral of Dwight L. Moody, the famous evangelists, was Rev. C.I. Scofield..." *Ibid.* It is worthy of the interested reader's time to read Canfield's book, *The Incredible Scofield...*

70. *Moody,* 518, *Scofield,* 155, *Roots,* 223.

organizer, but in the calendar of Fundamentalist saints no name is better known or more revered."[71]

It is interesting that on the opening page of The Scofield Reference Bible, two leaders of the movement emasculating American Christianity are listed among the eight "Consulting Editors:" James M. Gray and William J. Erdman. Erdman, a Presbyterian, was a *founding father* of the Niagara Conferences.[72]

Not only was Scofield a leader in the Darbyite movement, but he was also an important leader in the Keswick movement. His connection with Keswick's Perfectionism is obvious from his notes. Scofield combines Keswick and Irvingite-Darbyite teachings that perfection involves withdrawing from society in order to become more personally holy, more mystical. But the Scriptures are clear: "Christian perfection, therefore, is not individual or social alone, but the full self-realization of the individual **in society**..."[73]

Chapter 92

Various Men

The purpose of our present study is to trace the neutralization of victorious, world-conquering Christianity — its reduction to its present powerless place in society. There were several men exalted after 1850 who developed the idea that Christians are defeated in Christ, rather than *more than conquers.*

---

71. *Roots,* 224.

72. J.M. Gray (1851-1935) became the rector of the First Reformed Episcopal Church in Boston in 1879. In 1904, when Dr. R.A. Torrey began his worldwide evangelistic campaigns, he became dean of Moody Institute, which grew rapidly under him. He "manifested an interest in civic affairs, in national patriotism, in social betterment, in public education, and in prohibition." *Who,* s.v. "Gray, James Martin."

73. *Ethics,* s.v. "Perfection (Christian)." Emp. added.

H. W. Beecher

A key figure in defeating victorious Christianity, though not clearly connected with the Darbyite movement, was Henry Ward Beecher (1813-1887). His role in shifting the emphasis of the Gospel from its world-conquering message to a 'mystical, spiritual' message is so great that he cannot be ignored.

George Marsden gives an overview of America before victorious Christianity was withdrawn from society. He points out that "In 1870 almost all American Protestants thought of America as a Christian nation." The motive behind American Evangelical mission work of that day was the conversion of the world to Christ; the Evangelicals of 1873 sought to address every social issue of their day from the word of God; education was seen in the context of the Christian faith — Christian education was thus seen as the answer to the new urban problems brought on by the industrial revolution; the educational disciplines were seen in the context of the Scriptures; the sabbath was regarded as indispensable to the health, virtue and the Christian character of civilization; and Christianity was seen as indispensable to civilization:

> This was evident in the day devoted to "Christianity and Social Reform" at the 1873 Evangelical Alliance. "Christian Philanthropy," "the Care of the Sick," "Intemperance and its Suppression," "Crime and Criminals," "Industrial Schools... in the Prevention of Crime," and "the Labor Question" were on the agenda. Only the last of these dealt with a new American social problem and the advice given was that, although laborers had some legitimate complaints, the causes might be removed "gradually and safely, by wise and conservative legislation." Strikes "lead to ruin."[74]

In the 1860s and 1870s, Beecher was the most popular and widely-known preacher in America. He was a man of robust health and

---

74. *Fundamentalism,* 13. Marsden quotes from "William H. Allen, 'The Labor Question,' *EA* 1873, pp. 670-74." See also, *Christian Life and Character of the Civil Institutions of the United States,* F.B. Morris. George W. Childs, 628 & 630 Chestnut St. Philadelphia. 1864.

physical vigor, of strong courage and conviction, an oratorical giant, usually sweeping all before him. His messages were pre-eminently on the subject of love — love to God and love to man.[75] Though Beecher was not a theologian in a Biblical sense of the word (he claimed to have never read a book through), he was publicly perceived as one. He was thus the first "theologian" to adopt the full of evolution. Beecher's romanticism softened the implications of traditional doctrines without denying them altogether.[76] A forerunner of modern *Christian Psychology,* he interpreted God through human experiences, and held that even the Scripture should be subordinated to the authority of the modern age.

The 1870's saw American Evangelicals trying to grapple with the results of Darwin's Theory of Evolution:

> At the Evangelical Alliance meeting of 1873, the new direction was suggested by the most popular American preacher of the day, Henry Ward Beecher. Urging that American preaching should strive for such unassailable sentimental goals as "to inspire men with an idea of manhood," and to kindle the "nobility of a heart opened when God has touched it," the famed Brooklyn preacher had discovered a formula that would for many years allay the fears of respectable evangelical Americans concerning the new science and learning. "While we are taught," said Beecher, "by the scientists in truths that belong to the sensual nature, while we are taught by the economists of things that belong to the social nature, we need the Christian ministry to teach us those things which are invisible."[77]

Notice what Beecher said: leave science to the scientists — it is sensual, leave economics to the economists — it is social, and leave the spiritual to the ministry. Though no doubt unknown to each, Darby and Beecher worked together in withdrawing Christian light and salt from society. The American church was ready for a theology of defeat and retreat.

---

75. *Who,* s.v. "Beecher, Henry Ward"

76. *Romanticism* views things as one wishes they were, according to feelings, emotions and imaginations. *Romanticism,* as a 19th-century movement, emphasized imagination over intellect – it is closer to fantasy than fact. Aestheticism is a descendant of Romanticism.

77. *Fundamentalism,* 21-24.

H.A. Ironside

We cannot consider the Plymouth Brethren millennial movement without mentioning one of its most distinguished teachers of all time, Henry Allan Ironside (1876-1951).

In the first half of the 1900's, he was in tremendous demand as a conference speaker, speaking at places such as Gull Lake, Cedar Lake, Eaglesmere, Montrose, Ocean Grove and Colorado Springs. Wheaton College conferred an honorary degree on him in 1930.[78]

As with other Plymouth Brethren, his influence upon the church at large was through his vast number of books: over a million copies sold of his one hundred titles published. In addition, he had in circulation 750,000 booklets, pamphlets and tracts by 1976.[79] Ironside describes his feelings toward Plymouth Brethren doctrine:

> When it comes to expository works, I have no hesitancy in saying that I owe more to five writers of the so-called Plymouth Brethren school than to anyone else. C.H.M.'s *Notes on the Pentateuch,* together with six volumes of his *Miscellaneous Writings,* proved of inestimable value when as a young preacher I was seeking a firm foundation for my faith and a better grasp of Bible truth. Then a little later some unknown friend, to whom I shall be forever indebted, presented me with a set of J.N. Darby's *Synopsis of the Books of the Bible.* I remember well that I literally devoured these five volumes, giving almost every spare moment to them, so that I read them in two weeks' time. I think I am safe in saying that they opened up the Scriptures in their comprehensiveness in a way that nothing else has ever touched. Needless to say, I have familiarized myself with practically everything J.N. Darby wrote and I regard him as far in advance of any of the other commentators on the Bible... When it comes to theology itself, I owe more to the works of Grant, I think, than even to Mr. Darby and Mr. Kelly...[80]

Ironside was pleased to note that, as a result of his lectures on the book of Revelation to the students of the theological seminary in

---

78. *Ordained,* 164.
79. *Ibid.,* 176.
80. *Ordained,* 246, 247. Kelly changed Darby's writings to prove that Irving's ideas originated with Darby. Frederick W. Grant was a Plymouth Brethren writer, a colleague and disciple of Darby, *Roots,* 238.

Dallas, many of the students became interested in obtaining the writings of the Plymouth Brethren, C.H.Mackintosh, J.N. Darby and F.W. Grant.[81]

Let us also mention in passing a connection with Donald Grey Barnhouse. In July of 1932, Barnhouse, who was then the editor of the magazine, *Revelation*, was invited to sail on the *Revelation* Cruise with a total of eight speakers, including Ironside.[82]

Ironside's influence upon the church for the Irvingite-Darbyite system of theology is significant: his books are everywhere. His writings apply Darby's opinions in a modern perspective. Though a self-proclaimed follower of J.N. Darby, he is esteemed among Baptists as a great Baptist theologian.

---

81. *Ordained.,* 179.
82. *Ibid.,* 185. Barnhouse is also listed in *Keswick's Authentic Voice.*

Part X
Darbyism-Millennialism

Chapter 93
Starting Over

This section will develop several aspects of the millennial *faith*. The following tenets of that *faith* were revolutionary when introduced in the 1800s; they were considered heresy by the vast majority of church leaders. However, through the efforts of a few men such as Darby, these radical — even heretical — ideas became accepted Christian doctrine. Darby especially understood that the new millennial system militated against orthodoxy, and that a new system of *faith* was being established. Darby said, "My books are quite alarming..." Referring to the orthodox Christian *faith* of his day, he saw that "everything traditional..." was "crumbling to pieces."[1] He led in *digging down* the walls of 1500 years of Christian thought.

Before examining several of the non-orthodox Christian ideas propagated by Darby, we should notice this statement hidden within the many hundreds of his letters:

> God may permit, where there is much activity and labour, that Satan should raise up obstacles, in order that we may be kept in dependence on the Lord; but God never allows Satan to act otherwise than on the flesh. If we leave the door open, if we get away from God, Satan does us harm; but otherwise his efforts are only a test for faith, to warn us of some danger or snare, or of something that would tend to exalt us in our own eyes. It is an instrument for our correction. That is, God allows Satan to trouble the mind, and make the flesh suffer outwardly, in order that the inner

---

1. *Letters,* I.189, 1851. *Ibid.,* I.370, I.864.

man may be kept from evil... For "he that is begotten of God keepeth himself, and the wicked one toucheth him not."...[2]

"God never allows Satan to act otherwise than on the flesh"! This statement permits one to follow his *feelings* about a matter without questioning the source; it allows one to believe about anything he desires from Scripture, for Satan is not involved in moving the mind, feelings nor emotions; it allows one to be led by *circumstances* apart from God's word; it allows leaders with strong, charismatic personalities to lead sincere people anywhere.

Neatby's summary of *Brethrenism* shows us how thoroughly the Brethren faith has infiltrated the Church of the Lord Jesus Christ, rendering it close to powerless to stand against the world-wide rise of the spirit of antichrist:

> I am of course aware that the Brethren would have claimed to stand with the first in vindicating the spirituality of the secular; and their claim is good up to a certain point--but no further. To do the common things of life as under the lordship of Christ, and as so many acts of service to Him, was certainly the ideal of the Brethren, as it was of the Jansenists and of other excellent men whose High Churchism is not doubtful. But the Brethren, like the Jansenists, placed Christian perfection, and indeed Christian duty, in as total a seclusion as possible from the common pursuits of men, even in the case of pursuits that are lawful, and indeed necessary. To the Protestant this view suggests a dualistic theory, and seems hard to reconcile with the Divine origin and authority of Civil government in which, nevertheless, the Brethren very heartily believed. They believed, too, that the existing secular order — the administration of government, of justice, and so forth — was just as much divinely ordained as the Church itself. Christians ought, they said, to be very thankful for it, and to yield it a perfectly passive support; but they should remember that in its administration Christians, as a heavenly people, possessing a heavenly calling and citizenship, could not lawfully share.
>
> ...so far as the law left them a bare choice, they avoided all the offices upon which society depends for its maintenance. They filled

---

2. *Ibid.*, II.317, 318. Darby probably reached the conclusion from Job. This theory allows many "isms" to prevail – mysticism, romanticism, pietism, &c. It is strange that he would say this when he contended that Newton was led in the spirit by Satan.

no civil or municipal office, if they could help it; they never sat in Parliament, and if by some rare self-assertion one of them voted at an election, he was regarded with the most intense disapproval.

...to the Brethren their course was clear, as being derived from the essence of the Christian calling; and therefore, in the true spirit of the earliest and most genuine disciples of monarchism, they fled into the desert to establish a huge cenobitic fraternity, to pass their days in holy contemplation, and to await the Second Advent.[3]

The early developers of the millennial faith would have pronounced efforts such as stopping the slave trade (abortions!), "morally excellent," being "in full sympathy with its objects, but they thought it work that God had reserved for unclean hands; it was not for heavenly citizens to pass righteous laws for earth..."

They felt it was unlawful for Christians to promote popular liberties, *e.g.,* "emancipation of slaves, the suppression of drunkenness. These things were as the dead burying their dead; it was for the Christian to preach the Gospel. Philanthropy generally was under their ban. It aimed, as they held, at 'making the world better,' and this apparently innocent object was their special bugbear.":[4]

> The Brethren nevertheless inferred from the example of St. Paul that a Christian has the right to insist on the privileges allowed him by the political order under which he lives. They appear to have held that the apostolic example entitled them to claim their political privileges and to shirk their political duties; or, to put it otherwise, that the possession of a citizenship in heaven precludes the possession of a citizenship on earth, in respect only of the responsibilities of the earthly citizenship, and not of its advantages.[5]

Their monastic attitude not only controlled their attitude toward civil government, but it carried over into *secular* areas. There were

---

3. Neatby, *History*, 267-281.

4. *Ibid*. And we wonder why Christianity has been powerless to stop the abortion holocaust, the slaughter of the unborn. Finney, one of the leading millenarians in the destruction of America's Victorious Christian Faith, played a major role in giving a supposed theological foundation to the radical abolitionists in the War Between the States, for it was also a war against Calvinism. See Scott, *The Secret Six*.

5. Neatby, *History*, 267-281.

particular professions which were admissible, but the occupation of doctor and dentist were almost alone perfectly lawful. The legal bar and military were absolutely forbidden.[6]

The early Brethren even considered it "more or less a mark of lack of spirituality to read the newspaper." Neatby concludes that Darbyism formed a world of its own, which had a lasting effect upon Christian thought.

Socially, the Brethren were equally self-contained, limiting their friendships to members of their own group and to those they could possibly recruit. Marriage outside of their ranks was deemed blameworthy. But a word for the positive side: To other Brethren, the red carpet was rolled out anywhere in the world. To one another, they exhibited everything required by Scriptures, as long as the "guest" was in good standing with Brethrenism.

Chapter 94

Dispensationalism

Though modern dispensationalism was developed and injected into Christian thought by Irving-Darby, it was Marcion (died c. 160) who first,

> [P]ut Christianity into radical conflict with all previous revelations of God; as if God had neglected the world for thousands of years until he suddenly appeared in Christ.... (He taught that, *ed.*) The God of the Old Testament is harsh, severe and unmerciful as his law; he commands, "Love thy neighbor, but hate thine enemy," and returns "an eye for an eye, and a tooth for a tooth;" but the God of the New Testament commands, "Love thine enemy." The one is only just, the other is good. Marcion rejected all the books of the Old Testament, and wrested Christ's words in Matt. 5:17 into very opposite declaration: "I am come not to fulfil the law and the prophets, but to destroy them." In his view, Christianity has no connection whatever

---

6. Many of the formulators had been lawyers; thus they knew how to persuade people.

with the past, whether of the Jewish or the heathen world, but has fallen abruptly and magically, as it were, from heaven.... Marcion formed a canon of his own, which consisted of only eleven books, an abridged and mutilated Gospel of Luke, and ten of Paul's epistles.... Notwithstanding his violent antinomianism, Marcion taught and practiced the strictest ascetic self- discipline, which revolted not only from all pagan festivities, but even from marriage, flesh, and wine. (He allowed fish).... He had a very gloomy, pessimistic view of the world and the church, and addressed a disciple as "his partner in tribulation, and fellow-sufferer from hatred."... Constantine forbade the Marcionites freedom of worship public and private, and ordered their meeting-houses to be handed over to the Catholic Church. The Theodosian code mentions them only once. But they existed in the fifth century when Theodoret boasted to have converted more than a thousand of these heretics, and the Trullan council of 692 thought it worth while to make provision for the reconciliation of the Marcionites.[7]

Marcion holds the "honour" of being the first to mutilate — "dispensationalize" — the word of God down to basically the writings of Paul. And he was considered and dealt with as a heretic: "Justin Martyr regarded him as the most insidious and dangerous heretic of the day. Polycarp called him the 'first born' of Satan.'"[8] But the later followers of Marcion had what was earlier considered heresy accepted as part of Christian thought. Darby developed Marcion's heresy thusly:

> ...we are dead [in Christ, *ed.*] and the law cannot apply to a dead man: we have been crucified with Christ... The law was not annulled by His coming, but fulfilled: we are not under law but under grace. We do not sin because we have died with Christ; we have died to sin, to the law, by the body of Christ, [sic] This is true liberty, being made free from sin that we may live unto God...
>
> The absolutely perfect and living rule is the life of the Lord Jesus Christ. In Him all written rules are united in one solitary living example; but the written rule which ought to govern our whole life

---

7. *History,* II: 483-487.
8. *Who,* s.v. "Marcion." Marcion was "The son of a bishop, born at Sinope on the south coast of the Black Sea, where he became wealthy ship builder." About 139, he went to Rome where he made a generous gift to a church. He was excommunicated for erroneous doctrine about 144, and his gift returned to him. *Ibid.*

is the New Testament... We are called to walk worthy of the Lord so as to please Him in everything. We must know the Lord in order to walk thus — "worthy of God who hath called you to his kingdom and glory." This absolutely clear and perfect light is found in the New Testament alone; but the Old, if we have learned to distinguish between the dispensation under which the saints lived in those times, furnishes very fine examples of faith, of obedience, of subjection to the will of God, of constancy in His paths.[9] "As regards using Old Testament words as types, I quite agree that our imagination is to be held in check; nor can we ever insist on such as a doctrine. But there is a passage which may assist your mind on this point (1 Cor. x. 11), where the word "ensamples" is "types" or "figures," which gives the principle. Then we must only look to the Holy Ghost and divine guidance to use them soberly and aright."[10]

The law does not apply to New Testament Christians! The millenarians admitted that the Old Testament "furnishes very fine examples of faith...," but it contains no rule for action. The dispensationalization of God's word did not stop with simply separating God's word as found in the Old Testament from his word as found in the New. God's word was dispensationalized into many pieces, leaving basically only the writings of Paul for Christians.

Chapter 95

Paul's Writings

Excommunicating the Old Testament from God's inspired word, the millenarians still did not have a suitable word from God. Darby found only Paul's words acceptable for doctrine, correction, reproof and instruction in righteousness:

> ... But I have a full feeling that Christ did not send me to baptise; I leave to others activities on either side. The twelve were sent to baptise, but as to ecclesiastical matters, we are under Paul.

---

9. *Letters*, II.108, 109. From London, Dec, 1870. See also, *Ibid.*, I.395, II.396.
10. *Ibid.*, II.170. From London, 1872.

... Further remark, the commission to the twelve [*i.e.,* Matt. 28:19, 20, *ed.*] was not from heaven, nor consequently immediately connecting with heaven, but from Galilee, and a commission to bring the *nations* into connection with the accepted remnant of Jews on earth — not to bring Jew and Gentile into the body in an ascended Christ, which was Paul's commission especially, preaching withal [sic] reconciliation from heaven to every creature under it...[11]

Darby continually labored to separate the Christian from all Scripture except Paul's, *e.g.,* "As to baptising, Christ did not send me to baptise, and we are under Paul's dispensation."[12] Millennialism used "Roman Catholics and Puseyites" to justify its "otherworldliness."[13] Pointing to Rome's misuse of Peter, Darby justified using Paul alone for doctrine:

> The importance of judging church history, or the state it reveals, is daily more apparent to me. I am not at the bottom of it, but the change from scripture to prelacy, succession of bishops, so-called, has something mysterious in it, along with the fabrication of Ignatius, and perhaps Apostolic Constitutions, which are, I believe, heretical in their present state — a prelacy which is the basis of all subsequent Christendom till the Reformation, and now of high church, and even all clerical systems. But one things is clear, that all refer to Peter for the system, not one to Paul. The unity of the church as they view it is always based on him; Paul at best only comes in by the bye, swamped in Peter at Rome. And even as to detail, the rising up of scriptural conscience against image worship and evil was from Paul's writings, and the authors of it, called Paulicians. They had only his writings and the gospels — but this by the bye. This system presses stronger on me than even infidelity, dreadful as it is individually...[14]

---

11. *Letters,* II.47, 1869. From Elberfeld. See also, *ibid.,* 196. From St. Louis, Nov, 1872.

12. *Ibid.,* 56, 25, 196.

13. *Ibid.,* 48.

14. *Ibid.,* 55, 56, 1869. There are many hundreds of Darby's letters in the three volumes of *Letters,* and hardly one goes by without him passing his judgment upon something: "In my judgment..." There is, however, a serious, conspicuous absence of any Scriptural basis for his judgments.

Actually, Darby considered his doctrine Paul's doctrine revived. Writing from Toronto in 1865, he said:

> Here we are getting on pretty well: a good many have been added everywhere, and new meetings in birth. Our general meeting at Toronto was delicious.... One who may be very useful, got his soul all cleared, or rather filled with truth, at our meetings. He told me he saw plainly that what brethren taught was the recovery of Paul's doctrine. So it really is. I am daily more convinced that evangelicalism with partial truth is the abandonment of what Paul taught. I feel far more deeply the ground on which I am than ever...[15]

The speaker and Darby agreed that Paul's doctrine had been lost for eighteen hundred years until the Brethren came along and found it. However, when Marcion tried to present the dispensational idea as Paul's doctrine, he was dealt with as a heretic. How could 1700 years of church history — Marcion to the new millenarians — of using God's total word for doctrine, reproof and correction be so wrong? Thus the dispensational teachers followed in the footsteps of "the most formidable heretic" of the middle second century, Marcion. And many since have traveled Marcion's well-worn path.

Darby continually compares himself to Paul. He uses phrases as Paul used them, making himself sound as inspired and as great a church leader as was Paul: "In my judgment," "I judge," &c. Moreover, because he considered Paul totally unconcerned about civil matters, he held Christians should be also in order to be right with God.[16] He held that Paul's instructions from God were different than what the Lord gave to the Apostles in Matthew 28:19, 20:

> ... Hence Paul who was sent a minister to the church to complete the word of God was not sent to baptise.... The twelve who, though the church existed, had not this mission, but had been sent forth by Christ in connection with the kingdom... were sent to baptise... But this mission was not a mission for believers' baptism as it is called.

---

15. *Ibid.,* I.398. "Truth" was truth as Darby saw it. A common dispensational phrase is that it was Paul's doctrine.
16. *Ibid.,* I.78, 79, 81, 97, 1845. "... we are in another world as to our minds." *Ibid.,* 91. See also 253, 376, &c., 1846.

They were sent to disciple all nations, baptising them in the name of the Father and of the Son and of the Holy Ghost.[17]

Darby considered himself one of the few great establishers of Christian doctrine in church history. It was, therefore, sin to believe contrary to his *system:*

> It had been openly taught by N. and B. that the Lord did not now use poor uneducated men, as those He chose before His resurrection, but after that, such as Paul, Luther and Calvin, Wesley and Whitfield, and myself now.[18]

Darby dismissed St. John's books: "The latter is more John's doctrine than Paul's (Paul's more the liberty), though you may get the groundwork of it in Paul."[19] He even attempted to explained away the very words of Christ as recorded by St. John:

> ... What is John? "As the Father hath loved me, so have I loved you: continue [abide] ye in my love. If ye keep my commandments, ye shall abide in my love; even as I have kept my Father's commandments, and abide in his love." Then, "these things have I spoken unto you that my joy might abide in you and your joy might be full." If I take the context, I do not find a trace of what Mr. S. teaches, it is far and wide from it. Consequently I do not find in St. Paul exactly the kind of quietness and consistent triumph that Mr. V. speaks of and expects. I read, "I was with you in weakness, and in fear, and in much trembling": "without were fightings, within were fears; nevertheless God, that comforteth them that are cast down" — he repented of writing an inspired letter. I admit victory is ours, and to be "in nothing terrified by your adversaries." I recognise peacefulness of heart in entire confidence in the Christian's path down here; but I do not think a Christian can seek Christ up there, nor in connection with *His* interests and His service here without

---

17. *Ibid.,* II.278, 1874.

18. *Ibid.,* I.89. "N.", *i.e.,* Newton held that public dissertations of the word of God were no place for the novice, the unlearned and unstudied; Newton prepared beforehand, which Darby found reprehensible. Darby was firmly convinced that any disagreement with his ideas was satanic: "I have no doubt a direct power and delusion of the enemy was there, from which we have been rescued by the Lord's goodness." *Ibid.,* 90.

19. *Ibid.,* 398; II.47; III.40, 1879. Darby *had to* dismiss John's books, for he clearly requires obedience to God's Commandments, *e.g.,* Jn. chaps. 14, 15, 1 Jn. 3:4.

experiencing a deeper knowledge of self, and the subtleties of self and the flesh, and distress through the craft of Satan and the mischief he does, than Mr. S.'s system knows anything about.... It is peace in life, not the sentence of death in ourselves: and I hardly think rivers of water flowing forth mean speaking of one's self or of one's own joy, though it may sometimes in the first overflowing of it be natural and right. But to turn grace into this channel I am sure lowers Christianity.[20]

Not only does Darby dismiss Christ's command to obey his word because Paul does not give them, but he says that the distress caused by Satan through his craft and mischief counters any hope of victory. Thus Christ's words of joy are turned into defeat. However, Darby flees to Christ's words as they stand when fitting his purpose:

> Luke introduces the new order, the things in which we find ourselves, rather than the kingdom to come.... For my part I often go back to the gospels in order to study the precious Saviour Himself. They are full of the richest instruction. I have much enjoyed Matthew and Mark all this time. The Gethsemane of Matthew has just now interested me deeply: Jesus a victim without human resources; man completely fails Him...[21]

"Jesus a victim..."! How absurd, for Jesus was the Lamb of God slain from before the foundations of the world. "Gospels... are full of the richest instruction." In other words, not *all* of the Gospels are for instructions; rather, they *contain* instructions; Christians are thus able to pick and chose from what the gospels contain, according to the *way that seemeth right* to them. No two people will have the same instructions from God, so each is accountable only to himself.

The first chapter of *The London Baptist Confession of Faith of 1689,* OF THE HOLY SCRIPTURES, states that, generally, Christians before Darby believed the totality of Scriptures applied for all of God's people of all times. New Testament Christians are required to abide by the standard of right living as revealed to man through Moses. (1 Jn. 3:4.)

---

20. *Ibid.,* II.247, 1873.
21. *Ibid.,* 252. From Belfast, 1874.

The dispensational millennial *system* not only robbed every denomination of their godly heritage, but its destructive worms killed the idea of Christian victory as promised *through Christ who loved us.*

Chapter 96

According to Darby

Darby wrongly claimed he started the Brethren movement.[22] He wrongly claimed he developed the millennial faith that conquered world: "There were only four of us to do it at the first; not, I hope, in a spirit of pride or presumption..." From New York in 1877, Darby looked at the growing acceptance of Brethren doctrine, claiming it originated with him:

> At first, when I left the Episcopal church, there was no one with whom I could walk; I was led on and guided simply by the word of God. Afterwards four of us met together... The work extended, and that everywhere, and I am deeply convinced that it is a testimony which God Himself has raised up in these last days...

Darby typically takes credit for something that was not really his. He strongly implies God raised him up for the last days, giving him special revelations.[23] He warns about the speedy growth of acceptance of new faith. In an 1877 letter from Dublin, he said,

> I have the fullest persuasion that the testimony we have is God's testimony for the last days — the gospel Paul preached, brought out to light — what I never suspected when I began in this city, just fifty years ago now... Brethren are in a new position; attention is universally drawn to them. The Spirit of God is working, the emptiness of what is had in churches is felt: it is commonly owned that they have more scripture. This is a new, and in some respects, a dangerous position...

---

22. *Ibid.*, II.208, I.297, 298, 515.
23. *Ibid.*, II.438, 439. 386. We have reproduced a letter from Darby explaining the four basic principles of early Brethrenism.

More light! More scripture! Clearly, Darby held that the Brethren received new truth from God for the last days, and it spread out from them. Ironside held the same.[24]

Millennialism expanded by appealing to and converting dissenters to its *system*, rather than by converting sinners to Christ. Darby rejoiced when sinners were converted, but he was far more motivated by the hope he could convince someone to follow him: he enjoyed working against the odds.[25]

Within fifty years — 1827-1877 — millennialism infiltrated all Protestant Christendom. It was fifty years of hard, tireless work and sacrifice. Militating against the orthodox understanding of the many passages of Scripture and giving them "new light," the millenarians endured much ridicule and persecution. Because it was not yet being preached from the average pulpit, believers sought out millenarians during those fifty years to learn their unique doctrine.

Though presented as original, they, maybe unknowingly, were traveling well-worn paths. Many tenets of this faith had already been dealt with; they had been dismissed by the early church as heresies, *e.g.*, a "church/Israel distinction" and the heretical notion that God has one plan of redemption for Gentiles and one for Jews, depending upon which dispensation is presently at work.[26]

Darby acquired most of his ideas from outside of himself (Lacunza, Irving and Margaret), but he boldly claimed them as his own, wrote them down and popularized them, particularly in the area of prophetic opinions:

---

24. *Ibid.*, II.423, 400, 402. Irving held that *Ben-Ezra* was sent by God for the Gentile church. How many times have we heard millenarians say, "This is the doctrine Paul preached"?

25. *Ibid.*, I.44, 1841, II.129, 261, 230.

26. *Fathers*, I.207, "NO SALVATION TO THE JEWS EXCEPT THROUGH CHRIST"... 258, "CHRISTIANS ARE THE HOLY PEOPLE PROMISED TO ABRAHAM. THEY HAVE BEEN CALLED LIKE ABRAHAM"... 261, "RIDICULOUS INTERPRETATIONS OF THE JEWS. CHRISTIANS ARE THE TRUE ISRAEL"... 267, "CHRIST IS KING OF ISRAEL, AND CHRISTIANS ARE THE ISRAELITIC [sic] RACE" Justin's [AD 110-165] Dialogue with Trypho, a Jew, 194-270. The text is in caps as the headings for the various topics. Darby changed early church writings and hymns to support his theories.

The Jews and other Gentiles converted thereafter [after the "rapture," *ed.*] will never be Christ's bride: 'I deny that saints before Christ's first coming, or after his second, are part of the Church.' With breath-taking dogmatism Darby swept away what has previously been axiomatic in Christian theology:

> The assertion that His mystical body is the universal family of the redeemed, is unscriptural; all the declaration is founded on this gross and unscriptural error, that all the saved belong to the Church.[27]

Darby also claimed the idea that the Lord will come,

> [F]rom heaven to destroy the beast, and takes up the kingdom, and then out of Zion establish His kingdom on earth, the Assyrian [being destroyed]. This is connected with all His ways as to Israel, His being in the midst of the people or not; Israel owned or not owned. I apprehend the 1000 years will give ample time for the existence of the army at the end...[28]

The clergy of his day responded to these ideas as they do today when someone comes along with a system contrary to what they consider orthodox: "I am not surprised at the clergy being violent against the truth. It can hardly be otherwise, because their system is against the truth, and the truth offends them."[29] The tables are now turned as modern Darbyists violently react against what was then orthodoxy — a victorious Christian outlook on history.

Riots

The general population responded no better:

> "The tribulation is not at its close; last Sunday we had a formidable riot on our meeting in your apartment.... A furious crowd was before

---

27. *Hope*, 200. This is typical of the dispensational faith that is "widely popularized in the *Scofield Reference Bible.*" The church, "which comes in between the sixty-ninth and seventieth week of Daniel," "cannot be the subject of prophecy." *Letters*, I.131. He implies that the newly developed ideas concerning Matthew 24 and Daniel originated in his mind: "what I believe to be the successive states of the Church." *Writings*, II.582.

28. *Letters*, III.3, 137-138. Note Darby's inability to write and think logically.

29. *Ibid.*, I.523. He elsewhere defines truth as only those teachings emanating from his mind. Daniel according to Darby is what is taught today in every major Protestant college this pastor knows of, though he realizes there are exceptions.

the house, but this time the police, who were on foot, hindered them from attacking us, and protected us going out.... "Already, Friday, the transport of the benches by J.O. caused a real riot, of which J. supported the brunt without accident. They seized some benches from him, which they broke. I do not know if I told you that one Sunday morning the band entered my house also, penetrating close to my rooms where we were, several persons, and the Lord stopped them there..."

The riot was over the new *system* Darby presented in Lausanne. He continues:

"The next day the council of State had us requested through B. (its president), not to have our meeting all together at 22 St. Pierre [the house I lived in, where the riot was], in order not to expose the town to troubles whose issue could not be foreseen.... The Great Counsel is to be occupied to-morrow with the petitions relative to religious liberty.... The government seeks, in order to flatter the passions of the populace, to adopt a measure which deprives us of liberty, saving appearances as much as possible.... I do not expect to see religious liberty granted to the children of God in this country....[30]

His message was unique, and it created riots. In order to continue with his teaching, he pleaded for religious liberty and police protection. But when Newton taught something contrary to Darby's views, he was extremely hostile, as he was against the Baptists.

Not all millenarians held to all of Darby's views, and some even violently disagreed with him. But he viewed disagreement as departure from the Christian faith.

Chapter 97

Daniel

History/Theology Separated

Darby makes a remark concerning Revelation 17, which is foundational in the millennial faith: "History is not necessary in

---

30. *Ibid.*, 81-84, 1845. This letter is reproduced in App. A.

order to understand prophecy... History never explains prophecy."[31] In other words, only by ignoring history can one accept Darby's unique understanding of prophecy. When history is separated from theology, history becomes a series of unrelated, meaningless facts, which is totally unscriptural.

Thoughts on Daniel

Opening his remarks on Daniel, Darby said he threw out historic church teaching — "judgments" — on the book rather than build upon them: "I shall be short, my object being to throw out the grounds of judgment rather than to reason on them..."[32] His unorthodox ideas, such as the renewed sacrifice in Israel, are introduced with statements like, "I apprehend." Using Matthew 24, he placed most of Daniel's prophecies yet to be fulfilled. His thoughts concerning Daniel 12 were based on: "such as God has up to this time shown me," and "my conviction," "I apprehend," "It seems to me," &c.[33] His whole understanding that Daniel is yet to be fulfilled was based upon what seemed, felt, best to him.[34]

By ignoring history when reading *prophetic passages* from places such as Daniel and Revelation, one can deny that Jerusalem's destruction fulfilled prophecy. It permitted him to place Matthew 24 yet in the future:

> Now I do not believe that it is the time of trouble of Matthew xxiv. which applies more particularly to Judea and the Jews — the time of Jacob's trouble. This is far more extensive in its sphere, and precedes it in time; for that takes place on the setting up the abomination of desolation in the holy place, that is the last three years and a half. But there is a time of temptation which is to come upon all the world to try them which dwell on the earth, from which the true Church had been preserved, and from which these had not. This is, I apprehend, "the great tribulation," from the midst of which these have been saved...[35]

---

31. *Writings*, II.93.
32. *Ibid.*, 324. Darby was building on Lacunza's system.
33. *Ibid.*, 317, 322, 323.
34. *Ibid.*, 327-354. This section of Writings reads like Scofield's notes.

350 *Death of the Church Victorious*

Daniel's Stone

Though the new understanding of Daniel's Stone was previously and distinctly presented by Irving, Darby claimed it. This view of Matthew 24 and of Daniel permitted him to say that the Stone of Daniel 2 has not yet struck the image, for it, said he,

> "[S]hall break in pieces and consume those kingdoms" in their last form, *viz.*, under the ten kings who give their power to the beast. (Daniel ii. 40- 44; Revelation xvii. 11-14.) And here I must stop to remark upon a great error which prevails, *viz.*, that the little stone was the setting up of Christ's kingdom at the day of Pentecost, and that it has been growing into a great mountain every since; or, in other words, that the preaching of the gospel, in the present dispensation, is that which is to convert the world.[36]

Thus he saw "Christ's appearing is not at the end (as is supposed), but at the beginning of the kingdom." In other words, "Christ has not yet taken His kingdom.[37] Previously, the common belief was that Christ has already ascended to his throne, and is now ruling all things according to his own good pleasure. (Cf. Eph. chaps. 1 and 2.)

His view that the Stone has not yet struck the image permitted his next *logical* point: "The scripture does not speak of the universal prevalence of Christianity while the image subsists..." He taught that until Christ literally rules from Jerusalem on "David's throne," there is no hope for the gospel changing anything for God and godliness.[38] How sad when people become convinced that preaching the gospel of Christ cannot change society; they are left with no Christian hope for changing society for the better. Their only hope is a political hope, which must fail though they invest vast sums of effort and money in that effort.

Before Darby, the Christian view of the dry bones in Ezekiel 37 was the resurrected souls in Christ, the Lord's new army, the Gospel

---

35. *Ibid.,* 372. 373, 1843. Continuing, he says, "I judge that it refers to..."
36. *Letters*, III.185. See also, 121, 197, 199.
37. *Ibid.,* 172, 1843.
38. *Letters, III.*185.

Church of the Lord Jesus Christ. Darby led in its change to refer to a literal nation, Israel.[39]

Chapter 98

The Great Tribulation

With his new view of Matthew 24, Darby claimed to have developed the dispensational idea of "the great tribulation" and the church's removal before it started. However, *Ben-Ezra* had been in printed circulation since 1812, and Irving had already made "the great tribulation" *public domain* at Powerscourt. Darby, though, was the most influential man of the last century in spreading this system of faith. Falsely claiming originality, Darby gives the dispensational view of a tribulation according to Matthew 24 and Daniel's seventieth week:

> Now we learn from the gospels His ministry was as nearly as possible three years and a half, so that for intelligent faith there is only half a week left, and, in fact, only that of the great tribulation. For unbelief — the beast and the apostate jews — there is a week; and they enter into covenant for this time, but he breaks it when half through, takes away the sacrifice, and the great tribulation begins — that which is spoken of in Matthew xxiv. after verses 15, and Mark xiii. — and this only in the Revelation.[40]

Darby propagated world-wide the theory of a division between Daniel's sixty-ninth and seventieth week. He claimed that the division of the seventieth week when the sacrifice is stopped was his idea. He countered "Bagster's Lexicon" to make Daniel xii. 11 and Daniel viii. 13 support his unorthodox opinion.[41]

---

39. *Writings,* II.311. See Patrick Fairbairn, *An Exposition of Ezekiel.*
40. *Letters,* III.133-134. These letters are placed in the 1881 section of the volumes.
41. *Ibid.,* 315, 327. "... it would appear probable (I am inclined to suppose)...," was the basis of this theory, *Letters,* II.377, 1843.

His understanding of Matthew 24 — including the idea of the "Jews" reestablished as God's people — could only be supported by separating v. 15 from v. 16, "after verses 15..." The foundation for his ideas, however, was not God's word but his own personal thoughts about the matter: "it is evident to me", "seems to me", "I judge", "I think" and "I am disposed to think." "I will recall to your memories," said Darby, "my previous division of Matthew xxiv."[42]

The "belief in the coming of a personal Antichrist," along with a parenthesis in Daniel's seventieth week, was offered by both Morgan Edwards and Lacunza. However, Darby claimed credit for the idea:[43]

> But I cannot doubt that there will be a civil-religious power in Palestine, having the energy of Satan, and exercising the power of the beast, to whom Satan has given his authority, and this, I suspect, is much more properly the Antichrist, though there be many. But I present this, specially and avowedly, as a subject of inquiry of the saints and those content to learn and follow any increasing light our God in His goodness may see good to give; and certainly He will give all that may be truly profitable to His Church.[44]

His new view of Matthew 24:21, permitted him to say that,

> We are here absolutely in the time of distress (predicted in Dan. xii, and Jer. xxx. 7) at Jerusalem, to be followed by the deliverance of the people of Daniel, at least of the remnant, and by the establishment of the Jews in Palestine with David (Christ) as their king. But before this unequalled period of tribulation there will be "the beginning of sorrows." (Matthew xxiv. 8)[45]

And thus the modern understanding of "the great tribulation" developed:

> In Matthew is given the full development of Jewish dispensation, and this so much so, that I could not apply any of the statements in Matthew xxiv, or the like, to Gentile circumstances; whereas Luke explicitly opens the door, and brings them into the scene, as may be

---

42. *Ibid.,* III.356, 357.
43. *Ibid.,* I.6.
44. *Writings,* II. 345.
45. *Letters,* III.319.

seen in the close of chapter xxi. Whence also, I believe he introduces 'all the trees,' the fig-tree being the specific emblem of the Jewish corporate nationality.

Accordingly, Darby claimed the idea of the fig-tree being a future Jewish nation.[46]

The Church Ruined

Darby is wrongly credited with the "the ruin of the church" idea: "But ruin is found in this that the church such as God formed and fashioned it, *does not exist at all* save as He sanctions two or three meeting in the name of Jesus." "As to the ruin of the church, the theory came for me..."[47] So in the Darbyists' mind, "the ruin of the church" justified concerted effort to build their following out of already established churches, *e.g.*, "After all," would be the idea, "is not all organized religion in ruin? Therefore, we must use any means to get people out of it."

Preachers-teachers everywhere, because of public pressure, had to start preaching millennialism, but they did not use the "ruin of the church" theory in a way that might undermine their churches. They wanted to keep their people and the funds that came from the millennial system. Actually, they Americanized it, saying that the church is ruined; therefore, it is incapable of changing society for God and godliness. They were, accordingly, falsely relieved of any social responsibility except *soul-saving* and personal piety.

Chapter 99
Antinomianism

We beg the reader's indulgence as we deal more thoroughly with a serious aspect of the millennial faith, *i.e.*, antinomianism.

---

46. *Letters*, III.355.
47. "Meetings in the name of the Lord" was Darby's description of the Brethren, *Letters*, III.245, 1847. *Ibid.*, I.42, 1840.

Antinomianism holds that Christians are liberated from observing the moral laws when God's grace is active; rather than being subject to outward commands of "thou shalt" and "thou shalt not," it says Christians are to be controlled by their inward feelings about matters.

The millennial faith's foundation, laid down by Darby, militated against any firm command by God upon his people. It "maintained the insufficiency of the law as a guide to a life lived in the energy and illumination of the indwelling Spirit of God."[48]

Among A. H. Strong's 1907 charges against millennialism was that it denies "the moral law as the rule of life." In 1945, Ironside answered Strong's charge thusly: "Well, if 'Brethren' are heretics because they teach that *Christ*, not the law of Moses, is the rule of life, they are in excellent company — with many devoted and enlightened Baptist ministers who teach the same. Literature on this subject is abundant."

But Ironside did not refer to any "Baptist ministers." Instead he referred to one of the best known Brethren authors — "C.H.M.'s little booklet, 'The Law and the Gospel,' is clear and convincing. Any of the 'Brethren's' expositions on Romans or Galatians are helpful."[49] Ironside continues: "We are not under law (Rom. 6:14). We are neither saved by the law, nor under it, as a rule of life; we are not lawless, but 'under law (enlawed) to Christ."[50] Scofield's notes

---

48. Neatby, *History,* 234, 235. Darby claimed Galatians proves that it is "hateful to God" to apply the Old Testament law as the standard of life, *Writings,* II.475. Typical of false teachers of all ages, Darby used Scripture to support his heresy, Galatians in this case, but failed to point out that Paul is there dealing with those who sought to add the works of the law to *grace through faith* for justification-salvation. Mixing works with grace for justification is *legalism*. The issue in Galatians is *not* the law as a standard of holy living before God after salvation, Eph. 3. Scofield says that the new dispensation of grace that began with Christ sees, "no longer legal obedience as the condition of salvation...," *Scofield,* 1115. However, those who know Scripture know that "legal obedience" WAS NEVER a condition of salvation, for Abraham believed God, and it was counted to him for righteousness. *Ben-Ezra* was likewise antagonistic to the Law of God, *q.v.*

49. *Sketch,* 211. Note: compare Psalms 119:142 and John 14:6. Christ and the law cannot be separated.

under Galatians 6:24, read: "(5) Law neither justifies a sinner nor sanctifies a believer... (6) The believer is both dead to the law and redeemed from it, so that he is 'not under the law, but under grace... (7)... So far is the life of the believer from the anarchy of self-will that he is 'inlawed to Christ'...'" Ironside used Scofield's 1909 notes to refute Strong's earlier (1907) charge that Plymouth Brethren taught lawlessness.

Implied in the teaching of the "insufficiency of the law as a guide to a life" is that it is important that one obeys the law of the Lord only if his motives are right. It also fits in well with Darby's teaching that "God never allows Satan to act otherwise than on the flesh." However, the principle of obedience must always be the revealed word of God regardless of motives and feelings.

Privilege vs. Command

The millennial movement saw as its mission, "to emphasize the contrast between law and gospel, to insist on the freedom of Christian service, and to disparage the conception of duty in favor of the conception of privilege."[51] Though condemning the Baptist view of baptism, Darby describes his view of "the nature of Christianity:"

> ...The admission to a privilege cannot be a matter of obedience, though obedience gives privileges as such. But the real point is, the passages prove that it was the act of the baptiser, ["Acts viii. (verse 37 is not genuine)..." says Darby, *ed.*] not of the baptized. And this changes its whole nature. It is said, Where are children commanded to receive Baptism? of course they are not, nor believers. Ordinances are never the subject of commands. They are ordained and rightly used, but never obedience in Him who profits by them; it would deny the very nature of Christianity, and destroy the blessing for him who partakes of it.[52]

---

50. *Ibid.*, 212.
51. Neatby, *History*, 235.
52. *Letters*, II.49, date, 1869. Typically, Darby changed and removed Scripture to support his system.

The "nature of Christianity" did not see man's duty to obey God. Rather, obedience to God was taught as a privilege.[53] Having a good deal to say about God's Law-Word as revealed in the Ten Commandments, Darby held that neither the church nor Christians have any responsibility to the Commandments as revealed through Moses:

> For I cannot but feel that the religion of which we profess membership, is not an imposition of observance, a law of carnal commandments contained in ordinances (as indeed it would contradict the whole purpose and counsel of God), but an admission to privileges, exceeding great and precious promises... Nor is this any license to evil, because we are only so far become therein free, as in that we live we live unto God...[54]

Privilege vs. command: When one sees obedience to Christ and to God's Law-Word as a privilege, then that privilege of obedience can be forfeited with no harm nor consequences, as one might forfeit the privilege of using a modern convenience. But if obedience is seen as a duty, duty means discipline, responsibility, and answering to God — chastisement — if unfulfilled.

The letter presenting his view of the law was written before 1830 and before he came to Plymouth. Accordingly, the basis of his ministry was to free Christians from the confines of the law. (Cf. Ps. 2.) Darby deals specifically with the sabbath in that particular letter, contending that because Christians are not under the law, attempts to honour the sabbath are wrong — there is "no direction in the New Testament concerning it, and consequently, little notice of it in the early fathers..." Referring to the Jews' strict observance of the sabbath, he says, "how foreign to the perfect law of liberty!" Regarding the sabbath commandment, he states, "I think, on a much higher ground than formal ordinance."[55] Darby here is consistent

---

53. Darby was very widely traveled, and by the time he defined the "nature of Christianity," he had a huge following world-wide, having traveled by 1869 about 40 years.
54. *Ibid.*, III.225.
55. *Ibid.*, 228.

with his belief that Christians are not bound to obey the written law of God, being on a more *spiritual* plane. He, therefore, laid the foundation for forsaking the Christian sabbath.

The church, said Darby, has no responsibility to the Old Testament law, only love.[56] The Christian is simply controlled by the inwrought divine will as "The holy ghost directs..."[57] He clearly meant, however, that man's *control* is from the Spirit within, not from the written word without. Among the hundreds of letters Darby writes to individuals, extremely few suggest the person search the Scriptures for answers to personal problems.

Darby holds Christ as the model for life while excluding the written word from any instruction, leaving the followers of the millennial faith with no clearly defined standard of living. Rather, he gave them only some abstract standard. He held that one is sanctified by salvation, not by obedience.[58]

"But you have confounded, as is very common, law and gospel. The Gentiles have no law..." Nor can the law be made a measure for Christians: "You are all wrong as to making law the measure. It was the measure of human righteousness in a child of Adam... Nor is the blessing of Christianity... to be found in the Old Testament... Nor is the law the measure of human sin..." Darby thus confuses Christ's applied righteousness by faith to the sinner with the believer's right living according to the law. He contends that the Christian's promised blessings are claimed by obedience to God's will as written in the heart, not as written in his inspired Law-Word.[59]

> "How sad it is, how very sad, to see Christians, as we often do, tampering with such evil. Take, for instance, the Galatians: there were saints there who were tampering with Judaism, who wanted to

---

56. *Writings,* II.423, 424. This doctrine cuts off God's people from the Old Testament blessings and curses, *e.g.*, Deut. 28-32. It also requires ignoring the Old Testament context of passages such as 1 Pet. 2:9 (Exo. 19:6).
57. *Letters,* II.104, 1850. Is this not Scofield's notes for Galatians 3:24?
58. *Letters,* II, 160, 161, 1872.
59. *Ibid.,* III.21, 22. *Writings,* II.592.

bring in the law; it is not that they were not Christians, but they were mixed up with that which was utterly hateful to God."[60]

Despite Romans 3:20, &c., Darby did not see the necessity of the law in convicting of sin: "... But for many hearts [not all, *ed*.], or rather for many consciences, the law is a means of reaching them, and convicting them of sin."[61] Because Darby held the law was not binding upon Christians, especially the Gentiles, he had no firm Scriptural definition of sin.

Interestingly, Darby found the translations of Scripture of his day so corrupt that he had to issue his own:

> And besides, I have undertaken nothing less than correcting the whole Old Testament, working it from the Hebrew with all the helps I can. It is a service underground, but I trust will be a help to the saints. They are really without an Old Testament — either an excessively incorrect one, or by infidel translators... I accept my present work while it is so important in these last days that brethren should have the word of God, and that they should have it as pure as possible... And I feel I am serving the Lord in using the little knowledge I have of Greek and Hebrew, etc., in furnishing brethren who have them not, with the word of God as nearly as possible as it is.[62]

Concerning the word of God, one part of Darby's millennial "truth" imbibed by American Christianity is found in an 1870 letter he sent from London:

> ...The absolutely perfect and living rule is the life of the Lord Jesus Christ. In Him all written rules are united in one solitary living example; but the written rule which ought to govern our whole life is the New Testament. The Old Testament gives the most precious light, and illuminates the path of Christians by the light of divine faith working in hearts; still, before the rending of the veil, it could be said, "The true light now shineth," save in the life of Jesus Christ:

---

60. *Letters,* III.475. "To commit adultery is a common figure in scripture for tampering with evil..." *Ibid.,* 474. In other words, Darby implies that those "who want... to bring in the law" as a standard of life are adulterers.
61. *Ibid.,* II.73.
62. *Ibid.,* II.65. Because the then current translations would not support his view of the "truth," he translated, as mentioned in this letter, into German, French and English.

He was the light of the world. For this reason when the Holy Ghost gives as examples of walking in the path of faith, the faithful of the Old Testament, He adds, "Looking unto Jesus..."... We must know the Lord in order to walk thus — "worthy of God who hath called you to his kingdom and glory." This absolutely clear and perfect light is found in the New Testament alone; but the Old, if we have learned to distinguish between the dispensation under which the saints lived in those times, furnishes very fine examples of faith, of obedience, of subjection to the will of God, of constancy in His paths...[63]

Darby was very adamant that the Old Testament "judgements and destructions were on earth, and that they had nothing to say" about modern social matters.[64] And thus he taught that Christians are free from the Lord's Old Testament threats against sin. And God's people loved the message.

Chapter 100

Sin

Wading through Darby's confusing and "chaotic" doctrine, we find his corrupt view of sin. Admittedly, the following contains brief statements concerning sin, so we urge the interested reader to check the references. It is easy to see why his ideas were so popular then and continue to appeal to fallen men. He never defined sin, though he did agree that,

> Death entered by sin [Rom. v. 12]; sin is taken abstractedly, the thing, sin, even personified, which is the highest figurative form of abstraction...[65]

Speaking great, swelling words against sin and evil, Darby never defined sin: "Sin... is the highest figurative form of abstraction," and

---

63. *Letters,* II.108, 109.
64. *Ibid.,* I.402.
65. *Ibid.,* II. 101. From Lausanne, June, 1850. Also 139, 170, 272, III.42, 97, I.170, 1849. No wonder he caused a riot there.

then he fled to the Greek to justify his theory. The failure to define sin permits speaking great swelling words supporting "Family Values" without defining *values*. For when values are Scripturally defined, one runs the risk of offending others. He dismissed 1 John 1:5-10, as being abstract, explaining away v. 9 in a manner this pastor cannot follow.[66]

Strong stood against the expanding Darbyism of his day (1906):

> Gen.18:25; Deut. 32:4; Ps. 5:5, 7:9-12, 18:24-26; Matt. 5:48; Rom. 2:6; 1 Pet. 1:16. These passages show that God loves the same persons whom he hates. It is not true that he hates the sin, but loves the sinner; he both hates and loves the sinner himself, hates him as he is a living and wilful antagonist of truth and holiness, loves him as he is a creature capable of good and ruined by his transgression.
>
> There is no abstract sin that can be hated apart from the persons in whom that sin is represented and embodied. Thomas Fuller found it difficult to starve the profaneness but to feed the person of the impudent beggar who applied to him for food. Mr. Finney declared that he would kill the slave-catcher, but would love him with all his heart. In our civil war Dr. Kirk said: "God knows that we love the rebels, but God also knows that we will kill them if they do not lay down their arms." The complex nature of God not only permits but necessitates this same double treatment of the sinner, and the earthly father experiences the same conflict of emotions when his heart yearns over the corrupt son whom he is compelled to banish from the household. Moberly, Atonement and Personality, 7 — "It is the sinner who is punished, not the sin." [67]

In other words, sin cannot be separated from the sinner.

Though Darby's standard of perfection is continually an abstract idea of *being like Christ,* he fails to mention Christ's characteristics that one should follow. He does say, however, that Christ was totally "heavenly-minded," *i.e.,* unconcerned about anything of this world.

> The idea [sin, *ed.*] is abstract and absolute; it is the value and efficacy of the blood. It is not only restoration. It is an efficacy, moreover, which is never lost. My soul once washed, I am always before God according to the efficacy of this blood... I do not doubt

---

66. *Ibid.,* III.102, 103.
67. *Systematic Theology,* 290, 291.

that the light searches us; but here God does not see evil. He sees the man cleansed by the blood of Jesus...[68]

Thus those who have been washed in the blood have no sins to repent, no sins to be forgiven. 1 John is explained away in the same letter: "If sin has acted, we are brought to confess, not sin in the flesh, but what it has produced."

Chapter 101

Sin Defined

Darby did identify a few things clearly as sin:

> The world is the place of Satan's throne; and now corruption, pleasing to the flesh, associating the Church with the world is taught. The enemy is working within. "*Thou hast* them that hold the doctrine of Balaam."[69]

Based upon his idea that Satan has displaced the Lord as the king of the whole earth, Darby developed heretical definitions of sin that fit very well within the millennial faith.

Sin is: being concerned about worldly matters, *e.g.*, Christians who are involved in worldly matters are like Lot, and those above such matters are like Abraham;[70] defined as losing the emotion of heavenly-mindness, not in terms of public action and 1 John. 3:4;[71] captivity to superstition and errors by education that believes evil can be conquered by another means than by Christ's literal, supernatural intervention with a rod of iron;[72] when the conscience

---

68. *Letters*, II.139.
69. *Ibid.*, III.459.
70. *Writings*, II.464ff., 43.
71. *Ibid.*, 440.
72. *Ibid.*, II.311. He took many direct shots at the Reformers' "Postmil" teaching. The prevailing thought in Darby's day was that the Christian gospel would gradually convert the world, but misusing Daniel's stone, he sought to dash any such hope as a great error, *Writings*, II.185, *Letters*, I.257, 1858. He repeatedly condemns any desire for the conversion of the world to Christ.

is violated (thus, replacing God's law with man's standard);[73] desiring to bring in law as a standard of life — it is "hateful to God";[74] trying to instill Biblical justice in this world, including God's requirement of restitution;[75] involvement in established religion,[76] so, accordingly, his primary goal was to get people to separate from "sin" — that is, get them out of the established churches that refused to hold his faith.

Is it any wonder that Darbyism, with no dogmatic law for right living after one is converted, was and is so attractive to the natural man? It permits every man to do what is right in his own eyes as his own god, his conscience being his guide: "Under the new covenant of grace the principle of obedience to the divine will is inwrought."[77]

Personal Sin — following closely Irving's system, Darby held that a Christian is purified from sin by the hope of Christ's soon return, not by God's work of grace: "Suppose the thought of the Lord's coming to receive us to glory were very present to us, how many things would disappear!..." "'He that hath this hope in him purifieth himself, even as he is pure.'" The Christian has no sin in this life, nor does he have consciousness of sins.[78]

Social Sin — with no lawful definition for sin, Darby was left with only mystical answers for "sin." His answer for surrounding social evils was to become more withdrawn from his surroundings and more *spiritual*. The more evil progresses, said he, the more we feel the need of God's literal intervention to execute judgment.

---

73. *Letters*, II.141, 284.
74. *Writings*, II.475.
75. *Writings*, II.154. Writing on Revelation 21:21, he held that because Christians in this life live now above sin in the heavens, "One cannot mix together with grace the earthly justice, which says 'Eye for eye, tooth for tooth.'" Hence he makes righteousness a mystical experience — "The true character of the Christian is that of divine righteousness and holiness, and that of grace..." He totally ignores that redemption is based in the law of restitution, "Eye for eye..."
76. *Letters*, I.85, 1845.
77. *Scofield*, 1245.
78. *Writings*, II.417. *Letters*, II.146, 160, 398. 1 Jn. 3:3, but v. 4 is conveniently ignored. *Purity* is defined by *the law*.

Being powerless against evil, the Christian must not try to change his evil surroundings, for evil cannot be put in order until Christ returns with his *rod of iron*. Separation from evil was mystically defined as dwelling in Christ. The Christian's business is grace, not exposing social evils.[79] *Grace* was defined as God's power to just wait for HIM to do something about the surrounding mess — caused by indifferent Christians, we must add.

Darby did, however, have a clear vision of one particular sin: disagreement with his scheme of things, his version of "truth." He calls any disagreement with his "truth," among other things, blasphemy against Christ, work of Satan, and under God's judgment. He considered it evil to associate with other assemblies that did not totally accept his "truth."[80]

He also found a particularly sinful person, Newton, and the Brethren assembly under Newton at Bethesda was exceedingly sinful. Newton's disagreement with Darby earned him a special place in Darby's opinion as an outright sinner. Though never using Scripture to support his charges against Newton and Bethesda, Darby called him an evil, satanic, blasphemous heretic, an enemy of men's souls. He called Bethesda a work of Satan, and a propagator of evil doctrine.[81] Darby spent more words against Newton and the assembly at Bethesda than he did against any other one person or place, Baptists excepted. Though claiming to be above involvement in conflicts and hatred, he never missed an opportunity to condemn Newton and Bethesda as the very worst evil he had ever

---

79. Listed in order mentioned: *Letters,* III.158, I.328. *Writings,* II.311. *Letters,* I.328. *Writings,* II.598, 486, 535. *Letters,* III.59. *Writings,* II.569.

80. *Letters,* II.214-218, 220. Speaking of those who published papers attempting to correct his position, he said, "I am sorry those I have lived and walked with in charity should have fallen so much away from the path of simple faith..." *Ibid.,* I.465, from New York, Nov. 1866.

81. *E.g. Ibid.,* II.222, 1873: "A work of Satan has been going on, alleging that evil doctrine [at Bethesda, ed.] was no matter..." As time proceeds, Darby's venom against Newton and Bethesda becomes stronger. They seem to consume his thoughts more and more while Darby professes to be "clean" in the whole matter.

encountered. In fact, he implies Bethesda was not a Christian assembly because it followed Newton rather than himself.[82]

He does say, nevertheless, that "if any man sin," he has an advocate, 1 John 2:1, 2, but "It is abstract..." He held that justifying forgiveness was unknown in Old Testament: "Sin, as calling for it, was not properly known in the Old Testament..."[83]

Chapter 102

Sin and Judgment

Judgment of sin is spiritual, not physical, so there are no physical consequences for sin. He saw no sin in this life, holding that Christians cannot sin, nor can they have any trace of sin. Dead men are not accountable for sin, and Christians are dead in Christ. He does, nevertheless, mention that sin breaks communion with the Father, but worshippers once purged have no more conscience of sin, concluding that Christians will not be judged for sin. He does admit that "I remember sinning once upon a time."[84]

He held there must be a new heaven and earth before the effects of sin can be stopped. Though he saw an end to sin for Christians, he did not see that end for Jews: The Jews were set aside for the church

---

82. *Ibid.*, I.167, 168 (very bad), 181, 200, 205 (unholy), 218 (Darby always saw himself righteous in any matter, ibid., I.46), 219 (as bad as Rome — he held Baptists to be worse than Rome), 255 (deliberately supports evil), &c. Darby wrote several letters to others condemning Bethesda. *Ibid.*, II. 224 — Darby was clear: He was against the Brethren at Bethesda under Newton because they would not abide by his judgments. Darby also found Baptists and Baptist doctrine extremely hateful and sinful.

83. *Ibid.*, II.274, 275, III.10.

84. *Ibid.*, I.62, 1843, II.146, 170, 269, 459, 274, 447, 112. "This principle of judgment runs through them all [Rev. 2, 3, *ed.*]: 'I will give unto every one of you according to the use he has made of the privileges and grace in which the Church was at first set.'... "It is not condemnation as by the law...," *Writings,* II.424. Judgment is thus not according to God's written standard, but according to how one uses "privileges and grace" — defined as ability to wait.

(which in this system of faith is "unmentioned in prophecy"), but God will again deal with Israel as sinners.[85]

Darby had many confusing words to say about sin's judgment, but we will only mention a few here.

He saw spiritual rather than physical judgment for sin.[86] Judgment takes place in the conscience, not in any temporal events that might result from sins. The love of the Lord and the blood of the Lamb, he held, safeguards God's people against God's righteous judgment against sin.[87] The logical conclusion to this thought is that society does not reflect the Christian's irresponsibility to his social duties.

He was firmly convinced that the faithful saints (those who have learned to look up and to be unconcerned with worldly matters by God's grace) will be removed from the earth and miss "the great tribulation," during which time the Lord judges the wicked upon earth after he returns with his saints. Because only by his literal rule can the Lord straighten out the mess made on earth by sin, he allows sin to go unchecked during the present dispensation.[88] Hence, God's calling for his people is simply to wait unconcerned about surrounding evil, wait for the Lord to fix it all with his *rod of iron*. In other words, God's law of sowing and reaping is suspended during the present dispensation of grace!

Israel is the only one who will receive God's righteous judgments as the church only receives God's grace, "and it never gets out of this." Thus the faithful believers need not fear any judgment of God. The true church is gone during time of God's judgment against evil as recorded in Revelation. So believers have no reason for concern about surrounding evils. On the other hand, he taught that because

---

85. *Letters*, III, 12. *Writings*, II.265.
86. *Letters*, I.62, 1843.
87. *Writings*, II.441, 1852, 405.
88. *Writings*, II.369ff., 1843. *Ibid.* 385, 1853. See 383, *Letters*, II.196. *Writings*, II.544. Christ will not judge nations until he is on his literal throne at Jerusalem. Therefore, we need not worry about judgment for personal, national wickedness, *ibid.*, 597. He follows Lacunza's system very closely.

the professing church is not looking in unconcern for his coming, it will face judgment.[89]

The prevailing opinion until Darby was of a common resurrection of the just and the unjust, which he called "totally unscriptural." Darby's view of judgment is based upon his personal perceptions of the matter.[90]

Chapter 102

Conscience and Guidance

Effectively cutting off not only the Old Testament and all non-Pauline writings, the millennial faith leaves the Child of God with no standard of right and wrong:

> As to a convenient and comfortable means of knowing the will of God, as one might have a receipt for anything, no such thing exists — of knowing it, I would say, without reference to the state of our own soul.[91]

The Child of God is thus called to look inward for his guidance. This extremely active and perceptive man, Darby, convinced multitudes that they had no guide except the conscience of "the spiritual man" who is "near enough to God" to know God's will. He develops, "If thine eye be single, thy whole body shall be full of light," to say that if one is a Christian with a genuine desire to "walk in a way worthy

---

89. *Writings*, II.561. Remember his definition of faithful is "otherworldly" and unconcerned. *Ibid.*, 571. The Church will be judged according to how much it loved the Lord's return — that is, how much it remained unconcerned and otherworldly. Christians are free from judgment for sin, *Letters*, II.144. In fact, God cannot touch those who remain detached from the evil around them, *ibid.*, 490, 1852. The world's judgment does not start until Revelation 4, when John is called up into heaven, *Writings*, II.563, 1852. See also 597. Ignoring the clear teaching of Mat. chaps. 23, 24, of the coming judgment against those who killed Christ, Jerusalem, he contends that the subject of Revelation is God's judgment of the Gentile world. He followed Lacunza's break at Revelation 4.
90. *Ibid.*, 175, *Letters*, III.282. *Writings*, II.383, 385.
91. *Letters*, I.314.

Darbyism-Millenarianism

of Him," he will, accordingly, "grow in the knowledge of God's will" for his life. In other words, if one is a Christian with proper motive, God will guide him through his conscience. He makes no mention of God's word.[92]

Darby continues to make the point in another letter dated, 1875: "'He that is spiritual discerneth all things,'" *i.e.,* "If one is sincere in his motives, God's grace watches over him to lead in the proper path." In fact, when confrontations arose between Darby and others, he knew he was in the right because, in his words, "My conscience does not reproach me..."[93] Of the Holy Spirit speaking in the heart, Darby said:

> But all these things are given us in the word by inspiration, in order that we may know man and the ways of God. At the same time, God's own thoughts are also communicated to us, in order to enable us to judge all this according to His judgment.... For my own part, I do not doubt that a powerful effect of the Spirit of God is often produced, where the moral form with which that which produces it is clothed participates, [sic] to a very great degree, in all the thoughts of the class of persons who are the vessels and channels of it....[94]

Throughout the letters, it is obvious that Darby considered himself part of "the class of persons who are the vessels and channels of" communicating God's own thoughts to mankind. Might this be a reason Darby failed to emphasize God's word for instruction — he would be stripped of his power over people? Has this not over the centuries been a great motive for religious leaders failing to urge their people to seek God's will from his revealed word? The conflict between the Pharisees and the revealed Word of God was that he stripped them of their influence and power over God's people.

Darby continues to drive people away from the will of God as revealed in God's word:

> As regards *circumstances,* I believe that a person may be guided by them; scripture has decided that. It is what it speaks of as being

---

92. *Ibid.,* I.314, 315, 1856.
93. *Ibid.,* 323; I.74.
94. *Ibid.,* I.206, 207.

"held in with bit and bridle." "I will instruct thee, and teach thee in the way which thou shalt go: I will guide thee with mine eye" — such is the promise and privilege of him who has faith, is near enough to God to understand by a single glance from Him. God who is faithful, has given the promise to guide him thus.... and such it is to be *guided by circumstances.*[95]

This pastor questioned a young man concerning the young man's determination to become a pastor of a particular church upon graduation from one of the largest, best known fundamental Baptist "Bible" colleges in the world. The young man dogmatically defended his determination not from God's word, but from circumstances, saying, "The door is open, and I have peace about it" — that is, the *circumstances* are right for me to do what I want to do, so don't confuse me with the word and will of God.

The sin promoted by Darby of "Let your conscience be your guide" or "Do what you feel is right" has been around since Eve. The primary difference is that he gave it a cloak of Christian respectability by saying, "This requires spirituality, and abiding in communion with God. It is not to be guided by the circumstances, but to be guided by God *in* them, being near enough to God as to be able to judge immediately what one ought to do, as soon as the circumstances are there."[96] His "communion with God," however, was a mystical communion, not communion with God through his word; it was not, *Study to show thyself approved, a workman that needeth not be ashamed.* The words were godly — all the right ones were there, but the message was clearly demonic. "You are saved and desire to serve God; therefore, let your inner spirit guide you. If you are a Christian dedicated to serving the Lord, your conscience will not misguide you." *You can be and are like God, able to determine for yourself what is good and evil.*

He continues in his letter:

---

95. *Ibid.,* 316.
96. *Ibid.,* 316. Emp. his. He condemns others for making statements "without reference to scripture," yet he very seldom makes such a reference, *Ibid.,* 75.

> ...If I do something with the full certainty that I am doing the will of God, then it is clear that an obstacle is no more than a test of my faith, and it ought not to stop me. It stops us perhaps through our lack of faith; because, if we do not walk sufficiently near to God in the sense of our nothingness, we shall always lack faith to *accomplish* what we have faith enough to *discern.g*[97]

In other words, circumstances might be contrary to what a Christian is determined to do, but that is only Satan trying to hinder one from obeying "the divine will inwrought." This doctrine, along with "God never allows Satan to act otherwise than on the flesh," opened Christians to *devilish* activity in the spirit.[98]

Millennialism does not leave the Christian without a standard: "...do what Jesus would have done in such and such a circumstance." Good advice. Certainly, the gospels "are full of the richest instruction," but one needs sound, written, *black and white* instructions as found only in God's revealed will, his total Word.

There are a great many quotes revealing Darby's basic supposition concerning the word of God, sin, God's will, &c., but we will only give one more, then tie up the ends:

> To a spiritually intelligent mind, the word of God carries an authority beyond all cavils; and a poor, unintelligent man would pass over what is contrary to the mind generated by it, as evidently false, or as unable to understand it, so that he escapes what is false inserted by men in it. They shall be all taught of God; and when the conscience is reached, and the will subject, and therefore the mind silent, we have the peace which certainty gives (and uncertainty as to what is all important is misery), and blessed growth in what God Himself has revealed for divine blessing and joy.

The above excerpt from Darby's 1874 letter from London sounds like something every Christian could agree with, but notice his next statement:

> I do not receive the Bible, that is, a revelation of God from the hands of men. I receive paper and ink. The revelation I receive from God

---

97. *Ibid.,* II.317. Emp. his.
98. *Ibid., q.v.* See Scofield's notes for Galatians 3:24, 1245.

directly — "They shall be all taught of God." The revelation is the divinely- wrought conviction, and, I repeat, *in the conscience*...[99]

The man who laid the foundation for modern dispensational millennialism said that God did not speak to him through "paper and ink;" rather, God spoke directly to him through his *conscience* and through *circumstances*. Did he not here lay the foundation for today's Mysticism under the name of Christianity.

The devil's lie from the Garden is revived. The Christian is told he does not need God's command-word. As a Christian, you can let your conscience be your guide: "Under the new covenant of grace the principle of obedience to the divine will is inwrought (Heb. 10.16)."[100]

Chapter 104

Corrupted Words

The early millenarians used wonderful Biblical terms. However, the terms were corrupted, giving them totally different meanings from the Spirit's definitions. Reading material that uses common words, one may accept the writer as orthodox without realizing the writer's meaning, *e.g.*, "My, this writer is soundly orthodox — look at how he believes in God's *grace.*" Yet the word is redefined to an unbiblical meaning. Since the Garden, redefining words has been and continues to be a common practice by those desiring to cover their ungodly tracks while misleading sincere people.

Corrupted Biblical words can cause one to accept unique, unorthodox, even unbiblical, understandings of passages. One can

---

99. *Ibid.*, 297. Emp. his. Evidently, Darby's idea of "paper and ink" has survived, as his followers now see the Word as a series of confusing facts that they feel safe in rearranging to solve the "prophetic puzzle."
100. Scofield on Galatians 3:24. How many times has this pastor heard that the Commandments are no longer our standard of life? Rather, our rule is now according to how the Spirit guides us.

readily understand why much of Darby's millennial system has been accepted by the church.

Sanctification and Holiness

Darby agreed to the need to be "personally sanctified, set apart for God," but he saw it as an already accomplished fact: "In personal sanctification there is no progress, we belong wholly to Christ according to the value of His work and the claim which He has over us, according to the holy life which is the true 'I' of the heart." He did, however, hold to progressive sanctification, *i.e.,* "...through the operation of the Holy Ghost we become — we ought to become, at least — while looking at Christ glorified, increasingly like Christ, more holy, as regards practical holiness."

Practical holiness, though, had nothing to do with any kind of faithfulness to the revealed will of God as found in his word:

> Thus when Christians are called holy, it is indeed the expression of a relationship with God, but this relationship is formed by the gift of life, and founded on the fact that Christ has purchased them by His death. But there is no other relationship, and when a man calls himself a Christian he calls himself holy, consecrated to God, set apart from the world for God.[101]

Progressive sanctification and holiness were defined as becoming *more like Christ,* who was totally "otherworldly." But the standard was always an abstract idea of *Christ's likeness,* with no clearly defined "holiness." *Practical holiness* was no more than a mystical union with Christ by faith.

Faithfulness

Mixing with the world was considered unfaithfulness to the Lord, Revelation 16:10:

> If we give up waiting for Him, we prepare ourselves a part with the hypocrites. The waiting for Jesus was that which at the beginning

---

101. *Letters*, II.159-164, is a complete letter concerning sanctification, Mar., 1872.

detached the heart from the world, and rendered faithful. The christian religion has made its way into the world. [sic] in consequence of this faithfulness, and of this detachment from it.... God has patience towards the world, and waits, because He takes no pleasure in the death of the wicked. But the judgment comes sooner or later. I see evidently that men oppose the doctrine of the coming of Jesus, or at least that He is not coming so very quickly. This is the principle of the unfaithful servant, and this principle leads the Christian to mix with the world. God has had patience. He has given warnings; and, when these judgments strike men, men blaspheme. When the will is not subdued, the heart is always made bitter through chastisements.[102]

Thus faithfulness is identified with detachment from the world, which is in ruins,[103] detachment from organized religion (other than Darby's religion) and just waiting for the Lord's return. He repeats his definition of faithfulness many times.

The reader might find it interesting that Darby offered no definition for serving Christ.[104]

Evangelism

Darby rejoiced as non-Brethren laymen and ministers saw things his way. In fact, when he returned to the States in 1874, he was disappointed that millennialism was being promoted in America without the people coming out of their churches. Writing from Boston, he laments:

> ...The state of the churches is scandalous indeed: pious souls groan, but where are instruments to be found to guide them in the good way — God has raised up a few, several ministers even have left their systems, but it is a drop of water in the wide sea, and there is a great effort to keep souls in the various systems while taking advantage of the light which brethren have and preaching their doctrines. They do not even conceal it. One of the most active who has visited Europe [Moody, *ed.*] told ministers that they could not keep up with the brethren unless they read their books, but he was doing everything

---

102. *Writings*, II.85, 86.
103. *Letters*, II.242.
104. *Ibid.*, III.159.

he could to prevent souls leaving their various churches. It is a new wile of the enemy...[105]

Writing from New York, he continues:

> ...I believe God is blessing it, [*evangelization,* but "not the gospel, ordinarily so called." His *evangelization* was "the wide spread of brethren's truths." A term Darby used was, "awakening" to Brethren "truths," *ed.*] specially for gathering out in these last days, and it is healthful for an assembly that their hearts are engaged in it. At the very beginning it characterized brethren, and I trust still does, though it be more common now on all hands.[106]

Again from New York:

> In Brooklyn souls are making progress in the truth, and learning what it is to be a Christian... I have no doubt that evil is increasing, as we are warned of it, but I believe the getting into the truth of real Christianity — the light it brings — makes the darkness and evil more visible... "The word of his patience," and we as men that wait for the Lord, is what we are to have at heart.[107]

The "great general principles" of "truth" Darby *evangelized* with are basically defined in another letter from New York:

> ...I came here, though I thought I had done with these parts, because the last time I was here I found the doors opening among the Americans. The difficulty is that a diligent effort has been made to disseminate the truths we have been taught so as that people should have them, and not act on them — remain where they are. Eminent ministers preach the Lord's coming, the ruin of the church, [*i.e.,* American adaptation of the "ruin of the church" is that it is in a hopeless situation, unable to bring about Godliness into a corrupt society, *ed.*] liberty of ministry, and avowedly from brethren's books, and stay where they are, and there is a general deadening of

---

105. *Ibid.*, II.304. "[K]eep up with the brethren," *i.e.*, keep up with their newly developing, unique, dispensational, escapist understandings of Scripture. His complaint was that the preachers were teaching the Brethren's unique prophetic scheme while ignoring what he held important, "the ruin of the church." Sept. 27th, 1874.

106. *Ibid.*, 306. The Irvingite/Darbyite "truth" which "At the very beginning characterized brethren" was by 1874 being commonly dispensed from non-Brethren pulpits in the U.S. This *conversion* of the pulpits was seen by Darby as God's blessings upon his *evangelism*. Nov., 1874.

107. *Ibid.*, 307, emphasis added. 1874

conscience. Now people come, are interested, surprised at all the truth they find in scripture, but for the moment with most it ends there. This casts me on the Lord. It was so the last time out west; still the Lord called out some [out of other churches, *ed.*], and new gatherings were formed. It is His work, but the wide spread of brethren's truths alters the character of the work.[108]

The millennial "truth" was just be patient and you will escape the Great Tribulation that is about to come upon the earth because of sin. Introduced by Brethren immigrants from Europe and Darby's visits, it gained wide acceptance. American churches had to start preaching the "truth" or lose their people to the Brethren. They, therefore, took all the appealing aspects of millennialism, even Americanizing its "ruin of the church." Darby's version would cost them people and finances, but the America version simply meant that the Church of the Lord Jesus Christ was helpless and powerless in the present "dispensation" to change surrounding social evils. So the Lord would have to do it through his literal return and rule as a Jewish King from Jerusalem.

1874 was a time of the great immigration to America from Europe, and a major port of entry was New York. The once godly zeal that had reached the vast multitudes of immigrants for the victorious Kingdom of God was put to death, and millennialism provided the poison that spread over the land like The Black Plague. And America was *converted* to a new, powerless faith.

Hope, Blessed Hope, Peace

The hope and cheer of the saints is defined by millennialism as Christ's soon coming to remove them from the surrounding chaos. In fact, there was no hope for modern social turmoil, ills and darkness except escape through the Lord's soon coming, which was compared to Noah's ark. Darby defined the blessed hope as "the thought that Christ is coming to take me to himself," said in the context of escape from the terrible time he saw coming upon the

---

108. *Ibid.,* 309. Darby goes on to say, "The Roman Catholics in France I hear are discussing the Lord's coming, in consequence of the disasters of the country. It is a comfort to have settled truth. Protestantism is breaking up everywhere, but peace is our portion." *Peace, i.e., unconcern.* 1874

earth. He saw escape promised only to those remaining otherworldly.[109]

"The Blessed Hope" was seen as immunity from the imminent "great tribulation," and thus Titus 2:13 (*Looking for that blessed hope, and the glorious appearing of the great God and our Saviour Jesus Christ;*) was wrested from its context. Paul's words to Titus were meant to urge faithful obedience to the total of God's Law-Word in confronting the social evils of the day. The Lord Jesus soundly rebuked the servant, *e.g.*, Darby, who just waited for his Lord's return: *Thou wicked and slothful servant.*[110] "Bible readings" permitted words to be violently wrested from their context — the thought is hope, and the context of Titus 2:13 is unimportant.

The followers of the millennial faith have no hope of victory over the world, flesh and devil through faith in the risen Lord. It is, according to this faith, sin to get involved in trying to convert the surrounding society for Christ. (How can one convert souls without converting nations?)

In 1848, Darby saw peace the result of,

[T]he thought of the return of the Lord..., for He will restore happiness to the world, and re-establish moral relations according to His mind... But, I add, to me the Lord's coming is not a question of prophecy, but my present hope. Events before His judging the quick are the subject of prophecy; His coming to receive the church is our present, heavenly hope. There is no event between me and heaven...[111]

He taught that to be established in the faith is to be established in confidence that the Lord is coming soon to remove his people from the tribulations of life. He clearly saw his calling was not to seek

---

109. *Writings*, II.436. *Ibid.*, II.436, 440, 498, 545. *Ibid.*, II.550, 551. The "Saints' hope" he was convinced, was Christ's soon return. *Ibid.*, 584. "It is good, dear brother, that we should be brought to think of death. The coming of the Lord is our hope...," *Letters*, I.254, 1857. *Writings*, II. 576.

110. *Exposition*, 349-359. Mat. 25:26.

111. *Letters*, I.135. *Ibid.*, I.330. 1862.

sinner's conversion to faith in Christ, but to convert the saints to the millennial faith — the Lord's soon coming:[112]

> My work is more in setting souls free, and now in these last days, when all is going so fast to evil, getting, as the Lord enables me, the word of God in its contents and in its purity among those who profess His name...[113]

Grace

Grace is one of the more serious corruptions of Scripture. God defines grace as his power working in fallen man, giving him both the desire and power — ability — to do his will as revealed in his entire word. God's grace starts before salvation (Christian conversion), giving the desire and power to come to Christ and to please God. Grace is defined as the power of God to do God's work in society here on earth.[114] However, the "Bible reading" method of study allows the marvelous doctrine of grace to be corrupted beyond recognition.

Darby saw sovereign grace as the God-given ability which permits the church to fulfill her *responsibility* of just waiting for the Lord's soon return despite what is going on in the surrounding world.[115]

---

112. *Ibid.,* II.358. He rejoiced far more over conversions to his system than he did over conversions to Christ, *Writings,* II.164, 165. *Letters,* II.434, 498. *Ibid.,* I.34, 1840.

113. *Letters,* II.65, 1870.

114. Rom. 3:10ff. (Ps. 14), Phil. 2:13, 1 Cor. 15:10.

115. *Writings,* II.381, 467, c.1852. *Ibid.,* 164, 425. Grace is mentioned in salvation, but no mention of personal response in salvation. *Ibid.,* II.313, NY, 1874.

Chapter 105

The Great Escape

We must not overlook the most appealing, and destructive, aspect of the millennial system: escape from surrounding civil and religious turmoil, and escape from any responsibility to do something about them[116]— a religion of escapism. This idea (escape from a coming tribulation) was neither new nor unique with Darby: In its 1831 issues, *The Morning Watch* promised escape for the Philadelphia Church from the wrath to come from God upon the earth.[117]

The millennial faith, appealing especially to the lower classes, promised escape from present difficulties *if* one would fix his mind on heaven. Darby's refuge in trouble was mentally to escape, *i.e.,* heavenly minded or otherworldly — that is, detach one's self from surrounding troubling events. If one remains unconcerned about the world around him, the Lord will spare him from the "terrible time of trouble that shall come upon all the world, to try them that dwell upon the earth."[118]

> ...if I have bowed to the grace of the Lamb, then I have no connection whatever with that which will come under the wrath of the Lamb.[119]

Concerning Revelation 16, he said:

> What a blessing for the Christian to have assured peace, to know that, having kept the word of the patience of Christ, he shall also be kept from the hour of temptation; and the more the storm is raging outside, the more there is calm in tranquility in the house of God! We have on our side the immutability of the throne itself, from

---

116. *Ibid.,* I.5. The letter describing what took place at the 1832 Powerscourt Prophecy Conference is reproduced in App. A.
117. *Plot,* 76, 77.
118. *Letters,* I.91. From Plymouth, 1846. "Don't be conformed to this world." See 205 also. *Writings,* II.435, 1852; 550.
119. *Ibid.,* 561, 1852.

whence proceed these judgments, and these judgments do not touch us. This is the joy of the child of God. The peace of God keeps him in the midst of the awful times coming on the world.[120]

Darby was confident "that the faithful will escape judgment."[121]

Darby wrote just before his death that "they [the faithful of the Philadelphia Church mentioned in Rev., *ed*.] would accordingly escape the hour of temptation which would come on all the world. But the Lord said more, He was coming quickly, they were to hold fast what they had, that none took their crown." He continues: "And now, what I would beg of the brethren is, not to be occupied with evil...," *i.e.,* do not be concerned about challenging nor correcting any surrounding evil.[122]

Darby desired to "get as fast into heaven as I can."[123]

Let us conclude this section with Olson's observation:

> As the *Left Behind* books demonstrate, the power of the dispensationalist system rests in its offer of escape from suffering and tribulation, its claim to make sense of Scripture and history, and its invitation to be part of a chosen, knowledgeable few—true believers whom God will soon vindicate with wrath and power. As long as people want to know the future but not live in it, the Rapture will live on—a supernatural escape from an unbelieving world for those who long for a new and better world.[124]

Olson comments further:

> Fear and the desire to escape the world and its troubles are not the only—or even the primary—reasons that people are dispensationalists. Rather, it is their conviction that the dispensationalist teachers are accurately interpreting the Bible and the Bible itself teaches a pretribulational Rapture, a seven-year Tribulation, and a thousand-year millennial Kingdom on earth. Matching Scriptures with current events around the globe makes people feel they understand the Bible better. "It assures people that the Bible is true and historically accurate without any need to

---

120. *Ibid.*, 88, 1852.
121. *Letters*, I.58. From Lausanne, 1843. Also 179.
122. *Ibid.*, III.222. From London, 1882.
123. *Ibid.*, 39, 1879.
124. *Catholics*, 340.

grapple with the complex challenges of the Bible. It also frees the reader from any sense of obligation to improve or change significantly the culture, the arts, the political order, or any other aspect of society. The impending end of the world makes such pursuits trivial, even ridiculous—what matters is saving souls from the approaching tribulation." It is the ability of premillennialists to fit current events into their system that attracts large numbers of adherents.[125]

Darby's arrogance toward any disagreement of his system has been taken up by his followers who stoutly resist reasonable dialogue that might let their followers know there is another system.

Popular dispensationalist teachers have fount it quite profitable to play on people's fears and their desire to escape suffering and death for many decades, and LaHaye continues the practice. LaHaye writes:

> The Tribulation is a fitting consummation of the grand experiment of the ages from Adam to the Second Coming, giving individuals an opportunity to worship God voluntarily.[126]

And thus LaHaye teaches that God's grace is unable give man the desire to worship Himself, and hence the tribulation is God's way of granting humanity a second chance.

Chapter 106

Phenomenal Growth

The world was ready for what was offered by the millenarians. A means to escape from the turmoils of life and society certainly appeals to the natural man. It spread rapidly over the world like a cancer, astounding even Darby himself.[127]

---

125. *Ibid.*, 202, 203.
126. LaHaye, *Rapture under Attack,* p. 64, quoted by Olson, *Catholics*, 318-320.

1860 — in Lausanne, there was not enough room for the inquirers. 1863 — from London, he commented how the "truth" was spreading. 1869 — from London, again he said, "as to numbers and gatherings, they increase much... many young men, and a great and serious desire to hear; but with such a multitude as we have now..."1864 — from Pau, he said, "As to numbers, the increase is rapid enough..."[128]

Europe, especially Ireland, Germany and Switzerland, was overwhelmed with the system. Darby's statements about Nismes gives us an idea of the growth of the faith: "I have never had such large meetings, and such solemn ones." His reception at Nismes was quite different from years before: "But what a change since I was there some twenty-five years ago, just picking up here and there a soul, with a little company in a room to hear, and they uncertain."[129]

Darby also tells how ministers outside of the Brethren's millennial movement dealt with the problem of their people following the newly developing millennial system:

> Their minister [at Nismes, ed.], for they had one, though he disdains his place as chosen pastor, said honestly before us all (he came several days to the meeting), that he had learned almost everything from brethren, but then such always spoil it: he taught the Lord's coming, but made a strange mess of it — none of them in the church's place; they never can: however, my intercourse with him was fraternal and happy so far.[130]

In other words, the Christians of Nismes were so taken by Darby's theories that if the pastor expected to keep them, he had to accept those new dispensational, millennial theories. The pastor did, but did not really understand the new system, so Darby instructed him to a

---

127. *Letters*, II.261 — From Milan, 1874. We should remember, however, that Kelly had a way of stretching the truth, though we cannot deny that its spread was astoundingly fast and thorough.

128. *Ibid.*, I.300, 367. He identified his new ideas as the "truth." II.35. I.375. Also, 398, 413, 414.

129. *Ibid.*, II.117 [1871], 130, 156; 253, (1874), 273; 159, 1872. In fact, in 1874, people had to be turned away at Nismes. *Ibid.*, 260.

130. *Ibid.*, 261.

greater extent. The pastor was typical of what happened as millenarianism infiltrated the church.

The acceptance of the system was not limited to Europe. Even Darby expressed surprise at how swiftly people accepted dispensational millennialism as new groups sprung up everywhere with his system. Once his destructive seeds were planted in America, they grew rapidly, and multitudes flocked to the millennial meetings. Many others besides Brethren were drawn into the movement.[131] Darby himself pretty well sums up the growth of the system he presented:

> ...I am now in my seventy-ninth year. You will be interested to hear, as you find the opposition of the clergy, and especially to the Lord's coming, that in Constantinople they have preached against that and breaking of bread, and that this has set the Americans the inquiry as to both.... I do not speak of it now, when I do, as a point to be proved, but as a part of christian truth, as much as the atonement, though not like it the foundation of grace: but they were converted to wait for His Son from heaven. In that congress (at New York) as far as I know of it, the presence of the Holy Ghost was, says —, wholly left out. But these are the two truths brought out in these days, throwing much light on the truth of the first coming. They have been consciously my theme these fifty years and more. They started me on my path of service; the assurance of salvation came with them, and the christian character as of the new creation, "like unto men that wait for their Lord."... What set me free in 1827 is still the theme on which my soul dwells..."...Thus in the congress at New York there was the positive good of bringing the coming of the Lord publicly forward; but there were all sorts of heretics there, and persons deliberately hindering the truth in seeking to connect it with the world and the camp — avowing it, if the account is to be believed — leaving out the essential point of the presence of the Holy Ghost. Let us be content to be little and despised, but give out the full truth. The present great truth, redemption being known, is the presence of the Holy Ghost, what made it expedient Christ should leave the disciples; the future truth — in present hope — the coming of the Lord for the saints, and then in His own rights over the world.... In general, the work has made considerable progress in

---

131. *Ibid.*, I.533, 1868; II.15, 23, 1863, from Jamaica; I. 54 — 1843, II.83, 129, 144, II. 182 — 1872, 329, 330, 374 — 1876, 386, 390.

the United States. But all over the world the Spirit of God is working, and it awakes the bright hope that the blessed Lord is soon coming...[132]

At first, the millennial *truth* that people are simply "converted to wait" for the Lord's soon coming had to be "proved" with many Scriptures — "Bible readings." But fifty years later and over "the opposition of the clergy," the *truth* had become "as much as the atonement" "part of christian truth," not only in the United States, but all over the world.

Chapter 107
Conclusion

The "tiny religious sect" offered the Protestant Christian world an escape from reality; it offered escape from the Biblical responsibility to work hard, obey God's law-word, sacrifice and to convert the nations to Christ. The offer, though developed from insight rather than Scripture, was apparently supported by Scripture, making it even more appealing. One could be satisfied he was serving God when, actually, he was denying the Lord of the Bible as revealed through consistent, contextual study of Scripture. The result of the new, unique system of Christian thought was the deliverance of society to the spirit of antichrist by default. Though Lacunza's millennial system was not new, the anti-Christian fervor of the world today can be directly traced to the him, Irving, and to the "tiny religious sect" that Darby claimed as his own.

Though God's people many times love messages of irresponsible escapism, the task before the people of God is not hopeless, *For it is God which worketh in you both to will and to do of his good pleasure.*

---

132. *Ibid.,* 498, 499, 500, 1879. See also *Letters,* III.19.

The preceding document is offered to the reader with the prayer that God will work to give his people the desire to go *and teach all nations* — that is, Christianize the nations of the world, and develop the Christian faith into every area of life and thought.

Nay, in all these things we are more than conquerors through him that loved us.

(Rom. 8:37.)

Appendix A
Letters of Explanation

The following letters are included for the interested reader who is seeking to know the truth of matters we have discussed. However, the reader should keep in mind that: 1) Darby had a way of laying claim to other's ideas, *e.g.,* Lacunza's-Irving's, and stretching the truth to fit his purposes; and 2) his editor, William Kelly, changed Darby's writings to make them read like many of the new, unorthodox ideas originated with Darby. We will open with Irving's account of the 1826 Albury Park conference on unfulfilled prophecy.

Albury Park (1826)

Irving describes what took place at Albury where he no doubt introduced *Ben-Ezra*.

P.S. — I have said, that this work was to have been laid on the altar as my Christmas offering to the Church; and in the body of this Preliminary Discourse I have signified that it was written on that day, as indeed the substance of it was; and now two months have passted beyond the stated time. The cause of this delay I hold myself called upon to give; especially as I feel it will not be less agreeable to the Church to receive it, than it is to me to offer it.

There arose, in the beginning of last summer [this P.S. is dated, January 17th, 1827, *ed.*], amongst certain students of prophecy in London, a desire to compare their views, with respect to the prospects of the Church at this present crisis; and we held meetings during the summer, from time to time, as we could find opportunity. When one of our number, well known for his princely munificence, thought it well to invite by special letter all the men, both ministers and laymen, of any orthodox communion, whom he knew or could ascertain to be interested in prophetic studies, that they should assemble at his house of Albury Park, in Surrey, on the first day of Advent, that we might deliberate for a full week upon the great prophetic questions which do at present most instantly concern Christendom. In answer to his honourable summons, there assembled about twenty men of every rank and church and orthodox communion in these realms. And, in honour of our meeting, God so ordered it that Joseph Wolff, a Jewish Missionary, a son of Abraham and brother of our Lord, both according to the flesh and according to the faith, should also be of the number. And here for eight days, under the roof of Henry Drummond, Esq. the present High Sheriff of the County, and under the moderation of the Rev. Hugh M'Niel, the Rector of the Parish of Albury, we spent six full days in close and laborious examination of the scriptures, upon these six great heads of doctrine: First, The doctrine of the Holy Scripture concerning the time of the Gentiles. Secondly, The duties of Christian ministers and people, growing out thereof towards the Gentile churches. Thirdly, The doctrine concerning the present and future condition of the Jews. Fourthly, The duties growing out of the same towards the Jews. Fifthly, The system of the prophetic visions and numbers of Daniel and the Apocalypse. Sixthly, The scripture doctrine concerning the future advent of the Lord. And Lastly, The duties to the church and the world arising out of the same. Now these are points on which men are supposed to be wholly at sea, without chart, course, or polar star; and it is the common rebuke of the students of prophecy, that no two of them are agreed on any one matter: and therefore the thing which I am about to say, will appear the more wonderful; That though we were for the most part strangers to one another, of different churches and of different countries, and under no influence of one another, we were so overruled by the One Spirit of truth and love, as to have found our way to harmony and coincidence in the main points of all these questions. We believed in a common that the present form of the dispensation of the gospel was a time commensurate with the time of the Gentiles, which again are commensurate with the period of Jerusalem's being trodden under foot, and of the Jews' dispersion; that the restoration of the Jews would introduce altogether a new era into the church and the world, which might be called the universal dispensation of the benefits of Christ's death, while this is the dispensation to the church only, which is *few* compared with the *whole*. That the conclusion of the latter in great judgments, and the commencement of the former in great mercies, was hard at hand, yea even at the very door; all being agreed that the 1260 and 1290 days of Daniel were accomplished, and the remaining 45 begun, and the conclusion of which the blessedness will be fully arrived. And that during this judgment, which may open upon us any day, we are to look for the second advent of the Lord in person, to raise the dead bodies of his saints, and with them to reign upon the earth. All agreeing that in the view of these things, there was required of us the greatest vigilance at our several posts, and the most fearless constancy in affectionately warning and preaching righteousness to all; according as they are admonished be [sic] our Lord in the sixth vial, under which it was the universal opinion we are now living, ready for the last great and concluding vial of wrath.

These things I write from recollection, not caring to use the copious notes which I took, for it was a mutual understanding that nothing should go forth from the meeting with any stamp of authority, that the church might not take offence, as if we had assumed to our selves any name or right in the church. But there was such a sanction given to these judgments, by the fulness, freeness, and harmony which prevailed in the midst of partial and minor differences of opinion; by the spirit of prayer, and love, and zeal for God's glory and the church's good; by the sweet temper and large charity which were spread abroad; and by the common consent, that God was in a very remarkable way present with us; that I deemed it my duty to make known these great results to the Christian churches, which I have thus so early an opportunity of addressing; seeing, moreover, it is the just cause of, and the only apology for my delay.

Having said so much, I think it to be my duty further to state the godly order and arrangement according to which the Albury conference, concerning the second advent, was conducted: for to this, under God, I attribute in no small degree the abundance of the blessings with which our souls were made glad. We set apart a day for each subject, and resolved to give no more than one day to each; and as we were but six free days assembled, having met on the Thursday and parted on the Friday of the week following, we joined the fourth and the seventh subjects together, conceiving them to be closely connected with one another. And having apportioned a separate subject to each day, we proceeded to each day's work after the following method. We divided the labour of each day into three parts; a morning diet before breakfast, the second and principal diet between breakfast and dinner, and the third in the evening. The object of our morning diet, to which we assembled at eight o'clock precisely, as early as we could well see, was two-fold; first, to seek the Lord, for the light, wisdom, patience, devotion to his glory, communion of saints, and every other gift and grace of the Holy Spirit, which were necessary and proper to the labour, which was that day appointed us in God's good providence: this office was always fulfilled by a minister of the gospel. Secondly, one of the number was appointed over-night, and sometimes several nights before, to open the subject of the day in an orderly and regular way, taking all his grounds of argument, and substantiating all his conclusions out of the Holy Scriptures: and while he thus proceeded, the rest of the brethren took down the substance of what he said, and noted down the texts from which he reasoned. For we sat in the library around a large table provided with every convenience for writing and for consulting the Holy Scriptures. When the outlines, and divisions, and whole ground-word of the subject were thus laid out by the brother, strengthened by our prayers, we parted without at that time declaring any thing, and refreshed ourselves with breakfast, where we met the pious and honourable lady and family of our worthy host. Two full hours were allowed from the breaking up of the morning till the assembling of the midday diet, which was at eleven of the clock, in order that the brethren might each one try and prove himself before the Lord, upon the great questions at issue, and that we might come together with convictions, not with uncertain persuasions, and speak from the conscience, not from present impressions. And when we assembled and had shortly sought the divine favour to continue with us, and office generally performed by our reverend Moderator, he proceeded in due order to ask each man present for his convictions upon the subject which had been laid before us in the morning. And the rest diligently used their pen in catching the spirit of what dropped from each other's lips. No appeal was allowed but to scriptures, of which the originals lay before us, in the interpretation of which, if any question arose, we had the most learned eastern scholar perhaps in the world to appeal to, and a native Hebrew, I mean Joseph Wolff. In this way did every man proceed to lay out the nature and the ground of his conviction, which was done with so much liberty and plentifulness, and mutual respect and reverence of the Holy word, as much to delight our souls. Now this diet lasted oft four, and sometimes almost five hours, our aim being to gather the opinions of every one before we parted; and when we tired we refreshed ourselves with prayer, which also we regarded as our main defence against Satan. This diet also we closed with an offering of thanksgiving by any of the clerical brethren whom the Moderator might pitch upon. After dinner we again proceeded, about seven o'clock to the work of winding up and concluding the whole subject; but in a more easy and familiar manner, as being seated around the fire of the great library-room, yet still looking to a Moderator, and with the same diligent attention to order, each seeming desirous to record every thing which was said. This went on by the propounding of any question or difficulty which has occurred during the day, addressed to him who had opened the subject, or to any other able to resolve it; and so we proceeded till towards eleven o'clock, when the whole duties of the day were concluded by the singing of a hymn, and the offering up of an evening prayer. Such were the six days we spend under the holy and hospitable roof of Albury house, within the chime of the church bell, and surrounded by the most picturesque and beautiful forms of nature; but the sweetest spot was the council room where I met the servants of the Lord, the wise virgins waiting with oil in their lamps for the bridegroom, and a sweeter still was that secret chamber where I met in the Spirit of my Lord and master whom I hope soon to meet in the flesh.

Oh Albury! most honoured of the King
And Potentate of heaven; whose presence here
We daily look for! In thy silent halls
His servants sought, and found such harmony
Of blessed expectation, as did fill
Their hearts with lively joy: as if they'd caught
The glory of the cloud which bore their Lord,
Or heard the silver-toned trump of jubilee
Sound his arrival through the vault of heaven.
From thy retreat, as from the lonely watch-tower,
We had certain tidings of the coming night,
And of the coming day. The one to brace
Our hearts with dauntless resolution,
All sufferings to endure in his behalf,
Who for our souls did bear the ascendant dire
Of Satan's hour and power of darkness.
The other to delight our hearts with thoughts
And dearest joys which are not known to those
Contemptuous and unfaithful servants,
Who think not of the promise long delayed
Of thy most glorious coming, gracious Lord!
For me, and for these brethren's sake I pray,
That the sweet ordour of those hollowed hours
May never from our souls depart, till thou
Our glorious King thy standard in the heavens
Unfurlest, and commandst the Archangel strong
To make the silver-toned trump of jubilee
Sound thine arrival through the vault of heaven,
And quicken life within the hollow tomb.

So singeth my soul full gladly in the watches of the morning, which I have prevented, to recall these sweetest recollections of my life. And now I must conclude my labour by entreating thee, courteous reader, to weigh well such an unanimous voice of various divines; and to consider well ere thou scornest unheard, or unexamined dost reject the sum and substance of the great doctrine of the second advent, which thou shalt find expressed in this great work of God's favoured servant. The doctrine maketh most winged speed, I perceive, among the babes who are simple-minded, and among the strong men who are content to be accounted fools for Christ. But how is it I hear no account of any movement of desire and expectation of the common husband amongst the virgins who belong to my own quarter of the city, my dear brethren or kinsmen in the Lord, the children of the daughter of my people!

I said, the truth of his Son's glorious advent maketh winged speed in all the churches, as was evinced in the harmony and unanimity which pervaded those many long and laborious sessions of the divines and lay-men who met together from various quarters at Albury Park, for the end of consulting the Scriptures, and laying open their several convictions upon this great subject. Of which assembly the least that I can say is this, that no council, from the first which convened at Jerusalem until this time, seemed more governed, and conducted, and inspired by a Spirit of holy communion. I said it maketh winged speed in all the churches; but alas! that church to which I won my reverence as to a mother, a bountiful though somewhat a stern mother to me, giveth little heed that I can hear of, to this great immediate overwhelming truth. Do thou bless, O Lord, this second attempt of her unworthy son to awaken some of her fathers, some of her doctors, some of her ministers, some of her elders, some of her members, yea all, yea all, Oh my God, if so it might be pleasing in thy sight and according to thy will. For, that our fathers did heretofore witness a good confession to this kingly office of thy Son, the stones which cover their bones do testify, in the moors and solitudes where they fell martyrs to the doctrine of thy sole supremacy in thy house. Which these eyes can attest; for with unwearied foot I have visited them almost every one, and with keen eye spelt their moss-grown monuments, and do now delight to remember those the haunts of my early youth, upon this lonely watch tower where the Lord hath stationed me in his wonderful providence; — mine appointed post, from which, but the grace of God, I shall make known unto the Church whatever I hear and see; — fearing not, Oh my Lord, these Pharisaical and Sadducean enemies, with whom I am surrounded, not caring that I have not that communion of the brethren for which my soul longeth. For am not I thy servant, and the son of thine

Appendix A 391

handmaid, whose bands thou hast united — And to whom then is my light of knowledge, my life of conscience, and my freedom of speech and action due, but unto thee, O my God and King! my Head, the Head of thy Church, the Head of the worshipping universe! unto whom, with the Father and blessed Spirit, be honour and glory for ever and ever. Amen.
EDWARD IRVING
Caledonian Church,
January 17th, 1827.[1]

Note:

1) The strong emphasis on "Christian Zionism" [*i.e.,* a renewed and glorified Jewish state] was supported by Wolff, a "Jewish missionary." He was the only outside source for understanding Scripture, so he obviously confirmed the renewed Jewish hope from the prophetic passages being studied. Zionism was a key idea in Irving's and Lacuenza's version of the second advent.

2) The first Albury Conference was in 1826, and Irving's *Ben-Ezra* did not go to the printers until 1827. No doubt he took what his heart was overflowing with: Lacuenza's view of the second advent. Those at Albury welcomed his ideas.

3) Leaving Albury, Irving faced once again the hostile Christian world; even his own church ignored what he was trying to teach about the second advent.

Darby's Letters

Now we will list a few of Darby's key letters by their dates.

New Prophetic Theories Introduced

This letter is the second letter in Darby's Collected Letters. The reader will notice that the new prophetic speculations discussed at the first Powerscourt meeting are now accepted as "Apostolic" doctrine. The letter is unsigned, but Kelly assumed it to be Darby's, or he would not have included it. It reads:

---

1. *Ben-Ezra,* I.clxxxviii-cxciv.

It may be of interest to insert here the following account of the second meeting, for the consideration of subjects connected with Prophecy, held at Powerscourt House, from September 24th to 28th, 1832, at which this letter was commenced, with a list of the subjects. A comparison with the brief notice in the letter itself, suggests that it was from Mr. Darby's pen. It was addressed to the Editor of the Christian Herald, in which there is a Review of the Rev. W. Burgh's Lectures on the Second Advent, by Mr. Darby. (See *Collected Writings,* vol. xxxiii. p. 1.) (The first Powerscourt meeting was held on October 4th to 7th, 1831.)

To the Editor of the Christian Herald.

DEAR SIR, - If done with the delicacy due to a private house, the importance of the subject, and its association with that which so intimately affects the church, may justify some notice of the meeting held on the subject of Prophecy, and the truths connected with it, at Powerscourt. I shall venture, therefore, to send you some account of it, praying the Lord's blessing upon it; as, for my part, I feel very strongly its importance.

It would be, of course, impossible to go at large into the several subjects which were handled there; I shall endeavour merely to convey to you some character of the meeting. There were a number of Clergy, and several of the Laity, whose minds had been exercised on these subjects; and the Rev. Robert Daly, Rector of Powerscourt, as on a former occasion, unless casually absent, presided. The subjects you will be enabled to state below, should you feel it an object to your readers. The solemnity which characterized the meeting was broken only in a single instance, which needs only to be mentioned for the sake of truth. There was, besides at the opening and closing of each morning and evening assembly, much prayer made elsewhere for the meeting, and this even in England; and the remarkable recognition of the Spirit, I mean practically, was very striking; and, it appears to the writer, met by a restraint on the thoughts and feelings of man, which, considering the variety of the subjects, was very remarkable — more so even than the elucidation of scripture which was afforded. It appeared to the writer that the progress in knowledge and exposition of scripture was decided, but the practical apprehension of the subjects treated, yet more so. There was, of course, variety of view in so large an assemblage, but scarce anything which did not positively add to the information of all — subject, of course, to the correction which interchange of views ever brings, where there is unity in the general scope. There was but one individual who introduced anything which could have given pain to any on these subjects; and that was a reference to the reception of "the gifts" and the principles connected with it. Little, however, was said upon it; and while the principles were calmly inquired into by a few, it did not, I think, affect the meeting, otherwise than to direct the earnest desires and prayers of many, for the more abundant presence of that Holy Ghost, by which alone, error can be brought to light, and the believer guided into all truth. On the whole, this part of the meeting was, perhaps, the most practically profitable, from the elucidation of the doctrine of the Holy Spirit casually drawn out by it; and the presiding presence of the Holy Spirit most marked, by a careful observer; and several defective and erroneous views prevalent (to the writer's knowledge) in England, met by what appeared to be scriptural light.

The belief in the coming of a personal Antichrist was common, and that amongst many who, at a former meeting, had not received it at all; in this there was a very distinct and avowed change of opinion on the part of some. The discussion of the subject of Antichrist led to an extensive development of scripture, and to much very profitable detection of the spirit by which he might work in the nations; though no definite conclusion was come to upon this; while the recognition of his acting amongst the Jews, in Jerusalem, was more definitely recognized by those more conversant with the subject.

On Daniel a good deal of light was thrown, and though there was some, I think not so much, perhaps, upon the Revelation; though particular parts of it were discussed with considerable accession of knowledge. There was some very interesting inquiry as to the quotation of the Old Testament in the New; particularly on the point, whether there was any "accommodation," or whether they were quoted according to the mind of the Spirit in the Old; this gave occasion to some very interesting development of scripture. The progress of the Antichristian powers was very fully discussed.

This will give you, after all, but a very imperfect idea of the meeting. Even as to the extent of scriptural information brought forward, while it left the additional impression of how much yet remained to be understood of blessing and of truth, and left upon the minds of many a highly increased degree of value for the privilege of the word of God, many, I am sure, were humbled, and many refreshed; while light was afforded also to many, on points which are exercising the christian world so universally at the present day.

That all was perfect there, Sir, I suppose none there would be disposed to think; but this certainly struck the writer, how remarkably, as he has stated, the Spirit restrained, while it left the strengthened consciousness of all the imperfection and weakness which exists among us; and I think those in the church, who are really in earnest, must most deeply feel, on the whole, that, spread as that assembly will be over the country, the meeting was one of deep interest to the church of God at large. In the discussion on so many subjects, and many relating so much to the practical position in which Christians are, it cannot be doubted that the views advanced by some may have given pain to a few; but the effect, on the whole, was to knit, in the deepest interests of the church of Christ, the affections of many believers, and to unite them in the surest tie with each other; while the sense of the difficulties in which the church is now placed, would lead them individually (under God) to more earnest seeking the guidance and presence of God's Spirit, and that blessing upon the church, and presence of God's power with it, by which alone it can be brought, in the honour of Christ, through the perilous times in which it is now placed.

I remain, dear Sir,

Yours faithfully, X

Subjects for Consideration at the Meeting above referred to.

Monday Evening, Six o'clock, September 24th, 1832. — An examination into the quotations given in the New Testament from the Old, with their connections and explanations, viz.: --Matt. i. 23, Is. vii. 14; Matt. ii. 15, Hos. xi. 1; Matt. ii. 18, Jer. xxxi. 15;Matt. xi. 10, 14, Mal. iii. 1, iv. 5; Matt. xxi. 16, Heb. ii. 6, Ps. viii. 2; Matt. xxiv. 15, Dan. ix. 27; Matt. xxvii. 9, Zech. xi. 12, 13; Eph. iv. 8, Ps. lxviii. 18; Heb. ii. 13, Is. viii. 18; Heb. viii. 8, Jer. xxxi. 31-34; Heb. x. 16, Jer. xxxi. 33; Luke i. 73, Gen. xxii. 16; John x. 34, Ps. lxxxii. 6- John xix. 37, Zech. xii. 10; Acts ii. 17, Is. xliv. 3, Joel ii. 25; Acts xv. 16, Amos ix. 11, 12; Rom. ix. 25, Hos. ii. 23, i. 10; Rom. x. 5, 6, Lev. xvii. 5, Deut. xxx. 13; 1 Cor. ix. 9, 1 Tim. v. 18, Deut. xxv. 4; 1 Cor. xv. 55, Hos. xiii. 14; Gal. iv. 27, Is. liv. 1; 2 Pet. iii. 13, Is. lxv. 17, lxvi. 22.

Tuesday. - The Prophetical character of each book in the Bible; including the three great feasts of the Jews, the blessings pronounced on Jacob's sons, the Parables in the Gospel, and the Epistles to the Seven Churches in Revelation.

Wednesday. - Should we expect a personal Antichrist? If so, to whom will he be revealed? Are there to be one or two great evil powers in the world at that time? Is there any uniform sense for the word *Saint* in the Prophetic, or New Testament scripture? By what covenant did the Jews, and shall the Jews, hold the land?

Thursday. - An inquiry into, and a connection between Daniel and the Apocalypse.

Friday. - What light does scripture throw on present events, and their moral character? What is next to be looked for and expected? Is there a prospect of a revival of Apostolic churches before the coming of Christ? What the duties [sic] arising out of present events? To what time, and to what class of persons do 1 Tim. iv.; 2 Tim. iii.; Jude; Matt. xxiv. 23, 24; and 2 Peter iii. refer?[2]

Riots

We mentioned previously an eye witness account of Darby's new theories throwing Lausanne into confusion. The following letter is an account of that confusion. Please observe a few things: First, Darby presented many new, unorthodox ideas in Lausanne that have since become accepted doctrine. Second, the pleading for religious liberty permits us to safely assume the problems (riots) were over the new, unorthodox theories being presented at the meetings. Third, the riots recorded here were not the first, *viz.,* "but this time the police...." Fourth, Darby determined to avoid any civil involvement. Fifth, Darby tried hard to identify with Paul's situations, *e.g.,* the tumult had to be broken up by civil authorities, Acts 21:34.

> Dear _____,
>
> You have this account already, but it is so short I send it, still all for private reading. I could have sent you other parts, but I extract for everybody — it is only private sentiments I have not, but which would be very interesting in private. After acknowledging the receipt of what was sent, and thanking the brethren, in substance saying he had all and abounded, &c.
>
> * [*From Lausanne, editors note] "The tribulation is not at its close; last Sunday we had a formidable riot on our meeting in your apartment. The meeting passed in perfect joy; it was very numerously attended, scarce any one was wanting. A furious crowd was before the house, but this time the police, who were on foot, hindered them from attacking us, and protected us going out. After that, the people would have taken possession of the house, but the conservatoirs [sic] restrained them, and the gendarmes, who returned, succeeded in dissipating the tumult at past twelve o'clock. Since then our sisters M. have been guarded by the Lord, and nothing has happened to them.

---

2. *Letters,* I.5-7.

"Already, Friday, the transport of the benches by J.O. caused a real riot, of which J. supported the brunt without accident. They seized some benches from him, which they broke. I do not know if I told you that one Sunday morning the band entered my house also, penetrating close to my rooms where we were, several persons, and the Lord stopped them there. The brethren and sisters are generally happy. We go this morning to your room: the Lord knows what will come of it; in every case we are in His hands.... the persecution seems to arrive at a crises. Thanks be to God, who has saved us through Jesus Christ our Lord. How sweet to think that our brethren, and above all, Jesus prays for us. Adieu."

"Since my last letter, the Lord has permitted that we should pass tranquilly through sufficiently evil days. Our Sunday meetings had become for parties, the perspective of an engagement. The conservateurs [sic] pressed us to meet all together, and in case of need they would shew themselves and restrain the populace. From the moment that we became the occasion that parties seized to come to an engagement which might become a revolution, it seemed to me that our assembly was no longer simply a testimony, but a political affair, which we ought to avoid: the brethren were of the same judgment. The government were [sic] very uneasy, and we received overtures from members of the Great Council, who offered to ask for us from the Council of State, the German church in Mercerie, with the proviso of having us protected there.... I represented that in going there, we departed from the path of testimony, which offended the people, but was agreeable to the Lord — that this would be made use of throughout the Canton, to make our brethren go into the churches, and that our place was not to be protected but persecuted: the brethren were of this mind.

"The next day the Council of State had us requested through B. (its president), not to have our meeting all together at 22 St. Pierre [the house I lived in, where the riot was], in order not to expose the town to troubles whose issue could not be foreseen. This seemed to us a very simple direction (*indice*), and we agreed to disseminate ourselves on Sunday in small meetings — we had eleven in the course of the day. All were very tranquil. The Great Council is to be occupied to-morrow with the petitions relative to religious liberty. This question occupied it already Tuesday. The government seeks, in order to flatter the passions of the populace, to adopt a measure which deprives us of liberty, saving appearances as much as possible. It has shewn itself so illiberal, that the most radical of the Great Council (the government is the extreme radical) have expressed their surprise at it. I do not expect to see religious liberty granted to the children of God in this country. It is very sweet to know that that will happen as to it which our own Lord shall see good for the exercise of our faith. Men are occupied about us without consulting God; and the Lord when He is pleased to act for His children, defeats the designs of men. His counsels will be found to be very firmness itself. We are happy to be in His hands, and to have for our path Himself — not a path which men may make; though they may become the means of our trial, they cannot decide what is to happen to us.

"It is not probable that we can meet next Sunday all together. The government would not be sorry to have an occasion which would justify the measure it desires. People's minds are in a great fermentation. The Conservatives desire to stop this torrent of passions and violence which threatens everything with subversion. In case of a serious tumult, our meetings would be the spark which would set fire to the powder. We desire to rest strangers to all political conflict, and for that reason we prefer to break ourselves up into small portions while things are in this state. If there had been no danger to run but that of seeing our meetings assailed and our persons illtreated, the brethren were all encouraged to persevere. The Lord has sustained and encouraged and fortified us. He has made us find in the trial great subjects of joy and thanksgiving. The testimony has had blessed fruit. Hesitating souls have been established, and thus have joined us. The brethren are happy, and we see that Christ is precious to us in proportion as men reject us. Adieu, very dear brother; the brethren and sisters salute you. Not being able to write you word to-morrow what the Great Council shall have done as to religious liberty, if in any case some result is arrived at, I shall only write next week if the Lord permit.

"The grace of the Lord be multiplied to you.
"Your very affectionate, "G."
Somerton, May 27, 1845.[3]

---

3. Though signed "G.", this letter is in *Letters,* I.81-84. Its date, 1845, corresponds to the date Darby's new theories "threw Lausanne into confusion." If it is not Darby's, it is the only one amidst the many hundreds that are his. Another questionable letter is the one *To the Editor of the Christian Herald, q.v.* We mentioned in the text Darby's account of the Baptists' hostility toward his new theories.

Voting

This letter clearly delineates the stand against any political involvement whatsoever, as well as against any involvement in social matters. It reads:

[From the French]:

VERY DEAR BROTHER,
 I write a line in haste, having at heart the course of the brethren with regard to these elections which are about to take place. I found that the brothers at V. had scarcely reflected at all on the bearing of an act which was making them take part in the course of the world. Thanks be to God, from the moment when that was presented to them they saw the thing, and, I hope, clearly. This has led me to think that perhaps the brothers near you may not have reflected upon it either. It seems to me so simple that the Christian, not being at all of this world, but united to Him who died and rose again, has no business to mix himself up with the most declared activity of the world, by an act which affirms his existence as belonging to the world, and his identification with the entire system which the Lord is about to judge; [the soon coming judgment of God upon the world was a constant theme with Darby, starting in the late 1820s, *ed.*] that I think the truth has only to be presented in order to be acknowledged by those who have understood their position; so much the more that these events* [*The Revolution.] place the world more manifestly (not more really) on its own ground, but more really near the great catastrophe which is about to fall upon those who rise up against God [*i.e.*, the Great Tribulation from which the faithful Christians, defined as those who are "simply waiting for the Lord's return with no worldly activity," will be spared, *ed.*]. Oh how my soul longs that His people should be separated to Him, [*i.e.*, totally unconcerned about anything around them, totally otherworldly, *ed.*] and even with understanding of what is awaiting the world, and still more of what they ought continually to await themselves! May God give the grace to be faithful [*i.e.*, God's power to wait and not "mix it up" with the world, *ed.*] in bearing this testimony, and everywhere, according to the door that He will open, in season and out of season; for His own, so dear to Him, need it.
 Events are hastening on, dear brother, and yet as to us we are waiting for but one, that our Beloved, our Saviour should come. His coming becomes a resource, as it has long been a joy to us, and reality still more precious, and more near. May we expect it

continually; God alone knows the moment. The Christian takes cognizance of the events which are taking place, as a testimony to the one who understands; but his thoughts, his desire, his portion, is much more within the sanctuary than all that. But is it not true that this voting, as an act of identification with the world (in the very forms which it assumes in the last days), ought to be avoided as a snare by all Christians who understood the will of God and their position in Christ? Always true (I have been acting upon it for twenty years) [and spreading his theories all over Europe, later bringing them to America, we must add, *ed.*], it is doubly true now. May peace, grace and mercy be with you, dear brother, and be multiplied to you, and may the presence and joy of the Lord be with all the brethren who surround you. Probably I shall set out immediately for England, but in the hope of returning. Salute affectionately all the brethren.

Yours very affectionate.

I think that at the end of Philippians iii., the way in which we wait for Jesus Christ as Saviour, is to deliver us finally from the whole course of this world, such as it is [*i.e.,* waiting for Christ means total unconcern about the course of this world as total strangers passing through town with no interest in what is taking place in the community, *ed.*].

Montpellier, March 24th, 1848.[4]

Waiting

The following is from a lecture delivered in London, 1852. The ideas contained herein are important enough to place it in this section of Darby's letters:

> [Christ] is not now breaking the nations in pieces, but is sending forth His blessed gospel to gather souls out of the world; and the Holy Ghost is sent down to join them to Himself, thus forming the Church. But when He asks for the nations [Ps 2:8, *ed.*], it will be to dash them to pieces like a potter's vessel...
>
> ...The world must be set right and He will execute judgment upon it, and when He comes to do it, the Church will be associated with Him in it; but now she is dwelling where Satan's seat is, with evil on every side, and cannot touch it by way of setting it right...
>
> But meanwhile what are we to do as regards setting the world right? Nothing, and this the flesh cannot understand. We are not to

---

4. *Ibid.,* I.129, 130.

meddle with the raging of the heathen, nor yet to concern ourselves with the alliances of nations (while still remembering that we have to submit to the powers that be, as ordained of God, and obey them), for yet to defile ourselves by touching the evils of Jezebel, but to wait on God. "Keep my works unto the end" and wait patiently; for when Christ shall have the upper hand, so shall we. Our interests are His and His ours; they are so enwrapped together that they cannot be sundered. The force of that expression in Colossians — "If ye be dead with Christ from the rudiments of the world, why as though living in the world are ye subject to ordinances —"is just this: he is hid in God and so am I (that is the reasoning); His life is ours.[5] "Ye are dead, and your life is hid with Christ in God." He so refers our state to His, that, if He is hid in God, we are hidden too. And if His appearing is spoken of, "when he shall appear, we shall appear with him in glory." Thus, being entirely one with Christ while He is waiting on the Father's throne, we are called to wait with Him in spirit down here.

...Wherefore in the address to Philadelphia, we are called upon to keep the word of His patience, and if He is waiting, it is no wonder that we have to wait also; and it is *himself* that is the very best part of what we wait for.

This is the proper and peculiar portion of the Church — association with Him; the other, that is the power over the nations, is merely the fruit and consequence of it. He must judge, but to you He is the "morning star." Judgment is His "strange work." He is slow to wrath, but He must execute judgment, because He cannot allow iniquity to go on for ever; for He is going to take possession of His own throne, and He cannot have a throne in connection with Satan and his evil, and therefore He must put the evil down, for He cannot allow it; so that anti-christian power in the world must be cast down, as He cannot set up His own throne and let that exist. As it is said in Psalm xciv. 20, "Shall the throne of iniquity have fellowship with thee?" It could not be. Therefore He must do His strange work: but His proper work, so to speak, is to shine in His

---

5. Observe what Darby's system taught here for Col. 2:20. The *rudiments of the world* refers not to the evil around us, as Darby taught that it did, but refers to the Jewish rites and rituals done away with in Christ. Geneva: "And he uses an argument taken of comparison. If by the death of Christ who established a new covenant with his blood, you are delivered from those external rites with which it pleased the Lord to prepare the world, as it were by certain rudiments, to that full knowledge of true religion, why would you be burdened with traditions, I know not what, as though you were citizens of this world, that is to say, as though you depended upon this life, and earthly things?"

own heavenly brightness — our proper place to be associated with Him there.

These [the ones of Mal 4:2, *ed.*] were a poor despised few who were but little known and less cared for; but they were "waiting" for redemption in Israel, sensible of the ruin and of the evil, because alive to God's glory and to the privilege of being His people. In them, feeble as they were, we find a much brighter mark of faith than we do in Elijah when he was calling down fire from heaven. They were not setting the temple right, but were speaking together of God's thoughts. Elijah was setting outward things to rights, but had not faith for inside things. In God's unfailing grace to the remnant he had no just confidence. Law was the measure of his apprehension; but the Annas and Simeons had the secret of God in their souls ("the secret of the Lord is with them that fear him, and he will shew them his covenant"), and were waiting for the consolation in Israel. But were they content with the state of things? No; but in separation from evil, they waited for the consolation of Israel, which could alone set the evil right. And just so it is in our day. The Christian cannot change Jezebel, nor can he be mixed up with the mere temple-worshipers, the so-called religious systems of the day. He walks, while leaving them to the judgment of the Lord, far from violent attacks upon them, in quiet separation from all evil, patiently waiting and watching during the long dark night of sorrow for the morning star of the day of glory. "to him that overcometh will I give the morning star;" and this morning star is Christ Himself. And He is in this way known to those, who, though in the night, yet are not of the night, being children of the day. The morning star is gone before the world sees the sun, before the sun rises, before the day appears. But before the sun rises there is the morning star for those who are watching in the night. The world will see the sun; but the morning star is gone, as far as the world is concerned, before the sun rises. So we shall be gone to be with the morning star before the day of Christ appears to the world; and when Christ shall appear, then shall we also appear with Him in glory...

The prophecies, indeed, are plain, their warning clear; they guard me from being mixed up with the spirit of the world, whose judgment is announced... And I want the morning star in my heart (the hope of Christ before the day, coming to receive the Church to Himself — for the morning star is given to them that overcome) to cheer my soul through the long and dreary night, which is yet darker now than it was then, but still far spent, as the darkness of the night always thickens till again the dawn of another day rise beyond on the other side of heaven and the morning star appear to fix the eye of the watchful and waiting soul, and cheer the heart with a sure and certain hope... Do not you, therefore, go on mixing yourself up with the world and heaping up riches. What will you do with them when Christ comes? Remember the Lord is at hand...

...But beside and before all this, we have our portion in Christ; we are not of this world, we are redeemed out of it, and belong to the Lord Jesus Christ, and shall join Him on high before He is manifested for the judgment of this world; and therefore the thunders of judgment cannot touch us, because we are seated with Him in heaven, from whence judgment will come....we know our association with Christ Himself, as within that place from which the judgment proceeds.

...Plenty of things here are around in the world, plenty of bustle and turmoil; but it does not disturb the blessed calm of my soul; because nothing can alter our indissoluble relationship with a coming Jesus, as nothing should divide us in hope.

To see the coming of the Lord Jesus for the Church changes the character of a thousand scriptures. Take the Psalms for instance — those which speak about judgments on the ungodly, such as "the righteous washing their feet in the blood of the wicked." We are not the persons who say this. It is the language of Jews, and of godly Jews too, who will be delivered through the rod of power smiting their enemies, when all the tribes of the earth will wail because of Him... But as for me, I am going straight up to Christ in heaven. My place is in Him, while He is hid in God, in the nearest and most intimate union. I belong to the bride, a member of His body, of His flesh, and of His bones. When we have hold of this blessed centre, Christ, and with Him, therefore, of God Himself, then every scripture falls into its proper place; and we get a spiritual understanding of the Holy Ghost of things in heaven and our connection with them, and things on earth and our separateness from them; and, above all, our hearts get into their proper place, for, being set on Jesus Himself, we are waiting for Him. When He shall appear, we shall be with Him in glory, but we shall ever be with the Lord.

May the Lord give us such an apprehension of redemption and of our position in Him as may so fix our heart on Himself that we may be daily walking down here like unto men that wait for their Lord, who has promised to come and take us to Himself, watching in the midst of a night of darkness, aware that it is the night, although we are not of the night, but watching and waiting for the day, having the morning star arisen in our hearts!...[6]

Observe these key points promoted by Darby. They are very much with us today:

First, God's laws are not now in effect during the dispensation of grace, for we do not see him breaking the nations in pieces. The obvious conclusion is that Darbyite Christians have no hope of nor interest in changing the U.S. back to its godly foundation.

Second, strongly implied is that Christians are required to give unlimited submission to civil authority.

Third, the Christian's only calling is just to wait for the Lord's return. They are forbidden to set evil right. Patience is, accordingly, defined as just waiting for the Lord to come and straighten out the evil around us. In fact, Christians are hidden from, dead to, and unconcerned about surrounding evil. *Overcometh,* hence, is defined as overcoming temptation to "set evil right."

Fourth, Christians are exempt from God's judgment against sin, for "judgment cannot touch us."

Fifth, Christians are not to pass judgment on evil around them. That is the Lord's "strange work." Do we not hear this thought today in, "Judge not that ye be not judged?"

Sixth, the study of prophecy keeps one from trying to set evil right. Experience teaches that Darby was right in this area: it does prevent people from becoming involved in Christianizing the nations.

Seventh, the morning star is defined as the hope of a rapture out of the evil around us.

Scriptures' Character Changed

Eighth, "To see the coming of the Lord Jesus for the Church changes the character of a thousand scriptures." Using Lacunza's soon "coming of the Lord Jesus" and Irving's pre-trib rapture of the saints, Darby was able to change the character of "a thousand scriptures" while claiming to believe God's word. He showed how

---

6. *Collected Writings,* Vol. II, 482-494.

his system worked by referring to Psalm 58:4, "the righteous washing their feet in the blood of the wicked."

The early fathers of the dispensational millennial faith did not see the Lord visibly and literally exalting the righteous over the wicked in their day: "Christ is not now breaking the nations in pieces." Nor did they admit any chance that Christ would (or could) subdue the wicked in the gospel dispensation. They refused to see passages such as Psalm 58:10 in any kind of spiritual sense.[7]

The early dispensational fathers taught it was not only hopeless for Protestants to try to Christianize the nations for Christ (as was the general Protestant temper of the early 1800s), but they also taught it was sin. Consequently, they were left with some difficult prophetic passages to deal with: passages that spoke of the Lord exalting his people over the wicked before the end of all things, the second advent and one general resurrection. The Jesuit's idea of "the soon coming of the Lord," with an added rapture idea, solved the exegetical problems of those prophetic passages. It also solved Rome's problem of faithful Christians desiring to make Protestant Christian nations of the world. At his coming, Lacunza, Irving and Darby held, the Lord will exalt the Jews to do what the ruined church failed to do: subdue the nations to Christ. (Never mind that these men taught it was sin for the church to even try to Christianize the world.) The exalted Jewish nation would then literally fulfill, with a literal sword, the prophetic passages that spoke of God exalting his faithful people over the wicked. As Darby said, "We [Christians of the gospel dispensation, *ed.*] are not the persons who say this. It is the language of Jews, and of godly Jews too, who will be delivered through the rod of power smiting their enemies, when all the tribes of the earth will wail because of Him..."

---

7. We have already shown how the system required Psalm 45, and many other similar passages, to be literally fulfilled by a *blood and guts* ruler with a literal sword. Such views of those prophetic passages militated against any faith that the heathens could be Christianized through the preaching of the gospel. Remember, the French Revolution, the Napoleonic Wars and America's War Between the States established the temper of the day.

Lacunza's and Irving's followers, dispensationalists, using their "soon coming" system can thus deny any hope of Christianizing the world while, at the same time, claiming to believe God's word. Consequently, when challenged over their hopeless, faithless gospel, dispensationalists can respond with, "What! Don't you believe the word of God?"

Motivations

The below reproduced letter written by Darby around 1855 gives an excellent overview of the inner-most beliefs motivating his ministry. The astute reader will recognize in modern Christian thought many ideas developed and described by Darby below. We made no comments in the text, not wanting to interrupt Darby's flow of thought, so please check the footnotes for further documentation and important points.

> DEAR SIR AND Brother In Christ,* [*To Prof. Tholuck.] — Since I saw you, I have been continually on the move, so that it has been difficult for me to prepare the account which you desired to receive. It seems to me that the best way will be for me simply to mention the various circumstances as they transpired, in as far as I was personally concerned, at the time when this work of God first commenced. You will easily understand that numbers of others have laboured in that field, and many with much more devotedness than I, and with a far more marked result as regards the blessing of souls. But my concern now is with the work of God, and not our labours; so that you may gather from the account what will suit your purpose.[8]
>
> I was a lawyer; but feeling that, if the Son of God gave Himself for me I owed myself entirely to Him, and that the so-called christian world was characterized by deep ingratitude towards Him, I longed for complete devotedness to the work of the Lord; my chief thought was to get round amongst the poor Catholics of Ireland.[9] I was induced to be ordained. I did not feel drawn to take up a regular post, but, being young in the faith and not yet knowing deliverance, I was governed by the feeling of duty towards Christ, rather than by the consciousness that He had done all and that I was redeemed and

---

8. This letter contains an excellent example of Darby's pride over his humility and hard work. Almost every letter contains a mention of both.

saved; consequently it was easy to follow the advice of those who were more advanced than myself in the christian world.

As soon as I was ordained, I went amongst the poor Irish mountaineers, in a wild and uncultivated district, where I remained two years and three months, working as best I could. I felt, however, that the style of work was not in agreement with what I read in the Bible concerning the church and Christianity; nor did it correspond with the effects of the action of the Spirit of God.[10] These considerations pressed upon me from a scriptural and practical point of view; while seeking assiduously to fulfil the duties of the ministry confided to me, working day and night amongst the people, who were almost as wild as the mountains they inhabited. An accident happened which laid me aside for a time; my horse was frightened and had thrown me against a door-post. During my solitude conflicting thoughts increased; but much exercise of soul had the effect of causing the scriptures to gain complete ascendancy over me. I had always owned them to be the word of God.[11]

When I came to understand that I was united to Christ in heaven, and that, consequently, my place before God was represented by His own, I was forced to the conclusion that it was no longer a question with God of this wretched "I" which had wearied me during six or seven years, in presence of the requirements of the law. It then became clear to me that the church of God, as He considers it, was composed only of those who were so united to Christ, whereas Christendom, as seen externally, was really the world, and could not be considered as "the church," save as regards the responsibility attaching to the position which it professed to occupy - a very important thing in its place. At the same time, I saw that the Christian, having his place in Christ in heaven, has nothing to wait

---

9. In other words, one who has a *secular* occupation, *e.g.,* lawyer, cannot be completely devoted to the work of the Lord. All the early Brethren shared the idea that only missionaries, preachers, &c., can be 'full time Christian workers.' Their false notion clings tenaciously to Christianity today. Remember, this is in the 1850s.

10. His feelings motivated him, *i.e.,* Darby **felt** this is the way it should be; **then** he sought Scriptural support for his feelings about a matter, and his newly developed "Bible readings" provided that support. Not being a Christian who believed the word of God had to be the basis of all faith and action, Darby was clearly a **mystic.** "I have my 'Revelation' ready" he writes in an 1839 letter, *Ibid.,* I.30. See Mysticism.

11. Darby's accident and resulting solitude were the grounds for his newly discovered ideas concerning Scripture. He had great trouble with headaches from his accident on.

for save the coming of the Saviour, in order to be set, in fact, in the glory which is already his portion "in Christ."[12]

The careful reading of the Acts afforded me a practical picture of the early church, which made me feel deeply the contrast with its actual present state, though still as ever, beloved by God. At that time I had to use crutches when moving about, so that I had no longer any opportunity for making known my convictions in public; moreover, as the state of my health did not allow me to attend worship, I was compelled to remain away.[13] It seemed to me that the good hand of God had thus come to my help, hiding my spiritual weakness under physical incapacity. In the meanwhile, there grew up in my heart the conviction that what Christianity had accomplished in the world in no way answered to the needs of a soul

---

12. There are several basic themes of Darby's letters, and they are listed in the order of mention in his letters: 1) how humble he is; 2) how hard he works; 3) the mystical union with Christ; 4) the hopeless state of the church, and 5) the nearness of Christ's return. He also emphasized the other world and his longing for it, for he considered this world a wilderness to be endured with unconcern about its events. On the surface, his union with Christ appears proper, but we should keep it within his context: union *with the risen Christ* literally placed one's citizenship in heaven, leaving him totally void of any earthly responsibility or concern, *e.g., ibid.,* II.196. We saw in Groves the prevailing thought that one should not even provide for his own children: Why should he if his citizenship is in heaven? Death with Christ to the Brethren meant death to surrounding social events and turmoil; one's only concern and responsibility was "heavenly." His primary concern in this earth was that others would reach his state of unconcern. Darby remained single, and taught that if one will take care of the Lord's work, the Lord will provide for one's children. Moreover, he implies that one cannot follow Christ and take care of his family at the same time. *Ibid.,* I. 268. This writer has heard preachers dogmatically say that if one will take care of the Lord's work, "soul-winning," Sunday School classes, &c., the Lord will take care of his family. This heresy has been common in the Baptist "mega-church" movement.

13. Many times over, he speaks of "the ruin of the church" and its powerless state in the present world. One of his major life-goals was to convince world-wide Christianity of the church's ruined state. He lamented the state of American Christianity when he first arrived in the early 1860s because American Christianity still had the hope of converting the world to Christ, and worked to that end. He rejoiced when pastors especially saw the foolishness of trying to bring about a Godly social order. He did not use the term, "change;" rather, he considered his view of the powerless, defeated church as the "truth." Thus he rejoiced when others saw the "truth," *e.g., ibid.,* II.209-212. His goal was the "conversion" of Christians to his way of thinking; this goal far overshadowed any desire to convert the lost to Christ, *e.g., ibid.,* I.34. We say this because he rejoiced far more over interest in his new system of theology than he did over interest in the gospel of salvation.

burdened with the sense of what God's holy governmental dealing was intended to effect. In my retreat, the 32nd chapter of Isaiah taught me clearly, on God's behalf, that there was still an economy to come, of His ordering; a state of things in no way established as yet.[14] The consciousness of my union with Christ had given me the present heavenly portion of the glory, whereas this chapter clearly sets forth the corresponding earthly part. I was not able to put these things in their respective places or arrange them in order, as I can now; but the truths themselves were then revealed of God, through the action of His Spirit, by reading His word.[15]

What was to be done? I saw in that word the coming of Christ to take the church to Himself in glory. I saw there the cross, the divine basis of salvation, which should impress its own character on the Christian and on the church in view of the Lord's coming; and also that meanwhile the Holy Spirit was given to be the source of the unity of the church, as well as the spring of its activity, and indeed of all christian energy.[16]

As regards the gospel, I had no difficulty as to its received dogmas. Three persons in one God, the divinity of Jesus, His work of atonement on the cross, His resurrection, His session at the right hand of God, were truths which, understood as orthodox doctrines, had long been a living reality to my soul. They were the known and felt conditions, the actualities, of my relationship with God. Not only were they truths, but I knew God personally in that way; I had no other God but Him who had thus revealed Himself, and Him I

---

14. "In my retreat..." Darby retreated from a world gone awry, for he had no answers for the surrounding social ills. The only answer he could formulate, which he found in his retreat, was that there is "still an economy to come." Thus he is relieved from Christian responsibility to take Godly action to claim society for Christ, even holding that it was sin to make any effort to claim society for godliness, *Writings,* II.159, 459, 464., &c. Reading his letters, one must be impressed at how impractical they are. He never offers any kind of practical, active solutions for difficulties he is questioned about. All his answers tell the distressed questioners to identify themselves by faith with the risen Christ. His hatred for established churches, "All the pastors of the so-called churches — I abhor the name now...," caused him to see the primary answer to social ills as convincing Christians to remove from those churches.

15. He speaks several times of his new revelation from God, *e.g., Letters,* I.30.

16. The idea of a separate coming of the Lord to remove the church, *i.e.,* "Rapture," is claimed by Darby to have originated in none but himself. This "coming of Christ" was seen and developed by Darby as the answer to his surrounding social ills: ESCAPE. However, he usurped it from Irving who probably "discovered" it in the Jesuit's document, *Ben-Ezra, q.v.*

had. He was the God of my life and of my worship, the God of my peace, the only true God.

The practical difference in my preaching, when once I began to preach again, was, as follows: When a parson, I had preached that sin had created a great gulf between us and God, and that Christ alone was able to bridge it over; now, I preached that He had already finished His work. The necessity of regeneration, which was always a part of my teaching, became connected more with Christ, the last Adam, and I understood better that it was a real life, entirely new, communicated by the power of the Holy Spirit; but, as I have said, more in connection with the person of Christ and the power of His resurrection, combining the power of a life victorious over death, with a new position for man before God.[17] This is what I understand by "deliverance." The blood of Jesus has removed every spot from the believer; every trace of sin, according to God's own purity.[18] In virtue of His blood-shedding, the only possible propitiation, we may now invite all men to come to God, a God of love, who, for this object, has given His own Son. The presence of the Holy Ghost, sent from heaven to abide in the believer as the "unction," the "seal," and the "earnest of our inheritance," as well as being in the church, the power which unites it in one body and distributes gifts to the members according to His will; these truths developed largely and assumed great importance in my eyes.[19] With this last truth was connected the question of ministry. From whence came this ministry? According to the Bible, it clearly came from God by the free and powerful action of the Holy Ghost.[20]

At the time I was occupied with these things, the person with whom I was in christian relation locally, as a minister was an excellent Christian, worthy of all respect, and one for whom I have always had a great affection. I do not know if he is still living, but since the time I speak of, he was appointed to be archdeacon. It was, however, the principles, and not the persons, which acted on my conscience; for I had already given up, out of love to the Saviour, all that the world could offer.[21] I said to myself: "If the Apostle Paul were to come here now, he would not, according to the established

---

17. "connected more with Christ," *i.e.*, spiritually connected with no earthly responsibility, *q.v.*

18. Nor can we deny this definition of "deliverance," but "deliverance" cannot mean "deliverance" from societal responsibility as it seemed to mean to Darby.

19. "Developed" as he recuperated from his accident.

20. In other words, apart from ordination even by sound, Scriptural churches. The Darbyites held that ordination was wrong, and considered a man faithless for seeking ordination, *ibid.*, I.75.

system, be even allowed to preach, not being legally ordained; but if a worker of Satan, who, by his doctrine, denied the Saviour, came here, he could freely preach, and my christian friend would be obliged to consider him as a fellow-labourer; whereas he would be unable to recognise the most powerful instrument of the Spirit of God, however much blessed in his work of leading multitudes of souls to the Lord, if he had not been ordained according to the system." All this, said I to myself, is false. This is not mere abuse, such as may be found everywhere; it is the principle of the system that is at fault. Ministry is of the Spirit. There are some, amongst the clergy, who are ministers by the Spirit, but the system is founded on an opposite principle; consequently it seemed impossible to remain in it any longer.

I saw in scripture that there were certain gifts which formed true ministry, in contrast to a clergy established upon another principle. Salvation, the church, and ministry, all were bound together; and all were connected with Christ, the Head of the church in heaven, with Christ who had accomplished a perfect salvation, as well as with the presence of the Spirit on earth, uniting the members to the Head, and to each other, so as to form "one body," and He acting in them according to His Will.[22]

In effect, the cross of Christ and His return should characterise the church and each one of the members.[23] What was to be done? Where was this unity, this "body"? Where was the power of the Spirit recognised? Where was the Lord really waited for? Nationalism was associated with the world; in its bosom some believers were merged in the very world from which Jesus had separated them;[24] they were, besides, separated from one another, whilst Jesus had united them. The Lord's supper, symbol of the unity of the body, had become a symbol of the union of this latter with the world, that is to say, exactly the contrary of what Christ had established. Dissent had, no doubt, had the effect of making the true children of God more manifest, but here they were united on

---

21. "Love to the Saviour" is thus equated by Darby to mean abandonment of all worldly cares and responsibilities.

22. Notice his emphasis upon a "mystical" unity in heaven, rather than the physical unity as described in Hebrews 10. Darby did not deny the necessity of the physical assembly, but to him "Only the informal gatherings of Christians in Brethren fashion was compatible with the heavenly nature of the Church." Neatby, *History*, 208.

23. "Nothing to do but wait" for Christ's return, said Darby, and Christian social activity and involvement is thus labeled sinful.

24. Uses "Jesus" to justify his *other-worldliness*

principles quite different from the unity of the body of Christ. If I joined myself to these, I separated myself from others everywhere. The disunion of the body of Christ was everywhere apparent rather than its unity. What was I to do? Such was the question which presented itself to me, without any other idea than that of satisfying my conscience, according to the light of the word of God. A word in Matthew xviii. [sic] furnished the solution of my trouble: "Where two or three are gathered together in my name, there am I in the midst of them." This was just what I wanted: the presence of Jesus was assured at such worship; it is there He has recorded His name, as He had done of old in the temple at Jerusalem for those who were called to resort there.

Four persons who were pretty much in the same state of soul as myself, came together to my lodging; we spoke together about these things, and I proposed to them to break bread the following Sunday, which we did. Others then joined us.[25] I left Dublin soon after, but the work immediately began at Limerick, a town in Ireland, and then in other places.

Two years later (1830), I went to Cambridge and Oxford. In this latter place, some persons who are still engaged in the work, shared my convictions, and felt that the relation of the church to Christ ought to be that of a faithful spouse.

By invitation I went to Plymouth to preach. My habit was to preach wherever people wished, whether in buildings or in private houses. More than once, even with ministers of the national church, we have broken bread on Monday evening after meetings for christian edification, where each was free to read, to speak, to pray, or to give out a hymn. Some months afterwards we began to do so

---

25. Darbyism's primary growth was by converting dissenters to Darby's way of thinking, not from converting sinners to Christ, *e.g., Letters,* I.44, 205, II.9, &c., &c. Though he did not start the "Brethren" movement, he took the credit, *ibid.,* 515. He simply appeared at the right place in history to direct the dissenters to his way of thinking. "I was myself the beginning of what the world calls Plymouth brethren, though we began in Dublin. The name Plymouth arose from the earliest publications which attracted attention issuing thence, and was so far harmless, as no human name was attached to them; one cannot help the world giving some..." *Ibid.,* II.208. "We [Darby, *ed.*] began to meet in Dublin, Ireland, 1827-28... God was doing a work I had no idea of myself, and it spread over the world. It did not begin at Plymouth till 1832, where I went at Mr. Newton's request, then a fellow of Exeter College, Oxford..." *Ibid.,* I.515. Even Darby expressed amazement over the swiftness of the spread of his theories, *ibid.,* 54. Darby later viciously and relentlessly attacked Newton when Newton disagreed with Darby, calling Newton a tool of the devil to all who would listen.

on Sunday morning, making use of the same liberty, only adding the Lord's supper, which we had, and still have, the practice of taking every Sunday. Occasionally it has been partaken of more often. About that time also some began to do the same in London. The unity of the church, as the body of Christ, the coming of the Lord, the presence of the Holy Ghost here below, in the individual and in the church; an assiduous proclamation of the truth,[26] as well as the preaching of the gospel on the ground of pure grace and that of an accomplished work, giving in consequence the assurance of salvation when received into the heart by the Spirit; practical separation from the world;[27] devotedness to Christ, as to Him who has redeemed the church; a walk having Him only as the motive and rule; and other subjects in connection with these—all this has been treated of in separate publications as well as by means of periodicals and these truths have been largely spread abroad.

A good many ministers of the national church left nationalism in order to walk according to these principles, and England became gradually covered with meetings, more or less numerous.[28]

Plymouth being the place where most of the publications originated, the name "Plymouth brethren" became the usual appellation given to such meetings

In 1837 I visited Switzerland, and these truths began to be known there. I returned there more than once. The second time, Darbyism: I remained a considerable time at Lausanne, where God worked in conversions, and gathered a number of the children of God out of the world.[29] There were already, in Switzerland Dissenters who had suffered faithfully for the Lord during twenty years previously. But their activity had declined considerably, and it even seemed that the movement was about to disappear. The work of the brethren has, to a certain extent, by the goodness of God, filled the country, conversions having been numerous.[30] In German Switzerland, the work spread to a much less degree. On two occasions of my

---

26. Please remember that when Darby speaks of the "truth," he refers to his "truth," *e.g.,* ruin of the church and escape by a "rapture."

27. "Separation" is used in the sense that the Christian must not have any involvement in the practical things of this world.

28. As mentioned elsewhere, one of the things that Darby joyously mentions most often is pastors accepting his, in Ironside's words, "distinctive school of Christian thought."

29. Observe he is rejoicing over the conversion of Christians to his new line of "Christian thought."

30. Evidently, the conversion of sinners is not overlooked, but the emphasis of his letters is on the conversion of Christians to his way of thinking.

spending a protracted time in Lausanne, some young brothers who desired to devote themselves to gospel work spent nearly a year with me in order to read the Bible. We also partook of the Lord's supper together every day.

At the same time, quite independently of what was going on in Switzerland, a brother who was labouring in France had awakened an interest in a considerable district where the people were, in general, plunged in infidelity and darkness. Some also of the young brothers of whom I have spoken, and two or three others whose acquaintance I made, but who never stayed with me, went to work in France. Other labourers, belonging to societies, believing that they would be happier working under the Lord's immediate direction, and not as subject to committees, gave up their salaries, considering such arrangements to be unknown, both in fact and in principle, to the scriptures, since their very existence attributed to the possession of money the right to direct the work of the Lord: these began to work in simple dependence upon the Lord, trusting to His faithful care. God raised up others also, though it still remains true that "the harvest is great and the labourers are few." God has blessed these labourers by conversions, numerous, thank God, especially in the south of France. From the beginning I have visited these countries and shared with joy the troubles and fatigues of these brothers; but it is they who have actually laboured at the work. In some places, I had the first troubles; in others I have only visited, taken part and helped, when the work was, thank God, already begun. He gave us to be of one heart and one soul, mutually to be helpers of one another, seeking the good of all, whilst recognising our individual weakness.

Almost about the same time, in the eastern part of France, a like work had begun, independently of this one. It has also been visited, so that at the present time the work extends from Bale to the Pyrenees, with a fairly large gap in the districts of which Toulouse forms the centre. The country is more or less covered with meetings, and the work, by God's grace, is still going on.

I ought to say that I have never meddled in any way with the calling nor with the work of the brethren who studied the Bible with me. As regards some, I have the conviction that they had not been called to it, and they have, in fact, gone back into the ordinary routine of life. As to others, I only helped them in the study of the Bible, in communicating to them the light which God had given me, but leaving entirely to themselves the responsibility of their calling for the work of evangelisation or teaching.

We had the custom of gathering together occasionally for some time, when God opened the way for it, to study scriptural subjects together, or books of the Bible, and to communicate to one another what God had given to each. During several years, in Ireland and England, this took place annually in large conferences which lasted for a week. On the Continent, and latterly in England, they have been less attended; and consequently, with fewer numbers, it has been possible to spend a fortnight or three weeks studying some books of the Bible.

My elder brother, who is a Christian, spent two years at Dusseldorf. He is engaged in the work of the Lord, wherever he may happen to be at the moment. He has been blessed to several souls in the neighbourhood of Dusseldorf. These, in their turn, have spread the light of the gospel and the truth, and a certain number of persons have been gathered in the Rhenish provinces. Tracts and various publications of the brethren have been translated and largely distributed; and light as to the soul's deliverance, the true character of the church the presence of the Holy Ghost here below, and the Lord's return, has been disseminated.

Two years later, helped, I believe, by the knowledge of these truths, but entirely independent of this work, a movement of the Spirit of God began at Elberfeld. There was in that town a "Brotherhood" which employed twelve labourers, if I am not mistaken, whom the clergy sought to forbid from preaching or teaching. Enlightened as to the ministry of the Spirit, and moved by love for souls, they would not submit to this interdict. Seven of these labourers, I believe, and a few members of the "Brotherhood" detached themselves from it, and certain of them, with others whom God raised up, continued their gospel work, which spread from Holland to Hesse. Conversions have been very numerous, and many hundreds assemble at the present time to break bread. More recently the work has begun to get established in Holland, as also in the south of Germany. By means of other instruments, two meetings in Wurtemberg already existed.

Gospel preaching in Switzerland and England has led to the formation of some meetings amongst emigrants to the United States and Canada; the evangelisation of negroes led to others in Jamaica and Demerara, as also amongst the natives of Brazil, through a brother who went there and has since died. I am not aware of any other who knows the language sufficiently to continue this work, which has been blessed. The English colonies of Australia have also meetings; but this sketch will be sufficient for you.

Brethren do not recognise any other body but the body of Christ, that is to say, the whole church of the firstborn. Also they recognise every Christian who walks in truth and holiness, as a proved member of Christ. Their hope of final salvation is founded on the Saviour's expiatory work, for whose return they look, according to His word. They believe the saints to be united to Him already, as the body of which He is the Head, and they await the accomplishment of His promise, expecting His coming to take them to Himself in the Father's house, so that where He is, there they may be also. Meanwhile, they have to bear His cross and to suffer with Him, separated from the world which has rejected Him. His person is the object of their faith, His life the example which they have to follow in their conduct. His word, namely, the scriptures inspired of God, that is to say the Bible, is the authority which forms their faith; it is also its foundation, and they recognise it as that which should govern their conduct. The Holy Ghost alone can make it effectual both for life and practice.
185 —.[31]

The reader should note, "Isaiah taught me clearly, on God's behalf, that there was still an economy to come" Thus he took the ground of the great apostle Paul, claiming direct and distinct revelation from God because God himself taught him.

By Darby's own words above, we see that he was one of the most destructive men to Christianity to ever live.

Brethrenism Summarized

The next letter effectively sums up the Brethren's stand, as well as the world wide spread of its new doctrines. Darby takes the credit for laying the foundation for Brethrenism and for formulating what he presents herein. He also tells how he came to many of his conclusions. The reader will understand from the text of *Death of the Church Victorious* that Darby made many claims in his letter that simply were not true. The honest reader, however, must admit that he took little known, even unknown, doctrines, and converted the Christian world to his way of thinking. He turned Christianity upside

---

31. *Ibid.,* III.297-305.

down, into little more than a mystical experience while one simply waits for the Lord's return:

> We have been converted 'to wait for his Son from heaven.' (1 Thess. i. 9, 10)³² ... But it [baptism, ed.] is not what the Lord is occupying souls with, but separating His saints from the evil that is around them in a vast professing mass and to wait for His Son from heaven."³³

And thus the Christian is released from any responsibility to stand against evil and institute righteousness into society:

> [*From the French. To one of the Editors of the *"Francais,"* a Catholic newspaper. In a letter J.N.D. says, "I have given him in all simplicity what he asked for. He avowed himself a Catholic and devoted to Catholicism. His letter was simple and honest: I replied to him as a Christian."]
>
> Dear Sir,*
>
> My reply to the letter which you were good enough to address to me has been delayed by unceasing work which has left me no leisure. I have no difficulty as to informing you what my belief is, but a public newspaper is scarcely the place where I should wish to use my pen. I believe that the christian calling is a heavenly one, that the Christian is not of the world as his Master is not of it, and that he is placed down here as an epistle of Christ to manifest the life of Jesus amongst men, whilst waiting for the Lord to come to take him to be with Himself in the glory.
>
> As Editor of the *"Francais"* you will quite understand that articles written in order to inculcate such principles as these would little suit a political newspaper. Now I live only for these things — a life feebly realized I am quite ready to confess — but I live only for them. However, I will communicate to you what appears to interest you, namely, what has led me, and others with me, to take up the position in which we find ourselves as Christians.
>
> It is well perhaps, in view of the infidelity which is spreading everywhere, to begin by saying that I hold, and I can add that we firmly hold, all the foundations of the christian faith — that divinity of the Father, of the Son, and of the Holy Ghost, one God, eternally blessed — the divinity and humanity of the Lord Jesus, two natures in one person — His resurrection and His glorification at the right hand of God — the presence of the Holy Ghost here below, having

---

32. *Ibid.,* II.434.
33. *Ibid.,* 446.

descended on the day of Pentecost — the return of the Lord Jesus according to His promise. We believe also that the Father in His love has sent the Son to accomplish the work of redemption and grace towards men — that the Son came, in that same love, to accomplish it, and that He has finished the work which the Father gave Him to do on earth. We believe that He has made propitiation for our sins, and that after having accomplished it, He ascended to heaven — the High Priest seated at the right hand of the Majesty on high.

Other truths are connected with these, such as the miraculous birth of the Saviour, who was absolutely without sin — and yet others; but, you will readily understand, sir, that my object is not to give a course of lectures or a theological summary, but to make it quite clear that it is in nowise on the giving up of the great foundations of the christian faith that our position is based. Any one who would deny one or other of these fundamental truths would not be received amongst us, and any one who, being amongst us, adopt some doctrine which would undermine one or other of these same truths would be excluded, but only after all proper means to bring him back to the truth had been exhausted. For although these are dogmas, we hold them as essential to living faith and to salvation, to the spiritual and christian life of which we live as born of God.

But you wish, sir, to know not only the great truths which we hold in common with others, but also what distinguishes us from others.

Now, without in the least professing to give a course of christian doctrine in connection with the truths I have just pointed out, I am anxious, indeed I would heartily desire, to set them forth as the foundation, recognizing as true Christians and members of the body of Christ all those who, by the grace of God, and by the operation of the Holy Ghost who has been given to them, truly believing these things in their souls. Converted by the grace of God, I spent six or seven years under the rod of the law, feeling that Christ was the only Saviour, but not being able to say that I possessed Him, or that *I* was saved by Him; fasting, praying, giving alms — always good things when done spiritually — but not possessing peace, whilst at the same time feeling that if the Son of God had Himself forgiven me, I owe myself to Him — my body, soul, and means. At length God gave me to understand that I was in Christ, united to Him by the Holy Ghost — "At that day ye shall know that I am in my Father, and ye in me, and I in you" (John xiv. 20), which means that when the Holy Ghost, the Comforter, should have come, the disciples would *know* these things. With this were connected other blessed and reassuring truths — "There is therefore now no condemnation to them which are in Christ Jesus" (Rom. viii. 1.)

The promise of the Spirit is given to all those who have part in the remission of their sins, for "he that is joined unto the Lord is one spirit." (1 Cor. vi. 17.) Hence Christians are temples of the Holy Ghost — "Your body is the temple of the Holy Ghost who is in you." (1 Cor. vi. 19.)

I should say that at this time the word of God became for me an *absolute authority* as to faith and practice; not that I had doubted it previously, but it had now become such from conviction, implanted by God Himself in my heart. In this way the assurance of salvation through the work of Christ, the presence of the Holy Ghost dwelling in us, by whom "having believed, ye have been sealed for the day of redemption" (Eph. i. 13,14), salvation known and possessed, and this indwelling of the Holy Ghost giving us the assurance of it, constitute the normal state of the Christian. He is no longer of this world, save to pass through it peacefully, doing the will of God. Bought with a great price, he is to glorify God in his conduct.

This brings in the thought of the church and of its unity. For me the body of Christ was now composed of those who were united by the Holy Ghost to the Head — Christ in heaven. If we were seated in the heavenly places *in* Christ ("Even when we were dead in sin...hath he quickened us together with Christ — by grace ye are saved," (Eph. ii. 1, 5) what were we still waiting for? For Christ to come and place us up there in fact. "I will come again" said the Lord, "and receive you unto myself; that where I am ye may be also." (John xiv. 3.) "our citizenship is in heaven; from whence also we look for the Lord Jesus Christ as Saviour, who shall transform our body of humiliation into conformity to his body of glory." (Phil. iii. 20, 21.) We have been converted "to wait for his son from heaven." (1 Thess. i. 9, 10.)

Hence the presence of the Holy Ghost dwelling in him, and the attitude of waiting for the Lord constitute the normal state of the Christian. But all who possess this spirit are, by the very fact, one body. "For by one spirit we are all baptised into one body." (1 Cor. xii. 13.) Now, this baptism took place on the day of Pentecost. "Ye shall be baptised with the Holy Ghost not many days hence." (Acts i. 5.)

All those around me had not reached that point, at any rate they did not profess to have, and it was easy, reading Acts ii. and iv., to see how far we had got from what God had set up on the earth. Where was I to look for the church? I gave up Anglicanism as not being it. Rome, at the beginning of conversion, had not failed to attract me. But the tenth chapter of the Epistle to the Hebrews had made that impossible for me: "For by one offering he hath perfected for ever them that are sanctified... Now where remission of these is, there is no more offering for sin." (Heb. x. 14, 18.)

Then again it rendered impossible the idea of a sacrificing priesthood down here between me and God; seeing that our position, as the result of the work of Christ, is that we have direct access to God in all confidence. "Having therefore, brethren, boldness to enter into the holiest by the blood of Jesus." (Heb. x. 19.)

I am stating facts, sir; I am not entering into controversy: but faith in an accomplished salvation, and, later on the consciousness that I possess it, hindered me from turning in that direction; whilst having grasped the fact of the unity of the body of Christ, the various dissenting sects no longer attracted me. As to the unity to which, as we all know, Rome pretends, I found everything in ruins. The most ancient churches did not want to have anything to say to her, nor did protestants either, so that the great majority of those who profess Christianity are outside her pale. On the other hand, it was not a question of seeking this unity amongst the Protestant sects. Besides, whatever their ecclesiastical position might be, most of those who call themselves Christians are of the world, just as much as a pagan might be.

Now the 12th chapter of the first Epistle to the Corinthians shews clearly that there is a church formed on the earth by the descent of the Holy Ghost. "For by one Spirit we are baptisted into one body"; and it is evident that this is on the earth, for "Ye are the body of Christ, and members in particular." (1 Cor. xii. 27.) Besides, the apostle speaks of gifts of healing and of tongues, which only apply to the state of the assembly down here.

The assembly of God, then, has been formed on the earth, and ought always to have been manifested. Alas! it has not been so. In the first place, with regard to individuals, the Lord has pointed this out beforehand. "The wolf catcheth them and scattereth the sheep, "but, thank God, "No one shall catch them out of my hand," said the same faithful shepherd. (John x. 12, 28.)

But this is not all: Apostle Paul, bidding farewell to the faithful of Asia, said, "I know this, that after my departing shall grievous wolves enter in among you, not sparing the flock, and of your own selves shall men arise, speaking perverse things, to draw away disciples after them." (Acts xx. 29, 30.) Jude declares that already in his time, deceitful men had crept in among the Christians, and, which is of all importance, they are marked out as being the object of the judgment of the Lord when He comes again. "Certain men crept in unawares, who were before of old ordained to this condemnation, ungodly men." "The Lord cometh with ten thousand of his saints, to execute judgment upon all." (Jude 4, 15.)

These men were corrupters within the church, but there will be those who will entirely abandon the christian faith. "Little children," says the Apostle John, "it is the last time: and say ye have heard that antichrists shall come, even now are there many antichrists: whereby we know that it is the last time. They went out from us," etc. (1 John ii.18,19.)

But even this is not all. The Apostle Paul tells us, "Nevertheless the foundation of God standeth sure, having this seal, The Lord knoweth them that are his. And, Let every one that nameth the name of the Lord depart from iniquity. But in a great house there are not only vessels of gold and of silver, but also of wood and of earth; and some to honour, and some to dishonour. If a man therefore purge himself from these, he shall be a vessel to honour, sanctified, and meet for the master's use, and prepared unto every good work." (2 Tim. ii. 19-21.) Here is the church: it is a great house with vessels of all kinds and a call comes to the faithful man to purify himself from the vessels to dishonour. The following chapter is still more definite. "This know also, that in the last days perilous times shall come. For men shall be lovers of their own selves, covetous, boasters, proud," etc. (2 Tim. iii. 1-5.) These are almost exactly the same terms as he uses when he charges the heathen with sin (Rom. i. 29-31), but he adds here, "Having a form of godliness, but denying the power thereof." (2Tim. iii. 5.)

He warns us that "All that will live godly in Christ Jesus shall suffer persecution. But evil men and seducers shall wax worse and worse" (2 Tim. iii. 12, 13); but he gives us as a safeguard the knowledge of the person from whom we have learnt those things which we believe — it is the apostle himself; with the scriptures, which can make us wise to salvation by the faith which is in Christ Jesus. He assures us that "All scripture is given by inspiration of God, and is profitable for doctrine, for reproof," etc.

Thus we have the proof that evil, having entered into the church, would continue and would not be healed. "The mystery of iniquity," says the apostle, "doth already work: only he who now hinders will hinder until he be taken out of the way. And then shall that Wicked be revealed, whom the Lord Jesus shall consume with the breath of his mouth, and shall destroy by the brightness of his coming." (2 Thess. ii. 7, 8.) The evil which was already working in the time of the apostle was, then, to continue until the wicked one himself should be revealed. The Lord will destroy him then by His coming; and although it be not spoken of the church properly so called, the same thing is revealed to us in regard to Christendom, for we learn that tares have been sown in the place where the Lord had sown good grain. When the servants desire to pull up the tares, the Lord forbids them, saying, "Let both grow together until the harvest." (Matt. xiii. 24-30.) The evil done to the kingdom of God was to remain in the field of this world until the judgment. Christ will doubtless gather the good grain into His garner, but the crop is spoiled down here. You will tell me, But [sic] the gates of hell are not to prevail against that which Christ has built. Granted, and I bless God for it with all my heart, but we must distinguish here as the word of God does. There is on the one hand the work of Christ, and on the other what is done by men and under their responsibility. The enemy will never destroy what Christ built (we speak of the church of God), nor will he prevail against the work of the Lord. Whatever be the evil that has come in — for that there are heresies and schisms we do not deny — that which Christ works has endured and will endure for ever. It is the house which we find in 1 Peter ii., the living stones coming to Christ as to the living stone, and built to be a spiritual house. I find this house also in Ephesians ii. — "Ye are fellow-citizens with the saints, and of the household of God; and are built upon the foundations of the apostles and prophets, Jesus Christ himself Being the chief corner-stone; in whom all the building fitly frame together growth unto a holy temple in the Lord." (Eph. ii. 19-21.) Here it is again the work of the Lord Himself; living stones who come, a building composed of saints, growing to be a temple which is not yet completely built.

But, in scripture, the house of God on earth is viewed in another way also. "As a wise master-builder," says the Apostle Paul, "I have laid the foundation, and another buildeth thereon... If any man build upon this foundation gold...wood, hay, stubble; every man's work shall be made manifest: for the day shall declare it, because it shall be revealed be fire: and the fire shall try every man's work, of what sort it is. "Know ye not," he adds, "that ye are the temple of God, and that the Spirit of God dwelleth in you? If any man defile the temple of God, him shall God destroy; for the temple of God is holy, which temple ye are." (1 Cor. iii. 13, 16, 17.)

Here then I find the responsibility of man and the judgment of his work; the whole is called the temple of God, and the judgment of God commences there, at His house, says the Apostle Peter. Already, during the lifetime of the apostle, the time had come for that (1Pet. iv. 17), although the patience of God, acting in grace, still waited.

I recognise, therefore, the responsibility of the house of God, of the whole of Christendom. That which Christ Himself builds is one thing, and the fruit of His labours will not be lost; that which responsible man builds is another thing. At the beginning "the Lord added to the church daily such as should be saved." (Acts ii. 47.) Soon "false brethren" crept in, tares were sown, and the house was filled with all kinds of vessels, from which faithfulness was to purge itself; and with a form of godliness without power, from which the faithful one was to turn away.

This is what the word of God presents to us historically and prophetically in the New Testament: this word, addressed by the teachers to the faithful, is our resource when these perilous times should come; and, if that were necessary, the facts have borne out all that it says.

What is to be done? The word declares to us that where two or three are gathered to the name of Jesus, He will be in their midst. (Matt. xviii. 20) This is what we have done. There were only four of us to do it at the first; not, I hope, in a spirit of pride or presumption, but deeply grieved at seeing the state of that which surrounded us, praying for all Christians, and recognising all those who possessed the Spirit of God, every true Christian wherever he might be found ecclesiastically, as members of the body of Christ. We were not thinking of anything else, dear sir, than of satisfying the need of our souls according to the word of God, and we had no thought that the thing would have gone any further. We have thus found the promised presence of the Lord. Salvation through Christ has been preached, when there was gift to do so. The same needs caused others to follow the same road, and thus the work has extended in a way of which we had not the remotest idea.It commenced in Dublin, to spread in the British Isles, in France, where a great number of persons, open unbelievers, were converted: in Switzerland, where the work on the Continent had commenced, in Germany, in Holland, in Denmark, where it is commencing, in Sweden, where a great religious movement is going on at this moment. The path we follow has spread to a considerable extent in the British Colonies, and more recently in the United States, in Asia, in Africa, and elsewhere. The Spirit of God acts and produces needs of soul to which the religious systems offer no answer.

In a word, this is definitely the position of those brethren who rest on the authority of the word of God. Christ is seen, in the word, as the Saviour, in three different positions: — first, as accomplishing redemption on the cross; then, as seated at the Father's right hand, the Holy Ghost being thereupon sent down here; finally as coming

Appendix A

back to take His own to be with Himself. These Christians believe, these things have the assurance of their salvation, having faith in the efficacy of this redemption; and finally, being sealed with the Holy Spirit, who dwells in every true Christian, they wait for the Son of God from heaven without knowing the moment of His coming. "For ye have not received the spirit of bondage again to fear; but ye have received the Spirit of adoption, whereby we cry, Abba, Father!" (Rom. viii. 15.) We believe in the promise "I will come again, and receive you unto myself; that where I am, there ye may be also." (John xiv. 3.) Absolute faith in the efficacy of redemption; the seal of the Spirit which gives the assurance of salvation and the consciousness of being children of God; the attitude of waiting for the Lord — this is what characterises these Christians. Bought with a great price, they are bound to regard themselves as no longer belonging to themselves, but to the Lord Jesus, to please Him in everything and to live only for Him.

I do not mean to say, sir, that we all walk at the full height of the heavenly calling, but we acknowledge the obligation to do so. If any one fails openly in what becomes a Christian, in point of morality or in what concerns the faith, he is excluded. We abstain from the pleasures and amusements of the world. If we have evening parties, it is for the purpose of studying the word and of edifying ourselves together. We do not vote. We submit to the established authorities, whatever they may be, in so far as they command nothing expressly contrary to the will of Christ. We take the Lord's supper every Sunday, and those who have gift for it preach the gospel of salvation to sinners or teach believers. Every one is bound to seek the salvation or good of his neighbour according to the capacity which God has given him. Feeling that Christendom is corrupt, we are outside the church-world, by whatever name it is called. As to the number of those who follow this course I cannot tell you what it is: we do not number ourselves, wishing to remain in the littleness which becomes Christians. Besides, we reckon as a brother in Christ every person who has the Spirit of Christ.

I do not know that I have anything else to put before you. I am almost ashamed, sir, to have given such a long explanation of the principles which govern the walk of the Christians in question. We recognise that the church is one, the body of Christ: then, too, the house of God by the Spirit.

You ask me what is the advantage of this course. Obedience to the word of God suffices to decide us. To obey Christ is the first requirement of the soul which knows itself saved by Him, and even of every soul acknowledging Him as the Son of God who has loved us so much and has given Himself for us. But in fact, in obeying Him, in spite of weakness, faults and failures — which, on my part, I own — His presence manifests itself to the soul as an ineffable source of joy, as the earnest of a bliss where failures, blessed be His name for it, will no longer be found, and where He will be fully glorified in all believers.

You will tell me that these pages scarcely suit a newspaper. I admit it, but it is because the current of my thoughts scarcely flows in that line. I have explained to you in all simplicity what you asked me, and as well as I could. Having had to take up my work more than once owing to unavoidable interruptions, I much fear that it may contain some repetitions. Please excuse them and accept the assurance of my esteem.

1878[34]

Growth according to Darby

The following 1879 letter by Darby gives an overview of the tremendous growth and acceptance of this newly developing *faith*. Note that in this letter, Darby claims to have founded the *faith* that within 50 years conquered Christianity. (Starting in 1827, and by 1879, these ideas had conquered the Christian world.) Whether or not the theories originated with Darby, we must admit that he was the primary instrument of spreading this *faith* world-wide. H.A. Ironside was proud of the fact that the branch of Christianity he identified with, Brethren, originated the following ideas. Yet many Baptists refuse to admit that most of their doctrines came out of this movement:

> ***I was very glad to hear of and from you and of your work, the rather as it is not very likely that I shall get to America again, though in fine weather it is rather a rest; but I am now in my seventy-ninth year. You will be interested to hear, as you find the opposition of the clergy, and especially to the Lord's coming, that in Constantinople they have preached against that and breaking of bread, and that this has set the Armenians much on the inquiry as to both. I have no enmity, thank God, against any; but this character of opposition we must expect to meet. But there is One who "openth, and no man shutteth," and sets before the saints in the last days an open door, even if we have but little strength.... I do not speak of it now, when

---

34. *Ibid.,* II.431-440.

I do, as a point to be proved, but as a part of christian truth, as much as the atonement, though not like it the foundation of grace: but they were converted to wait for His Son from heaven. In that congress (at New York) as far as I know of it, the presence of the Holy Ghost was, says —, wholly left out. But these are the two truths brought out in these days, throwing much light on the truth of the first coming. They have been consciously my theme these fifty years and more. They started me in my path of service; the assurance of salvation came with them, and the christian character, as of the new creation, "like unto men that wait for their Lord." When man entered into the glory of God consequent on accomplished redemption, the Holy Ghost came down, till He comes to take us up. This connects the hope and the power of life and heavenly calling with accomplished redemption: Christ, Man at the right hand of God, is the central point. What set me free in 1827 is still the theme on which my soul dwells, with, I trust, much deeper sense of its importance — something much nearer to me, but the same truths. And blessed truths they are; and the hope, what a hope!

We have to seek, amidst all that is passing around us, to minister positive truth and blessing, Christ and what is eternal; and for that we must live of Him, and with Him too, and not much mind what passes around us, save as God brings it before our eyes. It is Christ? — the positive and good? — the world wants, and saints too. Thus in the congress at New York there was the positive good of bringing the coming of the Lord publicly forward; but there were all sorts of heretics there, and persons deliberately hindering the truth in seeking to connect it with the world and the camp — avowing it, if the account is to be believed — leaving out the essential point of the presence of the Holy Ghost. Let us be content to be little and despised, but give out the full truth. The present great truth, redemption being known, is the presence of the Holy Ghost, what [sic] made it expedient Christ should leave the disciples; the future truth — in present hope — the coming of the Lord for the saints, and then in His own rights over the world; to sinners — as plain and complete a gospel as possible, and the time is short. Meanwhile we have to watch, to walk in love and self-judgement in patience, to be enough with Christ to bring a love which is above the evil into the midst of the evil in holiness. That is what Christ was, and that we have to seek to be. I do not doubt, dear brother, God enables you to do it better than me, but I dwell on it as that which passes through my mind as that which we need.

England has tried me more than any one will ever know but One; but it has been good for me, and I have felt that we are to rejoice in the Lord always, and to be careful for nothing, and to count on Him who never fails, and He has not failed. How could He? I have unclouded confidence in His faithfulness to the end. With all this the Lord is working everywhere; and we have to think of what is of praise and is lovely and of good report, and find the God of peace with us.

In general, the work has made considerable progress in the United States. But all over the world the Spirit of God is working, and it awakes the bright hope that the blessed Lord is soon coming. The Lord be with you, dear brother, and with yours, and sustain you by His own presence in your work!

Ever affectionately yours in the Lord.[35]

The prophets prophesy falsely, and the priests bear rule by their means; and my people love to have it so: and what will ye do in the end thereof?

Jeremiah 5:31

---

35. *Ibid.*, II.498-500.

Appendix B
Various Meanings

Because this book is meant for the average reader who is seeking truth, this writer feels it wise to define some common terms used in the previous study.

We have mentioned that smell of *Death* was in the European air when Lacunza, Irving, Darby and the early Brethren came into history. We will, accordingly, glance at some of the other monastic, defeatist *Christian* movements that developed about the same time as Irvingism/Darbyism. It is amazing that *the smell of death* was rising from so many corners of Christianity.

This writer is firmly persuaded of God's Divine Providence continually working in history. So how is the rise of *Death* explained? Deuteronomy 13:1-5 presents the law:

> *... for the Lord thy God proveth you, to know whether ye love the Lord your God with all your heart and with all your soul. Ye shall walk after the Lord your God, and fear him, and keep his commandments, and obey his voice, and ye shall serve him, and cleave unto him....*

Then this law is applied to the Church in many New Testament passages, *e.g.*, 1 Corinthians 11:16:

> *For there must be also heresies among you, that they which are approved may be made manifest among you.*

In God's plan, for his sovereign purpose and for his own glory, he allows many men and events to rise to draw his people away from the final authority of his Law-Word. Biblical Christianity is a series of continual testings, proving one's love for and dedication to the Lord God. It appears that God's *provings* over the past couple of centuries have proved that man, though professing to love God and his word, would much rather be his own god, able to determine for himself what is good and evil. Fallen men desire Christianity's benefits without its social responsibilities.

Only the Spirit of God can change the hearts of men to again accept their Christian responsibilities before God. May the Spirit again draw men to himself through the preaching of the total Gospel of the Lord Jesus Christ. We will start at the place of the most controversy:

Millennial Views

We need to identify and define the three common millennial views as best we can in this short space.

Premillennialism

According to Gregg:

1. *Premillennialism* (once known as *chiliasm*, see p. 439) is the belief that the second coming of Christ will precede the millennial kingdom. Taking a mostly literal approach, premillenarians expect a period of one thousand years' duration, during which Christ will reign with his saints here on earth prior to the establishment of the eternal new heavens and new earth. The millennial reign will be characterized by international peace and justice resulting from the universal enforced rule of Christ over saved and unsaved alike. At the end of this time, Satan's brief period of freedom will put humanity to one final test just before the final judgment.

There are two principal varieties of premillennialism: *historic premillennialism* and *dispensational premillennialism* or, simply, *dispensationalism*. The latter differs from the former in its emphasis on the continuing centrality of national Israel in God's eschatological program and in anticipating a Rapture of Christians to heaven before the beginning of the Tribulation.

Premillennialism has been accused by its critics of promoting a pessimistic outlook for the temporal future—though, if this is what Scripture teaches, premillennialists can hardly be faulted for such pessimism. This view is most likely to be held by those adopting a futurist approach to Revelation (e.g., Walvoord, Ryrie, Gaebelein, Ironside, etc.).[1]

---

1. *Revelation*, 27, 28. See *Futurism*, p. 434.

Postmillennialism

2. *Postmillennialism* teaches that Christ returns after the millennial period. According to this camp, the millennial kingdom will be established through the evangelistic mission of the church. This enterprise will be so successful that all or most people become Christians, resulting in a thousand years of peace on earth before Christ's coming. Many great evangelical leaders, including Benjamin B. Warfield and Jonathan Edwards, were postmillennialists, as are a growing number of modern evangelicals, known as Christian Reconstructionists. Postmillennialists are often (though not always) inclined toward the *preterist* approach to Revelation (e.g., Chilton, Gentry, though not Rushdoony), since their optimistic view of the future works better if the disasters described in Revelation are seen as belonging to a time now past, rather than to the end of history.[2]

Christian Reconstruction

"Christian reconstruction," or *theonomy, i.e.,* "rule by the law of God," also fits here, teaching that the Kingdom of God will involve the complete transformation of culture, politics and institutions through the "application of biblical law."[3]

Postmillenianism dominated America until the wars, starting with the War Between the States, when secularism took over. America now sees itself dominating the world not through the gospel, but through military and economic strength.

Amillennialism

3. *Amillennialism* understands the thousand years of Revelation 20 to symbolize an indefinitely long period of time, which happens to correspond to the entire span of time from the first coming of Christ until his second coming. Most aspects of chapter 20 (like most aspects of the rest of Revelation) are believed to be symbolic. The binding of Satan happened spiritually at the Cross; the reign of the saints is the present age; the loosing of Satan is a final period of deception coming on the world in the end of the age; the fire from heaven that devours the wicked is the second coming of Christ.

---

2. *Ibid.,* 28.
3. *Catholics,* 133

Those of this persuasion have included virtually every theologian from Augustine through the Reformation, and there are many adherents today. Amillennialists have been found among adherents of several of the various approaches to Revelation, including the *historicist* (e.g., Martin Luther), the *preterist* (Jay Adams), and the *spiritual* (William Hendriksen), but only rarely of the *futurist* (Abraham Kuyper).[4]

Amillennialism can be credited to Augustine (354-430), who taught that the millennium is the time of the Kingdom on earth, the Church age, and will last an indefinite time, until Christ's return.[5]

It should be remembered that the various approaches to Revelation are not linked inseparably to any particular millennial position, so that one's eschatology does not necessarily dictate which approach to Revelation is to be preferred.[6]

"The early Church Fathers, whether premillennialist or otherwise, believed that the Church was the New Israel and that she— consisting of both Jews and Gentiles (Rom 10:12)—had Israel as God's chosen people.[7]

Note that *Amillennialism* is the only system that was not developed and introduced by Rome to defend itself from Protestant attacks against the pope.

The Revelation

Gregg lists four common views of the Revelation.[8] Since *historicism* excited the most response from Rome, causing her to develop the other views in self-defense, we will start with:

---

4. *Revelation*, 28.
5. *Catholics*, 135. See *City of God*, bk. 20, chap. 9. Thus, a 'thousand generations' is understood to mean 'all generations.' *City of God*, bk. 20, chap. 7. *Ibid.*, 137. Note that Christians are now seated with Christ in the heavens, Ephesians 2.
6. *Revelation*, 27, 28.
7. *Catholics*, 121.
8. *Revelation*, 34-46.

Historicism

1. *Historicist:* This view holds that God revealed the entire church age in advance through John's visions in Revelation. Thus, his prophecies have been fulfilled throughout history, and are still being fulfilled today. It represents the papacy (chapter 13) as "the beast," and the locusts as the Arab hordes. (See Trapp's statement, p. 41)

This view holds to a "year-for-a-day," that says five months (150 days) designates 150 years. *Historicism* claims for itself impressive success stories, *e.g.,*

> Sometime around 1690, it is reported, *historicist* interpreter Robert Fleming was invited before the English court of William of Orange, King William III, to lecture on Bible prophecy. The king asked the man of God when the temporal power of the papacy in Europe would fall. Fleming's reply was published in his 1701 book entitled *Apocalyptic Key*. Concerning the fall of the papacy as the ruling power in Europe, the prophecy scholar wrote: "I say this judgment will begin about A.D. 1794 and expire about 1848." This prediction was made approximately one hundred years prior to the projected dates. *Historicist* apologists point out that in 1794 the French Revolution's "Reign of Terror" occurred, which, they say, marked the beginning of the end of the pope's temporal power in Europe. In the year 1848, the pope was temporarily driven from Rome.[9]

Since the principle advocates of this view were the Reformers, a key, non-negotiable point is that the 'papacy is "Antichrist."' Thus, there are times when passages seem to be "forced" to maintain the diabolical nature of their opponents. Assuming their "identification to be correct, *historicists* see in all other approaches to Revelation satanically-inspired smoke screens to obscure the true identity of Antichrist."

Few, if any, modern commentaries hold to this view, but it survives in most of the classic commentaries of the past few centuries, many of which are still published. It was popular with well known men such as, John Wycliffe, John Knox, William Tyndale,

---

9. *Ibid.,* 35. See *Barnes* on Revelation 16:11.

Martin Luther, John Calvin, Ulrich Zwingli, Sir Isaac Newton, Jan Hus, John Fox, John Wesley, Jonathan Edwards, George Whitefield, Charles Finney, C.H. Spurgeon, Matthew Henry, Adam Clarke, Albert Barnes [See Barnes' *Preface,* vi-viii.], and others.

Though it has several weaknesses and justified criticisms, the *historicist* view is supported when one reads Gibbon's history of Rome: "... it was said that a missionary might go to heathen lands armed only with a copy of Gibbon's *Decline and Fall of the Roman Empire* in one hand and Barnes' *Notes on Revelation* in the other, and prove beyond question the inspiration of Bible."[10]

Being the strongest view against the papacy, the *historicist* view is the one that motivated the most defense of the papacy.

Preterism

2. *Preterist:* This view holds that most prophecies were fulfilled during the time of the Roman empire. Conservative, early-date preterism has had worthy advocates for several centuries. *Preterists* hold to a pre A.D. 70 date for Revelation. Thus they see Matthew 24 and Revelation basically fulfilled. *Preterism* can lead to saying that the Revelation has as much value to modern readers as does any fulfilled Bible prophecy.

Preterism was formulated by the Jesuit scholar, Luiz de Alcazar (1554-1613), and offered for the same reason as was *futurism*; that is, a Roman response to Protestants to take the pressure off of Rome. "After reviewing Josephus' description of the destruction of Jerusalem in A.D. 70," Eusebius (early fourth century) saw Matthew 24 as completely fulfilled–the preterist position.[11]

Preterism is thus credited as a response to Protestant's *historicism* claims that the papal system was the antichrist or the "beast." Accordingly, it shares common origins with *futurism*, which was formulated for the same purpose. However, there is proof that similar teachings as modern preterism concerning at least the early

---

10. *Ibid.,* 34-37.
11. *Ibid.,* 32, 39.

part of Revelation existed in the church as much as a thousand years before Alcazar, mentioned by men such as Eusebius, Andreas of Cappadocia (early sixth century), and also Arethas (also early sixth century).[12]

Conservative, or historical preterists have history on their side when one reads Flavius Josephus. His eyewitness account of the fall of Jerusalem strikingly corresponds with the details given in Revelation. Some understand Revelation as John's account of the Olivet Discourse. Though Matthew (ch. 24), Mark (ch. 13) and Luke (ch. 17, 21) each give their account of Jesus' answer to the question, "Tell us, when shall these things be? and what shall be the sign of thy coming, and of the end of the world?", John does not. Thus, Revelation can be viewed as John's expanded version of Christ's answer to the disciple's question.

While some preterists assume Jerusalem's destruction was the subject of both Matthew 24 and of Revelation, others, while saying Matthew 24 was fulfilled in A.D. 70, hold that only the first part of Revelation describes the fall of Jerusalem, the second part, the fall of the Roman empire, and the final chapters describe the second coming of Christ. Preterism depends on an early date for the Revelation, a claim that is not undisputed.

> "The first of these two counter schemes is the *Preterists',* which would have the prophecy stop altogether short of the Popedom, explaining it of the catastrophes, one or both, of the *Jewish Nation* and *Pagan Rome;* the second, the *Futurists',* which would have it all shoot over the head of the popedom into times yet future" (Elliott, iv. 529). The first of these schemes originated with the Jesuit *Alcassar* in A.D. 1614; the other with the Jesuit *Ribera* in A.D. 1558; and it is not a little remarkable, that both originated in the necessities of the Papal cause, oppressed by Protestant interpreters.[13]

---

12. *Ibid.,* 37-40.
13. *Barnes' Notes, Revelation,* Editor's Preface, xiii. Edited by Robert Frew, D.D. Baker Book House, Grand Rapids, Michigan. 1977 edition. Barnes spells the Jesuit's name "Ribera" while others spell it "Ribeira."

Some hold that ALL prophecies were fulfilled during the time of the Roman empire, *i.e., Full Preterism.* This idea can lead to thinking that the word of God, being totally fulfilled within the first century, was only for the first century Christians, though it continues to *apply* to Christians of all ages as do the fulfilled prophecies of men like Daniel. This extreme view is not unlike Marcion's, Darby's and Scofield's "rightly dividing the word of God" teaching that the Old Testament was for Israel alone before Christ, and much of the New was for Israel, which is distinct from the church. This dispensational view leaves only a few of Paul's books for the "Church Age." All the rest of Scripture outside of Paul's are only good for illustrations, but they have no binding effect upon God's people today.

Futurism

3. *Futurist:* This view holds that most prophecies are yet to be fulfilled. Holding that everything past chapter three is yet to be fulfilled and must take place after a rapture in Revelation 4:1, the rest of the events recorded in the Revelation are for a time when the church is not here.

Not all *futurists* are dispensationalists. As pointed out in Chapter 3, the system originated with a Roman Jesuit, Francisco Ribeira in his 1585 effort to refute the *historicist* claim that the pope was the "beast." "Protestants regarded *futurism* as a product of the papacy's self-defense against the claims of the reformers"[14]

The Alexandrian fathers, Clement of Alexandria, Tyconius, Augustine, and others, rejected millennialism. Origen (c. 185-254) rejected *chiliasm* as "Jewish."[15] Thus, the Protestants did not accept the *futurist* idea until Irving introduced the Jesuit Lacunza's (Ben-

---

14. *Revelation*, 42, 32.

15. *Ibid.*, 30. LaHaye's eschatological views bear a striking resemblance to those of the Watchtower Society and Armstrong's World Church of Tomorrow. *Catholics,* 61. Much to his mother's displeasure, this author was "hooked" on Armstrong. While driving the duty shuttle bus at night on a Washington, D.C. Naval base in 1961, he regularly listened to "The World Tomorrow." Because Armstrong was so close to what this author heard in Dispensational churches, he could, at the time, see nothing wrong with Armstrong's message.

Ezra) ideas at the 1826 prophecy conference, *q.v.* About that time, it picked up the pre-trib rapture idea.

In 1191, Cistercian abbot Joachim of Fiore (ca. 1135-1202) told Richard the Lion-Hearted that the Antichrist was already in the world, preparing for his rule. He also taught that the Antichrist, Gog and Magog, the beast and other puzzling elements should be understood as real people, institutions and places, rather than metaphorically. Joachim divided history into three parts: the age of the Father was the Old Testament; the age of the Son is the present age, drawing quickly to a close; and the age of the Spirit will be the age of "perfection, love, monks, and oil." Joachim's writings had an impact on philosophers of history such as Hegel and Marx, and continue their influence in dispensationalism. Another Franciscan, Peter Olivi (ca. 1248-1298) expanded on Joachim's ideas, and divided time into seven epochs. The Taborites of Bohemia, killed those they judged to be sinners (the Council of Constance burned John Huss [1371-1415] for his anti-papal views), believing that "such violence was necessary in order to bring about the second coming. The "Taborites were destroyed by the more moderate Hussites.[16]

The *futurist* view is the most prevalent among modern, popular commentators, evangelical writers, pastors and Bible teachers. Its influence in the last hundred and fifty years into every corner of Christianity shows its dominance of both Christian and "secular" media. The income generated by *futurist* books is astounding.

"Futurists, like *historicists,* often understand Revelation to be chronologically continuous, though some *futurists* see two parallel sections of Revelation (chapters 4-11 and chapters 12-19), both of which describe a future time of tribulation"[17]

Futurism, or modern *Dispensationalism,* alone has the freedom to take a very literal approach to Revelation:

---

16. *Catholics,* 147-149. How many times in the last 50 years have we been told by the prognosticators the same thing King Richard was told?
17. *Revelation,* 40.

The desire to understand Revelation literally may be the leading factor favoring the adoption of a *futurist* approach, although most of the elements of the scenario predicted by dispensationalists' appeal to the Book of Revelation do not arise from the literal application of any particular passage. For example, a major feature of the Tribulation expected by *futurists* is its seven-year duration, divided in the middle by the Antichrist's violating a treaty he had made with Israel and setting up an image of himself in the rebuilt Jewish temple in Jerusalem. Yet none of these elements can be discovered from the literal interpretation of any passage in Revelation. Similarly, there is no passage, which, literally applied, will yield a prediction of 200 million Chinese troops, cobra helicopters, a global cashless economic system, or nuclear war.

The *futurist* believes that Revelation 20 describes a period of world peace and justice with Christ reigning on earth from Jerusalem, though no part of this description can be found in the chapter itself, taken literally. This observation does not mean that this futurist scenario cannot be true. But it must be derived by reading into the passages in Revelation features that are not plainly stated.[18]

And thus the *futurists,* though claiming to base their faith on taking Revelation literally, actually take very little of it literally, a fact that even they themselves must admit. Thus, the *futurists'* condemnation of other positions that do not take the Revelation literally is very hypocritical, for they only apply it literally in areas that will support what they want to teach.[19]

Futurists are fond of "newspaper exegesis," which looks for current events to support what they see prophesied in Revelation. "In fact, every generation of futuristic interpreters for the last 150 years or longer has been able to find in Revelation a description of their own times."[20] "Newspaper exegesis" is very exciting and appealing to modern readers, but it leaves about 90 percent of Revelation irrelevant to the readers of the day it was written. And since *futurism* says the book is yet to be fulfilled after the church is gone, that 90 percent is also irrelevant to modern readers; why, may we ask, should they spend so much time studying something they believe

---

18. *Ibid.,* 41.

does not even apply to them, or why did God even record these future events if his people will not be here?

Gregg credits Francisco Ribeira with the development of futurism, and Samuel Maitland[21] with infiltrating the Protestant church with *futurism*, and credits Darby with the founding of dispensationalism in 1830. However, he overlooks Lacunza's and Irving's tremendous influence, which makes a far stronger claim on the roots of modern Dispensationalism.

---

19. Gregg quotes Walvoord, Ryrie and Henry Morris, all who admit that much of the Revelation must be taken symbolically. *Revelation,* 41, 42. Yet they condemn other systems for taking the Revelation symbolically. In other words, those who do not understand the symbolism as they do are not understanding the book properly. These men, *e.g.,* LaHaye, are very bold in their statements that these who do not see the "end times" as they do are biblically illiterate. *Catholics,* 27. LaHaye, in his *Rapture under Attack,* claims that both "'amillennialism and postmillennialism' use methods of Scripture interpretation similar to that of Christian Science, the Jehovah's Witnesses, Armstrong's World Church of Tomorrow 'and most of the cults'" Unable to Scripturally defend his prophetic system, LaHaye must attempt to discredit with name-calling and personal attacks those who will not follow his system. Men like LaHaye are the honest heirs to Darbyism, for when Darby was unable to Scripturally defend the new pre-trib, dispensational system as he developed it, he attacked those who disagreed with him by calling them things such as "tools of the devil," *qv.* Scofield said that those who do not follow his teaching and "divide" up God's word (reassemble it as you would a puzzle) are wasting their time studying Scripture, for their study will be in a "large measure profitless and confusing"... *qv.* Chafer "insisted that unless a person held dispensationalist beliefs he was doomed to teach a false gospel:...'", *qv.*

20. *Revelation,* 42. "In 1973 Hal Lindsey wrote: 'For those of us who know what the prophets have taught, picking up our morning newspaper is practically a traumatic experience. Headline after headline screams out a confirmation of these remarkable predictions.' (*There's a New World Coming,* pp. 99-100). Twenty years later, some dispensationalists still make the same kind of claims, though the headlines describe a very different political landscape today." *Ibid., 49.*

21. "(1792-1866), Church of England clergyman and historian, born in London, educated at St. John's and Trinity Colleges, Cambridge. Called to the bar in 1816, five years later took holy orders in the Church of England, although reared in the Non-conformist faith. ... Traveled abroad for some years, taking a keen interest in mission work among the Jews in Germany and Poland. A controversialist of no mean ability. Successfully combatted [sic] the "Year-day Theory" of Abbot Joachim (later taken up by Edward Irving". ... *Who,* 268. Note the appearance of yet another man in the dispensational foundation with special interest in the Jews.

It may be noted that, unlike the *historicist* and *preterist* approaches, the *futurist* approach cannot be tested from history. One may evaluate the *historicist* and the *preterist* approaches partially on the basis of their claims that actual historical events have occurred which correspond to their interpretation of Revelation's predictions. The *futurist* view, however, cannot be verified or falsified in this manner, since the things predicted, it is asserted, have not yet occurred. It can be argued in the absence of certain knowledge of the future that anything *might* yet happen to fulfill the *futurist's* expectations. The dispensationalists, in particular, do not stand ever to be embarrassed by future developments, since they believe that they will be raptured before any of the predicted events occur. Whether this invulnerability to falsification is an asset or a liability to *futurism* is not a matter of universal agreement.[22]

Spiritual

4. *Spiritual (*or *Symbolic* or *Idealist):* This view holds that most prophecies portray ongoing cosmic conflict of spiritual realities throughout history. Gregg applies this title "to include all approaches that do not look for individual or specific fulfillments of the prophecies of Revelation in the natural sense, but which believe only that spiritual lessons and principles (which may find recurrent expression in history) are depicted symbolically in the visions." This approach can be traced to William Milligan.[23]

Other names for the *Spiritual* approach are *nonliteral, allegorical* or *symbolic, poetic,* or *philosophy of history school.* "According to this view, the great themes of the triumph of good over evil, or Christ over Satan, of the vindication of the martyrs and the sovereignty of God are played out throughout Revelation without necessary reference to single historical events."[24]

---

22. *Revelation,* 40-42.

23. *Ibid.,* 43. "(1821-1893) Church of Scotland clergyman, born in Edinburgh, Scotland, educated at St. Andrews University, the University of Edinburgh, and Halle, Germany where he made the acquaintance of Neander. ... In 1860 became professor of Biblical criticism, and in 1870 chosen as one of the revisers of the New Testament. ..." He wrote at least four books on the Revelation. *Who,* 284, 285.

24. *Revelation,* 43.

[Spiritual] interpretations combine readily with those of the Preterists or of the Historicists, because any symbol, understood by them to refer to a certain force or tendency may be considered fulfilled in any event in which such a force or tendency is dominant.[25]

Evangelical commentators commonly "mix the *spiritual* approach with the *preterist* and then either call their view *preterism*, leave their view unlabeled or give it an original name."[26]

Gregg quotes J. Barton Payne:

> Allegorizing commentators may treat the Apocalypse according to principles of mystical interpretation ... or according to theories of liturgical, poetic, or dramatic literary forms such as have been proposed by modern critics; but all writers of this type unite upon reducing the book's 'real' teaching to certain matters of timeless truth, or at least to interpretations that are devoid of concrete, historical specification.[27]

A problem with all the views above, except the Preterist, is that John said several times over that the events recorded must shortly come to pass, Revelation 1:1, 19, and that John was told **not to seal** the book, Revelation 22:6, 7, 10. On the other hand, Daniel was told **to seal** his book, Daniel 12:4, 9. Daniel was opened after four to five hundred years, yet many say that Revelation is still sealed after two thousand years, a problem for which non-preterists have no answer.

Historic Chiliasm

Historic Chiliasm sees a literal millennial reign by the Messiah, King Jesus, upon this earth from a renewed Jerusalem in the literal land of Canaan.[28] It does not include a secret, pre-tribulation rapture. It is no more than a continuation of the old "rabbinical

---

25. Pieters, *The Lamb, the Woman and the Dragon*, p. 41. Quoted by Gregg, *Revelation*, 44.
26. *Ibid.*
27. *Encyclopedia of Biblical Prophecy*, p. 593.
28. *Chilioi*, a thousand: The doctrine that Christ will personally reign on earth during the millenium — *Webster*, second edition, unabridged. s.v. "Chiliasm."

dream" of a restored, exalted Jewish nation to rule the world again as it did under David and Solomon, *q.v.*

The common hope of Christ's day was for the Messiah to lead the Hebrew, Jewish nation from the bondage it had suffered since the time Babylon carried away Judah. Under this warlike Messiah, Israel would again be exalted over all the nations of the world.[29]

When Christ finished reading Isaiah 42 in the synagogue in Nazareth, he said, "This day is this scripture fulfilled in your ears." (Luke 4:16-21.) Throughout Christ's earthly ministry, he told Israel that he was the promised Messiah sent to free the people from bondage. However, Israel looked for a literal freedom from physical bondage – Rome at that time. Christ, though, said his freedom was from sin's bondage. Rome understood that Christ did not offer to free the Hebrew nation from its rule, so Rome found no fault in him. (Luke 23:4, 14, John 18:36; 19:4, 6.)

Looking for a literal, physical kingdom, the religious leaders could not understand that Christ was talking of a spiritual kingdom. (Luke 17:20ff., John 18:38, &c.) Even the Apostles looked for a literal restored Hebrew, Jewish kingdom until Christ finally opened their eyes to his spiritual kingdom. (Acts 1:6.)

Though Christ clearly presented the truth, the religious leaders who demanded his death retained their false hope of deliverance from Roman occupation by an Old Testament promised Messiah. *Judicial blindness* caused the religious leaders who called for Christ's death to continue in their rebellion, resulting in the total destruction of the Hebrew, or Biblical Jewish nation in AD 70, fulfilling passages such as Matthew 26:64 and Luke 21:20, *q.v.*

---

29. Isaiah 42:5, Daniel 2:44, Genesis 12:1-3, 22:18, Abraham receives the promise of the world's blessing through his seed, and Galatians 3:16ff., identifies that seed as Christ; Genesis 49:10, Jacob promises Judah the everlasting king and kingdom; 2 Samuel 7, David is promised an everlasting king and kingdom. These passages, with many other passages, *e.g.,* Psalms 72, Psalms 89, Psalms 110, Isaiah 9:6, 7, appear to promise a literal king over a renewed, literal Hebrew, Jewish nation, who will rule the world.

Appendix B 441

Though the Old Testament Israel was totally destroyed, and the early church generally dismissed the "rabbinical dream," it was renewed and, through the efforts various men, it has infected every corner of the church of the Lord Jesus Christ.

Two Views of Christ's Return

There has always been a great amount of speculation concerning this return of Christ. Basically, there are two views: One regards the second advent primarily as a spiritual experience already realized through the descent of the Holy Spirit upon the disciples after the resurrection of Jesus. This view is frequently supplemented by belief in a visible return of Christ at an indefinite historical moment in the far distant future, after the Gospel by its transforming power has gradually brought the world to a state of millennial perfection.

The second opinion insists that the promised return of Christ has not yet taken place, but may be momentarily expected. In the meantime, the world constantly deteriorates. Only by Christ's literal coming can the millennium be established and righteousness made to prevail upon the earth.

The latter opinion is commonly designated premillenarianism and the former postmillenarianism. Since the 'pre' sees Christ's return as an imminent event greatly to be desired, they have usually been much more diligent than 'post' in their efforts to determine the date and manner of the second advent. The belief in the imminent advent of Christ is a distinctively contemporary Jewish doctrine which has come over into the church of the Lord Jesus.

Throughout the 2nd and 3rd centuries, many Christians continued to cherish the hope of an early visible return of their Lord. Montanus (second century) was one of the better known figures who carried this doctrine to its logical extreme of sitting back and waiting for this glorious event. (Montanus was also the first to claim *tongues* after the Apostles.)

> *Chilliastic* views were held by Papias (c. 130), Justin Martyr, Irenaeus, Tertullian, Hippolytus, Methodius, Commodianus and

Lactantius (b. 320). The premillennialists believed the church would go through a time of tribulation and great turmoil. They did not see any kind of "snatching away."[30]

According to Hastings[31]

There was a general belief in the Early Church in the approaching end of the world, preceded by great troubles and by the revelation of the Antichrist. At Christ's advent, the Antichrist and the wicked would be destroyed. The chronology goes something like this: There are six periods of a thousand years each. Christ had come in the last thousand-year period, and his second coming would be at its close. The end of the 6000 years and the second coming would inaugurate the seventh period of 1000, the Millennium, for which the righteous dead would be raised to enjoy. The basic three dates of the start of the Millennium were set at A.D. 195, 200 and 250.

> In spite of the fact that, save in the Apocalypse, the New Testament did not speak of the Millennium, and that Christ does not connect the Parousia [coming of Christ, *ed.*] with the establishment of an earthly Kingdom, this belief had an extraordinary hold on the minds of Christians. Doubtless a misunderstanding of the Apocalypse gave the belief a certain authority, but it is rather from its Jewish antecedents that its popularity and the elaboration of its details are to be explained. [*Shepherd of Hermas*, Sim. ix. 16; *Acta Pauli et Thecloe*, § 28; *pass. Perp.* § 7; *test. Abrah.* § 14; Tertullian, *de An.* 35, 58, *de Monog.* 10, *de Cor. Mil.* 3.]
>
> The general picture of the millennial Kingdom on earth, 'the day of the supper of 1000 years' ('Boharic Death of Jeseph' [*TS* iv. 2. 142]), includes such features as that the earth would be renewed and Jerusalem re-built and glorified. Men would be perfectly righteous and happy, and would have numerous offspring. There would be no sorrow and no labour. The earth would produce abundantly, and a table would always be spread with food. A passage of Papias, cited by Irenaeus (*adv. Hoer.* v. 33), derives a picture of this fruitfulness from Christ Himself though it is now known to have been copied from a document (perhaps a midrash on Gn. 27.28 [Harris, *Exp.*,

---

30. *Catholics*, 118, 123.

31. This section is from *Ethics*, s.v. "Anabaptism," "Eschatology," "Second Adventism." See *Scofield's Rightly Dividing the Word of Truth* for an explanation of this theory.

1895, p. 448; *AJTh,* 1900, p. 499]), used also in *Apoc. Bar.* 29.5f., and in *EN.* 10.19 (see Charles, *Ap. of Baruch,* 54). The moon would have the brilliance of the sun, and the sun would be seven times brighter than the moon. Some of the wicked would be left on earth, subjected to perpetual slavery.

"This sensuous aspect of the Kingdom is directly taken over from Judaism" — "Protestant Zionism." Montanus also cherished millennial views of an unspiritual kind, seeing Christ speedily coming to establish an earthly Kingdom of the saints in the New Jerusalem, which would descend visibly out of heaven. There was strong opposition to this belief from early times: Justin says that many, who were otherwise orthodox, were opposed to it. Justin Martyr (A.D. 110-165), a premillennialist (or chiliast), in his *Dialogue with Trypho, a Jew,* writes:

> THE OPINION OF JUSTIN WITH REGARD TO THE REIGN OF A THOUSAND YEARS. SEVERAL CATHOLICS REJECT IT
>
> And Trypho to this replied, "I remarked to you sir, that you are very anxious to be safe in all respects, since you cling to the Scriptures. But tell me, do you really admit that this place, Jerusalem, shall be rebuilt; and do you expect your people to be gathered together, and made joyful with Christ and the patriarchs, and the prophets, both the men of our nation, and other proselytes who joined them before your Christ came? or have you given way, and admitted this in order to have the appearance of worsting us in the controversies?"
>
> Then I answered, "I am not so miserable a fellow, Trypho, as to say one thing and think another. I admitted to you formerly, that I and many others are of this opinion, and [believe] that such will take place, as you assuredly are aware; but, on the other hand, I signified to you that many who belong to the pure and pious faith, and are true Christians, think otherwise.[32]

Thus, there were many of the true faith who did not hold to premillennialism, and Justin did not regard them as heretics. Accordingly, Charles Ryrie is not being truthful with his sweeping statement that "Premillennialism is the historic fatih of the Church."[33]

---

32. Justin Martyr, *The Ante-Nicene Fathers,* I.239.
33. *Revelation,* 29.

A newcomer on the theological scene, the pretribulational Rapture is rejected by the vast majority of Christians world-wide. Recognizing that history is not on their side, dispensationalists have resorted to two different approaches: either denying history has any importance when it comes to "biblical doctrine", or denying that the pretribulational Rapture is only two hundred years old.[34]

Dispensational theology must be separated from history in order for it to stand: Separated from what took place in history to fulfill various prophecies it depends upon for its life, and separated from the historical stand of the church. As we mention elsewhere, Darby never tired of telling of his hard work, so he had no problem telling us how hard he worked to change history to support his ideas. Among other things, he changed orthodox church doctrine based upon his judgment, which included a coming "Great Tribulation."[35] He changed the Reformer's words for support.[36] He changed Scripture to support his view of Israel.[37] He changed the words of hymns for support.[38] He "corrected" Scripture, both the KJV and the Greek text, to support his ideas.[39]

More honestly, "the Alexandrian fathers rejected millennialism." The excesses of Montanism helped to discredit the doctrine in the East and to stamp it as Jewish rather than Christian. However, it was largely the influence of Alexander, Clement and Origen that gave the death-blows to it in the East.

> The Alexandrian fathers rejected millennialism. These fathers introduced a more spiritualizing approach to Revelation. Origen (c. 185-254) repudiated the literal interpretation of the chiliasts as "Jewish."[40]

---

34. *Catholics*, 325. Ryrie attempts to deny history: "history is never the test of truth—the Bible and only the Bible is. But they (those who say that dispensationalism is not historical, *ed.*) persist in using the approach and leave the impression that history is a partly valid test, if not the final test." Ryrie, *Dispensationalism*, p. 14. Quoted by Olson.
35. *Collected Writings*, II.372.
36. *Ibid.*, 370. *Plot*, 145.
37. *Collected Writings*, II.446.
38. *Letters,* III.45.
39. *Ibid.,* I.534, 380, 382.

Chiliastic views prevailed in the West until the time of Augustine (d. 604), who had himself once cherished them in a spiritual rather than a sensuous form. His attack against Chiliasm caused Millenarianism to become a heresy for many centuries.

According to Hastings, Augustine dismissed,

> [T]he view that Christ is yet to come to inaugurate a millennial reign upon earth. The Kingdom has already been established by Christ's first advent, when He bound Satan (Mk. 3), and His coming 'continually occurs in His church, that is, in His members, in which He comes little by little and piece by piece, since the whole Church is His body.' When the Church has reached the climax of its growth, the present world will be transmuted by a fiery bath transforming corruptibility into incorruptibility and revealing the New Jerusalem which is from heaven 'because the grace with which God formed it is of heaven.' The work of Augustine (q.v.) virtually eliminated all realistic Second Adventism from the main stream of Roman Catholic thinking, and his views have also been widely current in Protestant circles.
>
> Augustine holds that the 1000 years=the duration of the Church on earth; the reign of the Saints=the reign of the Kingdom of Heaven; the First Resurrection=the spiritual share which the baptized have in Christ's Resurrection (*de Civ. Dei,* xx.6f.). His theory regarding the duration of the Church, literally interpreted, gave rise to the view that the end would come in A.D. 1000.

There have been many attempts since Augustine to establish a date for the second advent of Christ. One of the latest attempts was 1988. Just about every generation has had its date setters.

The comparative ease with which millenarianism disappeared shows that, generally speaking, it had never interfered with the ethical and spiritual life of Christians. Millenarianism has appeared at various times throughout the history of the Church: When times are difficult, millenarianism gains popularity; when times are good, millenarianism fades into the background. It was revived in the Middle Ages by mystical sects, and after the Reformation, mainly by

---

40. *Revelation,* 30. Chiliastic ideas were held by Irenaeus, Tertullian and Lactantius

Anabaptists, c. 1500. The modern millennial view owes its development to Bengel.[41]

Many distinguished theologians have held millenarian views, but it is mainly in America that the doctrine had given rise to separate sects (Seventh Day Adventists, Second Adventists, etc.). These as well as the millenarians of the Early Church, believe that, at the close of the 1000 years, Satan will be unbound, and that he will make war against the Saints, only to be destroyed.

Tracing modern Second Adventism, Hastings says:

Wycliffe *(q.v.)* also regarded the papacy as the power of Antichrist and other signs of the times were taken to imply the nearness of Christ's advent. The reformers in Germany and Switzerland often spoke of the Antichrist papacy, but they did not as a rule draw the logical conclusion that the literal Second Advent was imminent. Millenarianism was branded as a Judaistic heresy by both the Augsburg and the Helvetic Confessions.[42]...

In Germany the Lutheran prejudice against adventist speculation was overcome by the Pietists. C. Vitringa, who drew largely upon the English interpreter Mede, was specially influential in reviving German interest in this subject. But J.A. Bengel did most to confirm that interest. From the figures and images of Revelation he concluded that a preliminary millennium would be inaugurated in 1836, when Satan would be bound for 1000 years. Then would follow the millennial kingdom proper, closing with the end of the world and the final judgment. Bengel exerted a powerful influence not only in his native land but also in England, when his commentary was translated at the special request of John Wesley. Thus advent speculations attained increasing popularity in various Protestant circles and have persisted down to modern times. The general method of the interpreter is to discover in Revelation a forecast of the entire history of Christianity up to his own day, noting especially those predictions that are believed to point to events of his age which convince him of the nearness of Christ's return to inaugurate the millennium...

The beginning of the 19th Cent. witnessed the rise of strong millennial sects in Great Britain. A movement was begun by Edward Irving, a popular Scottish Presbyterian preacher in London,

---

41. (1687-1752) A German Lutheran theologian, "He was one of the eminent Pietistic successors of Spener," *Who*, s.v. "Bengel, Johann Albrecht."

42. See art. *Confessions*, vol. iii. pp. 845ff., 859ff. Hasting's footnote.

which came to be known as the Catholic Apostolic Church (or the Irvingites). In 1823 Irving published a book [*Ben-Ezra, ed.*] which attracted considerable attention and led to the holding of a series of yearly conferences at the home of Henry Drummond, a wealthy London banker living in Albury. From these beginnings grew the idea of forming a new spiritual Church ready to receive Christ at His coming--an event which Irving had predicted for the year 1864. A kindred movement arising in Ireland and England between the years 1827 and 1831 received the name of Plymouth Brethren (or Darbyites). Its aim was to restore the simplicity and purity of primitive Christianity in preparation for Christ's imminent return. An elaborate scheme of events to take place in connection with the end of the world was derived from the imagery of Daniel and Revelation.[43]

Anabaptist millenarianism was closely connected with socialism (communal living), and contained the teaching of Lord's soon return, *i.e.,* Hans Hunt, c. 1526. Anabaptists of the Rhine regions, among other things, fixed the beginning of the reign of Christ on earth as 1533. They also held that the human nature of Christ was not derived from Mary. The state considered the Anabaptists dangerous for several reasons. Among other things, they refused to bear arms, to serve as civil officers or to take oaths. Their attitude toward property (communal), usury (against), certain forms of taxes (refused to pay war and ecclesiastical taxes), and their view of the law threatened the entire social order. An aberration of Anabaptist's doctrine was seen in 1534 when the entire city of Münster, Germany, was converted to that doctrine. The Anabaptists announced setting up of the kingdom, the New Jerusalem, and declared there should be no magistracy, no law, no marriage and no private property. Inside the city, murder, polygamy and crime ran rampant. In 1534, the terrible orgy ended in a massacre and cruel torture by the bishop and neighboring princes. The resulting shame upon the German Anabaptists shattered the movement. The German pieces were quietly regathered in 1536 by Menno Simons, all connections with the Münster fanatics was denied, and his new group was called

---

43. Ethics, s.v. "Second Adventism. 6. Revival of interest in adventism."

Mennonites as they went to Holland and America. Some persecuted Anabaptists possibly found their way into Independents, English Baptists and Quakers, all of whom now reflect some Anabaptist peculiarities.

Some Anabaptists, "at least, asserted the superior authority and sanctity of the New Testament over the Old Testament as the fuller, clearer revelation of God, thus approximating the modern view of a progressive revelation." Anabaptists held strictly to *believer's only* baptism, and some, "anticipating the modern Baptist position,... insisted on immersion as the only admissible form." They held to strong church discipline by democratic vote rather than by the officers of the church or by civil power, placing them in sharp collision with the State Church. Hastings:

> Glancing backwards over their views, we see that the Anabaptists were several centuries in advance of their age. They were the modern men of their tenets, then universally anathematized and persecuted, have been adopted by all civilized lands, *e.g.* universal religious toleration; others have been widely incorporated in the newer lands (America and Australia), and are making headway in the older societies, *e.g.* complete separation of Church and State; yet others are still objects of endeavour, only seen as far off boons, as, for example, abolition of war; some, as communism, are not likely ever to be adopted widely. It is remarkable that these simple people should have drawn from a fresh study of the Bible so many great ideas that still float before the trace as high and distant ideals.

Thus we see that the many doctrines being developed by these early Brethren were not new even though in their mind they were regarded as new. Several of their "unique" ideas had arisen many times in church history, had been dealt with and dismissed as unBiblical.

Gnosticism

> "the Gnostics took over only the ideal of a redemption through Christ, not the full Christian doctrine, for they made it rather a redemption of the philosophers from matter, than a redemption of mankind from sin." (*Early Church History to AD 313*, II, 20).[44]

---

44. Dr. Gwatkin, quoted by *ISBE*, s.v. "Gnosticism."

Dr. Orr writes, "Gnosticism may be described generally as the fantastic product of the blending of certain Christian ideas — particularly that of redemption through Christ — with speculations and imaginings derived from a medley of sources... Gnosticism was a species of *religious philosophy."* (*The Early Church,* 71) [45]

"Although it became a corrupting influence within the church, it was an alien by birth. While the church yet sojourned within the pale of Judaism, it enjoyed immunity from this plague; but as soon as it broke through these narrow bonds, it found itself in a world where the decaying religions and philosophies of the West were in acute fermentation under the influence of a new and powerful leaven from the East; while the infusion of Christianity itself into this fermenting mass only added to the bewildering multiplicity of gnostic sects and systems it brought forth." (Law, *The Test of Life,* 26.)[46]

"Gnosticism," says Dr. Gwatkin, "is Christianity perverted by learning, and speculation" (*Early Church History,* 73). The intellectual pride of the Gnostics refined away the gospel into a philosophy. The clue to the understanding of Gnosticism is given in the word from which it is derived — *gnosis,* "knowledge." Gnosticism puts knowledge in the place which can only be occupied by Christian faith....[47]

The profane babbling mentioned by Paul (1 Tim. 6:20) were,

[T]hat peculiar kind of religious speculation which originated in the East, but gradually spread westward to Asia Minor, Greece, and Egypt, and which bears the general name of Gnosticism, because of the predominant account it made of *gnosis,* or knowledge. It was this... which appeared one after another in the second and third centuries, and which, though courting alliance with Christianity, were always denounced as essentially antichristian by the Fathers.[48]

The church received the deposit of the Truth, with the responsibility to guard the Truth at all costs. Paul instructed Timothy to guard the *faith once delivered to the saints* from profane, unmeaning language and from speculative propositions opposed to Apostolic teachings.
[49]

---

45. Dr. Orr, *ibid.*
46. *Ibid.*
47. *Ibid.*
48. *Pastoral Epistles,* 254.

Montanism

Montanus — a Second century heretic — saw coldness, worldliness and laxity "creeping into the Church," so he attempted to call it back to purity. He "considered himself to be the passive instrument or inspired organ of the Holy Spirit" — that is, God spoke directly through him to a dead church, *i.e.*, mysticism. After attracting two "prophetesses" to himself (they left their husbands), his movement spread rapidly, gaining a large following, including Tertullian. Montanus was strongly chiliastic (teaching the speedy return of Christ), and laid great stress on miraculous gifts, including *tongues, prophecy* and progressive revelation. After the death of Polycarp (155), Montanus and the two *prophetesses* "went forth as prophets and reformers of the Christian life, and proclaimed the near approach of the age of the Holy Spirit and of the millennial reign in Pepuza, a small village of Phrygia, upon which the new Jerusalem was to come down.... The frantic movement soon... spread to Rome and North Africa, and threw the whole church into commotion." It caused the first Synods mentioned after the apostolic age. Though the bishops and synods of Asia Minor all agreed the movement was supernatural, they, though not with one voice, "declared the new prophecy the work of demons, applied exorcism, and cut off the Montanists from the fellowship of the church." Philip Schaff identified Montanism as "visionary MILLENNARIANISM," and he shows how Montanism is present in modern millennarianism. Thus millennarianism, along with the prophetic utterances and tongues, was dealt with in the Second century as heresy, "though not with one voice."[50]

Marcionism

"Marcion was the most earnest, the most practical, and the most dangerous among the Gnostics, full of energy and zeal for reforming, but restless, rough and eccentric." This is the famous

---

49. *Explanatory Analysis*, 92.
50. *Who*, s.v. "Montanus," and *History*, II.415-427. Caps his, 424.

church historian Philip Schaff's assessment of the man whose doctrine was considered heretical for the first 600 years of Church history. Though rejected by the early church, the 692 Trullan Council thought it should make provision for the reconciliation of the Marcionites, and Marcion's Gnosticism gained *Christian* legitimacy.

The Marcionites held to their Gnosticism; the church failed to contend for *the faith once delivered to the saints,* and Marcionite Gnostics have since become respectable Christian leaders.

Marcion (died, c. 160) was regarded by Justin Martyr as the most formidable heretic of his day. Polycarp of Smyrna, upon meeting Marcion in Rome, called him "the first-born of Satan." Marcion's own father, the bishop of Sinope in Pontus, excommunicated him. After his excommunication, he associated with Cerdo, a Syrian Gnostic, and soon founded a separate church that merged Gnosticism and orthodox Christianity. Widely traveled, Marcion dispersed his doctrine, making many disciples from different nations.

Marcion's Gnosticism was/is extremely dangerous because it subtly mixed pagan Gnosticism with Christianity. Marcion rejected Gnostic heathen mythology while accepting Christianity as the only true religion; however, Marcion's acceptance of *the Christ of Christianity* did not change the fact that he denied God's inspired word, a form of Gnosticism.Though Paul and Marcion are separated by many years, no doubt the Spirit warned pastors particularly (*i.e.,* Timothy), and the church in general, of false teachers like Marcion. But rather than protecting the Truth, the church allowed it to be mixed with pagan Gnosticism, hence Marcionism.

Old Testament vs. New Testament

Probably the most lasting Marcion Gnostic influence was his militancy against the Old Testament revelation of God. Marcion could see only superficial differences in the Bible, not its deeper harmony. Being utterly destitute of historical sense, separating history from theology, he put Christianity into radical conflict with all previous revelations of God. Marcion saw no connection whatsoever between Christianity and its Jewish past, *e.g.*, "The church is never mentioned in Old Testament prophecy." Marcion's work *"Antitheses"* was about what he saw as contradictions between the Old and New Testaments. His zeal was primarily directed toward enforcing what he saw as the irreconcilable dualism he established between the Gospel of Grace and the Law, Christianity and Judaism — Marcion would say, "We are under grace, not under law." The modern division many place between the Old and New Testaments can clearly be traced to Marcion's influence.

To support his dualistic system of Old Testament law vs. New Testament grace, he held that the God of the Old Testament is harsh, severe and unmerciful because he commands, "Love thy neighbour, and hate thine enemy," and he returns "and eye for an eye, and a tooth for a tooth." Conversely, the New Testament commands, "Love thine enemy." Therefore, Marcion's New Testament god was only a god of love, having no wrath against sin. With no required restitution, *eye for an eye* and *life for a life,* how can one develop and defend God's required substitutionary payment for sin, the Vicarious Atonement? Thus we see the development of *Easy Believeism.*

Hence, Marcionism is a faith as is humanism, Islam, Christianity, &c. His faith basically believes that God's word is divided into two parts: one identified as Old and the other as New. His faith then requires him to divide the One Sovereign Triune God of Scripture into two gods: one Old and one New. With two gods, he can assign different attributes to each: one law and wrath, the other love, mercy and grace. His faith in two gods provides two sets of standards: one set for his Old god and one set for his New god. Though professing to believe God's word, his two gods allow him to justify antinomianism and to deny the Sovereign God of Law. His faith permits "rightly dividing the word of God" according to one's personal liking.

Because Marcion's cannon of Scripture completely rejected God's word as present in Christ's and the apostle's day, the Old Testament (*cf.* 2 Tim. 3:16), he had to form a new canon to conform to his system of belief. First, he developed two divisions of the one total word from God, Old Testament and New Testament. Then he established an eleven book New Testament canon which would conform to his "two god" theory — an abridged and mutilated Gospel of Luke and ten of Paul's epistles. Marcion condemned Hebrews, Matthew, Mark, John and Acts.[51] Thus he removed God's threats and warnings against sin from the entire word of God, *e.g.*, Deuteronomy 4:24/ Hebrews 12:29, *God is a consuming fire.* Despite Marcion's denial of Hebrews and Deuteronomy, God is still a consuming fire against unrepentant sinners.

Marcionism not only permits but encourages antinomianism by removing Old Testament law from the realm of New Testament Christianity. The Marcionite is able, and even required by his faith, to ignore or excuse away any New Testament passage that might bring the Old Testament law forward to the New Testament Church. A good Marcionite can read passages like Romans 13:1-7 and never connect it with the practical application of God's Sovereignty in the Book of Daniel. Additionally, a Marcionite can read Romans 13:8-10 without connecting it with the Ten Commandments, for his misapplied passages permit him to separate vv. 8-10 from the church.

Though reducing Church Age Scripture to only ten or so of Paul's books, the Marcionite may still look to other books in both Testaments for good illustrations of faith.

Marcion supposed at least three principal forces: First, a good or gracious god whom Christ first made known — thus unknown in the Old Testament; second, the evil matter that is ruled by the Devil — heathenism; and third, the righteous creator — the finite, imperfect,

---

51. *History,* II.486.

angry Jehovah of the Jews. Marcion supported his militancy against the unchanging, Triune God of Scripture by corrupting Christ's words to make him say, "I am come not to fulfil the law and prophets, but to destroy them."[52]

His system of theology was more critical and rationalistic than mystic and philosophical — pure Gnosticism. Though violently antinomian, he practiced the strictest ascetic self-discipline, which not only revolted against all pagan festivities, but even from marriage, marital relations, flesh (except fish) and wine. Thus his followers may be recognized by their morality without Biblical basis, for they deny the validity of God's law upon them, yet they remain moral.

The Marcionites were very dangerous to the church because of their severe morality without God, and, unlike other Gnostics, they did not escape persecution. They had many martyrs.[53] Though they served dual gods and had a Christ after their own imagination (not the Christian Christ as revealed in both the law and the prophets, Lk. 24:44-47), their willingness to die for their faith in their false Christ gave an appearance of truth to uninformed onlookers.[54] Tertullian (c. 160-220), defending Apostolic Christianity against heretics and false teachers, identified and proved Marcion's dual god scheme "ABSURDLY DEFECTIVE," calling Marcion's dual god, "NO GOD AT ALL."[55]

Finally, Marcion had a very gloomy, pessimistic view of the world and of the church. He addressed a disciple as "his partner in tribulation, and fellow-suffer from hatred," holding that the Devil was sovereign ruler of the material world. Lacunza was not the first to present that corrupt idea of Satan to the world.

---

52. *History,* II.485. Mat. 5:17

53. *Ibid.,* 487. "Ambrosius, a friend of Origen, was a Marcionite before his conversion."

54. Marcion's false Christ is much like the modern *other Jesus* that is asked to come into one's heart for salvation, 2 Cor. 11:4.

55. *Fathers,* II.287. In *The Five Books Against Marcion,* Marcion's god was intentionally left in lower case by Tertullian to show it is no god at all.

Marcion was rightly regarded by the early church as the most formidable heretic of his day, "the first-born of Satan." Though the early church cast out Marcion's leaven many times, it continually works its way back in, causing many sincere people to serve two gods, a god for the Old Testament and a god for the New.[56]

Monasticism

Christian Monasticism separates life into two parts: secular and sacred. Monasticism is "Monastical... secluded from the temporal concerns of life and devoted to religion; as a *monastic* life; *monastic orders*."[57] Accordingly, monasticism is defined as placing one's self apart from all outside influences, e.g., monks behind closed doors.

Though there has always been a Monastic spirit within the church, our study attempts to focus on the modern, general Monastic attitude encountered in Christianity — withdrawal from the secular world to be more spiritual. If it is not dealt with, the antichrist will inherit the earth by default.

This false dualism led to the false doctrine of "separation of church and state." It prevented the church from influencing the state. However, God commands his people to bring *every thought, action* and *all things,* including the state, into *obedience* to his word.[58] Hence excluding from God's word any *secular* area of *life* and *thought* is a clear violation of the commands of Christ. He *sent them into the world.* (Jn. 17:18.)

Tracing monasticism (asceticism) from the middle of the second century, Schaff defines monasticism. He makes several excellent points found at the root of modern monasticism: 1) it "is based on an irreconcilable metaphysical dualism between mind and matter... the moral conflict between the spirit and the flesh," *e.g.,* life is divided

---

56. See: *History,* II.483-489; *Who,* s.v. "Marcion"; *ISBE,* s.v. "Gnosticism," and *Fathers,* III.270-423: At the end of *The Five Books against Marcion* is the translator's, Dr. Holmes, lengthy note showing how Marcion mutilated the word of God to conform to what he wanted to believe, 423-425.
57. *Webster,* 1828, s.v. "Monastical."
58. 2 Cor. 9:8, 10:5, Gal. 6:6, Col. 1:10, 1 Tim. 6:13, 2 Tim. 3:17, Tit. 2:7-10.

into two parts, sacred/spiritual, and secular/flesh; 2) it started as a reaction against the "secularizing state-church system and the decay of discipline," and 3) it was an effort to keep "the Christian church" pure "by transplanting it in the wilderness."[59]

The "secularizing state-church system and the decay of discipline" prepared hearts and minds for ready acceptance of the modern millenarians' spirit propagated by Irving. In fact, the term *wilderness* is frequent throughout Irving's and Darby's writings.

Spiritual/Sacred — Flesh/Secular:

> Pertaining to this present world, or to things not spiritual or holy; relating to things not immediately or primarily respecting the soul, but the body; worldly. The *secular* concerns of life respect making provision for the support of life, the preservation of health, the temporal prosperity of men, of states, &c. *Secular* power is that which superintends and governs the temporal affairs of men, the civil or political power; and is contradistinguished from *spiritual* or *ecclesiastical* power.[60]

A more modern definition:

> 4. pertaining to the world or to things not spiritual or sacred; relating to or connected with worldly things; disassociated from religious teaching or principles; not devoted to sacred, or religious use; temporal; nonecclesiastical; worldly; as, *secular* education, *secular* music.
>
> **Secularism,** *n.* **1.** secular spirit, views, *or* the like; especially, a system of doctrines and practices that rejects any form of religious faith and worship. **2.** the belief that religion and ecclesiastical affairs should not enter into the functions of the state, especially into public education.[61]

Any "system of doctrines and practices that rejects any form of [Biblical, *ed.*] religious faith and worship" as applicable to an area of life or thought is sin, antiGod, and is the work of the spirit of antichrist.

---

59. *History,* III. 151-154. "Eremite," or hermit. "Eremitical" — live like a hermit. *American Heritage Dictionary.*
60. *Webster,* 1828, s.v. "Secular."
61. *Webster's New Twentieth Century Dictionary,* Unabridged, Second Edition.

The plain fact is that the same weakness afflicts most Protestant attempts at educational philosophy that mars Roman Catholic educational philosophy — a neglect of the full reliance upon Scripture. And, let it be noted, this is true even of the theologically conservative groups; in doctrine they are thoroughly Biblical, but they have failed to see that the great truths of Scripture embrace even the so-called secular fields of knowledge. Despite their adherence to fundamental gospel truth, they have either not seen the unity of all truth in God or, recognizing this unity, have done little to make it a living reality throughout the whole of education. Thus much of evangelical educational thought has yet to move beyond a kind of scholastic schizophrenia in which a highly orthodox theology coexists uneasily with a teaching of non-religious subjects that differs little from that in secular institutions.[62]

Accordingly, the primary purpose of educating Christians is to equip them to take "fundamental Gospel truth" and Biblical precepts into every area of life and thought: family, work place, civil government, education, church, art, building trades, music, entertainment, crafts, &c. By default, Christian Monasticism delivers everything except *soul-winning,* prayer and dealing with inner attitudes to the ungodly.

Monasticism causes nationally known and respected Bible teachers, such as Chuck Swindoll, to say that it is unscriptural for a Christian to be involved in politics or to try to influence the world for Christ through political means. Absolutely nowhere, Swindoll dogmatically stated, in Scripture is there permission given for God's people to attempt such influence.[63]

Monasticism causes nationally known and respected Bible teachers to teach God's word from a subjective view to support their presuppositions. Their teachings, rather than influencing Christians to be salt and light in every area of life and thought, influence Christians worldwide to abandon all areas of society to the spirit of antichrist. Monasticism releases Christians from costly responsibility to God; it allows them to spend everything on personal peace and prosperity. Even the media, which wars against

---

62. *Introduction,* 41.
63. Chuck Swindoll, 8/9/86, over the Moody Broadcasting Network.

God, can place its finger on the problem of why society has lost its Christian influence, *i.e.*, "Premillennialism".[64]

Admittedly, salvation, Christian Conversion, cannot be legislated, nor can the world be influenced for Christ through political means. But Biblically sound laws, such as restitution, are the only laws that will restrain evil in society. Without proper laws, the freedom to preach the Gospel of Christ is lost. Only the Spirit through the preaching of the word will change men. Moreover, someone's morality will be legislated: either God's or Satan's.

Because of corruption in church leaders, Monasticism found grounds for renewal in the early 1800s. Its gradual development in the 1800s can be attributed not to its theological soundness, but to the overwhelming personalities and hard work of those involved. It further developed so that now, as of the beginning of the 21st century, Monasticism has come close to stripping the entire Church of the Lord Jesus Christ of its power and influence to change its surrounding society for godliness. In fact, that Monastic spirit stripped almost all hope from Christianity of bringing about any godly social change.[65]

Because of the zeal of the early formulators of modern Monasticism — "Premillennialism" — the movement was known for its missionary endeavors and evangelistic zeal. It went into every English speaking nation on earth, as well as many non-English nations with great power.[66] But with its message went its

---

64. *U.S. News & World Report,* Dec. 19, 1994, "THE CHRISTMAS COVENANT," rightly identified as modern "Premillennialism" the belief that Christian involvement in social issues is useless. They also identified Darby as the major founder in the Plymouth Brethren movement, out of which "Premillennialism" developed.

65. 44% of the general American population has the Premillennialists hope, or, should we say, *lack of hope:* "Americans who believe the Bible should be taken literally when it speaks of:... the Rapture of the church 44%." *Ibid.*

66. Though starting from different roots, the Keswick movement became very closely tied with the Brethren's Monastic movement: "In the first half he [the Apostle Paul] impresses upon us that the Church is other worldly..." *Keswick's,* 469. *The Secret of Power,* G. Cambell Morgan.

overwhelming pietistic spirit of otherworldliness and hopelessness.[67]

The result was that the dispensational ideas turned everything except *soul-saving* and personal *spirituality* over to the spirit of antichrist, the non-Christians. Socialism and Communism found extremely fertile grounds in the nations that received the Monastic gospel that viewed social involvement as sin.

Hosea answered effectively the modern doctrine of Monasticism (withdrawal), 8:4ff. God chides his people for ignoring his principles and laws in the area of civil government. In fact, as we follow through Hosea 8, we find that God's people were cut off for ignoring God's authority over civil government. Will we see the same?[68]

Pietism

Pietism! Is it bad or good? Judge for yourself.[69]

"Pietism was the reaction of the spirit against the letter. It sprang up in protest against the formalism of its day. But it represents a permanent spirit, for, much as tyranny provokes rebellion, and

---

67. The *Plot,* as revealed by MacPherson, succeeded in drawing attention away from dispensational premillennialim's originator, Irving, to its usurper, Darby. *U.S. News* reported the accepted version thusly: "It is the premillennialist view, with its elaborate timetables and graphic end-of-the-world scenarios, that has captured the most attention in recent years and that now has become the focus of scholarly scrutiny. While there are differences of opinion within the tradition, the dominant view, called dispensationalism, has its roots in the teachings of John Nelson Darby, a 19th-century Englishman and founder of the Plymouth Brethren. He taught that history is divided into seven ages, or dispensations, which will culminate in the final judgment and the end of the world. The dispensationalist scenario, popularized recently in evangelical writer Hal Lindsey's 1970 best seller, *The Late Great Planet Earth,* and by Dallas Theological Seminary Chancellor John Walvoord's *Armageddon, Oil and the Middle East Crisis,* is drawn largely from the Old Testament prophecy books of Ezekiel, Zechariah and Daniel and the enigmatic New Testament book of Revelation." In other words, though originating in Lacunza and Irving, modern dispensational teaching is recognized as basic Plymouth Brethren doctrine.

68. See also Acts 7:38.

69. The following from *Ethics,* s.v. "Pietism," "Revivals of Religion," "Sanctification."

licentiousness creates a Puritan reaction, so will formalism always call up some form of Pietism." It finds its roots in Philip Jacob Spener (1635-1705), 'The father of Pietism.' In his course of studies, he studied at Geneva. He there came under the "influence of A. Leger and Jean de Labadie, the ex-Jesuit, combined with the piety, mysticism, and strict discipline of the place [Geneva, *ed.*] to shape his character."[70]

> In 1675 Spener's Pia Desideria appeared in Frankfort. In it he advocated (1) earnest Bible study conducted in 'eccelsiolae in ecclesia'; (2) a lay share in Church government, as the proper consequence of the Christian doctrine of the priesthood of believers; (3) that knowledge of Christianity is practical, not theoretical, and shown in charity, forgiveness, and devotion; (4) that, rather than denouncing their errors, sympathetic treatment should be given to unbelievers, to win them, if possible, to truth; (5) that theological training should be reorganized and **emphasis laid on devotion rather than** on **doctrine;** and (6) that preaching should be more practical and less rhetorical. (Emp. added.)

Observe

First, Pietism was a reactionary move against the formalism of its day, particularly in the Lutheran Church — formalism in doctrine, one can quote the Catechism, so he is spiritual, and formalism in worship. By being a reactionary movement, Pietism went to the other extreme, and stripped Christianity of its outward discipline of holiness — as defined by the law of God and applied to all of society. Thus it removed the salt and extinguished the light from *secular* areas. Pietism, accordingly, replaced outward disciplines of holiness with inward communion with Christ, permitting the *secular* areas of life to depart from the law of God.

---

70. "In 1663, (Spener, *ed.*) became an assistant preacher at Strasburg; then (1666- 1686) engaged in preaching, teaching, and writing at Frankfurt. He called people together in semi-weekly meetings in his home for Bible Study, prayer, and discussion of the Sunday sermon. These meetings, known as *Collegia Pietatis,* gave to the people the mane of Pietists. *Who,* s.v. "Spener, Philip Jacob." Notice the appearance again of a Jesuit.

Second, Pietism "uprooted all sound theology" by stressing emotions and feelings over "correct knowledge in religion:" Feelings were exalted over theology. Pietism de-emphasizes Biblical doctrine and emphasizes personal emotions, feelings and relationships with Christ. Pietism preaches multitudes of sermons about the salvation of individual souls and conquering inner attitudes, but hardly, if ever, mentions applying God's Law-Word to surrounding social situations. It went hand in hand with the Brethren's otherworldliness and the Keswick emphasis on *personal holiness.*

Third, Pietism stressed the will in regard to conversion rather than the Spirit's work upon the understanding. The door is thus falsely opened for salvation, conversion, to simply be a matter of *accepting Christ* with no understanding of his substitutionary work for the sinner. Pietism, consequently, sees no need for solid Biblical instruction in the Gospel. Why is instruction needed if the will *makes a decision for Christ*"? One simply works on the will of the prospect to make him willing. There is no need to understand the Gospel nor understand one's actions.[71]

Fourth, Pietism emphasized "separation from the world" and all its problems and difficulties. It led to "acute repentance" — that is, excessive self-introspection.

Fifth, Pietism's withdrawal from the world led to "the formation of independent communities," further withdrawing Christian influence from society. This permitted society to go its own way because it was left without salt and light.

Sixth, Pietism permitted Christian liberty to become license. The indisputable result was that degeneration and evil of all kinds were accepted in the lives of Christians.

Seventh, "Pietism proclaimed a gospel of individual rather than universal salvation." In other words, like Irvingism/Darbyism, it

---

71. Note the clear violation of passages such as Rom. 10:14ff.; Eph. 1:13, &c. How, may we ask, can one trust in something he does not understand? Please see small booklet by this writer, *The Gospel Perverted.*

saw no hope for converting the world. It, therefore, reduced the Gospel to simply *soul saving;* it reduced Christianity to personal relationships with Christ. Now rather than all the world being conquered for Christ through the power of the Gospel and teaching of God's Law-Word, the conquering power of Christ is reduced to simply controlling inner emotions and attitudes.

Eighth, the result of Pietism's reduction of the Gospel to *soul-saving* was its tendency "to leave the Church and the world as evil and to seek purity in isolation." Consequently, Pietism defined purity and godliness in terms of withdrawal from the world, not as godly living in the midst of a crooked and perverse world and influencing the world for Christ.

Ninth, Pietism left every individual to determine his own course of action as his own god. It has no standard except the standard each establishes for himself according to the "divine will inwrought."

Tenth, Pietism "lowered conception of the church as the sphere and instrument of Christian salvation..."

Because Pietism was a reaction to the dead formalism of its day, it did bring with it some good points. It revealed the religious value of feelings and of practical Bible study. It removed conversion from purely an intellectual fact. It vindicated the rights of the layman who had been shut out by formal religion. It led to some improvement in the conduct of worship and a better liturgy as it produced and gave life to hymns. It brought a more intelligent form of worship. It emphasized the priesthood of the believer and the individual dignity of the child of God. It gave new life to philanthropic work — Francke established the famous Halle schools which educated between 2,000 and 3,000 poor children, and Pietism was a pioneer in foreign missionary activities.

Hastings points out that the Moravian Church was closely connected with Spener's Pietism movement, and the Moravians had a direct and determining influence on the origin of Methodism. Not only was its effect felt on John Wesley himself, but on his brother, Charles, and his friend, George Whitefield. All three were converted in the Moravian movement, and thus Spener's Pietistic, influence. The Moravian movement of Pietism was more spirited than Spener's as it cultivated hymn-singing that has stayed with the revival movements.

Therefore, when Darby and the early Brethren appeared with their opinions ("This is the way I feel it ought to be," and then they searched Scripture with "Bible readings" to justify their feelings), they practiced Pietism, a spirit already "in the air."

Revivalism

Revivalism is closely connected with Pietism.[72] We are not down-playing the importance of the conversion experience. But Revivalism places the emphasis upon an emotional experience, and it takes great care and makes great effort to heighten the emotions. (Moody showed modern revivalists how to work the emotions.) Then, far too often, the emotional experience is mistaken for conviction and a subsequent conversion experience. Worked up human emotions are many times mistaken to be the Holy Spirit conviction of sin.[73]

Revivalism places the emphasis upon an emotional experience with Christ, and the fact that the emotions were worked up is completely overlooked. Revivalism de-emphasizes sound Biblical doctrine, and emphasizes personal piety, personal emotions and feelings. Revivalism, no doubt, was a reaction to the prevailing dead, formal religion, but deadness cannot be the basis for a 'new method' of presenting the Gospel: Only God's word determines truth. An 1847 legitimate charge against Revivalism was that it "exaggerated individualism, no comprehension being displayed for the functions of the Church, the family, and the State…"[74]

---

72. Coad gives an excellent definition of Revivalism. *History,* by Coad, 279.
73. How many have traumatic emotional experiences when the genuine Gospel is not even present, nor is there genuine conversion as they return to the same sin after the emotion is gone.
74. *Ethics,* s.v. "Revivals of Religion."

Emotionalism was a consistent trait in Revivalism from Spener down through Wesley, G. Whitfield, R.M. McCheyne, D.L. Moody, H. Drummond and J. Edwards. Moreover, nearly all evangelists who have gone out since Moody "may be looked upon as his disciples and imitators, though some of them have developed novel methods in certain directions," *e.g.*, G.F. Pentecost, R.A. Torrey, J.W. Chapman, W.A. Sunday. They have followed in the Pietists-Revivalist tradition.[75]

---

75. *Ibid*. This work was published in the early 1900s. Many more Revivalists have followed since.

Appendix C
Manuel De Lacunza (*Ben-Ezra*)

Lacunza Y Diaz, Manuel De, Chilean theologian and Scripture scholar; b. Santiago, Chile, July 19, 1731; d. Imola, Italy, July 18, 1801. On Sept. 7, 1747, he entered the Society of Jesus and in 1755, he was ordained. On the expulsion of the Jesuits from Spain and its colonies in 1767, he went to Italy, where he led a retired life dedicated to meditation and study. This resulted in a book that later became famous, *Venida del mesias en gloria y majestad,* finished in 1790. It circulated in manuscript form before it was published in Cadiz, Spain, in 1812. It was later published in London, Mexico, Paris, and elsewhere, and translated into various languages. Lacunza used the Pseudonym Juan Josafat Ben Ezra. The book had, even among the Jesuits, fervent admirers as well as strong opponents. It was finally banned by the Holy Office on Sept. 6, 1824, and again on July 11, 1941, this time with specific reference to the book's moderate millenarianism. This was considered a fatal blow to the book among Catholics, although many of them, like Menendez Pelayo, believed before 1941 that the condemnation did not refer to millenarianism per se but rather to statements against the Roman Curia or statements offensive to the Fathers of the Church or in praise of Judaism. Among Protestants the book has become a symbol for some adventist sects. Lacunza's good faith and proper intentions cannot be doubted, although his mental health is questionable. His great reputation in Chile is based upon the depth of his thought, expressed in a polished style.[1]

Joseph Wolff

WOLFF, JOSEPH (1795-1862), missionary, the son of a Jewish rabbi of the tribe of Levi named David, by his wife Sarah, daughter of Isaac Lipchowitz of Bretzfeld, was born at Weilersbach, near Forchheim and Bamberg, in 1795.... When he was eleven his father became rabbi at Wiirtremberg, and sent him to the protestant lyceum at Stuttgart, whence he afterwards removed to Bamberg. While still a youth he learned Latin, Greek, and Hebrew. Leaving home on account of Christian sympathies, after many wanderings he was converted to Christianity in part through perusing the writings of Johann Michael von Sailer, bishop of Regensburg, and he was

---

1. *New Catholic Encyclopedia,* s.v. "Lacunza Y Diaz, Manuel De."

baptized on 13 Sept. 1812 [age, 17, *ed.*] by Leopold Zolda, abbot of the Benedictines of Emaus, near Prauge.... He arrived in Rome in the same year [1815, *ed.*], and was introduced to Pius VII by the Prussian ambassador. He was received on 5 Sept. 1816 as a pupil of Collegio Romano and afterwards of the Collegio di Propaganda, but about two years later, having publicly attacked the doctrine of infallibility and assailed the teaching of the professors, he was expelled from the city for erroneous opinions. After a visit to Vienna he entered the monastery of the Redemptorists at ValSainte, near Fribourg; but, disliking the system of the monastery, he shortly after came to London to visit Henry Drummond [q.v.], whose acquaintance he had made at Rome. He soon declared himself a member of the church of England, and at Cambridge resumed his study of oriental languages under Samuel Lee (1780-1852) [q.v.] and of theology under Charles Simeon [q.v.] He resolved to visit eastern lands to prepare the way for missionary enterprises among the Jews, Mohammedans, and Christians who inhabited them, and commenced his extraordinary nomadic career in oriental countries. Between 1821 and 1826 he travelled as a missionary in Egypt and the Sinaitic peninsula, and, proceeding to Jerusalem, and was the first modern missionary to preach to the Jews there.... While in England he met Edward Irving [q.v.], through whom he made the acquaintance of his first wife. About 1828 Wolff commenced another expedition in search of the lost ten tribes. He was twice married: first, on 6 Feb. 1827, to Georgiana Mary, sixth daughter of Horatio Walpole, second earl of Orford (of the second creation). By her he had a son, Sir Henry Drummond Wolff, G.C.M.G., who was named after his earliest English friend. She died on 16 Jan. 1859, and on 14 May 1881, he married, secondly, Louisa Decima, youngest daughter of James King (1767-1842) of Staunton court, Herefordshire, rector of St. Peter-la-Poer, London. Wolff was a singular personality. At home in any kind of society in Europe or Asia, he fascinated rather than charmed by his extraordinary vitality and nervous energy. He signed himself 'Apostle of our Lord Jesus Christ for Palestine, Persia, Bokhara, and Balkh,' and styled himself the Protestant Xavier. Xavier, indeed, was his constant model, and he 'lamented that he had not altogether followed that missionary in the matter of celibacy, such was the sorrow that their separation, but his frequent wanderings, brought on Lady Georgiana and himself' (SMITH, *Life of Wilson,* p. 124). Besides the work already mentioned, Wolff was the author of: 1. 'Sketch of life and Journal of Joseph Wolff,' Norwich, 1827, 12mo. 2. 'Missionary Journal and Memoir,' ed. John Bayford, London, 1824, 8vo; 2nd edit. 1827-9, 3 vols. 8vo. 3. 'Journal of Joseph Wolff for 1831,' London, 1832, 8vo. 4. 'Researches and Missionary Labours among the Jews, Mohammedans, and other Sects between 1831 and 1934,' Multa, 1835, 8vo; 2nd edit. London, 1835, 8vo. 5. 'Journal of Joseph Wolff, containing an Account of his missionary Labours from 1827 to 1831, and from 1835 to 1838,' London, 1889, 8vo. 6. 'Travels and Adventures of Joseph Wolff,' London, 1860, 2 vols. 8vo; 2nd edit. 1861; translated inGerman in 1863. [Wolff's Works: Gent. Mag. 1862, ii. 107-9; Burko's Peerage, s.v. 'Orford;' Burke's Landed Gentry, s.v. 'King;' Joseph Leech's Church-goer, 1847, i. 233-41; Memoir of Bishop Gobat, 1844, pp. 177-80; Smith's Life of Bombay, 1878, pp. 251-2.[2]

---

2. *DNB*, s.v. "Wolff, Joseph."

Works Cited

Listed below are only the more relevant works that have been used in forming the conclusions reached in the preceding text. This bibliography is by no means a complete record of material available on the subject discussed. This author urges the reader to continue the research into the important topic discussed in *Death of the Church Victorious*. The following references would be a good place to start.

In citing works in the notes, short titles have generally been used. Works frequently cited have been identified by abbreviations [text]:

Ben-Ezra, Juan. *The Coming of Messiah in Glory and Majesty*. 2 Vols. Translated by Edward Irving with a preliminary discourse by the Rev. Edward Irving. London: L.B. Seeley and Son, MDCCCXXVII. [*Ben-Ezra*] Ben-Ezra claimed to be a converted Jew—that is, converted to Romanism.

Biederwolf, William E. *The Second Coming Bible Commentary*. 1924. Reprint, Grand Rapids, MI: Baker Book House, 1985.

Bray, John L. *Morgan Edwards and the Pre-Tribulation Rapture Teaching (1788)*. Lakeland, Fl., n.d.

Bullinger, E.W. *The Apocalypse or "The Day of the Lord."* 1902. Reprint, Old Tappan, NJ. Fleming H. Revell Co., 1972

Carlyle, Thomas. *Reminiscence*. Ed. by James Anthony Froude. NY: Charles Scribner's Sons, 1881. Mr. Carlyle was personal acquaintance of Mr. Irving.

Coads, Roy. *A History of the Brethren Movement*. Great Britian: The Paternoster Press, 1968. Reissue, Greenwood, SC: The Attic Press, Inc., n.d. [Coad, *History*] Mr. Coad is fourth generation in this movement.

Darby, J.N. *The Collected Writings of J.N. Darby, Prophetic*. Vol. 3. Edited by William Kelly. London: G. Morrish, n.d. For the inquisitive and stout hearted, Darby's Collected Writtings can be obtained through used book stores or inter library loans. With Darby's permission, William Kelly "edited," i.e., changed, Darby's writings to not only make Darby say things he did not say, but to give him credit where credit was not due. See *The Rapture Plot*.

——. *Letters of J.N. Darby*. 3 vols. Oak Park, IL: Bible Truth Publishers, n.d. [*Letters*] Bible Truth Publishers probably were not the "official"

Plymouth Brethren publisher; apparently that "honour" belonged to Loirzeaux Brothers. Furthermore, there are many unidentified comments in the *Letters*, so the reader must assume that Darby's letters have been "edited," *i.e.*, changed, to support what the editor wanted the reader to attribute to Darby.

Edwards, Morgan. *Two Academical Exercises on Subjects bearing the following Titles; MILLENNIUM, LAST-NOVELTIES.* Philadelphia, PA: Morgan Edwards, A.M. And Quondam Fellow of R.I. College, M. DCC. LXXXVIII. [*Novelties*]

Ellis, William T. *"Billy" Sunday, The Man and His Message.* N.d. Reprint, Chicago, IL: Moody Press, 1959.

Gregg, Steve, editor. *Revelation, Four Views, A Parallel Commentary.* Nelson Publishing Company, Nashville. 1997. Mr. Gregg identifies the three millennial views, and gives a good history of various systems of interpretation of the Revelation. He also makes it clear that modern dispensationalism came from Rome to protect the pope. [*Revelation*]

Hastings, James, editor. *Encyclopedia of Religion and Ethics.* 13 vols. New York, NY: T & T Clark, 1908. [*Ethics*]

Hoffman II, Michael A. *Judaism's Strang Gods.* Coeur d'Alene, ID: The Independent History and Research Co., 2000.

Ironside, H.A. *A Historical Sketch of the Brethren Movement.* 1941. Neptune, NJ: Loizeaux Brothers, 1988. Ironside was an important figure in the Darbyite movement, and a staunch defender of the theories coming out of the 1825-1900 period of the Brethren. [*Sketch*]

Keil, C.F. and F. Delitzsch. *Commentary on the Old Testament.* 10 vols, n.d. Reprint, Grand Rapids, MI: Eerdmans, 1986.

Ladd, George E. *The Blessed Hope*, 1956. Reprint, Grand Rapids, MI: Eerdmans, 1983. [*Hope*]

LaRondelle, Hans K. *The Israel of God in Prophecy. Principles of Prophetic Interpretation.* Andrews University Press, 1983. Though a Seventh Day Adventist, LaRondelle does an excelent job proving that God's Word revolves around Christ, rather than around a renewed Jewish state. This author does not agree with everything in the book, but LaRondelle does an excelent job in *Prophetic Interpretation* this area. [*Israel*]

MacPherson, Dave. *"Deceiving and Being Deceived," The Biblical Examiner.* (Summer, 2001.)

———. *The Great Rapture Hoax.* Fletcher, NC: New Puritan Library, 1983

———. *The Rapture Plot.* Simpsonville, SC: 1995. [*Plot*]

Marsden, George M. *Fundamentalism and the American Culture. The*

Shaping of Twentieth-Century Evangelicalism: 1870-1925. NY/ Oxford: Oxford University Press, 1980.
McKibbens, Thomas R. and Smith, Kenneth L. *The Life and Works of Morgan Edwards.* NY: Arno Press, 1980. [*Morgan Edwards*]
Moody, William R. *The Life of D.L. Moody, by his son, William R. Moody.* 1900. Reprint, Murfreesboro, TN: Sword of the Lord Publishers, n.d. [*Moody*]
Müller, George. *The Life of Trust; being a Narrative of the Lord's dealings with George Müller, written by Himself.* A new edition brought down to the present time, including his visit to America. NY: John B. Alden. Entered into the Library of Congress in the year 1873, by Gould and Lincoln. Copyright, 1877. The first American edition was published in 1860.
Murray, Iain H. *The Puritan Hope.* Carlisle, PA: Banner of Truth Trust, 1975. [*Hope*]
Neatby, William B. *A History of the Plymouth Brethren.* London: Hodder and Stoughton, 1902. [Neatby, *History*]
Oliphant, Mrs. *The Life of Edward Irving–Minister of THE NATIONAL SCOTCH CHURCH, LONDON.* Illustrated by his Journals and Correspondence. London: Jurst and Blackett, Publishers. No date, but many first hand experiiences with Mr. Irving by the author starting before 1822. [*Irving*]
Olson, Carle E. *Will Catholics Be "Left Behind"?* Ignatius Press, San Francisco, 2003. Mr. Olson was raised in an anti-Catholic, Fundamentalist home, and for two years, attended a Fundamentalist college, following the dispensational, pretribulation rapture teaching into his adult years. He speaks of the fears that came with the dispensational view: fear of the possible future pain and terror, fear that computers may be used to implement the mark of the beast, and fear of other Christians who held non-dispensational views, for he was told that they were deceived by the Satan. Apparently, it was the unscripturalness of that dispensational system that influenced him to look elsewhere, leading him to Rome. Though he does defend Rome in some areas, he mentions them only in passing. He clearly attributes the idea of modern Dispensationalism to Roman theologians trying to take the Protestant pressure off the pope. (He points out that Post-Millennialism and Preterism were also offered by Rome for the same reason. Rome is Amillennial.) He attributes too much of the dispensational theory to Darby, and lightly passes over Irving. He deals with many of the same issues dealt with in *Death of the Church Victorious,* without making

the strong Jewish link to Millennialism. He does spend a lot of time on modern Dispensational writers, LaHaye, Lindsey, &c., effectively pointing out their hypocrisies, foolishness, inconsistencies and errors. [*Catholics.*]

Payne, J. Barton. *Encyclopedia of Bible Prophecy.* New York, NY: Harper & Row Publishers, 1973.

Price, Robert L. *The Rapture Cult, Religious Zeal And Political Conspiracy.* Signal Mountain, TN: Signal Point Press, n.d. [*Cult*]

Reese, Alexander. *The Approaching Advent of Christ.* Marshall, Morgan and Scott edition, 1937. Reprint, Grand Rapids, MI: Grand Rapids International Publications, 1975. [*Advent*]

Rowdon, Harold H. *The Origins of the Brethren. 1825-1850.* London: Pickering & Inglis Ltd., 1907. [*Origins*]

Sandeen, Ernest R. *The Roots of Fundamentalism. British and American Millenarianism 1800-1930.* Grand Rapids, MI: Baker Book House, 1970. [*Roots*]

Schaeffer, Francis A. *How Should We Then Live? The Rise and Decline of Western Thought and Culture.* Westchester, IL: Crossway Books, 1976.

Schuyler, English E. *Ordained of the Lord, H.A. Ironside.* Neptune, NJ: Loizeaux Brothers, 1976. A biography of Ironside, written by a personal friend at the request of his publisher, Loizeaux Brothers. Ironside was their best-selling author in the firm's history, and they reprinted this book in celebration of their fiftieth year. Loizeaux Brothers was the major publisher of Darbyite literature, publishing C.H. MackIntosh's material also.

Scott, Otto J. *Robespierre, The Voice of Virtue.* New York, NY: Mason & Lipscomb Publishers, 1974.

———. *The Secret Six, John Brown and the Abolitionist Movement.* Murphys, CA: Uncommon Books. Third printing, 1979.

Shedd, William. *Dogmatic Theology.* Originally Published in three volumes by Charles Scribner's Sons, 1889. Reprint in four volumes, Minneapolis, MN: Klock & Klock, 1979.

Smith, George. *The Dictionary of National Biography,* from Earliest times to 1900. Oxford University Press. (N.D.) [*DNB*]

Stevenson, Herbert. *Keswick's Authentic Voice, Sixty-Five Dynamic Addresses delivered at the Keswick Convention 1875-1957.* Selected and edited by Herbert Stevenson. Grand Rapids, MI: Zondervan Publishing House, 1959.

Strong, A.H. *Systematic Theology. Three Volumes in One.* Boston, MA:

The Griffith & Rowland Press, 1907.
Trapp, John. *Commentary on the Old & New Testaments.* 5 vols. 1865-1868. Reprint, Eureka, CA: Tanski Publications, 1997.
Webster, Noah, *American Dictionary of the English Language,* 1829. Facsimile edition. San Francisco, CA: Foundation for American Christian Education.
Moyer, Elgin S. *Who Was Who in Church History.* New Canaan, CT: Keats Publishing Inc., 1974. [*Who*]
Woodrow, Ralph. *Great Prophecies of the Bible,* 1971. Riverside, CA: Ralph Woodrow Evangelistic Association, Inc, third printing, 1979.

Various Other Works

These are works, some referred to in the text and some not, that the interested reader will find profitable for further study into the conclusions herein.

Anti-Nicene, Nicene and Post-Nicene Fathers. 38 vols. Grand Rapids, MI: Eerdmans. 1979 edition. [*Fathers*]
Armitage, Thomas. *A History of the Baptist, Traced by Their Vital Principles & Practices, from the Time of our Lord and Saviour Jesus Christ to the year 1886.* 1890. 2 vols. Wattertown, WI: Baptist Heritage Press, 1988.
Baron, David. *The Visions and Prophecies of Zechariah.* Grand Rapids, MI: Kregel Publications, 1918.
Blackstone, William. *Commentaries on the Laws of England.* 1753. Reprinted as *Jones' Blackstone*, Baton Rouge, LA: Claitor's Publishing Division, 1976.
Bridges, Charles. *Proverbs.* 1846. Reprint, Carlisle, PA: The Banner of Truth Trust, 1981.
Berkhof, Louis. *The History of Christian Doctrines.* 1937. Eerdmans. 9th printing, Granpid Rapids, MI: Baker Book House, 1988.
Canfield, Joseph M. *The Incredible Scofield And His Book.* Asheville, NC: Canfield, 6th printing, 1987. (Ross House Books, Vallecito, CA 95251.)
Crane, Frank. *The Lost Books of the Bible, and The Forgotten Books of Eden.* 1927. Reprint, n.p.: World Publishing, 13th printing, 1973.
Durham, James. *The Law Unsealed; Or A Practical Exposition Of The*

Ten Commandments. "Mr. James Durham, the late minister of the gospel at Glasgow. Printed by D. Schaw, Lawnmarket, 1802. To which are prefixed, the commendatory epistles of two famous English divines, Dr. John Owen [1616-1683, *ed.*] and Mr. Jenkyn." Mr. Jenkyn dated his note, "London, November 22, 1765."
Fairbairn, Patrick. *An Exposition of Ezekiel.* N.d. Reprint, Grand Rapids, MI: Zondervan Publishing House, 1960
———. *Fairbairn vs. Fairbairn, The Prophetic Prospects of the Jews.* Intro. by Mr. Pieters, 1930. Grand Rapids, MI: Eerdmans Publishing Co., n.d. Contains two messages by Fairbairn, one 1840 and another "about twenty-five years later."
———. *The Pastoral Epistles.* 1874. Reprint, Minneapolis, MN: Klock & Klock, 1980.
Finney, Charles. *Finney's Systematic Theology, 1846-47.* Ed. by J.H. Fairchild. Reprint, Minneapolis, MI: Bethany Fellowship Inc., 1964.
Gibbon, Edward. *The History of the Decline and Fall of the Roman Empire.* 1879. Notes by the Rev. H.H. Milman. 6 vols. NY: Harper & Brothers, n.d.
Hankes, J. Edward, editor. *An introduction to Evangelical Christian Education.* Chicago, IL. Moody Press, 1964.
Hengstenberg, Ernest Wilhelm. *Christology of the Old Testament.* 2 vols. 1864. Reprint, McLean, VA: MacDonald Publishing Co, n.d.
Josephus, Flavius. *The Life and Works of Flavius Josephus.* Trans. by William Whiston, Winston, NY: Holt, Rinehart and Winston, n.d.
Koch, Kurt E. *Occult ABC.* Grand Rapids, MI: Kregel Publications, 3rd printing, 1986.
Hanks, J. Edward, editor. *An Introduction to Evangelical Christian Education.* Chicago, IL: Moody Press, 1964.
Law, William. *The Power of the Spirit.* Edited by David Hunt. N.d. Reprint, Fort Washington, PA: Christian Literature Crusade, 3rd printing, 1971.
Lewin, Thomas. *The Siege of Jerusalem by Titus.* London: Longman, Green, Longman, Roberts, & Green, 1863.
Liddon, H.P. *Explanatory Analysis of St. Paul's First Epistle to Timothy.* 1897. Reprint, Minneapolis, MN: Klock & Klock, 1978.
The London Baptist Confession of Faith of 1689.
MacPherson, Dave. *The Incredible Cover-up.* Logos International, 1975.
Multimedia Encyclopedia Version 1, CDROM. The Software Toolworks, 1992.

Pierce, Larry. *Online Bible, CD ROM,* v.8.0. Ontario, Canada.
Provan, Charles D. *The Church is Israel Now.* Vallecito, CA: Ross House Books, Vallecito, CA, 1978. "Old and New Testament Scripture texts which illustrate the conditional privileged position and titles of 'Racial Israel' and their transfer to the Christian Church."
The Religions of the World. NY: Gray Brothers & Co, NY. 1883.
Salvian, the presbyter. *The Governance of God.* "Fathers of the Church, V. III." New York: CIMA Publishing Co., Inc., 1947. Fathers of the Church, V. III. Living about 400 AD, Salvian witnessed the fall of Rome.
Rushdoony, R.J. *The Institutes of Biblical Law.* N.p.: The Craig Press. 1973.
———. *World History Notes.* Fairfax, VA: Thoburn Press, 1973.
Scofield, C.I. *The Scofield Reference Bible.* 1909, 1917, 1937, 1945. Facsimile Series No. 2. Oxford, n.d. "With a new system of connected topical references..., and a new system of paragraphs."
———. *Rightly Dividing the Word of Truth.* 1896. Reprint, Neptune, NJ: Loizeaux Brothers, Inc., n.d.
Schaff, Philip. *History of the Christian Church.* 8 vols. 1910. Reprint, Grand Rapids, MI: Eerdmans, 1980.
Shedd, William. *Dogmatic Theology.* Originally Published in three volumes by Charles Scribner's Sons, 1889. Reprint in four volumes, Minneapolis, MN: Klock & Klock, 1979.
Stanley, Arthur Penrhyn. *Epistles of Paul to the Corinthians.* 1858. Reprint, Minneapolis, MN: Klock & Klock, 1981.
Spurgeon, C.H. *A Catechism with Proofs.* Reprint, Pasadena, TX: Pilgrim Publications, n.d.
———. *Lectures to My Students,* second series, reprinted from editions issued in England in 1875, 1877 and 1894 respectively. Grand Rapids, MI: Baker Book House, 5th printing, 1983
Taylor, Thomas, *Exposition of Titus.* 1619. Reprint, Minneapolis, MN: Klock & Klock, 1980.
Warfield, B. B. *Biblical and Theological Studies.* Philadelphia, PA: Presbyterian and Reformed Publishing Company, 1952.
———. *Perfectionism.* Ed. by Samuel G. Craig. Grand Rapids, MI: Baker Book House, 1958.

Index

Scripture Index

Genesis
 1:31, i
 12:1-3, 440
 15:13, 88
 18:25, 360
 22:18, 440
 49:10, 440
Exodus
 3:12, 216
 4:14, 216
 28:3, 202
 31:3-6, 202
 35:31-36, 202
Leviticus
 25:18, 202
 26:3-13, 202
Deuteronomy
 3:1-5, 427
 4:24, 453
 28, 29, 238
 28-32, 129
 29:29, 233
 32:4, 360
Joshua
 1:7, 8, 202, 239
 1:8, 105
 7, 205
2 Samuel
 7:12ff, 440
1 Chronicles
 22:8, 72, 119
 28:1-3, 119
Psalms
 1, 239
 1:2, 105
 2, 107, 120, 212
 2:8, 399

 2:9, 108
 2:12, 108
 5:5, 360
 7:9-12, 360
 14, 376
 18:24-26, 360
 19:7ff, 53
 22:27, 91
 45, 71
 58:4, 404
 58:10, 404
 72, 440
 89, 440
 91, 175
 94:20, 400
 102, 120
 110, 440
 110:1, 108
 119:9ff, 53
 119:142, 354
 119:151, 53
 149:7-9, 71
Proverbs
 13:22, 177
 18:13, 1
 18:17, 1
 22:3, 165
 27:12, 165
Ecclesiastes
 12:13, 14, 129
Isaiah
 9, 70, 75
 9:1, 2, 117
 9:2, 70, 77, 284
 9:5, 27
 9:6, 70, 284
 9:6, 7, 440
 11, 87
 11:6, 120
 11:9, 197

477

11:11, 9
24, 80
32, 96
35:1, 2, 120
42:5, 440
65, 120
66, 120
Jeremiah
5:31, 306, 426
8:6, 212
23, 165
30:7, 352
Ezekiel
37, 350
38, 9
38, 39, 8
39:12-16, 73
40-48, 74
43, 44, 8
Daniel
2:27, 82
2:34, 35, 228
2:40-44, 350
2:24, 440
7, 135
7:13, 70
7:18, 27, 8
9:27, 160
12, 92, 349, 350
12:4, 439
12:11, 351
13:13, 351
Hosea
8:4ff, 459
13:9, 216
Habakkuk
2:14, 197
Zechariah
13:9, 85
14, 73
Malachi
3:3, 85
4:2, 401

Matthew
4:14, 15, 77
4:15, 16, 70, 77, 106, 284
5:13-16, 216
5:17, 338, 454
5:48, 360
12:42, 72
12:45, 4
13, 234
13:24-30, 421
13:24-30, 36-42, 197
13:31, 32, 228
16:28, 8
18, 411
18:20, 422
20:21, 125
21-24, 68
21:41, 218
22:24, 108
23, 24, 86
23:36, 83, 106
24, 78, 83, 107, 246, 349, 350, 351, 432, 433
24:8, 352
24:15, 16, 352
24:15ff, 351
24:21, 352
24:23, 24, 142
24:36, 125
25:26, 375
26:64, 106
26:65, 106
27:51, 275
28:19, 20, 56, 242, 341, 342
Mark
3, 445
11:23, 24, 253
12:36, 108
13, 351, 433
14:62, 106
14:64, 106
Luke
4:16-21, 440

17, 21, 433
17:20ff, 440
20:43, 108
22:67, 106
23:3, 14, 440
24:21, 125
24:44-47, 454
24:44ff, 87
John
3:4, 101
3:16, 293
7:25, 78
10:12, 28, 419
10:16, 55
14, 254
14:3, 418, 423
14:6, 354
14:20, 417
16:7-11, 91
16:8, 146
16:13, 14
17, 12
17:17, 53
17:18, 455
18:36, 440
18:38, 440
19:4, 6, 440
21, 234
21:22, 8
Acts
1:5, 418
1:6, 71, 125, 440
2, 418
2:14, 83
2:27-36, 71
2:30, 71
2:35, 108
2:47, 422
4, 418
4:24-28, 71
7:38, 459
8:36, 270
15:14, 197
17:6, 180

19:2, 314
20:29, 30, 419
21:34, 395
26:18, 103
Romans
1:29-31, 420
2:6, 360
3:10ff, 376
3:19-30, 101
3:20, 116, 358
5:12, 359
5:14, 99
6:14, 166, 354
8:1, 418
8:15, 423
8:37, 383
9:2, 52
10:2, 299
10:12, 430
10:14, 461
10:17, 58
11, 116
11:25, 55
12:19, 27
13:1-7, 453
13:8, 239
13:8-10, 453
1 Corinthians
2:14, 175
3:13, 16, 17, 421
3:16, 72
6:17, 418
6:19, 418
8:13, 418
10:11, 340
10:31, 99, 106, 129, 244
11:16, 427
11:25, 26, 206
12:27, 419
15:10, 376
15:22ff, 99
15:24-28, 120
15:53-57, 71
15:57, 124

2 Corinthians
5:17, 101
6:16, 72
9:8, 455
10:5, 455
11:4, 454
12:14, 98
Galatians
3:24, 357, 369, 370
3:28, 86
4:24, 13
6:6, 455
6:24, 355
Ephesians
1:13, 461
1:13, 14, 418
1:20, 99
1:22, 23, 251
2, 430
2:1, 5, 418
2:19-21, 421
3:10, 251
4:14, 167
4:17ff, 103
6:18, 146
Philippians
2:13, 101, 376
3, 399
3:15, 4
3:20, 21, 418
Colossians
1:10, 455
2:20, 400
1 Thessalonians
1:9, 10, 416, 418
2, 45
4:16, 17, 56
5:4-7, 79
2 Thessalonians
2, 42, 112
2:1, 2, 146
2:3, 43
2:7, 8, 420

1 Timothy
1:19, 58
3:6, 175
4:2, 142
4:17, 58
6:5, 6, 151
6:13, 455
6:17, 3
6:20, 449
2 Timothy
2, 270
2:15, 220
2:17, 26, 58
2:19-21, 420
2:22, 172
3, 142
3:1-13, 197
3:1-5, 420
3:5, 420
3:12, 13, 420
3:16, 58, 453
3:17, 455
Titus
2:7-10, 455
2:13, 375
Hebrews
1:13, 108
4:11, 239
6:1, 2, 58
7:12, 114
8:6-9, 116
10:13, 108
10:14, 18, 419
10:16, 370
10:19, 419
12:27-29, 120
12:29, 453
James
1:22, 4, 128
1 Peter
1:6, 360
4:17, 422
2 Peter

1, 234
1:3, 93
3, 142
1 John
1:5-10, 360
2:1, 2, 364
2:18, 19, 420
2:18-22, 160
3:4, 116, 166, 344
3:8, 122
3:22, 238, 255
4:3, 361
4:4, 146
4:3, 160
Jude, 142
4, 5, 420
Revelation
1:1, 19, 439

3:10, 180
4:1, 69, 81, 112, 434
4:16, 17, 56
9:1, 85
9:3, 41
11, 109
13, 44, 135, 431
16, 135, 377
16:10, 97, 371
16:11, 431
17, 348
17:11-14, 350
19, 16
20, 54, 121, 436
20:2, 42
20:4, 5, 8, 211
21:21, 362
22:6, 7, 10, 439

General Index

A

Abbot Joachim, 437
Abolitionist Movement, 279
  See Finney, C.
Abomination of Desolation, The, 82
Abraham, blood ties to, 52
Adams, J., 430
Advent, Second, 31, 36, 37, 38, 42, 43, 45, 53, 63, 65, 79, 88, 91, 93, 94, 95, 96, 98, 100, 104, 105, 107, 111, 112, 118, 122, 132, 134, 135, 139, 148, 151, 213, 230, 244, 252, 255, 404, 446
  Already past, 441
  Augustine, 445
  Chiliasm & Strong, A.H., 233
  Christ's kingdom, 28
  Contrary to universal public opinion, 54
  Darby lectures on, 392
  Darby's view, 386, 387, 390
  Date set, 1843 or 1847, 264
  Imminent, 217, 325
  Irving, 34
  Jewish doctrine, 441
  Jewish glories, 28
  Just wait, 337
  Millenarianism, Chiliasm, 439
  Motive for expansion, 243
  Second Adventism, 228
  Speculations about, 132, 230
  Standard view, 18th century, 39
  Wait for, 337
  Wolff, Joseph
    Jewish hope, 391
    Preacher of, 140
Advent, Second. See Keswick; Prophecy Conferences; Revelation, views of
Aestheticism, 331
Albury Park. See Prophecy Conferences
Alcazar, 44
  See Jesuits
America
  Christian nation, 1870's, 330
  Christian spirit before/after Darby, 305
  Conversion
    To Darbyism, 303, 311, 373
  Darby in, 302
  Dispensationalism considered heretical, 263
  Resistance to Darbyism, 307
  Ruin of the Church, version of, 373
Amillennialism
  Defined, 429
  False charges against, 437
  Founder of, 430
  Kingdom of God on earth, 430
Anabaptist, 446, 448
  Baptists, English, 448
  Mennonites, 448
  Millennialism, and, 447
Anglican Church, temper of, 163
Ante-Nicene Fathers. See Church Fathers
Anti
  Clergy, 169
  Intellectual spirit, 169
Antichrist, 42, 43, 54, 57, 59, 74, 85, 105, 106, 112, 121, 122, 133, 148, 149, 160, 206, 252, 259, 336, 352, 382, 394, 436, 442, 455, 456, 457, 459
  Already alive (A.D.1200), 435
  Darby claims ideal of, 45
  Doctrine defused attacks against pope, 68
  Future
    Individual, 43
    Literal, papist fable, 43
    Newly placed into, 45, 57
    Rome placed him there, 41
  Idea introduced, 142

Many already here, 420
Nero, 44
Papacy, 43, 431
Personal
  Appearance of, 45, 54
  Developed, 393
  Introduced, 352
  Pope considered the, 41
  Richard (1135-1202) told about, 435
  Those who considered pope, 42
Antichrist. *See* Pope
Appearance
  Over Scripture, 70, 75, 118, 156
Areas Conquered
  America, 301
  British Guiana, 254
  British Isles, 241
  China, 196
  Eastern Europe, Russia, &c., 255
  Germany, 239
  India, 243
  Romania, 255
  Switzerland, 246
Armageddon, Battle of, 122
Armstrong, H.W., 434, 437
Augustine. *See* Church Fathers
Augustinian view of Millennium
  Rejected by Lacunza, 60
Authority
  Civil
    Involvement unlawful, 336
    Magistrate unlawful for Christian, 193
    Privileges, no responsibilities, 337
    Unlimited submission to, 400, 403
    Only in home, 193
Awakening
  Newly defined, 93, 214

B
Babbling, profane, 449
Babylon, 44
Baptism and sin, 271
Baptist, 11, 278

Anabaptist, 448
Brethren, difference between, 272
Confessions of Faith, 268
Conversion to Brethrenism, 11
Conversion to Darbyism, 265, 276
Darby's hatred for, 269
Darby's influence among, 291
Errors according to Darby
  Eyes on future, 268
  Seeing only one gospel, 274
  Heritage changed, 268
  Jewish nation restored, against, 274
  Nothing poorer than, 270
  Obligation to Lord's law, 268
Barnes, A., 432
Barnhouse, D.G. *See* Brethren
Beast, the, 16
Beecher, H. W., 296, 329
  Start of Christian Psychology, 331
Ben-Ezra document
  Given to conclude canon., 67
Ben-Ezra System, 47
  1260 years discovered, 102
  5 novelties of, 109
  A voice from Rome, 62
  Account of, Albury Park, 386
  America before/after, 305
  America's conversion to, 303
  Antichrist, Personal, 122
  Armageddon, Battle of, 122
  Becomes Darbyism, 161, 237
  Changes
    Character of Scripture to fit, 403
    Protestant view of papal power, 66
  Christ cannot satisfy, 86
  Christ not the end of prophecy, 86
  Contrary to orthodoxy, 76
  Conversion = proselytizing, 93
  Daniel's stone yet to come, 91
  Daniel's view of Christ's kingdom, 112
  Darby plagiarized, 185
  Darby's zeal spreads, 179

Index 485

David must return as literal king, 90
Defined, 46
Defines Jewish hope, 75
Denial of spiritual judgment, 106
Financed by Buenos Ayres government, 59
First Protestant defenders, 34
Fundamentalism, root of, 57
God exalts & glorifies man, 124
Heresy, charged with, 89
Hopeless, only political hope, 108
Imminent return, 92, 103
Introduced by Irving, 31
Irving acquires, 59
Jew/Gentile distinction in Christ, 86
Jewish dispersion/regathered, 106
Jewish hope restored, Josephus, 74
Jewish hope restored, Zionism, 60
Jewish restoration, 90
Josephus, 82
Law vs. grace, 113
Like no other prophecy, 67
Made Protestant, 56
Millennialism revived, 49
Millennialism, fountainhead of, 45
Motivated by Jews, 52
New understandings introduced, 77
Not new, 49
One vs. two resurrections, 102
Peace keepers, 119
Prophecy conferences, 110
Psalms 45 & 149, literal, 71
Purpose to exalt Jewish nation, 75
Purpose to exalt Jews, 52
Purpose to restore Jewish hope, 51
Rejected Augustinian view, 60
Roman document, 64
Rome, problem solved for, 41
Ruin of the Church introduced, 91
Summed up by Irving, 76
Supports popery, 73
Three goals of, 51
Three points of, 89
Two resurrections required, 102

Wait for Second Advent, 90
See Church/Israel distinction
See Futurism
See Revelation, views of
See Zionism
Ben-Ezra. *See* Jesuits
Bengel, J.A., 446
Bethesda and Darby, 209
Bible
   Always study with Church/Israel distinction, 286
   God confused when He gave it, 284
   Unscientific, misleading, 328
Bible Readings, 68, 77, 305
   America, new in, 294
   American style, 312
   Arbitrary & unhistorical, 282
   Dangers of, 283
   Darbyism's basic strength, 284
   Defined, 292, 294
   Developed, 282
   French Revolution, 283
   Millennialism's foundation, 205
   Moody's conversion to, 292, 294
   Pietism, 463
   Prophetic Puzzle, &, 284
   Prove dispensationalism, 281
   Solve God's problem, 284
   Spurgeon against, 24
Biola College discovered Millennial Money Machine, 2
Blackstone, Sir William, 164
Blessed Hope
   Escape from tribulation, 219, 220
   Misused, 375
Boehe, J., 13
Bolshevik Revolution and Millennialism, 256
Bounds, E.M., 265
Bradford, J., 42
Brethern
   Mackintosh, C.H., 21, 147, 265
   Moody's connection with, 297
Brethren

Anderson, Sir Robert, 22
Barnhouse, D.G., 22, 265, 333
Bellett, J. G., 143, 172
Bounds, E.M., 22
Chapman, J.W., 22, 265
Chapman, R.C. (1803-1902), 21, 199
China Inland Mission, 196
Craik, H., 143, 195
Cronin, E., 21, 172
Dixon, A.C., 25
Drummond, H. (1786-1860), 21, 129, 199
Evans, J.H., 199
Grant, W.F., 21
Groves, A.N., 21, 174
Hall, P.F., 21, 143, 193
Inter-Varsity, 22
Ironside, H.A., 5, 22, 265, 332, 428
  Barnhouse, D.G., 333
  Darbyite, 332
  Defends lawlessness, 354
  Presented Brethren doctrine, 189
  Statement by, 5
  Strong, A.H., vs., 354
Irving, E., 21, 171
Jukes, A., 21
Kelly, W., 21
Lang, G.H., 21
Mackintosh, C.H., 21, 297
McVicker, J.G., 21, 265
Moody, D.L., 22
Moorehouse, H., the man who moved Moody, 21
Müller, G., 21, 23, 143, 195, 265
  Against conversion of world, 196
  At Powerscourt, 198
  Departs from Baptists, 195
  Scriptural Knowledge Institution, 21, 196, 254
Murray, A., 22, 265
Nee, W., 21, 255, 265
Newman, F.W., 21, 189

Newman, J.H., 21
Newton, B.W., 21, 143, 190
Powerscourt, Lady, 21
Stanley, C., 21
Sudan Interior Missions, 22
Sunday, W.A, 265, 464
Sunday, W.A., 22
Taylor, H., 21, 196, 265
  China Inland Missions, 196, 198
  Scofield, C.I., 198
Torrey, R.A., 22, 258, 265, 464
Tregelles, S.P., 21, 200, 265
Vine, W.E., 21, 265
Wigram, G.V., 21, 143, 192, 265
See Darby, J.N.
See Moody, D.L.
See Scofield, C.I.
Brethrenism
  Baptist mix, 199
  Immigration, spread by, 240
  Origin of, 411
Bristol Academy, 7
Brookes, J.H.
  Darby, 312
  Scofield, C.I., and, 326, 327
Brothers, Richard (1757-1824)
  Anglo-Israelism, 171
Buenos Ayres government financed Ben-Ezra, 59

C

Calvin, J., 431
Calvinism
  Darby against Post view, 218
  Darbyism, vs., 180
  Irvingism's connection, 265
  Millennialism, 208, 312
Campbell, Mary, 148, 155, 157
Camping, H., 264
Cashless economic system, 436
Chafer, Lewis Sperry, 267
Changed Christ's words, 215
Changed meanings
  Christ's reign, 88

Daniel 12, symbolical to literal, 92
Faith, 104
Faithlessness, 103
Latter rain, 85
Overcometh, 401
Satan's work on earth, 103
Chapman, J.W. *See* Brethren
Chick, J., 126
Children, sinful to prepare for, 176
Chiliasm, 73, 146, 158, 211, 233, 326, 450
  Christ's reign literal, 439
  Early church's view of, 210
  Held by, 441
  Historic defined, 439
  Jewish Zionism, 136
  Literal interpretation repudiated, 444
  Protestant, 233
  Strong's (A.H.) view of, 233
  View until Augustine, 445
  See Millennialism
Chilton, D., 429
China Inland Mission
  Conquered China, 255
  Social withdrawal, 198
  Taylor, H., & death, 196
Chinese troops, 436
Christ Jesus
  Caiaphas, before, 106
  Common view before Irving, victorious, 27
  David's throne, on, 71, 88
  Failed in redemption, 123
  His mission, Lacunza's view, 122
  Imminent return of, 276
  Irving against victorious, 53
  Lacunza, against victorious, 70
  Leader of literal warlike Jewish nation, 70
  Nations exempt from Christ's judgment, 399
  Not now king, reason why, 117
  Not Prince of Peace until Millennium, 120
  Peace in literal reign only, 88
  Peace keeper, 119
  Powerless during church age, 109
  Reign spiritual only, 83
  Replaced with literal nation, 87
  Return of, 441
  Rule summarized, 118
  Victim, a, 344
  Victorious reign, 70
Christian
  Calling, just wait, 224, 400
  Defeatism, 427
  Mysticism, 15
    Müller, 238
  No judgment for, 403
  Reconstruction, 429
  Retreat from secular affairs, 169
  Retreat, immense peril of, 260
  Separated from world, 223
Christian Science, 437
Christianity
  Dead & unconcerned about evil, 400, 403
  Melancholy state, 213
  Neutralized, 56, 212, 224, 244
  Taylor's neutralized China, 199
  Turned into mystical experience, 224
  War against, 17
Christians
  Hopless during church age, 35
Church
  As seen by Marcion, 454
  Cannot reach world, 38
  Darby's view, 186, 231
  Dispensation failed, 204
  Early belief of, 442
  Failed, 84
  Forbidden to set evil right, 187
  Heavenly society only, 222
  Jewish must be reestablished, 232
  Jewish, new source of mission activity, 91
  Jewish, the true, 89
  Last enemies of, Muslims & Rome, 9

Moravian, 462
New Israel, 430
Newly defined, 80
No earthly use, 21
No place in prophecy, 186, 219
No responsibility to OT Law, 357
No worldly concerns, 187
Only Scriptures for, 267
Origin of, true, 220
Removal of, 251
Removal of, new idea, 247
Ruin of, 48
  Irving's idea, 80
  Wrongly credited to Darby, 353
State, separation of, 448, 455
Strength not in doctrine, 201
Through tribulation, 442
Useless, 222
Visible only, 232
Church Fathers
Adreas of Cappadocia, 433
Alexander, 444
Alexandrian
  Augustine, 434
  Clement of Alexandria, 434
  Origen, 434
  Rejected Millennialism, 434
  Tyconius, 434
Ambrose's, 154
Arethas, 433
Asterius Urbanus against tongues, 152
Augustine, 50, 444, 445
  Amillennialism, 430
  Anti-Millennialism, 445
  City of God, 430
  Eliminated Second Adventism, 445
  Millennial view rejected by Lacunza, 60
Believed Church is New Israel, 430
Christians are true Jews, 74
Clement, 444

Commodianus, 441
Eusebius, 433
Hippolytus, 441
Irenaeus, 441, 442
Jerome, 50
Justin Martyr, 74, 441, 451
  Chiliast, 443
  Trypho the Jew, 50
Lactantius, 441
Methodius, 441
Origen, 444
Papias, 441, 442
Polycarp, 450, 451
Tertullian, 441, 450
Tertullian against Marcion, 454
View of Matthew 24, Revelation, 82
Church/Israel Distinction, 1, 47, 57, 172, 247, 275, 285
Darby's version, 1840, 251
Defined, 47
Developed, 147
Doctrine, new, 246
Key to dispensationalism, 48
Lindsey's view, 127
Origin of, Lacunza, 80
Rapture added, 56
Required for Protestant Zionism, 48
Scripture studied accordingly, 48, 286
Those against are demonic, 48
Two gospels, results in, 239, 346
See Zionism
Civil. *See* Authority
Clarke, A., 432
Clergy vs. laity, 169, 324
Coming of the Lord
Darby's version, 96
Defined, 95
Commandments
Dismissed as the rule for life, 113
Common
Enemy unites various groups, 278
Public Opinion

One coming of Christ, 49
Communism. *See* Dispensationalism
Conferences. *See* Prophecy
Conferences
Conflict, Anglican-Roman, 223
Congregational Church order, 144
Conversion
 America's, 311
 Baptists to Irvingism/Darbyism, 266
 Darby defines as proselytizing, 93, 214, 269
 Presbyterians to Irvingism/ Darbyism, 266
 World's, hope of, geat error, 350

D

Dallas Theological Seminary, 267
Daniel
 69/70th week, 186, 232
 Developed, 220
 Parenthesis new idea, 351
 Beast, Rome changed to future, 66
 Book of, 285
 Image not smitten yet, 91
 Orthodox view changed, 112
 Powerscourt developed ideas, 393
 Vision's Stone introduced, 350
Darby, J.N., 21, 143, 179
 Against Baptists, 265
 Against obedience, 272
 Against Postmil Reformers, 187
 Against sermon preparation, 230
 Against voting, 398
 America converts, 302
 America, proselytizing in, 266
 Baptism, &, 271
 Calls Wesleyanism Satanic, 245
 Changes history, 444
 Changes reformers and Hymns, 204
 Changes words for support, 160
 Christendom failed, 247
 Church is not universal, 346
 Church splits excite, 308
 Claims credit for Antichrist idea, 352
 Claims inspiration, 369, 408
 Compares self to Paul, 340
 Confrontations, dislikes, 184
 Darbyite spirit dangerous, 24
 Defines Zionism, 75
 Divides Mat 24:15 from 16, 352
 Doctrine analyzed, 405
 Doctrine of escape, 250, 407
 Following grows, 263, 374
 Gives his background, 405
 Gospel, more than one, 275
 Great Tribulation, claims idea, 351
 Identifies with Paul, 395
 Imminent return, 213
 Ironside followed, 6, 332
 Just wait, 416
 Law/Commandments, view of, 356
 Matthew 27:51, 275
 Meets Moody, 291
 Most destructive to Christianity, 415
 Motives, 245, 405
 Mystic
  Feelings vs. Scripture, 406
  Not a theologian, 182
 Never defines sin, 359
 New doctrine caused riots, 247, 347
 New doctrine summarized, 405
 New insights discovered, 251
 New prophetic scheme, 252
 New view of Mat. 24, 351
 Newton, conflict with, 158, 178, 234, 247, 363
 Powerscourt, at
  See Prophecy Conference
 Proselytize, sees his calling to, 375
 Proselytizes in North America, 291
 Proselytizes new converts, 303
 Proud of his humility, 405
 Refused Matthew 18, 235
 Religious liberty, asked for, 395
 Riding accident, 189
 Risen with Christ defined, 407
 Satan, king of earth, 361
 Secular vs spiritual, 456
 Sin, answer for, 362

Sin, highest form of abstraction, 359
Sin, view of, 51
Spreads Millennialism, 447
Switzerland, in, 250, 412
Translation, motive, 180, 358
Darbyism
  America's early rejection of, 307
  Depends upon proselytism, 237
  Growth, Darby's account of, 411
  Money &, 306
  Preached in self-defence, 241
  Robs churches, 303, 375
  Robs pastors, 242
Darwin, C., 277
Dates
  Date setting, 263
  Important, 9, 190
  Important (1874), 374
Dead
  Burying of in Ezekiel, 73
  To this world defined, 309
  With Christ defined, 407
Death
  Air, in the, 12
  Emphasis on, 39
  Fascination with, 228
Demonic
  Being against Church/Israel Distinction, 48
  Utterances, tongues/rapture, 152
Denominations Conquered
  Baptist, 241
  Congregational, 241
  Mennonite, 241
  Pentecostal, 241
  Presbyterian, 265
Destiny of the Jews, 250
Devotedness defined, 303
Dispensationalism, 16, 25, 35, 38, 52, 56, 57, 66, 77, 118, 127, 134, 135, 146, 151, 152, 155, 159, 173, 220, 226, 228, 234, 235, 252, 257, 259, 261, 266, 267, 276, 277, 278, 284, 286, 287, 325, 340, 342, 345, 346, 350, 354, 359, 365, 380, 403, 405, 434, 435, 437
  Against Christ the Victorious, 70
  America considered heretical, 263
  Answer, become more spiritual, 314
  Attracts great wealth, 177
  Basis of modern, 68
  Bible Readings prove, 281
  Christ helpless, 374
  Church/Israel distinction required, 48
  Contrary to orthodoxy, 76
  Darby defends new system, 437
  Darby's scheme, 338
  Defined, 11, 257
  Defines Israel, 47
  Denies history, 444
  Depends on escape mentality, 378
  Developed while in seizure, 152
  Dispensational Premillennialism, 36, 45, 57, 58, 142, 163, 171, 404, 428, 459
  Avoided in America, 307
  Dispensations
    Another needed, 247
    Christian failed, 247
    Jewish, Church, 147
    Jewish-Christian developed, 251
  Distinctions, new, 251
  Divide Bible & conquer, 286
  Exalted Jewish Church, 59
  Fundamentalism, 284
  Glorifies man, 35
  Great Tribulation, 351
  Ideas not new, 339
  Lawless, 366
  Leads to Socialism, Communism, 459
  Literalism, 435
  Marcion, 338
  Marxism &, 257
  Millennialism, 381

Money Machine, 2, 206, 280, 379
Müller, 21
Neutralized Protestant attacks, 68
No answers, 408
No responsibility, 177
No Word from God, 340
Opposition to, 23
Outlandish ideas offered, 285
Plays on fear, 379
Power of, 378, 379
Protestant Zionism, 74
Proved by money, 176
Purpose to restore Jewish hope, 51
Rearranges Bible for better understanding, 284
Resists dialogue, 379
Revolves Word of God around Israel, 79
Scofield Reference Bible, 347
Scofield's seven dispensations, 324
Scofield-Brooks, 327
Scripture according to LaHaye, &c., 127
Solves God's problem, 284
Theories develop, 319
Why developed, 234
See also Millennialism
Dispensations
First time 7 are used, 435
Divine Providence, 427
Divine will inwrought, 357, 369, 370
Doctrine
Chaotic, impossible to follow, 182
Firm stand rejected, 24
Lacunza's
Added to at 1833 Powerscourt, 143
American's introduction to, 263
Changed Scripture's character, 403
New, Distinctive, 175
Worms contained in, 239
Drummond, Henry, 447
Drummond, Henry (1851-1897), 464
Moody &, 297

E

Earthly hope abandoned, 174
Economy still to come, 218
Education, against, 217
Edwards, J., 42, 429, 431
Great Awakening, 265
Edwards, Morgan (1722-1795), 10, 15, 19, 44, 47, 54, 59, 65, 77, 145, 185, 218, 352
Darby compared with, 9
Eschatology of, 8
First to offer Millennialism, 6
Last-Novelties, lectured on, 8
Ellis, F.M., 313
Emigration. See Immigration
Emotionalism, 464
Escape through prophecy, 231
Eusebius, 432
Evangelical
First use of name, 3
Evangelization defined, 320
Evolution, Theory of, 331
Exegetical problem solved, 284, 404
Ezekiel
Ch. 39 literal, a popery legend, 73
Dry bones, 350

F

Fairbairn, P., 70, 73
Faith
OT only contains examples of, 340
Redefined, 238
To be established in, defined, 375
Faithfulness, newly defined, 371
Faithless defined, 215
Family, concerning the, 407
Fear
Dispensationalism plays on, 379
Of non-Dispensational doctrine, 1
Fig Tree
Darby claims as his idea, 353
Finney, C., 19, 432
Ardent abolitionist, 279, 289, 337
Calvinism, against, 279
Fanned the Flames of War, 279

Revivalism, 278
First Resurrection, 445
Fleming, Robert, 431
Fox, J., 431
Freedom offered, 24
French Revolution, 16, 37, 212, 283, 304, 431
  Changed views of prophecy, 16
  Date, 15
  Effects on theology, prophecy, 15
  Fulfilled prophecy - end near, 31
  Fulfilled Rev. 13, 37
  Key to prophetic understanding, 135
  Liberalism, 18
  No answers for, 37
  Prepared way for millennialism, 10
  Prophetic speculations about, 129
  Rise of patriotism, 17
  War against Christian culture, 17
  World prepared by, 51
Frere, Hatley, 40
Fundamentalism
  Defined, 287
  Founded by Rome, 57
  Meaning of name, 3
  See Dispensationalism
Future
  Against working for, 191, 216, 244
  Evil of seeking to know, 233
  Work for forbidden, 98
  See Sin
Futurism, 43, 44, 57, 428, 433, 435
  (42 mo. &c.) system's origin, 60
  Attracts people, 58
  Darby, 59
  Doctrine of devils (Trapp), 41
  Early view of Protestants, 434
  Francisco Ribeira, 437
  History, cannot be tested by, 438
  Irving, 59
  Literal, 435
  Literal view hypocritical, 436
  Maitland, Samuel, 437

Money Machine, 435
Moody, 59
Müller, 59
Must be read into Scripture, 436
Newspaper exegesis, 436
Rome develops, Protestants accept, 57
Rome's problem solved, 41
Scofield, 59
System attributed to Jesuits, 44
View introduced, 41

G

Gaebelein, A.C. *See* Scofield
Geneva Bible comments on pope, 42
Gentiles have no law, 357
Gentry, K., 429
Gibbon's History, 432
Gifts, miraculous appear, 136
Gill, J., 43
Gnosticism defined, 451
God hates sinners, verses, 360
God's Word
  Confusing puzzle, 284
  Simply paper and ink, 369
Gog, 435
Gordon, A.J., historicist, 326
Gospel
  Cannot change society, 350
  False must be taught by non-disp, 267
  Great error, 350
  Müller's view of, 238
  Not for instruction, 344
  Reduced to soul-saving, 462
  Two gospels, 274
  Wait to be snatched away, 233
Grace insufficient, 379
Grant, W.F., 22
Great
  Awakening, 265
  Tribulation idea introduced, 351
  Tribulation, claimed by Darby, 351
  Tribulation, how idea developed,

352
Growth
By proselytism, 237, 307
Phenomenal, 204, 379
Guided by conscience,
circumstances, 366

H
Hagee, J., 126
Happiness & salvation supreme, 128
Healing, faith, 254
Heavenly
Citizenship, 337
Mindedness defined, 303
Mindedness, origin of, 259
Helicopters, cobra, 436
Hendriksen, W., 430
Henry, M., 432
Heretical, 48
Dispensationalism in America, 263
Higher Criticism
United all who believed Bible, 264
Historic vs. Ben-Ezra systems, 99
Historical, developed against Rome, 43
Historicist, 326, 431, 434, 438, 439
History
Divided into three parts, 435
Must be ignored, 82
Premillennial denied, 444
Theology separated from, 348, 451
Holiness
Motive for, 321
Through knowledge, 53
Hopelessness, results of, 261
Hunt, D., 126
Hunt, Hans, 447
Hus, J., 44, 431, 435
Hussites, 435
Hymns changed by Darbyites, 204

I
Idealist
View of prophecy, 438
If the Lord tarries, origin of, 161
Immigration
Emigrants receive Darby, 309
Great, to America, 281
Importance of, 290, 306, 310
Lax emigration policies, 59
Imminent Return
Ben-Ezra System, 92
Changed Christ's words, 215
Christ's, 206
Defined, 212, 213
Introduced, 31, 102, 103, 132
Irving, 171
Paul & John, 103
Serious implications, 213
Important Dates
1833-1845, Oxford Movement, 165
Before French Revolution, 59
Industrial Revolution, 330
Intellectual abilities unlawful, 172
Ireland, 168
Ironside, H.A. *See* Brethren
Irving, Edward, 41, 75
Against victorious Christ, 53
Condemns Public Opinion, 100
Deposed from ministry, 32
Influence of, 38
Introduced, 29
Introduced Defeat, 37
Knew Ben-Ezra was from Rome, 61
Lacunza's Ben-Ezra document, 447
Message of defeat, 45
Millennial message against Public Opinion, 34
Presbyterian, 29
Propagating heretical errors, 69
Removed from his church, 157
Spanish lessons, 62
Tongues, 32
Tongues introduced by, 32, 148
Translated Lacunza's document, 11
Irvingism/Darbyism, 427
Israel
Always Jews, never the Church, 16
Literal vs. spiritual, 57
National exalted, 35, 48

National exalted over church, 72
National renewed, 86
National replaces church, 86
Unconditionally given land, 252

J
Jeffery, G., 126
Jehovah's Witnesses, 437
Jenkins, J., 126
Jerusalem destroyed by Titus, 82
Jesuits
  Abbot, Joachim of Fiore, 435
  Alcazar, Luis de (1554-1613), 43, 44, 432, 433
  Antonio Vieira
    Exalts Jews, 55
  Ben-Ezra
    Converted Jew to Romanism, 46
    Manuel De Lacunza, 46, 434
    Voice from Rome, 62
  Cardinal Bellarmine, Robert, 44
  Euodio Papia
    Three comings of Christ, 54
  Franciscan, Peter Olivi, 435
  Labadie, Jean de, 460
  Lacunza
    Converted Jew, 46, 62
    Established new Orthodoxy, 64
    Exalts Jews, 52
    Identified, 46
    Neutralized Protestant attacks, 68
    Offered Millennialism, 7
    Refuted Revelation as history, 67
  Offered futurism 4 times, 59
  Papia, 59
  Peter Olivi (c. 1248-1298), 44
  Removed Protestant pressure, 41
  Ribeira, Francisco, 41, 43, 44, 59, 433, 434, 437
  Robert Bellarmine, 44
  Rome defended by, 41
Jewish
  Dream of literal kingdom, 72
  Errors, warning against, 8

False hope, 70 AD, 74
Hope by Ben-Ezra, Irving, 75
Hope Christianized, 81
Hope restored, 51
Hope taught by Darby, 75
Hope, renewed Zionist state, 82
Militant Messiah required, 75
Nation destroyed, 68
Nation exalted, 70
Nation restored, 74
Race, cannot trace, 52
Hope restored, see Zionism
Rabbinical dream, see Zionism
Jews
  Ben-Ezra exalted, 47, 52
  Converted, Lacunza, Manuel De, 46, 62
  Converted, see Wolff, Joseph
  Depressed state of, 52
  Destiny of, 250
  Financed Scofield
    Gaebelein, Arno C., 325, 327
  Given the land unconditionally, 203
  Number perished in 70 AD, 83
  Palestine, return to, 39
  Rabbinical dream, 9, 63
  Special interest in by Samuel Maitland, 437
Joachim of Fiore. *See* Jesuits
John's books dismissed, 343
Josephus, 74, 82, 432, 433
Judaism renewed, 443
Judgment
  Christ waiting to judge, 99
  Christians forbidden to judge, 400
  Nations exempt from, 399

K
Kelly, William
  Attributes rapture to Darby, 145
Keswick, 206, 317, 461
  American conference, 318
  Baron, D., 319
  Doctrines of, 321

First convention, 316
Heresy of, 315
Holiness defined, 316
Keswickism explained, 314
Leaders, origin, doctrine, 316, 319
Leads to Welfare State, 318
Let go & let God, 319
Meyer, F.B., 315
Millenarianism, 315
Moody's involvement with, 316, 320
Morgan, G.C., 315
Motive for personal holiness, 321
Murray, A., 315
Northfield Bible Conferences, 315
  Influence at, 315
Princeton, at, 267, 319
Scofield, C.I., 319, 329
Sincerity over obedience, 314
Social programs dangerous, 318
Sunday School Times promoted, 317
Taylor, H.
  Committed to, 198, 319
  SVM committed to, 320
Teachers, Bounds, E.M., Murray, A., 22
Thomas, G., 319
Trumbull, C. G., 317
Warfield against, 319
Key Events
  Millennialism, acceptance of, 37
  Millennialism, Post to Pre, 277
Killed
  Those with anti-pope views, 435
King William, III, 431
Kingdom
  Of God on earth, 430
  Of Heaven, 445
Kirban, S., 126
Knox, J., 42, 431
Kuyper, A., 430

L

Lacunza, Manuel De
  See Ben-Ezra System

  See Jesuits
LaHaye, T., 126, 127, 284, 379
  Darbyism's honest heir, 437
  Eschatological views, 434
Last days newly defined, 94
Latter rain is for the Jews, 86
Law
  Church has no responsibility to, 357
  Grace, vs., 193, 354
  Nations exempt from God's, 403
  New view of, accepted, 115
  Summarized, 115
Law, William, 1, 14
Lawlessness
  Ironside defends, 354
  Law does not apply, 340
  Scofield defends, 354
Liberalism, 18
Liberty
  Becomes license, 461
  From law, 339
  Religious, requested by Darby, 395
Lindsey, H., 48, 127, 284, 437, 459
  Compares Bible to Crystal Ball, 127
Literal
  Antichrist, Papists' fable, 43
  Christ
    Militant Jewish Messiah, 72, 75
    Must intervene, 253
    Must sit on David's throne, 119
    Not literal king, 117
    Not now reigning, 404
    Reign, 70, 71, 88, 101, 102, 103, 122, 350
    Reign with Saints, 171
    Reign yet to come, 35, 441
    Reign, soon to come (c. 1850), 104
    Return our only hope, 219
    Return, rule as Jewish King, 374
    Sword to subdue sinners, 198, 404
    Throne yet to come, 56, 81
  Ez. 37 changed to, 351
  Ez. 39, Popery, 73
  French Revolution fulfilled Rev. 13,

37
Fulfillment, Mat. 4:15, 16, 106
Future fulfillment of Mat. 24, Rev., 82
God must establish throne, 187
God must intervene, 89, 91, 362
Infallible tests of faith, 53
Interpretation, end in A.D. 1000, 445
Interpretation, Jewish, 444
Israel restored, Jewish-carnal view, 74
Jewish nation must be restored, 121
Jn. 21:22, Mat. 16:28, 8
Millennial faith restored, 211
Millennialism, Judaistic heresy, 446
Millennialism, new school of interpretation, 205
Nation replaces Christ, 87
New Israel, 57
Newly required for Daniel 12, 92
Only way to understand, 8
Prophecy must be fulfilled, 120, 203
Prophetic passages must be, 112
Reestablished Jewish nation, 107
Reign of Peace from Israel, 73
Revelation misinterpretations, 436
Revelation, Book of, 435
Rod of Iron, 15, 77, 308, 361, 365
God must intervene, 215
Scriptures must be understood, 458
Sought for in every Biblical prophecy, 16
Spiritual, contrasted with, 438
Thousand year reign, 6, 110, 428
Unless absurd, 16, 106, 285
Warning against too literal, 8
Zion restored, 44
See Chiliasm
Louis the Sixteenth, 17
Luther, M., 430, 431

M

Macdonald, Margaret, 11, 52, 152, 154, 155

First with tongues, 152
Tongues appear, 136
Mackintosh, C.H. *See* Brethren
MacPherson, D., 2, 205, 459
Magog, 435
Maitland, Samuel, 437
Jews, special interest in, 437
Man
A hopeless victim of Satan, 120
Exalted, 124
Marcion, 338, 342
Dispensationalism and Darby, 342
Dispensationalism, rejected OT, 338
Divided God's Word, 451, 452
Doctrine of defeat, 454
Marcion & Mat. 5.17, 454
Marcionism defined, 450
Most formidable heretic, 454
No God, 453
Marxism. *See* Dispensationalism
Material possessions renounced, 214
Mather, C., 42
Matthew 24
Fulfilled, 83
New view of, 352
V. 21, Darby's new view, 352
McCheyne, R.M., 464
McVicker, D.G. *See* Brethren
Menace to the Orthodox, 24
Mennonites
Menno Simons, 447
Origin of, 447
Messages, against prepared, 230
Meyer, F.B.
Heresy of Keswickism, 315
Millennial Money Machine, 2, 205, 206, 280, 379
Millennial reign summarized, 119
Millennial views, 428
See Amillennialism
See Chiliasm
See Dispensationalism
See Historical

Index

See Millennialism
See Postmillennialism
See Premillennialism
See Preterism
See Reconstruction, Christian
See Second Adventism
See Theonomy
Millennialism, 341, 381, 442, 444, 445, 450
  Absorbed Reformed churches, 206
  American, established at Northfield, 313
  Americanized, 263
  Anabaptist, 447
  Antinomianism, charges of, 354
  Attracts wealth, 205
  Augustine against, 445
  Baptist, Presbyterians resist, 264
  Calvinism, ties with, 266
  Changes Scripture to fit, 403
  Child of the times, 15
  Conquered world, why, 305
  Darby spread, 447
  Dead 1400 years, 50
  Death, and, 227
  Deep Jewish/Roman roots, 56
  Defined by Fr. Paul, 46
  Development of, 208
  Disaster for cause of Christ, 221
  Early Church Fathers against, 445
  Early church rejected, 211
  Emphasis death, 39
  Escape into prophetic study, 37
  Excitement, 190
  Excitement at Oxford, 37
  Exempts church from judgment, 159
  Financing of, 326
  Five points of, 85
  Foundation of, 52, 167, 174
  Fountain head of, 5, 45, 206
  Growth of, 206
  Hatred for Victorious Christ, 28
  Hopelessness justified, 405
  Hopelessness promoted, 211
  Hypocrisy of, 126
  Invades US, 212
  Irving founded, 446
  Jewish hope restored in Zionism, 443
  Jewish rather than Christian, 444
  Judaistic heresy
    Augsburg, Helvetic Confessions, 446
  Keswicks & Millenarians, 315
  Lacks serious study, 58
  Lacunza 1790 introduction of, 7
  Leaders Calvinistic, 25
  Loses sight of Christ, 79
  Millennial Money Machine, 126
  Missions, purpose of, 321
  Modern overwhelms Christianity, 36
  Moody, first training institution, 320
  Motive for Holiness, New, 321
  Neutralized enemies of Communism, 257
  New doctrine, 211
  Opposition to, 23
  Post-18th century standard view, 39
  Preached from self-defence, 209
  Pre-millennialism, 39
  Promotes Zionism, 139
  Rejected as Jewish, 434
  Renewed Judaism, 443
  Requires Church/Israel distinction, 47
  Rome offered, 56
  Rome revived theory, 49
  Rome's conclusion of, 46
  Rome's problem solved, 148
  Second Adventism, 439
  Secret rapture added, 54
  Secular view, 259
  Snatching away, 442
  Stoutly anti-Catholic before Ben-Ezra, 42
  Summarized, 178
  Supported by new exegesis, 205
  Ten Principles of, 167

Tongues & Rapture, 464
Why expanded so quickly, 346
See Darby, J.N.
See Pope
See Zionism
Millennium
Mentioned only in Apocalypse, 442
Start, three dates set, 442
Miller, W., 19, 263, 264
Milligan, W., 438
Missionary endeavors
1850, failed, 214
20th century enthusiasm, 199
Müller changed, 197
Modernism
Defined, 264
United all who believed Bible, 264
Monasticism, 26, 458
Asceticism traced, 455
Defined, 455
Hosea's answer to, 459
Spread, 458
Swindoll, Chuck, 457
Montanus, 149, 152, 153, 154, 441
2nd century heretic, 13, 450
Demonic, 154
Millennialism &, 443, 450
Women who followed, 154, 450
Moody, D.L., 21, 264, 265, 464
Abilities of, 290
American evangelists imitated, 287
Ardent Abolitionist, 289
Bible reading, 294
Conversion to Brethrenism, 22, 286
Conversion to Millennialism, 288
Conversion, Christian, 288
Darby & Moody, 291
Darbyizes US Christianity, 313
Denounced converting grace, 292
Encounters Bible Reading, 292
Introduced new methods, 290
Irish revival, 298
London meetings, 298

Methods to draw crowd, 298
Moody Bible Institute, 320
Northfield, 264
Northfield and Darbyism, 294
Planning or Spirit, 299
Qualifications to preach, 289
Revivalism, 463
Sermons described, 295
Student Volunteer Movement, 320
Study method, 295
Unites Irvingism/Keswickism, 315
Won by Moorehouse, 293
See Brethren
Moody, D.L. *See* Brethren
Moravian movement, 463
Morris, H., 437
Motives
Brethren's, 355
Darby's, 405
Missions, for, 243
Original unifying, 172
Müller, G. *See* Brethren
Münster, Germany, 447
Kingdom at, 7
Murray, A. *See* Brethren
Muslims, 3
Mysticism, 14
Christianity, a Melancholy state, 213
Defined, 12
Montanus, 13

N

Napier, J., 42
Napoleonic War. *See* War
Nation
Jewish exalted, 70
Jewish reestablished, 274
Renewed Jewish required, 79
Nations
No healing for, 110
See Areas Conquered
Nee, W. *See* Brethren
Nero, 44
New World Order

Opposition neutralized, 258
Newspaper Exegesis, 436
Newton, B.W.
  Darby, Conflict with, 178
Newton, Sir Isaac, 42, 431
Niagara Bible Conference. *See* Prophecy Conferences
Noah's Ark, 374
Non-Dispensational
  Followers teach false gospel, 267
Northfield Bible Conference. *See* Prophecy Conferences
Nuclear war, 436

O

Obedience
  No duty to, 356
  No requirement of, 272
  Privilege not duty, 356
Only two preaching messages, 226
Opposition
  Bass, C.B., 23
  Croskery, T., 23
  Dabney, R.L., 23, 24
  Fairbairn, P., 23, 24
  M'Vicker, J.G., 24
  Reid, W., 23
  Smeaton, G., 23
  Spurgeon, C.H., 23, 24
  Strong, A.H., 23, 24
  Warfield, B.B., 23, 24
Orberlin College, 279
Ordination unneeded, 174
Other-Worldliness defined, 14, 303
Oxford
  Darby &, 183
  Millenarian excitement at, 37
  Revival of 1833, results, 165

P

Pacifism, 193
Papacy. *See* Pope
Patience defined - just wait, 400
Paul
  Alone for Church Age, 340
  Reason for, 341

Ben-Ezra system, 103
Civil matters, unconcerned about, 342
Darby compares self to, 340, 395
Doctrine recovered by Darby, 342
Writings only, origin, 339
Peace keepers, 119
Pentecost, G.F., 464
Pentecostal, 11, 149
Pentecostalism
  Brethren, 254
  Start of, 129
Perfection - doing one's best, 314
Personal holiness emphasized, 461
Pietism
  Defined, 13, 459
  Devotion over doctrine, 460
  Feelings over theology, 461
  Good points of, 462
  Implications of, 460
  Lowered idea of the church, 462
  Origin, 460
  Priesthood of the believer, 462
  Salvation &, 461
  Sound Theology uprooted, 461
  Whitfield, G., 462
Pit, bottomless, 41
Plymouth Brethren, 42, 147, 447
  Foundation of, 11
  Influence on Christianity, 11
Political involvement
  Sin, 217, 240
  Treason, 217
Polycarp. *See* Church Fathers
Pope, 39
  Antichrist, considered as, 42
  Contact with Wolff/Drummond/ Irving, 140
  Defended by Millenarianism, 42
  Ezekiel 39, literal, absurd legend of popery, 73
  Gregory 7th, 42
  Joseph Wolff meets, 139
  Millennialism

Problem solved for, 57, 404
Papacy, 48, 148, 432
  Antichrist, 160, 184, 446
  Beast, 431
  Papal empire, 68
  Papal power defended, 433, 434
  Papal power is the Antichrist, 74
  Papal power's end prophesied, 431
  Popelings, churches' enemy, 9
  Popish doctrine out of bottomless pit, 41
  Protestant attacks against, 42, 434
  Removed from pressure, 48
  Vicar of Christ, 44
  Viewed by KJV translators, 42
Postmillennialism, 278, 437
  Defined, 429
  Dominate until wars, 429
  Prevalence in America, 265
Poverty
  Exalted, 214
  Proves sincerity, 18
Powerscourt. *See* Prophecy Conferences
Premillennial advent of Christ, 168
Premillennialism, 210, 278, 428, 458
  Beginning, from the, 6
  Defined, 428
  Historic, 146, 147
  Neutralized Christianity, 258
  Never dominant view, 51
  Not the historic faith, 443
  Promotes pessimism, 428
  Sit back and wait, 441
  Society's problem, 457
  Spiritual virus, 258
  Strong's (A.H.) view, 227
  Subversive, 258
Premillennialism. *See* Millennialism; Dispensationalism; Revelation, views of
Presbyterian, 11, 278
  Conversion to Brethrenism, 11

  Conversion to Irvingism/Darbyism, 265, 266
  Darby's influence among, 291
  Dispensationalism's major promoters, 267
  Finney, C., 278
Preterism, 43, 44, 45, 429, 432, 438, 439
  Defined, 432
  Full, 434
Pretribulation vs. Posttribulation, 325
Pretribulationism introduced, 146
Princeton
  Keswicks, 319
  Seminary, 283
Privilege
  Vs. Command, 273, 356
Problems
  Exegetical solved, 68, 77
  No answers, 194
Progressive revelation, 450
Prophecy, 450
  1260
    Days, 44, 67, 92, 109
    Years, 92, 102, 135
  Believers &, 58
  Ben-Ezra's summarized, 112
  Conferences develop millennial hope, 216
  Conferences on unfulfilled, 125
  Curious inquiry forbidden, 127
  Emphasized over doctrine, 58
  French Revolution, Rev. 11, 109
  Fulfilled, proves Scripture, 108
  Futurist system, origin of, 60
  Historic understanding denied, 137
  Ideal conditions for study of, 37
  Literal if at all possible, 106
  Literal required, 120
  Literal, figurative, 16
  Maturity, &, 108
  Millennialism's power, 173

Index 501

New prophetic speculations, 391
Pivot of Darby's work, 246
Progressive revelation, 450
Psalms 2, 108
Purpose, escape from reality, 37, 215, 231, 249
Study of will solve sin problem, 110
Unfulfilled, 219
  First conference for study of, 129
Prophecy Conferences
  Albury Park, 32, 37, 63, 69
  1st, 1826, 129, 132
  2nd, 134
  3rd summarized, 134
  4th (Irving), 155
  Changed the Christian faith, 37
  First on Unfulfilled Prophecy, 34
  Irving, 31, 37
  Purpose of, 129
  Disastrous results of, 125
  Drummond, Henry, hosted first, 130
  Moody's in America, 311
  Niagara Bible Conference, 38, 135, 266, 267, 307, 316, 326, 329
  Americanized Millennialism, 311
  Bible readings, 312
  Brookes, J. H., 311
  Calvinist Presbyterians, 312
  Needham, George, 312
  Niagara Creed, 276, 313
  Northfield Bible Conference, 135, 198, 288, 295, 313, 316, 317
  American influence of, 281
  Keswicks at, 315
  Millennial respectability gained, 264
  Promoted Darbyism, 294
  Scofield, 328
  Seminary at, 298
  Permit deceiving spirits, 128
  Powerscourt, 237
  1832, Darby's summary, 141
  Acount of prophecy meeting, 392
  Importance of, 143

  Ireland, prophecy conferences, 198
  Prophetic speculation at, 395
  Record of, 391
  Scriptures examined listed, 394
  Second meeting, 392
  Sponsor, Lady, 141
  Purpose of conferences, 136
  See Keswick
Prophetic
  New schemes introduced, 250
  Secret Puzzle Solved, 284
  Speculations, 70
  According to appearances, 78
Proselytize = soul-winning, 244
Prosperity renounced, 176
Protestants
  Against pope, 433
  Futurism
    Accepted, 434
    Early view of, 434
    Rejected, 65
Psychic power, 289
Public life, against involvement, 217
Public Opinion
  Condemned by Irving, 100
  Post-Mil., 100

Q

Quakers, 448
Quotes, why so many, 45

R

Rabbinical dream. *See* Zionism.
Rapture, Secret Pre-Trib, 8, 11, 14, 47, 52, 68, 75, 88, 146, 147, 148, 168, 171, 172, 185, 190, 221, 234, 235, 247, 252, 276, 326, 378, 428, 434, 438
  Added to
    Ben-Ezra at Powerscourt, 237
    Imminent return, 404
    Millennialism, 212
  Amazing spread of idea, 237
  America influenced for, 307
  Changes a thousand scriptures, 403
  Church out of world, 219

Darby, 221
  Attacks Newton over, 221
  Claimed idea for, 408
  Explains how he developed idea, 147
  Date setters fizzle, 177
  Defined as Morning Star, 403
  Gentiles converted after rapture, 347
  Imminent return, 215
  Indefensible, 234
  Introduced, 145
  Joseph Mede, credited to, 7
  Killed desire to convert world, 404
  New, novel and unique, 147, 158
  Newton challenged Darby, 235
  Offered by Irving, 56
  Only hope out of evil, 143, 403
  Powerscourt, 435
  Result in tortured Christians, 199
  Solves 3 Advents problem, 54
  Solves pope's problem, 160
  Supernatural escape from world, 378
  Tongues, ecstatic utterances, 464
  United with millennial hope, 205
  Victorinus, credited to, 7
  Vs Post-Trib, 325
  Wrongly attributed to Darby, 145, 221
Reactionary Movement. Anti
  Clergy, orthodox, intellectual, 168
Reconstruction, Christian defined, 429
Redemption's purpose. Exalt man, 35
Reduction of the Biblical faith, 202
Reformation, 2 great truths of, 43
Reformers, 127, 187, 192, 204, 431
  Against antichrist Papacy, 446
    Rome defends self, 434
  Darby against, 361
  Darbyites changed writings of, 204
Reign, spiritual hated, 71
Religion

  Reduced to individual matter, 128
Renewed sacrifice, 349
Resurrection
  First & second, 102
  Two, offered by Lacunza, 61
Revelation
  Early dating of, 432, 433
  Four common views, 430
  From history to prophecy, 67
  Historic vs. Future view, 160
  Irrelevant to its readers, 436
  John's Olivet Discourse, 433
  Orthodox view of changed, 65
Revelation, views of
  See Chiliasm
  See Futurism
  See Historicism
  See Idealist
  See Postmillenarianism
  See Premillennialism
  See Preterist
  See Spiritual
  See Symbolic
Revival, Irish, 298
Revivalism, 280
  De-emphasized sound doctrine, 280
  Defined, 14
  Emotionalism, 278, 463
  God's or man's spirit, 299
  Moody, D.L., 463
  Pietism, 463
Revivalism. *See* Finney, C.
Revivals, 301
Revolution
  Bolshevik, 256
  Second American, 256
  See French Revolution
  See Wars
Richard the Lion-Hearted, 435
Rightly dividing the Word of Truth
  Corrupt meaning of, 220
  Origin of saying, 220
Riots

Account of, 395
Darby's new theories caused, 247, 347
Robbers of churches, 241, 242
Robespierre, 17
Rod of Iron, 119, 365
  Ben-Ezra system, 77
  French Revolution, and, 15
Roman Empire, 432
Romanticism, 331
Rome
  Against Protestant conversion of world, 57
  Ben-Ezra
    Banned, 48
    Critiqued, Approved, 45
    Rome's gain, 56
    System approved, 48
    Voice from, 62
  Conquered Millenarians, 148
  Countered Protestant antichrist teaching, 42, 44, 160
  Introduced Futurism, 41, 160, 434
  Millennialism, 212
    Removed Pressure, 44
    Rome's Involvement, 54
    Solved problem, 404
  Supported by Darbyism, 184
  Taught Premillennial Advent, 44
  See also Futurism
  See also Jesuits
  See also Pope
Ruin of the Church, 146, 248, 412
  Americanized, 373
  Ben-Ezra system, 91
  Introduced, 91
Rushdoony, R.J., 429
Ryrie, C., 48, 428, 437, 443

S

Sabbath
  Darby's view, 356
Saints
  Not all belong to the Church, 347

Salary, Darby's view of, 218
Sanctification, newly defined, 371
Satan
  Adam, 123
  Bound, 429, 445
  Earthly work of defined, 103
  Goals of, 97
  Rule summarized, 122
  Rules, 120
  Terrors of introduced, 27
  Victims of, 99
  Victorious over Christ, 122
Scholastical abilities unlawful, 173, 175
Scofield, C.I., 23, 265, 323, 437
  2 Timothy 2:15, 220
  Against world's conversion, 324
  Connection
    Brookes, James H., 266
    Erdman, William J., 266, 329
    Gaebelein, Arno, 325, 428
    Ironside, 355
    Jews, 324
    Moody, 327
    Taylor, Hudson, 199
    Trumbull, Charles G., 318
  Degree "self-bestowed", 322
  Divides history, 11
  Divine will inwrought, 357, 369, 370
  Financed by Gaebelein, Arno, 326
  God's Grace fails, 324
  Keswicks, &, 329
  Points from his Introduction, 328
  Presented Brethren doctrine, 6, 189
  Reference Bible, 6, 10, 45, 322, 325, 347
  Scofieldism, 38
  Systematized Darbyism, 11, 180, 323
  World was ready for, 323
  Zionism, 325
Scriptural Knowledge Institution, 196, 197, 198

Neutralized Christianity, 199
Scriptures
 Darby changed character of, 403
 Prophetic examined at Powerscourt, 394
 Studied according to Church/Israel distinction, 48
Second Advent
 Common view before Lacunza, 93
 Just wait for, 337
 Two resurrections, 252
Second Adventism, 446
Second Adventists, 446
Secular vs. spiritual, 456
Self-denial defined, 226
Self-Esteem, 129
Separation from involvement, 412
Separation of church, state, 223
Sermon on the Mount
 Church removed from, 159
Seventh Day Adventists, 446
Sin
 2 gospels, Jewish/non-Jewish, 159
 Answer to, 362
 Christian magistrate unlawful, 193
 Conscience violated, 274
 Darby's view of, 51, 359
 End of, 364
 Expect world's Conversion, 252
 Judged, 365
 Judgment for, 364
 Law enforcement unlawful, 193
 Learn a trade, 218
 Making world better, 337
 Newly defined, 247, 361
 Political involvement, 217
 Prepared messages, 167, 178
 Read a newspaper, 338
 Riches, 193
 Seeking righteous laws, 337
 Sinless sin introduced, 359
 Social involvement, 459
 Study of math, 218

Voting, 337
Work for future, 216
Work for world's conversion, 214
Working for righteous laws, 337
Worldly pursuits, 222
See Darby, J.N., 51
Skills, secular, 218
Smith, C., 126
Socialism. *See* Dispensationalism
Solutions
 None offered, 225, 231
Soon Coming
 Darby defines, 213
Spener, Philip Jacob, 462
 Pietism's father, 460
Spiritual
 View of prophecy, 438
 Other names for, 438
Spurgeon, C.H., 23, 123, 292, 314, 432
 Bible readings, against, 24
 Darbyism, view of, 23
 Monasticism, against, 25
 Propecy, Bible reading, 206
 Prophets for profit, shuffling Scripture, 207
Star, Morning
 Rapture, defined as, 403
Stone, Daniel's still future, 92
Strong, A.H., 265
 Ironside against Strong, 354
 Millenarianism, view of, 211
Study forbidden, 230
Sunday, W.A. *See* Brethren
Supernatural illumination, 175
Surrounding turmoil, escape from, 377
Swindoll, C., 457
Switzerland
 Conversion to Darbyism, 412
 Darby introduces new insights, 246
Symbolic
 View of prophecy, 438

Index

T

Taborites, 435
Taylor, H. *See* Brethren
Temple of God, the, 220
Tests of faith, three, 53
Theology uprooted, 461
Theonomy defined, 429
Time devided into seven epochs, 435
Tithe & the Law, 144
Tongues, 11, 85, 151, 152, 157, 171, 254, 419, 450
  Appear, 136
  Darby rejected, 149
  Demonic utterances, 152
  Dispensationalism &, 149
  First heard, 148, 149
  Introduced, 32, 148
  Montanus, first to claim, 441
  Origin of, 148
  Prophecy, 155
  Rapture, 148
  Religious delusion, 149
  With Dispensationalism, 149
Torrey, R.A. *See* Brethren
Tradition, 53
Trapp, John (1601-1669), 8, 9, 41, 44
Tribulation
  Great, 436
  Post, 146
  Seven year, 378
  See also Great
Trullan council of 692, 339
Trumbull, C. G. Keswick involvement, 317
Truth newly defined, 374
Turks, 9, 39
Tyndale, W., 431

U

Ulrich, 431
Unconcerned, must remain, 377
Under grace, not law, 339
Unholy zeal, 221
Unworldliness defined, 303

V

Victorious, Christ the, 168
Victory, Christian vision lost, 276
Vine, W.E. *See* Brethren, 265
Visible/invisible church, same, 249
Voting, against, 398

W

Wait
  For Second Advent, 337, 403
Walvoord, J., 428, 437, 459
War
  Christianity, against, 17, 194
  Civil, 19, 59, 265, 279, 280, 302, 307, 337, 360, 429
  Bible Readings, and, 283
  Darbyism grows, 304
  Left hopeless attitude, 304
  Moody, D.L., 289
  Prepares way for Millennialism, 10
  See Finney, C.
  Independence, for, 10, 16, 59, 265, 307
  Napoleonic, 19, 37, 304
  Date, 15
  Ideal conditions, 37
  Prophecy, 131
  Public mood, 10
  Pacificist, 194
  Premillenarianism subversive, 258
  Satan against the Saints, 446
  WW I, 266
  See French Revolution
Warfield, B.B., 13, 429
  Against Keswickism, 319
Watchtower Society, 434
Wealth
  Dispensationalism &, 177
  Unchristian, 177
Wealth. *See* Dispensationalism
Welfare State
  Condoned by churches, 177
  Keswickism promotes, 318
  Rise of, 177
Wesley, J., 42, 431, 462

Whitby, D., 39
Whitefield, G., 431, 462, 464
Wigram, G. V. *See* Brethren
Wisenant, E., 264
Wolff, Joseph, 73, 75, 465
  Alone gave proper understanding to Scriptures, 63
  Converted Jew, 55, 63, 138
  Meets the pope, 139
  Rabbi's son, 140
Words
  Corrupted
    Blessed Hope, 374
    Evangelization, 372
    Grace, 376
    Peace, 375
    Redefined, 204
World
  Conversion of
    Forbidden, 196, 238, 324
    Hope for abandoned, 37
    Impossible, 404
  Do not meddle with, 399
Wycliffe, J., 431
  View of papacy, 446

Y

Year-Day Theory, 431, 437
Years, 3 1/2 fulfilled, 82

Z

Zeal replaces theology, 293
Zion
  Rome taught literal restoration, 44
Zionism
  Christian, 391
  Church/Israel Distinction, 141
  Defined, 141
  Defined by Darby, 75
  Denies Christ, 86
  Gaebelein, Scofield, 325
  Jewish hope Christianized, 81, 219
  Jewish hope restored, 39, 51, 63, 137, 141, 352
  Origin of, 137
  Political introduced, 139
  Political, Protestant defined, FN., 73
  Praised by Ben-Ezra/Darbyism/Scofieldism, 48
  Protestant
    Admittedly a Jewish idea, 82
    Introduced by Lacunza, 136
    Renewed Judaism, 443
    Requires Church/Israel Distinction, 48
  The Jews Society, 1818, 138
  Rabbinical dream, 9, 63, 439
  Rejected before Lacunza/Irving, 36
  Revived in premillennialism, 210
  Urged by Ben-Ezra System, 81
  Zionist cause, 139
  See Ben-Ezra System
Zwigli, Huldreich, 42, 431

www.ingramcontent.com/pod-product-compliance
Lightning Source LLC
Chambersburg PA
CBHW020727160426
43192CB00006B/139